Resu[illegible]

Through a case study of community organizing in the global city of London and an examination of the legacy of Saul Alinsky around the world, this book develops a constructive account of the relationship between religious diversity, democratic citizenship, and economic and political accountability. Based on an in-depth, ethnographic study, Part I identifies and depicts a consociational, populist, and faithfully secular vision of democratic citizenship by reflecting on the different strands of thought and practice that feed into and help constitute community organizing. Particular attention is given to how organizing mediates the relationship between Christianity, Islam, and Judaism and those without a religious commitment in order to forge a common life. Part II then unpacks the implications of this vision for how we respond to the spheres in which citizenship is enacted, namely, civil society, the sovereign nation-state, and the globalized economy. Overall, the book outlines a way of re-imagining democracy, developing innovative public policy, and addressing poverty in the contemporary context.

Luke Bretherton is Associate Professor of Theological Ethics and Senior Fellow of the Kenan Institute for Ethics at Duke University. Before Duke he was Reader in Theology and Politics at King's College London (2004–2012). His other books include *Hospitality as Holiness: Christian Witness Amid Moral Diversity* (2006) and *Christianity and Contemporary Politics: The Conditions and Possibilities of Faithful Witness* (2010), winner of the 2013 Michael Ramsey Prize for Theological Writing. In addition to publishing journal articles and books, he writes for the media on issues related to religion and politics. This book grows out of a three-year Arts and Humanities Research Council–funded project for which he was principal investigator (2008–2011).

This book [illegible] community organizing in the [illegible] [illegible] and [illegible] [illegible] [illegible] [illegible] [illegible] [illegible] [illegible] [illegible] [illegible] [illegible] [illegible] [illegible] political [illegible] based [illegible] [illegible] depth [illegible] study [illegible] [illegible] [illegible] [illegible] [illegible] secular [illegible] democratic [illegible] [illegible] [illegible] [illegible] [illegible] [illegible] [illegible] [illegible] [illegible] [illegible] and [illegible] the [illegible] [illegible] [illegible] [illegible] [illegible] [illegible] [illegible] [illegible] [illegible] [illegible] [illegible] nation-state, and the globalized economy. [illegible] [illegible] [illegible] [illegible] [illegible] [illegible] [illegible] [illegible] [illegible] [illegible] [illegible] [illegible] [illegible] and addressing poverty in the contemporary context.

CAMBRIDGE STUDIES IN SOCIAL THEORY, RELIGION AND POLITICS

The most enduring and illuminating bodies of late nineteenth-century social theory – by Marx, Weber, Durkheim, and others – emphasized the integration of religion, polity, and economy through time and place. Once a staple of classic social theory, however, religion gradually lost the interest of many social scientists during the twentieth century. The recent emergence of phenomena such as Solidarity in Poland; the dissolution of the Soviet empire; various South American, Southern African, and South Asian liberation movements; the Christian Right in the United States; and Al Qaeda have reawakened scholarly interest in religiously based political conflict. At the same time, fundamental questions are once again being asked about the role of religion in stable political regimes, public policies, and constitutional orders. The series Cambridge Studies in Social Theory, Religion and Politics produces volumes that study religion and politics by drawing from classic social theory and more recent social-scientific research traditions. Books in the series offer theoretically grounded, comparative, empirical studies that raise "big" questions about a timely subject that has long engaged the best minds in social science.

Titles in the Series

Luke Bretherton, *Resurrecting Democracy: Faith, Citizenship, and the Politics of a Common Life*
David E. Campbell, John C. Green, and J. Quin Monson, *Seeking the Promised Land: Mormons and American Politics*
Paul A. Djupe and Christopher P. Gilbert, *The Political Influence of Churches*
Joel S. Fetzer and J. Christopher Soper, *Muslims and the State in Britain, France, and Germany*
François Foret, *Religion and Politics in the European Union: The Secular Canopy*
Jonathan Fox, *A World Survey of Religion and the State*
Anthony Gill, *The Political Origins of Religious Liberty*
Brian J. Grim and Roger Finke, *The Price of Freedom Denied: Religious Persecution and Conflict in the 21st Century*
Kees van Kersbergen and Philip Manow, editors, *Religion, Class Coalitions, and Welfare States*
Karrie J. Koesel, *Religion and Authoritarianism: Cooperation, Conflict, and the Consequences*
Ahmet T. Kuru, *Secularism and State Policies toward Religion: The United States, France, and Turkey*
Pippa Norris and Ronald Inglehart, *Sacred and Secular: Religion and Politics Worldwide*
Amy Reynolds, *Free Trade and Faithful Globalization: Saving the Market*
Peter Stamatov, *The Origins of Global Humanitarianism: Religion, Empires, and Advocacy*

Resurrecting Democracy

Faith, Citizenship, and the Politics of a Common Life

LUKE BRETHERTON

Duke University

CAMBRIDGE
UNIVERSITY PRESS

32 Avenue of the Americas, New York, NY 10013-2473, USA

Cambridge University Press is part of the University of Cambridge.

It furthers the University's mission by disseminating knowledge in the pursuit of education, learning, and research at the highest international levels of excellence.

www.cambridge.org
Information on this title: www.cambridge.org/9781107641969

First published 2015

Printed in Great Britain by Clays Ltd, St Ives plc

A catalog record for this publication is available from the British Library.

Library of Congress Cataloging in Publication data
Bretherton, Luke.
Resurrecting democracy : faith, citizenship, and the politics of a common life / Luke Bretherton.
pages cm – (Cambridge studies in social theory, religion and politics)
Includes bibliographical references and index.
ISBN 978-1-107-03039-8 (hardback) – ISBN 978-1-107-64196-9 (paperback)
1. Community organization–Philosophy. 2. Citizenship. 3. Democracy. 4. Civil society. I. Title.
HM766.B74 2014
306.2–dc23 2014023800

ISBN 978-1-107-03039-8 Hardback
ISBN 978-1-107-64196-9 Paperback

For Isaac

So that there may be a world for you to laugh in

Contents

Figures

Acknowledgments

When I began researching this book in 2007, few people I spoke with had heard of either community organizing or the Corporation of the City of London, or had much to say on the relationship between the church and different forms of direct action and participatory democracy. Moreover, they thought their financial future was secure. By 2014, when I finished researching and writing the book, the president of the United States was a former community organizer, the Conservative Party in the United Kingdom had made it government policy to train 5,000 community organizers, the financial system was going through a systemic crisis, and a confrontation between St. Paul's Cathedral and the Occupy Movement in 2012 had not only made the church's response to direct action front-page news but also brought the Corporation of the City of London to national consciousness in the United Kingdom.

A further dramatic change of circumstances accompanied the production of this book. I began the research with my friend and colleague Maurice Glasman. The book was originally conceived as a joint project with him. But events took a different turn. Questions generated by our research and relationships he built through it led him to become a catalytic figure in the development of "Blue Labour" as a vision for the future direction of the Labour Party. In terms of mainstream political policies and practice, what felt like speculations on the impossible in 2007 became intense deliberations over the probable by 2011. The full story of Blue Labour must be told elsewhere, but it forms a tacit backdrop to this work because much of the thinking related to Blue Labour as a political project grew out of the thinking, conversations, and research that informed this book. So for his intellectual contribution, companionship, and sheer vitality of presence, I thank Maurice.

I extend deep thanks to Neil Jameson without whom Citizens UK would not exist and whose drive and commitment seem to know no bounds. His active support and openness to this work were crucial to its realization. In addition to Neil, this whole project would not have been possible without the trust, conversation, and friendship of Stefan Baskerville, Matthew Bolton, Julie Camancho, Bernadette Farrell, Mike Gecan, Arnie Graaf, Lisa Jamoul, Jonathan Lange, Mike Miller, Leo Penta, Gerald Taylor, Colin Weatherup, and numerous other organizers I had the great privilege to learn from and be tutored by. And I am grateful to Helen Bevan and Marshall Ganz for pointing me to other arenas in which organizing might be applicable, such as healthcare. A large note of thanks must also go to the leaders within Citizens UK who were willing to talk to or be interviewed by me, and whose commitment to the work of organizing is a wonder to behold given all the competing demands on their lives.

Alongside the organizers and leaders, a set of academic collaborators and conversation partners were crucial in generating and guiding the development of this book. Particular thanks must go to Harry Boyte, Jane Wills, and Richard Wood who were insightful and vital interlocutors all along the way. I must also thank David Ford, John Milbank, Mark Warren, and Jon Wilson for important discussions of different aspects of the work. For their support in developing the initial research proposal out of which this book emerged, I thank my former colleagues at King's College London: Alan Cribb, Jeremy Hodgson, Alister McGrath, and Christopher Winch. I am grateful to the Arts and Humanities Research Council for the grant that made the initial research possible. For their encouragement, comments on, and conversations about earlier drafts I thank Kate Bowler, Stanley Hauerwas, and Jeffrey Stout, as well as Charles Mathewes and all the presenters and participants in the workshop on a draft of the manuscript held at the University of Virginia's Center for the Study of Religion in 2013. For his help with archiving material and compiling data for the graphs I thank Brian Manchester. For help with the graphs themselves I thank Angela Zoss. I am deeply grateful for the invaluable editorial work and guidance provided by Jennifer Benedict and Judith Heyhoe. And for being willing to take a risk with a book such as this I thank the commissioning editors of this series (Richard Wood, Kenneth D. Wald, and David C. Leege) and Lewis Bateman and Shaun Vigil at Cambridge University Press.

Lastly, for the many late nights, early mornings, and absent weekends demanded by the research I must gratefully acknowledge the patience and goodwill of my wife Caroline and children Gabriel and Isaac. A measure of the cumulative impact of the research process on our family was that, toward the end of the research, when asked after church one Sunday what his father did, my youngest replied with earnest innocence: "He's a politician."

Parts of Chapter 1 have been taken, with revisions, from an article that appeared in *The Good Society Journal*, volume 21, number 2 (2012) under the title "The Populist Politics of Broad-Based Organizing." Parts of Chapter 3 have been taken, with revisions, from an article that appeared in the *Journal of the American Academy of Religion*, volume 79, number 2 (2011) under the title "A Postsecular Politics? Inter-Faith Relations as a Civic Practice." Parts of Chapter 7 have been taken, with revisions, from an essay that appeared in *The Oxford Handbook of Theology & Modern European Thought*, edited by Nicholas Adams, George Pattison, and Graham Ward (Oxford: Oxford University Press, 2012) under the title "Sovereignty." Parts of Chapter 8 have been taken, with revisions, from an article that appeared in *Modern Theology*, volume 27, number 3 (2011) under the title "'Love Your Enemies': Usury, Citizenship & the Friend-Enemy Distinction." Parts of the Appendix, with revisions, are from an article that appeared in *Modern Theology*, volume 28, number 2 (2012) under the title "Coming to Judgment: Methodological Reflections on the Relationship between Ecclesiology, Ethnography and Political Theory." The Scripture quotations contained herein are from the New Revised Standard Version Bible, copyright 1989 by the Division of Christian Education of the National Council of the Churches of Christ in the U.S.A., and are used by permission.

Lent 2014

Introduction

It was a clear, crisp autumnal morning in London, with just a hint of the previous night's dampness still in the air as guests entered the crystalline edifice of Allen & Overy, an international law firm. Its offices were part of a gleaming new complex built over what had previously been one end of Spitalfield Market, a site that used to mark the boundary of the financial district and the beginning of the East End. We gathered for coffee, croissants, and fresh orange juice, all served by demure and identically dressed waiters and waitresses, on the top floor suite. From the glass-walled offices one could look out over the raggedy bustle of Commercial Street and Brick Lane and glimpse Canary Wharf, a citadel of steel and glass beyond the teeming jostle of Whitechapel and Stepney, areas long associated with poverty, congestion, and intense religious diversity. We were gathered for a meeting of the Council of Christians and Jews, an organization set up in 1942 to foster better relations between the two traditions in the midst of World War II. It was now November 25, 2009 and a very different world crisis was prevailing: the unquiet specters of capitalism – scarcity, fear, and instability – haunted the news cycle with the prospect of a second Great Depression and the potential collapse of the global banking system. The theme of the breakfast meeting was "Ethical Capitalism" and the presenters were Stephen Green, chair of the global bank HSBC and an ordained minister in the Church of England; Lord Levene, chair of Lloyds of London, former Lord Mayor of the City of London and a major figure in the British Jewish community; and Lord Paul Myners, the then Financial Services Secretary for the Labour government and aspirant theology student (earlier that year Lord Myners, a Methodist, declared that on retirement he intended to study theology). Like exorcists gathered at the bedside of the possessed, they put forth their remedies for the troubled souls of the financial markets and those that traded in them.

Immediately below this gathering, and timed to begin just after it finished, another group was assembling in a coffee shop on Brushfield Street. This one was made up of middle-aged Jewish, Christian, and Muslim leaders in clerical dress mingling with fresh-faced and frenetic young community organizers who were taking orders for coffee and relaying these to the baristas serving behind the counter. They were assembling for a press conference organized by London Citizens, a broad-based community organization whose banners and literature proclaim that it "reweaves civil society" and that it is "building powerful communities to work together for the common good." The focus of the press conference was the announcement of an "accountability assembly" that evening at the Barbican Theater in the heart of the City of London in which politicians and bankers would be questioned about the need for anti-usury measures and other proposals required to address how the financial crisis was affecting ordinary people.

The Barbican assembly marked the beginning of a campaign by London Citizens that was to lead up to the General Election in 2010 and called for a response by politicians and bankers to the proposals outlined that evening. The campaign, the global financial crisis it was a response to, and the subsequent impact that campaign had on all involved, is the context and backdrop of this book. However, the context and events depicted here serve to dramatize a much larger set of debates about the relationship between democratic citizenship, religious beliefs and practices, and the power of money. The power of money refers to money as both a frame of reference for imagining social and political relations and the agency of those who control the means of finance and credit. It is the relationship between faith, citizenship, and money that is a primary focus of this book.

What the events of November 25 illustrate is that we live in a time of economic and political turmoil when the efficacy of democracy in bringing accountability to financial markets and ruling elites is being tested. It is simultaneously a time when the relationship between different faiths and political life is under intense negotiation at a local, national, and international level throughout the world. It is my contention that community organizing provides a lens through which to constructively address these concerns and understand better the relationship between religious diversity, democratic citizenship, and economic and political accountability. Through examining the relationship between them the book tackles a core paradox that confronts the conceptualization of democracy in modern political thought: that is, how democratic citizenship is seen as an expression of individual liberty, but its performance and defense is in great measure dependent on participation in a group. Without being embedded in some form of association, the individual citizen is naked before the power of either the market or the state and lacks a vital means for his or her own self-cultivation. Yet at the same time, the market and the state can help to liberate the individual from communal overdetermination. The relationship between different religious traditions and democracy encapsulates the triadic tension between market, state, and community within which the individual is located. State and market processes are seen to limit, challenge, and provide alternatives to those derived from religious obligations and identities, yet in an increasingly deinstitutionalized and atomized society religions provide one of the few corporate forms of life available for mobilizing and sustaining the ability of individuals to act together in defense of their shared interests. However, political thinking at both the popular and academic levels tends to perceive the vibrant religious groups operating in the contemporary context as antidemocratic and reactionary. This book explores whether or not community organizing represents a paradoxical politics that draws on religious associations to renew democracy, democracy to strengthen religious associations, and religious beliefs and practices and democratic politics together to limit the power of market, state, and community over the individual. Central to any such exploration is a problem that ancient and modern political thought has wrestled with: that is, how to coordinate the at times conflicting obligations demanded by faithfulness to the polity and one's fellow citizens with faithfulness to God and one's fellow believers.

"Faith" is used here to denote both an identifiable habitus of belief and practice (whether explicitly "religious" or not) as well as a virtue that entails loyalty, reliability, commitment, and trustworthiness. Such qualities can appear foolish, but treachery as the opposite of faithfulness still carries a sulfurous stench even in the nostrils of those schooled by a hermeneutics of suspicion.[1] We can recover the vitality of faith as a political virtue when we understand that it implies attentiveness to a world we did not make, as well as to people we do not control, but with whom we must order our relationships, whether we like it or not. The ordering of social, economic, and political relationships must of necessity entail acts of faith as such acts are part of coming to know and participate in the world around us. As an orientation to attentiveness and reception – best characterized by a posture of listening – faith is the precursor of shared speech and action and therefore the coming into being of a common life. As a condition for the possibility of politics faith is orientated to the specific. We cannot keep faith with everyone all at once in every place. We can only be faithful to these people, in this place, at this time. Thus, to modern cosmopolitan ears, faithfulness provokes a scandal of particularity: it demands boundaries and limits. Part of the tragic nature of political life is that we have multiple loyalties and therefore conflicting obligations and interests that must be navigated and negotiated in the configuration of a common life. This book examines the inherent interplay of faith – in all its dimensions – and citizenship as mediated through a particular form of democratic politics: community organizing.

DEFINING CITIZENSHIP

The concerns outlined so far all intersect with the broader question of what constitutes democratic citizenship. In order to clarify how community organizing contests and extends contemporary understandings of citizenship we must delineate the different uses of citizenship as a term.[2] Its first and primary use is to denote a legal status with certain civil, political, and social rights as granted and distributed by the institutions of a national government whose sovereignty is derived from the citizens themselves. In contrast to the subjects of a monarch, who receive rights from the crown, democratic citizens receive rights from a government for, by, and with the people, which entails a claim about the popular nature of sovereignty and the self-derived nature of rights and laws. Distinctions between citizens and denizens, resident aliens, guest workers, foreigners, refugees, and a constellation of "others" mark the boundaries and scope of who does and who does not have the legal status of being a citizen. Intrinsic to these demarcations is the link between citizenship and place: citizenship as a legal status is inherently tied to a bounded territory. However, while citizenship and place are interconnected, the nation-state is not the only bounded territory within which citizenship is performed. Part of what is explored here is the way in which constructions of place other than the nation-state enable different ways of performing citizenship.

The second usage of the term citizenship refers to participation in a system for representing, communicating, and legitimating the relationship between governed and government. In large-scale nation-states this process of authorizing cannot be done by popular assembly, and so involves a system of representation. To be a citizen is to be designated as someone who can participate in these kinds of mechanisms, whether as a voter or a representative or both. Democratic citizenship demarcates who is authorized to govern and the processes by which their authority is legitimized.

Third, to be a citizen of a polity is to identify or be identified with an "imagined community."[3] Imagined communities generate a sense of identity and belonging and may be national but can be sub- or transnational in scale. As a political identity that co-inheres with an imagined community, citizenship is not just a legal term; it has an affective and subjective dimension that is the result of cultural processes. Key questions to be asked about this aspect of citizenship are: What does a citizen look like? And who counts as a "normal" member of the body politic? In relation to these questions, issues of belief, race, gender, class, physical ability, and sexuality come to the fore. The work of the social theorist Michel Foucault has been of particular importance in highlighting how citizenship is not just a legal status and part of a system for relating the governed and their government, but, as an identity, citizenship is also a regime of governance, culturally produced through a matrix of institutional and social practices.

Fourth, and closely aligned with citizenship as a form of identity, is how citizenship necessarily includes the performance of a vision of politics. In this guise, citizenship involves doing certain things. However, the performance of citizenship is not reducible to formal mechanisms of representation or involvement with the apparatus of the state. Rather, it entails a mesh of beliefs, narratives, practices, bodily proprieties, habits, and rituals reiterated and enacted in contexts as diverse as the workplace, social media, and the street, and which together constitute a "social imaginary" of what good and bad politics entail, and thus what the good citizen should do.[4]

Lastly, citizenship names a political and moral rationality through which a "common sense" is forged and reproduced: that is, it is a way of discerning goods in common and a vision of the good life through which "we, the people" come to decide on how to live. In relation to this denotation of citizenship, the question is how should citizens talk and deliberate together and on what basis can they make shared judgments about what to do and how to do it? This question directly relates to debates about "religion" and politics because the issue of whether religious speech and practices can constitute forms of public speech and practice is vehemently contested. The construction of citizenship involves an ongoing debate about what constitutes the requisite kinds of moral and political rationality that make one capable of talking and acting with others in ways that build up the common life of a polity.[5]

Community organizing of the kind London Citizens represents is primarily concerned with the construction of citizenship as an identity, a performance of democratic politics, and as a shared rationality. Citizenship in these registers is not about possessing a set of rights but about having the capacity and virtues necessary to relate to and act with others in diverse ways and settings. As a form of citizenship it can include those without legal status, notably the undocumented and refugees, who nevertheless assume responsibility for and contribute to the life together and commonwealth of where they live. How community organizing builds this capacity contrasts with other constructions of citizenship and contradicts many widely held assumptions about what good democratic citizenship involves. Part of what community organizing contests is the idea that the nation-state is the arena most fitting for the ways in which citizenship functions as an identity, performance, and shared rationality. It may well be the primary vehicle for citizenship as a legal status and system of representation – for now – but this does not mean we should collapse all other dimensions of citizenship into the vessel and category of the nation-state. As an identity, performance, and shared rationality, citizenship can be subnational, national, and transnational simultaneously. Union membership, Catholicism, and environmental activism are cases in point: they are means for enacting citizenship at registers above and below that of the nation-state. As the example of London Citizens illustrates, a focus on community organizing locates democratic citizenship at an alternative scale to that of the nation-state but within an ancient and modern nexus of the formation of citizenship: the city. Attention to community organizing also attends to the importance of civil society and workplaces to constructions of citizenship. A focus on the urban, civil society and work allows for the interplay of subnational, national, and transnational processes in the construction of citizenship to be observed and analyzed. In addition, it foregrounds the conditions and possibilities of individual and collective agency at the heart of the concept of democracy, the meaning of which is, after all, derived from the words *demos* (people) and *kratia* (ruling power).

DEMOCRACY, POPULISM, AND CONSOCIATIONALISM

In struggling to make sense of how broad-based community organizing constructs citizenship, "consociationalism" emerged as a framework consonant with community organizing. The initial assumption was that community organizing would best be located within a conceptuality that built on the thought of the political theorists Hannah Arendt and Sheldon Wolin as many leading organizers explicitly draw from their work. However, it became necessary to make sense of the populist roots of community organizing and the institutional form that organizing embodies. While some consider Arendt as having an "idiosyncratically populist notion of the People," a consociational account of democracy suggested itself as allowing for a stronger integration of all the different elements that constitute organizing as a form of politics.[6] The term consociation is defined here to mean a mutual fellowship between distinct institutions or groups who are federated together for a common purpose.

The consociationalist tradition of political thought has been largely eclipsed on both sides of the Atlantic but at the turn of the twentieth century it represented an important and vibrant stream of conversation that ran between North America and Europe.[7] The work of the German legal historian Otto von Gierke and his "discovery" of the seventeenth-century political thinker, Johannes Althusius, were important components in the European side of the conversation. As were political movements ranging from anarcho-syndicalists to Guild Socialists and Christian Democrats, all of whom aimed at restoring the "federal multiplicity" of political life and upholding the priority of social relations over economic and political ones. It was also a conversation that bridged "secular" and theological concerns as evidenced in the pluralism of the British theologian and historian of political thought John Neville Figgis and the "anarcho-federalism" of the Austrian Jewish philosopher Martin Buber. The "dean" of community organizing, Saul Alinsky, directly interacted with this conversation through his relationship with the Roman Catholic philosopher and political thinker Jacques Maritain, but he brought to it a distinctly American and populist perspective and experience.

It would be wrong to falsely corral thinkers as diverse as Buber, Figgis, and Maritain into a unified position. However, they can all be seen as part of a broad alternative tradition of consociational democratic thought to that which begins with some notion of a social contract as the basis of good political order. This alternative tradition is as equally cautious about the liberal state as it is about capitalist markets, seeing them as two sides of the same coin. Moreover, as a pathway in the development of modern political thought it was not anti-theological or inherently secularizing; rather, it was always inflected and interwoven with theological currents and points of reference. My own account of consociational democracy and of community organizing as a performance of citizenship should be seen as a restatement of this broad tradition. However, the kind of consociational democratic politics I claim community organizing embodies differs markedly from the standard uses of the term "consociational democracy" in political science and its application to countries like Switzerland or power-sharing arrangements in contexts like Bosnia-Herzegovina. The distinction between my own conception of consociational democracy and its more common usage, one that is largely derived from the work of political scientist Arend Lijphart, is set out in Chapter 7.

Part I identifies and depicts a consociational vision of democratic citizenship by observing and reflecting on the different strands of thought and practice that feed into and help constitute community organizing. Part II unpacks the implications of this vision for how we conceptualize and respond to the determining and interwoven spheres in which citizenship is enacted, namely, civil society, the sovereign nation-state, and the globalized economy. Being consociational in form and rationality and populist in its performance and identity, community organizing refuses simplistic dichotomies and oppositions between the state and the market. Neither does it envisage itself as in opposition to them. Rather, it seeks to stand amid the tensions and shifting sands produced by asking several questions at once. First, what does the state need in order to be a means of establishing the conditions of liberty without crushing a just and generous common life? Second, what do markets need so they can genuinely be a market and not become an overweening substitute for the state and thereby usurp political authority and commodify social existence in order to be crowned king? And third, how can the market and state serve and prioritize social existence while providing the disciplining forces of law, mobility, and innovation so that social practices themselves do not ossify into structures of oppression but feed into the formation of a just and generous common life?

POLITICS, THEOLOGY, AND THE ANTHROPOLOGY OF THE SECULAR

To make sense of the kind of event described at the outset and of a consociational vision of democratic citizenship, it is necessary to reconceptualize what we mean by the term "secular." The past decade has seen a massive shift in academic thinking about the nature of secularization. The so-called "secularization thesis" that processes of modernization result in the inevitable decline in the public significance and presence of religious beliefs and practices is now largely rejected. In its place a more nuanced account is emerging of how religious and nonreligious commitments and practices interact over time and thereby constitute particular formations of secularity. Constructions of the public sphere as secular are understood to be as much a creation of theological beliefs and practices as they are of anticlerical ideologies and modern processes such as industrialization.[8] As the anthropologist Talal Asad argues, the secular "should not be thought of as the space in which *real* human life gradually emancipates itself from the controlling power of 'religion' and thus achieves that latter's relocation."[9] If anything, secularization is itself a religious process.[10]

What is clear now is that constructions of secularity vary according to cultural, historical, and religious context and institutional domain. So the form secularity takes in healthcare is different from its outworking in prisons or the military; likewise, how it emerges and develops in Great Britain is different to its construction in the United States, China, or India.[11] Building on this new theoretical standpoint, this book moves beyond binaries that pose a necessary and inevitable opposition between the "religious" and the "secular." This is not to say that such binary constructions of the public sphere do not exist: France's regime of *laïcité* is an example of exactly this. Butin contrast to such oppositional and binary constructions, this book portrays a form of secularity constructed as a meeting point of diverse and complexly religious and nonreligious positions. It is a form where the tending of the commons on which the flourishing of all depends constitutes secularity as plural and open. In this kind of secularity, commonality amid difference and the reality of people having multiple loyalties and identities sets the course, rather than everyone being determined by either a "secular" or "religious" identity. On this kind of account, secularity is not a universal teleological process leading to a uniform historical outcome but an ongoing work subject to multiple iterations and formulations. Visions and experiences of secularity are historically contingent and vary according to context. Community organizing is assessed as one way of constructing a form of secularity, the creation of which is mediated through a specific kind of democratic politics and which produces a realm in which those of different faiths and identities forge a common life. The "faithful secularity" that certain kinds of democratic politics generates allows for the public recognition and interplay of the myriad obligations and commitments that citizens keep faith with (whether "transcendent" or "immanent") and which must be coordinated and negotiated in order to generate a common life.

There is a methodological analogue to the theoretical debates about the nature of secularity. Part of what is at stake in this book is an attempt to move beyond overly materialistic assumptions that dominate political theory and which inherently construe religious discourses as epiphenomenal and therefore marginal to understanding political life. The arguments developed here represent a form of what some call a "post-secular," "asecular," or "sociotheological" discourse, but which I call a "faithfully secular" one wherein religious beliefs and practices co-construct and are interwoven with other patterns of belief and practice so as to constitute a genuinely plural pattern of secularity that is open to multiple configurations of time and space. In a faithfully secular account theological forms of analysis stand side by side with other modes and contribute to the coloring and texture of the overall picture. This faithfully secular analysis is in keeping with developments in the contemporary study of "religion" and "secular" politics, which, once viewed as academically distinct areas of concern, are now seen as intertwined, both in theory and practice.[12] Jürgen Habermas is but one example of a contemporary philosopher who now recognizes the importance of religious categories for the development of generative political thought able to address central dilemmas of contemporary human existence. However, although "post-secular" philosophers often draw from theological ideas, they are not very interested in the lived experiences, practices, and communities of religious people.[13] And for all the recent emphasis on "practice," a similar inattention plagues many theologians writing about politics.[14] Inattention to the actual embodiment and performance of religious beliefs and practices is deeply problematic as it replicates an ideological marginalization of religion to the private, the internal, and the subjective and thereby replicates methodologically many of the false assumptions about the nature of religious belief and practice that underwrote the secularization thesis. My use of an ethnographic methodology and attention to theological discourses is an attempt to overcome the myopia about religious belief and practice that shapes much contemporary political thought (whether theological or not).[15]

The analysis developed here builds on prior work that distinguished between two interrelated and symbiotic forms of civic life: a hospitable politics and the politics of a common life.[16] A hospitable politics relates to those situations in which religious groups are the initiator and lead in generating shared action and a faithful form of secularity. The hospice and sanctuary movements are instances of a hospitable politics I have examined previously. By contrast, the politics of a common life occurs when no single tradition of belief and practice sets the terms and conditions of such shared speech and action, and the generation of a faithful and pluralistic pattern of secularity is a negotiated, multilateral endeavor.[17] Both a hospitable and a common life politics can constitute performances of democratic citizenship and faithful secularity. In this book the particular focus is on the conditions and possibilities of a common life politics and the role of religious groups in constituting it.

DECIPHERING ALINSKY AND LOCATING COMMUNITY ORGANIZING

Community organizing is not new. As a formal practice it emerged in Chicago in the 1930s and was brought to prominence and distilled into a distinct craft by Saul Alinsky [see Figure I.1], who founded the Industrial Areas Foundation (IAF) in 1940. The history of its emergence and development is told in Chapter 1. Since his death in 1972, and beyond the specific work of the IAF, Alinsky's legacy remains hugely significant for numerous strands of democratic activism. It is seen by many as a direct influence on not only the development of community organizing as a practice, but also on the civil rights, student, and antiwar activists of the 1960s and the organizers of the environmental movement, feminism, and consumer activism from the 1970s onward.[18] Since the foundation of the IAF in 1940, numerous other community organizing networks have

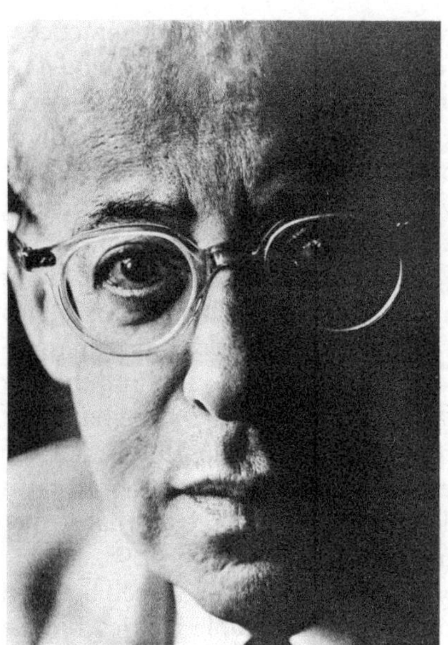

FIGURE I.1. Portrait of Saul Alinsky, 1968.

been founded. Those who initially worked for Alinsky established many of these. Among the most prominent are PICO (People Improving Communities through Organizing), DART (Direct Action Research and Training), the Center for Community Change, National People's Action, and the Gamaliel Foundation. At the time of writing, the IAF itself had sixty-three affiliate coalitions operating throughout the United States and in Canada, Britain, Australia, and Germany. Beyond the work of the IAF, a recent comprehensive survey of community organizing in the United States calculated that there are now 178 different coalitions involving 4,145 member institutions.[19]

In recent years, Alinsky came to renewed prominence in the 2008 U.S. presidential race and the election of Barack Obama. Obama not only began his political career as a community organizer in Chicago, but his highly innovative and successful election campaign drew on the ideas and practices of community organizing. Moreover, Obama ran against Hillary Clinton to win the Democratic nomination. Much was made both then and during her time as First Lady of her 1969 honors thesis written at Wellesley College, entitled "'There Is Only the Fight ...': An Analysis of the Alinsky Model." Clinton was allegedly offered a job by Alinsky but turned it down. After Obama's election, Alinsky and community organizing became the bête noire of right-wing commentators and Republican politicians who made repeated use of references to Alinsky's work to paint the new administration as subversive radicals bent on destroying American decency and democracy.

In response to the use of Alinsky as a bogeyman of the Right (and as a figure of historical curiosity to the Left), it is worth taking heed of Robert Bailey's comments, written in the early 1970s:

> Unfortunately the significance of the Alinsky approach to radicalizing the urban poor is obscured by the heated controversy surrounding the man. Most of those who have written about Alinsky agree that the Alinsky phenomenon has important implications for urban society and government. Yet there is not even consensus on whether the overall impact of the organizations is positive or negative. Part of the confusion stems from a lack of knowledge about Alinsky organizations and what they do.... [We] need to enhance public debate by providing reliable information about the Alinsky phenomenon.[20]

Echoing Bailey's sentiments, an aim of this book is to dig beneath the rhetorical deployment of Alinsky as a trope for socialism, Satanism, Marxism, and all that is wrong with a particular administration in order to understand something of Alinsky's actual political vision and the legacy of his work.

Beyond the North American context, the Alinsky approach to community organizing shaped many grassroots democratic efforts in diverse cultures. For example, the Reverend Herbert White helped set up community organizing in the Philippines, while Thomas Gaudette worked extensively in India.[21] Both worked directly with Alinsky. Currently, the Gamaliel Foundation operates in South Africa; PICO works in El Salvador, Guatemala, and Rwanda; and the European Community Organizing Network promotes community organizing in Central and Eastern Europe. Already mentioned are the IAF affiliates in Australia and Germany and there is a new organization being established in France. Although this book focuses on the work of London Citizens, it is situated in dialogue with affiliates in Australia and Germany and the historical legacy and continuing practice of the IAF in North America. In turn, the internationalization of the IAF's work provides a conduit for reflecting on transnational forms of grassroots and participatory democracy.

This book is the first to consider community organizing from an internationally comparative perspective and to locate it within debates about the possibilities of democratic citizenship under conditions of globalization. A key part of such an analysis is assessing how organizing is a response to and negotiates the context of "world cities" as sites for the production and convergence of processes of globalization. World cities are places of intense religious plurality, command points in the global economy, and centers of national political and civic administration. They are also key sites of democratic politics and the formation of new practices of citizenship.[22] The exploration of world cities as strategic places where questions about what it means to be faithful and what it means to be a citizen are intensely and creatively negotiated is the focus of Chapters 2 and 3. The particular case study through which this theme is examined is London and the work of London Citizens as an affiliate of the IAF.

What makes London so significant is the way it combines particular features of what it means to be a world city. Jerusalem is of far greater significance in the history and symbolism of Judaism, Christianity, and Islam; Los Angeles and Mumbai are greater centers of cultural production; and New York, Tokyo, Hong Kong, and Shanghai rival London as command points of global finance. However, it is how religious traditions, population, money, and cultural flows combine in London, along with the role of London as a regionally significant center of industry and academia and the national center of political, bureaucratic, and legal administration, that makes it both unique and a synecdoche through which to reflect on dynamics affecting the conditions and possibilities of political life within the contemporary context.[23] Moreover, attention to London highlights the contemporary interaction of "metropole" and "colony" in the formation of Western political life. For these spatial designations no longer mark mutually constitutive but geographically separated zones through which a carefully demarcated social imaginary can be articulated; instead, colonizing and colonial subject are now neighbors on the same street. And as a city rather than a nation, London creates a space for examining the consequences of globalization, repertoires of democratic citizenship, and the relationship between religious groups and politics from a perspective other than that of the nation-state. The urban perspective on faith and citizenship that London as a city provides is both an ancient one and one reopened and reconfigured by processes of globalization and the role of cities within them. So while this book is not about London, London is the soil out of which it grows.

DEBATING COMMUNITY ORGANIZING

The literature on community organizing relates primarily to the North American context. However, it is fair to say that, compared to other forms of political activism, community organizing remains an under-researched area. Alinsky was a controversial and widely known figure up to his death in 1972. But apart from the extensive journalistic coverage of his work, there were no systematic studies of the IAF or community organizing more generally.[24] Bailey, who produced the first detailed study of a particular community organization in 1974, noted that "Alinsky organizations are almost unmentioned in scholarly literature. During the past quarter of a century not a single article in the major political science or sociology journals has focused on the Alinsky phenomenon."[25] Thankfully the situation is somewhat better today. The existent writing on community organizing, much of it focused on the IAF, falls into seven overlapping and interwoven categories. Reviewing these will not only locate this book within wider fields of scholarship but also suggest why community organizing is a fecund and important topic to study.

First, there are those accounts of community organizing written by organizers themselves. These works attempt to describe the practices of and give a rationale for organizing. They are neither scholarly exposition nor "how-to" manuals, rather they seek to make accessible and inspire participation in the practice.[26] Foremost among these are Alinsky's two books: *Reveille for Radicals* (1946) and *Rules for Radicals* (1971). Following the example of Alinsky, later accounts make links to broader academic discussions of what ails U.S. politics and society and how community organizing represents part of the remedy. But the analysis is driven by stories and descriptions of actions that bring alive and make real the nature of organizing and its vision of how to change things for the better.[27] While they often discuss phases of organizing from earlier decades, all bar one of the accounts by organizers subsequent to Alinsky were published after 2000 and so are relatively recent.

Second are the biographical and historical accounts. Foremost among these is Sanford Horwitt's biography of Alinsky, which is written with an eye to how community organizing represents a response to a perceived decline in democratic participation and the professionalization of U.S. politics.[28] Published at a similar point in the late 1980s and early 1990s to Horwitt's biography of Alinsky were a number of historical studies that locate community organizing within the broader development in North America of social welfare provision, the alleviation of poverty, and the emergence of different forms of advocacy by and on behalf of the "have-nots."[29]

Third are those works focused on community organizing as representing a constructive response to the perceived crisis of U.S. cities and urban governance. For example, Bailey's 1974 analysis of Organization for a Better Austin in Chicago is written in the context of debates about the regeneration and redevelopment of U.S. cities in the face of deindustrialization, ghettoization, and "white flight." Bailey's work is the first in a series of accounts that sees in community organizing a vibrant although not unproblematic form of urban politics that is unusual in its ability to form cross-class and multiracial coalitions.[30] A parallel set of concerns among practitioners led to a debate that centered on the contrast between community development corporations, which were primarily focused on service provision and economic capacity building, and community organizing, the main focus of which was political action and generating the power, leadership, and strategies that would enable local people to change and improve their neighborhoods.[31]

Fourth are those that alight on community organizing in the context of the rightward drift of U.S. politics from the Reagan Administrations onward, its domination by professional lobbyists and corporate interests, and a perceived crisis in mainstream "progressive" politics. For these writers, community organizing is seen to provide lessons for remedying overly technocratic and elitist forms of progressive political activism.[32] This concern led to consideration of the use of religious discourses and the importance of churches in the repertoire of organizing as a form of democratic politics.[33] However, these accounts tended to reduce religion to an example of the need for progressive politics to recover an affective dimension and see "religion" as simply another cultural resource to be instrumentalized for political purposes.

The fifth category includes those scholars whose interest in community organizing is as a counter to the emergence of the religious right as the primary force connecting religious and political activism in the United States. The story of community organizing is seen to provide an alternative narrative to that which those on both "Left" and "Right" tell about the political potential of religion in U.S. politics. This body of work can also be located within the turn to civil society after the fall of the Berlin Wall in 1989 and broader debates about the importance of civil society for the health of democracy, renewed focus on the social dimensions of citizenship, and the recognition of religion as a resilient part of civil society. Seminal studies by the sociologists Mark Warren and Richard Wood emphasize how community organizers themselves generate theological reflection and outline the differential responses to involvement in community organizing within different kinds of congregations and denominations.[34] In a similar vein, the theologian Melissa Snarr gives an account of the Living Wage movement in the United States that draws attention to the vital role religious discourses, institutions, and actors play in helping to instigate and sustain such initiatives.[35]

This book builds on these prior studies; however, its focus is different from theirs. Snarr is particularly concerned with coalitions of "faith and labor," whereas Warren gives attention to the multiracial dynamics of IAF as a coalition and Wood examines the multidenominational and ecumenical aspects of organizing. By contrast, this book is primarily in conversation with a set of different theoretical frameworks, notably those of political theory, and is particularly concerned with the interfaith dynamics and the potential of organizing in contexts of intense religious diversity.[36] In the light of this focus, I will use the IAF's self-designation of their work as "broad-based community organizing" (BBCO) in order to specify and distinguish the primary subject of this study from other forms of community organizing.[37] Such a designation draws out the way in which the kind of community organizing focused on in this book can generate a common life not only across divisions of race, gender, sexuality, and class, but also among different faiths and between secular and nonreligious institutions.

Sixth is work that draws on BBCO to help illustrate and conceptualize a "post-liberal" account of democracy. A core concern is how BBCO constitutes a form of democratic politics that is open to religious discourses informing public deliberation about the good. Although a number of political theorists such as Michael Sandel have briefly pointed in the direction of BBCO as a sign of hope, it is Romand Coles and Jeffrey Stout who have given the most systematic consideration of BBCO within debates in political theory.[38] What distinguishes this book from those of Coles and Stout is that, for all the overlap on specifics, rather than let the practice and internal discourses of the IAF determine the theoretical framing, both Coles and Stout subordinate their understanding and framing of the IAF to a prior, theoretically established and superordinate conception of democracy. In Stout's case it is his particular conception of grassroots democracy and for Coles it is a particular conception of agonistic pluralism. By contrast, this book began with the experience of organizing and the theoretical resources already used by participants for framing and conceptualizing what they were doing. It was this beginning point that led to populism and a consociational account of democratic citizenship as primary points of reference.

Lastly there is an emerging literature that looks at the intersection of community organizing, institutional reform of public services, participatory democracy, and the renewal of "democratic professionalism."[39] The concern here is with the need to move beyond bureaucratic, technocratic, and faceless public services that only listen to credentialed experts and instead to create delivery agencies open to involving multiple stakeholders and sources of wisdom in their production and governance. If professions and their related institutions are about addressing shared problems – disease, ignorance, pollution, etc. – and realizing public goods – health, education, potable water, etc. – then it is vital that they actively involve those affected if they are to avoid becoming top-down schemes of social engineering. With this concern in mind, community organizing can be understood as contributing to democracy as a form of collective problem solving.[40] Conversely, this concern entails reforming professions such as medicine or education, and the institutions that sustain them over time, such as schools or hospitals, so that they can enhance the resilience and capacity of democratic politics and the public life where they are located.[41] Community organizing is seen as having something to contribute to the cultural and organizational change required to reorient professionals beyond, on the one hand, the pursuit of money, status, and power, and on the other hand, the reduction of their work to compliance with managerially and economically determined targets and performance indicators. It provides also a means of mediating relationships with a wider community of stakeholders, each of which has an interest in the construction, delivery, and governance of the service in question. Education and health are the primary areas of work in this category.[42] We can also add in here studies of attempts to reenergize trade unions through drawing from and linking up with community organizing in order to connect unions to place-based constituencies and to the union movements' own traditions of relational politics.[43] This concern with the co-governance and co-production of public services, democracy as a means of solving collective problems, and the democratic potential of professions can be nested within a broader commitment to revivifying the theory and practices of economic, participatory, and citizen-centered democracy.[44]

This book shares and synthesizes many of the concerns that motivated the scholarship surveyed here. Although they take specific form in the context of North America, concerns about the increasingly elitist and technocratic nature of politics and welfare professionals; the capture of policy by a narrow range of corporate and financial interests; the atrophying of civic and democratic participation; the governance and economic development of cities; the production and delivery of good-quality education, health, and welfare services in impoverished neighborhoods; and the negotiation of religious and ethnic diversity, particularly as this relates to the use of religious beliefs and practices in public life, are shared by all Western polities. This book extends and develops the work of each of the categories outlined and like them uses community organizing as a way to explore such concerns and their remediation. What is distinctive about the present volume is its focus on the conditions and possibilities of democratic citizenship within processes of globalization, its internationally comparative perspective, the use of a non-U.S. case study, and an emphasis on how organizing constitutes a form of interfaith relations. The book contributes also to emerging debates about the co-governance and co-production of social welfare, not only in the West, but also in response to the need for health, education, and other forms of service provision and poverty alleviation initiatives to reckon with the interconnections between the "Global South" and "the West." The rationale for attending to community organizing is that it is a point of convergence for democratic citizenship, the production of public services, urban and economic governance, and the interaction of the beliefs and practices of religious communities with processes of modernization.

CHAPTER SUMMARY

The structure of the book mirrors the research process undertaken to write it. It begins with a historical and ethnographic description and analysis that immerses the reader in the practice of community organizing. This is necessary in order to depict and thereby make comprehensible and plausible the subsequent theoretical claims. Methodologically, the ethnographic analysis of community organizing developed in Part I is necessary for identifying the categories and concepts at work in its historical and contemporary manifestations. These categories and concepts are then drawn on and expanded in Part II so as to develop a broader account of: first, the conditions and possibilities for a consociational, faithfully secular, and populist form of democratic politics in the interlocking spheres of civil society, the sovereign state, and the globalized economy; and second, the interplay between religious beliefs and practices and a consociational vision of democratic citizenship in limiting the power of money over our common life in each of these spheres. The structure of Part II mirrors a broader underlying argument that in the contemporary context it is not the sovereign nation-state that is the determinative context of political judgments but the globalized economy.

Chapter 1 examines the key traditions and historical contexts out of which community organizing emerged and which directly shaped its practice and political vision. Alongside the influence of the Shtetl Movement, the Chicago School of urban sociology, the labor movement, organized crime, Christian Democracy, and a broadly Aristotelian conception of politics in the formation of organizing, particular attention is given to the relationship between community organizing and the history of American populism. This first chapter gives the historical backdrop to the subsequent discussion and analysis of organizing. Chapter 2 locates the work of London Citizens within the context of London as a world city. Key themes of the book as a whole are interwoven so as to unfold a depiction of the complex, symbiotic relationships and global flows that are refracted through faith, democratic politics, and political economy in London. Mirroring the context, theology, social theory, and philosophical discourses are deliberately interlaced and shown to interpenetrate each other in order to generate an analysis that captures more richly something of the reality described. Chapter 3 is an examination of how community organizing as a constellation of democratic practices mediates the relationship between different religious traditions and democratic politics and reframes interfaith relations as a civic practice. Whereas the early chapters set out something of the history and traditions that have shaped community organizing and the urban, political, and religious context of London Citizens's work, Chapters 4 and 5 give an account of what community organizing actually involves as a performance of democratic citizenship. They develop an anatomy of organizing as a form of political action by focusing on how one particular campaign was developed and executed. Particular attention is given to how the various elements of organizing relate and interact with each other.

Part II shifts to a more theoretically focused mode of analysis. It opens with Chapter 6, which assesses how BBCO, as a craft, generates political judgments based on a "wily wisdom" through forging a sense of a common world of meaning and action between diverse traditions in a particular place. It then locates BBCO within broader debates about the nature of civil society in order to investigate the claim by London Citizens that they "reweave civil society." In doing so, a constructive reconceptualization of civil society as a "body politic" is developed. Building on this, Chapter 7 locates community organizing within debates about the nature and form of sovereignty in order to substantiate the thesis that BBCO is best understood as an embodiment of consociational democracy. Chapter 8 examines how a consociational vision of democratic citizenship is undergirded by a relational view of power and by patterns of gift exchange and mutuality. This is contrasted with more contractual conceptions of citizenship that emphasize patterns of sociality characterized by equivalent exchange. The chapter argues that, in the contemporary context, in relation to the vexed question of whether democratic citizenship can challenge the power of money in shaping our common life, it is gift-based visions of citizenship that need to be to the fore. To understand why this is the case and to draw out how liberal conceptions of social contract and rights are inadequate as the sole basis for conceptualizing democratic citizenship, the chapter assesses the relationship between debt and citizenship and why social relations characterized by gift and mutuality are vital to challenging the prioritization of profit over any other consideration.

The conclusion assesses the strengths and weaknesses of community organizing. Added to this, emerging developments within community organizing networks are pointed to as indicative of constructive future possibilities for "resurrecting" democratic politics, particularly the engagement with the health and education sectors, the forms of co-governance and co-production of public services BBCO can help enact, and the ways in which organizing can link to professional identities as forms of democratic agency. A point of further analysis is the efforts to take the lessons of community organizing and apply them directly to a national political party. Overall, the conclusion explores how insights generated from the ethnographic analysis of BBCO developed throughout the book may contribute to a post-social democratic and post-neoliberal vision of democracy.

PART I

I

The Origins of Organizing

An Intellectual History

We begin by excavating the philosophical and historical origins of community organizing. Giving this chapter the subtitle "an intellectual history" is something of a conceit, as community organizing is a set of practices rather than ideas. Nevertheless, the different sections of this chapter identify and discuss the key traditions out of which community organizing emerged and which directly shaped its practice and political vision. These traditions are populism, Judaism, the labor movement, and Christianity, with crucial insights being formulated through interaction with urban sociology, organized crime, Communism, and later, a broadly Aristotelian conception of politics. It was not just a relationship with different traditions of belief and practice that was important, but also how these traditions interacted with each other in a particular context: that of modern urban life and the processes of industrialization and deindustrialization that shaped it. The central character in this history is the figure of Saul Alinsky [Figure 1.1]. The main thesis is that Alinsky's approach to community organizing represents one of the most important forms of contemporary democratic politics available for two reasons. The first is that it addresses a primary problem apparent in most other forms of political mobilization and political theory; that is, it prioritizes social relationships and refuses to subordinate these relations to political or economic imperatives. The second is it constitutes a means of enabling ruled and rulers to arrive at political judgments together.

JUDAISM, THE SHTETL TRADITION OF COMMUNAL SELF-ORGANIZATION, AND POPULAR RELIGION

Born in 1909, Alinsky was a child of Russian Jewish immigrants and lived within a close-knit Jewish community in Chicago that had its origins in the Shtetl traditions of Eastern Europe. Central to the pattern of life in the Maxwell Street area where Alinsky grew up were traditions of self-organization and mutual

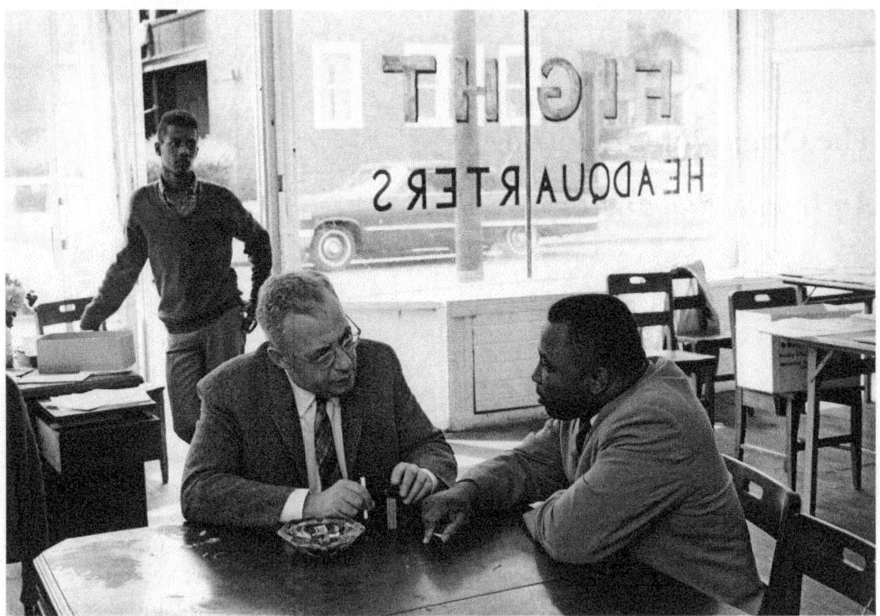

FIGURE 1.1. Alinsky at the FIGHT (Freedom, Integration, God, Honor, Today) offices in Rochester, NY, c. 1966.

care.[1] Given the history of state-directed pogroms and persecution experienced by the Jews who settled in this area, the first point of reference was to look not to the government to solve one's problems but to one's own community. Moreover, social and, crucially, commercial relations were subordinated to a ritual calendar, a set of customary practices, and religious injunctions that determined what was to be done, when, and in what order. The family, not the individual, was the basic unit of society and families were located within a series of interlinked institutions whose very development speaks of a set of clear communal priorities. The first Jewish institution in Chicago was the Jewish Burial Ground Society formed in 1845, followed by the first congregation that met above a shop in 1847, its first school in 1850, and the creation, in 1851, of both the Hebrew Benevolent Society to aid the sick and provide for burials and the building of the first synagogue.[2] Then they began to build institutions to help their Jewish neighbors, notably the B'nai B'rith lodges, the first one of which was established in 1857. Numerous other institutions followed. Alinsky was part of the last generation to grow up within this environment. By the time he left college, it had all but disappeared as the Jews of Chicago moved from "the shtetl to the suburbs." But, in its development and as Alinsky experienced it, we see exemplified the ancient pattern of Jewish diasporic existence as set out in Jeremiah 29:4–7:

Thus says the Lord of hosts, the God of Israel, to all the exiles whom I have sent into exile from Jerusalem to Babylon: Build houses and live in them; plant gardens and eat what they produce. Take wives and have sons and daughters; take wives for your sons, and give your daughters in marriage, that they may bear sons and daughters; multiply there, and do not decrease. But seek the welfare of the city where I have sent you into exile, and pray to the Lord on its behalf, for in its welfare you will find your welfare.

The Biblical reference is wholly appropriate, for not only is Chicago's Jewish context central to the formation of Alinsky's political vision, but his very mode of articulating that vision also draws from Biblical genres – notably universal rules embedded within highly contextual narratives, as exemplified in Exodus – and the rabbinic mode of debating Scripture: fiercely and with sharp contradiction of one's opponent. Indeed, organizing can be seen to embody a form of *Mahloket* or "controversy" that involves well-managed, creative conflict and debate. For Alinsky it was Judaism that constituted the beliefs and practices that helped form him. As will be discussed in Chapters 2 and 3, community organizing continues to have a symbiotic relationship with religious beliefs and practices, in particular those of Christianity.

Alinsky's experience of Jewish communal self-organization directly contrasted with the primary mode of neighborhood organization that developed from 1900 to 1930: that of the settlement houses. Inspired by Toynbee Hall in East London, settlement houses were founded in New York and other cities from 1886 onward. Most famous of all was Jane Addams' Hull House. Founded in Chicago in 1889, it continued long into the twentieth century but now is only extant as a museum. As in the London settlements, organizers were college educated and upper-middle class young men and women who provided various social and welfare resources such as athletic programs, neighborhood vegetable gardens, nurseries, laundry facilities, employment assistance, and legal aid in poor working-class neighborhoods. What they did not do was directly address structural political and economic problems. However, it is important to note this is not true of Addams and Hull House, something Alinsky explicitly acknowledged.[3] Through her work at Hull House, her political philosophy, social ethics, and role as public intellectual, Addams had much to say on political and economic matters.[4]

Alinsky shared with Addams two key assumptions about how to address poverty.[5] First, in contradiction to a European sociological conception of community as exemplified in the work of Ferdinand Tönnies, Alinsky and Addams did not see "community" as a static or inherited social formation that was subject to inevitable dissolution through processes of modernization. Rather, for Alinsky and Addams, a community was an ongoing project of social and symbolic interaction through which people form meaningful relationships with each other and develop a collective sense of identity and place. Second, poverty was not the result of individual pathologies; instead, it was produced through broader social and structural processes. Addressing poverty demanded tackling the environmental conditions that catalyzed and reinforced individual and communally self-destructive behaviors.[6]

Addams's involvement in helping establish a number of unions in Chicago, particularly in the textile industry, exemplifies her approach. She was a keen advocate both of union organizing and labor legislation, seeing both as necessary elements of a strong democracy.[7] In relation to the development of community organizing, Addams can be seen as contributing to a practice of organizing parallel to but distinct from that which Alinsky represents: the emergence of the civil rights movement. Addams was directly influential on Myles Horton, who established the Highlander Folk School, a crucial catalyst in the formation of the early civil rights movement and the subsequent training of organizers involved in both the Southern Christian Leadership Conference (SCLC) and the Student Nonviolent Coordinating Committee (SNCC). It was the Highlander Folk School where figures such as Rosa Parks were trained and which provided a platform for Septima Clark to develop her distinctive approach to citizenship education and local organizing.[8] Horton was mentored early on by Jane Addams while, like Alinsky, he was studying at the University of Chicago with Robert Park in the 1930s.[9]

In most settlement houses the social-welfare style of neighborhood organizing remained elitist, and, despite their ideals, they were top-down initiatives that tended to reinforce class divisions and ignore existing modes of mutual association and leadership.[10] In his seminal urban ethnography, the research for which was undertaken during the 1930s, William Foote Whyte notes:

> The [settlement] workers had no systematic knowledge of the social backgrounds of the people in their Italian homeland. Furthermore, they made little effort to get to know the local social organization except as it came to them through the doors of their institutions.... [T]he settlement was an alien institution, nevertheless the community was expected to adapt itself to the standards of the settlement house. Some people made this adaptation; most people did not.[11]

Whyte goes on to note: "The primary function of the settlement house is to stimulate social mobility, to hold out middle class standards and middle class rewards to lower-class people."[12] Whyte's work was done in Boston. Yet Robert Slayton's local history of the Back of the Yards neighborhood, where Alinsky first developed community organizing, comes to a parallel judgment on the University of Chicago Settlement House that was set up there. Slayton identifies the dense networks of mutual aid and associational life that developed in that neighborhood, and contrasts this with the settlement house, which struggled to embed itself within the community and paled in significance when compared to the role of the churches and ethnic associations.[13] Robert Fisher identifies the response of those the settlements aimed to help: "Instead of relying on settlements organized by upper-class outsiders, neighbourhood residents preferred to use their own churches, synagogues, mutual benefit associations, and ethnic, labor, and political organizations, not to mention informal networks of support, to advance their collective and personal interests."[14] In other words, most settlement workers were self-proclaimed leaders without any followers who nevertheless insisted they knew better how other people should live. In contrast, Alinsky grew up within an urban environment organized by religion where there were clear leaders and followers and the kinds of communal self-help that Fisher identifies as central to how poor families could make life better.[15] It is worth noting that this same conflict between the "progressive" liberal values and methods of external, "expert" welfare professionals and "conservative" communal and often religious self-organization is still a feature of contemporary urban social service provision.[16]

Admittedly, there were efforts in the provision of welfare to incorporate more democratic elements. Notable among these was the setting up of councils of social agencies for unified fund-raising and social planning efforts. By 1926 there were neighborhood councils in Milwaukee, Pittsburgh, Chicago, Boston, St. Louis, Los Angeles, Detroit, Cincinnati, Columbus, and New York. Such efforts involved organizing cooperative planning and consultation to ensure services were responsive to real needs and accountable to the population served, as well as organizing education about broader issues affecting a community. Early figures in the development of social work such as Bessie McClenahan and Eduard Lindeman were deeply concerned about the ability of communities to engage in democratic decision making and saw the role of the social worker as that of an organizer encouraging a community to recognize and solve its own problems.[17] However, as the historian Roy Lubove argues, the intensive concern with the machinery and financing of social welfare

> diverted attention from co-operative democracy and the creative group life of the ordinary citizen to problems of agency administration and service. It substituted the bureaucratic goal of efficiency through expert leadership to what had been a quest for democratic self-determination through joint efforts of citizen and specialist. Community organization had barely emerged as a cause before it had become a function absorbed into the administrative structure of social work.[18]

As will be seen, this was a recurrent problem in the history of community organizing that was not resolved until the social service provision elements were separated from the cooperative democratic and civic renewal aspects of organizing.

URBAN ETHNOGRAPHY AND ORGANIZED CRIME

Chronologically, the second key influence on Alinsky came in the form not of a tradition but of a method: that of ethnographic observation. Alinsky learned this method by studying another form of hierarchal, communal self-organization that was independent of the state: organized crime. Alinsky was trained in the Chicago school of sociology as it was developing in the 1920s and 1930s under the guidance of Robert Park and Ernest Burgess, two of the founders of urban sociology and, in particular, the emerging method of urban ethnography. Alinsky first encountered their work as an undergraduate when he took one of Burgess's courses.[19] Park and Burgess encouraged an eclectic approach and resisted over-rigid theories. Their focus was more empirical, being concerned with how to find appropriate ways of mapping and describing the urban situation and the social processes and transformations at work within the city. Where it did have a commitment, it was implicit and drew on the view most clearly articulated by the American philosopher George Herbert Mead in *Mind, Self, and Society* (1934).[20] The philosophy was pragmatist and anti-positivistic and its basic anthropology can be characterized as communitarian: "Each person becomes human through interaction with others. Institutional patterns are learned in communities dependent on shared language and symbols."[21] Influenced by Mead and John Dewey, it was an approach that viewed social science as having a special responsibility "to help create democratic decision making and political action, especially in the city."[22]

Park and Burgess encouraged intensive local studies of what they called "natural areas" or neighborhoods that encompassed particular cultures and lifestyles within which meaningful social identities and structures were forged.[23] The Back of the Yards where Alinsky set up his first community organization was identified as just such a "natural area."[24] The natural areas were then situated within a wider picture of the city as an "urban ecology" within which the areas were integrated and linked. Having studied organized crime for two years, in particular Al Capone's operation, Alinsky abandoned his doctoral dissertation in criminology to work for Clifford Shaw at the Institute for Juvenile Research, established by Shaw in 1926. This involved further study of criminal gangs, this time of teenage Italian gangs on the West Side of Chicago. Then in 1933 he worked as a staff sociologist at the state prison in Joliet, but returned to work with Shaw at the Institute in 1936.

Alinsky says of his time studying organized crime, "I learned, among other things, the terrific importance of personal relationships."[25] This was something that became a central feature of his political vision. For Alinsky, organized crime represented a form of community organizing. As he put it, only half jokingly: "I came to see the Capone gang as a huge quasi-public utility servicing the population of Chicago."[26] The stories he tells of how he first gained entry into the circles of both the Capone gang and the teenage gangs he studied illustrate the importance of building trust and relationships when working with the gangs. Trust and strong relationships, in addition to the threat of violence, are crucial to maintaining the effective management and power of any organized criminal group who necessarily operate outside the law and avoid transparent, accountable procedures. In his work in Back of the Yards, Alinsky sought to use the same emphasis on trust and relationship in organizing the poor to resist the power of organized crime, substituting the threat of violence with the threat of nonviolent means of exerting pressure, means he elaborates on extensively in his writings.

Arguably, Alinsky drew directly from his experiences working for Shaw's Chicago Area Project (CAP). Steven Bubacz, lead organizer from 1935 onward of the initial CAP project based in Russell Square, described the Russell Square Community Committee – the first of CAP's community organizations – as nothing less than a "vigilante organization." In addition to its youth club, its "vigilante" activities consisted of a wide variety of communally organized programs to address issues such as minors entering taverns, stopping the fencing of stolen goods, and neighborhood improvement schemes. These were aimed at reducing criminality, directing gangs into more productive activities, and developing a sense of pride in and responsibility for the neighborhood.[27] Alinsky discerned that for those without power and who cannot deploy either the resources of the state or the power of money to achieve their ends, relational power is the only means available through which they can act. To be effective – that is, for association to generate power – it demands the kinds of discipline and loyalty (or faithfulness) that Alinsky saw at work in the mafia. Faithfulness is vital for developing any kind of common life, whether civic or religious. Without it, trust cannot develop, promises are broken, commitments are not kept, and so the possibility of long-term reciprocal relations is dissolved. In short, faithfulness and relational power are inextricably linked.

Alongside organized crime, the other great model of community organizing based on loyalty, turnout, pragmatism, and personal relationship that Alinsky encountered was that of the urban political boss and the machine politics of the Chicago Democratic Party. Nowhere does he cite it as a direct influence, and ward captains and bosses were a frequent target for attack, but with his keen eye for how organizations work, Alinsky cannot have failed to take note of how the Party machine operated. Central to ward politics was loyalty and reciprocity: the Boss helps you and you help the Boss and together, through coordinated, disciplined action, you achieve the aims of the organization.[28] However, like the illegal capitalist corporations of organized crime, the ward bosses had no interest in either contesting the power structure, generating political opposition to the owners of the factories that dominated the living conditions of everyone in the area, or promoting unity between their own neighborhood's different ethnic enclaves.[29] Instead, they were clientalistic rather than participatory and preferred to preserve the status quo rather than transform it.

As part of his research, both for his doctoral dissertation and for Shaw, Alinsky engaged in the long-term study of criminal gangs, triangulating these observations to develop a detailed picture of the locality in which the gang operated. As with other "Chicago school" researchers shaped by Park and Burgess, Alinsky was actively encouraged to live in the area being studied, walk the streets, and include these autobiographical dimensions as part of the data collection.[30] The training Alinsky offered his early organizers such as Edward Chambers, Richard Harmon, and Nicholas von Hoffman was basically a version of the urban ethnographic method, as is evidenced from the extraordinarily detailed reports they produced for the Catholic Archdiocese of Chicago.

Alinsky required regular detailed reports from his field staff and insisted that they read a wide range of books in order to develop broader frames of reference. What urban ethnography gave to organizing was the importance of developing first hand, local knowledge through sustained attention to the people of a community while simultaneously developing broader accounts of the relationships and social transformations at work within those places.[31]

THE CHICAGO AREAS PROJECT AND THE BEGINNINGS OF NEIGHBORHOOD ORGANIZING

It was through working with Shaw that Alinsky developed a key insight that formed the basis of the Back of the Yards initiative. Shaw developed what is now called a "social disorganization theory" through his long-term observations of juvenile delinquents.[32] A key part of his work was examining the consequences of a community's inability to solve its own problems. He contrasted his own experience of growing up on a rural Indiana farm with that of the urban situation. He frequently recounted how as a child he stole stove bolts from a blacksmith and was caught, shaken upside down by the heels until all the bolts fell to the ground, and then helped by the same blacksmith to repair the toy wagon he had stolen the bolts for in the first place.[33] For Shaw the incident illustrated the role of community self-policing and intervention that was often absent in urban neighborhoods.[34] Shaw can be seen as a "missionary" and "agrarian conservative" who was "zealously hoping to kindle a popular return to hamlets and ethical humanism within the confines of the city."[35] In this concern, Shaw echoes other early developers of social work who, in the words of one such initiative, sought to restore "the advantages of village life to city people."[36] For Shaw, community organizing was a way to save the American city from its own self-generating forces of social disintegration.[37]

Shaw and his colleague Henry McKay argued that delinquency was not an individual issue, but a normal response to abnormal conditions.[38] If a community is not self-policing but imperfectly policed by outside agencies, some individuals will exercise unrestricted freedom to express their dispositions and desires, often resulting in delinquent behavior as young people seek alternative ways to meet their social and material needs. A key need was for recognition and respect, which, if not given by adults and those in authority, would be sought among peers and through delinquent behavior.[39] Alinsky's assessment of the Italian teenaged gangs he studied directly echoes this analysis.[40] Only by organizing itself could a community contain criminal action and provide viable institutional means by which to meet real needs. Crucial here was reconnecting young people to families and institutions that could "house" them instead of leaving them to form surrogate families in gangs. Ethnic diversity, lack of communication between different groups, and differences between first- and second-generation immigrants within the same family all exacerbated the problem of disorganization and so allowed greater scope for delinquent behavior. On this account, crime was correlated with poverty because poor people were disorganized.[41] But this did not mean that the urban poor lacked their own institutions and potential leaders; rather, they were often disconnected from or antagonistic toward each other, lacked direction, or were narrow or fragmented in focus. To organize them first required disorganizing them so that they could work together in pursuit of a common life instead of working against each other and their own best interests.[42]

The Back of the Yards Neighborhood Council (BYNC) began in 1935 as an initiative of CAP, which was set up by Shaw in 1934 to address juvenile delinquency. At its inception, CAP, which is still going, had a number of aims.[43] These included the following:

> (2) the area project stresses the autonomy of the actual residents of the neighborhood in planning and operating the program and contrasts this with the traditional organizations in which control is vested in the lay and professional persons who reside in or represent the interests of the more privileged communities; (3) the area project places great emphasis upon the training and utilization of neighborhood leaders and contrasts this with the general practice in which dependence is largely placed upon professionally trained leaders recruited from sources outside of the local neighborhood; (4) the area project seeks to utilize to the maximum established neighborhood institutions, particularly such natural social groupings as churches, societies, and clubs, rather than to create new institutions which embody the morale and sentiments of the more conventional communities; (5) the activities program in the area project is regarded primarily as a device for enlisting the active participation of local residents in a constructive community enterprise and creating and crystallizing neighborhood sentiment with regard to the task of promoting the welfare of children and the social and physical improvement of the community as a whole.[44]

Along with its self-organizing ethos went an emphasis on self-financing. CAP projects raised much of their money from and through local people.[45] The BYNC held its first formal meeting on July 14, 1939 and was attended by 350 people representing 76 institutions.[46] BYNC was in effect a forum where people could come together for common purposes.[47]

Although it had antecedents, notably the short-lived but influential Cincinnati Social Unit experiment (1918–20) and the Social Center Movement (1907–30), it was Shaw and the Chicago Areas Project that systematically developed key elements of what came to be Alinsky's analysis and approach.[48] But the differences between Alinsky and Shaw are also highly significant.[49]

Alinsky discerned the essential flaw in Shaw's approach to community organizing. While alert to the reality of how the people and land were subordinated to the demands of business and industry, Shaw's approach to neighborhood organizing did not address structural dynamics. Instead, the interpretation of the causes of delinquency stayed at the communal level and tended to ignore the economic and political sources of delinquency arising outside of the community, thereby leaving business and industry immune from any responsibility.[50]

This helps explain why Alinsky is so dismissive of his time with Shaw. He states:

Finally, I quit Joliet and took a job with the Institute for Juvenile Research, one of those outfits that were always studying the causes of juvenile delinquency, making surveys of all the kids in coldwater tenements with rats nibbling their toes and nothing to eat – and then discovering the solution: camping trips and some shit they called character building.[51]

In the CAP organizations, organization itself was "the dominant goal and the dominant good."[52] In effect, CAP organizations were apolitical and lacked any engagement with or analysis of power. Instead, following Park and Burgess, Shaw's analysis was governed by an ecological paradigm that envisaged urban development as a natural process; this rendered the creation of cheap labor, slum housing, and social disorganization inevitable.[53] It assumed that the expansion and prosperity of industry took ultimate precedence over the social flourishing of the people it affected.[54] Alinsky refused to see these outcomes as a result of a "natural" or inevitable process of evolution. For Alinsky, the haves were responsible for the immiseration of the have-nots and needed to be held personally accountable for their actions. After falling out with Shaw and frustrated with CAP's wholly social and apolitical focus, Alinsky set up the Industrial Areas Foundation (IAF) in 1940 to continue the work in the BYNC independently of CAP.

Alinsky learned much from Shaw's approach, but in order to learn political organizing and gain an understanding of and address directly the economic processes creating social disorganization, he turned to the labor movement.

LABOR ORGANIZING: COMMUNIST AND DEMOCRATIC

While working for Shaw, Alinsky began volunteering as an organizer with the Congress of Industrial Organizations (CIO), which was active in the Back of the Yards area.[55] This was a time of intense union activity and tumultuous and often violent labor relations. The origins of the labor movement lay in the craft unions that dated from the 1790s onward. The first recorded strike is said to have occurred in 1763 in Charleston, South Carolina, although earlier agrarian and urban rebellions against proprietary and royal restrictions on liberties and chartered monopolies can be seen as part of the early history of both the labor and populist movements in America.[56] To this archeology of resistance should be added the opposition and outright revolts by slaves; for example, in New York (1712) and Stono, South Carolina (1739). It was with the development of industrial manufacturing that a self-conscious labor movement emerged. The formation of the Mechanics' Union of Trade Associations in 1827 and the Workmen's Party in 1828 in Philadelphia are key moments in its inception.[57]

As in Judaism, and in its early history, the labor movement was built on inherited practices and the values of reciprocity, mutuality, and cooperation.

These values were central to building self-organized institutions that gave primacy to social relationships over and against the demands of the market and the state. We overhear such sentiments expressed in Abraham Lincoln's 1861 address to Congress: "Labor is prior to, and independent of, capital. Capital is only the fruit of labor and could never have existed if labor had not first existed. Labor is the superior of capital, and deserves much the higher consideration."[58] Unionization enjoyed high points in the 1830s, 1880s (with the rise and demise of the Knights of Labor), and during World War I; by the early 1930s, however, union membership was low.[59] Through the passing of the National Labor Relations (Wagner) Act in 1935, which guaranteed the right of employees to organize or join a union, followed by a series of other legislative measures in support of fair working conditions, space was created for a renewed effort in unionization.[60] From fewer than three million members in 1933, union membership rose to more than ten million by 1941.[61] A vital factor in union growth was the CIO's move away from the existing craft union approach of the American Federation of Labor (AFL) in order to develop industrial unions that included mass production workers in the auto, steel, and rubber industries. Although preparations had been going on since 1935, the first CIO convention was held in 1938, so Alinsky encountered the CIO at its foundation. It was through collaborating with the union organizers that Alinsky learned how to organize large assemblies, focus attention on the issues that were of central concern to the people living in an area, raise money, and recruit members.[62] Through this he came to know John L. Lewis, head of the CIO, from whom he learned a great deal in terms of the tactics and strategies of political organizing.[63]

Alinsky interacted with two distinct groups within the unions, both of which taught him the techniques of organizing. Arguably the most effective organizers at the time were the communists. Alinsky seems to have learned many of his militant, confrontational tactics from the communist organizers he met when volunteering for the CIO, mirroring their tactics in his own work but without adopting their ideology or party structure.[64] However, the group Alinsky identified with most closely was the non-statist democratic left. The democratic left found a distinctive voice in the life and work of the writer Upton Sinclair, whose 1906 novel, *The Jungle*, was famously set in the Back of the Yards neighborhood. Like Clifford Shaw's theory, Sinclair's novel also has an ecological metaphor, only his jungle is not natural; rather, it is a man-made inferno where nature is completely inverted. Unlike the sociology of Shaw, Sinclair's social-realist novel portrays the relationship between capitalism, political corruption, and social disorganization and how this produces crime and family breakdown. The industrial processing of food in the Chicago meatpacking industry serves as an analogy for what happens to social relationships under conditions of unfettered laissez-faire capitalism. In the novel, Sinclair presents union organizing as the road to both personal and social redemption for its central character Jurgis Rudkus. The basic tenets of its political vision are captured in John L. Lewis's 1937 "Labor and Nation" speech, which set out the rationale for the CIO:

> The workers of the nation were tired of waiting for corporate industry to right their economic wrongs, to alleviate their social agony and to grant them their political rights. Despairing of fair treatment, they resolved to do something for themselves. They, therefore, have organized a new labor movement, conceived within the principles of the national bill of rights and committed to the proposition that the workers are free to assemble in their own forums, voice their own grievances, declare their own hopes and contract on even terms with modern industry for the sale of their only material possession – their labor.[65]

Lewis, while seen as a radical and even accused of being a communist, saw labor organizing as the "middle way." For Lewis, the triumph of the Wall Street financial elite over ordinary workers (in other words, the subordination of workers' interests to financial interest) would lead to an industrial revolt that would result in either Communism or Fascism. It was on this basis that he argued for union support of the New Deal during the Great Depression. Lewis stated:

> If I may speak as a prophet, I … say that full organization on the part of free labor, with the free right to enter into collective agreements with employers, is bound to come sooner or later, if the economic system, as we know it, is to endure … Labor cannot, and will not, and should not ever be content until its partnership becomes a real one and is not merely one in theory. To oppose such a move is, to paraphrase an old saying, not only a crime against labor – it is a social blunder which may lead to the toppling over of our whole economic edifice.[66]

Alinsky shared much of this analysis and envisaged his organizing work as anti-Fascist and, while, like Lewis, he worked with communists, he was clear that his work was also deeply opposed to Communism.

For Alinsky, place-based neighborhood organizing was a complement to the work-based organizing of the unions, hence the name Industrial *Areas* Foundation, which drew on Shaw's emphasis on natural areas, yet located the emphasis not on the need for social control of the people in those areas but on organizing those people to address the real source of their problems: the industrial conditions under which they labored and lived. Focusing on this "external" target rather than exercises in character building was the best means of addressing delinquency. The first meeting of the Back of the Yards Neighborhood Council in 1939 voted to support the efforts of the CIO in reviving union membership in the meatpacking industry.

The rationale for Alinsky's opposition to Communism and his commitment to democracy can be illustrated by reference to another novel, John Steinbeck's *In Dubious Battle*. Written in 1936, *In Dubious Battle* tells the story of a strike in a California valley by apple pickers and the attempt by two organizers, one experienced and the other a rookie, to initiate and develop the strike and provide for the striking pickers. Many of the tactics Alinsky set out in his *Rules for Radicals* are articulated in the novel. Again, Steinbeck has an ecological paradigm shaping the novel – this time it is of how the individual becomes wholly subsumed to the collective organism and the loss of autonomy that ensues. The novel is clear-eyed about the instrumentalization of people for economic purposes and how organized money deliberately tries to oppose the organization of people. However, through the figure of the doctor, Doc Burton, who helps the strikers but who is pointedly not a member of the party, it constantly raises questions about how to uphold the dignity of the individual while neither instrumentalizing people for economic purposes nor subordinating them to a utopian political project.[67] The title of the novel itself indicates the ambiguity of the strike – it is a quotation taken from Milton's *Paradise Lost* and describes Satan's battle with God. The contrast for Steinbeck is between the communists' prideful usage of people for lost causes and Doc Burton's advocacy of more realistic change that recognizes the legitimate interests at work on both sides of the conflict. This may seem to be nothing more than an interesting period piece, but in the contemporary context we can substitute any number of utopian political projects for the communist organizers, ranging from political Islam and deep ecologists to free market and cultural libertarians.

Alinsky had similar concerns.[68] He rejected Communism as a form of enslavement that demands unqualified political loyalty, does not allow for self-government, and does not uphold the dignity of the individual.[69] What he wanted was a free society in which all may participate actively and in which the multiple loyalties of each individual are accounted for; that is, where social relationships are not subsumed to the needs of the state or the market and where there is scope for a more complex space. As Alinsky puts it:

> Democracy is that system of government and that economic and social organization in which the worth of the individual human being and the multiple loyalties of that individual are most fully recognized and provided for. Democracy is that system of government in which we recognize that all normal individuals have a whole series of loyalties – loyalties to their churches, their labor unions, their fraternal organizations, their social groups, their nationality groups, their athletic groups, their political parties, and many others.[70]

In contrast to the communist organizers for whom loyalty to the party was paramount, Alinsky envisaged the role of the organizer in the following terms:

> This, then, is our real job ... it is the breaking down of the feeling on the part of our people that they are social automatons with no stake in the future, rather than human beings in possession of all the responsibility, strength, and human dignity which constitute the heritage of free citizens of a democracy. This can be done only through the democratic organization of our people for democracy. It is the job of building People's Organizations.[71]

For Alinsky, the slow building of an organization by ordinary people pursuing their real interests and addressing concrete issues was preferable to chasing the ideological and idealistic goals of the communists of the 1930s and 1940s.

A parallel concern was the basis of his disenchantment with the student radicals of the 1960s. As Alinsky would say of the New Left, they wanted revelation, not revolution.[72]

In addition to the problem of instrumentalizing people for political purposes, Alinsky also came to be disenchanted with union organizing as a whole. The key point of contention focused on the differences of analysis about the real conflict between what he called the "haves" and the "have-nots." For Alinsky, both the democratic socialists and the communists had no account of a common life (the conflict was a class war or a necessary conflict of different sectional interests) and tended to reduce everything to the need for economic well-being. He called for a complete change of philosophy in the U.S. labor movement, stating that

> instead of viewing itself as a separate section of the American people engaged in a separate craft in a particular industry, it will think of itself as an organization of *American citizens* – united to conquer all of those destructive forces which harass the workingman and his family. The traditional union cry of "higher wages and shorter hours" then becomes one of a wide variety of objectives.[73]

Alinsky's analysis was not class-based. For Alinsky, the interests of the poor were not intrinsically opposed to those of the rich. His concern was the identification and pursuit of a genuinely common life premised on justice, understood as the right judgment to be made for the benefit for all. Hence, he was equally critical of the sectarian interest-group politics pursued by organized labor and business, and the identity-group politics pursued by religious groups and the Black Power movement, all of which, in his view, denied the possibility of such a good.[74] What Alinsky developed was a common life politics. Refusing to be bound by sectional interests and "community chauvinism," his approach was broad based. This is illustrated by the very first meeting of the Back of the Yards Neighborhood Council, which overcame deep hostility and mutual suspicions between different groups in order to draw together different ethnically constituted churches, unions, athletic clubs, and communists to pursue goods in common: a living wage and just working conditions.[75] Perhaps the most startling evidence for its broad-based character is the fact that it was an agnostic, ethnically Russian Jew who was organizing devout Catholic and probably anti-Semitic Poles, Lithuanians, Slovaks, and Irish. Herein is embodied an important distinctive feature of Alinsky's approach to organizing: the organizer has to respect and work within the experience of the internal culture, values, and structure of the institutions being organized and have relationships with the leaders of these institutions, but the organizer does not have to identify with or come from those institutions.[76] We can summarize this as the *relationship-but-not-identification* approach. The positioning of the organizer in this way constituted a refusal of identity politics and embodied the possibility of a common life.[77] So, for example, the IAF can be justly criticized for not recruiting enough African-American organizers, but not for reasons of representativeness. Rather, it is the need for white congregations in the U.S. context to learn from and be organized by African Americans.

For Alinsky it was through the interaction between democracy and Christianity that he was able to realize and articulate his common life politics and his distinctive approach to organizing.[78] Although the influence of Shaw and Lewis is significant, the majority of Alinsky's primary interlocutors throughout his life were clergy (for example, Bishop Sheil), theologically trained individuals (for example, Ed Chambers), or even theologians of major standing (for example, Jacques Maritain).[79] And it is churches of all denominations that have most intensively and fruitfully engaged with and funded Alinsky's approach to organizing, both during his life and subsequently.

CHRISTIAN DEMOCRACY, CATHOLIC SOCIAL TEACHING AND ORGANIZED RELIGION

Whereas Clifford Shaw, the former farm boy and Lutheran seminarian, had left the church and the country only to try and recreate agrarian moral communities in the middle of the city, Alinsky had grown up in a religious community in the city and understood that mutually responsible and faithfully committed relationships beyond the family required more than self-organization and socially beneficial activities.[80] Likewise, while union organizing had taught Alinksy that only organized people could oppose the power of organized money, he knew that a political organization could only serve as a salve and never offer salvation. To sustain faithful relationships and prevent their subordination to either politics or economics, moral traditions and institutions were required. It is in the churches that Alinsky found the moral basis for common action and the means of sustaining mutually responsible, committed relationships beyond political and economic self-interest. While often scathingly critical of churches, Alinsky nonetheless contended in 1966 that "the only major institutions fighting for justice, decency and equality in America are the churches. The labor unions are no longer doing it.... They've become part of the status quo."[81]

Alinsky's insight about the churches and his close collaboration with the Roman Catholic churches in particular builds on and is in many ways a fulfillment of Tocqueville's aspiration for Catholicism in America. Underlying parts of Tocqueville's book *Democracy in America* is a twofold argument.[82] On the one hand, he develops an apologetic on behalf of Catholicism, arguing that American democracy is best aligned with Catholicism rather than the deist tendencies of Protestantism, and on the other hand, he argues that French (and by extension European) Catholicism should reconcile itself to democracy.[83] It was an analogous appeal that lay behind the embrace of community organizing by certain sections of the Catholic Church in Alinsky's day. From the perspective of the Catholic Archdiocese of Chicago, involvement in Alinsky-style organizing represented a way of "Americanizing" their largely immigrant clergy and overcoming ethnic enclaves developing within the church.[84] It is important to

To Saul Alinsky
with my admiration and love
Jacques Maritain

FIGURE 1.2. Signed photo of Maritain sent to Alinsky.

remember that at this time many viewed Catholicism the way Islam is often viewed in North America and Europe today: inherently antidemocratic and subject to a foreign power. For the younger clergy, organizing represented a way of overcoming this prejudice, contributing to the "common good" and, at the same time, avoiding being co-opted by the Democratic Party machine. For Alinsky, it was the connection with the emerging expression of Christian Democracy and Roman Catholic social teaching, most notably through his relationships with Bishop Sheil and Jacques Maritain (Figure 1.2), that Alinsky found a political vision to complement and help him articulate his own. Christian Democracy was envisaged as a truly "middle way" between fascism, communism, socialism, and an anticlerical liberalism.

Maritain identifies a direct link between his political vision and that of Alinsky's. He comments in a letter to Alinsky concerning the latter's book *Reveille for Radicals*: "It reveals a new way for *real* democracy, the only way in which man's thirst for social communion can develop and be satisfied, through freedom and not through totalitarianism in our disintegrated times."[85] The editor of Alinsky and Maritain's correspondence, Bernard Doering, points to key areas of synchronicity between their conceptions of the relationship between Christianity and democracy.[86] They shared an emphasis on the centrality of the dignity of the individual, the priority of common over particular goods, and the principle of subsidiarity. Alinsky's neighborhood councils were in a way the embodiment of Maritain's vision of a personalist and pluralist pattern of social, economic, and political life that was a pre-condition of true democracy.[87] This positive vision was built on a trust in the practical wisdom of ordinary people as opposed to technocrats and ideologues.[88] This trust was coupled with the need to identify and work alongside the poor and marginalized, moving beyond charity and welfare paternalism. Yet at the same time, their opposition to injustice took as a given the ambivalence of the world and the sinfulness of human relations.[89] While Maritain chides Alinsky on his rhetoric of excess concerning the relationship between means and ends – with Alinsky at times seemingly taking the posture of an outright "Machiavellian" – they basically agreed that in the world as it is, one must, out of tragic necessity, occasionally resort to bad means for good ends.[90] The analogy here is with just war theory where the use of force is at times a moral imperative in order to truly love one's enemy and defend the innocent. Maritain pushes Alinsky to go beyond this and see a complementarity between what he advocates and the approach of Gandhi and Martin Luther King; that is, rather than constitute the use of bad means for good ends in exceptional circumstances, Maritain urged Alinsky to see his approach as the use of moral power to overcome evil.[91] The moral basis of this power is that the power used is relational rather than unilateral and seeks to respond to others as ends rather than as means, thereby avoiding instrumentalizing others as a means to a private, uncommon end. Lastly, both saw the need for prophetic figures that could awaken people from an unjust status quo. For Alinsky and Maritain, contentious political action was not simply appealing to an already existing moral register such as "American values." Community organizers, like civil rights activists, had to exercise a "prophetic imagination." Such figures were not propagating the false messianism of political revolution, forcing the people to be free, but were setting out new visions that call into question the existing political order while at the same time reformulating and deepening the justice and generosity available within it.[92] Robert Fisher clarifies how the organizer acts in such a "prophetic" manner, noting that

> [t]he organizer's most valuable skill remains the ability to challenge the accepted vision of things.... It rests with the sensitivity that brings people to recognize the ways in which a deep and authentic commitment to "human solidarity, mutual responsibility, and social justice" demands a profound re-examination of the values on which their society, and way of life, is based. Such transformations of consciousness do not emerge without intervention and engagement.... The task for organizers is to tie people's understanding of their grievances to an analysis that expands as well as addresses the problems, constituencies, and communities with which they immediately identify.[93]

A point of connection that Doering does not identify is the common concern for a more pluralistic body politic. It is this connection that has perhaps the greatest salience for contemporary political debates. Alinsky and Maritain advocate the need for a genuine institutional plurality as a means of holding in check the centralizing and totalizing thrust of the modern market and state. As Alinksy puts it:

The best insurance of an open society is a whole complex of voluntary organizations, each with a large following and each so involved in action that they deserve and derive strong loyalty from large sectors of the population. Such powerful organizations would resist the surrendering of their power and of the loyalties of their followers to a central power. Therefore strengthening your organization becomes a high priority for the reinforcement of the political openness of our society.[94]

Likewise, Maritain argues for a genuine plurality and a consociationalist conception of civil society as a way of limiting the power of the state and the market. Maritain describes the plurality of civil society as "an organic heterogeneity" and envisages it as being constituted by multiple yet overlapping "political fraternities" that are independent of the state.[95] Maritain distinguishes his account of a consociationalist political society and economic life from fascist and communist ones that collapse market, state, and civil society into a single entity *and* from collectivist and individualistic conceptions of economic relations.[96] Crucially, civil society constitutes a sphere of social or "fraternal" relations that has its own integrity and telos but which nevertheless serves the defensive function of preventing either the market or the state from establishing a monopoly of power, thereby either instrumentalizing social relations for the sake of the political order or commodifying social relations for the sake of the economy. Within this sphere there can exist multiple and overlapping and, on the basis of subsidiarity, semiautonomous forms of institutional life and association, forms that are not reducible to either a private or voluntary association. Indeed, in contrast to his overall theological framework, Maritain's account of a consociationalist body politic overturns the kind of divisions between public and private at work in, for example, John Rawls and late-modern liberalism more generally. As will be argued in Part II, Alinsky's approach displays what such a consociational political life that nevertheless seeks to discern and uphold goods in common might consist of in practice. Community organizing as Alinsky envisages it therefore offers an alternative imaginary to how Christian Democracy developed in Europe after World War II, as it turned to the state as both the sole keeper of the "common good" and as the primary or only means of addressing social and economic ills via legal regulation and welfare programs. What this alternative political imaginary entails will be set forth in Part II, but what can be said now is that Alinsky's approach points to what a non-statist, decentralized, and pluralist Christian democratic vision might look like in practice.[97] Indeed, Alinsky seems to have understood community organizing as just such an alternative.[98]

Before moving on from the relationship between Maritain and Alinsky to consider the later development of the IAF, it is important to distinguish between how Alinsky understood the relationship between Christianity and broad-based community organizing and how Maritain envisaged it. Maritain reads Alinsky theologically, refusing Alinsky's own contrarian self-descriptions. In a letter to Alinsky he states: "All your fighting effort as an organizer is quickened *in reality* by *love for the human being, and for God,* though you refuse to admit it, by a kind of inner *pudeur.*"[99] And in a letter to a third party describing Alinsky, he posits an inner theo-logic in Alinsky's work:

> Alinsky's methods may seem a little rough. I think they are good and necessary means to achieve good and necessary ends. And I know (this is the privilege of an old man) that the deep-rooted motive power and inspiration of this so-called trouble-maker is pure and entire self-giving, and love for those poor images of God which are human beings, especially the oppressed ones – in other words, it is what St Paul calls *agapé,* or love of charity.[100]

However, Maritain is perhaps too quick to claim Alinsky as a saint and in the process elides the ongoing tensions between Christianity and democracy. William Cavanaugh critiques Maritain's conception of church-state relations for so spiritualizing the church that he cedes too much ground to the state.[101] In effect, Maritain subordinates the church to the political order and converts Christianity into a civil religion, albeit one that conforms to Maritain's conception of a mediating "democratic secular faith."[102] On Maritain's account, democracy is not merely a set of mediating *practices* but a mediating *creed* to which all must subscribe if they are to gain entry into the public sphere.

In contrast to Maritain, Alinsky does not demand that the church should adopt democracy as an additional article of faith. Alinsky, as a careful reader of Machiavelli, is more alert to the tensions and temptations in the relationship between democratic politics and Christianity.[103] For Machiavelli, a prophet armed is far superior to an unarmed prophet. Christianity on his account makes humans humble, self-abnegating, and contemptuous of worldly things, and thereby enervates and undermines political order. By contrast, armed prophets such as Moses or Muhammad found civilizations that are strong and glory seeking and so foster robust political orders (whether or not Machiavelli's characterization of Moses and Muhammad is fair is another matter). It is in light of Alinsky's Machiavellian insights into the nature of politics that we should read his notorious dedication of *Rules for Radicals* to Lucifer as the first radical. Alinsky was making explicit the fundamental conflict between the pursuit of Christian virtue and the virtues demanded by republican politics. There is a constant tension to be negotiated between the transcendent, universalistic obligations and theological virtues of the Christian faith and the particularistic loyalties, materialistic ends, and potentially martial, self-glorifying virtues demanded by a place-based republican and democratic conception of citizenship.[104] Alinsky is thus more Augustinian than Maritain. For Augustine, there is an inherent division between the harmonious life of the City of God and the kinds of social peace available in the earthly city. Such an Augustinian view does not disavow the peace of the earthly city, but it does relativize, desacralize, and critique it as inherently oriented toward immanent, penultimate ends and as inescapably inflected with patterns of domination.

It is precisely this tension that the political philosopher Ronald Beiner argues lies at the heart of the emergence of liberalism as a response to the problem of the relationship between religious and political authority.[105] Underlying Beiner's genealogy is an argument for the solution liberalism proposes: the privatization and interiorization of Christianity so that it is politically neutralized and the acknowledgment that liberalism is not an impartial arbiter, but a project of "civil religion" – albeit a philosophically grounded one – that purports to provide the values, virtues, and vision needed to bind people together within a particular construction of political order. In contrast to Maritain and Beiner, who from very different perspectives propose the same kind of solution, Alinsky's approach to community organizing maintains the tension between Christianity and democratic politics in order to simultaneously relativize the claims and demands of citizenship and to recognize the need for both political and religious authorities to give space to multiple loyalties. Politics, as Hannah Arendt argues, is based on plurality; without this plurality, the many are subordinated to the one. Liberalism claims to stop religion's subordination of the many to a single religious authority, but in the process it mimics that which it opposes. For all its vaunting of pluralism, liberalism sublates difference within a univocal moral-political order and thereby consistently becomes antipolitical when it becomes hegemonic, taking a technocratic and proceduralist turn away from politics. In its commitment to being broad-based, community organizing thereby affirms a genuine plurality, the relativization of politics, and challenges all religions to see themselves as but one of many transcendent visions of the good that must negotiate a common life with others through democratic politics. It is the making explicit of this dynamic through an engagement with Arendt and a broadly Aristotelian vision of politics after Alinsky's death in 1972 to which we now turn.

LATER REFLECTIONS: FAITH, CITIZENSHIP, AND THE REJUVENATION OF POLITICS

If the counterpoints to community organizing in urban politics in the 1930s, 1940s, and 1950s were organized crime, organized labor, and organized religion, from the 1960s onward more movement- and network-based forms of social and political activism emerged. Today, community organizers seek to distinguish their work from these forms of political mobilization, campaigning, and "checkbook activism."[106] That being said, the need to embody and advocate a common life politics only intensified as single issue, interest group, and identity politics increasingly denied the possibility of such a good; and the state, aligned with "neoliberal" economics, transformed citizens into consumers and clients exercising private preferences rather than forging a common, public life. Another key contextual change with which community organizing had to contend was the shift from an industrial economy to rapid deindustrialization in many cities, as well as the emergence of post-Fordist, globalized forms of economic production. However, this did not undermine the relevance of community organizing – in many ways it reinforced its importance. Arguably, in the industrial economy the primary focus of organizing was the factory and workplace. Yet, in the shift to a postindustrial economy with a greater emphasis on service provision (e.g., retail, healthcare, and financial services), it is place-based organizing that becomes the dominant form.[107] This is illustrated in IAF's "Living Wage" campaign begun in Baltimore in the 1990s, which, in contrast to the Back of the Yard's, support of unions, was not focused on a factory or sector of industry but on a city, its local government, and an array of institutions within that place.[108] When capital and thence production facilities are highly mobile, then key targets and partners in organizing efforts are anchor institutions such as schools, hospitals, and universities. Within such anchor institutions, capital and people are tied to place (for example, Johns Hopkins University and its affiliated hospital cannot be moved from Baltimore). Moreover, the public officials and authoritative bodies in charge of these institutions can be identified, a meaningful relationship can be built with them, and they can be held accountable for the decisions they make.

From the 1970s onward, there has been a rapid splintering of community organizations and the development of many different – and what, in some cases, came to be rival – networks. Notable among these are PICO (People Improving Communities through Organizing), DART (Direct Action Research and Training), the Center for Community Change, National People's Action, and the Gamaliel Foundation. There emerged also a welter of more local initiatives, sometimes referred to as "neo-Alinskyite" groups. All these post-1970s groups trace their history back to Alinsky or a combination of involvement in the civil rights movement and an engagement with Alinsky's work. Moreover, a number of leading organizers in these networks were mentored by Alinsky himself, hence the description of Alinsky as the "dean of community organizing." However, this chapter continues to focus on the IAF as it is the IAF with which Citizens UK is affiliated and therefore, its story is the antecedent of Citizens UK's own story.

Provoked by the changing political environment the IAF engaged in a sustained, if ad hoc, process of critical self-reflection and experimentation. After Alinsky's death in 1972, two of the IAF's lead organizers, Ernesto Cortés and Edward Chambers, undertook a self-conscious engagement with Catholic social teaching and the theological basis of organizing and came to understand organizing as emerging from the intertwined values of family and religion.[109] A deeper engagement with the Bible was central to this.[110] The 1978 pamphlet *Organizing for Family and Congregations* represents the fruition of this process. Largely authored by another lead organizer, Michael Gecan, it was produced as a collegial statement from all the organizers.[111] Against the assumption held by many, including Chambers himself, that what it said represented a fundamental change of emphasis for the IAF, what should be clear from the previous sections is that the emphasis on families and congregations represented a systematization and rendering explicit of what was already central to the origins of the Alinsky approach to organizing.[112] However, from Alinsky's death onward, what the next generation of IAF organizers did (and particular credit must go to Chambers, Cortés, Gecan, and Arnie Graf) was to engage in an extensive process of experimentation with the forms and methods of organizing. Through this process a number of innovations emerged.

First, Chambers and the other organizers systematized the work and put it on a more secure financial and administrative footing. This enabled a longer term and more stable involvement with the community organizations that were initiated. This was a major departure from Alinsky who was skeptical about ongoing and long-term commitments to community organizations.[113] Second, they developed a commitment to institutional renewal involving popular education, systematic leadership development, and an emphasis on changing the organizational culture of local institutions so that they embody the desired changes. This involved a far more intentional focus on working with institutions as a whole rather than subgroups and informal associations within institutions that had, up to that point, been the primary point of engagement. Third, they began working in new contexts. Spearheaded by Gerald Taylor, this included organizing in the southeast. By contrast, Alinsky had explicitly rejected working below the Mason-Dixon Line. Enormously significant to the development of sustained models of organizing was the work of Cortes in San Antonio and the formation of Communities Organized for Public Service (COPS).[114] Fourth, there was an intentional focus on building multiracial coalitions and thereby deepening and extending the broad-based nature of the coalitions.[115]

Alongside these changes to practice were a number of conceptual innovations spurred on by a broader process of critical reflection. Cortés and Leo Penta were key catalysts in this. With funding from the Ford Foundation, Cortés organized regular seminars for Texas IAF staff with philosophers, theologians, and social theorists that included, among others, Benjamin Barber, James Cone, Charles Curran, Jean Bethke Elshtain, Robert Putnam, Theda Skocpol, Michael Walzer, Cornel West, and Delores Williams.[116] At the same time, on the East Coast, beginning with the clergy caucus of East Brooklyn Congregations, Leo Penta (along with Douglas Slaughter and Sr. Maryellen Kane) organized a series of retreats and seminars. These included reflection on selected texts and conversation with invited scholars such as Stanley Hauerwas and Walter Wink. These retreats culminated in the "IAF Reflects" sessions between 1990 and 1996. These sessions entailed sustained reflection on the "public philosophy" of the Industrial Areas Foundation.[117]

Through these parallel processes a wide variety of philosophical, theological, cultural, political, and sociological texts were engaged. On the theological side,

Walter Breuggemann's work was felt to be the most relevant and significant. The political theorists Hannah Arendt, Bernard Crick, and Sheldon Wolin were felt to best enable the organizers to make sense of their own work. Evidence for this is in the repeated referencing of their work both in training programs and in the writings of the organizers themselves. For example, in an interview, Chambers identifies Arendt as the most significant thinker for him and he calls Wolin "America's finest political teacher."[118] Central to the work of Arendt, Crick, and Wolin is an account of politics as the ongoing process through which to maintain commonality and recognize and conciliate conflict in pursuit of shared goods. And, following Aristotle, politics is considered as properly relating to what pertains to the general, comprehensive, or public order of a polity. This broadly Aristotelian conception of politics is contrasted with modern liberal and totalitarian forms of political organization, all of which seek to substitute politics for some kind of legal, bureaucratic, or market-based procedure. The focus here will be on Arendt and Wolin rather than Crick, whose work seems to have been less formative and had more of a crystallizing effect. That being said, the following statement by Crick can be read as a manifesto for what organizers mean by the term "politics":

> Politics arises ... in organized states which recognize themselves to be an aggregate of many members, not a single tribe, religion, interest or tradition. Politics arises from accepting the fact of the simultaneous existence of different groups, hence different interests and different traditions, within a territorial unit under a common rule. It does not matter much how that unit came to be – by custom, conquest, or geographical circumstance. What does matter is that its social structure, unlike some primitive societies, is sufficiently complex and divided to make politics a plausible response to the problem of governing it, the problem of maintaining order at all.... For politics represents at least some tolerance of differing truths, some recognition that government is possible, indeed best conducted, amid the open canvassing of rival interests.[119]

The point of politics within this account is to identify points of connection and mutuality between diverse interests and loyalties.[120] As political theorist and former organizer Harry Boyte notes, the aim of this kind of politics "is not to do away with ambiguity and the conflicts it entails. The aim is rather to avoid violence, to contain conflicts, to generate common work on common challenges, and to achieve broadly beneficial public outcomes."[121] The IAF organizer Gerald Taylor suggests that this approach to politics "means being able to negotiate and compromise. It means understanding that people are not necessarily evil because they have different interests or ways of looking at the world."[122]

The kind of conception of politics envisaged here is very different to that which tends to equate politics with legal and bureaucratic procedures and decisions. Such a vision restricts politics to pressure on and action by state agencies rather than the negotiation of a common life between multiple actors, with the state being only one among many players. Wolin developed the fullest articulation of the contrast between politics and proceduralism. He gives an account of the centralization of sovereignty in the nation-state and the subsequent attempt to overcome political conflict within liberal nation-states through a combination of rational administration, use of technology, and the demarcation of the economy as the sphere of free, uncoerced relations.[123] For Wolin, the vital task in the contemporary context is the recovery of what he calls "politicalness": the "capacity for developing into beings who know and value what it means to participate in and be responsible for the care and improvement of our common and collective life."[124] In Wolin's analysis, the recovery of politicalness depends, in part, on local patterns of association born out of cooperative institutions and what he calls "archaic," and, in many cases, very "conservative" traditions such as Christianity. These provide the means for the recreation of political experience and extend to a wider circle the benefits of social cooperation and achievements made possible by previous generations.[125]

Within this kind of account, community organizing constitutes an important way of rejuvenating politicalness. It acts as a "catalyst," providing what organizers often refer to as "agitation" for archaic traditions. As Penta and Chambers put it, IAF is a

> catalyst that brings into relationship and reaction elements which without it would not of themselves interact, or do so only partially or sluggishly. For the IAF the elements are the wounded and struggling institutions which mediate relationship: families, congregations, churches, workers' organizations. These are both out of relationship to one another and internally fractured, yet they are the potential collective, the potential initiators of action, the enfleshment of a new public space and a new public process. The role of IAF organizers is to bring these disparate elements into relationship with one another gradually but persistently weaving a network of new or renewed relationships. This means moving people beyond their usual limits and experiences.[126]

What the work of Arendt (along with that of the theologian, Bernard Loomer) did was help refine the understanding of the kind power through which the poor – and for that matter, any participant in an "archaic" tradition – could overcome their disorganization and act for themselves in public life. In stark contrast to nearly all other modern political thought, Arendt gives an account of relational power as a countervailing force to unilateral power or what she calls the "command-obedience model" of power. For Arendt, "[p]ower corresponds to the human ability not just to act, but to act in concert. Power is never the property of an individual; it belongs to a group and remains in existence only so long as the group keeps together."[127] Through acting in concert with one another in their families and congregations and self-generated institutions, the poor could resist the unilateral power of money and the state in order to establish public goods.[128] Such goods – housing, education, health, and so forth – were the basis of a genuinely common life as opposed to a practice of politics based on the individual pursuit of private interests. For Arendt, as for community organizing, politics requires a liberal legal-constitutional order to establish its conditions, but this order cannot be a substitute for politics itself. As Arendt puts it:

> The political realm rises directly out of acting together, the "sharing of words and deeds." Thus action not only has the most intimate relationship to the public part of the world common to us all, but is the one activity which constitutes it. It is as though the wall of the polis and the boundaries of the law were drawn around an already existing public space which, however, without such stabilizing protection could not endure, could not survive the moment of action and speech itself.[129]

Community organizing represents the recovery of this kind of account of politics as it arises out of common speech and action between ordinary people through one-to-ones, testimony, and a myriad of other forms of meeting. Alinsky's approach to organizing aims to stimulate the appearance of those who are depoliticized or excluded from the decision-making process, enabling them to appear and act on their own terms rather than be confined to either a private world of consumerism, a sphere of necessity where they are always responding to the actions of others upon them, or a disorganized arena of hostile, fearful, and broken relationships.

The more explicit, theoretical conception of politics contributed to another significant shift in IAF's practice. Prior to the 1980s, community organizing tended to combine political activism with service provision. This was the case right from its origins in the Back of the Yards Neighborhood Council. However, the development of The Woodlawn Organization (TWO) provides a salutary lesson in what can happen when political work and service provision are integrated within the same initiative. As Fisher notes:

> As a community development agency TWO was a success, the shining gem of all Alinsky organizations in the 1960s and early 1970s.... But TWO was now a neighbourhood development corporation, not a "People's Organization." It was run by a paid, professional staff whose attention was fixed on development and growth, organizational stability, and professional competence, not on social change or even on serving the needs of all the neighborhood people. Predictably, neighborhood resident participation declined as technical expertise grew to paramount importance. TWO became just another business in the community, a non-profit business almost as removed from many of Woodlawn's problems and needs as the profit oriented enterprises.[130]

In effect it had become co-opted and professionalized through a process of "institutional isomorphism," a phenomenon in which civil society organizations adopt the norms and structures of state bureaucracies and commercial organizations such that they conform to rather than challenge the norms and practices of the state and market.[131] This is a frequent developmental pathway for many "third sector" or nongovernmental organizations as they shift from confrontation to coexistence. The question of whether it is possible to combine community organizing with community development programs sparked a widespread debate among academics and practitioners in the 1980s and into the 1990s.[132]

Organizers addressed this problem head on by separating out service provision from the community organization. An example of this separation is Texas IAF's work with Project Quest (a jobs training and recruitment agency) that it had campaigned to establish with local government funding. The IAF had a close involvement with the project but did not directly manage it.[133] As the sociologist Mark Warren notes: "[T]he independent organizational capacities of the IAF proved essential to maintaining funding for the program and to keeping the agency true to the organization's priorities."[134] A similar pattern of maintaining a cooperative but critical relationship with service providers that emerged as a result of organizing efforts became the norm. However, developing and maintaining such distinct but related arrangements between community organizations and service providers have often proved very difficult in practice.[135]

The development of a more clearly articulated, broadly Aristotelian conception of politics by the organizers helped identify the key task for organizing as not providing for basic social needs, as these can be met by state or other service providers, but fostering politicalness and generating associational forms of power. What became clear is that what was lacking in most civil society initiatives was an emphasis on building power and doing politics. Through processes of isomorphism, the boundaries between civil society, market, and state collapse, leading to the subordination of civil society to the demands of state and market. To focus on service provision at the expense of more directly political-civic work is to collude with this collapse and fail to address the real need: the fostering of political judgment among both the powerful and the powerless and resisting the substitution of politics by proceduralism, whether the procedures employed are legal, bureaucratic, or market based. While developing existing community assets more effectively through "bottom-up" schemes or leveraging new resources into a community is important, the primary need community organizing tried to address was the development of an alternative power structure to that which already existed.[136]

COMMUNITY ORGANIZING AS POLITICAL POPULISM

Having identified the streams of thought and practice that formed community organizing, we can now locate its emergence within a broader historical topography. To this end I contend that organizing is best understood as an extension and development of American Populism. American Populism has its origins in the broad-based and fractious movement that emerged from the 1850s onward. It reached its high point in the 1890s with the formation of the People's Party that challenged the duopoly of the Republicans and Democrats but declined rapidly as a formal movement thereafter.[137] Yet, like an event of nuclear fission, its half-life continues to be felt long after its moment of greatest energy. The vital center of the Populist movement was the midwest, southwest and southeast, with particular concentrations of activity in Texas, Kansas, and

Oklahoma. While primarily an agrarian phenomenon, its political impact came through forging a farmer-labor alliance.

The link between Alinsky and Populism is conceptual, genealogical, and sociological, as well as the taproot that community organizing shares with certain elements of the civil rights movement and other forms of grassroots activism.[138] However, there are good reasons for rejecting such a linkage when it comes to Alinsky. Not least among these is the consistent failure and lack of relationship between the constituency that formed the Populist movement and the People's Party of the 1890s (primarily Protestant "yeoman" farmers in alliance with miners and railroad workers) and the urban and predominantly Catholic industrial workers of that era, a lack of relationship that is central to the failure of the People's Party to establish itself as a third force in U.S. politics.[139] It was precisely among the urban and largely Catholic workers that Alinsky developed his craft as an organizer.[140] Yet like the Populists, Alinsky consistently and insistently drew conceptually on the Jeffersonian tradition of democracy and the Federalist Papers, which were for him a key reference point in his teaching and writing, combining these with Biblical analogies and allusions. Related to this Jeffersonian vision of American democracy was Alinsky's use of Tocqueville, particularly Tocqueville's notion of "self-interest properly understood," the importance of association, and the need to resist the *noblesse oblige* of the rich while binding them into the democratic body politic.[141] Alinsky's references to Machiavelli can also be understood as a further point of connection. Machiavelli's treatment of Rome and his conception of an antagonistic republican politics where the people seek to limit the domination of elites, but which is itself vulnerable to the lure of "Caesarism," anticipates many populist themes.[142]

If Jeffersonian republicanism interwoven with religious frames of reference represents the conceptual point of connection, then Alinsky's relationship with the labor leader John L. Lewis represents the genealogical one. John L. Lewis should be interpreted as mediating the legacy of the Populist movement into the U.S. labor movement. As already noted, Lewis steered a middle path between capitalism and both socialism and communism. In 1933, he told a Senate committee on labor relations: "American labor ... stand[s] between the rapacity of the robber barons of industry of America and the lustful rage of the communists, who would lay waste to our traditions and our institutions with the fire and sword."[143] The key point to note here is the valuation given to "our traditions and our institutions," a valuation that directly contrasts with the class-based analysis of socialism and Marxism that viewed the sundering of people's traditional communal and place-based ties as the prerequisite of freedom and political agency. For example, Marx and Engels saw tradition as a great retarding force, from which industrialization enabled liberation. Freedom from tradition was the necessary precursor for the formation of the proletariat and thence the true liberation of consciousness. Such disdain for tradition has been a common feature of most left-wing and liberal political theories.[144]

In contrast, like the Populists before him and like Alinsky after him, Lewis worked with the values and traditions of the people, not against them. Populist discursive themes were the wellspring Lewis drew on by which to steer his middle course, themes that in the historian Michael Kazin's view had their roots in the "pietistic revivalism" and Enlightenment rationalism of America's formative Revolutionary period (as well as a third stream that Kazin misses: Calvinist covenantal discourses that shaped the "commonwealth ideal").[145] These themes came to fruition among the Populists of the 1890s and have been deployed in a multiplicity of ways in the ongoing tradition of American populism.

Kazin identifies four themes that shaped Populist discourse and the idioms of its inheritors. First, "Americanism," identified as an emphasis on understanding and obeying the will of the people. Second, "producerism": the conviction that, in contrast to classical and aristocratic conceptions, those who toiled were morally superior to those who lived off the toil of others and that only those who created wealth in tangible material ways could be trusted to guard the nation's liberties. This second theme was counterpoised to a third: the need to oppose the dominance of privileged elites (variously identified as government bureaucrats, cosmopolitan intellectuals, high financiers, industrialists, or a combination of all four) who were seen to subvert the principles of self-rule and personal liberty through centralizing power and imposing abstract plans on the ways people lived.[146] The final theme was the notion of a movement or crusade that was engaged in a battle to save the nation and protect the welfare of "real" America or the common people.[147] Lewis drew mainly on the first, second, and third themes, and for the first time in a populist movement, African Americans were seen as integral to the common people.[148] Lewis also embraced Catholics as key allies in the development of the CIO, quoting Papal encyclicals and giving a prominent place to Catholic clerics in CIO national conventions from 1938 to 1946.[149] Thus, where the Populist movement failed, Lewis was able to succeed in connecting populist sentiment with urban and largely Catholic industrial workers. Within Kazin's account, Alinsky can be seen as taking up Lewis's mantle and counteracting the rightwing drift of populism and the state-centric, technocratic focus of the unions that occurs from the 1940s onward. The four discursive themes Kazin outlines appear again and again in Alinsky's writing and in his genealogical roll call of who are the "radicals" he is seeking to "reveille"; he identifies the Populist Party (along with Thomas Jefferson, the abolitionists, the Knights of Labor, and other early labor activists) as their predecessors.[150]

To identify the sociological link between Populism and Alinsky, we must traverse the choppy waters of how Populism is interpreted and navigate the crosscurrents of its historiography. As with the interpretation of many social movements, treatments of the Populists tend to be refracted through the concerns and sympathies of the historian's own time.[151] The account given here confirms, deepens, and extends the case put forward by Boyte, who has done the most to suggest that community organizing represents a form of populism.[152] The contemporary consensus among scholars of Populism seems to be that it was neither predominantly socialist nor capitalist but constituted a broadly republican critique of the overconcentration of "money power."[153] This critique was combined with the language of Evangelical Protestantism, the Methodist camp meetings, and Baptist revivals in order to generate a powerful rhetoric with which to challenge the status quo.[154] It was a language that cut across the color line, being shared by black and white populists, but which, at the same time, alienated the predominantly Catholic industrial workers in the northeast.

Within their principally Jeffersonian vision, the Populists saw a need for government intervention. Such intervention was necessary to establish the conditions for fair access to public goods such as transport, credit, and a postal service (recognizing that such measures would of necessity involve creating modern centralized government bureaucracies). Elizabeth Sanders, in her history of the Populists and their legacy, summarizes their approach in the following terms:

> Its philosophy was anticorporate, though not *anticapitalist*. It sought, as recent scholars have established, not to turn the clock back on industrial development but to harness the new technological power for social good, to use the state to check exploitative excesses, to uphold the rights and opportunities of labor (farm and factory), and to maintain a healthy and creative business competition. The program was profoundly opposed to concentrated corporate power. Where concentration seemed inevitable, and for vital economic functions on which the well-being of the entire society depended, it was best that complete government control be established.[155]

At the same time, consistent with their Jeffersonian vision, they developed the rudiments of a "cooperative commonwealth" consisting of a huge range of autonomous institutions, educational initiatives, and mutual associations such as cooperatives in order to address their needs without being dependent on the banks or the state. Contrary to standard narratives about the inherent opposition between a localist civil society and a nationalizing government, the Populists understood that while the state must know its place, it most definitely had a place in securing a common life and that it was sometimes necessary to organize trans-locally and generate institutional forms at the appropriate scale in order to secure one's aims.[156] Inevitably in such a diverse movement there were a wide variety of people involved, ranging from doctrinaire socialists (of various sorts) to white supremacists.[157]

By the 1890s the Populists sought reform in three major areas: land, transportation, and money. These came to expression in what is known as the "Omaha platform."[158] Populists called for limits to land speculation; the nationalization of railroads, telephones, and telegraphs (as these were natural monopolies and so needed to be operated in the interests of everyone); the formation of a central bank directly responsible to elected officials; and a flexible currency through issuing paper money (greenbacks) and the free coinage of silver (those who supported this were known as the "silverites").[159] In addition, the platform endorsed measures such as the need to enforce the eight-hour workday, referendums in order to introduce elements of direct democracy into the system of representative democracy, and a graduated income tax. Populists also came to endorse the "sub-treasury plan," a Federally backed farm commodity price-support program after the failure of local and regional efforts to break the crop lien system that resulted in the debt bondage of both black and white farmers.[160]

What these measures amount to is, I contend, a countermovement against the effects of unregulated laissez-faire capitalism. The notion of a countermovement is drawn from the work of the economic anthropologist and historian of capitalism, Karl Polanyi. For Polanyi, the laissez-faire capitalism of the nineteenth century led to a process of "commodification" whereby unregulated, disembedded markets make goods that are not products – notably humans, nature, and money (the key planks of the Omaha platform) – into commodities to be bought and sold. The nineteenth-century alignment between the Republican and Democratic Parties and the northeast banking interest along with the subsequent imposition of the gold standard as the basis for a global market is an extension of exactly the process Polanyi describes. Polanyi argues that the formation of a global market system inherently led to spontaneous countermovements to re-embed market relations within social and political relations as populations and governments struggled to cope with the deleterious impact of an unregulated market on society and on nature. The introduction of regulation and statutory measures (for example, the New Deal as a response to the Great Depression) and political movements such as trade unions are examples of the kind of countermovement that Polanyi discusses.

Populism, which developed in parallel with the labor movement in North America, is another such countermovement. It sought to re-embed labor, land, and money within a wider social and political matrix and thereby inhibit the destructive effects of commodification on place-based political and social relations. In terms of the Populists' own frames of reference, laissez-faire capitalism seemed to be destroying the moral community and threatening the nation with God's judgment. The government, as the embodiment of the will of the people, needed to act to make things right.[161] Such a view was expressed time and again in Populist speeches and pamphlets. To quote but one example, Milford Howard writing in 1895 states: "The spirit of avarice is devouring the great heart of this nation. The greed for gain gets such possession of men's souls that they become demons. They rush into the maelstrom of money-getting, and soon lose all fear of God and love for their Fellow-men."[162]

As a countermovement, Populism was simultaneously "conservative" in that it sought to inhibit the liquefying thrust of "money power" and "radical" in that it called into question the status quo and tried to forge a new institutional and governmental framework within the processes of modernization, one that would pluralize monopolistic forms of economic and political power in order to generate a more complex or polycentric space.[163] As a countermovement, and like trade unions, Populism was both a creature of processes of modernization and a reaction against the deleterious impact of these same processes, and so it is both modern *and* an expression of modernity criticism that sought an alternative path of development. As a countermovement, we can see the sociological link between community organizing and the Populists.[164]

Framing both Populism and community organizing as forms of historical countermovement that share a conceptual, sociological, and genealogical link necessitates sounding a note of caution. Crucially, for Polanyi, countermovements can either be democratic or fascistic. Indeed, one of Polanyi's primary interests was explaining the rise of Fascism in Europe in the wake of the Great Depression. Polanyi himself identifies the American populist figure of Huey Long as an example of a fascist countermove that was an "ever given political possibility" in every industrial nation since the 1930s.[165] Polanyi's conflation of Populism and fascism is strange given his own sympathies with populist movements in both Russia and Hungary.[166] However, as will be seen, Polanyi's own account can be nuanced and enriched through its encounter with the historically specific phenomenon of American populism.

Historical forms of populism are themselves democratic or authoritarian and often combine elements of both. For example, Peronism in Argentina and Huey Long in the United States are both examples of the integration of democratic and authoritarian elements (rather than being straightforwardly fascist as Polanyi asserts). This is what makes populism (as opposed to fascism) such an ambiguous political phenomenon. The Populist movement was itself a mixed bag (hence the contentious nature of its historiographical reception). Conceptions of "the people" are always contradictory: the people are vicious and virtuous, irrational and bearers of a nation's true spirit, a threat to democracy and the holders of sovereignty. The categories "democratic" or "authoritarian" are perhaps too blunt as analytic instruments with which to explain the paradoxes of populism, tending more toward labeling and stigmatization than rigorous assessment. After all, as Tocqueville observed, democracy can turn into the tyranny of the majority and produce a distinctly democratic form of servility that substitutes politics for philanthropy and paternalism.[167] What is needed, then, is a more conceptually crisp way of framing American populism, and thence community organizing.

There have been various attempts to develop a comprehensive theory of populism. Following the pioneering work of the political theorists Margaret Canovan and Ernesto Laclau, I contend that rather than being deviant or marginal, populism is inherent to modern polities.[168] For Canovan it is a contextual phenomenon that reacts to whatever makes up the dominant power structure and ruling hegemony.[169] Canovan identifies democracy as having two faces: the "redemptive" and the "pragmatic." When democracy, which offers government by the people, of the people, and for the people (its redemptive face), is reduced to a mechanism for negotiating and resolving conflicts of interest and distributing power (its pragmatic face), populists "move on to the vacant territory, promising in place of the dirty world of party maneuvering the shining ideal of democracy renewed."[170] Canovan is right to see populism as an inherent possibility in modern democracy and as playing off tensions within democracy itself. However, while her theory helps explain in part the Populist movement in the United States and its relationship to community organizing – both are, in a sense, reactive – her theory fails to account for how populism is not simply a reaction but rather constitutes a mode of political rationality that draws on practical reason, hence its seemingly antitheoretical position.[171]

I propose that it is more helpful when discussing the Populist movement and other manifestations of American populism to distinguish between its "political" and "antipolitical" moments. Drawing from what has already been said in relation to Arendt, Crick, and Wolin, "political populism" embodies a conception of politics that works to reinstate plurality and inhibit totalizing monopolies (whether of the state or market) through common action and deliberation premised on personal participation in and responsibility for tending public life.[172] This can be taken as a summary of Alinsky's broadly Aristotelian approach to politics. This contrast between political and antipolitical populism seems to be tacit in the early training developed by the IAF. As Alinsky's biographer notes: "The trainees read Alinsky's biography of John L. Lewis and T. Harry William's study of Huey Long – and spent hours discussing how each had accumulated and used power."[173]

With reference to U.S. history, Alinsky frames his approach to politics as being both revolutionary and conservative.[174] It is akin to the kind of conservative radicalism advocated by Wolin, who argues for the intrinsic connection between "archaic" and diverse historic institutions, traditions, and patterns of local participation and the ability to "tend" democracy and resist centralizing and technocratic forms of modern power.[175] As already noted, the emphasis on the importance of existing traditions and institutions distinguishes this approach to that of liberal, socialist, communist, and the majority of modern political theories that view tradition with suspicion.[176] Wolin's account of democracy helps articulate the interrelationship between Alinsky's conception of democratic politics and establishing a contradiction to totalizing forms of dominatory power. Wolin states, in almost a direct echo of Alinsky, that the aim of democracy should be neither equality nor nostalgic preservation but the restoration of

> some measure of control over the conditions and decisions intimately affecting the everyday lives of ordinary citizens, to relieve serious and remediable distress and to extend inclusion beyond the enjoyment of equal civil rights by making access to educational and cultural experiences and healthy living conditions a normal expectation.[177]

Political populism and "democracy" as Wolin envisages it can be read as synonyms.[178] And it is as a form of political populism that we can reconnect community organizing with Arendt whose concept of "the people" (as opposed to the mob, the mass, or the tribe) converges with the concept of political populism developed here.[179]

By contrast, "antipolitical populism" seeks to simplify rather than complexify the political space. It advocates direct forms of democracy in order to circumvent the need for deliberative processes and the representation of multiple interests in the formation of political judgments. The leader rules by direct consent without the hindrance of democratic checks and balances or the representation of different interests. In antipolitical populism the throwing off of established authority structures is the prelude to the giving over of authority to the one and the giving up of responsibility for the many. The goal of antipolitical populism is personal withdrawal from public life so as to be free to pursue private self-interests rather than public mutual interests.[180] In antipolitical expressions of populism, personal responsibility is for improvement of the self, one's immediate family, institution (e.g., a congregation), or community disconnected from the interdependence of any such project of improvement with the care of the public institutions, liberties, rule of law, physical infrastructure, and natural resources that make up the commonwealth on which all depend.

Alinsky's approach to community organizing shares a number of elements with antipolitical populism. These include: the emphasis on strong leaders; the dichotomization and simplification of issues; the use and advocacy of direct forms of rule; a certain romanticization of the wisdom of ordinary people; the formation of cross-class coalitions; a localism that distrusts universalist ideologies and the prioritizing of international issues; a distrust of party politics, elites, and bureaucracy; a suspicion of theory and an envisaging of itself as pragmatist; the use of affective rituals and symbols to generate a sense of unity; a demand for loyalty to leader and group; and the mobilization of dissent through the organizing theme of ordinary people/non-elites as both the subject of grievance and the means of correction.

The key differences between political and antipolitical populism are fourfold. First, the orientations and sentiments in political populism are put in the service of forging a political space not limiting, subverting, or closing it down. Second, political populism invests in long-term organization and education (the role of the "lecturer" in the Populist movement and the "organizer" in community organizing). Third, political populism develops a broad base of local leaders rather than relying on one charismatic leader and short-term mobilization of people who are focused not on loyalty to each other and a common life but on the single leader and the cause or issue.[181] Lastly, while both political and antipolitical populists frame their proposals as moral imperatives, political populists believe that, in the words of Alinsky, "compromise is a key and beautiful word."[182] In short, political populism seeks to generate a common life as opposed to a politics dominated by the interests of the one, the few, or the many. Such a common life politics is encapsulated in the closing peroration given at an IAF assembly in Baltimore in 1987 by Reverend Grady Yeargin:

One day it will be said that in the city of Baltimore in the last quarter of the twentieth century, strange and unusual things began to happen. Well known somebodies with something from someplace began to meet with little-known nobodies from noplace. The upper crust began to meet with the middle crust and with those who have no crust at all. It was a peculiar people. A strange and unusual coalition that negotiated and fought and worked together.[183]

Kazin tells a declension narrative about the "conservative capture" of populism in the U.S. from the 1940s onward. By contrast, the historian Richard Hofstadter gives an ascension narrative about a move from populism to progress. The conceptualization of populism suggested here allows for a more nuanced account.[184] Populism in the U.S. contains political and antipolitical elements and sometimes these elements receive a greater or lesser emphasis within particular expressions of populism.[185] We can contrast the various expressions of primarily antipolitical populism such as Father Coughlin and the Coughlinites of the late 1930s, McCarthyism, Ross Perot, and most recently the Tea Party movement with the primarily political populism of the IAF and other broad-based community organizations such as PICO, Gamaliel, National People's Action, the development of "community unionism," and the self-described "new populists" such as Harry Boyte, Heather Booth, and, within the Roman Catholic Church, Monsignor Geno Baroni.[186]

Alinky's criticism of state welfare programs, the "apostles of planning," and nongovernmental charity illustrate his political populism.[187] He saw such endeavors as paternalism and the actions of elites that failed to address the real needs of people, which served to reinforce existing structures of injustice and undermined people's dignity.[188] Expressing central themes of populism, Alinsky's approach to social, economic, and political injustice aimed to empower those excluded so that they could take responsibility and act for themselves and thereby forge a common world with (rather than against) the existing power holders. This is summarized in the "iron rule" of community organizing: "never do for others what they can do for themselves" – a maxim that is almost a perfect distillation of populist political rationality. Nevertheless, the potential for community organizations to drift from political to antipolitical populism is illustrated by the history of the Back of the Yards Neighborhood Council, which by the 1960s had become vehemently racist and protectionist – a development that deeply grieved Alinsky. It is its populism that helps explain the constant apprehension and nervous responses that community organizing has provoked among liberals and the rhetorical basis of its appeal to "conservative" constituencies.

The roots of organizing in American populism are a hindrance when it is transplanted to other cultural contexts. For example, in the United Kingdom, the lack of available and identifiable populist idioms has meant that the training itself has become a kind of induction into a new language rather than an extension and redirection of an existing, readily available vocabulary.[189] The constant danger in the British context is not that there will be a drift into anti-political populism, but that community organizing will become reduced to a technique or method of political mobilization as it struggles to embed itself in the lived traditions and values of its member institutions, divorced as it is from any wider cultural-historical frame of reference with which participants can instinctively identify community organizing.[190] Within London Citizens, this is played out in the tension between using frames of reference steeped in the discourses of liberalism and human rights and those that draw from religious and historical narratives and analogies. Such tensions will be explored in greater detail in Chapters 4 and 5 through an examination of the repertoires of community organizing.

THRESHOLD

This is not the place to rehearse all the "rules" that Alinsky himself spelled out in his own writing. However, there are a number of salutary lessons that the origins of community organizing suggest for its future prospects. For in the formation of the practice we see displayed a number of temptations that constantly present themselves to organizing efforts and which have at times overwhelmed some IAF and other Alinsky-style initiatives.

First, organizing grew out of neighborhood organizing, and Alinsky judged place so important that he even included it in the name of the organization he founded: the Industrial *Areas* Foundation. There is a temptation to ignore the neighborhood and the city amid the clamor for regionally, nationally, or globally "effective" action. A consistent critique of all community organizing efforts is that they operate at the wrong scale to have any effective power: first it was said they were too focused on the neighborhood and ignored the city-wide scale, then it was argued that they ignored the national scale, and now contemporary critics say organizing efforts lack a sufficiently global scale to be effective. Yet if the people are the program, then one can only really listen to people and build relationships between them within particular places and the "natural area" in which they connect. Without sufficient attention to place, organizing ceases to be a relational politics; in fact, it ceases to be politics at all in the sense that Arendt, Crick, and Wolin define the term, and becomes just another form of proceduralism. The challenge for community organizing now is addressing how to maintain a place-based, relational politics that is at the same time attentive to the dynamics of globalization. This challenge will be addressed in Chapters 2 and 3.

Second, if urban ethnography emphasizes the importance of listening to and observing the people and places to be organized in systematic, in-depth, and disciplined ways, then the temptation is not to listen and really pay attention, but to engage instead in a shallow or rushed analysis of the social, political, and economic context. The mechanics of how to listen, develop an analysis, and thence forge public action appropriate to the context is examined in Chapters 4 and 5.

Third, over and above acting according to some predetermined program or agenda that claims to know better what people really need, there is the temptation to instrumentalize the people and institutions being organized, rendering them campaign fodder even while working within their experience. Here the problem is not giving enough attention to building relationships and honoring familial, religious, and other social obligations by turning everything into an opportunity for action. Organizing grew out of traditions such as Judaism, the labor movement, and Roman Catholicism that built institutions to support cooperative enterprises, mutual responsibility, and committed, faithful relationships as exemplified in the family. Nurturing and sustaining these relationships requires virtue and moral vision. However good its intentions, a politics without such piety is pitiless and impoverished. Conversely, piety without any politics is pitiful, as it has no means to challenge, protect, and pursue the very relationships it loves and values most in the face of their erosion and co-option by the market and the state. Chapters 6 and 7 examine the thesis that organizing efforts that fail to pay heed to the health of the moral vision, virtue, and associational life of its people and its organizers will leave untended not only the basis of its political vision, but also the basis of its ability to make rational political judgments.

Fourth, in Judaism and the early labor movement there was an emphasis on self-organization and not turning to the state as either the bearer of a moral vision or the first port of call to resolve problems or provide for needs. This was an insight the labor movement lost as it turned to the state and the national arena as the proper domain of political action and welfare provision. There is a constant temptation in organizing to go the same way and render itself unto Caesar first rather than encourage its constituent members to take direct responsibility for matters themselves and only turn to the state where it is necessary and appropriate. The implications of this insight will be explored in Chapter 8.

As should be clear, Alinsky's approach emerged as primarily an urban practice of politics. Yet, as the link to Populism suggests, its historical roots lie in forms of political action first developed among agrarian radicals of the nineteenth century. And early civil rights organizers such as Septima Clark and Ella Baker developed a parallel approach to Alinsky in the largely rural southern states. Moreover, those mentored by Alinsky adapted his approach to a variety of nonurban and non-Western settings. Therefore, community organizing is not an exclusively urban or Western phenomenon. However, it was within urban conditions that the kinds of processes to which community organizing is a response are felt most intensely and displayed most acutely. In Chapters 2 and 3 we turn from Chicago to London to discern how the practice of organizing that Alinsky crystallized has evolved and been developed to address the dynamics of globalization as they manifest themselves in a world city.

2

Faith and Citizenship in a World City

To see how Alinsky's legacy traveled and developed historically and geographically, we move from North America to Europe and, more specifically, to the context and work of London Citizens. The aim of this chapter and of Chapter 3 is to immerse the reader in one specific context – London – and some of the ways in which organizing was adapted to address the demands of working in that context. The chapters provide a backdrop and point of reference for the detailed description and analysis of how to organize, which is set out in Chapters 4 and 5, and the subsequent examination of the relationship between faith, citizenship, and the politics of a common life in the rest of the book.

We begin by picking up where we left off in the Introduction: the events taking place on November 25, 2009. The central figure of the press conference held at the coffee shop on Brushfield Street was Rabbi Natan Asmoucha. Rabbi Asmoucha's story is important because within it two worlds collided: the one represented by those gathered in the coffee shop and the other by those seated in the plush offices of Allen & Overy. Rabbi Asmoucha had hosted a gathering at the Bevis Marks synagogue on July 22, 2009. The Bevis Marks synagogue is Britain's oldest synagogue and centrally located in the City of London. This event marked the beginning of the process that eventually resulted in the proposals that were to be set out at the Barbican assembly. Given the history of the link between usury and anti-Semitism in Europe, it was felt to be symbolically crucial by London Citizens not only to involve the Jewish community from the outset (despite no synagogue formally being a member at this point) but also to launch any initiative from a synagogue so as to decouple the focus on usury and responsible lending from any association with anti-Semitism.[1] The initiating event involved Christians, Muslims, and Jews, as well as representatives from other members of London Citizens gathering at Bevis Marks before marching together the short distance to the Royal Bank of Scotland (RBS). Once at the bank, they tried to present its chairman with a copy of the Torah,

FIGURE 2.1. Action outside Royal Bank of Scotland July 22, 2009. Rabbi Asmoucha stands on the far left.

the Bible, and the Qur'an with passages highlighted in each text that discussed the evils of usury (Figures 2.1 and 2.2).

RBS was targeted for the action because, as part of its rescue package, the British government had purchased a majority share in the bank in October 2008 and subsequently increased its holding from 58 percent to 70 percent in January 2009. While being dependent on public money, RBS was seen to be charging exorbitant rates of interest on its credit card services. Despite prior agreement with officials from the bank that the Bible, Torah, and Qur'an would simply be handed in at the reception desk, the delegation was refused entry. This refusal was widely reported and commented on in the mainstream media with the issue of usury coming up again and again. Subsequent to the event, Rabbi Asmoucha was forced to resign from his position as rabbi at Bevis Marks in October 2009.[2] The stated reason given for his forcible resignation was that he had compromised the security of the synagogue. The unstated reason was widely known and much debated within the Jewish community itself. As the BBC reported, "[A] senior synagogue member said the march had upset members with links to the financial services industry."[3]

The Barbican event that evening opened with the following scenario to explain who London Citizens was and what the event was about. After two

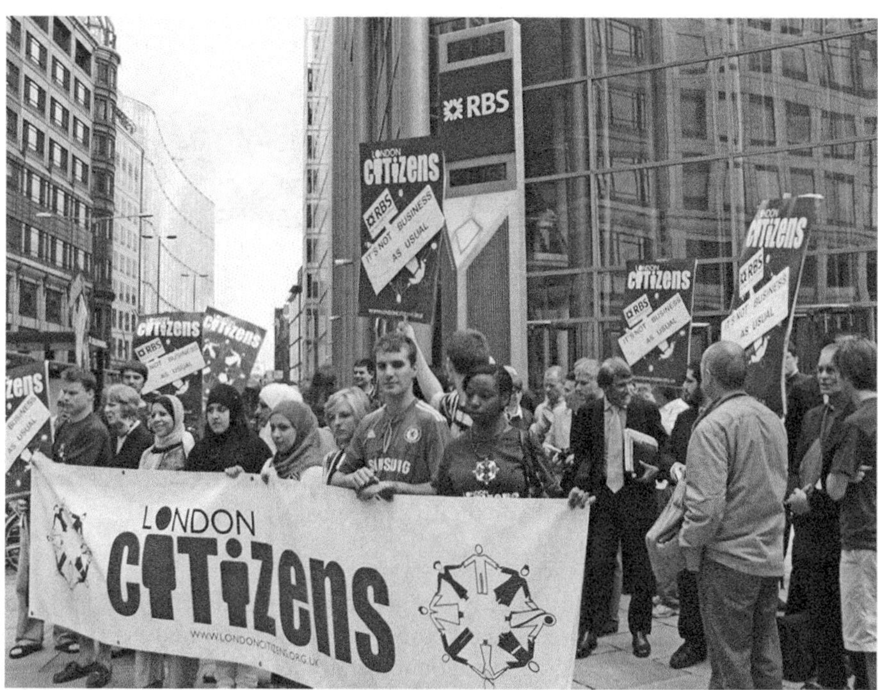

FIGURE 2.2. Action outside Royal Bank of Scotland July 22, 2009.

female members from the Pentecostal New Testament Church of God sang "Lean on Me," followed by a performance by a street-dance troupe called "Visionz," Sister Una McLeash, a former head teacher of a Catholic girls' school in East London and a trustee of London Citizens, introduced the panel of chairs and sought approval from everyone in the room for the authority of chairs to govern the assembly.[4] This consisted of asking the 2,000 participants (the total capacity of the Barbican) to say "Aye" and wave their programs if they agreed. As Sister Una did this, five religious leaders took to the stage to sit, positioned like a panel of judges, at the center back of the platform (Figure 2.3). These leaders came from non-Establishment traditions. They were the Roman Catholic vicar-general of East London, the head of the Muslim Council of Britain, the head of the Salvation Army, the senior rabbi of the Masorti synagogues, and the leading bishop of the New Testament Church of God (Figure 2.4).[5] After Sister Una finished, two young black comedians and children's television presenters named Ashley J. and Tee-J bounded to the front of the stage to provide a prologue to the proceedings.

Tee-J started by asking who was holding the assembly and how the proposals being put forward that evening had been developed. The response, which had been agreed on and edited with other organizers and leaders at a Sunday evening rehearsal three days previously, was that those gathered were 2,000

FIGURE 2.3. Assembly at the Barbican theatre November 25, 2009.

people representing London Citizens – a group comprised of more than 150 institutions, which represented some 50,000 people across London. The institutions were made up of schools, synagogues, churches, mosques, trade unions, university departments, and other civil-society institutions spread throughout London. The key sentiment expressed was that "we are people who take responsibility for ourselves, for our families and for the communities where we live. And we expect others to do the same, whether they be our neighbours, whether they be bankers, or whether they be politicians."

Tee-J then went on to ask: "So what is London Citizens' response to the economic crisis?" It was explained that London Citizens had been working with low-paid workers from across the capital for about ten years on the issue of getting them increased wages. From that experience it was decided to spend time learning what the impact of the recession was on the people in the member institutions and the places where they lived and worked.[6]

Prompted by Tee-J, Ashley responded to the explanation by saying: "Basically everyone here tonight is coming together and they have put their trust back in a democracy: getting people to come together and decide what they want to happen and creating a proposal and putting that towards the people who have the power to change these things." As will be seen, the reality of how the proposals came together was a less linear and more multilateral process than the one depicted at the assembly. However, Ashley's summation was accurate: the gathering was testimony to a renewed trust in democracy as a way of gaining some power to determine what was happening to the inhabitants of London.

The proposals set out at that assembly provide a window to many of the economic challenges participants in the work of London Citizens face on a daily basis and the responses seen to be necessary in order to address them constructively. The proposals set out at that assembly were also ones they hoped would make sense to the bankers and politicians they had cajoled and agitated into attending that evening. The first proposal was the adoption and promotion of the "Living Wage" as a commitment by all the major political parties in recognition that indebtedness among working families is often caused by poor pay. The Living Wage is an hourly payment over and above the statutory minimum wage; it is paid voluntarily by companies and designed to reflect the real cost of living when housing and transport costs are factored in. The second proposal was the curbing of usury through the introduction of a 20 percent cap on interest rates on unsecured personal loans by financial institutions (e.g., credit card companies, store cards, doorstep lending agencies). The measure would bring the United Kingdom in line with Germany, France, Italy, and Poland, each of which, at that time, had a 20–25 percent cap on the rate of interest that could be charged on unsecured personal loans. The third proposal was the expansion of local, mutual lending (e.g., credit unions) through infrastructural investment by banks and government to increase access to credit for the financially excluded. The fourth proposal was the development of a London Citizens' financial literacy project in partnership with the banks for use in schools and colleges – one in which what it means to be both a responsible borrower *and* a responsible lender is outlined. London Citizens' member schools would pilot this. Last, there was a call on all political parties to commit in their election manifestos to establish a statutory charter of responsible lending overseen by an established regulatory body. The charter would include measures such as a requirement for debt management plans, transparency of charges, and criteria for responsible marketing.

At the heart of the proposals was a call to restore responsibility to both borrowing and lending and to demand greater accountability from financial institutions. Hence the five proposals: (1) the Living Wage was seen as the best insurance against the working poor being forced into debt to make ends meet; (2) the cap on interest rates safeguards against the borrower being caught in a debt trap; (3) the recapitalization of local, mutual lending ensures that responsible, community-based forms of credit are available, thus breaking the monopoly of the banks on the one hand and the power of the loan sharks on the other; (4) financial literacy enables people to be more aware of the mechanisms of credit and the consequences of debt and to take responsibility for managing their money; and (5) a statutory code for fairer lending binds the financial services industry to greater accountability and transparency.

That morning, above the street, in the air-conditioned suite at Allen & Overy, the panel of bankers were asked a question about whether there was a need for the reintroduction of anti-usury legislation to curb the exorbitant rates of interest being charged on credit cards and other financial products. None of the panelists supported such a measure, and Lord Levene in his response asserted that usury was a "deliberately pejorative term" meant to imply that those who worked in the city were "rogues and vagabonds." A little while later at the coffee shop press conference, Rabbi Asmoucha told a Bloomberg journalist: "Usury is, I think, a proper term to use. Money is a tool to empower people, to create material prosperity that is for all people, as opposed to impoverishing people and making them completely dependent."[7]

Dependency on the banks and a need to rebalance the relationship between the power of money and the power of people was the central focus of the Barbican event on the evening of November 25. However, the concerns of London Citizens were not ones shared by Lord Levene. In his speech that morning he expressed how, in his view, the banks should be lauded for their philanthropy and for the positive impact of capitalism in lifting millions of people out of poverty (for which he cited the then Chief Rabbi, Jonathan Sacks, as an authority), and how the emphasis needed to be on reinforcing personal moral values among those who worked in banks, not on regulation and structural reform. Yet, Lord Levene did think there was need for greater responsibility, stating:

> Now is the time when we need to re-examine the great Victorian philanthropists and what they can teach us in this so-called post-religious age. They made huge profits but they considered a lot more than their bottom line. They managed to make money but stay true to often narrow religious dogmas. Now I would neither expect nor advocate a return of religion to the work place but what I think what we must learn from the Victorians is to rediscover a sense of responsibility. A strong ethical sense inspires and creates a sense of responsibility and the board members of a modern public company, regardless of their religious or moral beliefs, need to act responsibly to consider the consequences of the steps they take.[8]

In his emphasis on responsibility there appears to be a point of connection with the London Citizens event, which was itself entitled: "Taking responsibility in the economic crisis." But while the responsibility envisaged by Lord Levene is corporate, it is also utilitarian, self-referential, unmoored from any explicit moral tradition, and dislocated from and unaccountable to anyone or any place beyond those who make up the board of directors. In short, it encapsulates a vision for self-governance and self-regulation rather than public and transparent accountability. By contrast, the need to take responsibility spoken of at the London Citizens' assembly emphasized the mutual responsibility between banks and ordinary people in a particular place (namely, London) to ensure both personal responsibility in borrowing and fairness in lending. The link between the moral vision shaping the proposals, the proposals themselves, and practices of accountability were explicitly tethered to a "narrow religious dogma": a belief that usury (the charging of exorbitant interest) was a sin.

At the Barbican assembly, Nehemiah 5:1–13 was read aloud by Christian, Jewish, and Islamic leaders as a prelude to the cross-questioning of a senior representative of the City of London Corporation (Figure 2.4).[9]

In the Biblical passage, the leader of the people, Nehemiah, gathers an assembly in order to call on the elites of Jerusalem to repent from forcing their poorer neighbors into debt slavery. The reading dramatized the moral and political

FIGURE 2.4. The reading of Nehemiah 5:1–13 at the Barbican assembly November 25 2009.

conflict between the financial elites and institutions located in the City of London and their neighbors living in the boroughs around them. To understand the significance and historical backdrop to this conflict, we must better understand the history and nature of the City of London as a place and a polity.

THE CITY OF LONDON AND THE POWER OF MONEY

A "unique authority" governs the City of London as a place: the City of London Corporation.[10] The Corporation combines a role as the local municipal authority of the "Square Mile" with a national and global role as a lobbyist for "the City," which, as their website proclaims, is "the world leader in international finance and business services."[11] The City of London as a place must be distinguished from the metropolitan area of Greater London, which has its own mayor and municipal authority – the Greater London Authority (Figure 2.5). As the City of London website notes of its mayor, "The Lord Mayor in particular plays an important diplomatic role with his overseas visits and functions at the historic Guildhall and Mansion House for visiting heads of State."[12] At a meeting leading up to the November 25 assembly between leaders and organizers from London Citizens and the then Lord Mayor of London, Ian Luder, the Lord Mayor declared he spent most of his time meeting heads of state and representing the interests of the financial services industry around the world.[13] He was not boasting. In 2010 the Lord Mayor visited

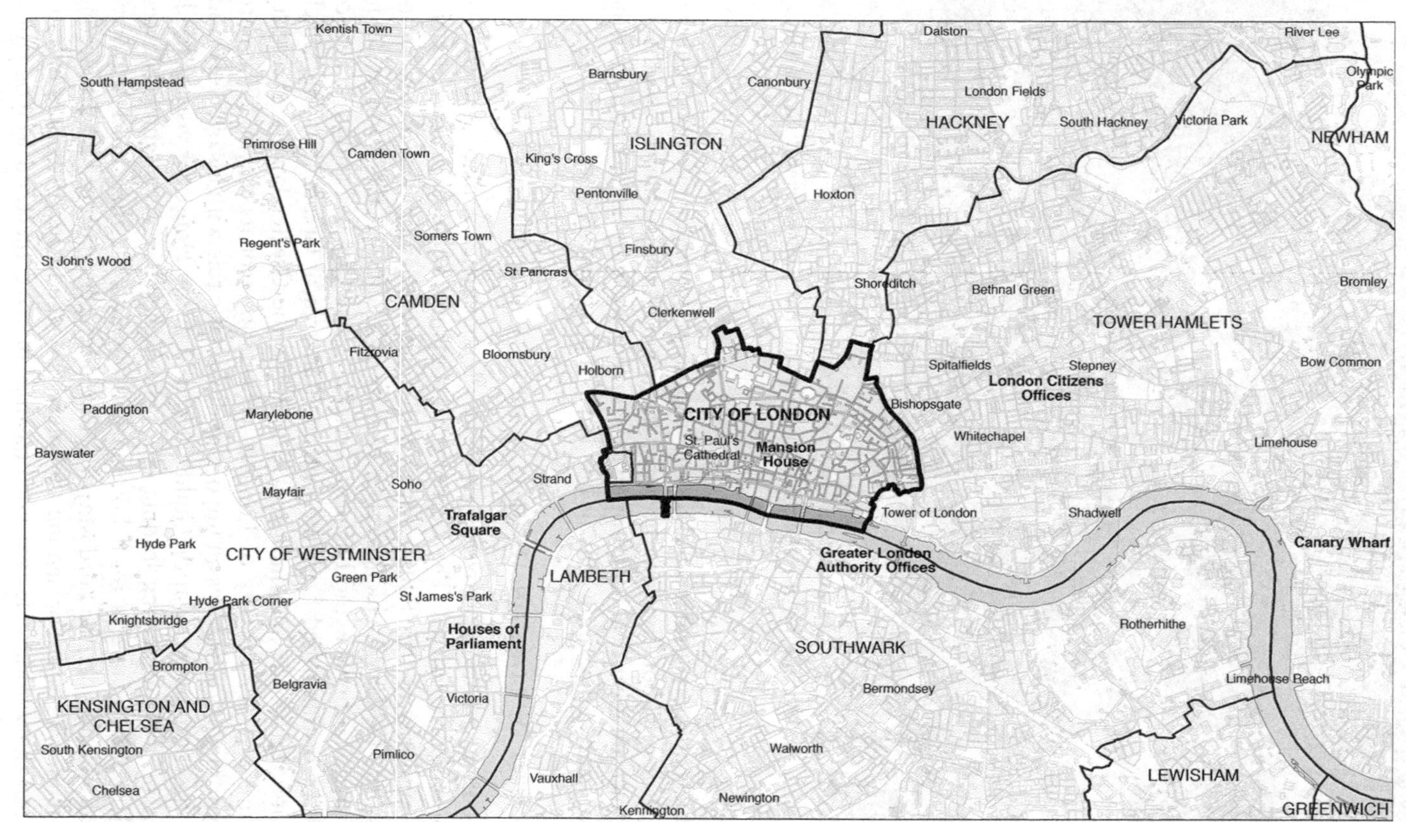

FIGURE 2.5. Boundaries and location of the City of London.

the United States, Qatar, United Arab Emirates, Saudi Arabia, Bahrain, South Africa, Romania, Indonesia, Singapore, Japan, Greece, Russia, China, Mexico, Columbia, Brazil, India, Oman, and Kuwait (in that order). The purpose of these visits was to

> encourage growing economies to raise capital in London; to open up new markets for city businesses, and to open doors at the highest levels for the accompanying business delegation. In private meetings and speeches, the Lord Mayor expounds the values of liberalisation and expands on those factors which have underpinned London's success, such as probity and transparency, open markets, corporate governance, Common Law [the City of London Corporation is responsible for managing Britain's central criminal court at the Old Bailey], welcome for skilled people from around the world, support for innovation, proportionate taxation and regulation.[14]

As well as owning large tracts of real estate in major cities around the world, the City of London Corporation as a polity also maintains permanent offices to represent its interests in Brussels, Mumbai, Beijing, Shenzhen, and Shanghai. The City of London Corporation is indeed a "unique authority," one that sits at the heart of local, national, and global politics and is a strategic and historic agent in processes of economic globalization. As the geographer Doreen Massey notes, "Globalization is made in places. The global is grounded. And one of the key localities where financial globalization was invented and orchestrated was London."[15] And the City of London Corporation sits at the center of this process of invention and orchestration.

As far as money is concerned, place still matters. Long after Great Britain ceased to be a global center of trade and industry, London has remained a command point in the global financial system.[16] London has more foreign banks than any other financial center and is the world's "biggest international – and offshore – financial hub."[17] While New York is the largest financial center, London is still more important in terms of international finance. Additionally, the City of London Corporation is central to creating and perpetuating a spider's web of tax havens or "secrecy jurisdictions" around the world that serve as feeders into the City. These "secrecy jurisdictions" or "states of exception" exist half inside and half outside the regulatory frameworks and political systems of Europe and North America and have been crucial to the development of economic globalization.[18] Because they are states of exception, banks and businesses – as well as despots and drug dealers – can do there what they cannot do at home: privatize their profits by shifting money to zero-tax havens and socialize their costs through nation-states who not only pay the bill when things go wrong but also provide the natural resources, infrastructure, education, and medical, political, and legal systems that are the condition and possibility of making the profits in the first place. The basis of the City of London's exceptional status goes back to the Norman Conquest in 1066 and the ways in which, over the centuries, it has created for itself a space outside the legal and political institutions of the rest of Great Britain. Its walled-off and protected status is symbolized by a ring of gates: Aldgate, Bishopsgate, Moorgate, Aldersgate, Ludgate, Cripplegate, Newgate, and Billingsgate mark the territory of its exception where even the monarch must wait to be invited in, and must surrender her sword (symbolic of her sovereignty) before she can enter.[19] The City is, in effect, a medieval commune whose ancient rights, privileges, and customary practices have formed the means through which to assert and consolidate an exceptional status that was then deployed as a command point of a "neoliberal" form of economic globalization.[20]

As stated already, the origins of the City's exceptional status go back to the Norman Conquest. William the Conqueror came "friendly" to London and recognized the liberties of its citizens in a formal charter.[21] Crucially, the charter granted nothing new; it only ratified existing rights and privileges.[22] Like all public authorities, William could not afford to overly antagonize the merchants and moneymen who were an important source of tax revenues and loans. From the reign of William I onward, a stream of charters and privileges that protected the City of London from royal interference and recognized the antiquity of its customs upheld the City of London's special status within the constitution. The status of London as part of the "ancient constitution" – that which existed prior to the Norman Conquest and therefore was partially outside of the jurisdiction of the crown – was formerly recognized in 1191 when the City became an independent commune.[23] The significance of this came to the fore at the Magna Carta in 1215 when not only were the rights of the "whole body" of citizens respected, but the Mayor of London (and by implication, the militias under his authority) was also designated as one of the twenty-five guarantors charged with enforcing the charter if the Crown should renege.[24] The combination of wealth, functioning democratic and legal institutions, as well as an effective system of civic militias meant that the Crown could never subordinate the City of London to its rule. Indeed, in 1135, the citizens of London claimed the right to choose the king and acclaimed Stephen of Blois as successor to Henry I. Richard I rejected this claim and caused a riot when it appeared that he rebuffed the leading citizens of London at his coronation. Despite such occasional snubs, London taxed itself, judged itself, and governed itself.

Echoing a Europe-wide pattern, London became a city that recognized guilds and professions as central institutions in the body politic.[25] The Corporation was built on the guilds as democratic units of the city and in the twelfth century the Guildhall became the center of the City's government. The crafts had a professional and public status because market entry was dependent on completing an apprenticeship, the reward for which was the granting of citizenship.[26] However, in the late sixteenth and seventeenth centuries, London began to diverge from other comparable European cities. Even while London expanded – largely as a result of becoming the home of those displaced by the process of enclosures in the North and Midlands – it lacked any unitary municipal authority. Despite attempts by Charles I both to assert sovereign control over the City of London and to establish civic government for its newly populated areas, the Corporation refused to countenance such measures.[27] Thus, from the seventeenth century onward, the general populace of London lacked civic representation, whereas businesses – particularly bankers – had the most ancient political institution in the kingdom at their disposal. All subsequent attempts to exert sovereign control over the City of London have failed. Despite its manifesto commitment, the 1945 Labour Government did not interfere with the political institutions of the City, but its prime minister, Clement Atlee, understood clearly the problem the City of London represented. He wrote:

> Over and over again we have seen that there is in this country another power than that which has its seat at Westminster. The City of London, a convenient term for a collection of financial interests, is able to assert itself against the Government of the country. Those who control money can pursue a policy at home and abroad contrary to that which has been decided by the people.[28]

Contemporary political theorists are fixated on political sovereignty and tend to view the nation-state as the only form of sovereign power. Attention to the City of London suggests an alternative view: economic power can constitute itself as an exception to the assertion of national sovereignty, creating for itself freedom from state-level and democratic accountability while massively limiting the ability of ordinary citizens to act politically and of governments to act juridically, thus eroding the civic and democratic life of political communities. The City of London is a paradigm for this dynamic. Capitalizing on its unique status, banks in the City built on the creation of unregulated offshore Euromarkets in the City of London in the late 1950s so that the City became a place in which U.S. banks could evade New Deal regulation.[29] Other bankers from around the world took their lead from the United States and headed to London. Subsequently, as the investigative journalist Nicholas Shaxson notes, the "Big Bang" of 1986 enhanced the City of London's offshore status and a reverse flow ensued whereby "regulatory competition from 'light-touch' London became a crowbar for lobbyists around the globe: 'If we don't do this, the money will go to London,' they would cry, or, 'We can already do this in London, so why not here?' The City emitted anti-regulatory impulses around the world, deregulating other economies and their banking systems as if by remote control."[30] When the then Lord Mayor visited Hong Kong, South Korea, and China in 2007, he met with senior officials from Tianjin, the Chinese city chosen as a pilot for national financial "reform." An official Corporation report noted that its mayor, Dai Xianglong, "placed great value on deepening cooperation with the City of London, which he dubbed 'the holy place' of international finance and globalization."[31]

LONDON: A WORLDLY CITY

Writing in the same month that London both suffered the July 7, 2005 bombings and won the bid to host the 2012 Olympics – a bid in which its cultural diversity was a major feature – the then Mayor of the Greater London Authority (note: not the Lord Mayor of the City of London) claimed: "London is the whole world in one city."[32] His statement reflects the way in which the status of London as a world city is based not only on its status as a command point in the FIRE (finance, insurance and real estate) sector, but also on its role as a global center of cultural production and its demography as one of the most religiously and ethnically diverse cities in the world. But what does it mean for London to be a "world city"? The term "world" refers to more than just the internal diversity of London's population and its role in processes of economic and cultural globalization.[33] The social science usage of the term "world city" can be collocated with an older, theological use of the term "world" (*kosmos*) as a synonym for the universal order of things and how, before the Day of Judgment, this order is coterminous with a worldly system opposed to God's ordering of creation: what Augustine called the "earthly city."[34]

As a world city, London is an earthly or worldly city, an instantiation of "Babylon." This is an insight first articulated in the nineteenth century with the rise of London as an imperial and industrial center. For example, Benjamin Disraeli identified London as a "modern Babylon" in his 1847 novel *Tancred*. His account was part of a widespread nineteenth-century sentiment that viewed London elegiacally through the prism of the great Biblical motif of imperial power: a prism encouraged in part by the discovery of the ruins of the original Babylon and the transport of artifacts from that ancient city to the British Museum.[35] London, like Babylon and Rome before it, was simultaneously the center of things and embodied the system as a whole, and thus stood apocalyptically under judgment. Like all imperial centers, it is awe-inspiring and capable of producing things beautiful and precious as well as decadent and damned. As with the depiction of Babylon/Rome given in Revelation, London stands for and is imbricated in a whole system of production, domination, and degradation. This manifests itself in how London has a tentacular spatial and temporal spread, with mutually dependent social, economic, political, and administrative relationships, reaching not just throughout Great Britain, but also around the globe. Already mentioned is its role as the central point in a network of tax havens. Another example of this is the dependence of London's health services on recruitment from overseas and how, in turn, the localities from which migrant workers come suffer from a "brain drain" while at the same time gaining from financial remittances from expatriates, improved training, and long-term professional networks.[36] What happens in healthcare is repeated across London's labor markets, from the menial to the managerial.[37] To rephrase the mayor's statement: the whole world is in London and London is in the world.

The negative influence of the whole world being in London and London in the world – or what can be called "globalization" for short – is overheard again and again in the kinds of problems facing leaders of institutions in membership of London Citizens. For example, Hugh O'Shea, a local trade-union leader involved in London Citizens, notes the changes in work he experienced in the hospitality industry:

I think previously in the industry you were all employees, so you would join on a permanent contract and you would all be, for better or worse, part of a team. You were the team in the hotel or the team in the restaurant. And everybody of course grumbled about conditions and that because it's always been a low paid industry, but here in my second incarnation as a hospitality industry worker, the system of agency work and casual work meant that you were a commodity. So you would be booked in for four hours, five hours, six hours, there was no certainty of work. And then after a while I discovered that not only weren't you certain of how much work you'd get, but if you raised any concerns your work would dry up. So basically you were brought in as a commodity to fill a half day or a day's shift, there was no continuity of work and you had no chance of having any impact upon your own working conditions, you were just a little cog in a very big wheel.[38]

What O'Shea identifies as the problem is a process of "commodification" – a central issue for nineteenth-century Populists. To reiterate what was said in Chapter 1, commodification is used here to denote the process whereby unregulated markets make goods that are not products (and therefore are non-fungible) into commodities to be bought and sold. These goods cease to be unique and irreplaceable and become goods exchangeable with anything else and of no greater value than anything else. In Polanyi's account of this process, it is not markets per se that are the problem; rather, it is when markets are no longer subordinated to and embedded within social and political relationships, and in turn subordinate human flourishing to the demands of the market.[39]

For members of London Citizens, the felt pressures of commodification and the critique of the market do not generate hostility to global capitalism per se. Despite occasional accusations to the contrary, community organizers do not identify with either Communism or Socialism and are highly critical of "anti-globalization" protesters as divorced from the concerns of ordinary people.[40] The issue for London Citizens is that, while the market has a place, it must know its place. As London Citizens lead organizer Neil Jameson puts it:

I've learnt it by experience and by just watching what happens. ... Maybe the market's a sort of solution but I don't think it is, really. Containing the market is the challenge. Holding ourselves accountable, developing our own power base, so that the market has to give. We know we can do that, 'cause we have done that with Living Wage certainly, but there's so much else to do because the market is so much more sophisticated and has got so much more money than we have and so many more organisers than we have.[41]

The challenge for community organizing as Jameson presents it in training and at evaluations is to humanize the market and limit the negative consequences of its untrammeled operation. A key way broad-based community organizing does this is through seeking to entangle market relations with place-based social relations; that is, it aims to ensure that companies remember that those they operate among, sell to, and employ are also their neighbors.

It is my contention that community organizing, from its origins in Chicago to its practice in contemporary London, can be seen as a way of re-embedding market relations within place-based social relations. Evidence for this interpretation can be seen in the way in which numerous campaigns are narrated.[42] For example, the Living Wage campaign is narrated at assemblies and in training as emerging not out of class conflict, or the need for equality, but as arising out of the need to enable families to flourish. Testimony is given at assemblies of how parents have to work several jobs to make ends meet and so never see their children, but payment of a living wage frees them up to spend more time with their family and in their church or mosque. As Neil Jameson comments, "[t]he fight for family time is very important to us ... And then, you know, Living Wage [is] to strengthen family."[43] The Living Wage campaign also seeks to decommodify labor relations by asserting the importance of place (through demanding recognition of locational factors in the calculation of the wage) and social relations (through forging relationships between civil society institutions and businesses). Analogous to the medieval conception of the just price, advocates for a Living Wage contend that market factors should not wholly determine the price. Rather, social considerations and a contextual judgment about what human flourishing requires at a particular time and place are taken to be a key consideration. In short, market exchange is not counted as the only determinative factor relevant to economic life; rather, a prior set of social and political relations must be accounted for.[44] What such an accounting process involves will be explored in Chapter 8.

A GLOBALIZED LOCAL POLITICS

The Nehemiah 5 passage read aloud at the Barbican assembly was also referred to at each of the local assemblies that led up to November 25 and at each of those, as well as at the Barbican event, all those gathered repeated the following line at the end of the passage: "And all the assembly said, 'Amen.'" At those prior assemblies Jameson, a Quaker, had taken to the stage and made the link between the passage, the contemporary economic crisis, and the democratic practice of assembling to hold those with power accountable for their actions. What Jameson said was directly inspired by a sermon on Nehemiah preached by a black Baptist pastor in a church in New York. The preacher was Johnny Ray Youngblood, a key leader in East Brooklyn Congregations, another broad-based community organization affiliated with the Industrial Areas Foundation (IAF). East Brooklyn Congregations became an important force in the urban politics of New York in the 1980s and pioneered the Nehemiah Homes project: a citizen-led and independently financed house-building program that was a key initiative in the renewal of derelict parts of Brooklyn.[45] Jameson did his initial training as a community organizer under the tutelage of Michael Gecan, lead organizer of East Brooklyn Congregations. After this training he returned to Britain to found the Citizens Organizing Foundation (the forebear of Citizens UK) in 1990. While in New York he formed a friendship with Reverend Youngblood, attending his church on numerous occasions and eventually arranged a number of visits by Reverend Youngblood to help build relationships between the Citizens Organizing Foundation and Black majority churches in Britain. The point of connection between Jameson and Youngblood was part of the emergence of a formal (as distinct from the ad hoc and occasional) international dimension to the Industrial Areas Foundation's network. In addition to the United Kingdom, the IAF now has affiliates in Canada, Germany, and Australia. These affiliations raise two questions: First, how are we to understand the relationship between London Citizens as a form of local politics and its simultaneous participation in a global network? And second, do the links between the IAF and its international affiliates constitute a form of "globalization from below"?

Each part of the IAF network engages in place-based forms of political action. But the IAF connects these place-specific forms of action and local foci to a broader process that shapes both the shared practices and the particular forms of action appropriate to specific contexts. This process is sustained through moments of *concentration* (for example, there are occasional gatherings that draw together IAF organizers from around the world to reflect on issues of common concern) and *dispersion* (for example, each affiliate is assigned an experienced U.S. organizer who regularly travels to mentor local organizers, consult on tactics, and help train leaders). Through this process of concentration and dispersion, shared stories, resources, and practices traverse national frontiers and cross-pollinate from one national political and cultural context to another. Over time the IAF has developed a network of transnational, organizationally linked broad-based community organizations.[46] However, this process is not always straightforward and the links between different sections are often thin with organizers in Australia, Germany, and the United Kingdom expressing a sense of detachment and exclusion from debates and developments in the United States. Although there is a network of broad-based community organizations formally affiliated with the IAF in a number of countries, the IAF network is neither focused on global issues nor a self-consciously "global" network.[47] Even though formal organizational, relational, and financial ties exist, each node in the network participates as a self-governing and independent organization.[48] The international network thus mirrors the local organizational structure in which independent institutions formally affiliate as part of an identifiable broad-based community organization.

The emphasis on institutions is a distinguishing feature of London Citizens and the IAF more generally. This is in contrast to many other forms of political campaign groups and organizations. One cannot join London Citizens as an individual; one can only take part as a participant in an institution in membership.[49] Yet strengthening the kinds of corporate allegiance and covenantal bonds that traditions and institutions embody and reproduce is seen by many social theorists to be swimming against the tide.[50] It is fair to say that the weakness of institutions in the face of processes of globalization is a key anxiety among organizers.[51] Indeed, London Citizens declared 2009 the year of strengthening institutions, focusing its annual retreat on this theme. In London the figures are stark: data indicates that ten out of London's thirty-two boroughs now have at least 50 percent turnover of population in a five-year period, with one borough, Westminster, having a 70 percent turnover in the same period.[52] A consequence of this kind of population "churn" (i.e., the rapid turnover of people from one place to another) is that the means of producing place-based forms of organization and action are constantly being dissolved.

Building a common life through making neighbors of strangers depends on shared knowledge, vision, and memory; this needs updating and reinforcing via socialization and induction into shared practices. Social flexibility and population churn (which means people are far more mobile and less tied to place and social relationships), a flood of knowledge (which overwhelms and erases memory rather than feeding and stabilizing it), and multiple sources of information (which means people receive contradictory messages about the world all at once) make generating a common world of meaning and action both within an institution and in a locality extremely difficult.[53] To address the socially liquefying effects of economic globalization and, in particular, the issue of population mobility, Jane Wills argues that within anchor institutions (such as religious institutions, schools, universities, workplaces, and community centers, etc.) a mobile population can be captured, albeit temporarily. The negotiation of a common life between such *institutions*, rather than between individuals, allows for a place-based politics to emerge. Yet, as the analysis set out here suggests, the need to organize is constant and the pressure relentless as the ground of such a place-based politics is constantly shifting. There does appear to be an inherent conflict between what it takes to sustain the values and vision of the institutions in membership of London Citizens and the demands of the market for dissolving place-based and social ties, which inhibit the flow of money. As Polanyi puts it, commenting on the power of global capitalism: "Labour and land are made into commodities, which, again, is only a short formula for the liquidation of every and any cultural institution in an organic society."[54] Part of the work of London Citizens is to enable its members to understand and confront this conflict.[55] In addition, organizers constantly reassert their commitment to strengthening the institutions in membership.

In light of what has just been said, it would be easy to frame the kind of work that London Citizens does as a form of "globalization from below," which pits the local politics of ordinary people against the political machination of global elites as represented by those gathered in the boardroom of Allen & Overy. However, as will be seen in Chapters 4 and 5, the connections between London Citizens and different kinds of elites suggest that the line between "above" and "below" is fluid as elite agendas and grassroot forms of insurgency contest and interact with each other. Moreover, if the division between "above" and "below" dissolves on closer inspection, so does another spatial division: that between "local" and "global."[56] Two conclusions are often inferred from framing community organizing within a story that pits a local politics against global elites: the story of community organizing is either a tragedy whose protagonist is fated to irrelevance because the local is an insufficient scale at which to act effectively or it is written as a hagiography, community organizing being sanctified by dint of its status as a form of local resistance to globalization. Neither genre is the right one: the story to be told about community organizing must necessarily be a complex drama involving all the ambiguity of politics, the fortitude and finitude of human being, and the possibilities and pitfalls of action in time.

To be true to the story of community organizing we must resist setting up false dichotomies and Manichean conflicts such as those that pit "local" against "global."[57] The experience of London as a world city suggests that global and local dynamics interweave and constitute each other.[58] Urban local politics operates in a number of registers – neighborhood, metropolitan, national, and global – with global and nonlocal political dynamics impacting a particular locality and local politics affecting or being interwoven with global or transnational political dynamics.[59] What this analysis points to is a need to move beyond the advocacy of thinking globally and acting locally. Rather, it is a question of how neighborhood, metropolitan, national, and global scales of action interact in particular places and what kind of action is therefore appropriate in that place and time. A contemporary world city such as London and the conditions and possibilities of democratic citizenship it represents call forth the need to articulate a new vision of the relationship between the construction of place and the practice of democratic politics.[60] Meaningful political action is not simply local or global but strategically located and site and time specific.[61] When assessing the impact of democratic political action the question of location, means of agency, and the strategic value of the target in that location are perhaps more significant than the numbers of people involved or the national or global breadth of involvement.[62]

Within the reconfigurations and refractions of globalization certain kinds of places re-emerge as globally significant locations of political action; cities are territories of this kind. Moreover, some localities generate globalizing processes more intensely and directly than others; as we have seen, London is one such place.[63] In these kinds of places local democratic politics is given both the opportunity and responsibility for greater impact. The question democratic politics and religious groups then confront is how to configure political action that is both place based and attuned to what is happening at other scales and in other places. This is not just a tactical question; it is also a theoretical one that requires paying attention to the spatial dimensions of politics.[64] Attention to community organizing in the context of a world city allows for analysis of what a politics that is both place based and simultaneously woven into broader dynamics might entail and draws attention to the spatial dimensions of democratic citizenship and the placed-based opportunities available to challenge the power of money.[65]

The question of how to configure political action that is both place based and attuned to what is happening in other places poses a particular challenge to the IAF, which could do far more to build relationships between coalitions located in different places, both in terms of its campaigns and in terms of constructing a genuinely confederal organizational form.[66] A good example of this kind of coordination was the successful action on Deutsche Bank regarding their involvement in foreclosures in 2012 through coordinating the actions of the IAF affiliates in the United States and Germany.[67] At the same time, organizers need to attend to the opportunities for reweaving civil society in other places afforded to them by their location in world cities and other strategic places. A good example of this is the work of London Citizens in training Zimbabwean and Congolese diaspora living in London in forms of distributed leadership and democratic organizing. The Zimbabwean Movement for Democratic Change and the Congo Support Group were members of London Citizens and became involved in local campaigns. Yet they were also eager to learn the skills of organizing so that when they returned to Zimbabwe and the Congo they could use what they learned to change what they saw as the anti-democratic political culture and "big man" vision of leadership in their country of origin. The process of learning was neither an imperialistic imposition nor a technocratic intervention; rather, it occurred between neighbors living together in the same place. However, the significance of the learning was not restricted to one place. Similar effects can be seen with organizers who were recruited, trained, and gained experience in London and then returned to their country of origin – be it France, Mozambique, Taiwan, or Columbia – and began doing organizing in one form or another in their home context. This kind of process needs to be engaged in and capitalized on far more intentionally by the IAF and other organizing networks.

What is proposed here is not the usual critique of organizing as ineffective because it operates at the wrong scale (citywide, national, or global). Rather, my critique is that organizing is often not local enough: insufficient attention is paid to how place is constructed, the opportunities available within a place for political action, and how different places are interconnected. Beyond organizing, thinking about how to strengthen democratic politics and civil society through working with the flows, circuits, and dynamics afforded by the global connections between places represents a challenge and opportunity not only for organizers, but also for the likes of international development and global health organizations. As with the strategic importance of London in the FIRE sector, analysis of the supply or value chains of an industry or organization is vital to identifying where action can be strategic. For example, to act in a way that affects the conditions and wages of agricultural workers or addresses obesity, it makes far more sense to act against a supplier such as Tyson Foods (one of the world's largest producers and distributors of chicken, beef, and pork) or a large-scale retailer such as McDonalds. Their ownership of and influence on entire supply chains is such that they can impact the terms and conditions of the production, distribution, and marketing of a whole industry.[68] These "value chains" can be acted on at specific points and in specific places with great effect. Conversely, action on the same company in another place might be almost entirely pointless as at that place no value is added and so nothing is really at stake.

THRESHOLD

Echoing Chapter 1's portrayal of the conditions and possibilities of community organizing within an earlier phase of modernization as experienced in Chicago, this chapter located community organizing as the response to a different moment of modernization in a different city. It was seen that London as a context of community organizing is one in which both ancient and modern political forms intersect to produce and refract processes of globalization. The chapter opened with London Citizens' November 25 assembly, an event that combined faith and citizenship in the attempt to bring accountability to financial elites. The context of the assembly was London, defined here as a world and worldly city in which the role and influence of the City of London is key. The City of London as a command point in the financial services industry was identified as a "state of exception" that constantly evades political accountability. The nature of London as a world city was located within broader debates about how processes of globalization shape the construction of place and the practice of politics in the contemporary context. The work of the IAF was shown to both participate in global flows through its own internationalization, and constitute a response to processes of globalization through enabling a particular kind of place-based politics. This place-based politics is conceptualized as a means of contradicting processes of commodification and re-embedding globalized economic relations. Anchor institutions were identified as central to establishing a place-based politics within a world city. It is to the role and involvement of religious institutions in broad-based community organizing to which we turn in Chapter 3 in order to further understand the nature of community organizing as a form of democratic politics and the context of London as a world and worldly city.

3

Reimagining the Secular

Interfaith Relations as a Civic Practice

This chapter focuses on an assessment of how community organizing as a practice mediates the relationship between "faith" and democratic citizenship and how democratic politics can mediate the relationship between different religious traditions. Understanding these relationships is central to understanding broad-based community organizing (BBCO) itself, as religious institutions are a key component of both London Citizens and the Industrial Areas Foundation's core membership.[1] Moreover, an immersion in the details and dynamics of how BBCO engages religious communities is a vital precursor to and point of reference for the broader, more theoretical analysis of the relationship between faith, democratic citizenship, and the power of money discussed in Part II.

To comprehend how London Citizens worked with and drew from religious groups, its work needs locating within a broader historical context. The interaction noted in Chapter 2 between Jameson, a white Quaker social worker from Bristol, and Johnny Ray Youngblood, a black Baptist preacher in New York, can be situated within a long historical process of religious mobilization running to and fro between Britain and North America from the seventeenth century onward. These transatlantic and now global processes of interaction within Christianity (as well as Judaism and Islam) feed into the dynamics of community organizing as a performance of democratic citizenship. To understand something of the impact of global processes in shaping community organizing in London, it is important to begin with the history of how BBCO came to Great Britain.

A BRIEF HISTORY OF CITIZENS UK

A 1984 study of the prospects of community organizing in Britain suggested that it could not work, yet by the early 1990s there were fully functioning broad-based community organizations in Bristol, Liverpool, Sheffield, North

Wales, and Birmingham set up under the auspices of the Citizenship Organising Foundation (later named Citizens UK).[2] The work of Alinsky was a source of inspiration in the training of social workers and teachers and among political activists in the United Kingdom from the 1970s onward. One Anglican clergyman recalls coming across Alinsky in 1976 as part of a course run by the Student Christian Movement entitled "Gestalt Orientation and Alinsky Training" or GOAT.[3] More specifically, Alinsky's work was an influence on the emergence of "community development" as a distinct field in the United Kingdom from the 1950s onward.[4] As well as their interwoven history, community organizing and community development share overlapping objectives.[5] Many see community organizing as but one approach within the broader umbrella of community development. However, as was suggested in Chapter 1, the Alinsky approach is distinctive and addresses directly one of the self-contradictions that has plagued community development since its inception: its espoused commitment to strengthening civil society and place-based forms of participatory democracy and yet, given it has been primarily a state-sponsored activity, its history of co-option by and collusion with top-down, state-driven policy agendas of community management.[6]

Despite the engagement with Alinsky's work in Britain since the 1950s, it was not until the founding of the Citizens Organising Foundation that a fully fledged broad-based community organization was developed. So although its history in the United States goes back to the 1940s, it is a relatively recent phenomenon in the United Kingdom.[7] Yet leaders and organizers within Citizens UK claim they are reviving traditions that have roots in British history. While the antislavery movement and Chartism (an early nineteenth-century working-class movement for political reform) are sometimes cited as part of the prehistory of community organizing in Britain, it is the 1889 London Dock Strike, which had a catalytic effect in the emergence of the Labour movement, that is most frequently held up as a key antecedent.[8] What is notable about both the framing of this imagined tradition and the actual history of Citizens UK is the role of the churches.

All the central figures involved in founding Citizens Organising Foundation/Citizens UK had strong religious affiliations and the churches, both institutionally and financially, were vital to its emergence. For example, Neil Jameson and Eric Adams, the leading figures in its early development, were Quakers with financial support coming from the Barrow Cadbury Trust.[9] The Citizens Organising Foundation (COF) was formally established in 1989 with the aim of setting up broad-based community organizations in which "faith institutions" were key players. The original trust documents even stated the aims of the organization were to work within the "Judeo-Christian tradition."[10] From the outset Jameson sought to build relationships with all the faith communities present in a city as well as with the unions, envisioning the work as "not faith led, but faith inspired" and at the same time "an alliance of faith and labour."[11] The founding of COF (which was renamed Citizens UK in 2009) was neither

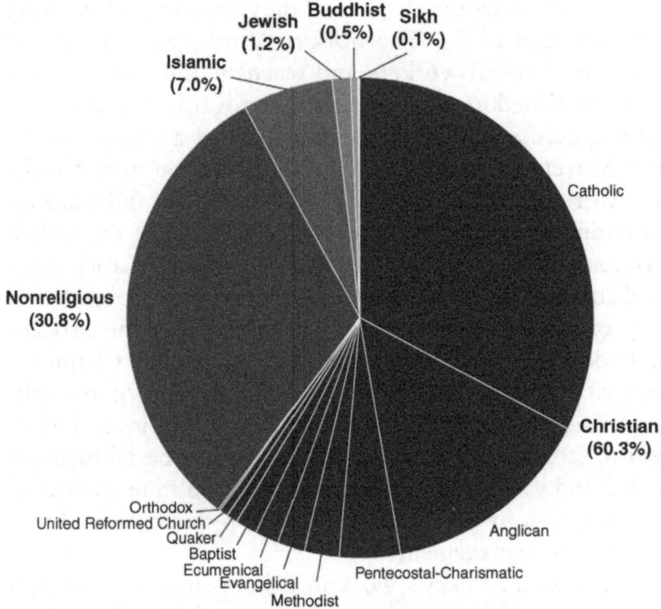

FIGURE 3.1. Religious affiliation of member institutions (2008–12).

a simplistically secular act nor a straightforwardly "religious" one; rather, as will be argued here, it was a faithful and pluralistically secular act in which Christianity played a crucial catalytic role, hosting what became in practice a common life politics. This is illustrated in the following representations of the membership institutions by type and affiliation from 2008 to 2012 and how they changed over that period [see Figures 3.1–3.4]. As is clear from the figures, Christianity is the most significant religious constituency involved and the most internally differentiated, while local congregations (whether Christian, Islamic, or Jewish) are the core type of membership institutions.

POPULAR RELIGION AND DEMOCRATIC CITIZENSHIP

The relationship between the religious groups and the innovative forms of democratic citizenship that Citizens UK represents is not new. As was suggested in Chapter 1, the Populist movement in the United States represents one historical precedent for the relationship between community organizing and religious groups in the context of resistance to the domination of the power of money. In the U.S. and British contexts, forms of popular, local self-organization and common action emerge within such movements as the antislavery and abolitionist movements, the Chartists, the suffragists, and the temperance movement. These were aligned and had a symbiotic relationship with popular religion.[12] In the British context, whether it was Methodism, working-class Catholicism,

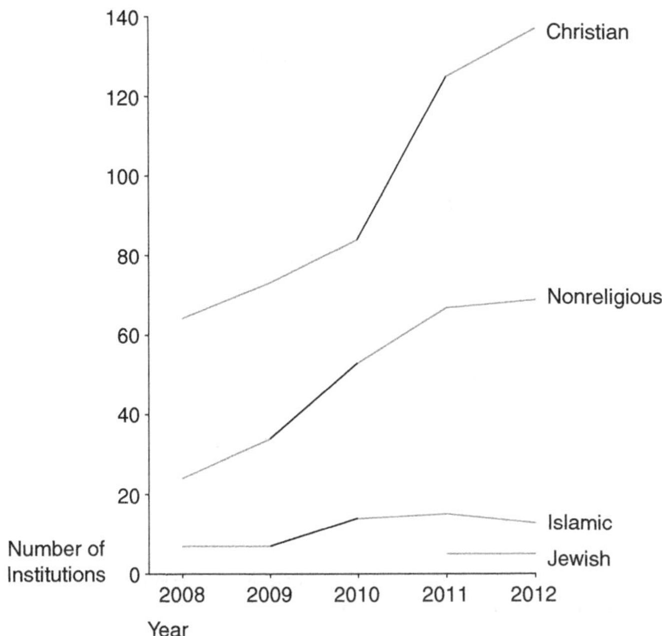

FIGURE 3.2. Religious affiliation of member institutions over time (2008–12).

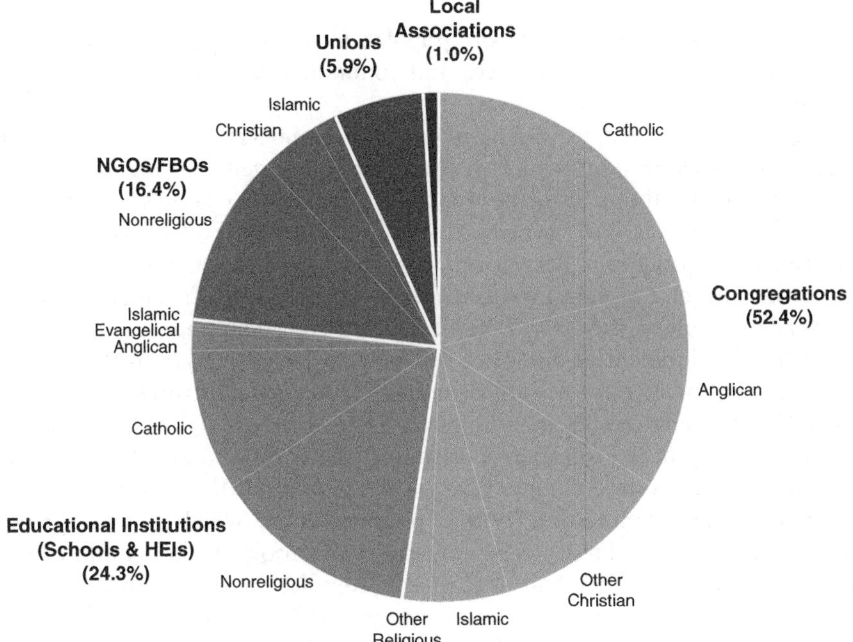

FIGURE 3.3. Type of member institutions (2008–12).

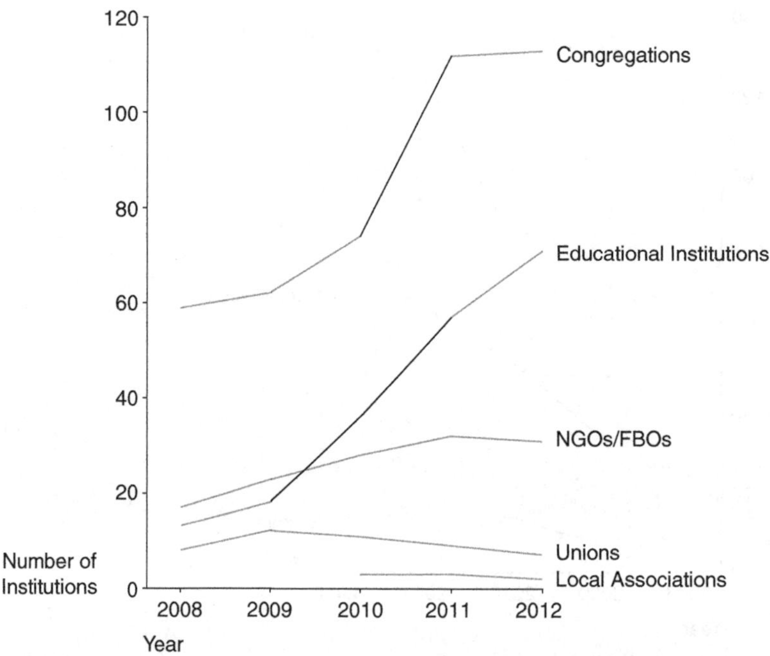

FIGURE 3.4. Type of member institutions over time (2008–12).

or the Shtetl movement in Judaism, popular forms of religiosity were a key social force generating the practices and common values vital for grassroots activism.[13]

In Great Britain, we see this confluence of democratization and popular religion embodied in figures such as Keir Hardie (as well as being founder of the Independent Labour Party, he was a keen temperance activist all his life), George Lansbury (as well as being a key figure in East End Labour politics and leader of the Labour Party from 1931 to 1935, he was an active member of the Church Socialist League and a teetotaler), and Cardinal Manning (alongside his role in the 1889 London Dock Strike, Manning was a key figure in the development of the Catholic temperance society).[14] In the United States, it is embodied most forcefully in the thrice-Democratic presidential candidate William Jennings Bryan (who ran in 1896, 1900, and 1908). A standard bearer of Evangelical Protestant Christianity, he was nicknamed "the Great Commoner" for his ardent support and championing of the "producing classes" against their exploitation by the "plutocracy," by which was meant the East Coast financiers. From 1896 onward, Bryan took on the mantle of the farmer-labor alliance that had shaped the Populist movement, pursuing its core elements to the extent that some argue the Progressive Era reforms of the early twentieth century mostly originated with Bryan's reform effort and his mediation of the populist creed.[15] Bryan exemplifies how Evangelicalism played a vital part in the democratization of nineteenth-century America.[16]

The challenge to the status quo represented by the Populists in the United States and the Labour movement in Britain took on the character of the moral crusades such as the temperance movement with which they were aligned. As Kazin notes, "[t]he notion that a democratic politics must concern itself with the enforcement of ethical standards, both public and private, was integral to the appeal of Populism."[17] What these movements represent is the assertion of the priority of social relationships, and the upholding of common values and a common life over and against their instrumentalization and commodification through political and economic processes.

The relationship between popular piety and the realization of democratic citizenship runs counter to many of the dominant interpretations of the relationship between religion and politics in the contemporary Western context. As outlined in the Introduction, many sociologists of religion no longer accept the secularization thesis that processes of modernization lead to an inevitable decline in the public significance of religion. Rather, modernization leads to a process whereby different configurations of belief and unbelief combine to form particular and entirely contingent constructions of secularity. There is, however, still a widespread assumption that the continuing public significance of religion is determined by a defensive reaction against processes of modernization (and globalization) rather than a critical appropriation of modern processes such as urbanization, industrialization, and bureaucratization.[18] In addition, popular religion is often identified with the phenomenon of "fundamentalism," which tends to be seen as antidemocratic and authoritarian.[19] This was reflected in how the November 25, 2009 event at the Barbican – and the work of Citizens UK more generally – was reported both in the newspapers and on blogs; there was an underlying anxiety expressed about the relationship between religion and politics at the event. But such negative constructions of the term fundamentalism do not exhaust the options. Some see fundamentalism itself as a form of modernization.[20] In a similar vein, I contend that the involvement in broad-based community organizing of religious groups, many of which could be classed as "fundamentalist," suggests that popular religion can and often does co-construct and critically engage with processes of modernization and that this co-construction can take the form of engagement in and renewal of democratic politics.

Contemporary movements for religious revitalization are at the vanguard of constructing and reproducing different iterations of modernity and secularity in different contexts.[21] Processes of globalization and material changes such as changes in religious demography have led to new moments emerging within existing configurations of the place of religion in the public sphere. As I have argued elsewhere, these moments are ones in which the relationship between religious groups, the state, and the market is undetermined and ambiguous while at the same time those from many different religious traditions and nonreligious actors are encountering each other in new and deeper ways within shared territory.[22] The contemporary context may be described as a postsecularist space as far as the state and certain elite groups are concerned – by this I mean that elites can no longer disregard the public presence of "religion." But it is better understood overall as a period in which, for the first time, different ways of being "modern" and "secular," each with their own construction of the relationship between belief and unbelief, are overlapping and interacting within the same shared, predominantly urban spaces. In responding to this context many groups judged "fundamentalist" are highly innovative and entrepreneurial in their critical appropriation and construction of both modern processes and their own religious traditions.[23] Moreover, each fundamentalism is as much a contested and negotiated space as any other part of a religious tradition. What is clear is that reformist, revitalizing, and radical movements within all religious traditions are utilizing all the dimensions of globalization, part of which entails manifesting themselves in particular ways in each locality. An engagement between very conservative elements and forms of democratic citizenship in one context is just as possible as the denunciation of democracy as unfaithful by the same group in another context. Moreover, as the lineup of corporate and banking luminaries with religious affiliations at the Council of Christians and Jews event suggests, religious actors are not simply in a position to react to globalization "from below" but are instead immersed and active agents within the enactment of a neoliberal vision of globalization "from above."

Even when a particular strain of religious belief and practice seems at first glance to be antidemocratic and authoritarian, it may well be a field of wheat and tares in this respect. For example, many dismiss politically active U.S. Evangelicals as right-wing conservatives with "theocratic" tendencies.[24] Yet as Jon Shields notes in his extensive study of the pro-life movement, one of the political ironies of the past few decades is that the Christian Right has been successful in fulfilling key goals of the New Left for U.S. democracy: first, by helping to mobilize one of the most politically alienated constituencies in twentieth-century America, and, second, by realigning public debate around contentious moral questions rather than the bureaucratic and technical issues that tend to bewilder and put off ordinary citizens.[25] The political scientists Clyde Wilcox and Carin Robinson confirm Shields's position. They note that in the 1972 National Election Study, white Evangelical voter turnout was 17 percent lower than other whites. Since 1992, however, voting rates among white Evangelicals hugely increased such that by 2008, they voted as often if not more than other whites.[26] Shields contends that the pro-life movement (as distinct from the Christian Right more generally) should be viewed as one of the most widespread and sustained expressions of participatory democracy in recent U.S. history, and that, contrary to its portrayal in the media and in pro-choice literature, it is often exemplary in its upholding of deliberative norms.[27] Of course, some readers will find the last sentence wholly implausible – but perhaps this raises more questions about them than it does about the phenomenon Shields analyzes. The story unfolded here represents another instance of a contemporary form of the relationship between popular piety and democratic citizenship. In telling it, I do not claim that the relationship between religious traditions and democratic politics is a necessary or inevitable relationship, but it is a historically and conceptually rich relationship and one that is too often ignored both in debates about the relationship between religion and politics and in debates about the future prospects and proper shape of democratic citizenship.

INTERFAITH RELATIONS AND THE RE-SIGNIFICATION OF SECULARITY

Key to identifying the dynamics through which broad-based community organizing mediates the relationship between religious beliefs and practices and the performance of democratic citizenship, as well as how religions may construct processes of modernization, are the linguistic practices and discursive themes used to frame political engagement. In London Citizens there is no translation between "public reasons" and "private" religious languages, nor is there a process of hybridization whereby different discourses are merged with each other.[28] Rather, different language worlds stand side by side, sometime collide and sometimes overlap. In contrast to John Rawls's advocacy of an overlapping consensus, which envisages a convergence between different worldviews (religious or otherwise) when it comes to basic law but demands the exclusion of religious and other "comprehensive" doctrines when justifying a common policy, the process of overlapping in London Citizens is one in which explicit "religious" language and beliefs are present alongside and feeding into "secular" public reason. This overlapping and, at times, colliding set of language worlds is best illustrated by an event held at the East London Mosque.

The event was a lecture by the secular Jewish political philosopher from Harvard University, Michael Sandel, jointly sponsored by *The Guardian* newspaper, London Citizens, and a foundation called the Citizens Ethics Network in 2010.[29] The broader context of the event was the scandal over the expenses of Members of Parliament and the disregard for probity and due diligence exhibited by bankers that contributed to the financial crises. Concern about "low morals in high places" led to a widespread public debate about the role of ethics in political and economic life. The work of London Citizens came to prominence within this context as it was viewed as a means to combine active citizenship within a moral framework and to undertake a "politics of the common good." But the event must also be situated within another discursive context: concern about the political role of religious groups and in particular Islam, a concern that takes specific form in relation to the East London Mosque.

The mosque's origins date back to 1910 but the first purpose-built mosque was developed in 1940 out of three houses on Commercial Road. It moved to its current premises on Whitechapel Road in 1985. The mosque is a founding member of The East London Communities Organisation (TELCO), the original chapter of London Citizens. The story of how they came to be involved is often repeated and celebrated in training and other events organized by London Citizens as exemplifying the advantages and strengths of community organizing. It was through TELCO that the mosque was able to overturn a planning application by a property developer to turn the building adjacent to the mosque into luxury apartments and subsequently secure the building for itself and build the London Muslim Centre. It was in the center that the event with Sandel was held. As an institution, the mosque is controversial. The Sandel event was held on Friday, February 26, 2010, and on the following Monday (March 1) a Channel 4 documentary program called *Dispatches* was aired entitled "Britain's Islamic Republic." The documentary noted that the mosque was linked to the Islamic Forum of Europe (IFE) – a group it labeled "fundamentalist" – that was based in the London Muslim Centre and suggested the IFE supported the Islamicization of Great Britain. Beyond this particular affiliation, the mosque is repeatedly accused of being dominated by the group *Jamaat-e-Islami* and of providing a platform for preachers such as Anwar al-Awlaki, who supported al-Qaeda and the use of violence in jihad.[30] The mosque maintains that it condemns entirely any resort to violence and, in the words of Dilowar Khan, Executive Director of the East London Mosque and London Muslim Centre, it is committed to "uphold an institution that is the most open and welcoming Muslim institution in the country. We take great pride in our pioneering projects that help Muslim men, women and young people to be active British citizens."[31]

To enter the building for the event we had to make our way through crowds of men, many in salwar kameez, gathered for Friday prayers. Making their way into the event were rabbis wearing a yarmulke and Anglican and Roman Catholic clergy wearing clerical dress. Along with religious leaders and lay people, also present were a clutch of journalists, the director of strategy and a number of other senior policy advisors from the Conservative Party, and the head economist from the Trade Unions Congress. As is customary with London Citizens events, the proceeding began with a reflection. That day the reflection was drawn from the Qur'an and from the Roman Catholic encyclical *Caritas in Veritate*. The Qur'anic reflection came first, with the following Suras being first sung by a cantor and then read out in translation: Sura 5.8, "Be just, justice is next to piety. Allah knows all you do"; Sura 4.135, "Stand out for justice, even against the King"; and Sura 16.19, "Render back trust. Judge with justice." Then the Anglican canon theologian of Westminster Abbey read a reflection from Benedict XVI's *Caritas in Veritate* on the "common good." After this Sandel gave an address based on his book *Justice: What's the Right Thing to Do?* and reflected on the work of London Citizens, giving a strong endorsement of its work.[32] During the question-and-answer session with Sandel, the muezzin began to recite the *adhan*, so against the backdrop of the call to prayer, the discussion ranged over topics such as community land trusts, living wage, and a cap on interest rates. No attempt was made to unify these discursive framings into a single framework or metanarrative. But neither did the event represent a form of postmodern bricolage. There was an overarching point of reference and set of common commitments within which different discursive frameworks were collated. The common point of reference was focused on the question of what it means to pursue justice (however conceived) where you live and alongside those who live beside you. What the event represented was a genuinely plural construction of secular space in which faithful speech, along with other kinds of language, was part of the formation of the *sensus communis* of London Citizens.

While representing one of a number of acts of generous hospitality by the East London Mosque, the event raises the question of the nature of the relationship between Islam and broad-based community organizing. This question is posed by the struggle, identified by Muslim leaders and organizers, to recruit other mosques.[33] The question is also posed by the contentious nature of views related to patriarchy, apostasy laws, and anti-Semitism that non-Muslim participants struggle with in relation to some of the Islamic institutions in membership.[34] These questions were pressed in an acute way from 2011 onward as synagogues came into membership of London Citizens for the first time. Tensions came to a head in June 2011 when a series of articles was published in *The Jewish Chronicle* drawing attention to support for the Palestinian political party Hamas and its military wing by Junaid Ahmed, deputy chair of London Citizens board of trustees and a member of the East London Mosque (the UK government designates Hamas as a whole a terrorist organization).[35] Beyond the specificities of Jewish-Islamic relations, the conflicts and tensions touched on here are instances of more generic dynamics relating to the negotiation of a common life between diverse institutions. For example, many trade-union participants have grave reservations about Roman Catholic attitudes toward women, abortion, and homosexuality; conversely, many Roman Catholic participants struggle with the overly permissive views of trade-union members on these same matters. The specific question in relation to Islam is whether, on the one hand, Muslims have good reasons for seeking a more mutual relationship with other religions and those of no religion, and on the other hand, whether Christians, Jews, and nonreligious groups have any choice but to engage and try to build collaborative relationships with institutions such as the East London Mosque with whom there are serious points of tension, conflict, and disagreement.

One way to frame this question, particularly as it pertains to religious groups involved in broad-based community organizing, is as a tension between the duties and responsibilities of being a member of a *community of faith* and those that come with membership of a *community of fate*.[36] What I mean by this is that in a world city you do not choose either whom you live next door to or who lives in the next block or neighborhood.[37] You find yourself living in relative proximity with people from whom you may be very different, whether individually or collectively. They may speak a different language, have different eating habits, or look at the world very differently. But whether one likes it or not, one shares the same fate as them. If the electricity is cut off, everyone loses power. If gangs rule the streets, everyone is under threat. Living in a worldly city shaped by global population flows and diverse patterns of life confronts religious and nonreligious constituencies with an intense sense of disjuncture between the common life they build as a "congregation" or collectivity to sustain their beliefs and practices and the common life they inherently share with everyone in their neighborhood or city. Gated communities, the phenomenon of "white flight" in the US, and de facto socioeconomic and racial segregation are prevalent kinds of response to living with others. Community organizing and other ways of building a common life are another kind. Practically speaking, the community of fate (law, roads, electricity, etc.) is necessary to make the community of faith possible; however, for some, patterns of belief and practice can locate the community of faith as prior to and the basis of the community of fate. So the question to be confronted for all groups is: How are the two to be related?

For many Muslims, building a common life to sustain the community of fate conceptualized in terms of interfaith relations would seem to be problematic: How can Muslims have a mutual relationship with Christians and Jews given that fundamental to Islamic belief is that Islam supersedes both?[38] On questions of belief and practice, a dominant position within Islam is that Christians and Jews are to be tolerated rather than afforded equal respect.[39] The mainstream of the tradition would seem to rule out approaching other religions as possible bearers of divine disclosure. The same problem affects Christian and Jewish relations, although a non-supercessionist view has become more widespread in the twentieth century.[40] Here we meet the incommensurable ways in which Islam, Judaism and Christianity understand each other "theologically" and more broadly the status afforded other constellations of belief and practice within different religious traditions, and thence the differing imperatives in relation to mission, dialogue, and civic cooperation.[41]

It does seem more possible from a Muslim perspective to build a common life with other religious traditions within the context of participation in the kind of democratic politics London Citizens represents.[42] Such participation can be understood as part of a broader collaborative pursuit of the "common good," a category familiar within Islamic jurisprudence.[43] As Dr. Abdulkarim Khalil, Director of the Al-Manaar Muslim Cultural Heritage Centre and Mosque in West London, notes of his center's involvement:

> It's one of our objectives actually around the Centre, is to try to contribute to the common good of the community really, and one way of doing that of course is to act through the platforms which are obviously sharing with others to promote, you know, what's really good for the whole community. So – and I think West London Citizens provides that [——] just that kind of platform. The second thing is the [——] promoting

the common good is actually an essential value in Islam and we [——] I mean really West London Citizens do us a favour by providing the – some sort of a venue or sort of gateway to really do that, because otherwise it would be difficult for us to participate, to contribute to that kind of thing.[44]

There are numerous resources that Islamic scholars are drawing from to conceptualize the question of the role of Muslims in civic and political life and the status of relations with non-Muslim others (both in majority non-Muslim societies and in Muslim majority societies with significant non-Muslim populations).[45] For example, Tariq Ramadan disrupts the historic opposition between the *dār al-Islam* and *dār al-Harb*, arguing that in a context of globalization and population churn, the division between a homeland and a "house of war" is no longer tenable. In its place he proposes a division between *dār al-ʿahd* – the house of treaty or negotiations – and *dār al-daʿwah* – the realm of invitation.[46] Within this conception, broad-based community organizing represents an embodiment of the realm of negotiation at a local level. Other proposals from within Islam separate democratic politics from Western conceptions of liberal democracy, which is identified as but one species of democracy, and give an account of forms of democratic politics, developed out of notions of *shūrā* and *maslaḥah*, that are consonant with Islamic belief and practice.[47] On-the-ground initiatives include the emergence of the Wasat (Center) Party out of the Muslim Brotherhood in Egypt from 1996 onward, which is committed to "equality between men and women in terms of political and civil rights,"[48] and the Gülen movement, primarily based in Turkey, but now active in 140 countries.[49] However, in the aftermath of the "Arab Spring" from 2010 onward, and the tumultuous political developments in Egypt and Turkey (and the Middle East more generally) that followed in its wake, it is not clear what the future holds for either of these initiatives.

To echo what has already been said, developments such as broader-based political parties and civil-society social movements emerging from Islamic groups that could be classified as fundamentalist constitute a constructive form of critical engagement with and development of processes of modernization, and this appropriation *can* take the form of engagement in democratic politics. The East London Mosque, among a variety of approaches it takes to political life, includes engagement with London Citizens, giving it a clear endorsement as a primary vehicle through which Muslims may participate faithfully in British politics. Although involvement in London Citizens is not the only option favored, it is available and officially endorsed and encouraged at the most senior levels. At a practical level, a number of Muslim leaders recognize that London Citizens helps Muslims negotiate the very difficult line between, on the one hand, not appearing to be "radical Islamists" in the eyes of political, bureaucratic, and intellectual elites and, on the other hand, not being seen by their own constituency to collude with governments perceived as hostile to Islam because of the international and security policies the British government pursues.

Citizens UK and the IAF have self-consciously sought to deepen the involvement of Muslims. This builds on long-term relationships with Muslim leaders in the United States and United Kingdom, and a self-conscious engagement with the more explicit tensions between Muslim and non-Muslim communities since 2001. For example, Chambers details how, in direct response to the 9/11 attacks, Chicago United for Power quickly organized an assembly of 4,000 Chicagoans drawn from institutions already in membership. Held on November 18, 2001, the assembly took place within only two months of the attacks. It was designed to depolarize Muslim/non-Muslim tensions, and its centerpiece was a twenty-five minute one-to-one session that paired Muslims and non-Muslims in face-to-face dialogue.[50] It would have been impossible to organize such an event at such short notice, and generate the turnout, without the prior trust and long-term relationship building that predated the 9/11 attacks. Building on this kind of work, the primary vehicles for the attempt to deepen and extend Muslim involvement in the IAF were two events for Muslim leaders in membership, which included those from the East London Mosque, to (1) discuss the relationship between Islam and organizing and (2) identify points of tension and connection. Held in Chicago (August 2008) and Berlin (September 2010) these meetings drew together Muslim leaders from across the IAF's international network and resulted in a statement entitled "A New Covenant of Virtue: Islam and Community Organising" that set out an Islamic rationale for broad-based community organizing.[51] The statement was written collaboratively between organizers with an Islamic faith or background and Islamic leaders and then endorsed by all the leaders involved in the process. It gives the following rationale for Islamic involvement in organizing:

> This paper aims to unpack some of the Traditions of the Prophet Muhammad (peace be upon him, hereafter implied) to consider what strategies and tools we have at our disposal to equip ourselves to organize our communities and build a stronger, more cohesive society. Using examples in the life of Prophet Muhammad we can see how his leadership involved working alongside his neighbours and fellow citizens in order to create a more just and tolerant society at a time when Muslims were a minority. An important element of this leadership involved building relationships with others in the community over a common agenda much like the original covenant of virtue signed by the Prophet before his Prophethood.

It then goes on to conclude: "Working to make a positive change in society is arguably the best form of service or *khidma* to others and invitation or *da'wa* to the peaceful message of Islam." The paper as a whole draws on a number of analogies between Islamic practice and belief and community organizing, but it is the example of the *Hilf al-Fuḍul* or "Covenant of Virtue" that informs the key narrative used to frame Islamic involvement in BBCO.[52]

In the context of London Citizens' work, the intensification of these efforts by Muslim leaders and organizers with a Muslim background and/or faith from 2010 onward ran parallel to the uptake of community organizing by the Masorti synagogues.[53] Matt Plen, director of the Masorti synagogues and a member of the New North London Synagogue, met Neil Jameson and Matthew Bolton in 2009, when they were actively exploring setting up a North London chapter of London Citizens. Plen was persuaded to attend the London Citizens's five-day training that year with a colleague from Noam, the Masorti youth movement. He saw its potential as a way of training leaders and renewing the organizational culture of the Masorti synagogues. This led him to approach my research colleague Maurice Glasman (who is a fellow member of the Masorti movement) in order to develop a Jewish version of the leadership training – something Plen felt was appropriate as he identified a strong resonance between some of the approaches of organizing and Jewish practices. As he put it in an interview, community organizing "doesn't come straight from the tradition, but it goes together very well."[54] The process Plen set in motion is directly parallel to one established by Rabbi Jonah Pesner, a leader in the IAF affiliate, the Greater Boston Interfaith Organization.[55] After piloting the training and taking feedback the Masorti program is now run regularly.[56]

No explicit link is made between the Masorti version of the London Citizens's leadership training and the need to be involved in London Citizens. However, a number of those who have attended the training do become involved in London Citizens. Something of the fruit of this process can be overheard in the following statement from an interview with a participant who had attended both the London Citizens training and the Masorti training, published in *The Jewish Chronicle* in anticipation of the founding of North London Citizens on March 30, 2011:

> The principles relate closely to Jewish values. So organising emphasises the importance of the one-to-one (chevruta), why turnout and a strong sense of self-identity are crucial (minyan), how to manage creative conflict and debate (mahloket), and how, through a shared agenda, we can fulfill our obligations to society (mitzvah). But it's not really surprising because the movement was created and in many cases continued by Jews. Despite that, organising has yet to be adopted on a significant scale within Anglo-Jewry. I hope the founding of the north London branch of Citizens UK means that will change. It's Jews, Muslims, Christians, students, trade unionists and many others working together for the common good. It's inspiring.[57]

If we look further back historically, we can see that developments in the relationship between Islamic institutions, the Masorti, and Citizens UK form part of a pattern in the relationship between the IAF and the religious traditions that constitute its primary membership. As was seen in Chapter 1, Alinsky engaged in a theological conversation with Roman Catholicism and, in particular, with Jacques Maritain that simultaneously enriched and informed yet also challenged both the practice of organizing and the practices and beliefs of the Roman Catholics involved. In the southwest IAF, where a number of leaders and organizers had experience working in Latin America, the engagement also included a focus on liberation theology.[58] This mutually critical dialogue between community organizers and religious authority figures, which at an interpersonal level was often rambunctious, continues to this day, notably through the teaching and writing of lead organizers such as Edward Chambers, Ernesto Cortés, Michael Gecan, Father Leo Penta, and Sister Christine Stephens – all of whom have strong allegiances to Roman Catholicism. In the United Kingdom, a parallel process has resulted in the publication of a formal study of the links between Catholic social teaching and community organizing.[59]

As more religious traditions became increasingly involved in organizing, a similar pattern of engagement took shape. Interactive dialogue with liberal Protestantism developed from the late 1960s onward as more mainline Protestant clergy participated, a particular point of reference being the work of Reinhold Niebuhr.[60] Although they had long been a bulwark of the IAF, it was not until the late 1970s and 1980s that there was intentional engagement with the historic black churches which resulted in the formulation of the statement entitled "The Tent of the Presence: Black Church Power in the 1980's."[61] Again, echoing the engagement with Catholicism, the formulation of the "Tent of the Presence" document inspired a parallel process in the United Kingdom with the formation of a Black clergy caucus in 2011 and an edited, Anglicized version of the Tent of the Presence statement being issued to the caucus for discussion.[62] In collaboration with former IAF organizer Mike Miller, Christian leaders and theologians such as Robert Linthicum, Stephen Mott, Marilyn Stranske, and Wally Tilleman, involved in the network Christians Supporting Community Organizing, have done much to frame community organizing in terms directly related to Evangelical and Pentecostal congregations in North America.[63] An independent but parallel process is emerging in Citizens UK with organizers and leaders trying to develop a strategy of theological engagement with Evangelical and charismatic congregations. The engagements with Islam and the Masorti are thus but two iterations of this broader pattern.

A key catalyst for constructively engaging with religious discourses can be the presence of an organizer from within a particular tradition for whom wrestling with the points of connection and contention between organizing and their religious beliefs and practices generates a more self-conscious process of engagement. But it is not a necessary condition. More significant is a robust relationship between key religious leaders and organizers such that open and critical dialogue can be engaged in between them and that religious leaders are given the opportunity to reflect on the relationship outside of the pressures of either political or pastoral work.[64] Part of this relationship involves organizers being committed to learning about what matters to those with whom they work.[65] Measures such as establishing clergy caucuses and undertaking theological reflection on the practice of organizing are vital for generating a process of mutually educational and individually and communally self-reflexive dialogue that challenges both the practice of organizing and the beliefs and practices of each particular religious tradition.

The motivations for engaging in this kind of dialogue are multiple and range from an instrumental desire to mobilize a particular set of institutions as "campaign fodder" to a quest to align organizing with deeply held values and theological beliefs. What can be said for certain is that the need to negotiate a common life with diverse traditions in an ambiguous and sometimes hostile political and economic environment necessarily provokes questions within religious traditions. It is my contention that broad-based community organizing is a form of democratic politics through which these questions can be explored internally and constitutes a way to negotiate these questions externally in collaboration with others outside of one's own tradition. The questions provoked will be specific to each respective tradition, while the environment and the practices of organizing will be shared across multiple traditions. A necessary condition for this kind of exploration within each tradition is that the practices of community organizing are not themselves ideologically overdetermined and that both organizers and religious leaders have demonstrated loyalty and trustworthiness to each other through a process of common action.[66]

DEMOCRATIC POLITICS AS THE MEDIATION OF A COMMON LIFE

The East London Mosque is but one institution among many that London Citizens works with as part of "reweaving civil society." Common work between Christians, Muslims, Jews, and many others is mediated through affiliation with London Citizens. This does not entail collusion with what are seen as unsavory or even "evil" views ascribed to other communities since each institution remains independent of others and is involved for very different reasons. London Citizens is clear that it does not necessarily endorse the views of its membership institutions. Rather, organizers hold the view that, in the world as it is, all those who live in a place need to be drawn into building up the common life of that place via politics rather than violence, whether that violence is intercommunal or monopolized by the state.[67] As Neil Jameson puts it:

> Our aim is for the constituent bodies of TELCO to see themselves not just as worship centres, schools or union branches, but institutions with their responsibility to train and develop leaders, to teach faith and its value system in the context of East London today which means coexistence and mutual respect if tolerance is to grow and prejudice be challenged. TELCO teaches that diversity is a political strength and that people have more in common than elements which divide. We can agree that all in work should be paid a fair wage, that families should be housed properly and antisocial behaviour challenged. We cannot, however, agree on approaches to God or partisan political positions, so the best TELCO leaders avoid these issues and build relationships of mutual respect around an agenda for action we can agree on and can fight for together. These will not, by definition, simply be Muslim issues or Christian issues etc.[68]

The political vision organizing encapsulates holds that if a group is directly contributing to the common work of defending, tending, and creating the commonweal then it deserves recognition as a vital part of and co-laborer within the broader body politic. It is the emphasis on participation and contribution to the building up of a common life that allows for a greater plurality and affirmation of distinct identities and traditions, as each is able to play a part in this common work.[69]

This kind of common life politics is distinct from an identity politics and from multicultural approaches because recognition and respect is not given simply by dint of having a different culture or identity. Rather, recognition is conditional on one's contribution to and participation in shared, reciprocal, and public work. Evidence of this approach in London Citizens is that those groups – often union branches – who paid their subscription but never turned up for meetings were either asked to leave or the renewal of their annual membership was not pursued or encouraged.[70] The long-term hope of organizers is that involvement in politics through community organizing creates space for the emergence of a shared story – not a "religious" story, but a civic and penultimate one – and a context for real relationship where all participants – however distasteful their views to others – can begin to touch on difficult issues in a place of trust.[71]

It can be argued that democracy is not necessarily tethered to liberalism, but is a tradition in itself.[72] However, it is perhaps more accurate to say that democracy is a constellation of practices that mediate between a wide variety of traditions. Through democratic practices a common life can be forged and some kind of mutual identification crafted between individuals and groups dispersed by class, sexual orientation, religion, ethnicity, and legal status. Neither should we frame democracy in terms of Christian democracy or Islamic democracy, and so on, but rather pay attention to the kinds of interactions that allow for a common life to be fashioned in contexts where a plurality of interests and multiple loyalties have to be represented and negotiated.[73]

In interviews and casual conversation, something of how the experience of politics carries over and frames the experience of interfaith relations can be heard again and again. For example, Reverend Stephen Sichel, Anglican vicar of St. Matthew's Church in Brixton notes:

> What I find fascinating about organising, if I think about it in terms of the interfaith dimension, is that ... there is something about what you believe having less importance [——] not less importance, but it assumes a different place, when you work with people from different traditions, it is the relationship somehow that is the cement. You think less about their otherness in terms of what they believe and it becomes less important. What becomes important is the fact that you can relate to them as another human being. So if I meet Safrez, I know he worships in an entirely different way to me, I know that he believes very different things from me, but when I look into his eyes and shake his hands and I'm going to go on an action with him, I feel a tremendous sense of solidarity with him in what we're doing together.... He's doing it because he really believes, you know ... and so do I, we have a different reasoning for that, we have a different imagination of why that is so, but it is so.[74]

Participants frequently commented on how they became involved because of the issues but stayed involved because of the relationships and the way in which London Citizens enabled them to get to know people they would never otherwise have met. However, generating such public action is no easy matter and throws up many difficult issues that have to be negotiated. These range from questions of etiquette to managing tensions generated by broader geopolitical and historical conflicts. For example, after actions, organizers and primary leaders will often meet in a pub to debrief and evaluate the action: this necessarily excludes Muslim and many teetotalling Pentecostal participants, yet a pub is often one of the few spaces available that is free and large enough to host such a gathering. Organizers and leaders do try to give due attention to these issues.[75] To navigate these kinds of tensions requires the time-intensive organizing, listening, and relationship building practiced in community organizing.[76] Although Sisyphean in nature, the task of organizing and its outcomes for interfaith relations and "reweaving civil society" are necessary, and, as the quotation earlier suggests, profoundly meaningful for all involved.

Politics as practiced by London Citizens represents a way of paying attention to others and thereby stepping out of one's own limited perspective and enabling new understanding to emerge.[77] As I have suggested elsewhere, community organizing can be conceptualized as a form of tent making where a place is created in which hospitality is given and received between multiple traditions.[78] There are some issues heard in the tent that can be collectively acted on and some that cannot, but the encounter with others and their stories informs the sense of what it is like to live on this mutual ground, to dwell together in a given and shared urban space. The hearing of others' interests and concerns in the context of ongoing relationship and the recognition that everyone in the tent occupies mutual (not neutral) ground fosters the sense that in each others' welfare we find our own. Such tent making is the precondition of what Crick calls the "political method of rule," which, as noted in Chapter 1, involves listening to others and ensuring that all groups have a clear and reasonably safe means of articulating their interests.[79]

Part of what constitutes BBCO as a practice of building a common life is the centrality it gives to questions of power, structure, and changing policy. But it is also profoundly concerned with moral character and the cherished values and beliefs of those who participate. Indeed, against those who identify the political with the juridical and bureaucratic, the nature of BBCO suggests that the definition of politics itself needs to be expanded to include the negotiation of a common life that takes seriously not just the need for material goods and power but also the moral and social dimensions of that life. One of the paradoxes this book explores is how BBCO, as a practice of democratic politics, seeks to protect the relative autonomy of the civil sphere from being either co-opted by the state, commodified by the market, or rendered overly political and competitive by identity politics through, on the one hand, inserting consideration of the social, moral, and "religious" dimensions of life into the making of political judgments, and, on the other hand, inserting political consideration into the making of social, moral, and religious judgments. In doing so, BBCO reasserts the limits of politics and economics and the boundaries between the civil sphere and either state, market, religious, and social processes, and thereby repairs the conditions and possibilities of a common life. The dynamics of how organizing enables the "binding and loosing" of the boundaries and connections between different aspects of our social, political, and economic life as part of how it "reweaves civil society" is examined more closely in Chapter 6.

BEYOND DIALOGUE TO A PLACE-BASED POLITICS

The kind of interfaith relations London Citizens embodies contrasts sharply with that which informs public policy, both in the United Kingdom and the United States. In the policy arena the tendency has been to conceptualize relations between different faiths in terms of either interreligious dialogue (characterized as "interfaith relations") or in terms of joint humanitarian endeavors. This call for and resourcing of dialogue is driven by state concerns about the need for "social cohesion" in response to ongoing questions about how to promote the integration of new migrant communities with strong religious identities and the real and perceived links between terrorist activities and some Islamic groups. In response to the latter, the promotion of interreligious dialogue as a strategy for generating social cohesion and greater political stability is an alternative to the parallel "securitization" of religion: the rhetorical construction of religious beliefs and practices as a direct security threat to the state that needs to be dealt with outside the normal legal and political processes within which religion is dealt with ordinarily.[80] The end result of both the promotion of dialogue and securitization is a deeper level of engagement between state agencies and many religious groups as the government seeks to understand and address internal dynamics within these groups – Islamic ones in particular – that might exacerbate or diminish any resort to violence.[81]

Neither an emphasis on dialogue nor humanitarian service leaves scope for politics. In occluding the need for politics, the inherent conflicts that arise in the process of negotiating a common life and the pursuit of shared goods are thereby submerged, as is the need for power in order to achieve change. Policies that emphasize the importance of social cohesion more often than not lack any account of how the kind of relationships valorized are increasingly subordinated to and undermined by the needs of the market and the state. An emphasis on dialogue and volunteerism ignores questions of political economy and the way in which the kind of globalized market pressures and processes of commodification already outlined serve to undermine the very possibility of acting together. Yet if you have to follow the money in order to find work, then you have to leave people and place behind and the kind of time-intensive social ties that form the basis of sustaining long-term associative power that can challenge the priorities of either the state or the market and thereby defend the interests of citizens, whether they have an explicitly religious faith or not.

There is a place for straightforward dialogue, although this seems more appropriate and sustainable at a specialist rather than at a "street" level.[82] But the experience of London Citizens would suggest that real encounters, dialogue, and understanding are, at the popular level, best generated as by-products of shared political action. In such shared political action the focus is neither on merely meeting face-to-face nor even on simply working side by side as volunteers. Rather, it is on the pursuit and protection of goods in common. Instead of trying to generate relationship either for the sake of relationship as an end itself, or for theological reasons, or to comply with state directives, the external point of reference – fighting for a living wage or a cap on interest rates – provides the basis of mutual collaboration out of which dialogue may emerge as a by-product. Jameson calls this the "persuasion of need" approach to generating a "conversation between faiths."[83] As Father John Armitage notes:

> I think one of the important things of something like community organising is there's a distinction ... we can't worship together because we don't understand each other at that level but we can witness together, we can stand on a common platform. We may not feel comfortable going into the, you know, into the mosque or the synagogue, but there's a big distinction between witness and worship.... And, you know, it's the common good [that] is in the witness, the particular thing that drives me to the witness is my own worship.[84]

In addition to the shared commitment to concrete issues of mutual concern, a shared commitment to a particular place provides further grounds for common action. Different faith traditions will have different overarching visions of the good life and often very different beliefs and practices; but simply by sharing the same mutual ground, they necessarily have a shared investment in the good of that place. For example, if the council sells off the school playing fields, none of their children will have anywhere to play. These are the interests they have in common; they are not selfish interests, but mutual interests. And, while each may give different accounts of why law and order or public spaces are good, a common commitment to place can foster a common commitment to the people who live there, despite their differences. Added to the mutual material interests that emerge within particular places there is also what we might call a "convivial interest": if we are going to be sharing space with people, we have an interest in maintaining friendly relations with them.

Through a common commitment to shared places (a place-based interest) and local people (a convivial interest), a shared story of belonging and a shared social and political life can emerge, one in which any immigrant tradition may be enfolded. Such a common commitment to place and people can foster a shared identity narrative by connecting each faith story to the story of the ongoing civic life in a particular place and develop a sense of mutual responsibility and commitment for the world around them. In the words of one participant, it involves being more concerned about the drug pushers on your doorstep than the politics of Israel-Palestine. Yet generating concern for the concrete and the local is hard work as the question "who is my neighbor?" is often constructed in ways that prioritize the needs of fellow believers (in which case the politics of Israel-Palestine looms large) or "the poor" in distant lands with whom there is no meaningful connection other than those mediated via charitable donations to humanitarian agencies. The challenge for organizers is to help participants put people before program, whether these programs are ideological, theological, or philanthropic. This involves connecting them relationally to those they live in close proximity to so they can see and hear the world around them as it is, not refract it through a lens focused thousands of miles away or on abstractions, both of which distort their perceptions and experiences of those they actually live near. Such re-neighboring work is part of the spatializing dimension of community organizing that makes politics possible.

BECOMING NEIGHBORS AND THE FORMATION OF MUNICIPAL *PIETAS*

The combination of a place-based and convivial interest can be combined and conceptualized as a form of civic *pietas*. The notion of *pietas* is drawn from Roman and Scholastic political thinkers such as Virgil, Cicero, and Aquinas and denotes the reverential concern for that to which one owes the condition and possibility of one's own development, be it one's family, city, or *patria*. Thus, by one definition, "patriotism" may be broadly equated with the notion that there is a duty, reverence, or *pietas* owed by each person to the civic community, the land, and the cultural environment to which one owes the conditions of one's own development. *Pietas* expresses itself in faithfulness to one's community. I did not create the language, values, and legal system or the environmental, economic, and political context on which I depend and so I owe care, respect, and loyalty to the people and place that made such gifts possible. This is as true for the refugee and economic migrant as it is for the native. The patriot – one possessing the virtue of *pietas* – recognizes the need to value his or her civic life and identity as a gift to be both cherished and passed on. However, this gift should not be overvalued or sacralized and is not determinative of all relations; for example, one's religious, familial, or professional loyalties may at times stand over and against, chasten, or place limits on one's civic obligations.[85] *Pietas* grows out of both a need for others – living in the same place one depends on them for one's flourishing (the place-based interest) – but also affection for those among whom one lives (the convivial interest). In pointing to the symbiosis of proximity and conviviality in the formation of *pietas* for a particular place, we can see that this place-based *pietas* is simply the analogue of instances of work-based *pietas* such as those found in a guild, trade union, professional association, or mutual partnership – all of which integrate utility and solidarity. Relationships with those whom one shares a life together involves both utility and mutual dependence, as well as shared practices and customs that can cultivate what is sometimes characterized as public or civic "friendship," but which I contend is better understood as a form of "neighborliness."

There is a long tradition that builds on Aristotle's way of framing good civic relationships in terms of "friendship." However, use of this term can over-freight what should be expected of relationships with fellow citizens and can occlude the conflicts between them.[86] It can also set up highly exclusive and excluding visions of citizenship (something that will be explored in Chapter 8). Characterizing citizenship in terms of neighborliness rather than public friendship allows for both less and, where appropriate, more intense forms of direct concern for others. Being a neighbor, unlike being a friend, is a vocation. Moreover, being a neighbor is not a condition or state of being or preassigned role. We discover who our neighbor is within contingent and contextual relationships that require that we listen to who is before us and this entails being attentive to the conflicts and differences between "us" and "them." Unlike such things as family, class, ethnicity, or gender, I cannot predetermine who my neighbor will be. Neighbors have neither assigned social identities (e.g., father, sister, etc.) nor institutionally constructed roles (e.g., doctor, postman, IT officer, etc.). On occasion the call of the neighbor supersedes prior commitments and loyalties – whether professional, religious, social, or political – and we can encounter a neighbor in any one of our roles. Conversely, we have to constantly learn how to be a neighbor. Encountering fellow citizens through such practices as community organizing is part of the curriculum of neighborliness. At the same time, envisaging citizenship as involving forms of neighborliness means it can encompass friend-enemy distinctions within the same body politic (something that will be examined further in Chapter 6). As in the parable of the Good Samaritan, the neighbor is the one who refuses to be wholly defined by the friend-enemy relations, yet whose status as a "Good Samaritan" depends on the recognition of the reality of friend-enemy relations. The sense of being a neighbor can be combined with – but is distinct from – a sense of *pietas* for one's locality, city, commonwealth, or res publica. They can be mutually reinforcing: mutual need gives rise to a sense of loyalty that in turn fosters a commitment to neighborliness. Conversely, the call of the neighbor can interrupt and overturn the settled loyalties and demands of civic *pietas*.

A place-based, municipal vision of *pietas* – or civic faithfulness – contrasts sharply with universalist and nationalist forms while, at the same time, it echoes but can be distinguished from certain republican visions of citizenship. A universalist liberal cosmopolitan conception of *pietas*, as found in Bentham and Kant, is one where *pietas* to humanity is understood as overriding and prior to the *pietas* owed to one's particular locality and community.[87] Such a universalistic conception of *pietas* fosters a "Mrs. Jellyby syndrome" that devalues and undermines local patterns of association.[88] What is proposed here contrasts also with nationalistic forms of *pietas*. While operating at a more intermediary scale, reverence for the imagined community of the nation is still working at a high level of abstraction and subordinates the local to the national interest. Moreover, its all-encompassing nature has too often led *pietas* for the nation to become a pietistic nationalism that shows no pity for those identified as enemies and sacralizes and makes an idol of a contingent political formation. Civic *pietas* should never become a fully blown piety: that is, a self-constituting and self-subsisting form of belief, practice, and devotion invested in either a polity or a form of politics, democratic or otherwise.[89]

My account of municipal *pietas* is closer to republican conceptions of citizenship. Both cosmopolitan and nationalist conceptions of citizenship posit a pre-political unity (the former of "humanity," the latter of ancestry, culture, or homeland). By contrast, modern civic republican notions of *pietas* for a place and a people rest on a shared fate rather than a shared history, is grounded in the recognition of multiple interdependencies constantly reiterated over time, and shared practices of self-government. A shared political life is not discovered but made and is open to numerous cultures and values being involved in its production. Civic republican conceptions of citizenship still look to the nation-state as the primary vehicle of citizenship and loyalty, and tend to subordinate all other loyalties and identities to the superordinate value of upholding the political community.[90] By contrast, I posit a municipal, urban, or metropolitan form of *pietas*.[91] In this account, living in London, Hamburg, Chicago, or Sydney becomes the basis for a shared identity and sense of loyalty that can sit alongside, interrupt, and contest (rather than replace) either national or universal commitments (whether religious, philosophical, or economic) and their oftentimes abstracting, de-spatializing, and depoliticizing orientations. Advocacy of municipal *pietas* is not a surreptitious way of promoting civil religion or converting democratic politics into a creed: it is a call for civic virtue, not a votive offering.

A number of broader reflections suggest themselves on the basis of the account given here of interfaith relations as a civic practice and how this can give rise to a municipal *pietas* and forms of urban citizenship. The first is that when the state becomes involved in promoting interfaith relations, these relations become problematic as the state cannot help but try to instrumentalize and depoliticize them; yet the very thing that would help promote a more convivial life emerging between different religious groups in particular places – the identification and common pursuit of shared goods through involvement in common political action – is often perceived as a threat to the political order and those in power. Second, interfaith relations as a civic practice can be understood as a form of civic *pietas*, but this *pietas* is extremely fragile, requires constant work to build up and maintain, and needs to connect to prior traditions of belief and practice in order to generate its own moral points of reference. Such is the work of organizing. Third, citizenship at a municipal level is an achievable project. Where diaspora or transnational religious communities are required to sign up to a national project of citizenship, a whole host of other loyalties begin to conflict with the loyalty and duties of care demanded by the nation-state. In the light of how London Citizens facilitates the emergence of a shared sense of citizenship between plural and divergent groups, what is needed is some conception of citizenship that can cope with multiple loyalties within a shared place. We shall explore such a conception of citizenship as involving multiple loyalties in Part II. Fourth, it is an obvious point, but one often missed, that the challenge of pluralism is as much an intra-faith issue in Christianity, Islam, and Judaism as it is an issue of their relations with each other and that these interfaith and intra-faith negotiations are themselves located within the negotiation of shared geographic, political, economic, and cultural spaces and flows. Therefore, relations between different religious groups, when negotiating a common life, have to be conducted on three fronts simultaneously: interfaith, intra-faith, and dialectically in relation to state policies and market processes.

The experience of community organizing suggests that there can be a partnership between the congregation and the demos that brings a mutual discipline to both. In the shared pursuit of common goods, the congregation has to listen to and learn from its neighbors. Likewise, the congregation, as a moral tradition with a cosmic vision of the good, brings a wider horizon of reference and relationship to bear on the immediate needs and demands of the demos. This mutual disciplining helps ensure that both congregations and community organizing (as a vehicle for the encounter with others) remain directed toward political rather than antipolitical ends and that the competing demands of faithfulness to God and keeping faith with one's fellow citizens can be coordinated constructively.

SECULARITY AND THE CONTRADICTION OF THE MODERN COMPACT

The sociological and discursive dynamics of how this kind of interfaith and pluralistic form of secular politics comes into being requires some further examination. In North America, broad-based community organizing connects to the language worlds of its religious institutions in membership. As was outlined in Chapter 1, Roman Catholic social teaching played a crucial role in Alinsky's development of community organizing. Similarly, the linguistic practices of Black preachers are critical to helping many organizing coalitions understand their mission and purpose. The role of Johnny Ray Youngblood in the East Brooklyn Congregations is but one such example. Another is that of Bishop Doug Miles of Koinonia Baptist Church for BUILD (Baltimore United in Leadership Development). However, in the United Kingdom it seems at times as if broad-based community organizing is disconnected from the language worlds of its religious members. A number of Evangelical and Black Pentecostal leaders commented that organizers often did not seem to "get them" or understand what they were trying to say. Other church leaders worry that some organizers have a wholly instrumental view of them and their institutions. Julie Camancho, lead organizer with West London Citizens and herself a communicant Roman Catholic who emigrated from Colombia, contrasted her experience of working as an organizer in the United States with her experience in the United Kingdom. She noted that before a one-to-one meeting in the United States they would always pray, whereas in the United Kingdom she would never dream of suggesting such a thing, even with an ordained minister. London Citizens is trying to address this sense of disconnection through establishing clergy caucuses – a common practice in the IAF in the United States – however, much more care and attention needs to be given to this dimension of the work.

London Citizens comes across as religious to many external observers. Media reports frequently cited London Citizens as a faith-based organization or alliance. Likewise many participants reported that others they worked with viewed London Citizens as "religious." For example, Hugh O'Shea, branch secretary of the Central London branch of the Union of London Hotel Workers, commented that when he was considering whether to take his branch into membership of West London Citizens he spoke to another union organizer "and I always remember what he said, he said, 'Hughie, a lot of people in the union think that if you join London Citizens you'll be there at the communion rail with your tongue hanging out every Sunday receiving Communion.' [laughs] As if it was compulsory!"[92] O'Shea noted the hostility of many of the senior union officials toward London Citizens, which he said they viewed as both a rival union and too religious. He took a different view: "I don't regard London Citizens as a religious organisation. I regard its ideals as based quite largely on faith-based ideals. But that doesn't mean to say it's religious. It's religious backed perhaps ... but the ideas are of social justice."[93]

London Citizens partly appears "religious" to nonreligious outsiders because of the large numbers of religious institutions in membership [see Figures 3.1–3.4]. This is not, however, necessarily determinative. Many faith-based organizations are directly affiliated with churches or other faiths but do not "feel" religious in manner and style.[94] Something more is going on. To understand this, we can draw a parallel between the linguistic practices of London Citizens and those of Jerry Falwell (1933–2007), the prominent Evangelical Christian leader and key figure in the emergence of the Moral Majority in the United States. The anthropologist Susan Friend Harding, in her study of Falwell's political work, notes how religious language functioned to draw in and consolidate insiders through a familiar set of narratives, motifs, and linguistic styles while simultaneously alienating and excluding those who were critical such as "liberals" and mainline Christians, playing to and reinforcing the negative perceptions of those outside the organization.[95] Broad-based community organizing can provoke a similarly hostile or suspicious reaction from outsiders through the discursive practices by which it generates a sense of unity among those in membership. A particularly acute example of this hostile reaction framed wholly in antireligious terms comes from Berlin. Leo Penta, the lead organizer of DICO, the Deutsche Institute for Community Organizing, reported that he and his co-workers were accused of being Scientologists and a religious cult when they began trying to establish a broad-based community organization. In the UK context, the hostility it generates mostly splits along ideological lines: the Left tends to view Citizens UK as "too religious" while the Right tends to focus on its policies and tactics. For example, the neoliberal Tax Payers Alliance branded London Citizens a "radical left-wing group."[96] Within the churches the issue that repeatedly provokes a negative response is that of the confrontational tactics used.

Meetings and assemblies are not monopolized by religious language: a wide variety of discursive frames of reference are invoked at them. Yet the style and language of organizing feels familiar to religiously affiliated members and often alien to the nonreligious. Religious institutions meet regularly in assemblies, tithe, demand an intensity of their commitment, are comfortable with an affective dimension to public gatherings, and have a strong set of moral commitments. Organizers themselves frequently note the parallels between the demands of democratic politics and those of religious affiliation and see the skills and practices of organizing as directly relevant to the institutional renewal of congregations.[97] It is not surprising then that nonreligious observers see organizing as somehow "religious" in some unspecified way; broad-based community organizing involves ways and styles of gathering and association not encountered much outside of religious congregations within the contemporary European political context. By contrast, owing to a higher degree of religious affiliation in the United States, this form of organizing feels more familiar and thence less overtly "religious" to external observers.[98] That being said, negative reactions in the United States follow an analogous pattern to that in the United Kingdom: the Left views such organizing as too bound by traditional values such as leadership and family, the Right considers it as radically left-wing or even crypto-communist, while churches often see it as unnecessarily confrontational and aggressive in its tactics and are nervous about the emphasis given to self-interest and building power in its training.

What broad-based community organizing does not do as a form of political action is reinforce a secularist demarcation of politics as a nonreligious sphere either by claiming only "public" reasons can be used or by claiming to be excluded because of an insistence that highly particularistic and idiosyncratic "Bible-believing" views hold sway in public conversations. It thereby contests the construction of religion as private and set apart from politics, resignifying both religion and politics through the performances of what it means to be religious and political.[99] Broad-based community organizing as it evolved in the United Kingdom simply does not recognize the terms and conditions of an ideologically secularist modernity. Instead, it overtly mixes piety and politics, secular and religious styles and cultures. It is thus post-secularist, or rather a plural and complex instantiation of a religious and secular space, not observing the rules and regimes of "public secularity" and refusing to let religious groups marginalize themselves by adopting a narrative of exclusion and victimization.[100]

It is my contention that broad-based community organizing is symptomatic of a broader rupture of notions of public secularity in the UK context. In its alignment of religious institutions and democratic citizenship, it represents a different co-construction of secularity between belief and unbelief, one in which the church qua church may play a part. The ways in which community organizing called on religious actors to behave politically contradicted self-marginalizing dynamics adopted by evangelical and charismatic Christians as well as mainline Christian denominations in the United Kingdom in their political engagements from 1945 to the 1990s.[101] Where the churches in the United Kingdom were active in public life they tended to self-censor rhetoric that they perceived to be supernaturalist.[102] Community organizing as a practice is able to break with and contradict such a stance because it is not derived from a British (and mostly white) Christian subculture and so is not constrained by a folk/faux memory of the exclusion of religion from the public sphere or the very real history of the Establishment's exclusion of both Nonconformists and Roman Catholics from holding public office. BBCO was introduced as a set of political and associational practices in the 1990s at the point of the post-secularist turn and the consolidation and coming into public life of religious minorities, notably Muslims, who were also mostly people of color. Yet these populations refused to be labeled as "ethnic minorities" and demanded access to state resources on terms of religious affiliation not ethnic or racial identity. These groups become visible politically through religious speech and action and are not constrained by the self-policing compact between Christianity and a simplistically secularist modernity whereby Christians along with liberal and neoliberal elites adopted the secularization thesis as a self-fulfilling prophecy.[103]

Broad-based community organizing emerged in the 1990s at the point where the supposedly teleological process of secularization was seen to be unfulfilled. The world began to appear as religious as ever and philosophers started to discuss what it meant to be "post-secular."[104] Although many conservative Christians in the United Kingdom remain bound and obsessed by prior, more religiously hostile constructions of public secularity, broad-based community organizing has taught churches in membership to relax and occupy a genuinely plural space in which religious rhetorics and styles are as legitimate contributions to political life as any other, while at the same time demanding that religious voices cannot be the dominant or exclusive voice. This is evidenced in interviews with religious leaders who note that community organizing allows them to be explicitly religious in public in a way they did not deem possible prior to involvement. Contributing to this sense is the call by organizers for religious leaders to look as "religious" as possible in assemblies and actions, and the use of religious speech alongside other discursive forms to narrate and frame issues. It is given voice in the following comment by Matt Plen, Director of the Assembly of Masorti Synagogues:

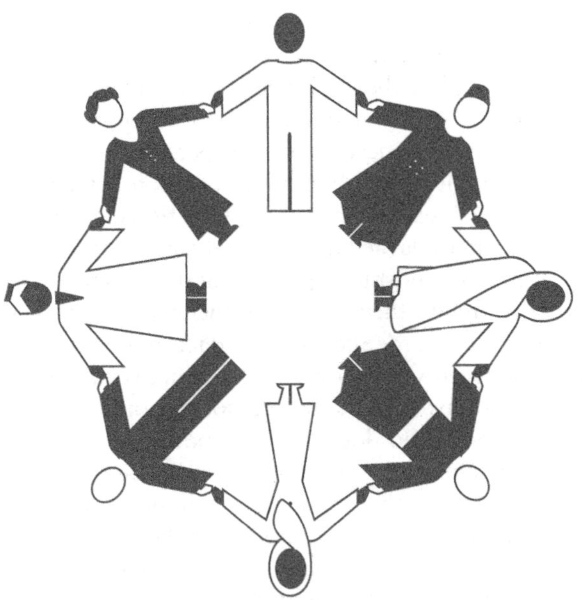

FIGURE 3.5. London Citizens' logo.

The thing that really attracted me to [London Citizens] is it's a place we can be out as a Jew. Like it's [——] you know you're out in the non-Jewish environment but you're there as a Jew and there's no question about it. There's always a [——] I mean in English society in my perception [——] I'm not the type to be paranoid about anti-semitism and that kind of stuff, but there is an undercurrent of anti-semitism in English society all the time. You're never quite sure when it's gonna come up. I imagine it to be like being gay. It's like you look the same as everyone else, you look, you know [——] you're white and you look the same as everyone else, but you have to decide when you're going to be out or not. And it's quite oppressive, there's something oppressive about it. Whereas here if you're out that's it. And you're welcomed. And everyone's pleased to see you and they know you're Jewish.[105]

This plural and complexly secular space is represented well by the London Citizens logo in which people in "religious" garb hold hands with others of nondescript and ethnic dress around a common space defined by their relations and nothing else [Figure 3.5].

The contrast between the faithful and complex secularity that London Citizens adopts and the self-policing, consensus-orientated approach that characterizes much Christian political and economic engagement is illustrated through the contrast between the Council of Christians and Jews (CCJ) event held in the offices of Allen & Overy and the November 25 Assembly at the Barbican. Each event encapsulates differing conceptions of religious responses to the power of money and notions of what it means to be a good citizen;

additionally, each represents how a simplistically secularist vision of the public sphere is either reproduced or deconstructed.

One kind of response, as displayed at the CCJ meeting, was to emphasize that markets were morally neutral. Where Christianity and other religious traditions intersected with capitalism was the need to provide personal moral values and motivations for good behavior rather than prescriptions for structural change. What religions do is offer visions for motivating the rational economic man or woman to spend his or her hard-earned money on altruistic rather than hedonistic ends. The church was to be a host to experts from the field to whom it respectfully listened in order to obtain their counsel rather than serve as an actor in the field who expected to be heard. Such an approach represents part of the self-censoring compact between Christianity and a simplistically secularist vision of modernity. Coterminous with the self-censoring compact is the evasion of questioning who does and who does not have power and why. In contrast, at the London Citizens assembly, the meeting took place quite literally on the street level or in a public theater rather than at an invitation-only event held in private offices and funded by corporate donors. Conflict and tension were not expected at the CCJ event; it was a polite exchange around a contentious issue rather than a contentious exchange around a public issue. The CCJ event represents the predominant mode of Christian social and political engagement with those who hold economic and political power (but interestingly, not with those who hold cultural power, primarily those who work in the arts and media who are often subject of vehement protest). What is said here is not meant to single out the CCJ, which is an extremely gracious and worthwhile organization that over the years has undertaken transformative interfaith work. It is simply to make explicit the pattern of its engagement with significant holders of power and the ways in which such an approach constitutes a form of self-marginalization in relation to the dominance of certain economic interests. Moreover, the CCJ event represents not only a failure to recognize but also a reproduction of the symbiotic relationship between capitalism and the construction of a disenchanted, secularizing form of modernity.[106]

The London Citizens event was different from the CCJ in a number of ways. Religious voices did speak "religiously" with a text from Nehemiah read out in what was a public, overtly political assembly. Religious leaders, in clerical dress, sat on the stage behind podiums, positioned like a panel of judges watching over the proceedings. These leaders came from non-Establishment traditions: Roman Catholic, Islamic, Salvation Army, and Pentecostal. (Despite repeated invitations, no Anglican Bishop attended or agreed to be a participant, although a number of Anglican clergy played key roles both in organizing the assembly and in its staging.) Unlike the CCJ event, which was chaired by the Anglican Bishop of Manchester, the religious leaders at the Barbican did not chair or claim any such neutral, host position within the proceedings. They represented an interest and had taken the side of the "have-nots" against the "haves." Explicitly religious figures and discourses were present, but these were combined with a number of other discourses and actors. The assembly itself was chaired by a cross section of representatives of different institutions. What was staged was not an encounter of passive listening but one of mutual accountability where holders of power were expected to respond to proposals that representatives from London Citizens pressed on them. But member institutions were also expected to respond, take responsibility, and act to address the issues raised. Unlike the CCJ meeting, we were not there to have an interesting discussion after which we were better informed so as to make our own individual judgments. We were there as delegates of institutions who were part of an ongoing process of personal, corporate, and social transformation and collective judgment making about what to do in collaboration with those with power over the communities where we lived. The dramaturgy of the assembly was not designed to uphold any pretence that everyone in the room was equal. Some were leaders, others were not; some held more power, some held less. What was needed was a rebalancing of power relations and that was what the event was meant to address. And it was expected that conflict and tension were part of the process. By contrast, at the CCJ meeting, conflict was curtailed in order to ensure the appearance of consensus and the "reasonableness" and relevance of religion. Yet in seeking consensus it reproduced, expressed, and crystallized an existing set of hegemonic power relations.[107]

KOSMOS VERSUS UNIVERSE: RECONFIGURING POLITICS AS A MORAL ENDEAVOR

The relationship between differing and interrelated patterns of belief and unbelief embodied by the event at the East London Mosque and the November 25 Assembly constitutes a reconstruction of secularity as genuinely plural and complex. This kind of space and the form of secularity it instantiates contrasts with attempts to exclude theological belief and practice from the construction of a common life and which predetermine the space in terms of a single, monolithic frame of reference or community of belonging. But to penetrate the heart of what is at stake in the kind of reconstruction of secularity I am pointing to, we must locate other ways of defining and imagining "secularity." One such way that is central to, yet largely obscured in debates about the nature of secularity in the West, draws from Christian belief and practice. A theologically attuned way of conceptualizing the kind of plural and complex embodiment of secularity the Barbican event represents can be derived from the New Testament usage of the term *kosmos*. The recognition of the finitude and fallenness of human judgments about the good, and thence the inevitable multiplicity of competing truth claims to determine the good, alongside the ongoing need to forge a common realm of meaning and action as a provisional participation in the good despite this plurality can be named theologically as a faithful instantiation of the *kosmos*.[108] And a Christian conception of cosmic order can in turn be distinguished from Platonic and modern conceptions of order and the temporal and spatial imaginaries to which each gives rise.

The New Testament usage of *kosmos* differs considerably and disrupts prior philosophical and largely Platonic usages of the term that denoted a wholly harmonious order, the antinomy and limit of which was chaos.[109] The multiple New Testament usages of the term *kosmos* resist a strict dualism between order and chaos. They can be combined to envision a single creation that is at once good but corrupted and subject to chaotic, nihilistic forces yet open to its healing and participation in God, and thence open to change.[110] On this account, engagement in politics is part of how we bear witness to a coming eschatological order.[111] Moreover, the New Testament usage deconstructs and offers an alternative to any attempt to write the political order into the natural order so that a historically contingent and fallen form of political rule is inscribed with an immutable character and posited as inevitable, "natural," and just the way things should be. The political and economic order of the day is not to be equated with God's *oikonomia*, however strong the temptation. From the writing of Genesis as an alternative creation mythos to the Babylonian *Enuma Elish*, and the refusal to bow the knee to the Roman emperor as the *kyrios* to the Barmen Declaration against the Nazis, it is a foundational (if often ignored) political insight of Christianity that there is a need to deconstruct and offer an alternative to any attempt to write a particular political order into the cosmic order.[112]

By its own theo-logic, Christianity posits the need to resist the ontologizing of social, political, or economic orders and refrain from according them too much significance – for good or ill.[113] For Augustine, this meant pointing to how slavery was a contingent and unnecessary form of relation (it was a result of the fall and thus an instance of sinful domination overcome in Jesus Christ) that would pass away. At the same time, Augustine recognized slavery as integral to and constitutive of the political, social, and economic structures of the world in which he lived.[114] In our own day, this means unveiling how capitalism is a contingent and mutable reality rather than a natural and inevitable one. At the same time, following Augustine, it means recognizing that we cannot extract ourselves from its influence or simply overthrow it by a revolutionary event or act of will. This side of Christ's return, capitalism, like any all-encompassing system, will not end via a revolutionary moment that comes from "outside" the system, nor can we posit an untainted subcultural politics of resistance "from below." Both postures presume forms of human speech and action capable of operating from a spatial and temporal register unconditioned by sin and patterns of domination. We must also resist the attempt to clothe an immanent political program in messianic robes and thereby claim for it a false innocence and innovation. Theologically, a more sober, yet at the same time more radical hope for change in this age, is to seek the *metanoia* or conversion of capitalism: that is, its reconfiguration from within by redirecting its discursive and structural apparatus to different, God-given ends.[115] Such sociopolitical *metanoia* is gestated through inventive tinkering and "mustard seed"-like improvisations across innumerable locations that together germinate an emergent order within and through the old.[116] Moreover, on a theological and Platonic account, real change involves a *metanoia* of the self and not just the material conditions of human relationships: cure of the soul is profoundly interrelated with the cure of the *polis*. A Christian conception of *metanoia* means not looking to a cataclysmic event or messianic leader from within history to make things come out all right, but to a conversion of self and others through time-intensive processes of building meaningful relationships one person at a time and the cultivation of ascetic and liturgical practices that redirect us to desire God first. Such a process helps foster a profound transformation of vision and subjectivity so that we learn to see temptations and idolatries for what they are and can turn instead to bear witness to the transformative actions of the Spirit who is the only one with the agency to irrupt a transfigured spatiotemporal register (a new heaven and a new earth) within the bounds of the old.

In addition to the distinction between a Christian and Platonic conception of the *kosmos*, a third distinction must be added. As Charles Taylor notes, a key shift into the modern period was the loss of a sense of what it meant to participate in and collaborate with a preexisting order, understood theologically or otherwise, and the emergence of a view of order as imposed *ab extra* on nature by the human will.[117] Taylor calls this the shift from cosmos to universe and it entails a change in how the world is imagined.[118] His account of this shift makes clear that in debates about different conceptions of secularity, what is also at stake are rival metaphysical constructions of order. Both a Christian and a Platonic conception of order entail a sense that the cosmic order provides meaning to those who participate in it and a sense of this meaning can be discerned through right participation, political or otherwise. Part of the shift into the modern period is a move to disengagement and disenchantment such that the cosmic order comes to be understood as mechanistic and morally neutral: it cannot disclose to us any sense of how we should live. As Taylor puts it: "The move to mechanism neutralises this whole domain. It no longer sets norms for us, or defines crucial life meanings."[119] However, Taylor also notes how the emergence of a "modern cosmic imaginary" from the eighteenth century onward reintroduces a sense of mystery, meaning, and moral significance through our participation in and kinship with nature and the "dark genesis" of humankind out of immeasurable time.[120] The environmental movement is but one expression of such a sensibility. For Taylor, "the striking fact about the modern cosmic imaginary is that it is uncapturable by any one range of views. It has moved people in a whole range of directions, from (almost) the hardest materialism through to Christian orthodoxy; passing by a whole range of intermediate positions."[121] Yet, what Taylor does not pay attention to is the continuing force of a mechanistic view of the universe in the realm of politics and economics where "Weberian" notions of politics as a rational legal order articulate the dominant political imaginary, whether it takes a liberal, neoliberal, or social democratic form.[122]

Part of the contradiction of the modern compact that broad-based community organizing represents is the reassertion of a moral order and a "cosmic imaginary" into the supposedly mechanistic and neutral realm of politics and economics. It implies also a rejection of procedural and bureaucratic forms of public reason that are correlative with a mechanistic vision. As will be argued in Chapter 6, in their stead, broad-based community organizing reasserts the need for practical reason as the basis of political judgments about common goods. Yet a reliance on practical reason assumes we live in a cosmos pregnant with meaning rather than a neutral and mechanistic one on which we impose meaning by dint of our will to power. A resort to practical reason assumes that, even though it can be opaque and demands a highly contentious discernment process, those in power can be held accountable on the basis of their shared participation in a common realm of meaning and action. Politics, on this account, is not reducible to a clash of opposing interests, wills, or classes. In other words, a common life is possible as it is premised on our shared participation in a cosmic order that has meaning. The diverse traditions involved in London Citizens, while having radically different visions of the good and different conceptualizations of the cosmic order, do share a sense that as humans we participate in a cosmos that is meaningful and this has public significance for our life together. Definitions of the good are plural but the good of political association (*politeia*) mediated via democratic practices enables the emergence of a common life shared across all traditions to be pursued as a good in itself. Broad-based community organizing refuses to separate morality and politics: the good that is a shared political life is premised on the possibility of shared moral goods. While other modes of political action – notably forms of environmentalism and contemporary anarchism – represent distinct but parallel contradictions of the modern compact, broad-based community organizing mediates a form where "traditional" religions provide a primary discursive frame of reference.[123]

Theologically understood, the non-eschatological order is a deeply ambiguous one in which the world is complexly faithful and unfaithful, loving and idolatrous; a time in which political authorities may both participate in the reordering of creation to its true end and be Antichristic that is, utterly opposed to God's good order. The language of "empire," "Antichrist," and the "principalities and powers" is language that reckons with the capacity of political, ecclesial, or any authority to act in wholly malevolent ways, with idolatrous cultural logics and regimes of governance that are something more than simply a distortion of a gift (or more properly something less if, following Augustine, we take evil to be a privation of the good). A Christian conceptualization of the world as *kosmos* (a moral order that simultaneously contains the possibility and moments of its own inversion and dissolution) helps capture the ambiguity of our participation in this order.[124] It allows us to see London/Babylon as having intrinsic value as part of the non-eschatological order of things in which we can perform the gift and vocation of being human but, at the same time, not be naïve about how London/Babylon is also an instantiation of a worldly system that can utterly desecrate this gift and vocation. Enabling life in the worldly city to be an arena in which this gift and vocation can flourish rather than be desecrated and distorted entails ensuring the prevailing political and economic order is neither made to bear the full weight of the meaning and purpose of being human, nor divested of any meaning and purpose and thus rendered a nihilistic vortex of dominatory relations.

For Christians, Christ is ruler over the *kosmos*, but this rule is not about increasing the size of the church, but rather seeks to heal and transform human social, economic and political orders so they can be the world (an arena of human flourishing to which the church can contribute) rather than worldly (the world turned in on itself so that social, political, and economic relations diminish our humanity and desecrate our dignity). Yet for the negotiation of a meaningful and penultimately good common life to be possible, some kind of common sense and moral vision needs to be developed among these people, in this place, at this time. Broad-based community organizing represents one such means, as it allows for multiple traditions of belief and practice to identify and pursue goods in common while recognizing these common objects of love are provisional and penultimate: that is, of the world but not necessarily worldly. A plurality of moral traditions in constructive relationship with each other becomes the basis of a genuinely common life as opposed to either a totalizing system that demands uniformity and claims for itself the ability to determine the end of history or a system that disaggregates and dissolves any form of common life and holds that there is neither meaning to history nor any moral life possible within the existing order of things.[125]

THRESHOLD

So far I have focused on the context of broad-based community organizing within the context of London. This chapter examined how community organizing as a constellation of democratic practices mediates the relationship between different religious traditions and politics itself. The brief history of how Citizens UK was established outlined its emergence in relation to transatlantic relationships and the initiative of Neil Jameson. Religious identities and discourses were seen to be a core component in both the initial and ongoing development of Citizens UK. Community organizing as a practice of democratic politics was then contrasted with and seen to contradict portrayals of the relationship between fundamentalism and democracy. Building on the account of the democratic possibilities of religious beliefs and practices, an account was developed of how Citizens UK's work constitutes a form of interfaith relations understood as a civic practice. Within this paradigm, consideration was given to how community organizing mediates relations between Jews, Christians, and Muslims and some of the tensions and issues pertaining to this process of mediation. The final section assessed the way in which broad-based community organizing reconfigures dominant notions of secularity and the relationship between moral and theological frames of reference and conceptions of political order. Having been immersed in the context that London Citizens operates within and discovered something of how the Alinsky approach to organizing is deployed within a contemporary world city, we can now begin to look with greater detail at how organizing works in practice. Chapters 1–3 are the foil against which the anatomy of organizing set out in Chapters 4–5 can be evaluated. Then, having seen where organizing comes from, what it does, and how it works, we will be able in Part II to make sense of organizing as a form of democratic politics and learn broader lessons for how we might think about the relationship between faith and democratic citizenship.

4

An Anatomy of Organizing I

Listening, Analysis, and Building Power

Previous chapters have depicted who is involved in community organizing, where it takes place, and how it emerged historically and intellectually. We turn now to the question of how organizing is done. What are its tactics, strategies, and rules? And what repertoires of political action does it employ? Answering these questions entails addressing the key political questions about *power* (who does what to whom and how do they achieve it?), *judgment* (how, when, and where should we act and what should we do?), and *legitimacy* (why should we act this way rather than that way, who gets to act, and what is the meaning and purpose of our actions?). I shall explore these questions by focusing on the initiation, development, and culmination of the campaign for responsible lending undertaken by London Citizens from 2008 to 2010. The account of the campaign provides a window onto the practices of broad-based community organizing (BBCO) and the dynamics and processes through which London Citizens as a particular instantiation of BBCO achieves its aims and fulfills its vision of democratic politics. This and Chapter 5 investigate what is involved for participants as they move through the sequences of a campaign and how the sequence itself embodies a distinct vision and performance of citizenship. We begin with how an issue is initially identified and a specific policy formulated. We then move on to consider how the capacity to work on an issue and bring about change through political action is developed.

INITIATING THE PROCESS

The story of how Citizens UK came into being was sketched in Chapter 2.[1] What is given here is an account of the emergent process through which a particular campaign and sequence of actions come into being. Although the campaign focused on is the responsible lending initiative, comparisons will be made to other campaigns in order to give illustrative contrasts and help develop a fuller sense of what community organizing can involve. In any account of something as multifaceted as a political campaign, there is always a degree of tidying up the narrative in order to communicate what happened succinctly and clearly, but as a result, there is a tendency to make things sound more linear than they were. I highlight this danger here in order to raise awareness of the problem in the ensuing examination.

The origins of the London Citizens responsible lending initiative go back to a number of parallel developments that converged and eventually crystallized to form the impetus for the campaign. Glasman and I initiated the first strand by encouraging the organizers to take seriously the role of the City of London Corporation in the politics of London. The concern was that the organizers talked about their role in building relationships with "power" in London but were not aware of the significance of the City of London Corporation and had no relationship with the corporation. At about the same time (2007–08) the financial crises began to unfold. This led to the organizers initiating what they called a "Governance of London" campaign. While primary leaders were involved in this initiative, it was not generated from the grass roots, although the campaign that subsequently emerged was. In a briefing note addressed to "Trustees and Key Leaders" from Jameson in January 2009, in which plans for the coming year were outlined, the initiative was explained in the following terms:

> THE GOVERNANCE OF LONDON; One reaction to the current economic crisis is for [London Citizens] leaders to both reflect on the causes and implications of the credit crunch AND develop a plan which protects our neighbourhoods, families and the services we rely on. It is logical to try and cement our relationship with the major power brokers in the capital – this includes Mayor Johnson [Mayor of the Greater London Authority], key business leaders and to seek a new relationship with the Corporation of London (the financial heart of the country).

Popular Education

The aim of the Governance of London campaign that emerged was twofold. The first dimension was an initiative in *popular education* aimed at primary leaders from across London Citizens member institutions and resulted in a series of workshops. A primary leader was understood to be someone who was in charge of or a strategic figure within a membership institution and who was also very involved or had extensive experience in campaigns and organizing.[2] As a form of popular education, the Governance of London campaign mobilized academic and media expertise in the service of leaders, many of whom had no tertiary education. This was vital for having informed participation in the development of London Citizens' response to the recession. In a sense it was a top-down initiative, but it was a crucial precursor to the formulation of the agenda that eventually came into being and was ratified at the November 25 Assembly. As noted in Chapter 1, a key part of an organizer's role is to be a catalyst or agitator and to take the initiative in educating those in membership. Indeed, Valley Interfaith (an IAF affiliate in Texas) refers to itself as a "university for the people."[3] For Ernesto Cortés, lead organizer of Southwest IAF and the organizer who has done the most to emphasize the crucial role of popular education in effective organizing, such seminars "are intended in part to provide ordinary citizens with access to information and expertise that has not been filtered through the biases of big business."[4] Reflecting on Cortés's work, Stout notes that part of organizing is ensuring equal access to information and direct access to experts in order to democratize the distribution of knowledge. And, we might add, it is necessary in order to strengthen the agency of primary leaders by developing their knowledge-base and interpretive capacity.

The "Governance of London" workshops were part of the preliminary process of issue identification and policy formulation. People are not always aware of the issues that affect them or able to identify what their real interests are as they have adopted the frames of reference and dominant scripts of the ruling hegemony. Organizers have to engage in a process of what Paolo Friere terms "consciousness-raising": informal or popular education that sensitizes those involved about their political, economic, and social conditions (which may or may not be ones of oppression and marginalization) and helps them imagine and move toward alternative ways of seeing themselves and their situation. Crucial to this process of sensitization is helping people critically reflect on their conditions through broader frameworks of interpretation. This is one area where London Citizens organizers were consistently weak: not giving time and attention to the educative aspects of organizing or helping leaders develop broader critical frameworks of analysis. Frierian approaches to organizing emphasize this more.[5] However, one of the differences between the approach of organizers and that specifically advocated by Friere is that Friere's approach draws almost exclusively on a Marxist conception of class relations as the framework of analysis.[6] This poses an inevitable and inherent conflict between the interests of the "haves" and the "have-nots." As noted in previous chapters, organizers are seeking a common life in which the interests of all can be fulfilled rather than the assertion of one set of interests over and against another. A further contrast to Friere is that organizers are far more eclectic in the frameworks of analysis they introduce to help people reflect on their conditions. As the "IAF Reflects" sessions outlined in Chapter 1 indicate, theology as well as a variety of economic, historical, philosophical, and social scientific sources are often used as a framework of analysis.

Research Actions

The second dimension of the Governance of London campaign was to build a relationship with the Lord Mayor and the Corporation. At this stage there was no talk of any specific proposals and the anti-usury element was not considered. Building a relationship with the Corporation of London involved simply asking them for meetings to discuss the nature of London Citizens's work and possible areas of collaboration with the corporation in its capacity as a local authority. This was an example of a *research action* through which a potential ally is identified. As well as listening to members, organizers instigate a process of listening to those with vested interests in the area concerned: some turn out to be allies and others, whom one may have presumed to be friendly, turn out to be hostile. But organizers cannot know this in advance and so meetings must be organized and relationships built. The introduction to the corporation was facilitated (and complicated by) the fact that London Citizens received sizeable grants for its work from the City Bridges Trust, the sole trustee of which is the City of London Corporation.[7] There was discussion of whether this placed London Citizens in a compromised and subaltern position in relation to the corporation. As it turned out, there was a certain irony in the trust facilitating the introduction because the largest grant received from the trust was to support and extend the living wage campaign and the City of London Corporation subsequently became a target for the campaign as it refused to pay a living wage to its street cleaners. The initial meetings eventually led to a roundtable with the Lord Mayor at the Mansion House on May 28, 2009.

The London Citizens team gathered before the meeting in the basement of a café to rehearse the running order, review the purpose of the meeting, and confirm the roles assigned to each member of the team. This is always something of a last-minute affair as organizers can never guarantee that those who said they would come will turn up and sometimes some turn up who were not expected. As it was, the team consisted of twenty-nine leaders and six organizers. The leaders included Roman Catholic priests, Anglican clergy, Methodist ministers, Evangelical pastors, school heads and pupils, student union representatives, academics, and representatives of congregations in membership. Such premeetings are an important feature of how organizers coach leaders in how to relate to those in power. These premeetings are built on the recognition that most ordinary people have little experience in negotiating with those in positions of authority and can often feel cowed by the surroundings, language, and way in which such meetings are conducted. When new leaders encounter the often disrespectful and alien nature of corporate, bureaucratic, and political power holders, and also discover their own inadequacy in responding, this is frequently a catalyst for becoming more involved in organizing and going for training.

The premeetings are part of the apprenticeship in politics. The coaching process entails such things as ensuring that leaders understand who will be in the room and know the agenda and interests of those they will face; that they possess sufficient knowledge and understanding of the issues to be discussed; what the aims of the meeting are; and how to react if things go badly or well. In theory, the organizers' work should end after the premeeting. While present at the actual meeting, organizers do not lead meetings on the basis of the iron rule that one should never do for others what they can do for themselves.

The success or failure of a meeting is often determined by how well leaders are prepared and the extent to which organizers have done their homework. Inexperienced organizers often fail to do sufficient preparatory work and end up speaking on behalf of their leaders in the actual meeting.

Sartorial Considerations

The team was told beforehand to dress "as if for a first date." Everyone was smartly attired with the head boy of St. Bonaventure's and St. Angela's School in his uniform and the religious leaders in clerical dress. The attention to sartorial details was not uncommon. There is a culture among organizers of wearing business attire and encouraging leaders to dress smartly or in formal clerical dress when attending meetings with politicians, bureaucrats, and corporate officials. Those external to the organization and who work in parallel areas can find this off-putting: a figure from a faith-based organization involved in political campaigns work commented that all the organizers he met looked like "Mormons." Three interrelated rationales can be identified for the adoption of the dress code. It is partly to credentialize leaders and organizers as of a similar status to the officials they meet; it is a self-conscious attempt to differentiate those involved in organizing from political activists, charity workers, and community groups who are perceived as dressing more casually; and lastly, it is a contextual and historic measure. The origins of the dress code go back to organizing black and white working-class communities in Chicago where looking smart was a symbol of status and aspiration while looking like a "hippie" or bohemian signaled someone who possessed the advantages of both class and racial privilege.[8] Looking well turned out was a way to simultaneously look like you mattered and a way of identifying with the people being organized. The one condition Alinsky insisted on before hiring his first organizer, Nicholas von Hoffman, in 1953 was that he "go out and get a haircut and buy ... a decent suit."[9] The same sentiment can be heard expressed to new organizers today.

After we made our way through the airport-like security process, the team was directed up a grand staircase with marble balustrades and into a large reception room. Soft drinks served by waiters were positioned at one end of the room, while at the other was a large horseshoe table set with thirty-three chairs around it. The corporation team included twenty people who all had seats assigned at the table. Their team included representatives from large, blue-chip solicitors' firms such as Clifford Chance and Linklaters, banks such as Deutsche Bank and Barclays Capital, and members of the Financial Services Authority, as well as senior figures from the City of London Corporation. The banks and solicitors had sent the people who handled their corporate social responsibility agenda. This was a subtle and probably unselfconscious act of marginalization: the concerns of London Citizens were not seen as calling into question their core business but were framed within their philanthropic and community engagement programs. Members of the London Citizens team who were assigned specific roles were also seated around the table while the others arrayed themselves along an outer circle of chairs. Sister Una McLeash chaired the meeting after negotiating this with the Lord Mayor. The initial act was a "rounds" in which a representative of each delegation from London Citizens introduced their section (the delegations were listed as religious leaders, student unions, sixth-form colleges, academics, community leaders, and organizers), while each member of the corporation's team gave an individual introduction. After the "rounds" and an overview of the corporation's community engagement work, there was a discussion of the impact of the recession on confidence in the banks with a range of contributions from both parties. The outcome of the meeting was an agreement to set up a joint working group to explore how a future relationship might be developed.

Learning the Topography of Power

After the meeting a tour of the Mansion House for the London Citizens team was arranged. As part of this tour, the team was shown the banqueting hall in which the Chancellor of the Exchequer gives the annual Mansion House speech on the state of the British economy. The dramaturgy of this annual speech is rarely if ever noted. However, in effect, it is not the bankers who appear before Parliament every year to give an account of their activities; rather, it is an elected representative who appears before the bankers to be held accountable for the government's policies.

In the banqueting hall were two stained glass windows. On one window was depicted the signing of the Magna Carta, for which the Corporation's militias provided the means of enforcement and in whose orchestration the mayor was a key figure [see Figure 4.1]. This was a celebration of the Corporation as a pioneer and defender of civic and market freedoms. The Magna Carta granted the City the right to elect its own mayor and specified "that the City of London shall have all its ancient liberties by land as well as by water." A central feature of the Magna Carta was provision for the free movement of goods and freedom from certain kinds of centralized taxation. Exactly opposite, on the other side of the hall, was a stained glass window depicting William Walworth, then Lord Mayor of London, slaying Wat Tyler, leader of the 1381 Peasants Revolt, at Smithfield outside the walls of the City [see Figure 4.2]. Walworth raised the city militias to defend the king against the rebels and their supporters among the citizens of London. The Corporation's self-representation in stained glass laid bare its dual role as, on the one hand, a defender of liberty and on the other hand, the sovereign power best able to act to defend the status quo and elite interests.

The impact of the meeting with the Lord Mayor was to impress on organizers and leaders the significance and power of the Corporation of London. No meetings with Mayor Johnson entailed anything approaching the munificence

FIGURE 4.1. Part of the "Royal Window" depicting the signing of the Magna Carta in the Egyptian Hall of the Mansion House, the City of London. Designed by Alexander Gibbs, the "Royal" and "City" windows were installed in 1868.

and business turnout as that encountered at Mansion House. But the question arose as to what was being sought from the relationship with the Corporation of London and what concrete issue was at stake in the relationship. The answer to this question suggested itself in a seminar room at London Metropolitan University that June. The seminar was part of a three-day colloquium that drew together organizers and academics from Germany, Australia, Great Britain and the United States to discuss different aspects of community organizing – in particular, the possibilities for organizing under conditions of economic globalization.[10]

FIGURE 4.2 Part of the "City Window" depicting the slaying of Wat Tyler by the Mayor of London, William Walworth, in 1381. Located in the Egyptian Hall of the Mansion House, the City of London.

At the seminar on June 16, after a discussion the evening before about the themes that were emerging in the United States through its house meetings, the issue of debt and usury were suggested as a way to frame the response to the recession and to the dominance of finance capital.

Listening Campaigns

There was already planned a commitment by organizers to undertake a thousand "one-to-one" relational meetings over the month of June among institutions in membership (the nature of the one-to-one will be explained later in this chapter). It was decided to combine this with a *listening campaign* to find out how the recession was affecting the membership and their friends and family, and then use these findings as the basis for identifying issues on which to take common action. This process was subsequently extended from June to September. Through the one-to-ones undertaken by organizers and house meetings undertaken by leaders in their institutions, a clear set of concerns and problems was identified. Echoing the findings in the United States, an issue that emerged quickly was how to cope with high levels of personal debt and what were felt to be punitive interest rates charged by loan agencies and credit card companies. In tandem with this listening campaign, a further process of research and relationship building with banks and other relevant financial institutions was initiated. This parallel initiative was launched with great controversy with the walk from Bevis Marks Synagogue to the Royal Bank of Scotland offices on July 22 in which Rabbi Natan Asmoucha played such a key role. This action in London was timed to coincide and be a part of the simultaneous launch of Metro IAF's "10% is Enough" campaign in New York; Washington, DC; Boston; Chicago; and Durham, North Carolina. The U.S. initiative explicitly called for the reinstatement of usury laws to cap interest rates at 10 percent for credit cards and personal loans, including payday loans and rapid-return tax refunds. Whereas the U.S. organizers billed the London action as part of a unified transatlantic campaign, in the United Kingdom, because of the lack of extensive consultation with membership institutions at that point, the launch was said to be calling for a national *debate* on the issue of debt and usury. Jameson was quoted in the media as saying:

> We are calling on the chairmen of banks, particularly those bailed out by the taxpayer, to have a formal meeting with citizen alliances.... There has been enough huffing and puffing about greedy bankers. Our job as a civil society alliance is to call for a national debate on the issue of debt, which includes the reintroduction of anti-usury laws in the UK.[11]

Types of Initiative

As is beginning to be clear, the responsible lending initiative emerged through a multifaceted process. However, two basic patterns of initiation can be identified in London Citizens' work and BBCO more generally. The first pattern is the *responsive-entrepreneurial* type and the second is the *adoptive-adaptive* type. The responsive-entrepreneurial type involves an event or condition that is identified either through a formal listening process or through coming to light in the media or via a network of established relationships. This event or condition calls forth a response, which then stimulates a creative and entrepreneurial process of policy formulation and common action. For example, the "Bin the Rats" campaign run by West London Citizens in Southall 2006–07 was a response to the linkage between poor provision for storing and collecting garbage and a growing rat infestation. This condition was identified as a source of considerable anger and frustration through a formal listening campaign conducted by member institutions in Southall. After identifying an issue of mutual concern, a creative solution was sought: this entailed lobbying the council to provide what are colloquially known as "wheelie bins" in which to store refuse before it is collected, the wheelie bins being effectively large, hard plastic rat-proof containers.

Another example of the responsive-entrepreneurial type of action is the "CitySafe" campaign. This grew out of a response to a particular event: the murder of Jimmy Mizen, a 16-year-old boy in broad daylight in Lee, southeast London, in May 2008. Jimmy was killed in a bakery shop when his throat was lacerated by a shard of glass from a dish that was smashed in his face when he tried to defend himself from an unprovoked attack. Jimmy's death fed into wider concerns sparked by a spate of such killings: between 2007 and 2009, seventy-three London teenagers died from street violence.[12] The Mizen family attended a Catholic church in membership with South London Citizens. The church leadership called on organizers and other membership institutions for support and to help formulate a response to the situation. After working with a group of teenagers from schools in the area, leaders and organizers from South London Citizens formulated the CitySafe Haven scheme, described by a BBC reporter as an "innovative project ... experimenting with a form of community self-policing."[13] The initiative involved teenagers going from shop to shop in specific areas asking them to become a CitySafe Haven. This involved the shop displaying a sticker in its window, declaring it to be a haven, and committing to locking the shop and calling the police should a child seek shelter and request help. It also involved shopkeepers agreeing to report crime 100 percent of the time to the police. The other dimensions of the initiative were building relationships, and hence trust, through face-to-face meetings between teenagers, police, and shopkeepers, where each could express their concerns. The scheme was subsequently adopted by other chapters of London Citizens.

The initiative also demonstrates a problem with the responsive-entrepreneurial model: overreach. There was an attempt to extend CitySafe into a wider neighborhood organizing effort; the aim was to mobilize and organize around the issue of street safety and take advantage of the high levels of anxiety this issue generated so as to build what were called CitySafe Neighborhood organizations. The hope was that these neighborhood organizations would eventually affiliate with London Citizens. While highly entrepreneurial, the move represented what military analysts term "mission creep" and was poorly conceived and never gained momentum. However, the stand-alone CitySafe Haven campaign was very successful with the two-hundredth haven being City Hall, opened by the then mayor Boris Johnson on November 19, 2009. Other organizations and institutions unrelated to London Citizens, such as supermarkets and train stations, are beginning to adopt the program, as are other towns and cities in the United Kingdom.

The adoption of the CitySafe campaign by other groups points to the second pattern of initiation: the adoptive-adaptive type. The "Living Wage" campaign is a good example of this type. The Living Wage campaign resulted from a responsive–entrepreneurial-type initiative in Baltimore in the 1990s by the IAF-affiliated coalition BUILD (Baltimoreans United in Leadership Development).[14] In 2000, on a retreat of primary leaders, it was decided to initiate a similar campaign in London. However, while it adopted the name and basic rationale of the campaign in Baltimore, it significantly adapted it to local conditions. In Baltimore it was a campaign for a citywide living-wage ordinance. In London, it became a campaign targeted at individual companies and sectors. This reflected the different kind of political economy at work in London.[15] The Living Wage has since become London Citizens' signature campaign.

The responsible lending campaign combined elements of both types of initiatory sequence. It was both a creative response to the financial crisis and adopted and adapted elements of an initiative from the "10% is Enough" campaign. In the United States, there had been a cap of 10 percent on interest rates in many states up until the 1980s and some states still had equivalent statutory measures in place. In England, by contrast, a legal ceiling for interest rates was set at 10 percent in 1571 (and reduced to 8 percent in 1624 and to 6 percent in 1651), but all such measures were abolished in 1854.[16] So it was decided that a realistic chance of winning a cap demanded setting it at around 20 percent as this was in line with the interest rate ceilings already in place in other European countries such as Germany, Italy, Poland, and France.[17] This process of adaption was not without conflict: U.S. organizers felt the 20 percent cap called for in the United Kingdom undermined the legitimacy of their call for a 10 percent cap in the United States. This could be read as an example of the difficulties of working internationally while undertaking a place-specific form of politics, except that the general opinion in the United Kingdom was that the United States would have had a more realistic chance of winning if they, too, had campaigned for a 20 percent limit.[18]

To understand fully how the responsible lending campaign came about, we must first examine how specific issues are identified and decided on.

IDENTIFYING THE ISSUE

The listening campaign through which common concerns are identified is a vital part of the organizing toolbox. It is a means of simultaneously putting people before program (a key rule of organizing) and building ownership of and capacity to act on a specific proposal that arises. The aim is to be relationally driven and not ask people to act on the basis of an abstract principle, or a predetermined program. It relates also to Alinsky's second rule: work within the experience of your people. For Alinsky the program for what he called the "People's Organization" was to emerge from the "principles, purposes, and practices which have been commonly agreed upon by the people."[19] As already indicated, developing such a program involves holding what are called *one-to-ones* and *house meetings*.

Relational Meetings: The One-to-One

The one-to-one is the cornerstone of organizing. Organizers in London Citizens are expected to undertake fifteen such meetings a week. Chambers claims to have invented the one-to-one or "relational meeting" after reflecting on the practices that were effective when he was working across deeply charged racial divisions on the south side of Chicago in the 1950s.[20] Whether this is true or not, the claim does reflect the way in which the one-to-one is a product of systematic evaluation and reflection on organizing and is invested with significance as a vital component and distinctive mark of community organizing. At its most basic, the one-to-one entails going and listening to family, friends, neighbors, and colleagues about what upsets or concerns them where they live or work. Gecan describes the one-to-one in the following terms:

> An individual meeting is a face-to-face, one-to-one meeting, in someone's home or apartment or workplace or local coffee shop, that takes about 30 minutes. The purpose of the meeting is not chit chat, whining, selling, gossip, sports talk, data collection, or therapy. The aim of the meeting is to initiate a public relationship with another person.[21]

He goes on to articulate the kind of rationale organizers often give for what Gecan sees as one of "universal tools of all effective organizing":[22]

> The commitment to listening to others means that the leaders who initiate them operate on the basis of several important assumptions. The first assumption is that the other person is worth listening to.... You are saying to the other person: you have values, ideas, dreams, plans, lessons, insights that are well worth listening to. The second assumption is that the person initiating the individual meeting – organiser, pastor, veteran leader – understands that the time devoted to individual meetings is more important than time spent in more conventional activities.... The third assumption, hinted at in the act of doing individual meetings but only proven over time, is that the corporate identity of the congregation remains in formation; that the newest member, the most recent arrival, is invited to join in the ongoing creation of the evolving local community. The relationship is not one-way, unilateral, provider-to-consumer, but two-way, reciprocal, and mutual.[23]

Cortés sets out how, within an ideal pattern, the relational meeting or one-to-one fits within the broader sequence of initiation:

> [T]he relational meetings lead to house meetings, whether they take place in a house or a school or a recreation centre or a church or synagogue or mosque. These small group meetings are about telling stories and developing narratives, but also about enquiring into the deep concerns affecting people's daily lives.... These small group conversations, properly directed and aimed, then lead to research actions to explore the dynamics, dimensions, and complexities of an issue, in order to prepare the public action. Through this process we learn to engage people who come from other contexts – business leaders, bureaucrats, union allies, and so forth. Properly conducted, these conversations

help people get inside one another's moral universe through sharing their stories and experiences.[24]

Relational Meetings: The House Meeting

The organizers Fred Ross and Cesar Chavez developed the "house meeting" in their work with Mexican-Americans in the late 1940s and early 1950s. It is simply a gathering of friends, neighbors, colleagues, or fellow congregants to discuss what matters to them, what they are angry about in their area, to tell their stories of the issues that affect them, and to listen to each other. In listening to each other they begin to hear that their story is not unique and so they can begin to discern issues of common concern. In hearing each other face-to-face they also begin to identify and empathize with each other's struggles.[25] As Gecan and Cortés indicate, in distinction from a pastoral or self-help group, the orientation of the meeting is out beyond the circle of meeting and the personal circumstances of those involved, toward public action with others.[26] This builds on Alinsky's original vision of community organizing as a process by which people are awakened or called out from a private world to participate in a public life.[27] Alinsky states:

> Through the People's Organization these groups discover that what they considered primarily their individual problem is also the problem of the others, and that furthermore the only hope for solving an issue of such titanic proportions is by pooling all their efforts and strengths. That appreciation and conclusion is an educational process.[28]

In the case of the 2009 listening campaign undertaken by London Citizens, this was marked administratively by the need to fill in a "house meetings tracking form" by those who led a house meeting. The form explained the aim of holding a house meeting as: "To strengthen relationships in and around CITIZENS member institutions; to focus on the impact and solutions to the economic crisis; to find new leaders who are prepared to act and do something about it." The form gave specific instructions for how to run a house meeting, suggested readings about the wider context and passages from the Bible and the Qur'an for use in any reflections on the economic crisis, and asked leaders to log the numbers, age, gender, and stories of those involved. In addition, it asked for potential issues, solutions, leaders, and people who would like to stay involved to be identified and noted. The results submitted from the house meetings were often haphazard and vague. However, all the forms were collated by organizers and used as the basis of identifying issues at a day-long workshop on September 26 held to determine a set of policy responses to the recession based on the listening campaign.

Anger as a Political Passion

A goal of the listening campaign is to identify what motivates people to act and energizes them, and conversely, to help people identify their real interests.

Central to all aspects of this discernment process is asking what makes them angry. Many commentators identify as a distinctive feature of the IAF's work the emphasis on and way of conceptualizing *anger*.[29] The "Tent of the Presence" document outlines what IAF teaches about anger in their training:

It is not temper, not the hot words exchanged when the driver ahead cuts you up. Nor does anger imply violence, as we have been taught to assume. No, anger comes from the old Norse word 'Angr,' which means grief. Grief implies that there is a vision – a vision of a good life that was or that could have been. Anger and grief are rooted in our most passionate memories and dreams – a father whose spirit has been tried by demeaning work or no work, a brother or sister lost to violence or alcohol or drugs, a church vandalised by an arsonist, a college career sabotaged by an under-funded and increasingly poor education system, a neighbourhood of shops and families and affections and relationships ripped apart because banks won't lend to it, because insurance companies wouldn't insure it, because local authority staff wouldn't service it, because youth wouldn't respect it, or because teachers wouldn't teach in it. Anger sits precariously between two dangerous extremes. One extreme is hatred, the breeding ground of violence. The other extreme is passivity and apathy, the breeding ground of despair and living death.[30]

As Chambers notes after quoting the U.S. version of this statement: "Effective public-life organizers and leaders feel that anger, listen to it, and act on it."[31] From its depiction in Sophocles' *Antigone* to the practice of the "mothers of the disappeared" in Argentina and on, personal lament, anger and grief have birthed public speech and action that contests the status quo.[32] However, the articulation of grief and anger goes against core commitments prevalent in the contemporary context: notably, political liberalism's rational consensus orientation, the emphasis among professionals on being an impartial expert, bourgeois notions of respectability, and dominant church cultures of being polite and deferential to those in authority. Drawing from Taylor, we can say that anger contravenes the modern social imaginary; an imaginary in which conversation based on mutual exchange between equals is the paradigm of sociability and civility.[33] The problem comes when this ideal becomes a straightjacket that precludes the need for politics, occludes questions about the distribution of power and who can and cannot act, and excludes certain behaviors and forms of symbolic representation that can revitalize and broaden who is incorporated into democratic politics. Instead of extending disciplines of dialogic quiescence to the "masses" and to the "religious" (who are often perceived by elites to be one and the same), organizers train ordinary people in disciplined anger. The ideal of a rational consensus is replaced by passionate contestation and the representation of conflicting interests in the negotiation of a common life. As Stout argues:

A politics of just anger aims to restore the *spirit* of democracy to democratic culture, a spirit disposed to become angry at the right things in the right way and use this passion to motivate the level of political involvement essential to striving for significant change. A politics completely emptied of the vehement passions, of spiritedness, tends in practice to be antidemocratic. It cedes the authority of decision making to elites – experts and social engineers – who characteristically present themselves as disinterested and rational agents, intent only on maximizing fairness and efficiency.[34]

Conflict and Conciliation

Another reason the consensus-oriented approach common to many church leaders, professionals, and political liberalism tends per se to be antidemocratic is that it refuses to take sides. Its advocates refuse to recognize themselves as one interest among many, claiming the role of an honest, impartial broker. Instead of making common cause with one side or another, the consensus approach – in some dim echo of patrician notions that consider genteel and magnanimous disinterest as the true mark of public virtue – positions itself as above the fray or outside of the conflict of competing interests.[35] Alinsky frames the problem with an emphasis on consensus, stating starkly:

> They will attempt to throttle a major independent militant organization of the poor by using the current con game gimmick of "consensus." Consensus is a word which is bandied about by those who are either political illiterates, and in this group we find primarily sociologists – or by representatives of the status quo who want to prevent any change and who are fearful of militant action. Their definition of consensus is not the compromise which ensues from negotiation between power organizations; the inevitable compromise which is the cost of human coexistence. Nor do they recognize that it is always conflict which leads to the negotiation table and to agreement or consensus. They attempt to introduce an artificial nonexistent dichotomy between conflict and consensus. To them consensus and conflict are simply defined; it is the definition always held by the status quo; that if you agree with the status quo you represent consensus and that if you disagree with them you represent conflict.[36]

The paradox Alinsky highlights is that in order to generate real dialogue, one must take sides and identify and recognize conflicts of interest and not mistake the dominance of a single interest for a consensus. What BBCO seeks is the genuine representation of all interests rather than the suppression or masking of interests in the name of a consensus. Helping people identify and express what they are angry about is a crucial way in which real interests – based on deep motivations and visions of a better life – can be identified and mobilized and a desire for greater recognition and respect called forth. In relation to the response to the financial crisis there was a palpable and already apparent sense of anger directed against the banks that organizers could tap into. More often than not, however, it is through the sharing of personal stories about how situations or institutions have affected them in negative ways that those involved in BBCO begin to discover their shared grief and desire for change.

To understand the relationship between conflict and conciliation, we must examine not just personal testimonies but also stories told about former enemies. Central to the narrative of successful campaigns are stories of conversion – tales of how enemies became friends. A good example is the narrative told about numerous employers, such as the bank HSBC, and the Living Wage campaign wherein initial opposition and conflict is transformed into a more neighborly relation where the managers extol the benefits of the living wage and London Citizens celebrates the company or institution for their action. However, while the process resulted in neighborliness, as a process it could not bypass judgment against and confrontation with the structures, institutions, and people who opposed a just and common life. In community organizing, building real public relationship must encompass judging your enemy to be an enemy and identifying the nature of the conflict or injured right that stands between you before there can be any possibility of the mutual recognition of a common life on which the flourishing all depends.

Research and Analysis

In parallel with the process of popular education and listening runs a process of research and analysis. As already noted, the initial part of this involves "research actions" to build relationship with relevant institutions and organization with expertise in a particular area. What often occurs is that after some hunting around, either an organizer or leader will identify an expert who has an in-depth analysis of the issues concerned. What the expert identifies in the community organization is a way of communicating their ideas to a wider audience. The expert may be an academic, a businessperson, or someone involved in a special-interest lobby group concerned with the problem London Citizens is trying to address. In the case of the responsible lending campaign, London Citizens had the good fortune to meet Damon Gibbons.

In 1999 Gibbons helped found "Debt on our Doorstep," a campaign to end extortionate lending and ensure universal access to affordable credit and other financial services. A number of other agencies were involved, including Oxfam, Church Action on Poverty, Help the Aged, and the National Housing Federation. The campaign did have successes and brought the issue of high-cost credit into policy debates.[37] However, in contrast to the approach of London Citizens, it was a campaign developed by a small group of experts and focused on lobbying central government rather than organizing and mobilizing a broad-based constituency. It involved advocacy on behalf of others rather than direct action by those most affected taking responsibility for change and speaking for themselves directly to the powers-that-be. Moreover, the campaign struggled to generate a public narrative that located the issue of a cap on interest rates within wider concerns about responsible banking. Instead, the issue was framed in terms of fixing a problem for a small percentage of low-income borrowers. Much of the inability to move beyond a narrow and rather technical framing of the issue was caused by the broader political and economic environment in which the financial services industry was endlessly portrayed as the "goose that lays the golden egg."[38] After 2008, new political opportunities arose as the goose had clearly fouled the nest, making it toxic for everyone else. London Citizens was poised to take advantage of the new opportunities. However, the effectiveness of a campaign is not solely attributable to political opportunity. Organizers recognize that the quality of the initial research and analysis can make or break a campaign.

Power Analysis

A central part of the analysis is not only understanding the technical background to the issues (in the case of the responsible lending campaign, these included knowing the different ways of calculating interest, the nature of banking regulation, studies of the linkages between debt and poor health, and so forth) but also what organizers call the *power analysis*. A "power analysis" is an assessment of who has power to change things (this may well be different from who is the titular office holder), and so who are the specific people to target in any public action, identifying what their interests, motivations, and constraints are, and finding out who they are in relationship with and thence who has influence over them.[39] Some of the information needed for a good power analysis can be developed through research actions, such as the meeting with the Lord Mayor at Mansion House, and some is accessed from either sympathetic insiders or experts in the field concerned. Ironically, experts are often unaware that they are repositories of this more relational, power-orientated kind of knowledge as they tend to be solely focused on the technical side of the issues.

Democratizing Knowledge Production

The process of research represents a democratization of knowledge production and a way to redress the asymmetries between those who have and do not have the knowledge and the power to utilize that knowledge. However, it is easy to miss the exact nature of the symbiosis between processes of expert and academic knowledge production and the dynamics of popular education and research. The IAF's own analysis of power, which insists there are only two kinds of power – "organized people" and "organized money" – can obscure from view this symbiosis.[40] However, it is not just organizers who suffer from myopia on this issue. In his analysis of the IAF's research-and-analysis process, Stout contends that what the IAF does challenges "the authority-claims of many experts holding appointments at prestigious universities."[41]

Stout is exactly right to point to the importance of the kind of self-generated information networks that the IAF generates, for they are a means of bypassing the media and the subsequent spin of dominant elite groups in politics and business. Such forms of knowledge production are vital for providing ordinary citizens with access to information and expertise that enables a democratization of intellectual authority and analysis. There is no doubt that the Internet has hugely aided this process. However, Stout misses the creative role academic institutions play and the generative relationship between grassroots activities and universities that figures in his own story. As he himself notes, "Cortés deepened his own grasp of economics by spending the 1997–98 academic year as a visiting professor at MIT in the Department of Urban Studies and Planning."[42] Likewise, Alinsky came from the University of Chicago and, as already noted, drew heavily from what he learned there. Universities inform and interact with grassroots activists in vital ways, providing them with intellectual resources and people and then helping to credential and communicate the story of their work to broader audiences. In turn, grassroots action enables academics to generate new insight and trade off the moral authority and authenticity of such "street" action within the academy – this book being a case in point. Grassroots democracy needs access to knowledge in ways undetermined by big business and political elites; but that does not mean it has the resources to generate this knowledge itself or that universities are necessarily aligned with the interests of plutocrats. Global information sharing and academic networks (and access to the funding they can mediate) are vital to enabling in-depth evaluation and to training the kind of people able to organize, translate, and mediate this analysis to the "street" so as to enable concerted action. Theory, scholarly analysis, and intellectuals (not just of Gramsci's organic variety) have always played a role in community organizing, despite protestations to the contrary from Alinsky onward. They make a vital contribution not only to popular education and research but also in contributing to the strategic thinking about what to do and how to do it.

This is not to suggest that universities are wholly virtuous actors and engines of democratic change. Their record is patchy at best and downright antidemocratic and dictatorial at worst. Some of Alinsky's most bitterly fought campaigns were against the property development policies of the University of Chicago in the 1960s. More recently, service learning and widening participation programs in most universities are merely philanthropic in orientation. Moreover, any vision of the university as an institution that contributes to strengthening the democratic life where it is located is subordinated to the pursuit of profit and status.[43] Aligned with and growing out of this pursuit, universities themselves are often exploitative employers. Throughout the time of working on the responsible lending campaign, the university I worked for at the time, King's College London, was subject to a Living Wage campaign by London Citizens. Indeed, the leadership team meetings in the run up to the November 25 and then the May 3 assemblies involved organizers and leaders gathering in the Old Committee Room at King's early in the morning and passing a number of the cleaners who were still polishing floors. These cleaners were also working on the campaign and so they would discuss the campaign's progress with those gathering. Similar campaigns were run against the London School of Economics; University College London; and Queen Mary, University of London; all of which, in addition to King's, are now committed to paying the living wage to their cleaning and security staffs. King's has gone even further, with the School of Humanities joining London Citizens as a member institution in 2011 and other parts of the university collaborating with London Citizens on strategies to address public health and the widening of participation to tertiary education. But in each case, academics within these institutions were key players in the campaign. In short, elite institutions are simultaneously part of the solution and part of the problem in relationship to grassroots democratic citizenship.

Generating an Interpretive Community

London Citizens' process of developing policy proposals contrasts sharply with most other forms of policy formulation. There is a real issue of what is called *policy* or *regulatory capture* in the contemporary context whereby politicians and bureaucrats overidentify with or only take into account the interests of particular groups within an industry, sector, or the population at large. This term was first put forward to describe the process by which statutory authorities come to be dominated by the very industries they were charged with regulating, so that instead of acting in the public interest, laws are created that primarily benefit the interests of industry.[44] Banking, health, education, the environment, security, and a range of other fields are now affected by regulatory capture. Think tanks are part of this problem, as they are largely funded by corporations, wealthy individuals, and foundations with a narrow range of interests. Added to this is the *problem of milieu*: whether liberal or neoliberal, political and economic elites tend to mix together socially, and in many cases they have been to school or college together and so reinforce each other's views. This creates a problem of groupthink.[45] This is particularly acute in Great Britain where elites tend to be concentrated in London and so, because of their socioeconomic and geographic position, are often insulated from the experience and views of the rest of the population. The BBCO process of policy development points to a very different approach and represents an alternative way to generate policy ideas from those that emerge via elite-driven, top-down approaches that use polling or focus groups. And contrary to narrow conceptions of what constitute "public reasons," the approach of BBCO is one that is open to a variety of sources of knowledge and experience, including the highly personal and the religious.

A feature of the broad-based community organizing approach to policy formulation is that it builds an interpretative community that has the agency to undertake the identification and analysis of the problem and the resources to develop the ability and strategy by which to act in relation to the problem. Officials would often respond to questions from leaders about a particular policy by saying that they had consulted widely and that was why they had adopted their current position. When pushed, however, the process of consultation varied from inviting a selected group of organizations in to discuss a predetermined range of options, to the use of polling and focus groups in relation to a prescribed set of questions. Interpretation of the results and of what constituted the range of possible policy options remained entirely in the hands of the bureaucrats and "experts" – who were often representatives of a professional group or business with a financial or professional interest in the outcome. In turn, this rendered citizens as clients, not active agents in the production of policy. By contrast, the approach of London Citizens did not denude ordinary people of agency in the interpretive and policy production process and trusted that they possessed knowledge and experience relevant to that process. London Citizens retained control over the means of producing an interpretation and determined its own direct relationship to centers of knowledge production. This meant there could be genuine forms of coproduction and cogovernance as those affected by a policy had the ability to present an alternative interpretation and course of action and negotiate with parity of knowledge. At one level, it was a way to make meaningful notions of informed consent in the policy process. An assembly is the arena in which two interpretive or epistemic communities come together to negotiate in public. Experts, officials, politicians, and managers are on one side and those affected on the other side. What takes place is a process of consultation where, for a brief moment, there is parity between rulers and ruled.[46]

A further contrast is between how citizens are asked to respond to party platforms and the approach of BBCOs. In relation to party programs (as distinct from the policies of businesses and bureaucrats), the options before citizens can be characterized by Albert Hirschman's typology of exit, voice, and loyalty: if we disagree we often exit, leaving the party or not voting for its program; or we can voice our discontent with a program presented as a fait accompli; or if we agree we can express loyalty by staying or voting for the program.[47] What we do not have the opportunity to do is establish a relationship with those in power where they listen first to a program generated by those outside the party machine and then respond. Yet this is exactly the order of events that London Citizens establishes: instead of a hustings in which local members of parliament (MPs) and councilors come to present their manifestos to a passive audience, London Citizens holds accountability assemblies in which politicians are asked to respond to a program developed by the citizens who are themselves actively involved in the assembly. This was the format of the May 3, 2010 General Election Assembly where each party leader had to respond to the Citizens UK "manifesto" rather than present a case for their own proposals.

We can see that the responsible lending campaign came together through an emergent process. Rather than being straightforwardly bottom-up or top-down, it began to flow out of the confluence of a number of inputs. It was partly as a response to the local conditions of the financial crisis, partly as an adoption and adaption of developments by the IAF in the United States, and partly the result of initiation by organizers, key leaders, and academics as a result of a broader strategic analysis of the situation. However, in any such process there is a tension between initiation and imposition. While there is a role for organizers and key leaders to be catalysts, the dangers of vanguardism and organizational oligarchy are ever present.[48] One key factor that exacerbates the aligned dangers of oligarchy and vanguardism in London Citizens is the scarcity of time and resources and the need to take advantage of political opportunities as they arise. Politics is about action in time and as such, it involves having the power to act (through having sufficiently organized money, people, and knowledge) and making the right judgment calls about when, how, and with whom to act. Amid the flurry of a campaign, the demands of acting in time as opportunities arise means that it is often difficult to involve a broad base of people in decision making and the day-to-day work. Under the pressures of time and with resources for organizing and involving members being scarce, it becomes necessary to centralize decision making in order to be either effective or entrepreneurial and so open up new opportunities for grassroots corporate action. However, the temptation is to lose the inevitable tension between a distributed and a concentrated form of leadership and start acting on behalf of others, thereby contravening the "iron rule" of never doing for others what they can do for themselves.

CUTTING THE ISSUE

The concerns that emerge from the listening and research process are often ones not addressed in the political platforms and debates of the day. When they are, it raises the tendentious question of whether the IAF/Citizens UK is prepared to work in coalition with other groups and networks. On the issue of the responsible lending campaign, Citizens UK did help form a coalition to address the issue with the Centre for Responsible Credit, Church Action on Poverty, and Compass. But this was, in effect, a new coalition to address a specific issue. The IAF/Citizens UK tends not to join broader coalitions addressing an already established issue. This can be seen as a weakness and results in accusations that they are aloof, exclusive, and uncollaborative. In the United States, unlike in the United Kingdom, Germany, and Australia, remaining aloof from broader coalitions is partly born out of competition between community organizing networks for membership institutions, funding, and reputation. Some, particularly grant-giving foundations, tend to see this competition as weakening all the networks on the assumption that it diminishes their overall voice. Others, particularly organizers, tend to see competition as strengthening the different networks. To date there is not evidence to support either view.

There is, however, a certain irony that those whose expertise is "reweaving civil society" have proved either unable or unwilling to weave strategic relationships between different networks and so remain disorganized. IAF organizers contend they are happy to work in coalitions but that such coalitions are necessarily temporary (they come together to focus on a particular issue or a particular context) and that a decision not to engage in a broader coalitions is born out of a concern that the forms of political organizing adopted by others (including other community organizing networks) are at best ineffective or at worst antithetical and undermining of how the IAF does politics. This, in turn, can generate accusations that IAF organizers are arrogant. While undoubtedly true in particular cases, what communicates itself as arrogance is often the manifestation of the chutzpah and swagger necessary to being an organizer in the first place. However, while the problems addressed by the IAF are common – poor pay, poor housing conditions, street safety, and so forth – the innovative policy proposals and ways of framing the issues they and other community organizing networks create are not necessarily ones already on the roster of public debate, advocated by lobby groups, or outlined in party manifestos. And, on occasion, the problems identified are themselves entirely absent from the debates of the day.

Issues, Not Problems

Crucial to generating the innovative policy responses is the process of what is called *cutting the issue*. Along with other community organizing networks, the IAF makes a distinction between a "problem" and "an issue." A problem is an amorphous, multifaceted, and generalized structural condition such as crime or poverty or a lack of affordable housing. In contrast to a problem, "an issue" is a specific and potentially "winnable" course of action or proposal targeted at identifiable people and institutions. Alinsky defines it with characteristic succinctness: "An issue is something you can do something about."[49]

To focus on problems is antipolitical because it generates apathy and fatalism and so drains energy for change and directs people away from public action toward making the best of their situation for themselves and their family. Focusing on problems privatizes the grief people feel by making it count for nothing and dislocating it from any identifiable and nameable community of witness. Helping people feel that their personal story of grief is recognized and heard, not only by others standing in solidarity with them but also by those in power over them, converts private lament into a broader process of public action.

The focus on issues is a turn away from structure to agency. People cannot choose the problems that afflict them but they can choose the solutions they think might help alleviate those problems. By contrast, much academic analysis focuses on structure and so has a disempowering and depoliticizing effect by emphasizing the enormity and depth of the problems. The work of Michel Foucault is a good example: his constructive proposals for change always look frail and thin beside his analysis of the structures and effects of power. This is not to say such analysis is irrelevant.[50] It can be extremely enlightening, but it is not the point from which to begin political action. A central insight of BBCO as a form of political action is that motivating and mobilizing people to act together for change entails identifying the possibilities for agency through breaking structural problems down into winnable issues. A simple but often neglected insight.

Connecting Issues to Moral Convictions and Lived Experience

There is a broader point at stake here. In political theory, advocates of deliberative and participatory democracy worry that strong moral convictions and the simplifying of issues degrade public debate and alienate "moderate" citizens. Amy Gutmann, Dennis Thompson, and other deliberative democratic theorists call for skeptical and morally tentative citizens who are "uncertain about the truth or their own position" and who "should not be dogmatic about their view."[51] The foci of concern for Gutmann and other deliberative democrats are moral issues such as abortion or same-sex relations, yet the practices of BBCO also run counter to their approach. Whether or not attention to such moral issues in political debates breeds decline in political participation is highly contestable. Shields argues there is no evidence for this and maintains that "[m]oral conflict seems to invigorate American public life."[52] Indeed, strong moral conviction and passionate commitment is crucial to generating widespread participation. As Shields notes: "Social movements, whether celebrated or not, all have been driven by strong convictions rather than provisionally held truths. Put simply, a dogmatic resistance to opposing ethical views may be the price of a more participatory democracy."[53]

BBCO avoids what it identifies as "wedge issues" such as abortion, where organizers and leaders know there is strong disagreement among different member institutions (although this does not prevent such issues being raised on occasions for active consideration by other members). However, rather than encourage tentative commitment and moral skepticism, BBCO as a political practice breaks down complex economic and political problems into clearly identifiable issues that are then identified with moral positions: for example, paying a living wage and introducing a cap on interest rates are not identified as solely economic concerns, they are also explicitly identified as moral issues. By constructing issues in this way, participants in BBCO connect the concerns of ordinary citizens with the vast commercial and administrative complex that shapes political life and the seemingly insurmountable problems and risks that face modern rulers. Breaking problems down into issues and framing these issues as moral and material links participants' values, institutions, and relationships to public life.[54] Such an approach also provides a means to build a broad base that involves those for whom the issue may not be of immediate material interest but is of moral concern and who see it as a matter pertaining to the common life of everyone who lives in a particular place.

The Tension between Advocacy and Activism

As debates over civil rights, abortion, the environment, and experimentation on animals make clear, passion and moral conviction are key parts of widespread participatory democratic politics; but such involvement can, at the same time, lead to violence and the diminution of a common realm of meaning and action as citizens talk past – rather than with – one another. BBCO as a practice tries to hold commitment to a common life and the need for common deliberation, compromise, and pragmatism in tension with the need for the moral convictions and passion required to mobilize people to act. Successful advocacy of issues necessarily involves both. Here we encounter the tension between *advocacy* and *activism*: the more one engages in successful advocacy, the more one requires consensus and cooperation with those in power in order to achieve something like one's ends, yet the more one seeks to widen participation and promote active engagement on an issue or agenda, the more one must polarize and personalize the public messages in order to mobilize turnout and generate commitment. This is not a dynamic much attended to by political scientists.[55] Yet it is something organizers have long understood as is reflected in the tension between Alinsky's imperative that "to the organizer, compromise is a key and beautiful word" and his rule thirteen: "Pick the target, freeze it, personalize it, and polarize it."[56]

Is It Winnable?

The criteria London Citizens use in cutting an issue are the following: Is it winnable? Does it build power? And does it develop leaders? The implications of these criteria can be illustrated in relation to the responsible lending campaign. At the strategy meeting on September 26, 2010, it was decided to focus the campaign on obtaining a commitment to introduce a cap on interest rates in the party manifestos. The power analysis suggested that in the context of the financial crisis, the political establishment was now open to the need to place limits on interest rates and in the run-up to the General Election on May 3, there was the opportunity to gain a hearing and extract a public commitment. The General Election also provided an external timescale and point of focus for concerted and sustained public action. Setting the goal more vaguely, such as introducing a cap on interest rates *tout court*, would have been too open ended, as it would not have created scope for targeted action toward specific people. Moreover, focusing on those in charge of writing the manifestos rather than a whole organ of government such as the treasury meant that clearly identifiable people with specific tasks could be addressed. To be winnable the issue had to connect to the actual experience of those in membership and had to be deeply felt (people had to be angry about it). In addition, the change proposed had to make an easily understood and concrete difference to those working on the issue. If it was too abstract, technical, or obscure, then it would be difficult to involve a broad base, generate turn out, and explain publicly.

Identifying Limits and Capacity

The issue picked meant that there was necessarily a national- and state-centric focus to the responsible lending campaign. This is not always the case. The Living Wage campaign targets particular companies and commercial sectors whereas the CitySafe campaign involves coordinated neighborhood-level action. However, the national and state-centric nature of the responsible lending initiative raises the question of the limits of BBCO as a form of political action. These limits become apparent if we fast-forward to after the General

Election. Despite winning a commitment to a cap on interest rates in the Labour Party manifesto and confirming a more limited commitment relating to interest rates on store cards in the Conservative Party manifesto, there came a point when proposals for national legislation had to be formulated. At this point, while concerted broad-based action continued to be needed to keep the pressure on, a highly technical and detailed case had to be made aligned with skill and knowledge in parliamentary and legislative procedures. Advocacy work by experts became absolutely vital. Fortunately, Stella Creasy, Labour MP for Walthamstow, in collaboration with Compass, a left wing pressure group, took on the issue from Citizens UK and could mobilize the necessary expertise and parliamentary support. However, they adopted a fundamentally different repertoire of political action focused mostly around mobilization via social media. Their work did generate the Consumer Credit (Regulation and Advice) Bill, a private members' bill that was given its first reading in the House of Commons on November 11, 2010. The transition from direct action to elite-led advocacy resulted serendipitously, although it did build on trust on both sides and a commitment to continuing collaboration. The shift from Citizens UK to Compass could be read as a positive example of how to combine parliamentary and extra-parliamentary politics. While there was a dialectic between the two, it was an accidental rather than a consciously adopted and coordinated strategy. The truth was that after the General Election, Citizens UK lost momentum on the issue as it had achieved its initial aims and needed to evaluate, reorganize, and reformulate its approach. Fortunately Compass, and subsequently the Labour Party itself, was there to pick up the slack.

The shift from Citizens UK to Compass and then the Labour Party points to the limits of community organizing. This limit is not only a result of its organizational form and repertoire of political action, it is also a structural limit arising from its being a form of political populism that trades off its status as an "outsider" to mainstream politics and institutions. Policy and structural change requires "insiders" with the requisite status and knowledge, yet to move onto the terrain of being an "insider" would undermine the credibility of Citizens UK as an unaligned voice of the people. That said, Compass and Creasy would not have taken on the issue had it not been for the prior work of Citizens UK in bringing the issue into mainstream political debate, changing the consensus on what was previously a marginal issue, and thereby creating a new political opportunity on which others might act.[57]

Identifying a Broader Public Narrative

Another aspect of an issue being winnable is whether it can be located within a compelling narrative. In BBCO such a narrative has two dimensions. The first is powerful personal testimonies that exemplify what is at stake in the issue and communicate the need for change. Testimonies are identified through the listening process or are actively sought by organizers (there was often an urgent scramble for relevant testimonies before a meeting or event). The second is a convincing broader analysis. This analysis must establish a case for why the change called for is both necessary and a solution to the problem identified. In the case of the responsible lending initiative, the issue was narrated as being but one element of a broader set of proposals. As a stand-alone issue, calling for a cap on interest rates was repeatedly dismissed as exacerbating the problem by driving high-cost credit users into the arms of illegal loan sharks. There was little evidence for this, but as a rationale for resisting caps it had a hegemonic grip on politicians, policy wonks, and civil servants. The rationale could only be countered and dissolved through locating the call for a statutory limit within a broader analysis. Thus, the narrative for the proposals outlined at the outset of Chapter 2 emerged as a way of linking together the testimonies and the proposals presented at the November 25 assembly.

Does It Build Power?

Collapsed into the question of whether an issue builds power or not is a nest of intertwined components and concepts of organizing. Key among these are a particular understanding of power, a focus on local institutions as the basis of power, and a recognition of the symbiosis of organizational development and political action. It is in this area that we really see the evolution of community organizing from its initial form developed by Alinsky.

Relational and Unilateral Power

Power is a contested term. However, at the most basic level it is the ability to act or make change in the world.[58] Within the IAF's conception, this acting can be done either unilaterally ("power over") or relationally ("power with").[59] Unilateral power is the only type of power most theories of power recognize and it emphasizes the capacity to get others to do your bidding against their will or coercively. In the training, "power over" is said to be the attempt to control and dominate others and is viewed as one way, private, and closed off from scrutiny. Unilateral power envisages power as a zero-sum game with winners and losers. By contrast, *relational power* ("power with") is said to emphasize a different dynamic – the "power to" get things done collectively. It is understood as interactive, two way, and involves identifying common, mutual interests rather than pursuing a special or selfish interest. It is public (for the commonwealth) and not private (for the good of one – tyranny; the few – oligarchy; or the many – democratic despotism). As Chambers puts it: "Relational power is infinite and unifying, not limited and divisive.... As you become more powerful, so do those others in relationship with you. As they become more powerful, so do you. This is power understood as relational, as power *with*, not *over*."[60] The distinction between unilateral and relational power is one constantly reiterated in the writings of organizers and a central feature of the IAF training program. A core related message is that power is not something restricted to the elite. Rather, everyone has relational power – however marginalized and impoverished they are – and it is normal to interact with those with more power, but such interaction needs to be habitual, public, analyzed, and evaluated so it can occur more effectively and constructively.

In the distinction between unilateral and relational power there is a profound insight. It is an insight that Alinsky articulated when he noted that the predicament of the poor is not only their poverty, but also their demoralized and disorganized condition and the self-destructive anomie that often goes hand in hand with poverty. For Alinsky, "[t]he complete man is one who is making a definite contribution to the general social welfare and who is a vital part of that community of interests, values, and purposes that makes life and people meaningful."[61] The predicament of nonelites is that they become depoliticized and disaggregated and therefore unable to make a contribution to the general social welfare on their own terms. Instead, they constantly have to accept the terms and conditions set for them by others, whether these are the banks, "welfare colonialists," or paternalistic and technocratic elites.[62] What they need is not revolution but reconstitution as a people capable of acting together in pursuit of its real interests. The rich and powerful dethroned would not result in the poor and downtrodden empowered. Moreover, the hatred of masters is not the same as a love of liberty. Alinsky discerned that the real battle is against an apathy that simply accepts the status quo and refuses to take responsibility for the situation. As he put it: "Persuading, persuading and persuading is the constant fight against apathy; against the feeling of anonymity of 'we don't count, nobody cares for us and we don't care for anybody but us.'"[63] New power – relational power – needs to be generated if the "have-nots" are to be able to act for themselves and freed from either dependency or relations of mimetic rivalry with the "haves." The creation of relational power relativizes and disenchants the power of the "haves," showing it to be impotent and incapable of producing a new situation.

Working from a Position of Strength

This relational view of power could be dismissed as idealistic and naïve, but it builds on and extends a deeply pragmatic view of power encapsulated in the use of the "Melian Dialogue" from Thucydides' *History of the Peloponnesian War* as an anchor point in the IAF training. Use of the Melian Dialogue is a consistent feature of IAF's induction since Alinsky, Chambers, and Harmon began a formal training process for organizers in 1969.[64] From that time on, the dialogue was linked to helping trainees understand the nature of power. The dialogue is "realist" in that it entails a strong endorsement of finding common ground with those with whom one disagrees. It is also a strident critique of those who would put program before people. Set within the context of the Athenian Empire's expansion, the dialogue reenacts the encounter between the Athenians and the besieged Melians and subsequent internal debates between the Melians about how to respond to their situation. Without consulting the populace or allowing the Athenians to speak directly to them, the

Melian leaders insist on defending their liberty and doing what is right (as they see it) rather than negotiating and coming to terms with the Athenians. The result is that the inferior forces of the Melians are defeated and the city's population is subsequently slaughtered.

In the London Citizens five-day training, the dialogue is role-played by all participants through multiple iterations. These performances are then evaluated and critically analyzed. The dialogue contains many of the themes explored through the rest of the training: the nature of self-interest and power, how to deal with the ambiguity of living in the tension between the world as it is and the world as it should be, the difference between pragmatists and idealists, the importance of compromise in politics, the need to keep an ongoing relationship with those in power and to make deals, the need to think strategically rather than being short-termist or absolutist, and the role of caucusing instead of diving straight in or letting those in power set the terms and conditions of the negotiation. The Athenians stood for those with power and the Melians for those in a position of weakness. The lesson to be learned was the need to recognize the strengths and weaknesses of one's position and develop a creative yet realistic strategy through which to build the necessary power to act rather than be acted on. In the parlance of organizers and leaders, to be "Melian" is a term of abuse denoting a group or person who has not come to terms with the weakness of their position or who is not arguing from a position of strength, but who insists on following a principle irrespective of the outcome or simply asserts the righteousness of their cause while ignoring the claims and positions of those they oppose.

Another dimension the Dialogue emphasizes is that politics is the alternative to war or violent struggle. However, this is not meant to imply politics involves neither conflict nor forms of nonviolent coercion. Part of the art of organizing is to introduce tension and provoke confrontation when necessary in order to gain recognition and respect, but to do so nonviolently and in a way that perpetuates relationships rather than ends them. In the training the word "confront" is shown to be derived from the Latin meaning forehead-to-forehead or face-to-face. In the IAF approach, politics is confrontational; that is, it entails face-to-face, personal encounters. However, the aim of such face-to-face encounters is to use the conflicts creatively in order to identify and address mutual issues.

The Vertical and Horizontal Dimensions of Building Relational Power

To ask whether an issue builds power or not means asking whether the issue deepens and extends the primary source of strength the "have-nots" possess: relationship. Thus, it asks whether an issue will unify or divide institutions in membership, strengthen connections within existing member institutions, and enable more institutions to be recruited. If this is the horizontal dimension of building power, the question is also asking whether an issue will build a relationship vertically by connecting with the interests of those confronted.

To discern this involves a detailed "power analysis." Specifying usury as the problem and a call for a 20 percent cap on interest rates in the manifestos as an issue attended to both the horizontal and vertical dimensions of building power. Horizontally it connected to the lived experience of those in membership and, crucially, each of the main traditions that made up the membership had much to say about usury. This included not just Islam, Christianity, and Judaism, but also the trade unions. Thus, as an issue, calling for a cap on interest rates enabled every distinct constituency of the network to contribute to the whole, each in their own way and for their own theological or other reasons, and thereby enabled an understanding to be built within and between each institution. Vertically, the challenge was to connect the issue with the interests and core values of each of the political parties and the particular people targeted within them.

It is the synthesis of interest, values, and relationally based organizing that gives the Alinsky approach its distinct conception of political action. It entails recognizing that democratic politics necessarily involves competition and conflict over interests, but also that it upholds the possibility for a common life based on "power with" rather than "power over" others. As a form of politics, BBCO builds on and echoes what political theorist Marc Stears calls the "radical democratic tradition" that developed in the United States. Stears argues that within this tradition, a conception of the "common good" is at the center of the democratic ideal while at the same time, action is undertaken that appears sectional or even coercive to others, in order to realize some approximation of that shared vision of the good within an imperfect democracy.[65] In concert with many advocates of participatory democracy, Stears asks whether radical democrats were justified in employing nondeliberative and even coercive means in their struggle for a better democracy.[66] But in identifying a tension between democratic ideals and the use of "coercive" means he establishes a false dichotomy. The use of relational power is not the same as the use of dominatory or unilateral power.[67]

Relational power has a coercive dimension, but unlike the state, the gang, or the bank (each of which can deploy its own agents of coercion – the police, armed groups, and bailiffs), the ultimate sanctions BBCOs can deploy to gain recognition or enforce a decision are themselves relational. These non-juridical, relational forms of discipline include rhetoric and deliberation; explicit noncooperation (as in a strike); forms of shunning, shaming, and ridicule; or nonviolent direct action (for example, a sit-in or demonstration). These are often highly confrontational and threatening but not dominatory; that is, they make neither a claim to possess nor do they attempt to exercise complete control over those being confronted. In contrast to other styles and repertoires of contention, in BBCO the aim of such action is to gain recognition and respect and therefore parity in the relationship, thereby establishing a common world of meaning and action. Forms of relational discipline presume the existence or possibility of a common world and have as their aim the (re)formation of such a common realm. By contrast, forms of unilateral power presume a disjuncture between the one commanding and the one being controlled. The threat of bad press through an action outside a hotel or inside a supermarket that pays its workers poorly is not coercive in a unilateral way; rather, it unveils and draws attention to the fractured nature of the common world between workers and managers and calls for the recognition and restoration of a common life in that workplace by paying a living wage.

Some proposals – for example, calling for a statutory cap of interest rates – do entail a call for the use of juridical and dominatory force by the state. Herein lies the real problem, one that leads to much confusion in discussions of power in democratic theory and involves a dichotomy between two conceptions of politics. The first conception draws on Greco-Roman notions of a political community as a self-governing polity or republic built on the capacity of citizens to participate in processes of collective self-determination. In this conception, debate, deliberation, action in concert, and collective decision making between those who are free and equal are all paramount and constitutive of public life and citizenship. Power in this first conception is generated collectively and through relationships. The second conception draws on Roman law and conceptualizes politics as being about the rule and dominion of a sovereign power.[68] What is "public" relates to the apparatus of this rule and the administration of its laws. The sovereign who represents public and legitimate authority stands above and acts on behalf of society, which is made up of "private" individuals who bear rights granted to them by the sovereign.[69] Power in this concept of politics is unilateral. Democratic citizenship sits on the cusp between these two different but historically interrelated conceptions of political power. There is a need for the exercise of sovereign power to protect or create the capacity to exercise nondominatory relational power. As with civil rights legislation or legislation protecting the right to form unions or freedom of worship, the aim of legislation proposed by Citizens UK is to inhibit the domination of vulnerable others and to ensure the basic interests of all are taken into account in any decision affecting them. The coercive sanction of legislation is thus used to preserve or create a common world of meaning and action within a polis in which all citizens may participate with relative liberty and equality.[70] Advocates of participative and deliberative democracy tend to valorize the first concept of politics to the exclusion of the second. Conversely, political liberals and social democrats tend to focus on the second to the exclusion of the first. A full-orbed conception of democratic citizenship needs to recognize the interplay of both. This is a theme that will be explored in greater detail in Chapters 6 and 7.

Does It Develop Leaders?

If building power does not necessitate generating the capacity to dominate others but rather, creating a common life through the exercise of relational power, then it does involve forming particular kinds of citizens. In BBCO the apogee of citizenship is conceptualized as *leadership,* hence the question: Does an issue develop leaders? The IAF defines leadership very simply: leaders are those who have followers.[71] On this account, leaders are not necessarily those who are elected or appointed. The criteria for identifying leaders is whether they have relationships of trust and loyalty with a number of others in their locality or institution and can mobilize these others to join with them in a public action. It is on the basis of their relationships and their ability to turn out people for meetings and actions that leaders can claim to be representatives of their institutions or their community. To be an office holder is not sufficient; without turnout a leader represents no one. But leaders are also seen to have relationships with power: that is, they are taken seriously and listened to by others in positions of authority, whether within the hierarchy of their church, union, or school or by local officials and business leaders. Leaders thus have an earned trust, respect and loyalty.[72] Within the BBCO their authority and legitimacy is a negotiation between their ability to sustain the loyalty of those who trust them in their institution and their ability to undertake and perform well the kinds of political action BBCO involves. Good performances in political actions and demonstrating commitment to the work and to doing good work eventually leads them to earn the respect and trust of leaders from other institutions and organizers.[73] The centrality of leadership to community organizing is marked by the fact that in interviews organizers consistently identified their primary role as recruiting and training leaders. The relationship becomes reciprocal over time as experienced leaders help train new organizers.

Training, Shared Language, and the Formation of a Common Life

The ability of leaders to perform well as part of a BBCO is the outcome of particular constellations of power relations, discourses, and disciplinary regimes that aim to shape (rather than coerce, control, or dominate) their conduct as citizens. In this respect BBCO is a form of what Foucault calls "governmentality" that determines how citizenship is practiced. The primary vehicle for inducting participants into the habits and practices of citizenship that Citizens UK encapsulates is the *training.* It is through the two- and five-day trainings that the ideas, symbols, narratives, and other interpretative resources that Citizens UK draws from in its political action are instilled. It is the training that forges a common language and points of reference that allow coordinated action among leaders of different institutions. This training is reinforced through one-to-ones between leaders and organizers and in evaluations after actions. This can sound cultish unless one realizes that all social welfare and philanthropic programs, as well as political organizations from formal parties to social movements, constitute forms of governmentality that instill particular habits, practices, and ways of seeing and doing citizenship. As political scientist Barbara Cruikshank argues, citizens, as those who are both "subjected to power and subjects in their own right," simultaneously construct and are constructed by the formations of citizenship in which they participate.[74] BBCO is simply one among many ways of constructing citizenship as an identity, performance, and shared rationality, although it is my contention that it represents a better form than many others.

The basis for suggesting that BBCO is normatively better than many other forms of democratic citizenship is that it entails a commitment to building a common life with others. It is by no means the only form of citizenship that entails this, but many do not: notably, state-driven, bureaucratically determined clientalism does not, nor does the construction of citizens as consumers who receive services, nor citizenship as constituted through identity and special interest groups. To be a democratic citizen is not simply to be a lone voter or volunteer, neither is it to be an individual and private consumer of state, business, or philanthropic services, even though all of these may contribute to our practices of democratic citizenship if constructed in such a way as to have a public, cooperative dimension. Nor is citizenship best instantiated by being a participant in a social movement or identity group. As Wolin argues in his critique of those who engage in identity politics and social movements, such forms of political action tend toward depoliticization because they construct what he called "groupies" not citizens. By contrast, for Wolin, "[t]he citizen, unlike the groupie, has to acquire a perspective of commonality, to think integrally and comprehensively rather than exclusively. The groupie never gets beyond ... the stage of unreflective self interest."[75] What Wolin fails to see, however, is that, contrary to his pessimism and his overly sharp distinction between public and private, there do exist practices of democratic citizenship that allow for a "perspective of commonality" to emerge and BBCO represents one such form. As a specific *ascesis* or disciplined regime of formation and training in democratic citizenship, BBCO enables a perspective of commonality to emerge precisely by enabling participants to move from being "groupies" with unreflective self-interests to citizens who are reflective about their self-interests and actively seeking mutual interests with others beyond their immediate identity or interest group. The training and participation in the distinctive form of political action the Alinsky approach entails is the means of ushering in this movement from being a groupie, client, volunteer, or consumer to being a citizen.[76] To ask whether an issue develops leaders is to ask whether an issue will facilitate the identification and recruitment of those willing and able to undertake this journey into public life and who can persuade others to follow them.

SELF-INTEREST RIGHTLY ORGANIZED

The link between *self-interest* and the building of a common life is an explicit feature of the IAF's leadership training program. However, along with the sessions on power, it is this aspect of the training that causes greatest concern and confusion among participants as the term has negative connotations, particularly for many of the Christian adherents taking part.[77] Contrary to what some contend, there is no great difference between Alinsky's account of self-interest in *Reveille for Radicals* and *Rules for Radicals*. In both he points to the ways in which "[w]e repeatedly get caught in [the] conflict between our professed moral principles and the real reasons why we do things – to wit, our self-interest."[78] Pointing to the hypocritical ways in which we are "white-washed sepulchers" is not a form of cynicism but of suspicion; that is, suspicion entails asking what motivates morality and what function morality plays in any justification rather than skepticism about morality as such.[79] This suspicion provides the basis for a critique of altruism and appeals to idealistic self-sacrifice as the basis for joining in cooperative activity. In its place, and in direct echo of Jeremiah 29:7, Alinsky points to how the pursuit of our own welfare is necessarily bound up with the pursuit of the material well-being of others.[80] As he states in *Reveille*: "The fact is that self-interest can be a most potent weapon in the development of cooperation and identification of the groups' welfare as being of greater importance than personal welfare."[81]

Alinsky's and the IAF's conception of self-interest is less "Machiavellian" and more Tocquevillian.[82] Tocqueville states:

> The doctrine of self-interest rightly understood does not inspire great sacrifices but does prompt daily small ones; by itself it could not make a man virtuous but it does shape a host of law-abiding, sober, moderate, careful, and self-controlled citizens. If it does not lead the will directly to virtue, it moves it closer through imperceptible influence of habit. If the doctrine of self-interest rightly understood happened to exercise complete domination over the world of morality, no doubt it would not be common to see unusual virtues. But I also think that gross depravity would be less common.[83]

Tocqueville is here drawing from notions of self-interest that came to the fore with Adam Smith and the Scottish Enlightenment. Yet against some prior conceptions, notably those of Hobbes, his account orientates self-interest toward virtue. Self-interest for Tocqueville can produce not simply prudential obligations but moral relations. His conception of virtue is, admittedly, a modest one, but it is nevertheless one that denotes more than either calculating self-regard or the acquisitive pursuit of material gain through commercial exchange. For Tocqueville, humans are not solely economic animals living as a "society of strangers" for whom politics is a necessary evil that inhibits the private pursuit of self-interest. Rather, within his conception, humans are political animals that need particular kinds of social relationships in order to live well. Building on Alinsky's Tocquevillian notion of "self-interest rightly understood," and, against those who envisage self-interest as meaning egoistic selfishness tempered by utilitarian calculation, in the training the term self-interest is identified as combining two Latin words *inter*, meaning "between" or "among," and *esse*, meaning "to be."

Self-Interests as Shared Interests

Within the IAF's conception, self-interests are the interests we have between us. They argue that as interpersonal beings or social animals, our natural interest in survival and preservation or our more complex need for recognition and respect can only be realized through and with others. The primary insight is that there is no necessary dichotomy between utility and mutuality: the warp of self-preservation is interwoven with the weft of neighborliness.[84] Self-interests are not necessarily private solipsistic concerns but can be matters of shared or public importance that form the basis for building and sustaining a common life. However, it becomes corrupted as a practice when it takes too literally the emphasis on self(ish)-interests as its aim and objective.

Chambers did much to develop this conception of self-interest through engagement with the work of Arendt. Arendt states:

> These interests constitute, in the word's most literal significance, something which *inter-est*, which lies between people and therefore can relate and bind them together. Most action and speech is concerned with this in-between, which varies with each group of people, so that most words and deeds are *about* some worldly objective reality in addition to being a disclosure of the action and speaking agent.[85]

For Arendt, as for the IAF, the focus might be material interests or matters of importance such as a living wage, but the pursuit of this interest unveils something beyond the material benefits sought. The insight here is that by having leaders focus on shared interests, most of which are material, those involved begin to actualize themselves as persons in relationship with others. Material interests are never simply materialistic; they are the currency of tangible relationships and visions of the world as it should be. As Arendt puts it: "The basic error of all materialism in politics – and this materialism is not Marxist and not even modern in origin, but as old as our history of political theory – is to overlook the inevitability with which men disclose themselves as subjects, as distinct and unique persons, even when they wholly concentrate upon reaching altogether worldly, material objects."[86] Identifying concrete "self-interests" in the form of "worldly, material objects" is the beginning of shared speech and action and therefore the reconstitution of a people with relational power who can appear in the world and act in relation with others. Crucially, what the experience and teaching of the IAF add to this Arendtian insight is the following: the best guard against self-interests becoming selfish-interests is the combination of cooperative institutions training people in the virtues and giving them the experience of self-rule, organizers linking these institutions, and a relational listening process through which self-interests can be recognized as mutual interests.[87] The IAF conception does not deny selfish interests are often to the fore: possessive and egoistic individualism and communalism is a reality organizers confront on a daily basis. However, in contrast to Hobbes, explicit in BBCO as a practice is the proposition that it is not the assertion of sovereign power that best prevents competition for resources erupting in violence, but politics, relational power, and organizing.

BETWEEN PUBLIC AND PRIVATE

While emphasizing the importance of a common life and the pursuit of shared interests, the IAF approach does not lose sight of the interplay and distinction between "public" and "private" as a politically significant boundary to observe. If its conception of self-interest counters a tendency in some modern political and economic thought to prioritize the private over the public, its conception of the relationship between public and private counters the equal and opposite tendency by others to subordinate the private to the public. Against the likes of Rousseau and those who would entirely subsume the personal and private to the demands of the general will, the state, or the public good, IAF teaching and training maintains that personal and communal interests are to be hallowed, respected, and distinguished from public or mutual interests. In the training the problem put before us was seeking in private relationships what one needs from public relationships (namely, recognition and respect) and seeking in public relationships what one needs from or is missing in our private ones (namely, affirmation and intimacy). This distinction between public and private is used to help leaders address care of self and the need for boundaries in their family, work, and political involvements.

The distinction is also used to train leaders to be alert to the ways in which they can be co-opted by those they confront. In one training session, Jonathan Lange used the story of the labor leader Sidney Hillman refusing to accept a gold watch as a present from those he was negotiating with because this would introduce an element of private obligation into what was a public relationship. Likewise, experienced organizers insisted that leaders only use official titles or formal names with politicians and business leaders in negotiations: use of the informal subtly converts a public relationship into a personal one and thereby makes it harder to introduce tension and conflict. Both Ken Livingston and Boris Johnson, the incumbent mayors of the Greater London Authority over the period of the research, would ask leaders to call them by their first names in negotiations or in assemblies but leaders would stick to calling them Mayor Livingston or Mayor Johnson. This was in order to reinforce the sense that Livingston and Johnson were there neither as individuals who we were trying to befriend nor as patrons we were approaching as clients in need of a favor, but in their capacity as holders of public office with duties and responsibilities for which they were accountable.[88]

In the IAF/Citizens UK's distinction between public and private there is a tendency to create a false dichotomy that belies the actual practice of BBCO. In the discourses that constitute BBCO as a political practice, a far more differentiated account of the relationship between public and private is operative than the dichotomy presented in the training would suggest. Four basic uses of the term "public" can be identified:

(1) As a synonym for civil society and the realm of active citizenship (as in "public life" and "public action");
(2) A term denoting the state and its administrative structures (as in "public authorities");
(3) In reference to relationships that occur in business: contractual and professional commitments, and the broader obligations of institutions and businesses (as in "public responsibility" and "public institutions");
(4) Marking the realm of sociability and meaningful relations beyond the home encountered in house meetings, one-to-ones, and assemblies, celebrations, and parties (as in "public relationships" and "public space").

All these uses of "public" are counterpoised against a positive notion of private denoting the realm of domesticity, intimacy, and personal friendship that may or may not be interwoven with the public realm, and against a negative notion of private denoting relations characterized by anomie, apathy, despair, calculating self-regard, and disorganization. "Private" in the negative sense meant an individual or organization was isolated and unrelated and thus powerless. The multivalent use of "public" and "private" disrupts any simplistic dichotomy between them but, at the same time, the distinction is not abandoned altogether. The IAF approach does, however, refuse any attempt to map divisions between public and private onto some account of what is political/nonpolitical. In the practices (if not the formal writings and training) of the IAF/Citizens UK, all these "public" and "private" realms may at times become sources of political life: the "private" grief of the mother who hardly saw her children because she was working three jobs to make ends meet or that of a sister whose brother was murdered is no less political than the "public" anger directed toward irresponsible bankers. Deeply personal testimony was often a catalyst for public action. At the same time, insofar as elements within each of these public and private realms cease to be connected to a wider sense of commonality, they are depoliticized. The key factor in ensuring whether relations are "public" or not – whether in a school, business, state agency, or church – is whether they are characterized by mutuality and connected to a common world of meaning and action. The real conflict is not between different spheres (state, economy, family, and so forth) but between patterns of relationship turned inward and those turned toward others.

CREATING THE CONTRADICTION

Central to the art of cutting the issue is creating a contradiction or, as Alinsky's twelfth rule puts it, the price of a successful attack is a constructive alternative. Rather than opposition or protest, part of the art of organizing is having the "prophetic imagination" to create an issue that points the way beyond both the rivalries of competitive group interests and the popular consensus to an expansive vision of a common life in which all may flourish. This entails imagining a contradiction. By contradiction I mean the attempt to show forth a pattern of relationships contrary to that existing in a particular hegemony.[89] Political actions for Alinsky exist in order simultaneously to declare the unjust way to be untrue and present a possible alternative through which all may flourish. His insistence on having a constructive alternative means that the declaration of a "no" to something is always premised on the prior celebration and upholding of a "yes" to another way, a way in which both oppressor and oppressed are invited to participate. Examples of this dynamic are seen in numerous IAF campaigns: for example, the Living Wage campaign is not against poor pay, but *for* a living wage that brings benefits to both the employer and the employee as well as the wider community. The contradiction is neither an act of assertion over and against what exists nor does it set itself up as in competition with what exists, nor is it a straightforward contrast, but through first listening and then deliberating on what could be the good in common, it discovers a way of reconfiguring what exists so that all may benefit.[90] Moreover, requiring participants to formulate a constructive proposal ensures that leaders will take responsibility for the situation and grow in political judgment and experience as leaders. The alternative is a politics of protest that never moves beyond critique but only forges an identity built on being in opposition and so becomes locked in mimetic rivalry with that which it opposes.[91]

In Chapter 5 we turn from the repertoires through which relational power is forged, popular education undertaken, and issues identified to the actual performance of political action.

5

An Anatomy of Organizing II

Rules, Actions, and Representation

FUNDING THE WORK: SOFT AND HARD MONEY

A distinctive feature of the IAF/Citizens UK's work is that they do not take money from the government. In an interview, Chambers said he considered this the "critical distinction" between the IAF and other organizing networks. It was certainly what distinguished Citizens UK from the organizing work undertaken by Church Action on Poverty and Locality in the United Kingdom. This is a grey area, but the emphasis on not taking government money does signal how the IAF sees organized money as a form of power. In the IAF training the importance of being self-funded was highlighted as a means through which to build ownership of the work, foster independence, and ensure accountability of organizers to leaders and leaders to their institutions. Money generated from dues-paying institutions was called *hard money* and that from foundations was deemed *soft money*. Hard money was "hard" because it was difficult to generate and secured real power. As can be seen in Figure 5.1, between 2008 and 2012 only 16 percent of London Citizens' funding came from membership dues (Figure 5.2), while 83 percent came from soft money. This is comparable with the experience of other IAF affiliates (with the exception of Sydney Alliance).[1] Organizers rationalized this by saying that soft money from foundations comes from civil society. More difficult to square with the emphasis on independent sources of funding was the fact that the dues paid by schools and other publicly funded institutions was generated, albeit indirectly, from the state.

Money generated from foundations was also problematic and was recognized as such. The IAF organizer Jonathan Lange notes:

> The biggest problems in organizing ... is unlike other senses of organizing, in particularly union organizing, we don't generate enough of our own money, therefore we're too dependent on soft money. The temptations to tailor our activities and our campaigns to the whims and desires of the foundation are really, really strong.[2]

FIGURE 5.1. Financial sources (2008–12).

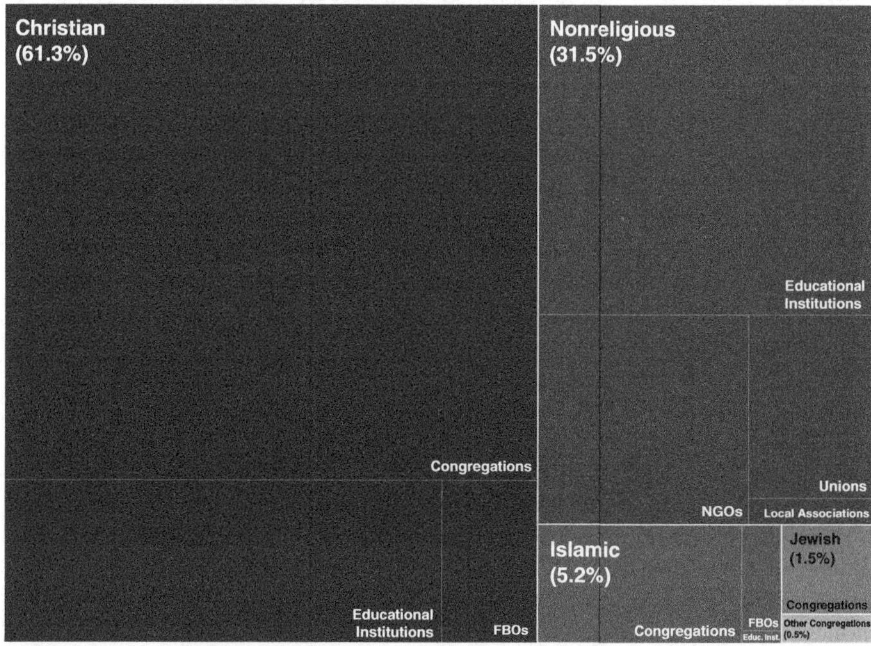

FIGURE 5.2. Membership dues (2008–12).

This was much in evidence in the responsible lending initiative. In 2008, Citizens UK received grants from a number of foundations to undertake work with the primary aim of rebuilding public support for asylum seekers.[3] These grants were given in response both to the foundations' aims of supporting refugees and changing the perception of asylum seekers, and to support the recommendations of the Citizens UK Independent Asylum Commission.[4] The Asylum Commission grew out of a local initiative by South London Citizens to improve the levels of service at Lunar House, the headquarters of the

Immigration and Nationality Directorate. This local initiative was developed in response to a listening campaign that revealed members of South London Citizens had been poorly treated by staff and procedures at Lunar House. The soft money from the foundations created a new, nationwide initiative called Citizens for Sanctuary.

Although the issue had originated in a listening campaign, by 2008 the link to membership institutions was tenuous. This is not say that the issue did not have strong support among numerous members. However, what was a local initiative became a national one, and its funding generated "soft-money organizers" whose targets and accountability were set by the foundations – not by membership institutions – who had no relationship to place and who were focused on a single issue. In an impressive and skilled piece of work, these organizers set up fifteen campaign action groups throughout the United Kingdom. In the 2010 General Election the focus of these action groups was to have local members of parliament and each party make a formal commitment to what was called "The Sanctuary Pledge," the primary practical commitment of which was to ask for support for "policies that will end the detention of children and families for immigration reasons." The campaign made its strategic focus a call for the ending of child detention in immigration removal centers. The campaign was judged to be successful: after the election, in July 2010, the newly elected Deputy Prime Minister Nick Clegg (Liberal-Democrat) announced the closure of the family unit at Yarl's Wood Detention Centre and confirmed a commitment to ensure no children are held in detention centers in the United Kingdom.

At particular points in the run-up to the May 3 General Election assembly there were moves by the soft-money organizers to make the Sanctuary Pledge and the issue of asylum, rather than the response to the recession, the lead issue in the assembly. Yet this contravened the central rationale of the whole assembly, which was to take forward the agenda that had been voted on at the November 25 assembly, and the fact that it was the economic agenda that was generating the real energy and commitment among London-based leaders who were directly involved in organizing the assembly. The tension between "soft-money" and "hard-money" organizers in relation to the run-up to the General Election illustrates how BBCO can itself suffer from a particular form of policy capture: rather than be driven by the concerns of membership institutions, the agenda is monopolized by the interests of grant givers.

STRATEGIC CAPACITY

When an issue is cut, the next stage is to appoint an *action team* to develop the campaign strategy. Marshall Ganz, drawing directly from the work of Alinsky and his own experiences of community and union organizing, has developed an extensive account of what makes for effective strategy and leadership if, to use his terms, David is to beat Goliath.[5] Ganz argues "that the likelihood that a leadership team will devise effective strategy depends on the depth of its motivation, the breadth of its salient knowledge, and the robustness of its reflective practice – on the extent, that is, of its strategic capacity."[6] For Ganz, a leadership team's strategic capacity derives from both biographical and organizational resources, which refer to the political, economic, and cultural/moral assets actors can use to realize their goals. Biographical resources consist of the diversity of the identities, social networks, and tactical repertoires a leadership team can draw from to interpret and act in a situation. Alongside these are the organizational resources, which include funding sources, accountability structures, and the openness or otherwise of deliberation and decision-making processes.

Ganz suggests that strategic capacity and creativity, particularly the ability to improvise in order to adapt and make the best use of the opportunities that are provided, depend on the diversity and range of both biographical and organizational resources. As he negatively puts it: "Organisational changes that increase homogeneity, reduce accountability to constituents, suppress deliberative dissent, and disrupt cycles of learning can diminish strategic capacity, even as an organisation's resources grow."[7] On this account, the ability of London Citizens' leadership teams to include people from diverse religious, ethnic, and socioeconomic backgrounds who themselves had varied political, moral, and vocational commitments, networks, and organizational experiences greatly enhanced their strategic capacity. Moreover, Ganz's analysis further supports the importance of being broad-based and the insistence that organizers do not have to be identified with those whom they organize. Not only do such measures resist an identity politics, but they also inoculate against groupthink and ensure a heterogeneous leadership team can be formed to tackle any issue. Strategic capacity is further enhanced by the openness and diversity of inputs into the policy formulation process and ongoing processes of decision making. The fluidity, flexibility, and informal nature of these deliberative processes contrasts with more procedural repertoires that involve minutes, points of order, and voting. Decisions generally arose through a relational process of interaction normed by commitments to the equality of everyone as able to contribute, rather than a formal procedure such as voting that aggregated individual choices.[8] When votes did occur they tended to be an acclamation of a consensus already attained rather than a way of deciding a problem in need of resolution. This meant the deliberative process was at once more open and interactive: whoever turned up could contribute.

Navigating Difference: Geography, Class, Gender, Ethnicity, and Education

Diversity of organizational and biographical backgrounds was reflected in the action teams that came together to plan both the November 25 and May 3 assemblies and through these the responsible lending campaign for which the assemblies were the primary point of action. The action teams would meet every other week and then, closer to the event, every week at King's College in the cafeteria and then later in the Old Committee Room: a high-ceilinged chamber on whose walls hung portraits of all the previous principals of the college. Its appeal as a venue was that I was able to offer it for free and the room could be booked directly, at short notice, and was outside any byzantine timetabling process. It was also because King's was centrally located and easily accessible from any part of London. Attendance at these meetings ranged from ten to thirty in size, with numbers increasing closer to the event.

Early on, the majority of those attending were organizers. Alert to the possible dominance of organizers in deliberations about what to do and how to do it, a system was instituted in the run-up to the May 3 event whereby leaders sat in an inner circle with organizers in an outer ring of chairs. This caused some tension between those who felt it important to have the people with the most knowledge steering things and those who were more committed to leaders taking responsibility for and leading the process on the principle that one should never do for others what they can do for themselves. The leaders who regularly attended came from Roman Catholic, Anglican, Methodist, Vineyard (a Charismatic-Evangelical network of churches), Muslim, and Masorti institutions, as well as UNISON (the public-service union). In the case of the Christians, they were a mixture of laity and clergy. In addition, there was occasional attendance by leaders from the Congo Support Group, the Zimbabwean Movement for Democratic Change, the Salvation Army, University of London Students' Union, schoolteachers, academics, and various journalists. Those in attendance were predominantly white and the great majority of all those taking part either had or were participating in tertiary education. And although there were a majority of men at all the action team meetings, the gender divide was fairly evenly spread, with women holding significant positions of authority within the team: most notably, the lead organizers of the main chapters (West, South, and East London) were all women. The team also included a mix of skills and interests. Meetings would divide into a team dealing with the "political" side of the event and one involved in stage managing the event and orchestrating the music, dance, and drama. Again, women and men were fairly evenly spread across both of these teams.

Although the organizers were diverse, closer analysis suggests a uniformity of educational background. Despite coming from various parts of the country and other countries (including Poland, France, and Colombia) and being mixed in terms of gender, ethnicity, and socioeconomic background, all of the organizers employed between 2009 and 2011 had attended college, with more than 60 percent having attended an elite, Russell Group university.[9] A key catalyst for this recruitment pattern was the Summer Academy for students, which offered summer positions to work on different campaigns at London Citizens.[10] These experiences give many a taste for community organizing. Such initiatives were vital in recruiting high-quality organizers: the inability to recruit and train organizers was identified by Jameson as an important reason for the early failures in establishing BBCO in Birmingham and elsewhere. As Osterman notes in his study of the IAF, a finding that was confirmed in my own interviews, "[a]lthough the pay is decent and the work stimulating, finding an adequate number of organizers is difficult, and the relative scarcity of organizing talent is seen by senior IAF staff as one of the major constraints on the growth of the network."[11]

Organizers across the IAF network are generally formally educated. However, education is not the key to becoming a good organizer. Rather, as Alinsky saw it, a key factor is "ego": motivated and able graduates are the kinds of people who have enough chutzpah to think they have the ability to go into an area and organize it.[12] Yet they must not have so much that they either start doing everything for others or make themselves the center of attention. Good organizing involves making leaders and not organizers the stars of the show. The task thus involves a delicate dance between assertion (and the attendant qualities of self-confidence and initiative) and self-effacement. Evaluating levels of "ego" through conversations about whether an organizer had either too much or too little was a marker as to the abilities of someone as an organizer. The irony was that other organizers viewed certain senior organizers in the United States, both within the IAF and in other networks, as blowhards with overinflated egos. But this seemed to function as a way of saying that they were past their prime as organizers and should retire or do something different. Those who knew Alinsky in the later part of his life frequently made comments about him along these lines.

Local Knowledge and Serendipity

The diversity of those involved in the leadership team meant a variety of formal and informal information sources were available. Some leaders had links to the Conservative Party while others had established relationships with the Labour Party. Those with local knowledge complemented those with knowledge of Parliament and central government. For example, attending a meeting after the November 25 assembly to discuss a cap on interest rates and proposals for a "People's Bank" with Greg Hands (then shadow treasury minister for the Conservatives) were leaders from large institutions in his constituency, including the Anglican vicar who baptized Hands's daughter and who was also a leader within West London Citizens. Sometimes these local contacts led to highly serendipitous relationships. For example, prior to the November 25 assembly, the team was struggling to obtain any response from the Conservative Party. However, in an unrelated initiative – a project to establish a community land trust so as to build affordable housing for low-income families – a relationship was developed with an architect who became very committed to the project. It transpired that her partner was a senior policy advisor with strong ties to both David Cameron and George Osborne. She jokingly offered to "withdraw bedroom privileges" until her partner ensured the Conservative Party responded to requests for someone to attend the assembly. Within twenty-four hours, Greg Hands agreed to attend.

Having attended the November 25 assembly, the team of Conservative Party advisors who came with Hands realized that London Citizens represented a political opportunity for them to articulate their own "Big Society" policy agenda. This agenda emphasized the importance of civil society in the production and delivery of social welfare services. A relationship was then pursued on both sides, which culminated in a visit by David Cameron to the offices of London Citizens on March 31, 2010 before he went on to give a speech launching the "Big Society" vision that afternoon. In the speech he explicitly identified London Citizens as an example of what the "Big Society" represented. Cameron's speech and visit constituted major national recognition for London Citizens. When he entered the room amid the crush of photographers and journalists, Cameron tried to dominate the space, but the chair, Kaneez Shaid, the dynamic hijab-wearing Director of Marketing from Sir George Monoux College in Walthamstow, reestablished control. During the rounds the religious and diverse nature of London Citizens was emphasized. Prior to the meeting there was a hurried and heated debate among the leaders present as to whether to be confrontational with Cameron and push him to attend the May 3 assembly (his office had said he was too busy to attend), and it was agreed that Nick Coke, a softly spoken Salvation Army officer, would ask him. As it happened, Ruhana Ali, the equally dynamic, hijab-wearing organizer for Tower Hamlets, took matters into her own hands and asserted that if Cameron really cared about creating a Big Society and wanted to demonstrate leadership he should be the first party leader to accept the invite to attend the assembly. It was clear that Cameron had not understood the nature of the invite but warmed to it when it was explained it would be an assembly with all three party leaders. He formally agreed to attend an assembly if not before the election then afterwards – his diary permitting. Obtaining even the tacit agreement of Cameron was the key to lobbying the other party leaders to attend the assembly.

Political Geography and Strategic Locations

Part of what these series of interactions with the Conservative Party point to is the dominance of London and the "Westminster village" in the political geography of Great Britain. Despite an espoused antipathy to party politics, London Citizens was necessarily focused on building relationships with all the political parties during the campaign. More broadly, despite billing itself as an alternative to Westminister-focused politics, Citizens UK has struggled to develop organizations outside London. Initial efforts in Liverpool, Bristol, and Birmingham in the early 1990s all collapsed owing to a nest of financial and organizational constraints and interpersonal conflicts. At the May 3 assembly the London-centric nature of Citizens UK was only modulated through the Citizens for Sanctuary groups from around the country providing some sense of Citizens UK being a national organization. The British context is different from that of Germany, the United States, and Australia where historically there was a much greater measure of power devolved to the state/regional level through a federal system of government. The outworking of the different political geographies in the United States and the United Kingdom is that in the United States, the IAF is criticized externally for failing to develop sufficient capacity to operate at a national scale because it focuses its energies in regional and metropolitan areas. Citizens UK, however, is criticized internally by local leaders for being either too concentrated in London or too focused on central government and campaigns with a national focus. Yet the experience of Citizens UK suggests these criticisms can be addressed.[13]

As outlined in Chapter 2, there is a need to move beyond a "scalar" social-spatial imaginary so that a false dichotomy between local and national (and global) is avoided. It is not a question of scale but one of place, albeit one oriented to a sense of place as a "microenvironment with a global span." The political questions to ask are: Where is the effective place of action given the issue addressed and how can an action be done in a relational and meaningful way? There is no reason the IAF could not develop Washington Interfaith Network as an equivalent to London Citizens, with a dual focus on both the city of Washington, DC and the organs of federal government. Meanwhile, Manhattan Together could take a particular responsibility for focusing on finance capital concentrated on Wall Street; or Durham CAN (Congregations, Associations and Neighborhoods) could become the global command point of the biotech and pharmaceutical industry concentrated in the Research Triangle Park area of North Carolina. Such a dual focus to these IAF affiliates would cohere in that their actions would be premised on the attempt to have nationally or globally focused organizations such as banks or departments of state recognize they are also local, anchor institutions with neighbors.

TACTICS AND ACTIONS

London Citizens deploys a variety of tactics and actions to achieve its aims. The determining rule taught for what is appropriate is that *the action is in the reaction.* By this it is meant that the appropriate action to take is the one that will provoke the reaction one is looking for. The repertoire of actions includes neighborhood walks (which connect members of an institution to residents in a local area), commissions (such as the one about Lunar House), assemblies, and various forms of direct action. Tactics demand innovation, creativity, and coming up with unexpected moves. As Alinsky notes: "Tactics are not the product of careful cold reason ... they do not follow a table of organization or plan of attack. Accident, unpredictable reactions to your own actions, necessity, and improvisation dictate the direction and nature of tactics."[14] A measure of virtuosity in organizing is the ability to improvise well given the constraints and opportunities of a particular context. However, there is a tendency among organizers to be repetitive and work from a limited palette of actions. Other experimental forms of direct democracy, such as citizen juries and participatory budgeting, are not considered as they represent forms of action developed outside of the IAF network. That being said, the IAF styles of direct action do share two common features with alternative approaches (such as anarchism, from which it otherwise differs markedly): (1) attention to the intersection of place and politics and (2) an emphasis on the "festive."[15]

Learning to Participate in Public Space

A crucial aspect of the spatial dimensions of democratic citizenship is familiarity with the political landscape, both geographic and symbolic. Buildings and institutions represent physical maps of political life: the Houses of Parliament, Buckingham Palace, the Guildhall, and Lambeth Palace are symbolic places both individually and collectively, representing as they do a history and nexus of power relations. Within the geographic-symbolic space, public relationships are formed and political life is conducted. But to participate effectively in any particular geographic-symbolic space requires knowledge of how to navigate the terrain: literally where to go, who to talk to, and how to undertake a public, political relationship.

In a context where such knowledge is often limited to elites, London Citizens trains people in how to conduct political relationships in particular places and is a means of reconstituting a place-based politics. This work can be seen in how it: (1) respatializes and renders visible an institutional and physical political and civic life within its public performances; and (2) trains people in how to conduct public relationships within particular political terrains. Dynamics of *despatialization* and modes of *respatializing* power physically and symbolically will differ from context to context.[16] However, spatializing power is vital for democratic politics in order that people can see and hear their relational power amid the disaggregating churn of the city and the isolating effects of state procedures and market processes on them.

A London Citizen's assembly manifests a vision of "the people" and represents those who "stand for the whole" to the power holders London Citizens is seeking to hold accountable. In many cities, including London, the symbolic and physical importance of gathering in a central square to democratic political action functions in the same way: the physically gathered people stand in a politically symbolic and geographically central place and thereby both manifest an expression of people power to the people themselves and call to account those in power. Demonstrations in Tiananmen Square in Beijing and Wenceslas Square in Prague in 1989, and Tahrir Square in Cairo and Mohammad Bouazizi Square (formerly November 7 Square) in Tunis in 2011 are all cases in point. Similarly, London Citizens made use of Trafalgar Square for its Strangers

FIGURE 5.3. May 4, 2009, "Strangers into Citizens" rally in Trafalgar Square.

into Citizens marches in 2008 and 2009 in order to give a sense of power in numbers to its members and to call for change to a particular policy: the difference between this event and those in Tahrir and Mohammad Bouazizi Square was that the London Citizens event was largely unnoticed by those in power [see Figures 5.3 and 5.4].

For London Citizens, the twofold work of (1) spatializing and representing this place-based political landscape and (2) manifesting the people's power to itself and to those in power is done most forcefully and effectively in the city-wide assemblies, and in particular through the roll call. In the roll call, a map of London is used to represent each area in which an institution is based as its name or borough is called out. Participants in the assembly are asked to stand up when the institutions in their area are announced. They then stand together with everyone from their borough so attendees can see who at the assembly lives near them. This moment of standing together with those from other institutions in your area is a moment where society and a sense of place, normally abstractions, are made concretely present to participants. The locations of these assemblies are themselves important: they are often held in town halls and in centers of power that draw people into the geography of politics and gives them the confidence and experience of participation beyond their immediate locality. At the same time, political and economic office holders also in attendance at the assembly see and hear representatives of the people physically gathered in significant numbers and feel pressured to answer to them.

FIGURE 5.4. May 4, 2009, "Strangers into Citizens" rally in Trafalgar Square.

The Festive in the Political

BBCO includes festivity in its public assemblies, the carnivalesque in its political actions, and celebrations and parties in its internal gatherings. As mentioned in Chapter 2, the November 25 assembly included dance troupes, choirs, drama, testimony, clapping, cheering, and audience responses as well as a high level of participation in the events on the stage. As has been suggested, all of this contributed to the "religious" feel of the event to outside observers. Such festive elements are a common feature of all London Citizens assemblies and the carnivalesque is a regular feature of its actions. However, they were not always present. A good measure of the efficacy of an action in terms of how the participants felt about it was whether anyone laughed or cried at the event or action. Often London Citizens' actions were humorless and fell into a kind of modern, disenchanted perfectionism: they were earnest, efficient, and instrumental, and lacking any sense of camaraderie or joie de vivre. The inclusion of a festive dimension helps resist such political perfectionism and the self-importance that goes with it. The need to have a laugh and the dangers of the puritanical in the political was overtly recognized by Alinsky who made having fun a measure of good organizing. As Alinsky put it in his sixth rule: "A good tactic is one that your people enjoy."[17] The carnivalesque and trickster dimensions of BBCO are echoed in Alinsky's fifth rule, which advocates ridicule as a potent weapon; rule four, which deploys the ironic gesture of forcing the enemy to live up to their reputed value system; and rule one, which advocates tricking your opponent into thinking you have more power than you have.[18] Indeed, organizing at its best manifests trickster-like elements.[19]

Something of this festive, tricksterish, and carnivalesque spirit comes through in the following action that was part of the Living Wage campaign focused on hotel workers.[20] The central drama of the action took place outside the Andaz Hotel (part of the Hyatt chain) next to Liverpool Street station and entailed singing carols.[21] Approximately fifty participants and eight organizers were involved. Most gathered beforehand at St. Ethelburga's Church nearby to practice and for a briefing. We stood on one side of the main hotel entrance to sing, accompanied by trumpets and other instruments. Police community officers stood in pairs on either side of the group, while organizers stood around the edges in high-visibility vests handing out bits of paper explaining the nature of the action. Meanwhile, a journalist from *The Evening Standard* did interviews with participants and hotel workers within the group through the course of the action. It was difficult to gauge whether it had any effect on anyone in the hotel, but the constant and large stream of commuters passing by on a cold Wednesday evening in December showed active interest and the signs and banners made clear who was staging the action. One of the carols sung was the following:

> God rest you merry gentlemen,
> Let nothing you dismay,
> Remember Christ our saviour
> Was born on Christmas Day,
> To save us all from Satan's power
> When we were gone astray.
> O tidings of comfort and joy, comfort and joy,
> O tidings of comfort and joy.
>
> Now he is come to all the world,
> This lesson to impart:
> If we're to show his love
> There must be action on our part
> To feed the poor, protect the weak,
> Show kindness from the heart,
> O tidings of comfort and joy, comfort and joy,
> O tidings of comfort and joy.
>
> God rest you weary labourers,
> Who need a living wage
> And places healthy, safe and clean
> And just eight hour days

To save us all from corporate power
And values gone astray
O tidings of justice and rights, human rights,
O tidings of justice and rights.[22]

The action could be viewed as an instance of politicized worship.[23] This would be a mistake. Carol singing is a popular cultural form in England that many nonchurchgoers will participate in over the Christmas period, yet carols retain explicit theological language and most carol concerts in London take place in churches. Part of the motivation for its uptake is that it is fun and highly participatory: people enjoy corporate singing. It has strong associations with Christmas festivity, and mulled wine and mince pies are virtually de rigueur accompaniments to any such event. The London Citizens action represented a borrowing, merging, and adaptation of the Christmas folk tradition of carol singing into a piece of festive and carnivalesque street theater. Yet, at the same time, carol singing derives its symbolic power from its reference to a wider, directly theological signification: the Christmas story.

Echoing Alinsky's rules, the action worked within the experience of the people (rule two) but at the same time wrong-footed the opponents by going outside their experience (rule three): carol singing with a message was not what the Hyatt executives were expecting. Contextual judgments must be made about what cultural forms are appropriate given both the set of traditions, customary practices, and institutions of the people involved in the action and the reaction one is seeking to provoke. The interfaith dimension of London Citizens' work means it is not always easy to decide which cultural forms should be inhabited or whether combinations and fusions can be made. Carol singing is native to some and alien to others, and Muslims were notably absent from the action (whether this was because it entailed carol singing was not clear). Some combinations do not work and others are profound – getting it right entails a high degree of artistry and inspiration. Through incorporating the festive, the action recognized that life exceeds the political and the economic, but also that certain political and economic conditions are necessary to live a life. It thereby inhabited the dichotomy that man cannot live by bread alone, but bread is necessary to live. In contradiction to the Weberian vision of politics that dominates so much contemporary political activism, it embodied the recognition that political life needs to engage us in all dimensions of what it means to be human and not simply as rational, rights-bearing units of production and consumption.

Celebrations and Parties

Added to the festive, tricksterish, and carnivalesque elements in organizing is the emphasis placed on celebration. For example, every year after the Annual General Meeting (AGM) – required by UK charity law – there is a ceremony and party where numerous awards are handed out [see Figure 5.5]. These include awards for such things as "New Community of the Year," "Student of the Year," and "Champion of the Year." The award ceremonies have a kind

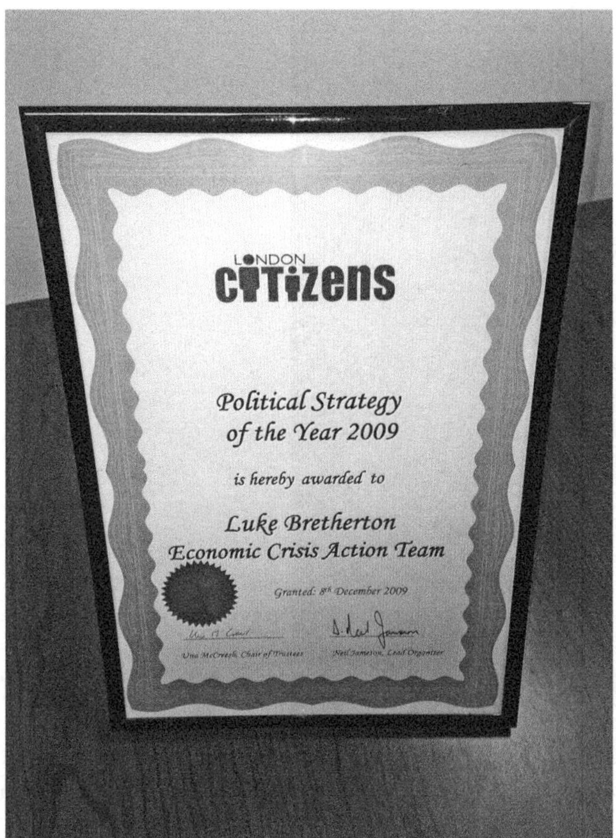

FIGURE 5.5. London Citizens award certificate.

of "end-of-term prize-giving" feel to them. People brought their families to witness their receipt of the award, although some of the corporate and institutional winners left as soon as they received their framed certificate. The ceremony served to recognize the dedication and commitment of leaders within the organization, reinforcing these values among participants but also holding up examples of good practice for others to follow. Public officials and business leaders were celebrated in the same way at the large assemblies. For example, at a South London Citizens assembly in 2009, representatives from the UK Border Agency in Croydon, who thanked South London Citizens for helping to secure £800,000 to build a new reception center for asylum seekers, were in turn vociferously clapped, hugged, and garlanded in recognition of their good work and cooperation [Figure 5.6]. After the AGM prize-giving ceremony there was a large cold buffet that included a range of ethnic cuisines, along with wine and soft drinks. Some of this was bought by the organizers and some brought as contributions by leaders. The parties tended to have the

FIGURE 5.6. TELCO assembly 2008. Garlanding a business executive for paying a living wage.

feel of a respectable but relaxed office Christmas party with high noise volumes from animated conversation and slightly harsh strip lighting given the kind of venues where they occurred.

The Festive as Cultural Work

There are a number of ways to interpret the *festive, trickster-like, carnivelesque, and celebratory* dimensions of London Citizens' work (or what, in summary, I refer to as "the festive"). It is widely recognized that the expressive and affective dimensions of collective political action are crucial in generating commitment and shared identity. Alongside resource mobilization and political opportunity, such cultural work is now identified as a vital part of collective political action in social movement theory.[24] In the case of London Citizens, these dimensions seem to function in a number of ways: they incorporate and fuse participants' political and religious identities, ritually contest asymmetric power relationships by demonstrating a comic disregard for political and social conventions, and enable a choreographed seizing of the space that reframes power relations and deflates the pompous self-regard of those in power. At the same time, they can be used to depolarize relations between "targets" and participants and prefigure alternative visions of the political and economic order that all may share. These dimensions also allow participants to do justice to, yet at the same time transcend, denominational and religious divisions. Essentially, these elements, particularly of festive and celebratory action, are as significant as the seemingly more "political" work. For power lies not only in formal political and legal systems and decisions, but also in the cultural and religious discourses and imaginative possibilities that construct social reality; to be sustained, BBCO, along with all forms of political action, must pay attention to these. However, while these dimensions are neither simply expressive nor instrumental, neither are they just part of the cultural work that helps produce shared meaning and identity among participants.

There is a danger that the festive elements might be reduced to a form of politicized, strategic action if they come to be seen only as a form of cultural work.[25] A richer conception of this dimension of BBCO's processes and repertoires identifies in such moments the deepest "religious" significance of BBCO (and it is here that BBCO is often more profound in its cosmic sensibility than many of the religious institutions involved) and where it poses the greatest contradiction to the modern social imaginary that envisages politics as a rational, technocratic order that is bureaucratically and legally mediated. The festive elements constitute the deeper cosmic grammar of London Citizens' events and actions. Against both a rational Weberian vision of politics and an epic, dualistic vision of politics as an apocalyptic battle between good and evil, these elements of BBCO disrupt claims to have the answer and help ensure politics is a penultimate and necessarily plural enterprise by introducing a comic acknowledgment of the limits of even the best-conceived social and political order. Tongue-in-cheek actions such as carol singing or "trick or treating" in Halloween costumes at the Department of Children, Schools, and Families as part of the Living Wage campaign are examples of such action [Figure 5.7]. The power exercised is not straightforwardly political power; rather, it is the power of imagination – that is, the power to reframe or reimagine reality in terms other than those defined by the representatives of the state or the market.

The Festive as Symbolic Exchange

Beyond cultural work and identity formation, the emphasis on the festive is a resort to the logic of symbolic gift exchange. I shall explore the nature of gift exchange and its implications for conceptualizing democratic citizenship in more detail in Chapter 8. Suffice it to say, the resort to ceremonial gift exchange is a way of demanding recognition in the absence, omission, or failure of bureaucratic, contractual, or rights-based approaches to securing public recognition. This is accomplished by recourse to the festive as a means of demanding respect. Rather than contractual or economic bargaining, the festive entails forms of symbolic exchange. The symbols offered at an assembly

FIGURE 5.7. "Trick or treating" at the Department of Children, Schools, and Families, London, October 31, 2009. Neil Jameson stands on the far left.

or action include physical goods and gestures such as a garland, dance, or song [Figure 5.6]. In offering these gifts, even in a comic manner, something precious is offered as a pledge that calls for a response. As we shall see, for BBCO, it is through rituals of commitment that those in power reciprocate this pledge through making a "counter gift" of public recognition.

Before proceeding to examine the operation of this ritual we must note the symbiosis of democracy and festivity in BBCO. The festive, conceived as a form of ceremonial gift exchange, and democratic politics, understood as the negotiation of a common life between those with multiple loyalties and diverse interests, both articulate and in BBCO, mutually reinforce the claim that there is a common life that all, despite their differences, are called to recognize and contribute to. Given the place of conflict in the repertoire of BBCO it is important to bring to the fore this basic orientation to the possibility of a common life. Indeed, on this account, the reduction of BBCO's repertoire to the airing of grievances and earnest protest, with the loss of any offer of a constructive alternative or festive gift, is a sure sign that something is wrong with the practice. In its reduced and dysfunctional form conflict is seen as more basic than commonality and the other emerges as somehow less than human.

Rituals of Commitment

The distinctive culture of the IAF lives in tension with the wider culture and the internal cultures of the institutions in membership. This tension often expresses itself in relation to different ways of handling confrontation. Reverend Joe Hawes, a Church of England minister in Fulham who was an active leader within London Citizens, notes:

At the accountability assembly, even though I was one of the chairs of it I was feeling a bit uncomfortable that we'd be hauling these candidates up saying, "Will you deliver?" "No, no." "Will you deliver?" "No, no." "Will you deliver?" and, you know, on my particular bit, which is on the whole housing thing, the land banks, Ken Livingstone was saying, "It's not as easy as that."[26]

Part of the antipathy expressed toward the conflict and contention that forms part of the work of community organizing is generated by broader cultural factors. As Monsignor John Armitage, Roman Catholic Vicar General of Brentwood Diocese and a long-term leader within London Citizens, puts it:

It's not the English style ... but I can see that certain times it works. Before every assembly I'm always a bit nervous, especially if I'm in the chair, you know, I'm not good at confrontation yet I can see it's a method that works. What happens then is that sometimes people who are not part of community organising see TELCO or Citizens or whatever as quite aggressive and certainly I know some of the people who we haul through the coals certainly see it as aggressive.[27]

But the Vicar General's reflection on the combative style of London Citizens suggests that beyond a cultural antipathy to confrontation there may be a number of factors that generate the apprehensiveness about using confrontational approaches. The first of these factors relates to how London Citizens constructs public accountability. Here Armitage makes the point:

So when someone holds them to account and, you know, and probably aggression is the wrong word, probably assertiveness I think is probably the right word, when someone is assertive, when someone comes out with a pat answer ... we won't just take any old crap off someone, and as politicians deal with a lot of crap a lot of the time they don't like to be challenged, and so you get it, for example, when they want to come [—] when we invite them to an assembly, if they've not been before they think they're coming to talk about their issues and they get quite miffed when we say we don't want you to talk, you can have two minutes to talk about what you want to talk about, but before you talk about that we want you to address our concerns.[28]

There is a constellation of issues here that needs unpacking, all of which pertain to the relationship between conflict, public accountability, and the rationale for particular forms and repertoires of action.

In the quotations just cited there is an anxiety about the simplifying and narrowing of complex problems into a program to which yes-or-no answers are demanded, a process that inevitably produces the heat of conflict but is felt to damp out the light of insight. Refusal to address an issue by those with responsibility to do so puts them in opposition to those making what is called "the ask." Officials can complain when they are asked to give a yes-or-no answer to what they conceive of as a complex problem. An example of this occurred in a preparatory meeting with some senior Conservative Party officials in preparation for the May 3 General Election assembly. The first proposed ground rule for the assembly stated: "Clear and unequivocal replies are best – Yes or No." Virtually the first request the party officials made was that a demand of such a yes-or-no response would sour any future relationship and that they would strongly prefer it if no such pressure was put on the party leader during the assembly.[29] However, as Stout argues, there is a role in public life for what he calls "rituals of commitment":

> An accountability session, like a wedding, is an opportunity not to give speeches, but rather to declare one's commitments in a way that fully clarifies a significant relationship and the obligations that flow from it. An unwillingness to say "I do," without further elaboration, when asked for a public commitment to enter an important relationship, is itself a significant act, which has consequences for all involved. But to say "I do" is to enter a relationship, to take on the obligations of the relationship, and thus to license the broader community to hold one accountable in the future for failures to meet those obligations.[30]

Conversely, as Stout points out, those with power, whether a public official or business leader, can refuse to make a commitment and have ample opportunity and means by which to explain their refusal at a later date. Non-elites lack such means and opportunity and need clarity from those with power over them so they can hold them to account. A public accountability session and the conflict and tensions played out within it are an attempt to rebalance the power relations between the "haves" and "have-nots" through ritualized ways of forming and taking control of public space. Such assemblies constitute a way in which those who are generally acted on can develop relations of parity and demand action by power holders who act on them. The clear public commitments – as distinct from a manifesto pledge that few read or a private commitment behind closed doors – enable the power holder to be held accountable at future meetings or in the press and at the same time generate a public invested with both the authority and commitment to keep the power holder accountable.

Actions as Political Communication

A central aspect of the Alinsky approach to organizing is that all actions are constructed so as to bring about a reaction – as the organizing adage puts it: "the action is in the reaction." These actions are thus forms of political communication. This may seem obvious but not all actions that claim to be political are. To draw out this point, we can contrast social media-based forms of political mobilization with those of community organizing. In training and other settings a contrast is often drawn between what is rhetorically portrayed as the impersonal world of online and electronic communication and the face-to-face transformative possibilities of one-to-one meetings.[31] However, this critique misses a more significant difference. Some see blogging, tweeting, and participation in other social media as forms of political action rather than as mediums of exchange that enable action. They confuse the means for the ends and so displace politically communicative action by the exchange of communication. Social media thereby serve as a distraction, offering the illusion of having participated in politics while at the same time diverting people from forms of cooperation that can bring about change. This is not to say that social media cannot be used to amplify and facilitate organizing and thereby be used as highly effective tools for political mobilization. Indeed, this is an area where organizers need to engage much more strategically. However, for something to constitute an act of political communication there has to be an expectation of a reaction: one acts in such a way as to provoke a reaction by those whose minds or policies you are seeking to change. Yet, online communication that is an end in itself means there is no reaction: despite its political content, online communication uncoupled from contexts of interpersonal action simply adds to the pool of circulating content; it does not expect or elicit a response. As an act of communication it thereby becomes politically useless.[32] By contrast, London Citizens' actions are targeted at specific people within specific contexts of action and application. A great deal of energy is expended in trying to ensure that relationships are established with the right people: that is, with those who are able to receive the communication and who have the power to react in the desired way in a particular place or institution. On this criterion, the May 3 General Election assembly was a success: all three party leaders attended and substantially positive reactions were elicited in response to the issues campaigned on.

In the emphasis on *political* communication (i.e., communication directed to changing the common life of a particular place or institution) we can discern an important dimension of the conception of democracy BBCO embodies. Given its practices of leadership, relational power, and listening; its commitment to building a common life and putting people before program; its conception of public action; and its commitment to work through the mediation of institutions and their internal discourses, traditions, and structures, BBCO is founded on a tacit conception of democracy that prioritizes political communication rather than representation, deliberation, or even participation. Rather than being defined in terms of the rule of a majority or the equal representation of different interests, democracy is defined by the extent and quality of decision making that results from interaction between the agent of rule (whether economic or political) and the ruled.[33] Moreover, in BBCO, communication that leads to political action is prior even to participation. Forms of democracy can enable a great deal of participation, but if it fails to lead to truly political action that changes the common life of everyone concerned, then its value ceases to be political and becomes moral and social. Rather than representative, deliberative, or participatory democracy, the nearest conceptual connection is with the tradition of consociational democracy. This is a tradition in which in addition to participation and deliberation, political communication is highly valued, and rather than individual involvement being the only point of focus, the institutional and corporate is also emphasized.

Economic and Administrative Corporations as "Estates"

Those who participate in BBCO seek to communicate with "non-political" representatives. Implicit in the practice of BBCO is the claim that representatives may be elected office holders, such as an MP or mayor, but they can also be those who hold real power to act within or on behalf of a community such as a business office holder or a public administrator. Those who need to be included in the process are those who have power over a place and with whom the people of that place are identified, whether they want to be or not, but whose office holders are not publically accountable for that power and the representative nature of the office they hold. Supermarkets such as Tesco's or Walmart, factories, schools, government offices, universities, and so forth are all "estates" or powers within a place, yet ones whose "office holders" (managers and executives) more often than not have no meaningful relationship with or actively disavow connection to the people in that place.[34] Managers and executives see themselves as purely economic or bureaucratic actors answerable solely to shareholders, internal institutional commitments or abstract procedures, rather than office holders of anchor institutions that have a direct impact on strengthening or weakening the civic life of an area and its social and political resilience. Yet when personal identity, social relations, and civic participation are often produced, mediated, and expressed through brands, patterns of consumption, sponsored activities such as sports clubs, and access to the goods and services of anchor institutions such as education or healthcare facilities, then it is vital that the offices holders of the "estates" (that is, corporate forms of power and status bearers in a place) identify with and listen to the people of that place. BBCO is one means through which to agitate and cajole such "nonpolitical" office holders into recognizing their broader social and civic duties of care.

STANDING FOR THE WHOLE

A frequent point of tension was the question of whether it was elected politicians or London Citizens who best represented the views of local people. The contrast between different forms of generating legitimacy and representativeness can be overheard in the following comments from Quentin Peppiatt, a Labour councilor and ordained Anglican minister in Newham:

> [P]arty politics is the way to organise things. I think actually doing it through the democratic ballot and putting yourself up to the electorate is the way to get that legitimacy. Now community organising and the Alinsky approach is very good at getting the grassroots mobilised over issues and doing the single issue campaigns which may

be the way forward. Greenpeace and all the rest of it, I've got nothing against it. I suppose when I get frustrated is when I meet them and I say, "Yes that's a point of view and I agree with you on the minimum wage, living wage, and I agree with a lot of your campaigns, but I'm not going to sign on the dotted line because actually I stand on a ticket which isn't that ticket." If I was wanting to be chosen as a party for those sort of things ... then I would stand on that and you would put people up and we would have a fight over that particular agenda, and that's fine, I've got no problem with that but they're not willing to engage in that democratic politics as I see it in the wider community.... [I am] happy for them to claim, or for anyone to claim, like Greenpeace or whatever, that they are pressure groups to make things happen and that is absolutely fine. I think what I find frustrating is when they claim more than that, that they represent community and therefore have a mandate. They don't have a mandate I'm afraid, the mandate comes from the ballot box.[35]

Peppiatt's sentiments were not uncommon among the local councilors and MPs with whom London Citizens engaged, and they signal a contrast between the authorizing processes of representative democracy and those of a populist and consociational democracy of the kind that BBCO embodies. Peppiatt's comments raise the question of the nature and form of the legitimacy and representativeness of London Citizens and the platforms it develops such as those presented to politicians at the November 25 and May 3 assemblies.

The IAF's reflections on this question are contained in a document produced in 1990 and entitled "Standing for the Whole." There are a number of aspects to how the legitimacy, representativeness, and "mandate" of the IAF's work is conceived.

Representing the Experience and Wisdom of Ordinary People

First, the representativeness of an IAF coalition is seen as being grounded in the experience and reflections of the thousands of ordinary people involved. The legitimacy is not based on specialist or technical knowledge or electoral mandate but the fact that the IAF is a vehicle through which the untapped talent, wisdom, and leadership of parents, bus drivers, secretaries, "dignified people on public assistance," and the like can be harnessed and brought to bear on the decisions that affect them. Key here is the sense that the IAF's legitimacy is partly premised on being a means through which the experience and insights of those who are the subjects of failed programs and policies determined by others can be included and learned from in the formulation of new programs and policies. However, the emphasis on the wisdom of ordinary people goes beyond the romanticization of "hardworking, simple folk" present in many forms of populism because BBCO actively involves a meaningful process of listening to and learning from "the people."

Representing Civil Society

Second, the IAF is said to represent an alternative voice to both commercial interests whose primary point of reference is generating profits and the "bureaucratic state" and its elected representatives, who deploy state processes to achieve narrowly defined party platforms. The IAF is presented as a token of the "third sector," which is said to give the market and state their meaning: "This sector is where we grow and see our children grow. This sector is the soul of the whole."[36] Explicitly rejected is the characterization Peppiatt gives of London Citizens as a special interest or single-issue group, equivalent to Greenpeace. Rather, as a body that encapsulates the "soul of the whole" the IAF/London Citizens perceives itself as representing a vision of the "common good" beyond sectional interests of either commerce, party politics, or special interest groups.

Representing Civic Agency and Common Work

Lastly, in contrast to a heroic model of leadership in which the enlightened official, technocratic specialist, elected representative, charismatic personality, social entrepreneur, or philanthropic CEO will deliver change, the legitimacy and representativeness of the IAF is taken to rest on involving and building a distributed form of leadership in which everyone, including ordinary citizens, takes responsibility for building change. Again, this is a key point of contrast with other forms of populism and is a vision encapsulated in the slogan: "We are the change we've been waiting for." The IAF/London Citizens presents itself as a catalyst for this broad-based and comprehensive conception of public responsibility and political freedom. As the document puts it, "[w]hat matters to us is not consensus, but a stake in the ongoing dynamic of controversy, resolution, and change. We do not want to dominate. We do not want to *be* the whole. We want and will insist on being recognised as a vital part of it – and as capable as others of standing for it."[37]

Popular Participation, Deliberation, and Discrimination

There is a tendency in modern political theory to view ongoing popular involvement in the formation of political judgments with some suspicion. It is a suspicion that elected representatives seem to share and one that is reflected in Peppiatt's remarks. Symptomatic of this suspicion is the account of democracy given in Joseph Schumpeter's seminal *Capitalism, Socialism and Democracy* (1947). Schumpeter's account is part of a broader tendency to justify democracy on the basis that it provides a mechanism for aggregating preferences in a competitive electoral process and thereby provides legitimacy to whichever party wins. Self-interest and economic advantages are the proper basis of party platforms for which individuals can express a preference through voting.

On Schumpeter's account, popular participation in the making of decisions is to be discouraged since it is thought to have dysfunctional consequences for this kind of system. Stability and order are to result from compromise among elected politicians and the interests they represent rather than from encouraging participation in the discernment of goods in common. As political theorist

Chantal Mouffe suggests, a consequence of this is that democratic politics is separated from its normative moral dimensions and is viewed from a purely instrumentalist and utilitarian standpoint.[38] Yet it is when it is understood simply as a system of aggregation that democracy is dysfunctional. With democracy reduced to an electoral procedure for collating individual preferences and interests, the consultative, deliberative, and discriminative aspects of making democratic political judgments drop from view. However, as theologian and political thinker Oliver O'Donovan contends, "[f]or representative action to have moral depth, the representative needs a comprehensive sense of what the people at its best, i.e., at its most reflective and considerate, is concerned about."[39]

In a democracy, wisdom is not seen to rest with the one or the few but with the many. To sustain good political order, the contention of democracy is that the widest possible net must be cast to catch wisdom and experience in the formulation of good policy. This is exactly the argument of "Standing for the Whole," which, echoing Alinsky, valorizes the dignity and practical wisdom of ordinary people. If the distinctiveness and particularity of this experience is lost because it is collapsed into an aggregation of individual preferences, then the demos becomes a crowd or mass. As O'Donovan points out:

> Aggregated in a mass, their separate contributions lose their distinctive basis in experience, and are reduced to a fraction of a decibel. The power of the crowd is the power of none. The price paid for strengthening its voice is for everyone to lose his own. "Demagoguery" was the name given to the reductive technique of political management that appealed to the crowd rather than the people, suppressing the relational structures that made for common practical reasonableness.[40]

Consultation, Communication, and Acclamation

Against aggregation, BBCO emphasizes the consultative, communicative, and acclamatory moments in democracy, allows for the wisdom of each to be heard in its particularity rather than be lost in the mass, and enables the people's considered views to be put forward and deliberated on. This is the basis of the IAF/London Citizens mandate to represent "the whole" and is what distinguishes its approach from what were named in Chapter 1 as forms of antipolitical populism. It is also how BBCO sustains the public realm as an arena of political freedom and guards against an elective despotism emerging wherein representatives, once elected, simply do as they see fit.[41]

An assembly and the processes through which it comes into being enable a diverse community to grasp imaginatively and practically a unifying vision of itself as possessing goods in common. In his reflections on representation, O'Donovan notes:

> A people is a complex of social constituents: of local societies, determined by the common inhabitation of a place; of institutions, such as universities, banks, and industries; of communities of specialist function, such as laborers, artists, teachers, financiers;

of families; and of communities of enthusiasm such as sports clubs and musical organisations. To have identity as a people is to be able to conceive the whole that embraces these various constituents practically, as a coordinated agency. When it is no longer possible to discern the constituent elements within the whole, each with its stock of tradition, its reserves of memory, and its communal habits of practice, then the whole dissolves before our eyes. It also dissolves when it is no longer possible to think of these elements as acting, in some sense, together and for one another.[42]

O'Donovan is here pointing to the aspirational sense of the term "people" as denoting the whole, as distinct from its factionalist use as a term for one section of the whole, the "have nots." The aspirational use of the term emphasizes the heterogeneity rather than homogeneity of the people.[43] This whole is not monolithic. Rather, it is a complex, intricate, and differentiated body. It is significant that the IAF emphasizes standing for the whole rather than representing the one community, nation, culture, or interest. An emphasis on wholeness rather than oneness encourages a vision of citizenship as about mutual exchanges between different parts of the whole. As classicist and political theorist Danielle Allen notes: "The metaphor of wholeness can guide us into a conversation about how to develop habits of citizenship that can help a democracy bring trustful coherence out of division without erasing or suppressing difference."[44] For wholeness to stand there is a need to find common interests, and democratic politics is the ongoing way in which to do this. BBCO is a practice through which to inhibit the dissolution of the whole and reweave a sense of a common life. In the absence of a common tradition or a well-established collective identity (which, in any case, tends to emphasize oneness and therefore demand homogeneity), BBCO provides a means through which those involved in a place can grasp imaginatively the whole. Its constituent elements can be seen and heard as possessing a common life for which those being ruled and rulers (whether economic, social, or political) are publicly and mutually accountable.

For democratic legitimacy to be sustained, the people must be able to see reflected in the goods upheld by their representatives something of their own sense of the good of the whole. If there is too great a sense of disparity, trust will break down and a crisis of representation will ensue. The frustration Peppiatt expresses in his remarks indicates a failure to grasp how representativeness is an ongoing project of imagination. An election is but one moment of communication and mandating. Participating in assemblies is another. It aids democratic representation because it strengthens and makes more meaningful the sense of identification and communication between office holders and the people they represent. Moreover, an assembly is a piece of political theater that plays out a far richer drama of democratic representation than the pageant of an electoral rally or the passive reception of a party agenda at a hustings, both of which operate on the logic of one-way acclamation (the people recognize the ruler) rather than reciprocal recognition (ruler and the ruled acclaim and respond to each other's concerns).[45] Stout notes that earning recognition of one's representative authority comes from one's responsiveness to the experience, concerns, proposals, and reasons of those one claims to represent.[46] The public accountability that comes from earned authority is the guard against vanguardism: that is, the claim to stand for the whole based either on a self-selecting group claiming to incarnate the popular will or a specialist gnosis that discerns the true direction of history and so claims to already know how everyone else should live.

The practices of BBCO detailed here encapsulate a vision of democratic representation as involving a communicative process through which representatives and those they represent are drawn into ongoing relationships of reciprocal and affective recognition. In representative democracy, where the act of legitimacy is conferred by an electoral procedure, this procedure is often conflated with the equally important moments of consultation and identification through which "the people" can be imagined as a meaningful entity. Yet if this is done, important elements are thereby eclipsed. Consultation involves listening and responding to one's constituents. This is often done on an individual basis through responding to letters and "surgeries" or in an aggregative way through elections, opinion polls, and referenda. What is missing in these modes of listening is the connection between consultation, identification, and acclamation of the kind that takes place in an assembly. In an assembly, the demos recognizes itself as a demos through the roll call and in turn offers acclamation to its representatives, who reciprocate by recognizing and responding to the people and corporate rather than their individual concerns. It is thus a moment of collective self-discovery that involves an affective ritual through which "the whole" or the "people" is visualized, experienced, and represented.

THRESHOLD

As a form of political action, BBCO is focused on practices and learned sequences. Mastery is transmitted in and through practice, without necessarily requiring a high level of conscious verbalization or rational deliberation – despite plenty of words being used in the formulation and outworking of the practice. Rather than cognitive recognition and verbal articulation, what is important in community organizing is the sequence of things and the skillful deployment and performance of a repertoire of actions and practices in order to provoke the desired reaction: one-to-ones, caucusing, assemblies, power analysis, evaluations, and inventive forms of contention are the ingredients of a successful sequence. As a sequence of practices, community organizing constitutes a public or common work. This sequence should be distinguished from the formal campaigns that are run, for example, to promote a living wage, stop the detention of the children of asylum seekers, or to introduce a cap on interest rates – all of which require cognitive and conscious assent to the issues. Without bringing about a new understanding of the concerns being addressed – that is, changing hearts and minds – the campaign fails. The same can be said of all issues-focused political activism. Consciousness raising and education are keys to such work: people need to understand the issues. However, the primary desired outcome of community organizing (as distinct from its campaigns) is organized people, leadership development, and "reweaving civil society." In organizing, the "program" or issues are not the main focus – the people are. Rather than winning a campaign (although this, too, is an important part of what makes a sequence good or not), what matters is the artful deployment of a repertoire of actions to form a particular sequence within a distinct context and among particular people. Crafting a good sequence enables the identification and training of leaders, the building of relational power, and the reweaving of civil society.

Identified in this chapter and Chapter 4 are a number of the core practices and concepts that the Alinsky approach to community organizing uses. These are shared with many of the other networks. In terms of concepts, there are distinct conceptions of:

- self-interest
- power
- anger
- the relationship between confrontation and conciliation
- public action
- leadership

Aligned with these is an emphasis on:

- working through institutions
- being broad-based
- popular education
- generating an independent community of interpretation
- a distinct, listening-based and relational approach to formulating "contradictory" policies
- the incorporation of the "festive" in the political
- democratic politics understood as a craft with "rules" – akin to a monastic rule – that one is apprenticed into
- democracy understood as a process of communication and acclamation, not just a system of representation

These elements combine so as to constitute a distinct practice of politics that can be symbiotic with a range of traditions.[47] BBCO, as a form of populist democratic politics, is a repertoire of practices that enables intersubjective engagement, understanding, and connectivity across diverse traditions of belief and practice (whether religious or not). At the same time, it requires the involvement of traditions with "cosmic" visions of the good so as to ensure that more universalistic ends shape and at times interrupt the pragmatic pursuit of material goals through political means.

By way of closing the circle, I should say that the upshot of the sequence described here was that, three days before the 2010 General Election, 2,500 people gathered in Westminster Central Hall for what the media billed as the "fourth debate" between the three main party leaders. Unlike the previous debates, this one took place in public and was neither organized by a television company nor micromanaged by party officials. It was put together by Citizens UK and it was ordinary citizens who chaired the event and questioned the party leaders. After months of organizing, Citizens UK had secured the attendance of the then Prime Minster Gordon Brown, future Prime Minister David Cameron, and the future Deputy Prime Minister Nick Clegg. And when the party leaders spoke, it was not to sell their manifestos but to respond and answer to a "citizens manifesto" formulated by the membership institutions. Journalists noted it was the largest and most lively public meeting of the whole election. That evening, the BBC made the event its lead story on the ten o'clock news, noting "the organisation behind this event is a testimony to the power of citizens." The months of political work had secured more than just a media-friendly event. It secured significant policy commitments by all three party leaders.[48] All this from an organization a journalist commenting on the event for *The Telegraph* says he had never heard of and found slightly disturbing.[49] Beyond the world of party politics, the practices of community organizing were already beginning to inform debates about the production and delivery of health, education, and welfare services.[50]

After the election the Labour and Conservative parties increasingly adopted community organizing within their own policy discourses. For the Conservatives, its adoption was framed within its advocacy of the "Big Society" and the need for civil society to play a greater role in social welfare delivery. On the Labour side, interest in community organizing took many forms, but most notably it included the initiation in June 2010 of "Movement for Change," which describes itself as "the home for community organizing inside the Labour movement, and a genuinely bottom-up organization which aims to ally the party and wider movement more closely with communities."[51] Of greater significance was the emergence of "Blue Labour" as a discourse about the future direction of travel for the Labour Party in the wake of its election defeat. Blue Labour was itself a response to the experience of involvement in the work of Citizens UK and the questions this raised about whether it was possible to reestablish a more relational, place-based politics within a political party and develop a "progressive" politics that did not disdain commitments to "family, faith, and flag."[52]

The story of the campaign for a cap on interest rates ends well. Although London Citizens lost momentum on the issue, as already noted, others carried on the fight. New energy was brought to the broader campaign by the appointment of the new Archbishop of Canterbury, Justin Welby, who made numerous very high-profile interventions on the issue of usury and exploitative lending. The result of all these combined efforts was that the Conservative-Liberal government made a number of amendments to the Banking Reform Bill in November 2013 to place limits on high interest rates and curtail key elements of the business practices of sub-prime lenders. The vital symbolic issue here was the enshrining in law of the principal that it is parliament that sets limits to the power of money and not vice versa.

The analytic description of what community organizing involves in this and Chapter 4 sets the scene for an analysis in Chapter 6 of how BBCO constitutes a form of practice-based, as opposed to theoretically driven, politics. The account of organizing in all the chapters so far depicts how engaging in such a practice-based politics necessarily involves an apprenticeship into a particular repertoire of actions. As will be made explicit in subsequent chapters, organizing is better conceptualized as a craft rather than a technique for doing politics.

To understand how community organizing is both a craft and constitutes a practice that mediates between and feeds off other traditions we must locate it within a wider account of the kinds of rationality a practice-based politics entails and how organizing generates political judgment. It is to this we now turn. It should also be noted that in the following chapters there is less ethnographic description and analysis and a greater emphasis on mining what has been said so far in order to develop broader conceptual categories and theoretical frameworks. As outlined in the Introduction, Part I was vital for making plausible the broader account of the conditions and possibilities for a consociational, populist and faithfully secular form of democratic politics. In Part II, the politics of a common life described so far is further conceptualized and its implications enumerated for how we understand the distinct yet coinhering domains of contemporary democratic citizenship: civil society, the sovereign state, and the globalized economy.

PART II

6

Civil Society as the Body Politic

This chapter assesses how broad-based community organizing (BBCO) generates a common world of meaning and action between diverse traditions in a particular place. This *sensus communis* enables political judgments to be made on the basis of a shared practical rationality. The chapter opens by reflecting on how, as a practice-based rather than a theoretically driven form of politics, BBCO is able to incorporate multiple traditions of belief and practice. It then considers how the modern urban condition presents a crisis to political life – in particular, to the ability to make reasoned political judgments – and how BBCO, as a response to this crisis, constitutes a means of demanding and enabling political judgments to be made. Building on this, the chapter examines the interdependence within BBCO of democratic politics, practical reason, and the existence of communities of virtue.

Until now I have been working with a conception of politics derived from the internal discourses of the IAF and which explicitly draws from the work of Arendt, Aristotle, Crick, and Wolin. We have also consistently seen how the Alinsky approach to community organizing engages in conflict and confrontation as well as conciliation and has implicit within its practice a critique of conceptions of politics that are overly wedded to dialogue and consensus as the normative image of what constitutes "good" politics. In this chapter I will further develop the theoretical conception of politics used by organizers but also try to supplement and enrich it by taking seriously the conceptions of public action, power, anger, and confrontation that BBCO incorporates and that were discussed in Chapters 4 and 5. This supplementing will be done by integrating the broadly Aristotelian view of politics used by organizers with a conception developed by the German political philosopher and jurist Carl Schmitt who envisaged political relationships as defined by the distinction between "friends" and "enemies." Schmitt's conception of how the "friend-enemy distinction" is constitutive of truly political relations helps articulate the very real sense of danger and threat at stake in many of the conflicts over issues that community organizing addresses. However, contrary to Schmitt, political relationships will be located not in the relationship between states, but as located in civil society. To make the case for this, I draw on the work of the contemporary sociologist Jeffrey Alexander in order to see what it might mean to "reweave" civil society by taking seriously the friend-enemy distinctions at work within it. In the chapters leading up to this one, we have seen the ways in which BBCO exemplifies how civil society can be an arena for the exercise of citizenship. In this chapter we analyze why civil society is the domain in which democratic citizenship is exercised as an identity, a performance, and a shared rationality. The portrait of BBCO in the previous chapters provides the anchor and inspiration for the arguments developed in this chapter, in particular those set out in the closing section where it is suggested that civil society is best understood in terms of being a "body politic."

ORGANIZING, ANARCHISM, AND THE POROUSNESS OF A PRACTICE-DRIVEN POLITICS

The rules of organizing as first articulated by Alinsky and subsequently developed by other organizers are rubrics for common action, not a prescription for how or what to think. Indeed, any such prescription would be to act against key rules of organizing, such as working within the experience, traditions, and values of the people and never doing for others what they can do for themselves. Rather than advocating a particular political ideology, community organizing – or more specifically, Alinsky's approach to organizing – has a particular practice of politics and public action. But, contrary to most modern political theories, its practitioners portray it as deliberately pragmatic, anti-utopian, and antitheoretical. This is evidenced in the often anti-intellectual stance of many organizers who emphasize action over theory and doing politics over talking about politics. The conception of politics in the Alinsky approach to organizing is derived not from some prior principle or schema. Instead, it is one born out of immersion in the context to which it is a response. Its "universals" are developed through close attention to particular places and people and based on practical rather than theoretical reason. Drawing on Aristotle, the moral philosopher Alasdair MacIntyre argues that practical reason is always embedded within a particular tradition. Each tradition has a determinate vision of the good life that it is trying to embody and establishes the particular practices and virtues that enable its adherents to fulfill the good and institutions that sustain the tradition across generations. BBCO is best understood as a prudential politics that draws on practical reason embedded within particular traditions and the interaction of these different traditions with a particular condition: namely, urban life and the forces of the market and the state brought to bear on social relationships within the urban context. Through this *interaction*, community organizing – as a particular conception and performance of democratic politics as a place-based negotiation of a common life in pursuit of shared goods – has developed as a way of structuring relations between different traditions so as to enable the mutual pursuit of goods in common. This is exemplified in the engagement between organizing as a practice and the different religious traditions it incorporates and the way in which, as outlined in Chapter 3, the practices of organizing mediate a common life between diverse traditions.

By identifying community organizing as a performance and vision of politics that grows out of practical rather than theoretical reason we can make sense of a seeming dichotomy in organizing between, on the one hand, the need for contextualization, and on the other hand, the advocacy of "universals" or "rules" to organizing. Within a prudential politics derived from practical reason, "rules" are judgments derived from particular contexts and actions that have an "exemplary validity"; that is, while retaining their particularity, and without reducing or subsuming them to expressions of a prior universal, the particular and local provide insight into the generality or the guiding rule or criteria that should govern future practice in other locations.[1] Different contexts provide scope for further specification of the generic rule guiding what the appropriate political judgment to be made is among these people, in this place, at this time. I contend that organizing needs to be understood first and foremost as a practice for making good political judgments as against the refusal of judgment by the imposition on the world as it is of an abstract, impersonal, and theoretically derived principle or procedure.

BBCO is not alone in the modern period in being a practice-driven and ideologically open or undetermined form of political action. The labor movement, populism, and arguably, anarchism, represent parallel political forms. The labor movement in Britain and Australia, and to a certain extent in the United States, is often associated with Socialism. However, Socialism itself is a hydra-headed phenomenon involving myriad ideological programs. But more importantly, as a movement, in its early history at least, the labor movement did not demand commitment to Socialism of any particular variety.[2] Methodists, Roman Catholics, and a host of others who never considered themselves socialists were involved in the development of unions, cooperatives, popular education, and other forms of working-class self-organization that formed the basis of the movement. What it did demand was solidarity and loyalty to one's fellow workers and a set of practices for organizing corporate political action and cooperative forms of self-help. In the British context it can be argued that this ideological porousness becomes increasingly obscured and then eclipsed by the demand for conformity to a narrow spectrum of ideologies, ranging from Fabianism to Marxism. As articulate theories rather than practices of organization and common action, these ideologies battled to determine what Labour stood for as a party, and were state-orientated and elite-driven political programs as against a grassroots movement of self-organizing affinity groups. The claim regarding anarchism, however, needs a bit more explaining.

David Graeber, in his extensive ethnography of anarchism as it developed since the 1980s in Europe and North America, argues that as a movement anarchism has no central ideology. He identifies strong ideological influences such as Situationism; however, for Graeber, contemporary anarchism is better understood as a set of practices for democratic decision making and repertoires of direct action.[3] On Graeber's reading, contemporary anarchism aims to prefigure a certain vision of democratic possibility.[4] Graeber's study reveals there to be myriad ideological visions informing involvement in anarchist politics; from the explicitly religious ones of Wicca, the Quakers, and other Christian pacifists to the avowedly atheist ones of Maoists and Marxists. The practices of direct democracy developed by contemporary (or "second wave") anarchists allow for mutual exchange between different visions of the good. The primary emphasis in contemporary anarchism is on direct action.[5]

Graeber's work provides a helpful insight into the nature of the Occupy movement that emerged in 2011 as the movement may be seen as taking on the mantle of the anarchist politics that evolved within the alter-globalization movement from the early 1990s onward. Graeber, who was himself involved in the early development of Occupy, contends that from its outset the movement was based on "anarchist principles."[6] In London, the primary point of focus of the movement was the encampment around the front of St. Paul's Cathedral. This was initiated as a response to a call on October 15, 2011 from *Los Indignados* who had begun widespread protests in Spain on May 15 of that year. Borrowing a term from the anarchist poet and essayist Hakim Bey (the nom de plume of Peter Lamborn Wilson), what was created around the Cathedral and in other Occupy encampments such as the one in Zucotti Park, New York, can be characterized as "temporary autonomous zones" or TAZs.[7] These TAZs are meant to give people an experience of direct democracy, including not only the experience of autonomy, but also of the exchange of ideas and a spontaneous social order in a space free from control by capitalist corporations or state authorities. The free library (made up of donated books) and the tented university, which constantly ran teaching sessions and workshops, were but small indicators of this. The primary point of focus at the Cathedral and other encampments was the daily general assembly where all matters were decided, anything could be proposed, and anyone could take part. The primary point of the assembly was not necessarily to come up with ideas to make the current system work better (although these were raised as well) but to give people the experience of a completely different space and time so that they were freed to see the oppressive nature of the reigning economic and political system.[8] As the initial statement by Occupy London Stock Exchange put it, "[t]his is what democracy looks like. Come and join us!"[9] The invitation was to enter, if only for a day, a new space and time, one beyond the current liberal-capitalist order of the West. Utilizing both an intensive commitment to consensus decision-making and through embodying imaginative alternatives to a neoliberal vision of globalization, the hope was that constructions different from the political system, patterns of property ownership, and capitalist modes of production and exchange could be generated.

Graeber notes that in contemporary anarchism there are frequent conflicts between those committed to direct democracy and direct action but open to building broad-based coalitions and those who began with a particular ideological program to which they expect everyone else to conform. He characterizes this as a contrast between "vanguardist" and "contaminationist" approaches.[10] Vanguardists see themselves as having the correct analysis of the world situation and so they should provide direction and leadership because their prior analysis means they can determine the right thing to do in any given situation, whereas those committed to direct action and direct democracy refuse to predetermine what to do, trusting that the process will generate the right outcome and that the practices involved are infectious, contaminating and transforming anyone exposed to them. Vanguardist political programs entail a kind of gnostic elitism wherein a small group claim to know better how everyone else should live. By contrast, a commitment to direct action and direct democracy that characterize the majority of anarchists entails the view that: "Ordinary people are perfectly capable of governing their own affairs on the basis of equality and simple decency."[11]

The distinction between vanguardists and contaminationists points to a profound division over the role of theory in politics. Many have noted the lack of high theory in anarchism. Anarchists, even those considered to be its founding figures such as Bakunin, Godwin, Kropotkin, and Proudhon do not produce works of systematic philosophy or detailed works of political economy. Indeed, a lack of theory was the basis of much of the scorn poured on anarchism by Marxists over the years. However, anarchism is not anti-intellectual. Rather, in its self-understanding it is more a moral project than a project of theoretical analysis. Graeber states that "[t]he basic principles of anarchism – self-organization, voluntary association, mutual aid, the opposition to all forms of coercive authority – are essentially moral and organizational."[12] Graeber goes on to argue that the founding figures of anarchism did not see themselves as creating a new grand theory, but as articulating a certain kind of common sense, which drew on existing modes of practice, notably those of peasants, skilled artisans, or even to some degree, outlaw elements such as "hobos" and vagabonds. For Graeber, the key factor was that the demographic from which anarchism mostly drew had a degree of control over their own lives and work conditions.[13]

I contend that as a way of doing democratic politics, anarchism, like BBCO, prioritizes practical rather than theoretical reason. And, as will be seen, the connection between craft modes of production and political action will be important when we consider the relationship between political judgment, virtue, and citizenship. The emphasis in anarchism on practice and organization over theory is indicated in the names given to different forms of anarchism. In contrast to Marxism, types of anarchism are not traced back to thinkers. Instead of Trotskyites, Gramscians, and Althusserians, there are associationalists, syndicalists, and platformists. As Graeber notes, "divisions are based on difference of organizational philosophy and revolutionary practice."[14] Graeber sees anarchism as a set of practices in which theory only ever has a secondary function. In this sense it is parallel to community organizing, which is also a practice-driven form of politics. Differences between organizing networks, such as IAF and PICO, pertain to emphasis of organizational form rather than differences of philosophy or analysis.[15]

Graeber's account of anarchism points to another parallel: while theories of human nature or political economy play a role, so equally – if not more importantly – do what Graeber calls "the sacred" or that which provides the basis for inspirational visions and alternative social imaginaries. In anarchism, these sacred visions take myriad forms, ranging from the anticlerical millenarianism of nineteenth-century Spanish anarchism and Proudhon's sense that all politics is at root theological[16] to Hakim Bey's emphasis on the magical, the ecstatic, and the marvelous, and the celebration of the Earth Goddess and the Green Man in pagan anarchism. In his history of anarchism, Peter Marshall contends that anarchism is not necessarily atheistic. Commenting on what he sees as the intricacies of the relationship between anarchism and religion, Marshall states:

> It should be clear that despite the opposition of many of the classic anarchist thinkers to Christianity in the nineteenth century, and the close historical link between the Church and the State, anarchism is by no means intrinsically anti-religious or anti-Christian. Indeed, its forerunners were inspired by the minor libertarian and communal trend within Christianity, especially in the Middle Ages and during the Reformation. ... As with the other major world religions, Christianity has left a mixed legacy, but it has been a source of great inspiration to anarchism as well as to socialism, and no doubt will continue to be so in the future.[17]

As the examples of Nicholas Berdyaev, Dorothy Day, Jacques Ellul, and Leo Tolstoy testify, there is a rich legacy of Christian anarchist reflection and practice coterminous with and feeding into the emergence of anarchism. Moreover, the genealogy of much direct action and direct democracy used by contemporary anarchists has its roots in Quaker and other forms of Christian pacifism.[18]

For Graeber, it is a sense of the sacred that lies at the heart of the contemporary anarchist conception of power. He states:

> Immanent in activist practice, I would say, is a theory that the ultimate form of power is precisely the power of imagination. It is this power that creates sociality and social form; the experience of concocting a chant and witnessing it become a collective project becomes an immediate experience of such power. But this power is a sacred force that can only, possibly, be represented by ridiculous self-mockery.[19]

This self-mockery is represented in direct actions through the use of huge puppets and street theater that constitutes a kind of symbolic warfare that aims to reframe reality in terms other than those defined by the representatives of the state, most notably the police.[20] As is apparent from Chapter 3, in contrast to contemporary anarchism, BBCO draws on formal religious traditions and institutions for its alternative social imaginaries – traditions most contemporary anarchists see as hopelessly patriarchal, homophobic, and authoritarian.[21]

The attention given here to anarchism – of which the Occupy Movement's political repertoire is a contemporary expression – is important because it serves both as a contrast to BBCO as a form of democratic politics but also as a parallel. Both BBCO and anarchism are ideologically open or undetermined, practice-driven forms of political action. They are forms of politics in which the patterns of action entail certain commitments to prefiguring a more democratic culture of politics within the constraints of the existing system (as distinct from a democratic system for legitimating the existing political structure). Anarchism is also pointed to for purposes of methodological comparison. As Graeber argues, the practice-driven nature of anarchism is what makes ethnography the most appropriate tool of analysis because ethnography is precisely a way of teasing out "the implicit logic in a way of life, along with its related myths and rituals, [in order] to grasp the sense of a set of practices."[22]

The insight about the importance of ethnography in understanding anarchism and community organizing generates a further insight into the contrast between community organizing and other repertoires of political activism. Not all, but many repertoires of political action begin with theoretical positions and therefore place a high value on discursive conformity and adherence to a particular viewpoint or ideology. This is evidenced in the vehement debates about the "orthodox" understanding of, say, Communism and the policing of views within rival groups. The scene from Monty Python's *Life of Brian* where the members of the People's Front of Judea harangue as "splitters" the "Judean People's Front," the "Judean Popular People's Front," the "Campaign for a Free Galilee," and the "Popular Front of Judea" is a good parody of this phenomenon.

Community organizers are keen to distinguish what they do from "movement politics" and "single-issue campaigns"; however, such rhetorical distancing can be misleading.[23] A comparison of the early civil rights movement and later forms of antiracist activism illustrates why organizers' distinction between organizing and movement politics is a false dichotomy. Both the civil rights movement and later forms of antiracist cultural politics were part of the same social movement, but the former has a direct affinity with BBCO whereas the latter can be clearly distinguished from it. The early civil rights movement, as exemplified in the work of Septima Clark and Ella Baker, had a strong focus on organizing and building grassroots leaders and shared a repertoire of actions similar to that used by community organizers.[24] Ensuring conformity to a particular ideology or worldview was not a priority of their work. Indeed, the early civil rights movement had a remarkably diverse conglomeration of viewpoints. However, the shift toward an emphasis on "Black Power" in SNCC (Student Nonviolent Coordinating Committee) and CORE

(Congress of Racial Equality) – two key civil rights organizations – in the late 1960s led to a rejection of the "open, discursive and participatory structure of old."[25] Ideological conformity and an emphasis on difference and separation became paramount. As well as interpersonal and contextual rearrangements and conflicts, this represented a shift to a different repertoire of political action. In the new cultural politics heralded by Black Power, the emphasis was on changing discourses – or what Foucault calls "knowledge regimes" – rather than organizing and mobilizing large numbers of people. In other words, it became more vanguardist than contaminationist.

Noting the cultural turn in the approach of SNCC and CORE should not be heard as a condemnation. In the context of North America in the late 1960s this shift represented another, and at the time, innovative way to construct an alternative community of interpretation to that which undergirded the racist status quo. An alternative community of interpretation is vital if resources are to be generated through which to recode and re-signify certain groups or kinds of behavior deemed polluted or illegitimate by the existing discourses circulating within and constituting public opinion. Reframing such discourses is essential if excluded groups (e.g., "gays" or the "disabled") are to be incorporated as full members with equal standing to that of existing members. As Alexander notes, "[t]hese new discursively created identities become the basis for political resistance and the movement for civil repair."[26] Alexander identifies the formation of what he calls "counterpublics" as an important feature of the feminist and civil rights movements and of multiculturalism as a strategy of civil incorporation. The end game of most cultural politics and the formation of counterpublics is that an out-group previously deemed untrustworthy and incapable of political responsibility be counted as full participants of the body politic.[27] In the repertoire of engagement that focuses on changing discourses, the emphasis is on reframing social imaginaries, first in enclaves and subcultures, and then in the mainstream media, educational institutions, and other arenas of cultural production. Hence arises the importance of engaging in the arts and media both to challenge negative depictions and stereotypes and to create new alternative portrayals. Such cultural work literally creates new political possibilities as people begin to see and hear the world differently.

The interpretation of counterpublics given here should not be taken as reducing them to forms of subcultural or countercultural politics – even if they self-identify as such. As Alexander notes, to do so is sociologically naïve as it ignores the dual identity of participants in counterpublics as simultaneously members of the surrounding civil society and how this duality "pushes the orientation of social movements not only to conflict, but also to integration."[28] Given this duality, counterpublics draw from broader forms of popular culture and refract discourses and symbolic representations and practices already available within civil society. A Gay Pride parade is a good example as it draws on traditions of carnival and Mardi Gras, pop-cultural references and music, and prior repertoires of symbolic protest. Moreover, the LGBT (lesbian, gay, bisexual and transgender) movement frames its claims for incorporation and acceptance in preexisting terms such as equality and human rights. Demands for recognition and the assertion of difference are more often than not premised on universalistic conceptions of solidarity and justice. When social movements succeed it is not simply because they have engaged in activities that contest the dominant hegemony, but also because they have linked their particular interests and grievances with the moral commitments already accepted in the public sphere.[29] Although different ideologies inform and shape different countermovements, within Western cultural politics the struggle takes place not between rival ideologies – say, capitalism versus Socialism – but on the terrain of an already established hegemony, which is then critiqued or valorized, exposed or expanded, elaborated or radicalized as is consonant with the demands, traditions, and interests of the groups concerned. In Alinsky's terms, they hold those in power to their own rulebook to gain entry to the club and in the process "convert" the nature of the club and the rulebook.

Forms of cultural politics are different in kind, if not necessarily in intent, to the repertoires deployed in BBCO. The difference in kind relates to the nature of the counterpublics or communities of interpretation each approach generates. The communities of interpretation constructed by cultural politics are necessarily less broad based and tend to be focused on single issues. BBCO does not focus on enabling out-groups to either become in-groups or on establishing a realm of autonomy. Rather, BBCO combines in- and out-groups together. It draws together clergy and communists, blacks and whites, the undocumented and the citizen, Christians and Muslims, the low-paid and the well-paid to form a broad-based organization. It then draws from the existing "rulebook" within the civil sphere to hold those with power to account but does so by stepping outside of what is considered legitimate behavior through its agitational tactics and outré discourses of power, self-interest, and anger, thereby pushing participants into a liminal in-/out-group zone that confuses established boundaries. At the same time, and as part of the formation of this in/out community of interpretation, it enables existing members of in-groups and members of an out-group to identify areas of shared interest and thereby foment a common life.

The resistance over many years of organizers to countenance "organized knowledge" as a complement to "organized people" and "organized money" as forms of power encapsulates a right intuition: that an emphasis on "organized knowledge" to the exclusion of "organized people" represents a shift to a different repertoire of political action, one that is in some tension with the current form of BBCO. However, as Richard Wood notes, cultural work is an important adjunct to the work of training and organizing people so they can participate in public life.[30] But when cultural work becomes the *primary* emphasis, it involves different repertoires and sequences of action and leads to a demand for greater ideological conformity. Community organizing lacks the need for discursive conformity and, to date, it has not invested in creating distinct forms of aesthetic representation through media, the arts, and formal educational programs. Even though there is a canon of rules (for example, never do for others what they can do for themselves), these rules are not about generating conformity to a prescriptive ideology or a particular position on, say, race, sexuality, gender, or economics. They are rules of action, not ruling thoughts. Thus, community organizers often sit lightly to what many "progressives" view as sexist, patriarchal, and other discriminatory discourses at work in membership institutions. However, it is also what enables the community organizer in Milton Keynes to establish Citizens MK (Milton Keynes) in 2010 with a mosque, a Roman Catholic Church, and the local chapter of Stonewall (the lesbian, gay and bisexual lobby group) as founding, dues-paying membership institutions all committed to common action and a shared platform. In community organizing, as outlined in Chapter 3, if membership institutions are prepared to build relations and demonstrate loyalty to a common work and commit their people, time, and money to learning how to deploy a sequence of actions in craftsman-like ways, then that is a better measure of mutuality and commitment to building a common life (and its democratic potential) than any ideological conformity to a particular view. BBCO should be seen as a practice that enables the forming of a common life in particular places between those with frequently conflicting moral visions. As such, it embodies a truth of profound political importance: people we agree with often do bad things to us, to others, and to themselves, yet people we vehemently disagree with can often show us love and kindness beyond what we expect or deserve.

This is not to say community organizing is value or commitment free. As outlined in Chapter 1, it grows out of a specific vision of democratic politics. However, unlike many forms of campaigning and party-based politics, community organizing does not demand everyone who disagrees with the issues leave the room before the discussion begins. Rather, leaders and organizers seek to engage as many people as possible in political action, trusting that participation in the practices of organizing will generate a shared vision of a common life within which all may flourish. No philosophical scheme, utopian ideal, or aesthetic depiction can prefigure the political life that community organizing seeks. Instead, it is the quality of the relationships generated by the artful improvization of particular kinds of action that "articulate" and embody it. However, as argued in Chapter 1, this does not mean community organizing has a proceduralist account of politics equivalent to that developed by John Rawls; rather, it envisages politics as a way of crafting a common life. The practices of community organizing are a means through which to enable shared political judgments to be made by those with the power to rule and those who are ruled. And it is the power of the ruled to demand political judgment by rulers and represent their interests in the process of deliberation and decision making that is a core feature of democratic politics.

To understand better why it is necessary to demand judgment, we turn to the crisis of judgment from which BBCO emerged.

DEMANDING JUDGMENT: THE URBAN "CRISIS" AND POLITICAL THEORY

As described in Chapter 1, Alinsky's political vision is one born out of interaction with a number of distinct traditions and in response to modern urban life. Its formulation of a cogent, urban-democratic politics is in itself a remarkable achievement. Its relevance to urban contexts is important for the wider significance of BBCO, for, as the geographer David Harvey points out, "[t]he twentieth century has been *the* century of urbanisation. There has been a massive reorganization of the world's population, of its political and its institutional structures and of the very ecology of the earth."[31] Yet while urbanization was particularly intensive in the twentieth century and continues to be so today, cities have always been important sites of political, economic, legal, and cultural innovation, which then become catalysts for more widespread and trans-urban developments.[32] Whereas the medieval city offered one set of political opportunities and challenges, the modern and now world city offers an assemblage of material and social conditions for a different set. The Paris Commune of 1871 differs in kind from the Arab Spring of 2011, yet for both the city was a crucible of their political struggle and the strategic site of their claims. However, unlike classical and medieval thinkers, modern political philosophers have relatively little to say about the relationship between politics and urban conditions, as their primary focus is the nation-state.

Modern cities can be seen as paradigmatic of the modern condition. However, we must avoid establishing a false dichotomy between the rural and the urban as political spaces. For example, industrialization has affected the shape of rural life just as much as it has urban life. Rather, it is a question of intensity. State and market processes are most acutely and intensively felt within urban life. For example, in Chicago, such was the interrelationship between political authority and the market that the local government redirected the flow of the river rather than challenge the commercial practices that led to its pollution.[33] The issues that the IAF, Citizens UK, and other community organizing networks have engaged with read like a roll call of urban problems: for example, the need for decent working conditions and a living wage, slum landlords, affordable housing, urban-suburban conflict and "white flight," mass immigration and the integration of new migrants into the fabric of civic life, schooling, delinquency, policing and street safety, restrictive banking and credit provision, and machine politics. Alinsky himself explicitly identifies community organizing as essentially an attempt to forge a democratic politics appropriate to conditions of modern urbanization.[34]

Modern urbanization can be seen as presenting a crisis to political judgment. The scale of the infrastructure needed, the cultural and religious diversity of the populace, and the rapid demographic changes driven by people leaving behind more settled and largely rural social arrangements all combine to eviscerate shared moral visions, community building customary practices, and widely held criteria of evaluation. The sense of rupture, vulnerability, and lack of control modern urbanization induces is profoundly disorienting to those who experience it and to those tasked with governing urban spaces. It is the question of how to make judgments when there are no precedents or shared criteria of evaluation that lies at the heart of the crisis that urbanization presents to politics. What community organizing represents is a means of reconstituting, from the ground up, a *sensus communis*, which can then form the basis of a practical rationality on which shared judgments can be made. It does this through assembling a "middle ground" out of the existing traditions, customs, and habits that have poured into the city.[35] The practices of community organizing create the conditions through which a shared world of meaning and action can emerge – albeit one often based on partial misunderstandings and misconceptions. Yet, whether on the Left or the Right, those who would seek to do without a shared life and resort instead to technical, bureaucratic, legal, and market-based procedures of control and risk avoidance consistently oppose organizing and thence the creation of a middle ground.

In fairness to those who pursue strategies of control and invulnerability, there is a sense in which the problems cities face are so huge and all-encompassing that democratic politics seems an inadequate response to them. However, the real problem is what happens when the exceptional circumstances – the crises – becomes the norm? That is, when what is normal – crime, job insecurity, terrible housing, and so forth – is only ever responded to as if it were the exception, as a short-term crisis of an otherwise healthy system. In such a situation, everything and anything is justified. For example, the political theorist Margaret Somers details how Hurricane Katrina was dealt with as an exception that then justified denying basic rights and services to the poorest citizens of New Orleans whereas in actuality, the impact of the hurricane was the result of the long-term neglect and degradation of these populations.[36] When everything is treated as a crisis or an exception, crisis and disorder become means of governing.

Framing something as an exception justifies two parallel responses. The first is the closing down of due process, proper accountability, and collective self-rule: the crisis demands immediate action rather than taking the time to formulate reasoned and collective political judgments. The second is to claim the problems are so overwhelming and so urgent that they are beyond the scope of widespread deliberation and human judgment and instead a "neutral," top-down procedure must be found to address the crisis. This can involve leaving it all up to the market to decide or trying to find a one-size-fits-all, technocratic, administrative solution (for example, huge housing projects) that just eradicate the problem in one go.[37] This second response displays what can be seen as *the* modernist prejudice: the need to abandon tradition and eviscerate rather than reform existing institutions in order to inaugurate the "new," "the modern," or the "progressive" solution. However, in urban life drug addiction, lawlessness, poor education, family breakdown, and so forth have been an everyday reality since the industrial revolution; but generating reasoned, accountable, and collective political judgments to these ongoing urban "crises" is rare. Decisions about such issues are often made within the context of moral panics and in response to controversial events. Alinsky's approach refuses the crises motif and seeks to *convert the crises into politics*. In Alinsky's approach, the urban condition is "the world as it is," and holds that the generation of political wisdom and constructive, incremental ways forward are best achieved through practicing democratic politics as the means of addressing social problems. Urban poverty is not the exception to be dealt with by exceptional means or a "war on poverty," but is part of the world we live in and a matter about which the urban poor, who experience the "crisis" as a daily reality, might have some solutions to propose.

Paradoxically, community organizing converts the crises into politics by trying to create a sense of crisis among participants in order to generate action. Those for whom the urban "crisis" is normal need to discover it as abnormal, as not "the world as it should be." But herein lies the tension in community organizing between, on the one hand, its emphasis on relationship building, training leaders, and building strong institutions, and on the other hand, the need to undertake action to effect concrete change at a micro, meso, and macro level. If there is too much emphasis on generating a sense of crisis, then organizers burn out the relationships and the institutions. Yet if there is too much emphasis on training and relationship building, then no change is generated and organizers simply accommodate people to the status quo.

POLITICAL JUDGMENT, PRACTICAL REASON, AND THE PROBLEM OF RELIGIONS IN PUBLIC LIFE

If BBCO constitutes a means to demand and contribute to judgments from rulers and convert what is viewed as an exception into an arena of politics, then the question arises as to what the basis of such judgments should be. The question of how to create a shared realm of meaning amid contested truth claims so as to be able to come to shared political judgments is a central dilemma that confronts not just urban politics but modern political philosophy as well. And it is one in which religion acts as a lightning rod. Philosophical anxiety about the relationship between religion and politics centers on how theological truth claims are perceived as undermining the possibility of coming to shared political judgments. For example, within the political liberalism of John Rawls, "religious" or any comprehensive doctrine must be confined to the private sphere so that it does not pollute public decisions. In order to detoxify their claims and participate in deliberation about public goods, religiously motivated actors must "translate" their reasons for advocating a particular policy into "public reasons"; that is, reasons all may accept because they accord with an ostensibly neutral conception of justice that stands apart from any particular comprehensive doctrine.[38]

Political liberalism is not alone in worrying about the relationship between religion and politics in the generation of shared judgments. In Christian political thought there is a different but parallel concern about the need for a single tradition or shared realm of communication being necessary for political judgments to be possible. The focus here is not the exclusion of religious truth claims but the need for a single comprehensive doctrine as the condition and possibility of political judgment.[39] In response to these concerns some eschew the need for an overarching tradition or neutral conception of public reason and give a self-consciously pluralist and agonistic account of the relationship between diverse truth claims and the generation of common political judgments.[40] Romand Coles specifically aligns community organizing with such an agonistic account of the problem, identifying in community organizing a non-foundationalist and "nepantalist" vision of politics: BBCO operates in the space torn between multiple traditions, a space that is in constant transition, and through which these traditions interact and thereby develop contingent notions of justice.[41] My account of BBCO is closest to but also at variance with that of Coles.[42] I contend BBCO is best understood as representing a politics of a common life in which multiple traditions, through participation in the practices of BBCO, create locations within which a *sensus communis* is forged; this *sensus communis* is then the basis of shared political judgment. What the rules and practices of organizing define is the space of politics: that is, the process through which to maintain commonality and recognize and conciliate conflict with others in the mutual pursuit of shared goods. And it is the formation of a shared political life through particular kinds of democratic practices rather than a single tradition, neutral procedure, or agonistic relations that is able to foster self-restraint and the conciliation of different interests and visions of the good within a particular place.

BBCO can be read as forging a faithful and pluralistic kind of secularity through enabling the formation of shared speech and action that forms a public arena of communication between diverse traditions. This communicative realm is the basis of political judgments as such judgments arise out of the *sensus communis* within a particular context.[43] Judgments on and within each location are necessarily contingent but that does not make them subjective or relativistic. Rather, such judgments can be located within a particular account of reason, namely, practical reason. However, in the modern period, it is practical reason that has come under threat. According to MacIntyre, practical reason has been usurped by "technique" so that political judgments are understood to be about "making a better world" through efficient and effective procedures for managing resources instead of about determining goods in common through communal and contested reflection and deliberation.[44]

Judgment, as an outcome of practical reason, does not seek universal validity. Rather, it appeals to those participating and present within a public realm where the situation or objects to be judged appear.[45] By contrast, Plato represents a mode of theorizing in political philosophy where an account of political life is derived from first principles in order to construct an ideal that is then related to practice.[46] For Plato, we come to know the world through rational contemplation of ideal forms and so political knowledge must be developed through systematic philosophical analysis based on contemplation of ideals. Political knowledge can be separated from the world of flux and change and a rationally demonstrable truth of political life can be developed. The ideal ruler is thus the philosopher king who can make judgments about what to do in accord with rationally derived principles. In short, Plato puts program before people.[47] However, accounts of political judgment that prioritize theory over practice (whether Platonic, Kantian, or utilitarian) fail to reckon with the nature of politics itself. Politics is, as Machiavelli discerned, about action in time and as such it involves questions of power (the ability to act), historicity (the temporal and temporary nature of action), and wily wisdom (the local knowledge, cunning intelligence, and practical skills necessary to respond appropriately to a constantly changing and ambiguous environment).[48] The ideal ruler is not a philosopher king, but a ship's captain who is able to safely navigate the tumultuous and mercurial sea by means of experience, craft, and quick-wittedness.[49] The unpredictable and unstable nature of political life directs attention away from universal principles and general historical patterns toward particular historical settings.[50] There is a need to act in a way appropriate to the time/*kairos*, and hence the need for judgments about what is best for these people, in this place, at this time. As action in time, politics requires a means of coming to judgment suited to putting people, place, and history before any particular theory or program. As should be clear by now, practical reason (*phronēsis*/*mētis*) is that means.[51]

It is the task of political theory to reflect on already established practices and the presuppositions that inform them in order to develop an account of what is the case and theorize out of that to generate wider prescriptions and criteria of evaluation. The patriarch of such an approach is Aristotle. Aristotle links the study of politics and practical reason.[52] This is necessary for Aristotle because the nature of politics means it cannot be reduced to questions of *epistēmē* (politics is always particular and contextual) or *technē* (politics as the pursuit of a common life always concerns questions of morality and ends rather than simply questions of technique or skill).[53] In contrast to Aristotle, what is often missing in modern accounts of politics is any account of how we come to learn how to make appropriate and contingent political judgments based on practical reason. Instead, politics is either about the application of universally valid principles or reduced to wholly technocratic and bureaucratic considerations that, of necessity, bracket out a huge range of "local" factors in order to simplify, standardize, and rationalize what is going on so as to make it more amenable to counting and controlling by schemes of scientific management.[54] However, something that modern accounts of politics do focus on that is underdeveloped in Aristotle is an account of power.

Political life always involves questions of power. Augustine's conception of the lust for domination implies that not only is our ability to do the right thing impaired, but so is our ability to think rightly about the good. The economic geographer Bent Flyvbjerg recognizes the need for such an account in Aristotle and seeks to nuance it by combining *phronēsis* with a stronger notion of how good or bad choices are deemed good or bad in relation to certain values and interests. Drawing from Foucault, he analyzes how the operations of power affect the process of decision making and what gets to count as common sense. Any analysis needs to face the reality of power relations and how certain knowledge regimes are legitimized and others marginalized to the benefit of some and the detriment of others. Nevertheless, for Flyvbjerg, the lesson to be learned from Foucault (and, we might add, from Augustine) is not that all moral claims in politics are hypocrisy but that the first step toward a more moral politics is recognizing our own complicity with structures of domination.[55] The next step is to establish the representation of other interests and voices in the decision-making process in order to reflect the contested nature of knowledge and judgment: an assembly, not a polite conversation, should be the paradigm. However, this does not of necessity warrant either a species of liberal interest-group politics or the kind of subcultural micro-politics that Foucault seems to advocate.[56] It can undergird a common life politics where, paradoxically, goods in common and the mutual interests they fulfill are realized through a combination of nonviolent conflict and shrewd political action. This combination of antagonism and wiliness involves destabilizing and disrupting the selfish interests of the one, the few, or the many in order to identify genuine goods in common. The paradox entails using conflict and cunning not to reject one's opponent, but to reweave or convert the situation and enmesh a more powerful adversary into a transformed relationship.[57] It is my contention that broad-based community organizing, at its best, represents precisely such a practice of politics.

While modern accounts of politics are laden with critiques of power, the analysis can often be highly abstract. In order to avoid abstract analysis of power and open spaces for judgments about what constitutes good and bad action, there is a need to focus on issues. Without attention to concrete issues and the ways people are able to act in concert and form a *sensus communis* through public practices of speech and action, we have little to say other than that wolves eat sheep, power corrupts, and the strong triumph over the weak. Moreover, to focus only on a critique of power in the abstract or to make critique an end in itself, primarily through a turn to the discourses and idioms of Continental philosophy, results in ever-diminishing returns: critique is no substitute for a constructive alternative.[58] Although power and sin must be accounted for, not all power is bad and David (possessor of dexterity, sureness of eye, and sharpwittedness) sometimes beats Goliath (possessor of overwhelming force). Overly deterministic accounts of unilateral power and the domination of structural forces such as capitalism do not allow for the reality of the kinds of agency constituted by relational power and wily wisdom, which in turn can form the basis of a more equitable common life.

A key insight of Alinsky-style organizing is that the only places in which to listen to others and learn judgment and responsibility for goods in common and from which to contradict, demand, or contribute to the judgments of political and economic power holders is within the kinds of non-pecuniary, tradition-situated institutions of which congregations are paradigmatic examples. The institutional basis of BBCO is crucial that the institutions provide a legal, organizational, financial, moral, social, and physical place to stand. Its membership institutions are places constituted by gathered and mobilized people who do not come together for solely commercial or state-directed transactions, but who instead come together primarily to worship and care for each other. Alinsky's insight, and the real potential of community organizing, is that it recognizes the importance of institutions, especially in urban and rural spaces where institutions that can organize people and money for effective public action have been decimated. Such institutions are the building blocks of a more complex space that inhibits the totalizing, monopolistic thrust of the modern market and state that seek not only to instrumentalize persons and the relationships between them, but also to subordinate all other interests to a single, dominant interest. This is not to deny that building or strengthening such institutions is extremely difficult and that there is a constant need to innovate, recruit, and form new kinds of institutional and associational life. As already noted in Chapter 2, the weakness of institutions in the face of globalized markets is a key anxiety among organizers.

MEANS, ENDS, AND THE VIRTUOUS PURSUIT OF DEMOCRATIC POLITICS

Attention to practical reason/wily wisdom (*phronēsis/mētis*) also helps makes sense of an ongoing anxiety not only about Alinsky, but also about BBCO more generally: that is, the relationship between means and ends and the seemingly instrumentalist dynamics of organizing. Alinsky is much criticized for being overly "Machiavellian" and utilitarian in his approach to the relationship between means and ends. Statements by him such as "[t]he tenth rule of the ethics of means and ends is that you do what you can with what you have and clothe it with moral garments" would suggest this is a correct reading.[59] While plausible, the critique itself needs questioning as it is built on a false dichotomy between instrumental thinking and the pursuit of good ends. Through attention to the ways a broadly Aristotelian account of practical reason relates means and ends we can exonerate Alinsky from the charge of utilitarianism and offer a reparative rather than a simply critical reading of his approach. Such a reparative reading has wider lessons for how we understand the interrelationship between virtue, political judgment, and democratic politics. This is because the critique of Alinsky's utilitarianism needs to be located within a much broader debate about the nature of politics. On the one side are those supposed "realists" who would simplify politics, rendering it as only about selfish-interest, competition, and material benefit; on the other side are "idealists" who would overinvest in politics as the arena of human self-realization and solidarity. As already noted, community organizing points to an older, practice-based form of politics as experienced in guilds and corporations, where craft, utility and solidarity, far from being opposed, are integrated in the pursuit of a common life.

The critique of Alinsky's supposed utilitarianism must also be located within a related anxiety among advocates of participatory and deliberative democracy about the colonization of what Habermas calls the "lifeworld" by the "systems world." The lifeworld is shorthand for the shared common understandings, including values, which develop through face-to-face contacts over time at various levels of social life, from the family to the public sphere. The systems world denotes the ways of organizing human life governed by a bureaucratic, instrumental, and technocratic rationality where values such as efficiency, calculability, predictability, and control are primary. Such anxieties are well placed. As well as forms of organization derived from factory-based systems of production colonizing the lifeworld, other symptoms of this colonization include the commodification and managerialism experienced in familial, religious, educational, and other spheres.[60] However, this does not necessitate the need to insulate the lifeworld from the systems world as Habermas suggests. Echoing the division between realists and idealists, Habermas's advocacy of a separation between the two seems to rest on his view that strategic or instrumental action and speech are inherently oriented toward "egocentric calculations of success."[61] Consequently, according to his view, strategic action and speech should be excluded from the lifeworld because it undermines free and uncoerced communication. For Habermas, strategic means-oriented thinking is private rather than public (although it can be justified if made visible to public scrutiny and debate). Writers on social movements that draw from a Marxist tradition take the reverse position to that of Habermas: for them, public action is necessarily strategic and calculating and discontent must be "manufactured." Such accounts of popular protest tend to ignore the moral and affective dimensions of political mobilization and reduce politics to an instrumental calculation.[62] However, not all strategy and calculation is the same.

Alinsky vehemently opposes the separation of expediency and morality, calling it a "basic fallacy."[63] Rather, for Alinsky, the question should never be the abstract question of does the end justify the means but the concrete and contextual one of does this *particular* end justify these *particular* means?[64] In his account of the relationship between means and ends he discusses various case studies of historical political judgments and assesses whether, given the context, particular ends warranted particular means and therefore whether the judgments made were appropriate. If one pays attention to the trajectory of what he says, and disentangles this from the rhetorical excess and agitational intent, Alinsky's approach is better understood as Aristotelian rather than utilitarian.

Aristotle argues there is a difference between a strategy that serves shared human ends and is consistent with these ends and a strategy that serves solely technical ends to the exclusion of all others. For Aristotle, as for Alinsky, shrewd political leaders must deliberate about what means will achieve the best end that is possible in existing circumstances.[65] Alinsky is clear that any form of political leadership requires attending to the strategic, result-orientated dimension of political judgments as well as the espoused moral ends. In short, he is calling for a form of wily wisdom. By way of comparison, it is arguable that just such a combination of virtue and cunning is advocated in Jesus' paradoxical command to be "wise as serpents and innocent as doves" (Matthew 10:16) and exemplified in Jesus' own nonviolent, trickster-like behavior.[66] The inclusion of strategic thinking and shrewdness in practical reason does not make it immoral; it simply demands that good, that is, moral, political judgments attend to the world as it is. Without thinking strategically, being wily, and paying attention to the context, there is no meaningful action and without meaningful action the community organization dies. On this account, in Thucydides's Melian Dialogue used in Citizens UK training, the Melians were as immoral as the Athenians subsequently proved to be. For all their high ideals, the failure of the Melians either to consult their people or take seriously the interrelationship between means and ends in determining what constitutes good political judgment means they made an immoral (because imprudent and irrelevant) political judgment. The Melians were not martyrs whose death was forced on them, but fools whose destruction resulted from unaccountable, naïve, and imprudent choices.

We can specify further the relation between virtue and *phronēsis/mētis* by attending to MacIntyre's development of Aristotle's understanding of the relationship between *poiēsis* (production) and *praxis* (action). Aristotle held that production was inferior to action since it was a realm of necessity and merely a condition of human flourishing rather than constitutive of it. It was only ever a means rather than an end. We find something of this division echoed in both the work of Arendt and Habermas. The implication of the division is that the realm of work and labor is segregated from the realm of political life and citizenship and thus those without the leisure to participate in political life and who were restricted to the *oikos* (house), the realm of necessity – notably women and slaves – could not therefore be citizens. Yet, as MacIntyre argues, this division owes more to Aristotle's prejudices than it does to any need for theoretical consistency. Rather than seeing them as mutually exclusive, MacIntyre argues that the logic of Aristotle's own position demands seeing *poiēsis* as constitutive of *praxis*. The realm of manual labor and modes of craft production helps form us into the virtues that make us people capable of good practical judgment in political life.[67] MacIntyre holds up practices such as farming and fishing as exemplifying how we come to inhabit the virtues.[68]

Although the virtues we need to be a citizen are not necessarily the same as those we need to be a good human (and by implication, we can be a competent citizen without being a morally good person) there is a relationship between the two: good politics needs good people, and the formation of good people needs a good politics. Moreover, to come to *good* or wise political judgments requires a combination of practical reason and wiliness, but to acquire this combination and to ensure they serve ends beyond selfish interests requires training in the virtues. By MacIntyre's account the kind of arenas through which we come to be formed in the virtues are schools, forms of craft production, congregations, or any form of local society that aspires "to achieve some relatively self-sufficient and independent form of participatory practice-based community."[69] These are also institutions shaped by a broader ethos and vision of the good – in short, exactly the kinds of institutions that constitute the membership of London Citizens. On this account, the pursuit of the virtues through forms of institutionally mediated practices with substantive goods is a prerequisite for being a good citizen: one who has the understanding and the ability to rule and be ruled and is able to make just and generous political judgments. But although such experience is a necessary condition, it is not a sufficient one.

The sense of what it means to be a *zōon politikon* developed here is perhaps better described as Althusian rather than Aristotelian.[70] Althusius rejected Aristotle's distinction between natural domestic rule and the political rule among free and equal citizens. For Althusius, all forms of social life, whether in the family or the guild, may participate in the formation of political life. However, this does not mean that Althusius totalitizes the political sphere so that every aspect of life is subsumed within it as is the case in Fascism and Communism. Rather, as political theorist Thomas Hueglin clarifies:

> For Althusius, each consociation or political community is determined by the same principles of communication of goods, services, and rights. The essence of politics is the organization of this process of communication. Therefore, families and professional colleges are as much political communities as cities, provinces, or realms insofar as they participate in this political process through their activities. What distinguish cities and realms from families or colleges are not their exclusive political character, but the public scope and dimension of their structures and goals. Althusius defines with precision that private consociations are simple consociations held together by the particular common interest of their members, whereas public consociations are all-inclusive orders (*politeuma*), consisting of several private consociations for the purpose of establishing general rules of communication and participation.[71]

In contrast to Aristotle, who overly separates public and private, and most modern conceptions that separate social plurality from the public sphere in order to maintain political unity, Althusius allows for the pluralization of political order so as to accommodate and coordinate the diversity of social and associational life, whether economic, familial, or religious. To be a political animal is to be a participant in a plurality of interdependent, self-organized associations that together constitute a consociational polity. In such a compound commonwealth, federalism is societal and political rather than simply administrative.[72]

As MacIntyre notes, for Aristotle political rule as the negotiation of a common life requires the right kind of experience of politics and reflection on that experience. Alinsky quotes Tocqueville to make a parallel point:

> It is, indeed, difficult to conceive how men who have entirely given up the habit of self-government should succeed in making a proper choice of those by whom they are to be governed; and no one will ever believe that a liberal, wise, and energetic government can spring from the suffrages of a subservient people.[73]

Arenas of cooperative self-organizing – whether a union, a congregation, school, disability support group, or small business – enable us to learn how to rule and be ruled. Moreover, customary practices and shared patterns of judgment making are means by which communities discern and name those individuals and groups who pursue political power for private ends. Standards of truth are communally shared and provide criteria to judge which characters and views are the most trustworthy. Without shared criteria of evaluation a society is open to the manipulation of individuals and groups whose positions are self-serving and whose programs are corrupting. However, although a prerequisite, experiences of self-government in and of themselves do not necessarily generate good democratic citizens. As Alexander notes against the likes of Robert Putnam who hail the importance of associations for the health of democracy, the mere fact of associating does not determine whether a group will be civil or uncivil, democratic or antidemocratic. As Alexander puts it: "It is not the existence of a group per se, even if the associating it spawns is enthusiastic and face-to-face. It is whether the group is orientated to issues outside of itself, and whether in relation to these it displays communicative intent."[74]

As with the difference between political and antipolitical populism, the crucial factor in determining whether an association is democratic or not is whether it is prepared to contribute to and communicate with others in order to build a common life. The experience of BBCO suggests that for such an orientation to emerge, what is needed is the catalyst of community organizing and therefore the experience of ruling and being ruled in pursuit of goods in common *between* diverse institutions. Without this kind of experience institutions can either be co-opted by and subsumed within the state, subordinate that which gives them purpose and meaning to the logic of capitalism (and thereby become commodified), or turn against each other in competitive and intercommunal rivalry.

The task of the organizer and the role of the broad-based community organization are to furnish those trained in the virtues, and with some experience of cooperative self-organization, with the experience and reflection necessary to make them capable of *good* democratic citizenship. It is the interinstitutional experience of ruling and being ruled that enables a resilient common life to be forged and sustained between diverse institutions and forms of association.

In short, they need to learn the architectonic craft of politics. The craft of politics, as MacIntyre argues, constitutes an overarching, integrative form of activity, the purpose of which is to enable diverse communities to approximate a just and generous common life. As a craft, politics is the means by which the goods of other forms of activity and institutions are ordered toward the pursuit of goods in common.[75]

In making the connection between MacIntyre's reworked Aristotelianism and the Alinsky approach to community organizing, we cannot simply rest there. What is needed is a movement beyond MacIntyre's construction of a "politics of virtuous resistance" to a constructive common-life politics.[76] It is to this I shall turn in subsequent chapters. However, what can be said now is that the form of political action intrinsic to the work of London Citizens, and to BBCO more generally, is one that enables the reconstitution of the conditions necessary for prudent judgment about goods in common. Furthermore, BBCO generates a local common life politics through creating a practice that enables the negotiation with regional, national, and global conditions that work counter to the operations of practical reason. I contend that the work of London Citizens points to a way that repairs and enhances MacIntyre's own work and suggests that his pessimism about modernity is too monolithic: other trajectories of modernity are present and BBCO represents the fruit of one such pathway. BBCO inserts deliberative processes based on practical reason into political processes otherwise dominated by rational choice, deontological, and utilitarian conceptions of political reasoning, inviting those operating within these kinds of rationality to participate in an alternative mode of political reasoning, one that enables them to consider how to pursue a common life among these people, in this place, at this time. Whether or not they accept the invitation is another matter.

REWEAVING CIVIL SOCIETY

Attention to practical reason and the need for citizens who are connected to some tradition of virtue and cooperative self-organization in order to make prudent political judgments demands a way of conceptualizing social life as an arena of moral formation and how it is related to politics and economics. As already noted, there is a tendency to overly bifurcate and compartmentalize social and political life, either consigning "the social" to the realm of necessity and thence unfreedom, or seeking to insulate the social from invasion by what Habermas calls the "systems world." Yet in BBCO the personal, the social, and the life of production or making (*poiēsis*) is a vital generator and basis of political action while at the same time is distinct from it. To address the problem of how to relate the social, the economic, and the political we need to first understand what is meant by the term "civil society," and second, to analyze how civil society mediates the relationship between the social, political, and economic realms. I shall address this need through an assessment of differing conceptions of civil society and then argue that it is only through incorporating some notion of the friend-enemy distinction into an analysis of civil society that we can make sense of it as a realm constituted through communication, cooperation, and conflict. In light of the conceptualization of civil society developed here we can understand better the claim of Citizens UK to "reweave civil society" through community organizing and political action.

In order to develop a conceptual framework that distinguishes analytically between state, economy, and society and yet also accounts for the interplay and interpenetration between all three we turn to the work of Alexander.[77] Building on and adapting Polanyi's notion of the double movement, Durkheim's conception of communicative democracy, and Mary Douglas's anthropological work on notions of pollution and purity within social systems, Alexander develops an account of the relationship between civil society and democratic politics. Importantly for the purposes of this book, Alexander's conceptualization of civil society grows out of and is grounded in wide-ranging empirical work and specific case studies.[78] More broadly, and in keeping with a central commitment of this book, he refuses to accept the standard dichotomy in sociology between tradition and modernity. Alexander conceives of civil society as a sphere or subsystem of society that is analytically separable from what he calls the "non-civil" spheres of the state, economy, family, and religious-intellectual life.

Building on Alexander we can trace a three-part sequence of how civil society was conceptualized historically. What Alexander calls "civil society I" (CSI) was developed in response to conditions that emerged in the eighteenth century. At that time, various thinkers – most notably, Andrew Ferguson, Rousseau, and Adam Smith – developed diffuse accounts of civil society as including emergent capitalist markets, religious, public, and private associations, public opinion, legal norms and institutions, and political parties.[79] The institutions of the capitalist market were seen as largely benign since commercial exchange was perceived as a means to restrain arbitrary rule and enhance international peace, domestic order, and political equality.[80] As Alexander notes:

> Capitalism was understood as producing self-discipline and individual responsibility. It was helping to create a social system antithetical to the vainglorious aristocratic one, when knightly ethics emphasized individual prowess through feats of grandeur, typically of a military kind, and descriptive status hierarchies were maintained by hegemonic force.[81]

In this conception, capitalism was experienced as aligned with processes of emancipation and cultivation of the virtues. We overhear something of this in Montesquieu's statement that "[c]ommerce cures destructive prejudices, and it is an almost general truth that everywhere there are gentle mores, there is commerce, and that everywhere there is commerce, there are gentle mores."[82] Montesquieu saw a direct relationship between the rise of "economic commerce" and republican forms of government. Contemporary advocates of capitalism continue to align it with the values of freedom and equality and see it as a moral as well as an economic project.[83] Less sympathetic commentators observe how capitalism is always dependent on a larger moral ethos or "spirit" and consistently incorporates critiques of itself as a system in order to sustain and legitimize itself.[84] For many today the emergence of capitalism is still perceived as a force for liberation and aligned with democratization, especially where it breaks the bonds of an authoritarian state, or oppressive clan, caste, or familial structures.[85] The justification and experience of capitalism as a moral project that fulfills liberal ideals is a dynamic its critics rarely take seriously. This leads to myopia around the coinherence of liberalism as a political and cultural project to promote personal freedom, tolerance, and equality and neoliberalism as an economic project to promote market freedoms and individual choice. That being said, capitalism as it evolved in Europe and the Americas through the course of the eighteenth, nineteenth, and early twentieth centuries was experienced by many as profoundly exploitative and a generator of intense domination, both within the "metropole" and the "colony."

The association of civil society with capitalism rendered civil society subject to radical critiques. As Alexander notes, the second conception of civil society (CSII) evacuated civil society of any of its alignment with the increase of cooperation and democratization. Marx is the leading exponent of this second conception of civil society. For Marx, industrial capitalism seemed only to consist of markets, the social groups formed by markets, and market-protecting states. For Marx, civil society ceased to be seen an arena of amicable strangership and became viewed instead as a battleground of class war. Society in the collective and moral sense was epiphenomenal. In response to CSII there was a turn to the state among both radical and conservative thinkers, and centralized bureaucratic management and regulation appeared to be the only counterbalance to the instabilities and inhumanities of market life.[86] What Alexander fails to note is that the turn to the state was in many ways the rendering explicit of a dynamic inherent in the symbiotic yet antagonistic relationship between conceptions of individual freedom, the liberal state, and laissez-faire economics. The political theorist C. B. Macpherson identifies Hobbes as the first to articulate this self-contradictory dynamic:

> The market makes men free; it requires for its effective operation that all men be free and rational; yet the independent rational decisions of each man produce at every moment a configuration of forces which confront each man compulsively. All men's choices determine, and each man's choice is determined by, the market. Hobbes caught both the freedom and the compulsion of possessive market society.[87]

In short, both Hayek and Marx are right and Hobbes prefigured both. Capitalism ushers in a freedom of action beyond the constraints of hierarchy and tradition while at the same time introducing competition with and oppression of others as labor is exploited and its surplus expropriated. The Atlantic slave trade, and the emergence of finance capitalism that undergirded it, is but the most horrendous example of the process whereby a newfound economic and political agency for some is built on the degradation and domination of others.[88]

For the Right, the identification of civil society and the market meant ignoring (or treating as "externalities") society, tradition, and custom and letting social relations be wholly determined by contractual relations and voluntaristic market exchanges. This necessarily entailed an increasingly central and centralizing role for the state in order to stave off market failure, defend property rights, break up corporate monopolies, and protect individual liberty. There is an equal but opposite dependency on the state by the Left whose identification of civil society with the market led to calls for abolishing markets and private property altogether and collapsing everything into the state. For the Left, as Alexander summarizes it:

> If civility and cooperation were perverted and distorted by capitalism, the latter would have to be abolished for the former to be restored. In this way, the big state became the principal ally of the left, and progressive movements became associated not only with equality but with stifling and often authoritarian bureaucratic control.[89]

Because of its negative association in CSII, civil society could not be considered as part of a democratic project and advocates of civil society tended to be seen by those on the Left as stalking horses for an unrestrained capitalism. However, undocumented by Alexander, but important to note for the purposes of this book, was the very different position developed by the non-statist Left. This trajectory was exemplified in France by the syndicalism of Pierre-Joseph Proudhon, Georges Sorel, and the Confédération Générale du Travail and in Britain by the various strands of Guild Socialism.

From the 1930s onward, this non-statist tradition became a minority, if not quite a forgotten voice. However, as Burawoy argues, the seeds of a renewed critique of capitalism, one that took civil society seriously, emerged in the work of both Gramsci and Polanyi. In contrast to Marx and most post-Marxist theorizations of the relationship between state, capitalism, and civil society, Gramsci and Polanyi see civil society (or what Polanyi called "active society") as both an adjunct of capitalism and the modern state and a source of resistance and autonomy.[90] For Gramsci, civil society colludes with the state to contain class struggle, while at the same time, its autonomy from the state can promote class struggle. Likewise, for Polanyi, new forms of social relations are made possible by the emergence of capitalism and the modern state, while at the same time society is in a contradictory relationship to capitalism, continually seeking to embed market relations in social and political relations and defend itself from the process of commodification.[91] Burawoy notes that:

> For both … "society" occupies a specific institutional space within capitalism between economy and the state, but where "civil society" spills into the state, "active society" interpenetrates the market. For both, socialism is the subordination of market and state to the self-regulating society, what Gramsci calls the regulated society.[92]

The key difference between Gramsci and Polanyi is that whereas Gramsci sees civil society as inherently tied to the interests of capitalist hegemony, Polanyi sees society as representing the grounds for solidarity among all classes. Any class, including the aristocracy or bourgeoisie, when it becomes the agent for resisting the commodification of land, labor, and money, could stand for the whole, representing and pursuing the general interest shared by all.[93]

With the collapse of Communism there was a more widespread and positive appraisal of civil society, but this appraisal was largely conceptualized in terms of CSI.[94] Contrary to CSI, and echoing Gramsci, Polanyi, and Alexander, there is a need to differentiate capitalism from civil society rather than conflate them as notions of "social capital" tend to do.[95] Conceptualizing civil society in terms of CSI privatizes it, leaving the state as the only public authority and fails to reckon with the symbiotic relationship between the liberal state and capitalism.[96] For Alexander, those who did attempt to move beyond CSI – to distinguish capitalism from civil society (notably Habermas and Jean Cohen and Andrew Arato) – failed to conceptualize how civil society both drew on and yet was also distinct from arenas such as culture, religion, ethnicity, and the market.[97] They insisted on too great a separation between the rational discourse that constituted the public/civil sphere and the traditions that constitute social life.[98] Alexander notes:

> Private property, markets, family life, and religious ideals might all be necessary at some point or another to create the capacities of the civil sphere, but they are by no means sufficient to sustain it. Rejecting the reductionism of CSII, but also the diffuse inclusiveness of CSI, we must develop a third approach to civil society, one that reflects both the empirical and normative problems of contemporary life.[99]

He calls this civil society III (CSIII) and suggests: "We need to understand civil society as a sphere that can be analytically independent, empirically differentiated, and morally more universalistic vis-à-vis the state and the market and from other social spheres as well."[100] We will need to question some of the implications of Alexander's position outlined in this statement, in particular the assertion of a clear boundary between civil society and other spheres. However, Alexander's account of civil society does avoid flat, homogenizing conceptions of "the social" and thereby circumvents Arendt's critique of the social – and by implication, civil society – as a depoliticized sphere.[101] Moreover, CSIII opens a space beyond simplistic pro- or antistate positions to ones that envisage how the state is both part of the problem and an important means of defense against the liquefying effects of the global financial markets. This dynamic will be explored in greater detail in Chapter 8.

Within his account of CSIII, Alexander conceptualizes civil society as:

> A solidary sphere, in which a certain kind of universalizing community comes to be culturally defined and to some degree institutionally enforced. To the degree that this solidary community exists, it is exhibited and sustained by public opinion, deep

cultural codes, distinctive organizations – legal, journalistic and associational – and such historically specific interactional practices as civility, criticism, and mutual respect. Such a civil community can never exist as such; it can only be sustained to one degree or another. It is always limited by, and interpenetrated with, the boundary relations of other, noncivil spheres.[102]

As suggested in the quote, the division for Alexander is not between public and private but between civil and noncivil spheres. The civil sphere is to be distinguished from the spheres of economic cooperation and competition, family life (which at times Alexander extends to include all forms of "primordial community" such as ethnicity, kinship, and clan), and what he identifies as the unitary sphere of intellectual and "religious" interaction and exchange.[103] The logic of Alexander's position means the state, and its administrative-bureaucratic processes, constitutes a fourth, noncivil sphere. As he put it:

States are, of course, essential, but they are, in their modern forms, simply Hobbesian organizations that have succeeded in monopolizing the means of violence and, thereby, in creating societal pacification. As such, states have nothing to do with justice in the democratic sense, but everything to do with order, with creating public, abstract, and universalizing standards that allow efficient, top-down, bureaucratic control. ... [S]tates provide arenas for rational, power-oriented actors. Without a vast complex of moral-related communicative and regulative institutions stationed on the boundaries of this arena, struggles for state power remain amoral and instrumental.[104]

As the quote suggests, distinctive symbolic frameworks, discourses, constructions of power relations, and patterns of interaction and interdependency regulate the state and constitute other spheres. For Alexander, even though the civil sphere depends on and is determined by its relationship to noncivil spheres such as the family and the economy, it has a relative autonomy – which means it can be studied in its own terms.[105] This is basically right, but Alexander tends to overemphasize the autonomy of the civil sphere. There is a constant danger in any such account of reifying particular spheres rather than seeing them as specific ways of institutionalizing and organizing human relationships that are then interlaced and interdependent with other institutionalizations. What has to be faced in the modern period is the extent of differentiation and specialization. What reification does, particularly in relation to the market, is grant a false autonomy and priority to one sphere so it is seen to generate its own patterns of sociality unaccountable to wider considerations. To avoid the problem of reification, my own position is that the sense in which the autonomy of the civil sphere is emphasized needs toning down. While the civil sphere is more than the sum of its parts, like the convergence area of a Venn diagram, it is not a wholly distinct sphere; rather, it is both related to and interpenetrated by, as well as differentiated from, other spheres [see Figure 6.1]. Civil society is constituted as the nexus of convergence and communication through which other spheres discover their limits and possibilities. At the same time, each sphere is a distinct yet mutually constitutive and co-inhering arena of communication

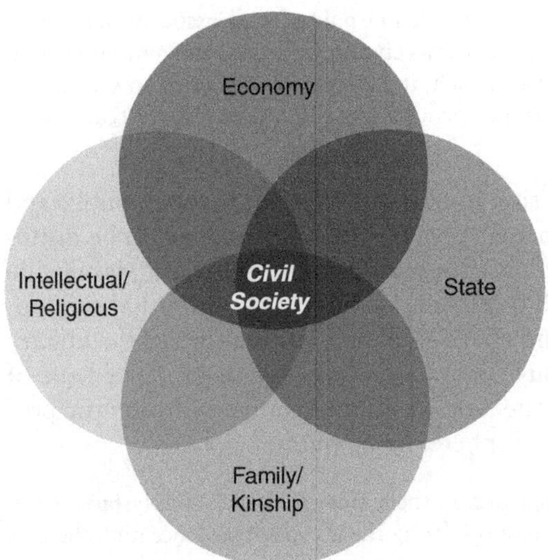

FIGURE 6.1. Venn diagram of civil society as a nexus of communication.

and responsibility in which humans take up the tasks, offices, and vocations through which we may discover others as neighbors.

Like Hegel, Alexander envisages noncivil spheres as having particularistic and sectional ends rather than universalistic and societal ones. Unlike Hegel, for whom the state was the arena through which universal solidarity was actualized, Alexander argues that civil society is that realm in which solidarity across difference emerges. However, in keeping with a well-established tradition of political thought from Hobbes and Rousseau onward, Alexander is too quick to see other realms as overly sectional. Other spheres have different practices for building links across difference. The administrative-bureaucratic procedures of the state create certain kinds of connection, whereas the contracts and exchanges of the market create others; religions (whether universalistic and missiological in orientation or not) can establish ways and means for building up a shared life with those not of the same faith, whereas kinship and clan networks create complex forms of linkage and obligation across difference through marriage, the obligations of hospitality, and patterns of gift exchange. Conversely, all of these spheres are comprised of hierarchies of value and structure that often conflict with the processes of building up a common life that connects all spheres and interests, and the relational patterns and practices of each sphere can be sources of division and disaggregation. The civil sphere is the point of convergence, cooperation, and communication that emerges out of, builds connections between, and upholds the specificities of the different spheres; in short, it is a form of the commons. When patterns of solidarity amid diversity break down there is a need for "civil repair": public acts that are designed to reweave relationship across difference and rebuild broad-based forms of solidarity and trust. The civil sphere is constituted by those processes and practices that can enable civil repair; that is, patterns of communication and sociality that facilitate the emergence of a common life. Democratic politics of the kind exemplified in BBCO is a way of "binding and loosing" each sphere so appropriate differentiation and interdependence is maintained between them.[106] It helps reconstitute the conditions of human flourishing through enabling judgments about when and what is alienated or broken apart, and therefore needs binding, and when and what is in bondage or falsely tied together, and thus needs loosing. It is a means of preventing the overdetermination of one or another of the spheres by a different sphere and the claiming of a false autonomy by one or more of the spheres. Moreover, as part of the civil sphere, democratic politics can be a means of "neighboring": that is, countering the dynamics of exclusion, whereby the other emerges as an enemy, and erasure, whereby the otherness of the other is denied or subjugated.

The process of binding and loosing entails noncivil spheres providing resources of critique and repair for the civil sphere and conversely, the civil sphere at times "invading" other spheres in order to demand certain kinds of reforms or change within them.[107] By this reading the living wage and the responsible lending initiative drew on the familial and religious/intellectual spheres to repair the civil sphere, whereas feminist groups draw from the civil sphere to critique and repair the familial and religious/intellectual sphere. Whether one sees the civil sphere as distinct (as Alexander does) or as a nexus of convergence and communication (as I do), what one can point to is how there is a reciprocal relation between the civil sphere and other spheres when it comes to civil repair. For Alexander, the civil sphere is about realizing more extensive forms of solidarity that create points of connection and relationship beyond particular ties. These can be threatened when one sphere or another comes to dominate all others and thereby begins to dissolve the very resources of critique and repair necessary to holding such domination in check.[108]

Domination can occur when the codes, practices, bodily proprieties, and interpretative frameworks of one sphere overdetermine another sphere. This can be seen, for example, when a family or university becomes remodeled and managed as a business and the goods intrinsic to family life or academia are delegitimized and corroded. On Alexander's account, in order to repair the distorting and disaggregating dominance of the economic sphere, people must act in order to:

> broadcast appeals through the communicative institutions of civil society; organize social movements demanding justice through its networks and public spaces; and create civil associations, such as trade unions, that demand fairness to employees. Sometimes they employ their space in civil society to confront economic institutions and elites directly, winning concessions in face-to-face negotiations. At other times, they make use of such regulatory institutions as parties, voting, and law to create civil power and to force the state to intervene in economic life on their behalf.[109]

However, against CSII, what is true of the economic sphere can apply to other spheres as well through processes of cultural production. What is outlined here refines and extends Polanyi's conception of the double movement and extends it to a more generalized process of civil repair. This process can be political or antipolitical, radical or conservative. And just as one sphere can dominate another, so the processes and practices of civil repair can be, and often are, monopolized by particular interests or groups and thereby used to project messages of civil competence and incompetence that favor one section of the population, such as whites over blacks.

The modified form of Alexander's conception of civil society developed here provides an account of what "reweaving civil society" entails, one that echoes and illuminates the experience of BBCO. For Alexander, processes of civil repair result in forms of "universalizing solidarity." However, Alexander avoids a Whiggish sense of historical progress by making clear that the civil sphere can be suppressed as well as enhanced. He steers clear also of a Hegelian logic that would make civil repair and the corrective effects of civil power an immanent and inherent sociological and historical process. As he puts it: "civil repair is not preordained but contingent."[110] Yet, instead of Alexander's "universalizing solidarity," I talk of a common life and the pursuit of goods in common as this better reflects the political nature of civil society.

Underdeveloped in Alexander's account is the way in which the resources of critique and repair within the civil sphere draw from multiple traditions and their respective beliefs and practices. His normative universal ideals seem to be self-constituting and to exist apart from particular traditions of belief and practice. In short, Alexander lacks a sufficient account of the interrelationship between tradition, virtue, and political action in the process of civil repair and in the formation of the civil sphere more generally. There is a danger that Alexander is so focused on the structure, processes, and form of civil society that he forgets that a repaired and virtuous civil society can only be brought about by loving and virtuous people. As Martin Buber notes, in relation to debates about the best way to bring about real social, economic, and political change:

> [t]wo views concerning the way stand irrevocably opposed to each other. The one demands that one begin by changing the "relations" [structures of production or power], for only out of their being different can a change of men and their relationships to one another arise. The other explains that the new orderings and institutions in the place of the old will not change one particle of life so long as they are carried by unchanged persons. This alternative is false. One must begin at both ends at once; otherwise nothing can succeed. What new relations really are, even in their operation, depends upon what kind of human existence is put into them; but how shall a new humanity persist on earth if it is not preserved and confirmed in new orderings? The world of man without the soul of it in addition is no human world; but also the soul of man without the world in addition is no human soul. At both ends at once therefore – but that it may avail, a third is needed that cannot be among us without the breath from another sphere: the

spirit. ... To me, it is as if two choruses stride about the arena there, the chorus that calls for the orderings and the chorus that calls for the men; their call will not reach its goal until they begin to sing in one: *Veni creator spiritus*.[111]

Echoing Buber's insight, if institutions – whether civil, noncivil, or anti-civil – are to become capable of civil repair there is a need to pursue, simultaneously, changed persons and changed structures.[112] The experience of BBCO suggests that this interpersonal and structural civil repair depends on (1) the formation of virtuous people capable of exercising and demanding political judgment, (2) the build up of relational power and trust as the means through which to mobilize the institutions of civil repair, (3) organizers who can be a catalyst for building a common life between diverse institutions and orientating these associations to public action, and (4) interpretative communities that have the capacity to act independently of and call on elites to change.[113] These four ingredients are vital to generating the creative spirit of change to which Buber points. The symbiosis of virtue and structural change raises the question of how Alexander conceptualizes the role of religions as traditions of belief and practice that help or hinder the formation of virtuous people in relation to civil society.

It could be contended that Alexander's discourse of multiculturalism is a trope for discussing religious diversity and Islam in particular.[114] For example, his fellow sociologist Bryan Turner asserts: "The unspoken assumption of Alexander's study of the civil sphere and its politics is that the public remains a secular domain."[115] Alexander refutes this criticism pointing to the centrality of his case study of how Jews became incorporated into the U.S. civil sphere as encapsulating how to build a common life between diverse religious groups without demanding conformity to superordinate secular norms.[116] The account of BBCO given here and the conceptualization of interfaith relations as a civic practice in many ways exemplifies Alexander's arguments by pointing to the need for and possibility of drawing from multiple traditions within the civil sphere in order to secure, repair, and expand it as the arena of democratic politics; that is, the sphere in which we negotiate a common life and identify and pursue goods in common amid diverse interests. Turner asks: "Can universalism be a sacred rather than a profane domain and if so can it tolerate a struggle between competing gods?"[117] The analysis of BBCO suggests the answer is that yes, under certain conditions and mediated by particular kinds of practice, the constitution of the civil sphere can "tolerate a struggle between competing gods" and necessarily involves the "sacred" as well as the "profane," but also that there is a need to resist establishing false dichotomies between sacred and profane as Turner's question implicitly does.

The account given here of civil society and the role of democratic politics as a form of civil repair can reconcile both "realist" and "idealist" concerns about democracy. Realist critiques of democratic theory tend to revolve around three concerns: (1) the need to take seriously deep differences between citizens and how these differences can be mobilized to exclude and stigmatize others, (2) that people act for reasons of self-interest and material benefit and not in order to fulfill ideals, and (3) that there are enormous asymmetries of power that inhibit the ability of many to act.[118] Meanwhile, idealists worry that without some kind of shared commitment to ideals compatible with democracy, democracy itself is impossible.[119] The account of civil society given here can encompass all these concerns. Civil society is a sphere plagued by the *libido dominandi* so that even universalistic ideals become mechanisms of exclusion and where the pursuit of particular loves and desires generates conflict and competition. Yet, as the analysis of BBCO suggests, civil society is also a context in which neighborliness is extended, civic virtue is realized, and people act together on mutual interests to effect change. The civil sphere is thus a point of communication and convergence in which different normative commitments and forms of life are negotiated and contested in dynamic interdependent relationships with each other. The Alinsky approach to community organizing represents a means through which to forge an aspiration and sense of shared responsibility for a common life while also allowing what is common to be conceptualized in terms intrinsic to particular traditions of belief and practice.

FROM CIVIL SOCIETY TO A BODY POLITIC

At the heart of civil society, Alexander identifies a binary logic. Following Carl Schmitt, I call this the friend-enemy distinction. For Alexander, there is no civil discourse that does not conceptualize the world into those who deserve inclusion and those who do not.[120] Nation-states, and the civil societies embedded within them, divide the world into those who do and those who do not deserve freedom and communal support. If we analyze debates about the deserving and undeserving poor, immigrants and refugees, public recognition of same-sex relations, abortion, or responses to Islam in the West, we can see this binary logic at work and how it divides the world into those who are considered worthy of inclusion in the civil sphere and those who are not. This binary logic is an inescapable feature of civil societies that take form within nation-states.[121] What Alexander analyzes is how universal ideals at the heart of democratic civil societies within a bounded polity inherently create friend-enemy distinctions, but also how what counts as civil and uncivil and who is in and who is out is constantly under negotiation and contested. For Alexander, the regulative institutions of the civil sphere are public opinion, voting, office, political parties, the mass media, law, social movements, and civil associations. It is through these that the civil sphere regulates access to state power. As Alexander notes, "[t]o do so, [the civil sphere] constitutes a new and different kind of power of its own. To the degree that society is democratic, to that degree regulatory institutions are the gatekeepers of political power, it is civil power that opens and closes the gate."[122] This may seem implausible in relation to, say, the banks, yet even the financial services industry has to engage in the civil sphere in order to capture policy and secure the domination of its interests. Insofar as civil power becomes fragmented and unequally distributed, then noncivil spheres such as the state, the economy, or kinship structures will function in a hegemonic, anticivil way. Hence the need to reweave civil society in order to strengthen and renew the mechanisms of "civil power" defined as the regulatory institutions of law, party politics, office, cooperative institutions and associations, public opinion, media, and so forth.[123]

A better term than "civil society," one that highlights the need for "civil" power, is the more ancient one of the "body politic." To talk of "civil society" is to underplay the political conflicts and power relations inherent in the processes and practices necessary for forming a common life between different conceptions of the good and also the paradoxical way in which such conflicts can generate a living, interconnected body of people. Yet, as my discussion of Alexander should indicate, my use of the term "body politic" in place of the term "civil society" should not be heard as advocating the kind of organic vision of society in which each part is subordinated to a larger whole. The body politic is a constructed, fractious, and fragile artifice that requires something like the practices of community organizing in order to constitute and reconstitute it out of its disparate elements. It is a constant work in progress rather than a spontaneous, natural phenomenon.[124] The internal dynamics of the body politic can be brought to the fore by examining further the friend-enemy relations at work within it.

THE BODY POLITIC AND THE FRIEND-ENEMY DISTINCTION

The way in which universalistic ideals generate binary friend-enemy distinctions is something Schmitt identified. Schmitt conceives of the political as determined by the friend-enemy antithesis.[125] As Schmitt puts it,

> The political enemy need not be morally evil or aesthetically ugly; he need not appear as an economic competitor, and it may even be advantageous to engage with him in business transactions. But he is, nevertheless, the other, the stranger; and it is sufficient for his nature that he is, in a specifically intense way, existentially something different and alien, so that in the extreme case conflicts with him are possible.[126]

Otherness for Schmitt represents a latent threat to one's own way of life because it represents a form of life that can replace or supersede one's own. This threat becomes operative when the other becomes an adversary who "intends to negate his opponent's way of life and therefore must be repulsed or fought in order to preserve one's own form of existence."[127] For Schmitt, while political conflict is inherent between humans there is at the same time a universal human society of which all are members. However, we can only come to this universality dialectically through conflictual encounter with others. This helps explain Schmitt's insistence that, although they represent a threat, the other/enemy should not be demonized, treated as evil, or rendered as subhuman and so outside the human community.[128] The distinction between political and moral judgment could be seen as Manichean, yet it appears to be a measure to ensure the moral status of the other while also recognizing the existential nature of the conflict between different forms of life.[129] Schmitt does not therefore separate the moral and the political as liberalism does.[130] Rather, a condition and possibility of the political is the cohabitation by friends and enemies in the same moral universe.

Schmitt saw the friend-enemy distinction only as operative between states. A central point of contention for Schmitt is denying the plausibility of pluralist and consociative conceptions of sovereignty.[131] For Schmitt, it is the "indirect" powers of the church and of interest groups, which in his view are reiterated in the nineteenth century as modern political parties, trade unions, social organizations, and what he calls the "forces of society," acting independently of the state under the banner of freedom of conscience, that Schmitt points to as the primary threat to the indivisible and transcendent sovereignty of the state.[132] Schmitt sees the real threat coming not from an overmighty state but from over-powerful groups whose rivalry would destroy the political order.

The analysis of civil society and BBCO developed here provides an alternative to Schmitt's denigration of "indirect" powers and his claim that "only states, and not just any domestic and international association, are the bearers of politics."[133] Contrary to Schmitt, what applies to state power must by implication relate to a people or any corporate entity utilizing the same means to exercise political power over others – whether this association or corporation exists within or without a state.[134] And Alexander's account of civil power as the gatekeeper of state power helps us see how civil society is also a sphere of political relations. A more pluralistic, consociational account of sovereignty of the kind Schmitt criticizes in Gierke and the Guild Socialists allows us to use Schmitt's insights in relation to how the friend-enemy distinction operates within the body politic and not just in international relations. Such a consociational conception of sovereignty will be developed in Chapter 7.

Where Schmitt continues to be helpful is in his account of the friend-enemy distinction and how this enriches a conception of the body politic.[135] Each universal horizon or discourse establishes a different friend-enemy distinction within the civil sphere; thus, for example, the discourses of human rights have a different binary logic to that of the Islamic Ummah or Christian eschatology. Divisions between "we, the people"/everyone else, bourgeois/proletariat, rational/irrational, saved/unsaved, and so on, have distinct temporal and spatial divisions built into them and create different formations of politics as a negotiation of a common life between friends and enemies. These same universal horizons also provide resources of critique and repair to draw from when seeking to credientialize and legitimize one's claims by reference to cherished self-images, values, and ideals circulating in the body politic. For example, the responsible lending campaign in the United Kingdom could draw from Christian, Jewish, and Islamic Scriptures, the story of the Labour movement, liberal ideals of fairness and equality, and neoliberal ideals of freedom of choice and competition in order to communicate in the body politic as part of its attempt to limit the domination of "money power."

Politics is the negotiation of a common life between – and at times the reconciliation of – these divergent and multiple kinds of friend-enemy distinction and the visions of the good they instantiate. Rival universalisms, and their respective friend-enemy distinctions, are the basis of the plurality that Arendt, following Aristotle, sees as the condition of politics. The body politic is a mélange of these binary distinctions generated by universalistic horizons. The dominance of one or another sphere (state, religious-intellectual, familial, or economic) can lead to countermovements that mobilize particular constructions of the friend-enemy distinctions and these countermovements, as the history of populism suggests, can be antipolitical and political at the same time. The body politic is thus a profoundly ambivalent arena, a field of wheat and tares, capable of displaying good, evil, and indifference in equal measure. Wily wisdom is needed in order to navigate this ambiguous and ever-changing environment.

Envisaging citizenship as involving neighborliness rather than "public friendship" means it can encompass the need to identify and address constructively the dynamic interplay of friend-enemy relations necessary to sustaining a democratic body politic. Being a neighbor does not necessitate being either friends or denying differences and conflicts, but neither does it mean being wholly defined or overdetermined by them. Being a neighbor entails recognizing enmity and difference (and their consequences and costs) while at the same time acknowledging that "we" exist in a common world of meaning and action and then acting in ways that broker a common life amid enmity and move toward reconciliation and reciprocity. As will be explored in Chapter 8, such neighborly gestures can range from radical kenotic dispossession to mutual aid. As discussed in Chapters 4 and 5, BBCO displays something of how friend-enemy relations might be addressed constructively so as to forge a more neighborly common life.

The ambivalence of the body politic and the ways in which it is riven with friend-enemy relations born out of rival loves is a necessary counter to the organicism with which the term is often associated. My more "bio-political" vision of the body politic can be contrasted first with an Aristotelian organicism that sees the body politic as a polity governed by natural laws capable of being apprehended by the virtuous statesman who thus possesses the appropriate capacity to reason rightly and make good judgments about how to direct the body; second, with a Newtonian organicism that sees the body politic as a mechanism with internal systems, principles, and procedures governing its actions that the social scientist and technocrat can measure and mold on the basis of the right method and evidence in order to ensure the machine runs smoothly; and lastly, with a Humean (or better, Darwinian) organicism in which the body politic is an ecosystem in which atomized and disaggregated elements, each pursuing their own self-interest, generate a spontaneous order that seeks equilibrium – an order in which the remit for political rule is largely limited to maintaining the rules defining property rights and intervening to make minor, incremental improvements.[136]

The account given here of the relationship between the friend-enemy distinction and civil society as the arena of politics (and hence the use of the term "body politic" in place of civil society) is clarified by Mouffe's distinction between "politics" and "the political." As she puts it:

> By "the political," I refer to the dimension of hostility and antagonism that is an ever-present possibility in all human society, antagonism that can take many different forms and emerge in diverse social relations. "Politics," by contrast, refers to the ensemble of practices, discourses, and institutions that seek to establish a certain order and to organize human coexistence under conditions that are always potentially conflictual because they are affected by the dimension of "the political." This conception, which attempts to keep together the two meanings of *polemos* and *polis* present in the idea of politics, is, I believe, crucial for democratic politics.[137]

I see her distinction between politics and the political as complementing and further specifying my distinction between "political" and "antipolitical" given in Chapter 1. According to Mouffe's terms, my conception of "political" as that which seeks to establish a common life in relationship with others is better termed *politics*. Politics is the attempt to construct a common life by moving beyond the friend-enemy distinction through processes that respect the otherness of the other, and recognizes the conflicts of identity, vision, and interest between friends and enemies. What is *political* refers to attempts to build a common life without moving beyond the friend-enemy distinctions by attempting one-sided determinations of the terms and conditions of a common life through processes of exclusion and erasure such as coercive assimilation, subjugation, or sheer indifference. But what is missing from Mouffe's distinction is a third term: the "antipolitical." The *antipolitical* denotes that which refuses the possibilities of a common life and is orientated toward personal or communal withdrawal from public life so as to be free to pursue selfish interests rather than public mutual interests. What is needed to uphold politics in the face of the political and the antipolitical are forms of public action that do not deny friend-enemy distinctions or try and transmute them into some other kind of category such as a commercial, moral, or aesthetic relation, and thereby depluralize and depoliticize the creation of a common life. But at the same time, if friend-enemy distinctions become too cemented, then, as Schmitt rightly discerned, civil society becomes civil war by other means. Rather, *the need is to mitigate and mollify the hostility, suspicion, and fear intrinsic to political and antipolitical responses to the other through the practices of democratic politics that generate a more neighborly polity*. As portrayed in the previous chapters, community organizing exemplifies a process that enables this to happen. It constitutes a practice that converts the absolute antagonism of friend-enemy relations – an antagonism that plagues many forms of populism – into paradoxical ones wherein conflict is the precursor of a common life. In light of Mouffe's account we can more properly distinguish between a populist politics and political and antipolitical populism.

For Mouffe, participation in a pluralistic democratic politics of the kind I am arguing is exemplified in BBCO enables one to see one's opponent not as an enemy to be destroyed, but as an adversary whose existence is legitimate and must be constructively engaged. In Mouffe's account the political and politics entail two different kinds of relations: one of "antagonism" between enemies – that is, "persons who have no common symbolic space" – and the other of "agonism" between adversaries or "friendly enemies" – that is, "persons who are friends because they share a common symbolic space but also enemies because they want to organize this common symbolic space in a different way."[138] As Mouffe puts it: "We could say that the aim of democratic politics is to transform an 'antagonism' into an 'agonism.'"[139] Although agreeing with Mouffe up to this point, the account given here of BBCO points beyond what she calls "agonistic pluralism" to the possibility of a common life politics, a possibility that Mouffe rejects.[140]

With Mouffe I assume a common life is always politically constructed. However, the difference is that for Mouffe, the order that arises though agonism is only ever a temporary settlement; a truce in an otherwise prior and ineradicable conflict. By my account, the conversion of the political and antipolitical into politics is the way to participate in a common world of meaning and action that always, already exists yet which, because we are fallible, fallen, and finite creatures, we misconstrue, disaggregate, and degrade. The shift from antagonism to agonism is not a defensive measure, as it is for Mouffe, but a generative one: we need others – and their otherness – so that we ourselves may participate rightly as part of a whole, a whole made up of differences in relation. These differences in relation constitute the body politic. Yet, given the epistemologically relative and finite nature of our knowledge of the whole, any human construction of the whole will place someone on the outside. Although fallible and often fugitive, epiphanies of wholeness are possible and these moments are transfigurative events that open up new conditions and possibilities for a common life through which those on the outside may be included.

THE SECULARITY OF THE BODY POLITIC

A related point of distinction between my own account and that of Mouffe's is her a priori rejection of what she calls "religious fundamentalism" from inclusion in the kind of democratic politics she articulates. Mouffe is committed also to a strict separation of church and state.[141] As should be clear, in contrast to Mouffe, I see "religious fundamentalists" and religion more generally as just as capable of being the bearer of a democratic politics as any other group. Moreover, alongside Mouffe's intuitions about religious groups converting political differences into Manichean conflicts between good and evil must be laid the tendency of secularist utopian and perfectionist ideologies to remake the world through immanent projects of salvation. These ideologies struggle at least equally, if not more so, to encompass the shift from antagonism to agonism. By contrast, the ability to imagine an eschatological end to antagonism can make possible the conversion of the political and the antipolitical into politics because this world is not all there is and so does not have to be the bearer of all meaning and purpose. If politics is simply a contingent, this-worldly, "secular" endeavor that is nevertheless located within a cosmos that has meaning and purpose, then I can relinquish control trusting that the other and I exist in what Mouffe calls a "common symbolic space." I can thereby compromise without compromising the end of history. As a fallen and finite human who participates with others in a penultimate yet common world of meaning and action, I can trust that the other may well have something to teach me about how to live well and that even if I profoundly disagree with them, a common life is still possible: in short, we might not be friends but we can be good neighbors. When religiously motivated actors do convert material conflicts into Manichean conflicts of good and evil and refuse to either listen to and learn from others or reject the possibility of a common life in the face of disagreement it is because they are not faithful enough. They are themselves overinvested in this-worldly projects of salvation. The theological term for this kind of overinvestment is idolatry and in the Jewish, Christian, and Islamic traditions, idolatry is unequivocally condemned as sinful.

DEMOCRACY AND LEADERSHIP

As already noted, Schmitt was very critical of advocates of pluralist and consociational visions of democracy. Moreover, he completely ignored the historical experience of countries such as the Netherlands and Switzerland and the successful development of pluralist and consociational forms of political order in those contexts.[142] Yet his concerns about the negative and destructive impact of "indirect power" on the liberal-constitutional state were not misplaced. He lived through a period in Germany when "indirect powers" destroyed the condition of their possibility. As he notes, this happened when the "wonderful armature of a modern state" and "the organisations of individual freedom" were used "like knives by anti-individualistic forces to cut up the leviathan and divide his flesh among themselves."[143] However, as Schmitt himself came to realize, his proposed authoritarian solution of reasserting sovereign power under strong leadership and closing down the civil sphere was no solution at all. Instead of fulfilling its duty to protect humans from being wolves to each other in exchange for their obedience, the state itself became the wolf.

Rather than an authoritarian solution, what is needed are ways of building a common life between diverse groups and interests while recognizing the threat each poses and equally the ways in which universalistic ideals themselves have an exclusionary logic that can be deployed to code certain groups – blacks, women, Muslims, the poor, and so forth – as uncivil and incapable of political responsibility. Moreover, Schmitt was not completely wrong about the need for leadership. His fault was to invest it in the one instead of distributing it to the many. Arendt's advocacy of "democratic elites" shares Schmitt's insight that, if politics rather than either proceduralism or the dissolution of political life into civil war is the way to address conflict, then there is a need for some to exercise leadership and responsible judgment.[144] As noted earlier, the place to learn leadership and how to make good judgments is through the experience of ruling and being ruled in cooperative institutions and forms of association. BBCO represents one such means for identifying and training leaders, building reciprocal relationships between them, and instilling a commitment to democratic politics as the way of negotiating a common life. As a constellation of practices, it embodies the claim that it is not a strong state, a messianic leader, or a rational administration that can provide a sure foundation for a peaceable and humane political order, but only a common life politics that combines a broad base of local leaders and meaningful relationship between diverse institutions and their often competing interests and visions of the good. As such, BBCO is a form of civil repair that incorporates diverse groups while also upholding distinct identities and substantive visions of the good, naming and engaging but not being bound by friend-enemy distinctions. The paradoxical aim of BBCO is to use wily wisdom, multiple institutions with different visions of the good, and nonviolent conflict to convert antagonism into a constructive common life.

THRESHOLD

This chapter opened by identifying how community organizing was driven by practices rather than theory. It shares this characteristic with a number of other forms of democratic politics, notably the early labor and civil rights movements and contemporary anarchism. Being practice based rather than theory driven means that BBCO is more open to the participation of multiple traditions and to its own configuration within them. The foundation of a practice-based democratic politics is practical rather than theoretical reason. Yet the ability to generate political judgments based on practical reason was seen to be what was threatened and undermined by modern cities where a crisis motif was used to justify circumventing the generation of democratic political judgments. BBCO was identified as a response to the conditions of urban politics and the need for ordinary people to demand and contribute to judgments that affect them. BBCO does this by generating relational power in order to contest the domination and determination of what constitutes "common sense" by a narrow range of interests. The institutional basis of BBCO is crucial not only for generating this relational power, but also for providing the arenas in which people learn how to rule and be ruled and so are able to make good judgments based on practical reason/wily wisdom. The religious institutions that make up the majority of the membership of the IAF point to the importance of the connections between training in the virtues, practical reasoning, and the proper relating of means and ends in democratic politics. Contrary to those who separate utility and solidarity, BBCO as a practice of politics extols the need for political judgments to incorporate a strategic, cunning dimension if they are to be considered good.

The Aristotelian account of politics, attention to wily wisdom, and the need for citizens who are connected to some form of virtue tradition and cooperative self-organization in order to make good political judgments outlined in the first section was then related to a Schmittian account of the political via a particular conception of civil society as the body politic. The work of Alexander was drawn from and adapted to historically locate and conceptualize the emergence of civil society. This conception of civil society enabled a consideration of how BBCO constitutes a form of civil repair that restores relations of trust and solidarity across difference and thereby prevents civil society disintegrating into civil war. Through linking the account of civil society to Schmitt's conception of the friend-enemy distinction, an account of the body politic was developed so as to allow for the full ambivalence not only of the market and state but also to account for civil society itself. This ambivalence rests on how the universal ideals that are mobilized to generate solidarity simultaneously generate forms of friend-enemy relations. Drawing from the work of Mouffe, democratic politics was identified as the means by which to convert political and antipolitical friend-enemy relations into those that could sustain a common life and which, at the same time, respect and contend with the otherness of the other that one encounters within the body politic.

Questions about the priority of social relations, training in the virtues, and the experience of ruling and being ruled necessary to form good political judgments that integrate strategic and moral considerations raise further questions about the possibility of forming a body politic under conditions of economic globalization. Having developed in this chapter an account of civil society as the body politic, democratic political judgment as a form of practical reason, and a common-life politics as the neighboring of friend-enemy relations, and having seen something of what this can all look like in practice in previous chapters, we turn in Chapters 7 and 8 to consider how what has been said so far may be extended so as to reconceptualize the nature of democratic citizenship in the context of the sovereign nation-state and the globalized economy.

7

Sovereignty and Consociational Democracy

Broad-based community organizing (BBCO) is seen as anomalous in contemporary politics because it operates with institutions, traditions, and customary practices. To understand the significance of its approach and why it stands in contradiction to so much contemporary political thought, we have to locate it within broader conceptions of sovereignty. When we do so we discover that the standard view is to see sovereignty as indivisible, monistic, and transcendent. The implication of such a view is that autonomous or semiautonomous corporate bodies necessarily appear as a threat to the indivisible and transcendent authority of the political sovereign. The primary corporate body that has been a lightning rod through which this sense of threat is projected is the church and, in the wake of religious plurality, other religious groups. Yet religious groups are not alone as being perceived as a threat to the cohesion and stability of the sovereign state; other forms of corporate body, notably trade unions, suffer the same suspicion. In this chapter, I will argue that a view of sovereignty as derived from and distributed among a number of sources is both closer to the reality of the world as it exists and is open to forms of consociational democratic practice of the kind that broad-based community organizing represents. Having surveyed debates about the nature of sovereignty and defined more clearly what is meant by the term "consociational democracy," not only can we delineate a more precise, theoretical definition of community organizing, but also, we can better understand the incomprehension of BBCO as a political form by external observers that we witnessed in earlier chapters.

INDIVISIBLE, MONISTIC, AND TRANSCENDENT CONCEPTIONS OF SOVEREIGNTY

We return to the anomalous nature of BBCO within the context of Anglo-American liberal democracy. To understand something of the challenge that

BBCO, as a form of consociational democracy, poses to standard accounts of democratic citizenship, we must locate it within broader accounts of the relationship between sovereignty and citizenship. At the same time, we can excavate the simultaneously "secular" and theological nature of discussions of political order so as to further challenge simplistic assumptions about the relationship between religion and politics in modernity.

Modern European thought on sovereignty sees itself as superseding earlier medieval understandings of political authority. On closer inspection, however, modern European conceptions of sovereignty trace over and reproduce many aspects of earlier conceptions. Against overly disjunctive readings of the relationship between past and present political thinking, Quentin Skinner and other historians of political thought have prevailed in their arguments that we cannot understand modern political concepts without understanding their foundations in the medieval and early modern period. Carl Schmitt went beyond making a point about intellectual history and contended that all modern political concepts are secularized theological concepts and so continue to carry a trace of their original imprint. In the wake of Schmitt, Jacques Derrida and Giorgio Agamben have done much to trace this theological imprint in modern notions of political sovereignty. For Derrida there is always "some unavowed theologeme" at work in even the most secularized societies, and when it comes to claims to sovereignty, we cannot escape the inherently theological dimension to such claims.[1] On Derrida's account we have not replaced God with something new. Rather, we have simply displaced God but left the structural analogy intact so that in God's place is put an autonomous, sovereign individual with an indivisible will who issues laws to him- or herself. Parallel to notions of God's sovereignty and nature, what is sovereign is taken to be what is legitimate and moral. Yet the paradox is that, at the very point at which the supreme sovereignty of the self-governing individual is posited, the individual is increasingly seen to be "bare life" (that is, life excluded from participation in and the protection of the rule of law) and who is subject to what Foucault calls "bio-politics" (the control of entire populations through numerous and diverse techniques for achieving the subjugation of bodies and the production of subjectivities consonant with a homogenized national political order).[2]

To make sense of the continuing theological imprint in modern conceptions of sovereignty some theologians and intellectual historians point to the emergence of voluntarism and nominalism.[3] The theologians John Duns Scotus (c. 1265–1308) and William of Ockham (c. 1288–1348) are identified as central to the shift from a participatory metaphysics to one in which God's sovereign will is the ultimate principle of being (voluntarism) and the adoption of the view that universals do not refer to real things but are merely mental concepts (nominalism). For example, John Milbank identifies Scotus and Ockham as the beginning point of a genealogy from which modern notions of individual and state sovereignty emerge. The shift to voluntarism and nominalism is a shift from seeing God as Logos (that is, as loving, relational and Trinitarian divine presence in whose created order humans can participate creatively through reason) to seeing God as a sovereign (a univocal being whose omnipotent will is unbounded, absolute, infinite and indivisible).[4] In the former, good order comes through right participation within the limits of creation and patterns of social relations that seek first communion with Father, Son, and Holy Spirit mediated through participation in Christ's body, the church.[5] In the latter view, order and social peace come through obedience and subordination to the sovereign and indivisible will of God and those who represent God on earth, whether pope or emperor, church or state. There then ensues a conflict between ecclesial and political authority over who is the true vicar of Christ on earth.[6]

Whether Scotus and Ockham really are the progenitors of more voluntaristic conceptions of sovereignty is open to debate.[7] However, what can be said is that when God is primarily understood as a willing agent who delegates his authority to a human representative, various solutions present themselves as to how to resolve the conflict between ecclesial and political authorities over whose sovereignty is supreme. One solution was to create not two swords, each of which has a coequal and reciprocal role in shaping the political order, but two distinct domains – "spiritual" and "secular" – within which ecclesial and political authorities exercise sovereign authority without threatening each other. This solution was not without precedent. Writing in the fifth century, Pope Gelasius outlined the basic position:

> Once the true priest-king entered on the stage of history, there was no ruler who assumed the name of priest, nor any priest who laid claim to the royal sceptre. For through the members of Christ, the true priest-king, partake of his nature, and so are said all-encompassingly to have assumed the two aspects of it ... he has mediated this privilege by an all encompassing manner of distributing it. Mindful of human weakness, as befits his care for his own, he had made a distinction between the two roles, assigning each its sphere of operation and its due respect. ... Christian emperors were to depend on priests for their eternal life, priests were to profit from imperial government for their historical existence. Spiritual activity must have distance from routine interruptions; so God's soldier does not involve himself in secular affairs, while those involved in secular affairs are seen to have no charge of divine affairs.[8]

However, for Gelasius what was envisaged was the independence of the church to decide its own affairs during what Augustine called the *saeculum*: the non-eschatological, historical order that exists between Christ's ascension and return. In the modern period, however, the "spiritual" becomes private and interiorized whereas the "secular" pertains to what is public and material (i.e., social, economic, and political) such that the body is ruled by the state whereas what happens to the soul is a "religious" and thereby immaterial matter.

Coming in the wake of the shift toward nominalism and voluntarism is the shift from complex or gothic space to simple space.[9] After the American and French Revolutions the paradigmatic modern polity is taken to be the republican nation-state whose citizens determine their own laws. Arguably, this paradigm has its origin in the conception of the "Hebrew Commonwealth" and the notion of the ideal polity being constituted by one people, one religion, and one law under God.[10] The bounded nation-state with a single law, single people, and indivisible and transcendent source of rule, which at the same time is unbounded in the exercise of its sovereign will within its own borders, contrasts with the complex and overlapping jurisdictions of medieval Christendom in which the sovereign authorities of the pope, emperor, kings, abbots, bishops, dukes, doges, mayors, and various forms of self-governing corporations were interwoven with each other and spanned disjunctive spaces (noncontiguous territories) and overlapping times (the eschatological and the *saeculum*). This kingdom, seemingly divided against itself, could be encompassed within an overarching vision of the providential ordering of the whole wherein each authority participated in and contributed to the governance of the single economy of God's kingdom.[11] The analogues of complex spaces were customary forms of measurement, evaluation, and practical reasoning that were "decidedly local, interested, contextual and historically specific" and were thereby highly resistant to centralized forms of either state administration and taxation or commercial exploitation.[12] But modern political thinkers began to view this mixed economy of political forms and customary practices with increasing incomprehension. In its stead, as Benjamin Constant observed when reflecting on Napoleon, "the conquerors of our days, peoples or princes, want their empires to possess a unified surface over which the superb eye of power can wander without encountering any inequality which hurts or limits its view. The same code of law, the same measures, the same rules, and if we could gradually get there, the same language; that is what is proclaimed as the perfection of the social organization.... The great slogan of the day is *uniformity.*"[13] The standardization of political space, time, law, and measurement was the prelude to homogenized conceptions of citizenship.[14]

In the shift to the nation-state as a singular and simple space with an indivisible and transcendent sovereign authority (whether monarchical or democratic), a key debating point was the legitimacy or otherwise of constitutional pluralism and in particular the status of the Germanic Imperial Constitution.[15] As commitment to singular constitutional forms gains preeminence, the Germanic Imperial Constitution – the most prominent vestigial form of medieval Christendom's complex space – comes to be seen as a problematic exception rather than a norm. In this regard, the Germanic Imperial Constitution has its analogue in the rejection and suppression of all forms of political order that derive their authority from a mesh of custom, tradition, and common law, whether they be the aboriginal forms of the Americas, Africa, and Australasia or the medieval forms of Europe. Behind the shift in the European context lies the rejection of Aristotelian political thought, which saw constitutional pluralism as the ideal: the idea that the best form of government involved monarchical, aristocratic, and democratic elements. Jean Bodin's *Les Six Livres de la République* (1578) is the prototype and catalyst for a rejection of Aristotle and a conception of sovereignty as indivisible, transcendent, and monistic.[16] Bodin directly attacks the Germanic Imperial Constitution. For Bodin, sovereignty is absolute by which he means that the sovereign must not be subject in any way to the commands of someone else.[17] Bodin can locate sovereignty in a single person, in the people, or in a section of the people. However, to combine these elements in a mixed constitution is "impossible and contradictory, and cannot even be imagined. For if sovereignty is indivisible … how could it be shared by a prince, the nobles, and the people at the same time."[18] He distinguishes sovereignty, which is indivisible, from governmental power, which can be divided and distributed to many parts – a distinction that flows into many streams of modern political thought. But, as Jacques Maritain noted in his critique of modern conceptions of sovereignty,

> [w]hen Jean Bodin says that the sovereign Prince is the image of God, this phrase must be understood in its full force, and means that the Sovereign – submitted to God, but accountable only to Him – transcends the political whole just as God transcends the cosmos. Either Sovereignty means nothing, or it means supreme power separate and transcendent – not at the peak but above the peak – and ruling the entire body politic *from above*. That is why this power is absolute (ab-solute, that is non-bound, separate) and consequently unlimited, as to its extension as well as to its duration, and unaccountable to anything on earth.[19]

For Carl Schmitt, this indivisible, monistic, and transcendent conception of sovereignty is to be celebrated not decried.[20] A counter voice to Bodin is that of the early seventeenth-century Dutch Protestant political thinker, Johannes Althusius. Althusius systemizes the medieval constitutional view and catalyzes the emergence of modern confederal and consociational views of sovereignty as constituted by the commonweal or body politic as a whole and not derived from a monistic source of sovereignty whose authority stands over and above the people and their forms of association.[21] For Althusius, it is the body politic that delegates authority "up" to the sovereign and not vice versa. However, with the defeat of absolutist monarchies and the passing of the ancien régime, republican and democratic self-government increasingly comes to be seen as the only form of legitimate (and God-given) rule. Such a form of rule could involve a separation of legislative, judicial, and executive elements, but sovereignty is still taken to be indivisible and derived from a monistic, Olympian source (e.g., the "general will" or the "nation"). Bodin rather than Althusius sets the course. It becomes a matter of common sense that "a Kingdome divided in itselfe cannot stand."[22] The theory of sovereignty and the political form of the nation-state come to mirror and justify each other. By contrast, for medieval constitutionalists, sovereignty was shared among all the estates in proportion to their contribution to the body politic, which, as a body, was necessarily made up of many parts and could be one and many or, echoing the Eucharistic body, catholic and distributed simultaneously.

What I hope is clear already from this brief sketch of developments in conceptions of political sovereignty is that it is at once a theological and "secular" story. But also, it is a story in which corporate forms of life other than the nation-state inherently emerge as problematic. The problem is not religion per se. Rather, the problem is one of how, when sovereignty is understood as transcendent and monistic, intermediate and autonomous groups must necessarily appear as a threat or rival. To excavate this dynamic further I turn now to three key thinkers who have shaped modern conceptions of the relationship between sovereignty and citizenship: Thomas Hobbes (1588–1679), Jean-Jacques Rousseau (1712–88), and Georg Wilhelm Friedrich Hegel (1770–1831).[23]

HOBBES, SCHMITT, AND THE SOVEREIGNTY OF THE ONE

Modern discussions of sovereignty operate in the shadow of Hobbes. Debates about the exegesis and context of Hobbes's own writing continue. However, I will focus less on the specifics of what Hobbes did or did not mean and the context of his work in seventeenth-century England and more on the reception of Hobbes in contemporary discussions. For this purpose, Carl Schmitt stands as a crucial figure. Schmitt both looks back to the constitutional debates of the sixteenth and seventeenth centuries out of which Hobbes emerged and stimulates a renewed attention to Hobbes in contemporary Continental philosophy.

Based on Schmitt's reading, the core purpose of the state for Hobbes is to protect its citizens. Conversely, the primary duty of the citizen is to obey the sovereign. As Schmitt puts it: "The *protego ergo obligo* is the *cogito ergo sum* of the state.... [H]uman nature as well as divine right demands its inviolable observation."[24] Thus, the relationship between citizens and the sovereign is a reciprocal one: the citizen gives obedience and receives protection in return. The obedience is given to an abstract sovereign who can be monarchical, democratic, or aristocratic in form but whose sovereignty is absolute, indivisible, and transcends the immanent political order. For Schmitt, the mark of sovereignty is the ability to decide the exception. He contends that for Hobbes: "The sovereign is not the *Defensor Pacis* of a peace traceable to God; he is the creator of none other than an earthly peace. He is *Creator Pacis*."[25] Unlike the divine right of kings' theory, this sovereignty is not derived from God above but is an omnipotence that flows up from below via a covenant entered into between individuals. Echoing my earlier distinction between cosmos and universe, Schmitt argues that

> [t]he decisive element of the intellectual construction resides in the fact that this covenant does not accord with mediaeval conceptions of an existing commonwealth forged by God and of a preexistent natural order. The state as order and commonwealth is the product of human reason and human inventiveness and comes about by virtue of the covenant. This covenant is conceived in an entirely individualistic manner. All ties and groupings have been dissolved. Fear brings atomised individuals together.[26]

Here we encounter the anti-Aristotelian element of Hobbes. Humans are not inherently political animals and there are no "natural" intermediate elements between the individual and the state. All groups, especially the church, must be made to serve the state and are subsidiary or incorporated under state sovereignty. In Rousseau's estimation:

> Of all Christian Authors the philosopher Hobbes is the only one who clearly saw the evil and the remedy, who dared to propose reuniting the two heads of the eagle, and to return everything to political unity, without which no State or Government will ever be well constituted.[27]

In individualist-contractualist theories of sovereignty, from Hobbes onward, the church is the primal enemy as it is the paradigmatic form of an alternative source of sovereign authority that relativizes the claims of the political sovereign. For all his espoused Catholicism, Schmitt sees this clearly and is adamant about the need to "de-anarchize" Christianity.

Yet obedience to the sovereign is conditional. For Hobbes, if the sovereign does not protect its citizens then any duty to obey is dissolved: citizens cannot swap the fear of the state of nature for the fear of a "Moloch." It is the latent right of resistance in Hobbes's account of sovereignty, combined with Hobbes's distinction between public and private belief that led Leo Strauss to postulate against Schmitt that Hobbes vindicated limited government and should be seen as a liberal rather than the prophet of authoritarianism. Schmitt agreed, but for Schmitt this was the pathos of Hobbes. For Schmitt, Hobbes fatally undermined his own political philosophy by incorporating the right of freedom of thought and belief into his political system. As Schmitt contends, Hobbes's thought "contained the seed of death that destroyed the mighty leviathan from within and brought about the end of the mortal god" because it created a whole area of independent activity over which the state had no authority.[28] Revealing his anti-Semitism, Schmitt identifies the Jewish thinkers Baruch Spinoza, Moses Mendelssohn, and Johann Georg Hamann as those who saw this opening and turned it from a crack into a fatal fissure. Schmitt objected to the distinction between inner freedom of faith and outer conformity of confession and behavior. But while this may be the conceptual objection he cites as undermining Hobbes's theory of state, it is the "indirect" powers of the church that Schmitt points to as the primary problem. This is a problem Schmitt sees as reiterated in the nineteenth century through modern political parties, trade unions, social organizations, and what he calls the "forces of society," which, under the banner of freedom of conscience, act independently of the state. These "forces of society" threaten the indivisible and transcendent sovereignty of the state.[29] By way of contrast, where Schmitt sees the emasculation of Leviathan, Foucault and Agamben see its triumph. On their account, the constitutional liberal state turns out to be the "bio-political" state. It no longer needs external threats because, far from constituting a realm set apart from state power, conscience constitutes the extension of state power into the heart, mind, and habits of citizens. On this account, we no longer need a sovereign Leviathan because we have internalized its ways.

ROUSSEAU AND THE SOVEREIGNTY OF THE MANY

We find in Rousseau an attempt to resolve the question of sovereignty that offers an alternative to Hobbes. Instead of resolving the rivalry of independent, individual wills by postulating the renunciation of their independence in order to be directed by the one indivisible will of the sovereign, Rousseau envisaged each indivisible will as directed to choose the general will. Rousseau rejected Hobbes because Hobbes's conception of the protection-obligation of the social contract does not lead to sovereignty but despotism: just because the Leviathan produces peace does not make it legitimate. As Rousseau says, there is peace in a dungeon but that does not make it inviting.[30] For Rousseau:

> To renounce one's freedom is to renounce one's quality as man, the rights of humanity, and even its duties. There can be no possible compensation for someone who renounces everything. Such a renunciation is incompatible with the nature of man, and to deprive one's will of all freedom is to deprive one's actions of all morality.[31]

Although Rousseau shared Hobbes's conception of sovereignty as inherently indivisible and transcendent, he sought an account of sovereignty that maintained the freedom of the individual and a foundation for political order on something other than egoistic self-interest. Rousseau conceived of sovereignty as a property of a people rather than as an aggregate of individual wills. The transcendent and indivisible sovereignty of the many is expressed through the unified *volonté générale*. As Rousseau states: "Each of us puts his person and his full power in common under the supreme direction of the general will; and in a body we receive each member as an indivisible part of the whole."[32] Each one becomes subsumed within the monistic will of the many.

To make sense of the concept of the general will it is necessary to locate it within a specific set of theological debates. Rousseau, drawing from a distinctively French contribution to moral and political thought, developed the notion of "generality" as a point midway between particularity and universality. The general interest is good whereas particular interests are sectional and therefore bad. Justice is linked to generality and opposed to "particular" exceptions and interests. A strong case can be made that Rousseau's notion of generality arises out of seventeenth-century debates about predestination.[33] The notion of the general will was subsequently developed as a moral philosophical distinction by Pascal for whom the particular will leads to disorder and self-love (*amour propre*) and that "not to incline toward *le général* is 'unjust' and 'depraved.'"[34] Rousseau transmutes a theological and then moral distinction into a political one: the general will of the citizen to place the good of the republic above his or her particular will becomes not only the basis of good political order, but also of the "salvation" of egoistic individuals through converting *amour propre* (self-regarding concern) into *amour de soi* (appropriate concern for oneself). In the process, the church comes to be seen as a particular interest that threatens to divide the sovereign, general will of the people. For

Rousseau, what must be promoted instead is some form of civil religion that bolsters the general will. However, Rousseau's advocacy of civil religion was itself deeply ambiguous and contradictory.[35] Yet, as with Hobbes, what threatened the indivisibility and transcendence of sovereignty was the public pursuit of "private" interests and this is exactly the danger "religion" represented when conceptualized as a private and particularistic interest.

HEGEL AND THE SOVEREIGNTY OF THE STATE

Hegel was an avid reader of Rousseau during his seminary education in Tübingen. The questions of how to achieve unity and how to overcome the division (and the role of religion in the division) of the political community were ones that haunted Hegel as they did Hobbes and Rousseau. Like Rousseau, Hegel found Christianity problematic and in his early writings contrasted it with an idealized Greek *Volksreligion* that enabled integration of and harmony between political, cultural, and religious life rather than creating a disjuncture and compartmentalization between a private, otherworldly, and individualistic belief and practice and the obligations of citizenship. Hegel held that Christianity had politically enervating effects, and saw these as symptoms of a more fundamental lack of freedom that could only be overcome through the formation of a rationally administered and socially unified nation-state.

For Hegel, Christianity teaches people to look to heaven for their fulfillment and this in turn trains them to accommodate themselves to their political and economic alienation. Thus, an otherworldly eschatology is the enemy of political and economic freedom, a theme picked up by Marx. Hegel blamed religion for the rupture of the Holy Roman Empire of the Germanic Nation and this itself was a manifestation of the broader problem of the assertion of particularity against universality. In contrast to the unified nation-states of France and Britain, the Holy Roman Empire of Hegel's day was a mosaic of 300 more-or-less sovereign territories: there were the monarchies of Prussia and Austria, several prince-electors, 94 princes (both ecclesiastical and secular), 103 barons, 40 prelates, and 51 free towns.[36] This gothic constitution that so troubled Bodin and other early modern constitutionalists was still in operation, only now these overlapping and intersecting sites of sovereignty were viewed by Hegel not as a constitutional anomaly but as an anomaly to the spirit of the age. The problem was not conceptual and legal but absolute: it should no longer exist, was an obstacle to the realization of human freedom, and what was needed was a unified nation under a supreme sovereign. For Hegel, the state as a unity is alone the bearer of sovereignty. The medieval society, as a mere conglomeration of factions, does not possess the harmony and unity of functions characteristic of the state.[37]

By way of contrast, those contemporary thinkers who advocate complex space over simple space take a very different view from Hegel's. After the historical experience of totalitarianism, the complex sovereignty of the Holy

Roman Empire, where ecclesial and secular rulers had to negotiate and limit each other's sovereignty, looks attractive. It is the unified and sacralized nation-state that appears to be the problem, not the solution. In the wake of gulags and death camps, the concerns of Hobbes, Rousseau, and Hegel for a monistic and transcendent sovereign authority with the power to secure and guarantee order against the disorder and chaos of particular interests (whether of the individual or the group) have been reversed. The transcendent sovereign is now the wolf we need to defend against. Agamben's work illustrates this inversion. He turns Schmitt on his head so that, far from the sovereign deciding the exception being the answer to the problem of lawlessness, the lawless state of exception – the paradigmatic form of which is the death camp – has become the true *nomos* of the modern state.[38] Given a state where this kind of exception is the norm, multiplicity and diversity are no longer the problems but the solutions.

For Hegel, different constitutional forms – monarchy, aristocracy, and democracy – must be understood as historically contingent.[39] Given the evolution of history, these forms are inevitably subsumed within and superseded by the modern state and its realization of universality in historical existence. All division is converted into internal differentiation rather than substantive difference. Hegel divides the powers of the state into three: legislature, executive, and crown. However, this division is one of functional differentiation and does not represent any division of sovereignty. It is not so much a separation of powers as a division of labor. As Hegel puts it:

> Where there is an *organic* relation subsisting between members, not parts, then each member by fulfilling the function of its own sphere is *eo ipso* maintaining the others; what each fundamentally aims at and achieves in maintaining itself is the maintenance of the others.[40]

The state is now the substantive unity and all particular powers are simply moments and different manifestations of its univocal nature.

For Hegel, the hereditary monarch is the personification of the constitutional state's indivisible and organic unity. On one reading, Hegel's account of hereditary monarchy is Christological in shape and origin: the idea of the unity of the state has to be realized in a particular individual in order to manifest its universal presence in history and move beyond being an abstract idea to objective realization.[41] The monarch is a type of god-man: through the monarch, the implicit unity of the universal spirit and the particular natures and interests of civil society become real and assume a definite existence. The monarch, having a hereditary position, had an unfounded, noncontractual basis to his sovereignty and so the authority of the sovereign transcended the immanent political order.

If the monarch is the personification of the divine will, it is the nation-state that supersedes and sublates (cf. *aufheben*) religion because it becomes the vehicle for fulfilling the universal element in the human spirit. Within Hegel's overall schema, the state replaces the church as the bearer of salvation wherein a people can realize their freedom and catholicity. For Hegel, "[t]he state is the divine will."[42] Christianity is but one stage along the way in the realization of freedom in history. The organic unity of the state and its actualization of freedom is the fulfillment of the divine will. It is a manifestation of the kingdom of God within history as opposed to an eschatological kingdom that interrupts history.[43] The unity of the state overcomes the division of space and time. Rejecting the "two swords" tradition that stems from Gelasius, Hegel is highly critical of the view of the church as the vestibule of the kingdom of God and the state as representing the earthly kingdom. For Hegel, this is a false dichotomy. Church and state should not stand in opposition to each other. Although there is a proper difference of form, the content of both are truth and rationality.[44] The state, of which the church is a part, is not a mere "mechanism" or means to an end. Rather, to participate in the state is to participate in the rational life of self-conscious freedom.[45]

In terms of political theory, Hegel is Janus-faced. He looks back toward Hobbes and Rousseau and the assertion of a transcendent sovereign authority and forward toward the division of governmental powers. For Hegel, the state is both one and sovereign, with each part contributing to the whole; at the same time, the need for a single sovereign authority is superseded as the state and its constituent elements realize rationality in history and so with particular interests transcended through the rationally and juridically administered state, the need for a transcendent sovereign authority to hold together particular interests is no longer necessary. Yet Hegel anticipates in some ways what Arendt seeks, which is the reestablishment of space and time for political judgment through the reinstitution of plurality. The political system Hegel envisages builds in and accepts a plurality of interests and a unified public sphere that is not subordinated to economic and social life but represents the arena of free and universal action in which being human is realized. However, as a vision of a sovereign state exercising its authority over all aspects of a population's life, Hegel's sovereign political system can also be seen to contain the seeds of Foucault's panoptical state in which the sovereignty of a single public authority (such as a monarch) remains but at the same time is superseded by and dispersed within a field of relations, discourses, and technologies that habituate those within the state to conform to its order. Power is no longer exercised over the body by an external authority but becomes "bio-power" exercised within, throughout, and around the body such that sovereignty becomes an internalized and self-administered regime of "governmentality."

More directly, Hegel anticipates much of what emerges in the post-World War II European nation-state. While some interpret Hegel as the progenitor of the Communist and Fascist totalitarian state, he is better seen as the anticipator of that all-encompassing hybrid, the liberal-capitalist/social-democratic nation-state. Political parties, a single public and administrative authority (*Polizei*), a two-chamber legislature, public opinion, a constitutional ruler, organized corporate/professional interest groups (*Korporationen*), *Stände*/class interests (although notoriously, Hegel did not include the working class among these), a nonpartisan, meritocratic, and well-educated civil service, public education, and public office as a site of rule-bound and accountable obligation rather than personal fiat – all of these contribute to and constitute but are sublated within the rational and just political order that represents the guarantor and objectification of universal human freedom.

CUSTOM AND THE MEDIATION OF CONSENT

Obviously, Hobbes, Rousseau, and Hegel do not represent the only voices in modern political thought and the interpretations of them given here can be contested. However, their work does illustrate the ways in which corporate forms of life – of which the church is paradigmatic – become seen as problematic when sovereignty is understood as indivisible, monistic, and transcendent. At the same time, this is as much a theological problem as it is a problem of political philosophy. There are other theological and philosophical resources available for thinking about this problem, ones in which the church – or any corporate or culturally distinct entity – appears not as an anathema but as a legitimate and proper part of political order. Ironically, these other resources tend to begin not with a Trinitarian doctrine of God but with human nature and, more specifically, with the recovery of an Aristotelian sense of humans as political animals and attention to customary practices, gift relations, practical reason (phronēsis/mētis), and the traditions necessary to secure a common life. Such a beginning point is in stark contrast to most modern political thought – even in its conservative strands – that not only begins with the individual as the primary point of reference but also sees tradition, custom, practical reason, and gift relations as of the past and in conflict with what is new or modern. The Weberian rationalist-legal order that is the dominant political imaginary shaping both "Left" and "Right" banishes tradition, custom, and gift relations to the realm of the private. In doing so it simultaneously renders practical reason an illegitimate and illegible means of public deliberation. What the modern state requires are universal and uniform modes of reasoning on which to base standardized and centralized forms of measurement, taxation, policy, and administration.

For medieval constitutionalists, custom mediated consent, and established historical practices, such as the use of common land or rights to claim sanctuary, set limits on what could or could not be done by a sovereign authority.[46] This view carried over into the early modern period: a hugely significant case in point being debates in Stuart England about the "ancient constitution" and the demand for the king to publically recognize and respect the liberties and privileges enjoyed by custom and lawful precedent from time immemorial. These customary practices were not set in stone, but rather, following the pattern of common law, they constituted arenas of negotiation and enabled discretionary judgments built on apprenticeship into particular habits of action and contexts of application. They allowed for innovation but also the recognition of distinct forms of self-governing association (i.e., political associations that could claim and grant rights without claiming a full measure of sovereignty). As political theorist James Tully notes:

> The convention of the continuity of a people's customary ways and forms of government into new forms of constitutional associations with others is the oldest in Western jurisprudence.... It is the spirit of ancient constitutionalism, expressing the view that customs and ways of people are the manifestation of their free agreement. To discontinue them without their explicit consent would thus breach the convention of consent.[47]

In Tully's view, Hobbes, Locke, and Kant – and, we might add, Rousseau and Hegel – represent theories and justifications of discontinuity.[48]

The "convention of consent" was derived from the principle of Roman law *Quod omnes similiter tangit ab omnibus comprobetur* (Justinian's Code VI.59.5.2): in summary, what touches all ought to be tested by all. In practice this meant that all those who have legal rights at stake in a decision are entitled to be present or at the very least to be consulted in the decision. The principle was particularly applied to taxpayers. It is this principle that formed the basis of both Houses of Parliament: from the thirteenth century onward, when the monarch needed to raise money he gathered both the aristocracy, in what became the House of Lords, and the gentry and freehold commoners, in what became the House of Commons, to consult them on the uses to which their money would be put.[49] Just decisions, particularly in relation to the use of money for things that affected everyone, required the representation of all the relevant interests in the decision-making process. The modern form of the British Parliamentary system emerges from a fierce debate in the seventeenth century, mainly led by Puritans, which radicalized the principle into a demand that what touched all required the consent of all.[50] It was this same principle that lay behind the rallying cry of the American Revolution: "no taxation without representation." As we shall see, there is a deep irony in the demand by American colonists that this principle of consent be applied to them but was then denied by these same colonists to the existing aboriginal nations, the sovereignty of which the British Crown had already formerly recognized through a series of treaties.[51]

INDIVISIBILITY AND IMPERIALISM

Western conceptions of political order that build on rather than reject medieval conceptions of sovereignty take time, gift relations, place, tradition, practical reason, and customary practices as having public force. They thereby create greater scope for dialogue and ad hoc commensurability with non-Eurocentric and aboriginal conceptions of political order and thereby create the possibility of forging more diverse, "glocal" enactments of citizenship.[52] This may seem an outlandish claim, but in order to illustrate its basis we can observe a curious parallel between the conquest of Italian city-states by Napoleon Bonaparte and the perception of the status of Native American "republics" during the process of U.S. nation-building and westward expansion. Part of the justification given by contemporary supporters of Napoleon for his conquest of the millennia-old republic of Venice in 1797 was that it was primitive, brutal, and in need of dismantling so it could be incorporated into a modern, rational political order that accorded with historical progress. Likewise, the aboriginal nations in North America were taken to be a relic of an earlier, "savage" stage in human development in need of "liberation" by modernization and assimilation into a singular constitutional order. This kind of view contrasts with the pre-1776 approach established in law by the British Crown through numerous treaties with aboriginal nations.[53] The approach the British Crown took was based on one developed by Bartolus of Sassoferrato for the recognition of the Italian city-states as sovereign entities by the Holy Roman Empire in the fourteenth century.[54] In the Bartolian approach (which can be traced back to Augustine and Aquinas), customary practices of self-government had the status of common law and needed to be recognized as having continuing validity.

The dismissive attitude toward earlier forms of constitutional settlement, whether medieval or aboriginal, was of a piece with notions of constitutional order as singular and sovereignty as transcendent and indivisible. Tully draws out how the rejection of constitutional pluralism and an emanatory and distributed vision of sovereignty had its analogue in the rejection of customary practices and traditions as means of mediating consent in processes of colonialism. He states:

> The vision of modern constitutionalism legitimates the modernizing processes of discipline, rationalization and state building that are designed to create in practice the cultural and institutional uniformity identified as modern in theory. These processes include the construction of centralized and uniform constitutional systems over the legal and political pluralism of early modern Europe, the implementation of similar systems by European colonization, the extension of these by post-colonial states over Indigenous populations and customary law, the imposition of linguistic and cultural uniformity, and countless programmes of naturalization, assimilation and eugenics to construct modern states and subjects.[55]

By this account, the internal colonization of regional, religious, and other forms of association and self-government in modern projects of nation building were the analogue of external programs of colonial subjugation. Tully argues that from Locke to Kant and onward, aboriginal and medieval political orders were the "other" against which modern social-contract theories of political order defined themselves. The delegitimization and dismantling of both was seen as a morally and historically necessary project in order that "mankind" might progress in "manners" toward a universal vision of cosmopolitan citizenship. They were also necessary in order to dispossess those whose claims to the use and title of common land and other common-pool resources were based on customary practices and traditions rather than a written legal contract. The post-Marxist theorists of globalization, Michael Hardt and Antonio Negri, go so far as to argue that the expropriation of the commons, the imposition and defense of an absolutist conception of private property, and what they call the "modernity-coloniality-racist complex" constitute the basis of modern liberal republicanism and cosmopolitan conceptions of citizenship.[56] Whereas Hardt and Negri direct their critique primarily toward capitalist forms of modernity, Buber presents a trenchant critique of state communist and state socialist forms of modernization, arguing that the destruction of customary and traditional basis of common ownership such as the Russian *mir* was intrinsic to the development of such forms.[57]

The work of John Locke illustrates and exemplifies the broader connections between visions of modernization as progress, regimes of private property, and justifications of colonialism. In the case of Locke it is a proto-liberal vision of modernization that is put forward.[58] In contrast to those who recognized the aboriginal peoples as having jurisdiction over the territories Europeans came to settle, in his *Two Treaties on Government* Locke developed arguments to reject these claims.[59] In the first place, Locke locates the aboriginal peoples as existing in a "state of nature" and thus at a primitive stage of human history in contrast to civilized Europeans. Such a condition had political and economic implications. Politically, rather than existing as self-governing, sovereign nations they lived as individuals in nonpolitical forms of association. Economically, their only property rights relate to what they hunt and gather and not the land on which this activity takes place. As Tully notes, two hugely significant consequences follow from Locke's conception of the state of nature. First, Europeans do not need to form treaties with the aboriginal peoples as there is no sovereign authority with which to deal. Moreover, European settlement could not be objected to and if it was, then the aboriginal people may be punished as "wild Savage Beasts." Second, Europeans can take over the land they want without the consent of the people already there because anyone can appropriate uncultivated land. Underlying this argument was Locke's theory of original appropriation whereby claims to property are derived from mixing one's labor with what is used. Dominion fell to those able to cultivate land to its fullest capacity: an argument that, as Tully points out, specifically favors European agriculturalists over aboriginal hunter-gatherers and pastoralists.[60] Europeans were not dispossessing aboriginal peoples; they were undertaking a task that a barbarian people had failed to fulfill properly. Lastly, Locke justifies the nonrecognition of the title and sovereignty of aboriginal peoples on the grounds that they will be better off as a result of European settlement as they can progress away from their state of nature and benefit from assimilation to a commercial system of agriculture and the protection of private property. Locke's view came to be enshrined in U.S. law as exemplified in the 1823 Supreme Court ruling in the *Johnson v. M'Intosh* case.[61] More broadly, ever since Locke, economic development and assimilation to a particular economic and political order seen as more advanced and rational has been a powerful and frequent justification for the forced assimilation of colonized peoples.

CONSOCIATIONAL CONCEPTIONS OF SOVEREIGNTY

A rival conception that builds on rather than rejects medieval notions of sovereignty can be termed "consociationalist." "Consociation" is a term derived from the work of Althusius and literally means the art of living together.[62] In contrast to Hobbes, Rousseau, and Hegel, Althusius allows for the pluralization of political order so as to accommodate and coordinate the diversity of associational life, whether economic, familial, or religious. In his account, to be a political animal is not to be a citizen of a unitary, hierarchically determined political society. Nor is it to participate in a polity in which all authority is derived from a transcendent, monistic point of sovereignty. Rather, it is to be a participant in a plurality of interdependent, self-organized associations that together constitute a consociational polity. The singularity and specificity of each is constitutive of the commonwealth of all. Such an approach entails a strong affirmation that there is a commonwealth and it is this affirmation that sharply distinguishes it from the antipolitical visions of "minarchist," "states-rights," and neoliberal approaches.

In a consociational commonwealth, federalism is societal and political rather than simply administrative.[63] In contrast to constitutional federalism as a way in which to limit the governmental power exercised by a sovereign authority (as exemplified in the dominant interpretations of the U.S. Constitution) but which leaves undisturbed the top-down, transcendent, and monistic nature of that authority, consociationalism envisages a full-orbed confederalism whereby the authority of the sovereign arises from the whole or commonweal that itself is constituted from multiple consociations.[64] For Althusius, sovereignty is an assemblage that emerges through and is grounded on a process of mutual communication between consociations and their reciprocal pursuit of common goods and in which unity of the whole (i.e., a common life) is pursued as a noninstrumental good.[65] This unity is premised on the quality of cooperation and relationship building and is not secured through either legislative procedure, the transcendent nature of sovereign authority, a centralized monopoly of governmental power, or the formation of a unitary public sphere premised on a homogeneous rational discourse. The definitional judgment of the sovereign is not deciding the exception but the discernment and weighing up of common goods that emerge through the complex weave of social relations and customary practices that constitute the body politic and then adjudicating what should be done in order to fulfill these goods. On a consociational account, sovereign authorities should not impose order but discover it.

The consociational approach is not as alien as it may first appear. Hobbes's and Hegel's theories are one thing; historical practice is another. The medieval gothic order did not wholly disappear with the advent of a "Westphalian" order of nation-states. Rather, it was displaced and redescribed so that forms of political community became relocated and renamed as "economic" or "social." For example, the joint-stock trading company – the early modern archetype of the contemporary capitalist firm – was an explicitly political community based on the concept on the *corpus politicum et corporatum* or *communitas perpetua* that went back to Roman law. The paradigmatic example of the early modern mercantile "republic" (and which basically invented modern office life) was the East India Trading Company which, as a colonial proprietor

> did what early modern governments did: erect and administer law; collect taxes; provide protection; inflict punishment; perform stateliness; regulate economic, religious, and civic life; conduct diplomacy and wage war; make claims to jurisdiction over land and sea; and cultivate authority over and obedience from those people subject to its command.[66]

Yet the nature of the company as a political and sovereign institution – and of all analogous company-states – is viewed as either anomalous or denied. Such entities are labeled "economic," not political. For example, the World Bank is bound by its charter to deal only with economic or technical issues, yet its work has directly political consequences and severely affects the actions of other sovereign authorities. Contrary to how it is often presented, legal and political pluralism is the norm rather than the exception in contemporary societies. Most nations are a series of overlapping political associations with varying degrees of self-government, intersected by a number of legal jurisdictions (local, national, regional, and international) and deploying various strategies of devolution, decentralization, federation, cross-border linkages, and ways of recognizing "non-territorial" collective autonomy in order to navigate "internal" plurality. Sovereignty is an assemblage that opens up different conditions and possibilities for agency depending on where one is located. Moreover, the relationship between the governed and regimes of governance is never one of unilateral control; it is always a more open-ended negotiation involving the interplay of different performances of citizenship and the procedures and institutions of governance.[67]

In the realm of theory, it is as variations on a consociational conception of sovereignty that we can make sense of a theologically and philosophically diverse yet interlinked tradition of political reflection. If Althusius is its progenitor, then another antecedent is Tocqueville's *Democracy in America* (1835 and 1840). However, a key mediator is the German legal historian Otto von Gierke (1841–1921), who directly influenced the "English Pluralists" and the subsequent development of "Guild Socialism."[68] Schmitt, who saw them as the alternative and threat to the position he was trying to establish, directly criticized Gierke and the Guild Socialists. The Guild Socialists advocated a decentralized economy based on the noncapitalistic principles of cooperation and mutuality and proposed a radically confederalist and politically pluralist conception of the state.[69] Sovereignty was not something that could be appropriated by a single agency or institution. Rather, it emanated from differentiated and distributed authorities that compose the body politic. In distinction from the anarcho-syndicalists, the Guild Socialists thought there was still a need for a public power but its role was severely circumscribed. A key concern of the Guild Socialists was the question of how to maintain the freedom, specificity, and self-development of all forms of association, particularly the churches and trade unions.

A further strand of consociationalist thought can be identified in the conception of sphere sovereignty developed by the Dutch Neo-Calvinists, Abraham Kuyper, and Herman Dooyeweerd.[70] For them, the sovereignty of independent spheres such as the family, schools, and workplaces are expressions of the sovereign will of God. Each sphere has a relative autonomy and specific character that needs to be respected. Government has a role in ordering and protecting the general good, but it does not have the authority to interfere with or determine the character or telos of each sphere. In turn, the state is bounded by the sovereignty of other spheres. It was in the Netherlands that notions of sphere sovereignty overlapped with and found a parallel expression in the emergence of Catholic Christian Democratic thinking. Central to this current were Jacques Maritain and the development, from the papal encyclical *Rerum Novarum* (1891) onward, of Catholic social teaching. Maritain's pluralist conception of the body politic was already outlined in Chapter 1; but briefly put, the advocacy of subsidiarity and a form of constitutional consociationalism are central to Maritain and Catholic social teaching more generally.[71] This view was a rival to and eventually displaced the "throne and altar" authoritarianism that informed much of Schmitt's work. Animating the Christian consociationalist tradition of which the Guild Socialists, Neo-Calvinists, and Catholic social teaching are a part is the sense in which we participate in a cosmic order that can disclose to us some measure of meaning and purpose. It is this cosmic social imaginary that distinguishes the Christian consociationalism of Figgis, Kuyper, Maritain, and others from their immanentist confreres, notably Emile Durkheim and the contemporary political theorist, Paul Hirst.[72] That being said, consociational approaches can equally produce a simplistically secularized vision of political order. For example, Maritain's own conception of the relationship between the church and state tends to replicate the marginalization of the church as a self-governing and public body of the kind we observed in Hobbes and Rousseau.[73] And a consociational vision can easily become state-centric as happened with Christian Democratic parties in Europe after World War II.[74]

When BBCO is located within rival conceptions of sovereignty, we can begin to see why so many view it as problematic; however, we can also discern where it fits within a broader pattern of political thought. Alinsky's critique of "welfare colonialism" outlined in Chapter 1 and the resistance of BBCOs more generally to top-down, rationalizing programs of urban regeneration or community development can be seen as part of a much larger, but largely hidden, struggle for self-determination based on the recognition of existing customary practices. The use of theological discourses, festive proceedings, and ceremonial gift exchanges outlined in Chapter 5 as part of democratic politics represent the reassertion of customary practice, tradition, and practical reason as having public force. However, whether BBCO and consociationalism more broadly are as anomalous as they may first appear is another matter. As the history of the Corporation of the City of London outlined in Chapter 2 suggests, even in a polity as highly centralized as Great Britain, things are not always what they seem and semi-autonomous corporate bodies continue to exercise considerable power and have customary practices and traditions of self-government legally recognized.

The question is why some kinds of corporate power and customary practice are perceived as acceptable (notably, "economic" forms) but other forms (in particular, religious, cultural, and political ones) are viewed with deep suspicion. The survey of conceptions of sovereignty outlined here gives some sense of why certain forms of corporate life – namely, those that defend and perpetuate the priority of contract over custom, gift relations, and tradition – will be looked on with favor within liberal/neoliberal frameworks. The paradox is that such forms often uphold and defend customary practices, practical reason, and gift relations within their own corporate life while denying their public force more generally, the Corporation of the City of London being a case in point. Whether one subscribes to a consociational approach or not, my analysis of sovereignty suggests that if non-economic forms of self-governing association are also to be given their due, then contemporary political thought needs to give greater consideration to the recognition of customary practices (and the kinds of gift relations and practical rationalities they embody) as having public significance and mediating consent and the ongoing existence of "bottom-up" and polycentric forms of sovereignty.

One response to the continued existence of "estates" – religious, economic, or otherwise – is to develop a more consociationalist position that opens them to the representation of diverse interests in their governance and to practical reason as a means of deciding policy, and immerses all forms of corporate life in democratic politics. This is the approach BBCO exemplifies through, first, the kinds of mutually committed and at the same time critical dialogues it establishes between a particular vision and practice of democratic politics and different streams of Catholicism, Protestantism, Judaism, and Islam; and, second, the way it constitutes a practice for enacting a critically constructive relationship mediated by practical reason between economic and political power holders and those whose interests their decisions affect as part of reweaving the civil sphere. It is not alone in taking such an approach. On many fronts a consociationalist position seems to be an increasingly prevalent, if tacit, recommendation. For example, in response to processes of globalization and the increasing cultural diversity of nation-states, some legal theorists are advocating what amounts to a more consociational approach.[75] In the realm of social policy there is a shift toward the advocacy of the co-governance and co-production of services such as education and healthcare. With this move there is recognition that the state and the market do not define or exhaust the parameters of provision.

Noncommercial and self-governing institutions and patterns of association must be involved in the construction and delivery of public goods. Beyond the world of social policy and legal theory, Elinor Ostrom's work on "polycentric governance" as a form of economic and political management can also be seen as an example of the consociationalist approach sketched here. Her work highlights the complex interweaving of state, market, and forms of self-organized and self-governing associations in policing and managing common-pool resources such as fisheries, forests, irrigation systems, and groundwater basins.[76]

DEBATING CONSOCIATIONAL DEMOCRACY AND CIVIC REPUBLICANISM

Standard accounts of consociational democracy build on the pioneering work of the Dutch political theorist, Arend Lijphart. Lijphart's initial reflections were born out of trying to understand the paradox of the Netherlands, which, on the one hand, had deep social and religious cleavages, yet, on the other hand, was a notable example of a successful and stable democracy.[77] However, Lijphart's conception of consociational democracy is state-centric and aims at creating a consensus between a "cartel of elites" through engineering highly technical power sharing, voting, and constitutional arrangements.[78] Lijphart's work has been much criticized, mainly for the lack of conceptual clarity and theoretical depth and its empirical inaccuracies.[79] Part of the problem with Lijphart's approach is that he does not pay sufficient heed to what originally inspired it: the work of Althusius and its subsequent development in Roman Catholic and Calvinist political thought.[80] In short, for all the richness of Lijphart's insights, he turns a diverse tradition of political thought into a technocratic set of procedures. Rather than draw from Lijphart in order to locate BBCO within a conception of consociational democracy, we must instead return to the beginning points of what constitutes a democracy.

This is not the place for a review of democratic theory.[81] However, if democracy at its most basic level means collective self-rule by the people for the people rather than rule by the one, the few, or the mob, then we must ask what the nature and form of this self-rule should be and how the people are constituted as a people or a whole rather than a disaggregated crowd. Many accounts of democracy conceive of self-rule as an extension of individual autonomy. A form of political order is democratic to the extent that it enables individual liberty and curtails forms of domination that limit the choices individuals may make within the context of personal and circumstantial constraints. Popular sovereignty is derived from the sovereignty of the individual and is considered indivisible and singular. Democratic legitimacy is premised on each individual having an equal say in the decisions that affect everyone. This "say" can be organized in a variety of ways, hence debates about different ways of organizing collective self-rule. The adjectives "representative," "deliberative," and "direct" placed before the term "democracy" denote different forms of organizing collective self-rule and constituting individuals into a people. For example, deliberative democracy constitutes a people by generating a consensus through processes of rational deliberation to which all may contribute, the consensus itself being the basis of the collective self-rule. Each form of organization is given priority according to different ideological and normative accounts of what the nature and form of self-rule should be under certain conditions and within particular contexts. However, by conceiving of collective self-rule as an extension of individual autonomy, what is lost from view is the intrinsic relationship between collective self-rule and the forms of association in which the art of ruling and being ruled is learned and performed. It is through associations coming into relationship with each other that the people as a whole is constituted and it is the negotiation of the different interests and visions of the good between associations that forms a common life – this common life being what constitutes the people qua people.

An alternative beginning point for democratic theory to individual autonomy is to start with the relationships between individuals. If democracy is the rule of the people by the people, then at its most basic level it demands relationships between people. Without some kind of meaningful relationships between people then there are merely individuals and an atomized and disaggregated crowd, whether at a local, national, or transnational level. If one is to begin with relationships – and therefore their mediation via custom and gift relations – then one has to take seriously the forms of social life through which individuals develop and sustain relationships over time and in which they learn the arts of ruling and being ruled. This starting point for thinking about democracy is not in opposition to individual liberty but recognizes that individual liberty depends on and is mediated by multiple forms of association and differing kinds of relationships.[82] As Arendt notes, "[a] body politic which is the result of covenant and 'combination' becomes the very source of power for each individual person who outside the constituted political realm remains impotent."[83] Much political theory has moved beyond the sterile dichotomies between "liberals" and "communitarians" to take seriously the symbiosis between individual freedom and communal formation in democratic politics. Yet beginning with the relationships between individuals it is still a narrow, if busy path.[84]

Perhaps the most developed theoretical position that begins with relationships rather than the individual is the modern restatement of civic republicanism.[85] Modern republican political theory focuses on how interdependent citizens may deliberate on and realize goods in common within a historically evolving political community. Amid the great diversity in modern civic republican thought, there is a common emphasis on freedom, civic virtue, participation, and recognition and how each of these is constituted through patterns of human interdependence.[86] But this interdependence is not based on similarity or homogeneity but on shared action and communication in a public realm. For civic republicans, rather than the upholding of individual rights, it is commitment to and participation in a shared political project of collective self-rule and pursuit of the virtues required to sustain that project that best guarantee and secure individual liberty. This approach is summarized in the following statement from Sandel: "I am free insofar as I am a member of a political community that controls its own fate, and a participant in the decisions that govern its affairs.... The republican sees liberty as internally connected to self-government and the civic virtues that sustain it."[87] However, the restatement of republicanism has remained a largely theoretical enterprise. Although running in parallel with the theoretical rearticulation of civic republicanism as a counterpoint to political liberalism there has been a growing sociological engagement with the practice and performance of citizenship in civil society and social movements.[88] This engagement was provoked by the antistatist democratic revolutions of 1989 onward in Central and Eastern Europe and the role of civil society to the exercise of democratic citizenship in these events.

The dark side of this way of thinking about democracy, the side that rightly worries liberals, is the way in which such a beginning point can lead to an emphasis on the collective taking precedence over and oppressing the individual. At a minimal level, the emphasis on relationships, and the necessary particularity of such a beginning point, is felt by some to threaten universalistic and egalitarian conceptions of citizenship.[89] Beyond this normative concern, and as Tocqueville and Montesquieu observed, there can be despotism of the people as well as that of a despot. Beyond even the problem of democratic despotism are those forms of political order that inherently subordinate the individual to a collective vision of peoplehood, as is the case with nationalist, fascist, state socialist, and state-communist regimes. Polities characterized by one or other of these regimes may include democratic elements, but instead of the demos being understood as constituted through politics, it is perceived as grounded in a supposedly pre-political species of peoplehood such as the *ethnos* or *Volk*. However, by beginning with the relationships between individuals, collectivist, homogenous, and monistic conceptions of peoplehood and popular sovereignty can be challenged. In accounts that link individual liberty with patterns of sociality a different set of adjectives come to the fore as ways of describing the organization of rule by the people, for the people. The adjectives used foreground how relationships between individuals take multiple forms and the complex rather than simple nature of social and political space. Key is the sense that the existence of diverse centers of social formation and political power not only provide a check on totalizing forms of power, but also make meaningful the ability of individuals to foster multiple loyalties.[90] The IAF/Citizen UK's practice of community organizing demands a similar starting point as their work is founded on building relationships between associations, and rather than recruiting individuals, it is structured around and seeks to ensure the flourishing of distinct membership institutions, each of which is recognized as possessing its own integrity. It is my contention that the adjective that best describes the IAF's kind of democratic politics is "consociational." It prioritizes the relationship between distinct but reciprocally related "consociations" or communities or forms of life together as the best way of generating the collective self-rule of a people/demos conceptualized as a non-natural, political community.

DEFINING COMMUNITY ORGANIZING

We can at this point define community organizing within a field of political concepts that draws from and grows out of all that has been said so far. In Chapter 1, Alinsky's approach to community organizing was identified with American populism. Yet this ascription was shown to need further specification. Use of the term "political populism" was an initial step that was in turn refined in Chapter 6 by drawing from Mouffe's work to develop a threefold distinction between a populist politics and political and antipolitical populism. In the light of the account of sovereignty given in this chapter, I am suggesting that it is more accurate to identify BBCO as a realization of democratic citizenship that is consociational in form and rationality and populist in its performance and identity.

I take the term *community* in the term "community organizing" to denote a coming together by mutual agreement of distinct institutions for a common purpose without loss of each of their specific identities or beliefs and practices. As an *organization*, it is consociational in structure: that is, it is a federated alliance of institutions with often divergent and conflicting beliefs and practices that nevertheless form a single union and in which authority is constituted from the consent of each participating institution rather being derived either from some preexisting or superior authority or aggregated from the votes of individuals. The community or *koinon* is founded on the identification of mutual need for each other, shared interests, and the pursuit of goods in common, which includes a commitment to democratic politics as a shared good. The recognition and pursuit of their mutual need, interests, and substantive goods gives rise to mutual obligations to support, aid, and defend each other (what was referred to in Chapter 3 as a "municipal *pietas*"). The common life of the community organization is shaped by a common rule and set of practices. This rule is not legal or contractual in nature but covenantal and can be renounced or opted out of at any time. Like a monastic rule, the rules and practices of community organizing, first articulated in a systematic way by Alinsky but subject to ongoing improvisation and innovation by other organizers, defines and structures the common life of the federation and provides the measure or standard of excellence among institutions in membership. It is sustained through education and training in the disciplines and mores necessary to uphold the practices. It is its consociational structure, a structure that allows BBCO to combine unity and plurality, which provides the best defense against organizations becoming either overly political (that is, establishing a common life by attempting to subjugate or assimilate "enemies") or antipolitical (that is, withdrawing from or refusing to acknowledge the possibilities of and responsibility for a common life with "enemies").

THRESHOLD

The advocacy of consociational democracy outlined here is not intended to imply that a consociational and populist democratic politics constitutes a wholesale replacement for or alternative to more widespread forms of representative and participatory democracy. Rather, consociational and populist forms of democracy – of which broad-based community organizing is one example – are envisaged as both reparative of and supplementary to already existing forms. As will be outlined in Chapter 8, a consociational approach is reparative to existing forms of democratic politics as it brings to the fore particular patterns of social relations that are necessary to resist significant forms of domination, notably debt bondage, which other realizations of democratic citizenship frequently fail to address because of dynamics intrinsic to them. Yet consociational and populist forms of democracy are only ever supplementary because they themselves have problematic dynamics that other forms of democratic politics help correct and keep in check. The necessary interplay of different approaches and of the forms of sociality each approach embodies is analyzed in Chapter 8.

8

Economy, Debt, and Citizenship

Previous chapters have displayed how broad-based community organizing (BBCO) does not operate with a contractual or rights-based vision of citizenship. Rather, it was shown to be consociational in form and rationality and populist in its performance of democratic citizenship. This chapter builds on the analysis and description given so far in order to contrast the gift-based forms and patterns of relationships that shape BBCO with those that undergird contractual, rights-based conceptions of citizenship. Modern political thought has tended to valorize contractual conceptions rather than the gift-based or covenantal visions of citizenship of the kind that underwrite BBCO. Yet, in the contemporary context, in relation to the vexing question of whether democratic citizenship can challenge the power of money in shaping our common life, it is gift-based visions of citizenship that need to be at the fore of the debate. To understand why and draw out how liberal conceptions of social contract and rights are inadequate as the sole basis for conceptualizing democratic citizenship, we must examine the relationship between debt and citizenship and why forms of gift and mutuality are vital means of challenging the prioritizing of profit over social relationships. In examining the linkages between debt and notions of citizenship, we discover that the problems of usury and debt slavery – the problems we began with in this study – turn out to be ones that are paradigmatic for democratic citizenship, and ones that democracy, from its very origins, was a means to address.

In order to examine how a gift-based vision of citizenship helps challenge the "power of money" (i.e., money as both a frame of reference for imagining social and political relations and as a source of agency for those who control the means of credit), this chapter takes three cities as both allegories for and generators of historical responses to this challenge. The first city is Athens as a point of origin of democracy and as a symbol of the need to set limits to the power of money via a participatory democratic politics. The second city is Jerusalem as a trope for how Judaism, Islam, and Christianity emphasize the need for legal limits and reciprocal relations in order to ensure lending and borrowing contribute to the flourishing of the body politic. The third city is Vienna of the interwar period, which is taken as an illustration of the liberal, social democratic yet precarious state in danger of being captured by either totalitarian forces or elite interests, or collapsing into relativistic and violent chaos.

ATHENS: DEMOCRATIC POLITICS AS THE MEANS TO LIMIT THE POWER OF MONEY

In ancient Athens there was a direct link between property and citizenship. Only property-owning men could be full citizens. There were also strict regulations on how land could be bought and sold and a key outcome of the fight for democracy was that if you were a citizen you could not be made a debt slave. It is a matter of scholarly dispute whether democracy emerged as a result of a rapid increase in debt slavery caused by a break down in law and order or disputes between wealthier landowners and poorer families who had lost, or were in danger of losing, their land and who therefore risked being forced into debt slavery.[1] What is clear is that debt and the emergence of democracy were inextricably linked. This linkage is reflected in Aristotle. Writing nearly 300 years after the reforms that laid the foundations of democracy in Athens, Aristotle sees the demand for an amnesty of debts and an ending of debt slavery as central to the origins of democracy.[2]

For Aristotle, politics was, in part, a means through which the common institutions of self-government preserved the sense of community necessary to subordinate the power of money to the pursuit of the "common good." Aristotle's condemnation of usury should be seen in this light. It is born out of a concern for the maintenance and health of the body politic and is not a reductively economic concern.[3] Lending and borrowing were to be situated within relations of *koinonia*/fellowship that reflected the obligations of citizenship and were not to be subordinated to the pursuit of money as an end in and of itself.[4] For Aristotle, usury led to the fracturing of the proper relationship between citizens.[5] Aristotle condemns the usurer: like a pimp, he takes more than he ought – from the wrong sources and for reasons of sordid gain.[6] He discusses the usurer under the category of "meanness," defined as deficiency in giving and excess in taking, which is to say that the usurer is someone who lacks what is required to be a good citizen. Amid the recent serried banking scandals and the seemingly endemic corruption in the financial services industry, it is difficult not to see the continuing salience of Aristotle's insight.

Aristotle's treatment of usury fits within his wider interrogation of the relationship between commercial trade, money, and citizenship. Unlike Plato, Aristotle admits the necessity of a seaport and commercial trading, yet says the activities of merchants should be strictly limited, lest they undermine the pursuit of justice that should be the telos of the polis. This view is even more pronounced in Plato who, deploying the language of disease, thought it necessary to keep the contagion of maritime trade quarantined from the land-based city economy: "The sea is pleasant enough as a daily companion, but has indeed also a bitter and brackish quality; filling the streets with merchants and shop-keepers, and begetting in the souls of men uncertain and unfaithful ways – making the state unfriendly and unfaithful both to her own citizens and also to other nations."[7] Aristotle and Plato are not idiosyncratic in this regard: the "port of trade" was a common phenomenon in the ancient world and acted as a permeable but protective membrane mediating between the ancient maritime economy of unregulated commercial trade and the land-based, legally regulated forms of economic exchange.[8] This buffering was mirrored in the advice given to merchants by Cicero on how to make their earnings respectable: "just as they have often left the high seas for the harbour, now leave the harbour itself for land in the country": that is, buy a country estate and begin farming, which was for Cicero the most pleasant and worthy occupation of a free man.[9] The heart of the problem for both Plato and Aristotle, however, was not commercial trade per se but money or, more specifically, the pursuit of money as an end in itself. The pursuit of money as an end in itself, through either usury or unregulated commerce divorced from any prior commitment to the good of a social and political community, led to a disturbed form of desire: *pleonexia* or insatiable desire.[10]

Money, *Pleonexia,* and the Dissolution of the Body Politic

Money has no natural limit. The law of diminishing marginal utility does not apply; it can be pursued without end and, in the process, everything else is subordinated to its accumulation. Although money is necessary as either a medium of exchange, a store of value, or a means of accounting, the practice of chrematistics or money making (as distinct from production and trade) threatens the polis because it makes the pursuit of profit an end in itself and in doing so not only turns money from its natural end but also, through *pleonexia*, becomes the enemy of citizenship as it undermines the pursuit of civic virtue and justice. As the philosopher Marcel Hénaff outlines, for Aristotle, "[t]he individual who is dedicated to the pursuit of financial profit can no longer be a true citizen (or has never been one, as in the case of many retailers who were either foreigners passing through the city or metics), since this acquisition without reciprocity amounts to acquisition without justice."[11] For Aristotle, the pursuit of money as an end in itself tended to instrumentalize and commodify all other relationships and arts, even philosophy.[12] The pursuit of money as an end rather than as a means of exchange or an aid to production undermines the virtues of courage and justice necessary to pursue the truly good life and sustain the freedom of the city/body politic that is the condition of the pursuit of such a life. The collective liberty of self-governing citizens and their virtuous pursuit of the "common good" are undermined by commercial and competitive values that prioritize the self-interested pursuit of property and consumer goods.[13]

JERUSALEM: GIFT AND LAW AS THE BASIS OF A COVENANTAL VISION OF CITIZENSHIP

We find an analogous set of concerns in the Bible. At the heart of the salvation narratives in both the Old and New Testaments we discover that the power of money and liberation from debt slavery are central concerns. A primary narrative template for understanding salvation is given in the book of Exodus where the central dramatic act is liberation of the Israelites from debt slavery in Egypt. The canonical structure of Genesis and Exodus in the ordering of Scripture makes this point. The book of Genesis closes with the story of Joseph. At the end of this account, although saved from famine, the Israelites, along with everyone else in Egypt, are reduced to debt slavery.[14] This is a "voluntary" process entered into in order to receive the grain from Pharaoh's stores that the people had given to Pharaoh for safekeeping in the first place.[15] The inhabitants of Egypt come before Joseph and pledge their bodies and their land as security for the grain they borrow (Genesis 47:18–19). Therefore, they lack both the means to repay the debt and someone to pay it for them (as everyone is now indebted). The inevitable consequence is debt slavery on a massive scale. The first chapter of Exodus opens with a new Pharaoh who takes advantage of the Israelites' debt slavery to exploit them. So the Israelites are not depicted as prisoners of war or chattel slaves; but as debt slaves undertaking forced labor on behalf of the ruling elite.[16] It is this condition from which the Israelites are redeemed.[17]

Exodus is one of the key framing narratives that shape the presentation of Jesus' life, death, and resurrection in the Gospels. And the notion of redemption or Jesus paying with his life in order to liberate humans from our debt of sin is a leitmotif in the New Testament (Mark 10:45; Romans 6:21–23; Colossians 3:5–6). Indeed, the declaration of Jubilee – that is, the release from debt bondage – forms the basis of how Luke frames Jesus' announcement of his purpose and mission (Luke 4:18–19).[18] And what Luke then depicts in Acts 2 as a direct fruit of the outpouring of the Holy Spirit is the enactment of the Jubilee community where no one has debts because "[a]ll who believed were together and had all things in common; they would sell their possessions and goods and distribute the proceeds to all, as any had need" (Acts 2:44–45). Thus, the admonition that we cannot serve both God and Mammon (Matthew 6:19–24) is not a trivial matter: the central drama of salvation history is an act of liberation from debt bondage.[19] To put the pursuit of money before the welfare of people, and use money to dominate and exploit people – especially the poor and vulnerable – is to turn your back on God's salvation and deny in practice the revelation given in Scripture of who God is. However, to use money to strengthen the commonwealth, and in particular to relieve the poor, is a mark of having received salvation.[20]

Usury, Redemption, and Legislative Limits

This brings us to the specific Scriptural teaching on when and how to lend. Indicative of the direct teaching on lending is the following from Exodus 22:25: "If you lend money to my people, to the poor among you, you shall not deal with them as a creditor; you shall not exact interest (*nešek*) from them."[21] As is set out in Psalm 15, not lending at interest is directly equated with righteousness.[22] In the Torah at least, usury can be used as a synonym for charging any kind of interest and is condemned as immoral between those subject to covenantal obligations.[23]

To profit from a loan to a fellow Israelite with whom one has a kinship relation is to make God an enemy. To engage in usury (in the absolutist sense of receiving any profit from a loan) is not only to have no fear of God, but also to oppose oneself to God through treating God's elect as an enemy: that is, to act as one whose manner and way of living is directly opposed and a threat to God's covenantal ordering of life. This political action against God and his people can only result in death to the usurer (Ezekiel 18:10–13). Locating oneself as an enemy of God and his people is not exclusive to the sin of usury. Bribery, theft, adultery, and other sins equally place one in opposition to God's order. However, the proper ordering of lending and borrowing and their effects on the right ordering of communal relations are of at least equal if not greater concern in the various legislative codes. This is because the proper relationship between the land and the people is at stake.[24] The land and fellow Israelites were nonfungible goods given by God as gifts for the flourishing of all. Possession of land (nahălâ) did not entitle the holder to exclusive use; rather, it was a nonexclusive usufruct. Human ownership and use of created goods was limited because ultimately it was God's homeland: humans are trustees and priests of what they have received from God.[25] To convert land or people into fungible goods of no greater value than anything else is not only to instrumentalize them for one's own benefit, and so place one's one welfare above the good of all, but also to usurp God. In modern parlance we call such a process "commodification": the treating of that which is not for sale as a commodity to be bought and sold. The extensive manumission laws of Exodus, Leviticus, and Deuteronomy relate to debt slavery and are measures to keep in check such a process of commodification of land and people.[26] For example, in Leviticus, the Israelite who cannot pay back his loan cannot be made a debt slave but becomes instead a hireling of the creditor until he can amortize his debt, thereby remaining free and continuing to be a fully-fledged member of the body politic.[27]

Treatment of the poor is a touchstone that marks whether relations of faithful, mutual responsibility that encompass the whole people are adhered to or not. The turning of people and land into property capable of being traded within a monetary economy is a direct threat to the proper ordering of economic, social, and political relations and the concrete ability of all the people to participate in the covenantal order as members with equal dignity. The key issue at stake here is not usury per se (as will be seen, there is no absolute prohibition on usury in Scripture) but the nature of the relationship between the lender and the borrower as fellow members of the people of God. Land and people together constituted the People of God and were not to be expropriated for personal gain or monetized as commodities to be bought and sold. The Jubilee legislation (whether historically enacted or not) served as an imperative that disrupted any justification to expropriate land permanently through debt.[28] The land/property was to be used to provide the means of life, not converted through exploitation or monopolization into a means for either the death or the enslavement of one's neighbor.[29] This is the context for the passage read at the London Citizens assembly on November 25, 2009 in which Nehemiah calls the "nobles and officials" to repentance and, in particular, to stop charging interest on what they were lending and make restitution (Nehemiah 5:10). Legislation in Scripture concerning lending frames it as a good thing to do as a response to someone in need.[30] But central to Jewish and Christian Scriptures is the imperative that on no account should another's misfortune be turned into an opportunity to exploit them for selfish gain. The prohibitions against usury in the Qur'an and Islamic law can be read in a similar light.[31]

Usury and Covenantal Relations

The Scriptural concern about lending and the proper treatment of those in debt can be heard as simply pertaining to the proper ordering of economic relations. However, this is to decouple in a peculiarly modern way what we might call the status of the "citizen" from questions of economics. As depicted in the Bible, participation as a full member of the covenantal community or organized body politic required a land holding. Land is portrayed as providing the basis for the right and obligation to participate in the legal assemblies, to act in common ventures such as defense, and to be present representatively at the festivals.[32] Possession of land was a necessary condition for participation in the assembly of tribes (the *edah*) and the sociopolitical organization of the tribe (the *shevet*), as well as the means to fulfill the obligations of the covenant with God and the duties of care owed to one's fellow Israelites.[33] To be without land meant one was without the necessary power/agency in relations of mutual responsibility and therefore, one was unable to fulfill one's covenantal obligations. This in turn affected the holiness of the people as a whole because the quality of covenantal relations broke down because *tzedakah u'mishpat* (justice and righteousness), the term for the meshwork of obligations and rights that were the basis of the God-given social order, could no longer be fulfilled.[34] Thus, the land in general, and familial land holdings in particular, were central to the organization and identity of ancient Israel as a body politic. To make those subject to covenantal obligations into debt slaves and permanently expropriate their land was seen as simultaneously undermining the political order and the character and identity of the people.

Within the theo-political vision of "Jerusalem," land – and, by extension, property – were communicative and not absolute goods. It is in this communicative vision of property relations as the basis for a shared life premised on the ability of each having agency within the whole that we find the root of an alternative vision of property relations to both privatized and socialized conceptions and even some recent reconceptions of the commons. It is a vision echoed in many reflections on what is necessary for a stable republic.[35] Obviously, the negative side of this is that, within historical forms of such a system, restrictions on who can own land (mostly adult men) and the distribution of land holdings (often restricted to a particular class) are thus directly linked to who has political agency. Nevertheless, such visions do take seriously the link between material and political agency that are central to notions of "social citizenship." In the modern period, when people no longer have land and are dependent on employers for money and banks for credit, there is a question of how people may undertake independent political action in collaboration with others when they no longer have economic autonomy. This question will be explored later in relation to "Vienna."

A Social View of Property

Property envisaged as a communicative rather than private good can be helpfully contrasted with Hardt and Negri's conceptualization of the commons. In their view, both capitalism and socialism represent related systems through which the commons is enclosed and expropriated and neither can encompass the kind of "bio-political economy" that generates the commons. Moreover, rather than either public or private ownership constituting the basis of freedom, it is the relational basis of the commons and the interactions of nature and culture in the production of a commonwealth that is the locus of freedom and innovation.[36] The basis of the "bio-political" commons – knowledge, language, scientific techniques, community relations, and so forth – are produced through social, cooperative processes that are autonomous in relation to and in excess of public or private ownership and material means of production. For Hardt and Negri, public and private means of management and production increasingly threaten and undermine the kinds of encounter, cooperation, and communication necessary for innovation within and the reproduction of the commons. A case in point is contests over the patenting of genetic information and the question of whether it should be possible to claim specific DNA of wheat that evolved through innumerable human interactions over millennia as the "intellectual property" of a single company.

The commons, however, cannot be wholly separated from forms of public and private ownership. Rather, following the economist Elinor Ostrom's more empirically based account, its formation as a cultural-political construct is the fruit of a negotiation between and interweaving of public authorities, market processes, and non-pecuniary forms of organization and association based on customary practice and tradition. Part of the problem with Hardt and Negri's conception of the commons and their critique of property is that they never countenance that there may be noncapitalistic conceptions of property that prioritize the communicability and sharing of goods rather than their private or exclusive use.[37] One such alternative conception is Thomistic, which represents a synthesis of Athens and Jerusalem. This social conception of property is derived from a notion of the prior common gift of the earth to all humanity, the contingent status of ownership arrangements as the result of historical, human, legal developments, and the telos of property in serving the "common good."[38] It is a tradition of conceptualizing property that finds clear expression in later strands of Catholic social teaching and is encapsulated in the following statement from the encyclical *Laborem Exercens* (1981):

> Christian tradition has never upheld this right [to private property] as absolute and untouchable. On the contrary, it has always understood this right within the broader context of the right common to all to use the goods of the whole of creation: *the right to private property is subordinated to the right to common use,* to the fact that goods are meant for everyone.[39]

Thomistic conceptions of property, unlike that of Hardt and Negri, do not establish a dualistic opposition between property ownership and the cultivation of civic and economic virtue. Echoing "Jerusalem," Thomistic accounts can envisage property ownership as a necessary condition for the development of moral and civic responsibility and the building of a common life. Furthermore, the opposition Hardt and Negri establish between the commons and property relations seems to close down the space for an account of the relationship between forms of social and personal ownership and the commons as mutually constitutive: enclosure and the production of the commons are not *necessarily* opposed to each other.[40] Such an account is necessary in order to make sense of the actual practice of such initiatives as Creative Commons licensing.[41] Nevertheless, some kind of social conception of property is a vital means of limiting the power of money and curtailing regimes of indebtedness.

Usury as a Political Act

There is no absolute condemnation of usury in Scripture. Usury is licit when it comes to foreigners (Deuteronomy 15:3, 23:20; Leviticus 25:39–54). The distinction between the prohibition of usury in relation to those subject to the laws of Israel and its licitness when it comes to foreigners has long troubled Christian interpreters. A common way of reconciling the seeming contradiction is through some kind of contextualization that thereby relativizes the distinction. For example, some scholars argue that because Israel was a peasant economy, most loans were distress or consumption loans rather than loans for investment. By contrast, loans to foreigners were commercial loans relating to trade.[42] However, a solely economic explanation is too reductive. The real issue was one of power and the question of whether the fraternal relations of mutuality that were to pertain among the Israelites could be expected between the Israelites and foreigners.[43] If the charging of interest to fellow Israelites positioned one as an enemy of God, then the charging of interest to foreigners was a correct identification of the foreigner as a possible adversary of God's good order. It is at this point that Schmitt's conception of the political clarifies what is at stake. Foreigners were enemies (latent or actual) against whom Israel was prepared to wage war. Foreigners were not necessarily evil or immoral; indeed, they may well conform to the Noahide covenant. Nevertheless, they were enemies who represented a real threat to the existence of Israel and its way of life. Conversely, if usury is a political judgment on one's relations with another, one is not to treat one's own people as enemies but as neighbors.

The Deuteronomic double standard suggests that, unlike murder or lying, charging interest does not constitute an absolute moral prohibition or exceptionless moral norm.[44] Rather, charging interest is morally ambiguous. Similar to a drug (*pharmakon*), usury is both a poison and a remedy.[45] Its ambiguity and double-edged nature, rendered explicit in the Deuteronomic double standard, is what makes the analysis of usury such a contested and confusing field. To offer credit at interest is to serve an essential need in the monetary economy. As the history of capitalism suggests, profit from interest-based credit and the levels of exchange it facilitates is a potent driver in the creation of monetary wealth, technological innovations, and the provision of state-driven and philanthropic welfare. Moreover, the effect of usury is to draw into ongoing relationship people who ordinarily might have nothing in common or who are deeply suspicious of each other and have no shared ends. Indeed, Hayek's concept of "catallaxy" (the coordination and reconciliation of divergent and conflicting interests through market exchanges) is premised on the notion that market exchange transforms the enemy into a friend.[46] At a concrete level, one fruit of modern economic globalization is just such an increase in trade between enemies. However, as well as enabling exchange, debt also gives enormous unilateral power to the creditor and its effects can be hugely destructive on social and political relations. The immiserating impacts of debt repayments, whether at a personal or national level, are instances of this destruction. Myriad personal testimonies recount how the burden of debt leads to family breakdown, depression, and, in some cases, suicide. It may be nonviolent, but usury can be a most effective form of coercion. It is my contention that the exercise of consociational forms of democratic citizenship at the points of production, distribution, and exchange are the antidote to the toxic effects of debt and its use to control and manage the indebted.

Debt as Domination

Contemplating the relationship between debt, money, and citizenship in Athens and Jerusalem unveils how debt can be a form of domination. By way of contrast to my emphasis on the oppressive consequences of indebtedness as a particular problem that democratic citizenship helps address, Stout identifies hereditary chattel slavery as *the* paradigmatic form of domination that modern accounts of citizenship, particularly in North America, are tackling.[47] For Stout, all forms of domination subsequent to hereditary chattel slavery – patriarchy, heterosexism, and so forth – are framed as analogous to chattel slavery. But the emphasis on hereditary chattel slavery tends to occlude domination by the power of money and debt as a form of domination. This is because the forms of domination that arise from indebtedness (debt slavery and debt bondage) are not analogous to hereditary chattel slavery since they are voluntarily entered into and the relationship is seen to result from a form of free exchange. This free exchange is itself located within a spontaneous and "natural" order and so perceived as legitimate. Within such a context, the history of usury is important because it opens up an imaginative and conceptual space through which the mythos of the capitalist economy as the sphere of spontaneous and natural relations of free and equal exchange can be contested.

Arguably, ending modern chattel slavery (that is, the predominant form it took from 1444, the date of the first auction of slaves from Africa by Europeans, to 1888, when slavery was abolished in Brazil) did not require a fundamental change to the emergent political economy of industrial and finance capitalism. Rather, although hereditary chattel slavery is a constitutive part of the early development of capitalism, industrialization did eventually undermine it as a form of economic production.[48] By contrast, challenging the nature of financialized credit and debt relations and placing limits on interest rates does challenge the fundamental structures of contemporary capitalism. This is because financialized debt instruments and charging interest are a basic component of capitalism in a way analogous to how chattel slavery was integral to much of the ancient economy. Limiting access to credit or the ability to borrow and imposing excessive interest payments are ways of oppressing and controlling subject populations in both the ancient and modern world. The irony is that reflection on debt in the ancient economy and examination of the biblical and medieval debates about usury can teach us better how to understand the political implications of financial debt and processes of financialization precisely because it was not as basic – it was not the water they swam in – and therefore the threat it posed to building a common life could be seen more clearly.[49] Such an examination is also important as it helps forge a language through which to discuss alternatives to current forms of capitalism – one that runs with the grain of the Jewish, Christian, Islamic, and Greco-Roman legal, philosophical, and theological traditions from which so much of our political and economic lexicon has emerged.

Slavery and Citizenship

Stout frames community organizing, and what he calls "grassroots democracy" as a response to domination. As already noted, the paradigm example of domination in his view is hereditary chattel slavery.[50] Stout draws on the political philosopher Philip Pettit's conception of freedom as nondomination in order to develop a critique of capitalism. Stout sees the unequal relationship between employer and worker as having potential for domination and exploitation. However, rejecting Marx, Stout does not see this as a necessarily and inevitably dominatory relationship. Rather, when it is dominatory, this domination represents a distortion of the system rather than part of the economic system itself. The state is necessary in order to ensure such distortions either do not arise or can be compensated for.[51] His concern with the current U.S. political system is that, rather than preventing or correcting these distortions, the state has been captured so as to serve the interests of capitalist elites so that the United States has become a plutocracy rather than a democracy. In such a context, capitalist relations become relations of domination as power is exercised arbitrarily over workers and "outside the bounds of mutual accountability."[52]

Accountability is crucial because for Stout "power minus accountability equals domination."[53] Following Pettit's conception of freedom as nondomination, it is the arbitrary, unaccountable use of the power, not the unequal possession of power itself that is the problem. For Stout, capitalist relations may not involve physical coercion and the contract of employment may be entered into voluntarily (and therefore notionally be free); however, the political system is so manipulated that workers are unable to stop employers from exploiting to their unfair advantage the necessity of their employees to work in order to live. Workers operate in a captive rather than a free market. But what is an unjust relation is then ascribed to market forces that are viewed as natural processes but which in actuality are relations of domination. On this interpretation, community organizing is a means by which ordinary citizens/workers, who are "weakly grouped," may become organized and thereby attempt to restore nonarbitrary and accountable relations to the system. For Stout, democracy literally "resides in these relations of accountability."[54]

Within Stout's narrative of how the United States came to be a democratic and constitutional republic, the rejection of hereditary chattel slavery and the way in which chattel slavery frames subsequent emancipatory discourses is key. All forms of relations that are morally analogous to chattel slavery must be excluded from the polity. For Stout, the particular experience of the United States is symptomatic of a universal struggle to avoid domination by others.[55] Since the abolition of slavery, these struggles take the form of who should and who should not count as a citizen: that is, as one who is not in a relationship of domination analogous to chattel slavery. As he puts it: "The landmark conflicts in democratic republics since Lincoln's time tend to be about which relationships sufficiently resemble the master-slave relationship to be ruled out absolutely. And this question often comes down to whether the power being exercised in the contested relationship is rightly regarded as arbitrary."[56] In order to rule out domination, sufficiently substantive notions of freedom must be developed and legally enforced. Liberal conceptions of freedom as noninterference are insufficient for two reasons: first, in the legal sphere they leave the dominated with no determinate legal and ethical norms to apply to the arbitrary actions of the strong; and second, in the "associational context, they leave ordinary people without the sort of group ties and differentiated roles that could generate counterpower over against the power of elites."[57] Stout combines a legal and constitutional state committed to a republican vision of freedom as nondomination with a recognition of the need for a strong associational democratic politics, one driven by organized groups with determinate visions of what is "sacred." A strong associational democratic life is essential if the potential of legal safeguards against domination are to be actualized.[58]

While I largely agree with the account Stout gives, it needs strengthening and supplementing through attention to another, and arguably more basic and pervasive form of domination: debt bondage. The International Labor Organization notes that debt bondage is a particularly prominent feature of contemporary forced labor situations and in 2012 it estimated that there were more than 20.9 million people worldwide in situations of forced labor.[59] This figure excludes many of the more subtle forms of debt bondage of the kind London Citizens identified in its listening campaign: practices such as redlining that control access to credit, how sub-prime debt is a way of making ends meet in low-wage economies, and the conversion of "social rights" into credit-debt relations and their subsequent financialization (e.g., student loans, voucher schemes, and private insurance). To generate a sufficiently robust critique of capitalism there is need to take seriously debt bondage as a primary form of domination and the ways in which indebtedness and access to credit determine who has power over whom, at both an interpersonal and a global level.[60] Chattel slavery foregrounds certain kinds of relationships as "horrendous" contraventions of what is held to be "sacred" (namely human dignity); but when it becomes the only or paradigmatic form of domination, it masks how debt relations can become another, more widespread form of domination. Attention to debt bondage also raises questions about the very conception of domination Stout uses. If chattel slavery is the paradigm of what constitutes domination, then the forms of sociality at work in contractual relations within a capitalist economy appear unproblematic as long as they are not arbitrary or too unequal.[61] However, when the contractual relation and the forms of equivalent exchange that undergird it are viewed through the prism of debt bondage, we discover that they inherently establish relations of domination if they are the only relational pattern in operation because they undermine the ability to act within a common realm of meaning and action. The dominated are left with no power to act together because the social bonds that bind them are dissolved and they are thus wholly subject to the demands of others on their time, energy, and resources.

Debt Bondage and the Desecration of a Common Life

The paradox unveiled by debt bondage is that contractual equality can establish nonrecognition of parity within a common life. What debt bondage reveals is that power can be exercised in a wholly accountable, nonarbitrary manner without physical coercion and on the basis of a presumed equality, yet it can entirely strip one of dignity and recognition as a fellow human. Whereas chattel slavery operates by violently ripping people from their contexts so that they are thoroughly dehumanized and removed from all that constitutes them as persons in relation to others, debt bondage constitutes a form of intense, internal exile. Indebtedness is like digging a well for much-needed water only to have the sides collapse as one digs, causing one to be buried alive by the very means through which alleviation is sought. Every time you turn on the light, buy food or clothes, get on the bus, or heat the house, you exacerbate the debt and make matters worse. One's means of living and existing socially becomes the means through which one is dominated and isolated. And, more often than not, all of this occurs "voluntarily" and legally.

The evolution of usury as a term illuminates the interrelationship between voluntary action and coercion in the production of debt bondage. From the twelfth century onward, in both the Christian and Jewish traditions, there emerge distinctions between the legitimate charges on loans and usury; that is, the act or intention of taking profit on a loan. There is a wide-ranging and complex historical debate about how usury as a term evolves and changes throughout the medieval period.[62] Key developments include the emergence of banking, processes of urbanization, and the religiously motivated attempt "to frame the intellectual and moral conditions under which credit might justly be extended."[63] What is clear is that beginning in the twelfth century, concessions to the prohibitions on usury emerged. Crucially, however, the common thread in all the concessions was the continuing subordination of economic to social relations and the distinction between legitimate profit and selfish gain.[64] If mutual reciprocity could be maintained, as in the sharing of risk, then a profit could be made. Usury theory, along with notions of a just price, was a way of conceptualizing the embeddedness of market relations within wider and prior moral and legal relationships.

Where lending at interest does not threaten to reintroduce coercive relations and can maintain relations of reciprocity, then it is licit. Crucial here is whether the exchange involves compulsion or not. And here, the Scholastic debate over usury is directly relevant to contemporary concerns as it was focused on the question of the relationship between need, free will, and compulsion. Responding largely to Aristotle, the key image was that of a ship's captain who has to throw his cargo overboard in a storm in order to save his life and his ship. Although it was an act of free will, it could hardly be said to be voluntary in any straightforward sense. At best such action was forced by need and involved a "mixed will." Likewise, the one who agreed to pay interest by dint of necessity or at a time of distress acted under duress.[65] In such cases, lending at interest was an act of unjust coercion. More difficult was the case of interest where there was no necessity and, thence, no coercion involved in the exchange. A factor determining whether the relationship was usurious or not was whether ownership of the money had been transferred or whether, as in the case of a partnership (either in the form of a *societas* or a *foenus nauticum*), the creditor retained ownership of the money.[66] Profit was legitimate in these latter cases.[67]

On the account developed here, a proper debate is to be had about noncoercive and commercial lending and the kinds of interest and charges that can be made on such loans. The key issue is whether the relationship involves reciprocity, equitable relations, and shared risk.[68] Theologically, as part of the penultimate political economy of the *saeculum*, the charging of interest, where it is noncoercive and involves just relations and mutual benefit rather than selfish gain, is licit. When it becomes coercive and fundamentally alters the relationship between lender and borrower, however, it pertains to the public order of a polity and the question of who legitimately can exercise coercive force. At this point, legislation is required in order to protect the needy and weaker party in the exchange. The most consistent and long-standing example of this kind of protection is a cap on interest rates. Legislative limits on interest rates are necessary to stop indebtedness from being converted into debt bondage and thereby dissolving the conditions for equitable relations between members of the same body politic. Without such limits, there is no end to the power the usurer may exercise.

In contrast to the kinds of borrowing relations cultivated by cooperatives and mutuals, debt-bondage converts relations of equality into ones of domination. As Graeber notes:

> Debt is a very specific thing, and it arises from very specific situations. It first requires a relationship between two people who do not consider each other fundamentally different sorts of being, who are at least potential equals, who *are* equals in those ways that are really important, and who are not currently in a state of equality – but for whom there is some way to set matters straight.[69]

He goes on to point out that during the time the debt is unpaid, the logic of hierarchy takes hold and reciprocity ceases.[70] Giving does not in and of itself generate debt; the gift can simply be part of ongoing mutual aid or reciprocal recognition. To make the gift a debt transforms it and the relationships from those of either equality or reciprocal recognition to those of unequal hierarchy. Debt is thus the inversion of gift. The subsequent conversion of debt into debt bondage, and eventually debt slavery through the imposition of usurious interest rates, is to render the condition permanent and make repayment – setting the matter straight – infeasible. Not only does this condition make dependents of one-time equals, but it also makes an honorable relation into one of shame and immorality (honoring one's debts/obligations to others being a basic feature of most moral frameworks) and, in certain contexts, it is criminalized.[71] Those who should be neighbors become strangers at best or enemies at worst. But what is acutely galling is that an emergency measure – a state of exception – to provide what another lacks in a time of need becomes a permanent ordinance that indentures someone all the while wrapping itself in the cloak of benevolence: a real need for credit is being provided by the usurer and is being accepted voluntarily. It is no wonder that the cancelling of debts is a central demand of innumerable popular uprisings and rebellions from the dawn of civilization to the modern world.

Debt and Citizenship

In ancient Israel, to be either a lender or a borrower was a good thing as it entailed being situated within economic relations of interdependence, cooperation, and mutual responsibility that reflected the God-given pattern of covenantal relations. To lend or borrow was to be drawn into relationships that demanded the negotiation of a common life in which the flourishing of the individual was dependent on the flourishing of others. A contrast can be drawn with Athens. Arguably, in ancient Athens, given the ideal of self-sufficiency, to be a lender was a good thing (although lending operated more on the principle of donation than reciprocity), but to be a borrower was to be located in a dependent rather than a mutual relation and therefore constituted a diminution of status.[72] Moreover, in contrast to the patron-client relations established through lending in Athens, the aim of lending in ancient Israel was to create conditions in which the recipient would no longer be dependent and thereby reestablish the covenantal equality of lender and borrower before God and each other.[73] Maintaining economic relations so they reflected the reality of interdependence and mutual responsibility required legal limits to ensure that the vulnerabilities involved in being a lender or a borrower did not become occasions for exploitation, oppression, and abuse. It was to this need that the legislation concerning usury was addressed and it was the order of fraternal interdependence and mutual responsibility that the act of usury opposed, making of the usurer an enemy of God and his people. Likewise, whether in the Athenian polis, ancient Israel, the Christian *ekklesia*, or the Muslim *Ummah*, debt was a public issue as it related directly to the conditions of membership and the health of the commonwealth. In the Christian world, up to and including the time of the Reformation, debates about usury understood the linkage between debt and the ability to sustain citizenship as a form of *koinonia*/fellowship.[74]

In the social contract tradition of modern political thought, from Hobbes and Locke onward, there is a gradual shift away from a view of citizenship as a form of *koinonia* – in which property was a communicative good – toward a more contractual view based on the exchange of equivalents and in which property is seen in terms of absolute and exclusive ownership.[75] A key backdrop to this conceptual change is the gradual shift from natural rights to subjective rights.[76] Citizenship eventually becomes located within a vision of "possessive individualism" in which freedom is a zero-sum game and not about mutual relations in which the individual's freedom and fulfillment is constituted by relations with others.[77] When freedom is based on absolute property rights rather than understood as the fruit of particular kinds of equal regard, *koinonia*, and good government, then freedom can be alienated, sold, and exchanged. The paradox of freedom understood as an absolute right to dispose of oneself as one chooses, analogous to an "exclusivist" view of property relations, is that we cast ourselves as both master and slave simultaneously. Within this framework there is nothing wrong with either debt or wage slavery if these are seen to arise from a legitimate because "voluntary" contractual exchange.

With the shift to a contractual basis for political order, the need to place limits on debt, usury, and the uses of money wanes as a primary public concern.[78] For example, the founder of utilitarianism, Jeremy Bentham, writing in the 1780s, expounded the influential view that anti-usury measures are unnecessary and irrational.[79] In the contemporary context, personal and national debt are not necessarily seen as threats to good citizenship and political order. Instead, the citizen is often conceptualized as a consumer and the economy, not civic life, is demarcated as the sphere of free, uncoerced relations.[80] Wolin argues that liberalism identifies freedom with private interest rather than the pursuit of common action and shared advantage. The corollary of this is to grant the economy maximal scope and priority over either the requirements of good government or the internal goods of any institution, whether it is a family, a farm, or a factory.[81] Economics becomes the queen of the sciences that can best tell us about how to order our common life.[82] As a result, social harmony and a rational political order are no longer seen to issue from and be embedded within a prior set of social, institutional, and historical arrangements but are now understood to flow from the spontaneous equilibrium of economic forces. Within such a vision the status of the citizen becomes absorbed into that of the producer, consumer, and debtor. Modern performances of citizenship tacitly envisage debt as the condition of good citizenship as debt sustains the dominant political order and its analogue: a mortgaged, highly speculative, and debt-driven economy in which social relations are mediated and represented through consumerist modes of common action and identity formation. It would be tempting to see in this shift the complete inversion of Athens and Jerusalem. However, we must resist simplistic declension narratives and look instead for patterns of continuity as well as change.

Land and Sea

The symbiotic yet antagonistic relationship between conceptions of individual freedom, the liberal state, and laissez-faire economics goes to the heart of the social contract tradition of citizenship. As suggested in Chapters 6 and 7, the sovereignty of the individual in the marketplace is the correlative of the rise of the indivisible sovereign political authority, which is needed to control the social forces unleashed by possessive individualism. When the institutions of the market are disembedded from prior social relations (and tradition, custom, mutuality, loyalty, and trust are replaced by contract), not only does everyone becomes a stranger to each other, but the stronger and more centralized one has to make state power. In the process, the standardizing and instrumentalizing rationalities by which state authorities evaluate and make judgments come to the fore, while more contextually sensitive and practically wise forms of making judgments are not only marginalized, but also delegitimized. Paradoxically, this process of disembedding renders the Hobbesian Leviathan, the monster from the sea, the only means by which to hold back the watery chaos that threatens to flood life on the land; that is, the unregulated, disembedded financial markets that exist beyond and outside of sovereign nation-states (as distinct from local, embedded markets that are part of the land-based political economy).[83] The population churn discussed in Chapter 2 exemplifies the consequences of this flood. Made visible and reiterated in every crisis of capitalism is the paradox of the Leviathan: the mythic symbol of chaos that comes from the sea is nevertheless called on to reestablish the borders between "land" and "sea." Welfare provision and the regulation of markets, whether in response to the Great Depression of the 1930s or the Great Recession of 2008 onward, are the manifestations of this paradox. The liberal state is simultaneously a symptom of and a defense against the rendering of human lives into commodities and collateral. Rather than being in opposition, the modern market and state are two sides of the same coin.[84] As with the coins in our pockets, one side – "heads" – bears the symbol of the sovereign authority whereas the other side – "tails" – specifies its value as a token of commercial exchange.[85] Yet coins only have value when embedded in and serving a set of preexisting social relations. When those same social relations are entirely subordinated to the service of either side of the coin, we should, following the book of Revelation, see this as a monstrous inversion of the purposes of both.[86]

The ambiguous nature of the modern state/Leviathan can be understood more clearly if we reflect further on the symbolic division between land and sea. Schmitt builds on ancient myths, philosophy, and history that portray human life as founded on the threshold between the restless sea and the stable ground to suggest that the primordial division between land and sea is crucial for understanding the nature and development of different kinds of political order.[87] Schmitt draws from the work of philosopher and geographer Ernst Kapp to suggest that the great shifts in human social and political organization are accompanied by a series of temporal and spatial revolutions.[88] For Kapp, the first large-scale political formations were based along and around rivers: for example, the association between the Babylon, Sumerian, and other Mesopotamian Empires with the Tigris and Euphrates; the Gupta Empire in India with the Indus and Ganges; Chinese empires with the Yellow River and the Yangtze; and the Songhai Empire with the Niger. Fluvial space and time was then superseded or threatened by empires that mastered and controlled the sea: for example, the Mediterranean was vital to the Athenian, Macedonian, Roman, and eventually the Venetian Empires; and the Persian Gulf and the Black, Arabian, and Red Seas were vital to the Ottoman Empire. From 1492 onward, the shift to oceanic trade represented a third temporal and spatial revolution. The Spanish, Portuguese, and Dutch spearheaded the development of this now planetary form of rule. But the first truly oceanic empire that encompassed a unified planetary space and time in a single economic and political realm was the British Empire, even though as an empire it was still imagined in contradistinction to imperial "others"/enemies, whether contemporaneous (France, Spain) or ancient (Rome, Babylon).[89] A key driver in its emergence was the City of London and its combination of finance and "corsair" capitalism that enabled it to simultaneously plunder and make itself indispensable to the world.[90]

The fourth spatial and temporal revolution was the shift from the oceans to the air. Exemplified in the "space race," the United States was the leading power in this revolution. Although it took the end of the Cold War for a truly global consciousness to emerge, globalization on this reading is the turn to look at the land from the perspective of the sea and then the air.[91] The land ceases to be a home or *terroir* and becomes instead a point of resupply in the flow of trade, a node in a communication network, and a resource to fuel the relentless need for movement necessary to sustain a now unified, planetary political and economic space and time. To paraphrase Marx: it is the melting of all that is solid into the constantly circulating and immaterial ambit of air and water.[92] Or to use a meteorological image, globalization is constituted by interactions simultaneously occurring at three levels: the planetary flows, circulations, and networks that constitute the global financial, political, and cultural climate, which are mediated through and interacting with regional and national economic, political, and cultural weather, which is in tension with and responsive to the needs and limits of social, economic, and political life in the neighborhoods where we live, work, and worship. Political authorities are always having to mediate between the competing and mutually refracting demands of these three levels, but particularly between the dissolving and quickening effects of global finance and trade ("the sea") and the requirements of stable, place-based, political relations ("the land"). The type of account given here enables us to refute simplistic pro- or antistate positions to ones that envisage how the state is both part of the problem and an important means of defense against the liquefying effects of "the sea." It is to such accounts that we now turn.

VIENNA: ECONOMIC DEMOCRACY AND THE NATURE OF FREEDOM IN THE MARKETPLACE

We shift now from Athens and Jerusalem to "red Vienna." Vienna was governed from 1918 to 1934 as a social democratic municipality – hence the label "red" – but was overthrown after a brief civil war in 1934, with the Nazis eventually taking control at the *Anschluss* in 1938. While it lasted, red Vienna anticipated much of what came to characterize the welfare provision that emerged from the New Deal in the United States and Europe after World War II, in particular the provision of public housing, healthcare, and education.[93] Apart from being an example of municipal *pietas* contesting a broader national configuration (albeit fleetingly), red Vienna is also of interest as it was the site of a now obscure but highly significant chapter in the history of economics: the socialist calculation debate. Responses to this debate have in large part determined the range of public policy responses to capitalism. On one side of this debate were Ludwig von Mises and Friedrich von Hayek, the patriarchs of neoliberalism and the Chicago school of economics; on the other side were various advocates of socialist thought, ranging from those who recommended command economies to those who took a more syndicalist line that favored exchange in kind.[94] The debate set the tone for what were to become the economic differences between market Socialism and Marxism. The primary question, however, was whether a centralized state authority could plan and control the economy. Mises and Hayek argued that no centralized authority could plan the economy because it could not gain sufficient information to set prices or predict outcomes. According to Hayek's view, any attempt to do so would lead not only to disastrous economic consequences, but also to totalitarian forms of government.[95] Given conditions of scarcity and finitude of knowledge, only a market mechanism can efficiently perform the allocative function of distributing capital and other resources to where they are needed most. If the price mechanism was to function properly, freedom for individual initiative was needed at the points of production, distribution, and exchange. Leaving aside the technicalities of the debate and the variation between Mises's and Hayek's position, the key point to note here is that for them the market system was spontaneous and self-regulating.[96]

Taking part in these debates was Karl Polanyi who was later forced to leave Austria in 1933 with the rise of Nazism. Polanyi took a view different from that of Hayek and Mises *and* from that of the state socialists and Marxists. It is his view that draws together Athens (the need for both a participatory democratic politics and buffers between "the land" and "the sea" in order to set limits to the power of money) and Jerusalem (the need for legal limits and embedding credit-debt relations in reciprocal relations to ensure lending and borrowing contribute to the flourishing of the body politic) in relation to Vienna (the liberal yet precarious state in danger of being captured by totalitarian forces or elite interests or of collapsing into relativistic and violent chaos).

Polanyi agreed with Mises and Hayek that the price mechanism rather than a centralized authority should determine the market. Concurring with Hayek, Polanyi realized that anything else was inherently totalistic and gave too much power to technocratic elites.[97] Thus, for the early Polanyi at least, the state socialists and social democrats were wrong. But the implication of the position

Polanyi developed was that Mises and the early Hayek were naïve in their view that market relations were spontaneous and could be self-regulating. Hayek himself came to advocate the need for legal limits to the market and moderate government-welfare provision. Hayek's state-centric approach was questioned by John Maynard Keynes who pointed to a paradox at the heart of Hayek's position: "You admit here and there that it is a question of knowing where to draw the line. You agree that the line has to be drawn somewhere, and that the logical extreme [i.e., laissez-faire] is not possible. But you give us no guidance as to where to draw it." Keynes goes on to say, "as soon as you [Hayek] admit that the extreme is not possible, and that a line has to be drawn, you are, on your own argument, done for, since you are trying to persuade us that as soon as one moves an inch in the planned direction you are necessarily launched on the slippery slope which will lead you in due course over the precipice."[98] While Hayek wrestled with this dilemma and came up with a variety of responses in his writing, and despite his own commitments to democracy, he could never accept the kind of approach Polanyi advocated, as it would have meant revoking basic assumptions he worked with, most notably, that markets were self-regulating.

Building on the work of the Guild Socialists, the implication of Polanyi's position was that economic freedom and individual initiative at the points of production, distribution, and exchange should be complemented by associational freedom and democratic politics also situated at those same points. The system Polanyi advocates is far too cumbersome to be implemented.[99] However, the basic point stands: an efficient and balanced economy – if it was to remain so – needed economic democracy as much as it needed market freedoms. Crucially, in Polanyi's view, Hayek and Mises truncated their analysis. The information that needed to be communicated was not just economic but also social and political. Polanyi saw that markets and money are not neutral; they tend to crowd out nonmarket values and considerations, which in turn has massive social and political consequences. Hayek's proposal for dealing with these consequences through locating political decision making in the state contradicts the logic of his own argument. If all political judgments are left to a centralized authority, then the system is inherently technocratic and totalistic. We see this self-contradiction reflected in the state-driven, highly centralized, and homogenizing "reforms" of education, healthcare, and welfare provision by right-wing governments. Marching under the ideological banner of marketization they enact utopian schemes of social engineering. Forms of participatory and economic democracy are a way of ensuring that more consociational, decentralized, and agency-centered forms of coming to political judgment are embedded within the means of production, distribution, and exchange (whether in the "private" or "public" sector) so as to ensure they contribute: (1) to the commonwealth not just the wealth of the few, (2) to a more even distribution of power, and (3) efficient and accurate accountability at the appropriate location.[100] As we shall see, in order for this to be possible, contractual property relations backed by the state urgently need supplementing with the institutionalization of the means for producing relational power and phronēsis/mētis; that is, consociational organizations that embody relations of reciprocity, mutuality, and gift.[101] Without countervailing forms of democratic association, judgment making, and means of communication to signal both variations in context and points of social and political conflict, then the power of those with money dominates all aspects of life.[102] As set out in Chapters 1 and 2, it was just such an insight that drove the Populists in the nineteenth century, the work of John L. Lewis in union organizing in the 1930s, the aligned work of Alinsky in community organizing from the 1940s onward, and the proposals London Citizens presented at the Barbican assembly in 2009. This is not a coincidence; it's a pattern. Moreover, this kind of framework echoes the conceptualization of civil society as a sphere of communication, cooperation, and conflict given in Chapter 6.

As in Athens and Jerusalem, legal limits, a participatory democratic politics, upholding the dignity of labor, and the re-embedding of market relations in social and political relations of reciprocity are needed if money, markets, and property are to serve socially and politically productive purposes. The implication of Polanyi's account is that we need to extend economic democracy through such measures as the representation of workers on pension remuneration boards; active trade union and shareholder involvement in corporate governance; alternative and local financial institutions such as credit unions, regional banks, and Local Exchange Trading Schemes (LETS); and consumer associations. Such measures depend on reciprocal relations being maintained and operate with a mixed economy of gift relations that are reflected in the self-ascribed names such ventures adopt in the modern period: *friendly* societies, *cooperatives*, *mutuals*, credit *unions*, and *social* insurance. These institutional forms of structuring production, distribution, exchange, and the dispersal of assets provide an alternative to capitalistic forms and thereby ensure that competition is meaningful and that there exists a genuine market. This alternative is not one that exists in a different region or across a border – as in the Cold War – but on Main Street. Alternative institutional forms and patterns of ownership need appropriate legislative frameworks in order to secure legal space for their establishment. This requires legal recognition of alternative economic arrangements (e.g., the UK's Credit Union Act of 1979), anti-usury measures, and regulation (e.g., the Glass-Steagall provisions within the 1933 U.S. Banking Act) that create a semipermeable membrane that prevents the fragile nexus of people, place, and money from being sucked into and commoditized by the unregulated global finance economy ("the sea"). But as well as a ceiling (legislative limits and frameworks), and furniture (the dispersal of assets, different forms of credit provision, and noncapitalistic institutions of production, distribution, and exchange), a room to live in requires a floor. In the contemporary context, a floor is constituted by a legally enforced minimum wage so that people are not dependent on redistribution mechanisms of the state to make a life but can act for themselves in relation to others.[103] A floor below which people cannot fall is needed in order to ensure there is a level and secure base from which all citizens can act.

The Rise of Capitalism, Social Citizenship, and the Re-Embedding of Markets

Writing in the 1940s and, like Hayek, trying to understand the rise of fascism, Polanyi analyzed the history of how laissez-faire capitalism emerged. Contrary to Hayek, Polanyi contended that capitalism historically resulted from intentional state action. The end result of which was the formation of a capitalist global-market system in the nineteenth century, which led not to greater social harmony (as Hayek supposed), but to social and political conflict and turmoil. In response to the deleterious impact of social relations being embedded in market relations, democratic and fascistic countermovements emerged.[104] In short, it was not centralized economic planning that paved the road to serfdom but unregulated and disembedded capitalism. Echoing Aristotle, Polanyi discerned that chrematistics – whether in ancient Athens, Weimar Berlin, or contemporary New York – leads not to self-regulating financial markets or an economic equilibrium, but a range of economic distortions and instabilities driven in large part by *pleonexia*.[105] In the terms of Chapter 6, what Polanyi identifies is the process by which the economic sphere simultaneously disentangles itself from the fabric of the civil sphere and then comes to overdetermine every other sphere.

Polanyi identifies three ideal-type mechanisms that coordinate economic production with the institutions of social and political life: *reciprocity*, *redistribution*, and *exchange*.[106] For Polanyi, reciprocity is a form of gift exchange in which goods are shared for the sake of building or upholding relationships. This sharing is symmetrical, interpersonal, and takes place over time so that today's giving will be recompensed at some point by the receipt of something proportional on another day.[107] By contrast, with market exchange the relationship is entered into solely for the sake of the commodity exchanged and expects an equivalent return there and then. Polanyi notes that "[b]arter, truck, and exchange is a principle of economic behaviour dependent for its effectiveness upon the market pattern. A market is a meeting place for the purpose of barter or buying and selling."[108] By Polanyi's account, reciprocal gift exchange undergirds forms of social institutions such as the family whereas commodity-focused exchange gives rise to a distinct institution: the market. Yet the nonrelational focus of the market means that "the market is of overwhelming consequence to the whole organization of society: it means no less than the running of society as an adjunct to the market. Instead of economy being embedded in social relations, social relations are embedded in the economic system."[109] Drawing from Aristotle, Polanyi distinguishes production for gain from the production and distribution of material goods within the household or for patterns of gift exchange. For Polanyi and Aristotle, these latter forms, which are a nexus of intention and institution, are wholly distinct in kind from the market. He states: "In denouncing the principle of production for gain as boundless and limitless, 'as not natural to man,' Aristotle was, in effect, aiming at the crucial point, namely, the divorce of the economic motive from all concrete social relationships which would by their very nature set a limit to that motive."[110]

In contrast to market exchange (and its intentional corollary, production for gain), but similar to reciprocity, redistribution also enmeshes the exchange of material goods in social relationships. However, unlike reciprocity, the exchange is not symmetrical, distributed across multiple points, and interpersonal, but rather is hierarchal and centralized in some way such that the "production and distribution of goods is organized in the main through collection, storage, and redistribution, the pattern being focused on the chief, the temple, the despot, or the lord."[111] The distribution of material goods moves away from or toward a central authority and tends to undergird and reinforce the institutions of a sovereign political authority.

By Polanyi's account, the separation of the production and distribution of material goods from social and political institutions is a pathology in need of constant remediation by institutions and movements to re-embed the economy.[112] The re-prioritizing of reciprocity and redistribution are two such means and both can be understood as undergirding particular expressions of citizenship. In Athens and Jerusalem, owning land was the means through which one gained economic and therefore political agency. Such agency enabled one to act with others without being dependent on their charity, a client of their patronage, or becoming either a debt or a chattel slave. In the contemporary context, land has been replaced by other kinds of social goods or properties. Thus, according to T. H. Marshall's influential account of "social citizenship," rights to such goods as free or affordable healthcare, education, housing, and pensions are a prerequisite of civil freedom; formal civil rights are meaningless without the educational, economic, and personal resources or properties necessary to be the kind of person capable of accessing and acting on civil rights on equal terms with others.[113] Similar to Marshall, Polanyi (and to a certain extent, Hayek) came to see redistribution via the state as the means through which to realize "social citizenship," deal with market-driven exclusions and inequalities, and re-embed capitalism.[114] One way of reading the emergence of social democracies and welfare states as ways of addressing the needs for "social citizenship" is that they have tended to focus primarily on redistribution as the means of remediation to the detriment of reciprocity.[115] The principle of redistribution emphasizes centralized authority rather than either the principle of subsidiarity or a more distributed, consociational vision of sovereignty, and downplays the role of civil society in the production and provision of welfare. In light of the manifold failures and problems that attend a redistributive approach, problems that Alinsky's work was partly a response to, we must question its sufficiency. I shall do this via a more detailed examination of the kinds of relationship a covenantal view of citizenship entails.

A Reciprocal Economic and Political Order

Two contemporary Italian economists suggest a different direction to that given by Polanyi's later work and the emergence of social democratic welfare regimes in the West. Luigi Bruni and Stefanos Zamagni focus on reciprocity as a mode of re-embedding economic relations as well as the implications of reciprocity for welfare provision, civil society, and economic production and distribution. Rejecting the attempt by the intellectual descendants of Mises and Hayek to apply economistic forms of analysis such as rational-choice theory to interpersonal relationships, they reverse the direction of travel and conceptualize the market and economic relations as a social institution maintained by specific norms, cultural matrixes, conventions, and social practices.[116] Consequently, they see economic modes of production and distribution as potential means of generating virtuous and politically significant social relations and institutions. The key to this project is reciprocity understood as the gratuitous and free exchange of gifts between distinct persons, each of whom is presumed to have intrinsic worth. Its aim is to build up "fraternity," which they contrast with "solidarity." Fraternity is said to emphasize the ways in which social relations involve differences in relation rather than a unified and abstract form of community where differences are erased in the name of everyone being identified as the same.[117]

They distinguish *gift-as-reciprocity* from the parallel but equally important and necessary principles of *exchange of equivalents*, *redistribution*, and *gift-as-*munus.[118] The exchange of equivalents, which they identify with contractual relations, aims at efficiency and equality in the exchange of goods and services, whereas the principle of redistribution aims at justice. In distinction to both of these, gift-as-*munus* denotes both a present and an obligation or duty. As such, the exchange of gifts is not a free act but is one that obliges the recipient to return a counter-gift or be indebted or even subservient to the giver. Their paradigm for this is the kind of competitive gift giving Marcel Mauss outlines in the phenomena of potlatch and *kula*.[119] Gift-as-*munus* is compatible with and can be expressed through individualistic forms of philanthropy and donation that expect no return and seek instead an increase in one's prestige and status.

Bruni and Zamagni contend that all four principles are necessary for human flourishing in complex societies, but the problem comes when one or two are emphasized to the exclusion of others. So what they call the "benevolent state" (which they take to be the dominant form in Europe) emphasizes redistribution of wealth produced efficiently by the market on the basis of an exchange of equivalents. By contrast, "philanthropic capitalism" (which they see as characteristic of the United States) emphasizes exchange of equivalents in the market tempered by gift-as-*munus* where the wealthy individual or foundation rather than the state is the benefactor. In contradistinction to the benevolent state and philanthropic capitalism are the historic forms of "civil economy" where gift-as-reciprocity is the primary principle. In their account of civil economy, civil society is rendered neither a not-for-profit sector (as in philanthropic capitalism) nor a nongovernmental sector (as in the benevolent state), nor a voluntary sector, but the sphere in which political, economic, and social relations are held in tensional, mutually constitutive relations and thus give rise to institutions that blend political, economic, and social commitments and outcomes. What Bruni and Zamagni's analysis helps describe are all sorts of institutions such as universities, schools, hospitals, and so forth that are already "civil enterprises" but which are under constant pressure to become that which they are not: institutions operating wholly according to the logic of either equivalence, redistribution, or *munus*.

Taxonomies of Sociality

Democratic citizenship should not only be conceptualized in contractual terms, but also as involving forms of gift relation. This contention necessitates acknowledging the role of Christian conceptions of "the gift" in what follows.[120] In acknowledging this debt, I am doing no more than making explicit what is implicit in nearly all deployments and discussions of such terms as gift, love, solidarity, and friendship as forms of political relation. These are terms, for better or worse, whose genealogy is profoundly shaped by "Jerusalem," even if they have subsequently become "secularized." Furthermore, in making explicit the theological roots of the taxonomy developed here I am following the precedent of Polanyi, Bruni, and Zamagni who, in their work, are all explicitly in dialogue with Christian theology.[121]

While deeply indebted to theological discussions of love and gift, what follows is also developed in dialogue with a particular strand of economic thought: namely, economic anthropology.[122] It is also one in which reflection on the nature of gift relations is central. Moreover, contemporary economists increasingly note the importance of particular forms of sociality to economic growth and that a breakdown in social relations has an adverse economic impact. This is reflected in the use of such categories as "well-being," "trust," and "happiness" in relation to economics. Following the work of the political scientist Robert Putnam, the use of the term "social capital" is one prominent way of interrelating forms of sociality with economics and has even been used to frame the meaning and purpose of community organizing.[123] Yet social capital, along with such terms as "well-being" and "happiness," tends to homogenize very different patterns of sociality and mask the tensions between different patterns of relationships. So while owning a certain specificity of tradition in how the different types of relationships are conceptualized (Hindu, Confucian, or Buddhist starting points, for example, would draw out different things), what follows is put forward as a richer, more differentiated account of interrelated but distinct kinds of sociality.[124]

Equivalent Exchange

Before exploring further how a conception of reciprocity can be the basis of democratic citizenship, it is necessary to question Bruni and Zamagni's schema as, like Polanyi's before it, it conflates a number of distinct forms of sociality. The term "sociality" is being used here to denote a distinct and recognizable pattern to the protocols, etiquette, bodily proprieties, and expectations that shape, structure, and orientate particular sequences of social interaction. In light of broader anthropological, theological, and philosophical discussions of gift exchange, we can be more affirming of gift-as-*munus* and more critical of gift-as-reciprocity as forms of sociality, while expanding and differentiating further the schema of ideal types Bruni and Zamagni outline.

The first ideal type of sociality is *equivalent exchange*. We can identify this type with commercial, legal, and other forms of contractually governed exchange. At its best, equivalent exchange is a means through which to achieve commutative justice. However, equivalent exchange generates its own corruption when it becomes an exclusive mode of conducting relations, one that subordinates all other social and political relations to its pattern.[125] The internal logic of equivalent exchange, if unchecked, is oriented toward processes of commodification and instrumentalization whereby persons become fungible objects to be exchanged, quantified, or subordinated to the demands of an "impartial" program or procedure rather than attended to as ends in and of themselves.

Redistribution

Following Polanyi, Bruni, and Zamagni, we can observe that another widespread pattern, habit, and way of organizing relationships is *redistribution*. This form of sociality ensures that each person is given a proportional share of the whole as a member of the wider community. At its best, redistribution is a means through which to achieve distributive justice. However, if redistribution is emphasized exclusively, then it tends toward forms of collectivism in which the good of the individual is entirely subordinated to the whole. Both redistribution and the exchange of equivalents depend on and presume the existence of a centralized authority for their enforcement. Although the exchange of equivalents is based on a form of reciprocity (a type of minimalist golden rule), rather than strengthening interpersonal relationships, it prioritizes the goods or services exchanged, resulting in the need for a third, independent, and sufficiently authoritative party able to impose sanctions if the contract is not fulfilled. Thus, we are back to C. B. Macpherson's argument about Hobbes: citizenship envisaged in solely contractual terms not only necessitates a strong, centralized sovereign authority, but also presumes that equivalent exchange is the basic and only politically salient form of social relation. Forms of noncontractual cooperation and exchange are excluded as either irrelevant or redescribed as forms of equivalent exchange.

Gift Exchange

Third, there is *gift exchange,* which blurs the line between gift-as-reciprocity and gift-as-*munus* as Bruni and Zamagni conceive it and which includes such things as ceremonial gift exchange, potlatch, and hospitality (understood as an asymmetric exchange between guest and host). No less present in modern than in archaic societies, gift exchange aims at the recognition between giver and receiver that they exist in a common world of meaning and action.[126] It can entail enormous asymmetry between the gifts received and what is offered in return, and what is offered may only be a symbolic gesture such as a dance or song. Yet the exchanges are tokens of *recognition*. As a means of forging or maintaining social bonds, it is not in opposition to justice but is rather a necessary condition for determining what each is due. As Hénaff notes, the purpose of gift exchange is not to distribute goods, measure wealth, or right wrongs, but rather, it is "[t]o honour a partner; to assert oneself in the order of esteem, glory, and honour; to confirm one another according to the requirements of dignity, fidelity, rank, and sometimes allegiance; and, above all, to express reciprocal attachment."[127] However, the corruption of gift exchange results in forms of paternalism and clientelism (and the injustices these reinscribe), or can trigger a degenerative cycle of mimetic rivalry (or negative reciprocity) leading to processes of scapegoating, victimization, and violence.[128]

Gift exchange is not a relationship between humans mediated by things – this is to conflate gifts with the exchange of equivalents. Rather, it is a relationship mediated by symbols.[129] As noted earlier, these symbols may be physical goods, but can also be such things as a gesture, word, song, or feast. That which is offered is presented as both a mark of respect and a demand for reciprocal recognition from the other; a demand that presumes the possibility of a common life. The demand for and offer of reciprocal recognition entails a simultaneous challenging of and a generous reaching out to another. As Hénaff contends:

> Above all, [gift exchange] remains governed by the triple obligation to give, to receive, and to reciprocate the gift. This is a paradoxical obligation, not only because it is at the same time free and required but also because for the partners it constitutes the reciprocal recognition of their freedom. The giver recognizes the other's freedom by honoring him, but he also claims his own freedom through his offer of munificent gifts, which amounts to a challenge for the other to do the same. This agonistic relation is first and foremost an equal one.[130]

Mauss was the first to suggest that ceremonial and public gift exchange is an agonistic yet peaceful means of generating mutual recognition between distinct groups in contexts where there is no centralized, sovereign state. With the advent of the modern state, public and mutual recognition between strangers becomes increasingly mediated and guaranteed through law and bureaucracy.

Modern polities seek to function without recourse to ceremonial gift exchange, relying instead on civic bonds defined by law and bonds generated by commercial exchange. Gifts then assume a more voluntaristic, private, disinterested character as their political functions are progressively taken over by state institutions. Yet, as Hénaff suggests, "the price to pay for this is a symbolic deficit that constitutes the major problem of modern democracies" as neither law nor commerce recognizes the infinite dignity of the person as a priceless and incommensurable gift.[131] Without the kind of public recognition generated by symbolic exchange in which gifts from one's customs and traditions are offered as a way of calling forth reciprocal recognition, then the kinds of social bonds such gift exchange can generate between diverse and potentially hostile groups is absent and an entirely administrative and commodified way of organizing and constituting social relations is in danger of dominating political and social existence. The result is that persons become treated as things.

As noted in Chapter 4, the resort to ceremonial gift exchange is a way of demanding recognition in the absence, omission, or failure of bureaucratic, contractual, or rights-based approaches to securing recognition. In community organizing, this is accomplished by recourse to the "festive" as a means of both demanding respect and offering acclamation. As a form of "protest," it presumes, invites, and challenges the other to participate in a common world of meaning and action. As a means, it touches on the "sacred" as it presupposes there are things deserving of recognition that are given rather than made, that are priceless and beyond an instrumental, administrative way of organizing and directing relationships. Resorting to the festive articulates the claim that before any legal, administrative, or economic exchange can occur between humans, a gift has been received that makes such exchange possible. This prior giftedness needs recognition and valuing within the ordering of political and economic life. The basis of this gift is what a community holds to be "sacred": that which derives its value from the symbols of a community's being, its very heart, that which it most treasures, and what represents its basic commitments and orientation through time. For religious groups these "sacred" things are originally gifts of or offerings to the gods. In offering gifts derived from these sacred things, even in a comic manner, something precious is offered as a pledge that calls for a response. Of course, the offering of a gift can be misinterpreted, particularly within a capitalist context, so that we confuse symbolic tokens of recognition for payments in kind and thereby convert gift exchange into the exchange of equivalents.[132]

Grace

Fourth is *grace* or *agapē*. This involves benevolent giving without either conditions or the expectation of a direct return or counter-gift. It is also premised on inequality: one individual or group has more than the other. Yet it aims at recognizing participation in a common world of meaning and action *despite* conditions of inequality, regarding the other as of intrinsic and inestimable worth without regard for material and other inequalities. The word grace (*charis*) is appropriate to use for this kind of act as grace refers to the act of someone with unilateral power – normally a patron – showing favor or giving something to another person or group out of sheer generosity, mercy, or compassion.[133] It is a move beyond forms of gift *exchange*. However, although grace is not earned or necessarily merited and operates outside of patterns of gift exchange, once it is bestowed there is an expectation that an appropriate response will be given.[134] What is the appropriate or fitting response to a gift of grace? In the Greco-Roman world a number of things could be expected (but not necessarily obligated or demanded) of those who received an act of grace.[135] The first was to show gratitude expressed through thanksgiving to and praise for the giver, but also through virtuous living, which was to behave in a way worthy of having received a great and unmerited gift. The second was to demonstrate loyalty or faithfulness, as the point of an act of grace was to establish a bond between giver and receiver. The third expectation was that one would circulate or pass on what was received: the act of grace was not supposed to stop dead but to initiate a cycle of generous gift giving (rather than gift exchange). The last was to render services to or on behalf of one's benefactor at the appropriate moment.[136] This pattern of conduct sequences many aspects of life. For example, as Bruni suggests, artists operate with this kind of "unconditional reciprocity." Their acts are gratuitous and understood to be acts intrinsic to the vocation of being an artist and their art is given irrespective of the response of others and without expectation of a counter-gift. Yet the artist hopes his or her contribution will generate an appropriate response and will inspire others to go and do likewise. Noncommercial blood donation can be seen in a similar light. So although grace is an unexpected, unconditional, and gratuitous blessing, the aspiration is that it will bear fruit.[137]

At its best, relations of grace are what the church historically called "works of mercy" and in their self-consciously secularized form, one divorced from any cosmic horizon of meaning and purpose, they become humanitarian aid.[138] Such provision is a means of recognizing another as a human, as an individual who is the same as oneself, and thereby communicating to one in distress or peril that he or she is not rejected, abandoned, or forgotten but exists in a common world. This is especially necessary at points of crisis – natural disasters and famine being paradigm instances – when others find themselves without the necessary resources to act for themselves. In the Christian tradition, following the pattern of Christ's incarnation and crucifixion, acts of grace may necessitate forms of radical renunciation or *kenosis* on the part of the giver so as to enable a deeper, intimate, and more meaningful relationship to be forged (an element almost entirely absent in notions of humanitarianism and altruism).[139] One can see something of this in the witness of monks and nuns through the centuries whose way of life points the broader body politic to the ongoing need to renounce idolatrous ties to property, kinship, comfort, and status if meaningful relationships to God and neighbor are to emerge. In stark contrast to practices of personal and material renunciation, the corruptions of grace take the forms of noblesse oblige and philanthropic donation, both of which emphasize rather than bridge the distance between giver and receiver and leave intact the structures of inequality or privilege that grace should be the first step in remediating. Added to that, its corruptions tend to sentimentalize and infantilize the "have-nots," perceiving them as victims or passive recipients rather than as active (or at least potentially active) agents within the ongoing formation of a common life. A further danger attends acts of grace: that we do not give or receive the gift as a generous blessing to be passed on so as to extend the circle of charitable relations but instead convert the gift into a debt. Again, we take a form of gift relation and turn it into the exchange of equivalents.[140] As in such notions as "venture philanthropy," instead of giving freely, we demand a return on our "investment." Instead of blessing, we count the cost.

Communion

Beyond gift exchange and grace is the fifth type of sociality: *communion* or mutual sharing. Communion is paradoxical: it is the gift that is not a gift because it is just what friends and family do for each other. Communion means literally a sharing or bringing together of gifts: *com-* meaning "with" or "together"; *munia* meaning "gifts." Communion denotes a common life built up of generous sharing of what we have. This sharing takes place between those one considers part of one's common, ongoing, and future life. Communion is neither an exchange, nor unilateral, nor a relation of debt and obligation, but rather is one of mutual aid and sharing according to need.[141] It characterizes the at-times perichoretic sharing between family, friends, or neighbors. Those one shares with may be considered equals (as between friends and neighbors) or unequal (as between parent and child).[142] The key is not the relative status or value of each within the whole but the ability of each to proportionally participate in and contribute to the whole according to need and ability.[143] The corruptions of communion are manifold and result in its ossification into exclusive and excluding forms of communalism, factionalism, sectarianism, or tribalism in relation to other groups and a move toward nepotism and the clannish overdetermination of members' identities and life in relation to "insiders."

The Necessary Interplay of Different Types of Sociality

All five types of sociality are necessary for human flourishing in complex societies and their interlacing is constitutive of a pluriform social, economic, and political order. Moreover, although there is no necessary opposition between the relational patterns, habits, and forms of gift exchange, grace, and communion and those primarily operative in law and commerce, in practice they often conflict. Part of political judgment is discerning when one type should be emphasized to the exclusion of others in order to ensure the flourishing of the whole. At the same time, the absence of one leads to dysfunction in the others as each can discipline and repair the distortions and corruptions in the others. When a single form of sociality is emphasized to the exclusion of the others, not only do its corruptions go unchecked, but also it becomes cancerous – overproducing itself and undermining the conditions and possibilities for other forms of sociality to operate. In the contemporary context, it is the exchange of equivalents that is emphasized to the detriment of the others, in the absence of which its minimalist version of the golden rule remains untempered and so in economic relations it collapses into the pursuit of selfish interests and, in legal and administrative relations, into a *lex talionis* untempered by mercy.[144] As the philosopher Paul Ricoeur notes: "The golden rule, given over to itself, sinks to the rank of a utilitarian maxim, the rule of justice, given over to itself, tends to subordinate cooperation to competition, or rather to expect from the equilibrium of rival interests the simulacrum of cooperation."[145] Contemporary understandings of citizenship need to expand beyond the framework of contract – and therefore the exchange of equivalents – to encompass gift exchange, grace, and mutual sharing, none of which should be confined to the realm of the private and each of which is necessary to temper equivalent exchange and redistribution.[146] In short, neither contract nor catallaxy are sufficient to generate a tolerably peaceable polis; also needed are forms of covenant.

Even though the taxonomy established here is simply a heuristic framework, it nevertheless helps bring to the fore certain dimensions of social and political life that are obscured in some of the dominant prisms through which democratic politics is interpreted.[147] It is to a number of other frameworks and how they compare and contrast with the taxonomy outlined here that we now turn.

Citizenship, Self-Interest, and Mutuality

In light of the previous analysis, we can specify further the nature of the social basis of democratic citizenship and how it constitutes a means of countering "money power." Part of our problem in conceptualizing democratic citizenship in consociational terms so that it can include covenantal forms of relation is that gift relations have become a private, personal matter, reserved for the protected niches of family, friendship, and neighborhood. The incursion of gift relations into public relationships is either seen as an added extra superfluous to their proper functioning or as an improper form of exclusive attachment that threatens to corrupt the equal and neutral application of laws, rules, and procedures. Appropriate public concern is conceptualized in terms of altruism and humanitarianism – the dispassionate sympathy for generalized and non-particular others – which at the same time, is apolitical and impartial. Moreover, the ideal of the public "man" – and the gendered nature of public and private distinctions becomes key at this point – is of an autonomous, self-reliant individual rather than one who is interdependent. What Weber called the "religious ethic of fraternity" is envisaged as something wholly distinct from the rational, juridical, and bureaucratic world of government and public administration. This view reflects a vision of modernization as a story of rationalization and the crowding out of modes of gift relation and neighborliness from public life; a story that is parallel to one of increasing and inevitable secularization. If this were the only problem, then it would be simply a case of overturning a false teleology and pointing to the continued existence of forms of gift exchange, grace, and communion in civic and political life.[148] But there is a more substantive problem with linking forms of gift relation and democratic citizenship: they appear to operate with contradictory patterns and habits of sociality.

There are a number of problems with trying to frame democratic citizenship as a form of gift relation. I shall address issues related to linking friendship and citizenship later in dialogue with Derrida's account of political friendship. For now the focus is on gift relations and citizenship. On many accounts, the receipt of a gift creates not simply a relationship between giver and recipient, but also a relationship of dependence and inequality. Practices of benevolence and altruism, in which the good action of the donor are to be responded to with heartfelt gratitude on the part of the recipient, are seen as an offense to the sensibilities of a democratic people: to accept charity is beneath the dignity of free, equal, and self-reliant citizens. This is a sentiment expressed in the oft-quoted words of Mary Wollstonecraft: "It is justice, not charity, that is wanting in the world."[149] It is a sentiment that Alinsky shared. He contends:

> There are those ... who come to the people of the slums under the aegis of benevolence and goodness, not to organize the people, not to help them rebel and fight their way out of the muck – NO! They come to get these people "adjusted": adjusted so they will live in hell and like it too. It would be difficult to conceive of a higher form of social treason – yet this infamy is perpetrated in the name of charity. It is any wonder that the men of the slum snarl, 'Damn your charity. We want jobs!'[150]

As indicated in Chapter 1, BBCO emerges precisely as a protest against and rejection of philanthropic donation and "welfare colonialism" as responses to poverty. Alinsky envisages democratic politics as an alternative solution that builds on and enhances the power, agency, and dignity of "the poor." Indeed, the "iron rule" of community organizing (never do for others what they can do for themselves) can be read as a direct rebuttal of benevolent and altruistic gift giving. And as noted in Chapter 4, organizers directly contrast self-interest with self-sacrifice in the training. However, the previous discussion of self-interest and its definition as connoting a form of mutuality points a way beyond the seeming incommensurability between forms of gift relation and notions of democratic citizenship. What is rightly rejected by the likes of Wollstonecraft and Alinsky are corruptions of and overemphasis on one form of gift relation: grace.

The tension organizers posit between notions of self-interest and self-sacrifice can be located within a long and complex history. This history includes both Christian theologies of charity and atonement and conceptualizations of self-interest that reach back to the likes of Hobbes and Pascal and before them to Seneca's *De beneficiis*. However, debates about self-interest come to the fore in discussions of social and economic cooperation in the work of Adam Smith and David Hume.[151] As evidenced in the work of Rousseau, Hegel, and Marx, the question of whether self-interest (and civil society more generally) is inherently particularistic and competitive or whether modes of self-interest can form the basis of more universalistic patterns of solidarity is one that is central to reflections on the basis of social order throughout modern political thought. Suffice it to say, there is a world of difference between *amour propre* or self-love (and the pride and *libido dominandi* that the Christian tradition beginning with Augustine sees as its inevitable corollary) and an appropriate love of self that is the correlative of neighborly love and human participation in divine love.[152] That being said, distinguishing between and relating the two in theory and practice has long troubled theologians and philosophers.

The problem goes beyond distinguishing between love of self and self-love. Framing the problem in terms of the contrast between a political order based on love as against one based on self-love suggests the issue is the character and telos of the sociopolitical order in which we are participating. But this is not how the problem comes to be conceived. By the time we reach Adam Smith, the language of love is abandoned and with it the sense of what it means to participate in a common world of meaning and action built on the pursuit of either virtuous, other-oriented relations or vicious, self-oriented ones. Moreover, lost from view in Smith and most modern conceptions of self-interest are notions of gift exchange as symbolic means of establishing reciprocal recognition.[153] Instead, with commercial trade mediated through money becoming the dominant framework and experience of interpersonal exchange beyond the confines of the family and neighborhood, the expectation of a return comes to be seen as necessarily operating according to utilitarian calculation. Anything exchanged ceases to be a symbol of a more fundamental social relationship and becomes viewed as a means of gaining material benefit for an autonomous individual. With this shift the usurious and utilitarian language of "interest" becomes the predominant way to describe political and economic relations with its logic of ownership, debt, and obligation and the expectation that one should seek a return or compensation above and beyond what one gives.[154] Within this context kinship and neighborliness is hived off from economics and politics and, rather than being understood as forms of mutual aid necessary to sustain interdependent relationships, the giving of a gift comes to mean altruistic benevolence that expects no return.[155] As the anthropologist Jonathan Parry points out:

> Those who make free and unconstrained contracts in the market also make free and unconstrained gifts outside it. But these gifts are defined as what market relations are not – altruistic, moral and loaded with emotion. As the economy becomes progressively disembedded from society, as economic relations become increasingly differentiated

from other types of social relationship, the transactions appropriate to each become ever more polarised in terms of their symbolism and ideology.[156]

In short, the modern, nonreligious ways of conceptualizing loving concern – notably, humanitarian aid, philanthropic donation, and altruism – goes hand in hand with the rise of capitalism and the modern state. The association of benefit/interest with commerce soils the expectation of a return as part of the give-and-take of a common life in which the flourishing of each is dependent on the flourishing of all. To be moral, giving must be free from benefit.[157] Of course, while *homo economicus* and his or her mirror image, the altruist, came to dominate theoretical discussion, this was not the only conceptualization available in practice. Friendly societies, mutuals, cooperatives, unions, professional associations, and other modern forms of economic, religious, and vocational organizations maintained the link between utility, recognition, and solidarity while patterns of gift exchange, grace, and communion continued to undergird myriad forms of social and political relations. Durkheim and Mauss were the modern social theorists who did the most to uphold the ongoing salience for political life of these forms of relationships.[158]

Organizers do not refer to wider debates surrounding notions of self-interest. However, the IAF's conception of self-interest represents a distinctive position.[159] By explicitly putting self-interest in tension with self-sacrifice, organizers point to a real juxtaposition between a notion of shared interest, which entails patterns of mutuality, and a notion of grace/sacrifice as a one-way, philanthropic or altruistic donation. Philanthropic donation or altruism involves unilateral assertion because it expects nothing in return and reinforces the status of the giver as at one remove from the recipient.[160] The further effect of philanthropic donation that expects no return is not only to position the recipient in a subservient position of dependency but also, by refusing to receive back in some way, the recipient is rendered irrelevant to the giver and no social bond is furthered. Thus, Wollstonecraft and Alinsky point to an important political insight: philanthropy corrodes citizenship. As Wolin caustically summarizes it: "Philanthropy is the symbolic act by which dependency is privatized and superiority publicized."[161] But as we have seen, philanthropy is not the only form of gift relation.

Citizenship as Generalized Reciprocity

As our meditations on Athens, Jerusalem, and Vienna suggest, citizenship is premised on the basis of a common life, a shared set of goods, and a reciprocal interdependence that requires each to play his or her part and contribute to the building up of the whole on which the good of each depends. Notions of citizenship as involving forms of generalized reciprocity are attempts to articulate something of this basis for citizenship. A notable modern example of this approach is that of the political philosopher John Rawls. Rawls saw generalized reciprocity as the basis of a well-ordered society, envisaging reciprocity as lying between mutual advantage and altruism.[162] The commitment to reciprocity as a foundational basis for democratic citizenship is a consistent theme in the evolution of Rawls's work. For Rawls, reciprocity involves the mutual recognition by persons of each other as free and equal and is thus a condition of both justice and fairness for it ensures that only that which can be reasonably acknowledged by persons who are free and equal will be accepted. He states:

> Reasonable persons, we say, are not moved by the general good as such but desire for its own sake a social world in which they, as free and equal, can cooperate with others on terms all can accept. They insist that reciprocity should hold within that world so that each benefits along with others.[163]

According to Rawls's account, reciprocity would seem to function as a version of the golden rule to do unto others as one would have them do unto you.

Of course, viewing citizenship as a form of generalized reciprocity raises many questions about justice and how those who are not able to contribute – such as the very young, old, or profoundly disabled – are then to receive their due. This problem has sparked a lively debate. However, what is notably missing from this debate is the kind of wider taxonomy of social forms set out here. Neither is a sense of reciprocity as involving symbolic exchange envisaged.[164] In addition, the discussion tends to ignore how generalized reciprocity involves recognition of participation in a common life in which we give today but will receive back from someone else on another day. Bruni and Zamagni call this characteristic of reciprocity "transitivity" in contrast to the direct transfers of equivalent exchange.[165] Instead, while Rawls upholds the need for redistribution, he reduces reciprocity to equivalent exchange and renders the kinds of reciprocal relations operative in gift exchange, grace, and communion as wholly private.[166] Implicit in his account is the need for something like differentiated patterns of neighborliness, yet he thinks justice is wholly independent of them.

Democracy as Sectarianism

The previous taxonomy helps us see that a covenantal or gift-based conception of citizenship is not a panacea. A key problem for the intersection of gifts relations with democratic citizenship is the exclusivism these relationships generate. Derrida states the nature of this problem forcefully. Similar to Rawls, he tacitly affirms that democratic citizenship involves some kind of generalized reciprocity but, unlike Rawls, he sees this as the heart of the problem. For Derrida, democracy involves drawing some and not others together in a circle that thereby excludes those on the outside. We call the circle "the people" and democratic government is said to be of, by, and for – and therefore entirely enclosed within – this circle of people. The logo of London Citizens of an enclosed circle of people holding hands neatly depicts this [see Figure 3.5]. A generalized form of familial relation – namely, fraternity – is then taken as the sign or figure that is paradigmatic for political relations within the circle.[167] By linking the political relation with the blood relation, the imagined and constructed political community is thereby rendered natural and necessary.

In part, Derrida is responding to Schmitt's conception of the political as defined by the friend-enemy relation.[168] Derrida concurs with Schmitt to the extent that he agrees that those inside the circle constitute the friend/fraternal relation and everyone outside it is then seen as an actual or latent enemy (albeit one "acknowledged and recognized against the backdrop of a common history").[169] But Derrida seeks to contest the implications of Schmitt's conclusions and to reopen the circle to others. However, like Schmitt, Derrida ignores the role of intermediate and overlapping consociations in pluralizing politics: as for Schmitt, so for Derrida – there is only one circle. Derrida's strategy for opening up and pluralizing the circle is to contend that the circle constitutes only one pole of democracy. Its other pole is the absolute value placed on equality and the singularity of the one. These two poles are in tragic relation to each other. As Derrida puts it:

> There is no democracy without respect for irreducible singularity or alterity, but there is no democracy without the "community of friends" (*koina ta philōn*), without the calculation of majorities, without identifiable, stabilizable, representable subjects, all equal. These two laws are irreducible one to the other. Tragically irreconcilable and forever wounding.[170]

It is the "forever wounding" quality of the relations between these two poles that opens the way for a more pluralistic democracy "yet to come." The value placed on the irreducible singularity of each one, and the universal horizon this opens up, means democratic politics is able to include others outside the circle. The broader implications of Derrida's demand that we are hospitable to the otherness of the other are drawn out by John Caputo who states:

> [Derrida] does not mean simply to destroy or annul community. Rather, he calls for communities that are pressed to a near breaking point, exposed to the danger of the non-communal, communities that are porous and open-ended, putting their community and identity at risk, like the risk one would take ... if one practiced an unconditional hospitality and issued an open-ended invitation to every wayfarer.[171]

In order to realize this kind of open-ended, hospitable democracy, the affinity of democratic citizenship with fraternity must be severed. Contrary to the account given by Bruni and Zamagni, fraternity in Derrida's view demands homogeneity. This is the problem with the revolutionary cry of "liberty, equality, and fraternity" – and, by extension, with modern conceptions of citizens as free and equal; such postulations are premised on citizens being the same (fraternity). Against such a view, Derrida envisages citizenship being constituted through difference.[172]

While we may laud Derrida's attempts to reinstate plurality to democracy and make it hospitable to excluded others, we must question the strategy he adopts for doing so. His argument is premised first on what I take to be a false dichotomy between the one and the fraternal many within democracy. A consociational, populist, and municipal vision of democratic citizenship does not do away with the problem of fraternity as Derrida conceives it, but it does inherently render contingent the claim to make of the democratic polity or nation a singular, natural, and necessary fraternity. Rather than emerging from a single circle of brothers, democracy is made of negotiating a common life between many bands of brothers and sisters and myriad other identity relations besides. No single group can claim to constitute the whole, but each can contribute to the good of all. Exclusionary tendencies are inherent in each circle, but if relations between each circle can be organized and woven together, then the advantages of "fraternity" (sociality) and its disadvantages (identity as sameness/friend-enemy relations) can be held in tension while at the same time democratic citizenship is de-ontologized and rendered a contingent, constructed, neighborly, and more open-ended political relation.

For Derrida the possibility of more pluralistic and hospitable forms of democracy is intrinsic to it. He states: "Democracy is the *autos* of deconstructive self-limiting."[173] Democracy's ability to open the circle is for Derrida immanent within the unstable, wounded, and therefore deconstructive impetus of democracy itself. However, Derrida displays too much faith in the self-corrective abilities of democracy. Counter to Derrida, I contend that it is the interaction between democracy and various forms of universalism and eschatological horizons that opens the circle and asserts the opposite pole – a pole that is not intrinsic to democracy per se but one that is carried by different world religions and by cosmopolitan liberalism. However, all universalisms – religious or otherwise – need the particularizing and pluralizing practices of democracy in order to stop them from falling into either a false abstraction that puts programs before people or an exclusionary factionalism that refuses a common world of meaning and action with others. As was argued in Chapter 6, different universal horizons establish different friend-enemy distinctions within the body politic. Divisions between "we, the people"/everyone else, bourgeois/proletariat, saved/unsaved, and so on have different temporal and spatial divisions built into them and so operate very differently and create different formations of democratic politics as a negotiation of a common life between friends and enemies. Politics is the negotiation of a common life between these divergent and multiple kinds of friend-enemy distinctions and the ideals/visions of the good they instantiate. Rival universalisms, and their respective friend-enemy distinctions, are the basis of the plurality that Arendt, following Aristotle, sees as the condition of politics.

The way to appropriate Derrida's critique of conceptions of democratic citizenship as a politics of exclusion is to locate it within a broader account of gift relations. Derrida's account of hospitality is, within my taxonomy, a call to emphasize a radical, kenotic, and unconditional grace as the basis for a form of hospitality in which guest and host both recognize and mutually learn from each other. For Derrida, this unconditional, self-dispossessive grace is the key to opening up the closed circle of friends; it is a type of relationship that stands in a dynamic and deconstructive tension with the other ways of answering the call to be a neighbor to another. As Derrida puts it: "What gives deconstruction its movement ... [is] constantly to suspect, to criticize the given determinations of culture, of institutions, of legal systems, not in order to destroy or simply to cancel them, but to be just with justice."[174] At the same time, we cannot live without a configuration of social and political life. The problem for Derrida is the absolutization of either multiplicity or unity: "You see, pure unity or pure multiplicity – when there is only totality or unity and when there is only multiplicity or dissociation – is a synonym of death."[175] The paradox Derrida's work highlights is that to be hospitable we have to come from somewhere – we must have a home/circle of friends – yet such a circle depends on acts of exclusion. Acts of self-dispossession are one way through which to open the circle but they are not the only way and they too are problematic.[176] The kind of consociational, populist, and municipal democratic politics that community organizing embodies is, I contend, another way of being a good neighbor.

Contract, Covenant, and Citizenship

In contrast to Derrida, who examines the linkages between equality and sameness/identity, Hénaff raises the question of whether notions of universal justice and equality are conceivable outside of monetary relations. He suggests that the monetary measurement of goods is one of the essential conditions of equity and thus of democracy.[177] Hénaff sees money as providing the ability to conceptualize each individual as the same and as exchangeable with others in an abstract way. Money allows us to account for justice: we can give each his due; we can pay each one the debt we owe in an exact manner. He states:

> In the city ruled by law, the exchange of useful goods is no longer a mere matter of subsistence but has become a fundamental aspect of justice and, more precisely, of equitable relationships between citizens. This is the seat of what will be the problem of modern societies in which political life can no longer be separated from economic life.[178]

But while the conceptualization and instantiation of distributive and commutative justice may have evolved coterminously with monetary forms of exchange, if the exchange of equivalents becomes the only paradigm of social and political relations, then that which binds a polity is itself undermined. Moreover, within the framework of equivalent exchange, customary practices and gift relations cannot but appear arbitrary and unfair: they allow for no common measure and establish non-fungible, unequal relationships.[179] Yet customary practices and gift relations are the very means of practical reason/wily wisdom: that is, of making discriminating judgments appropriate to local and contextually variable conditions.

One way of reconciling these conflicting patterns and ways of organizing social relationships is to examine more closely how money allows us to account for justice. Among myriad theories about the origins and meaning of money, Keith Hart and Geoffrey Ingham suggest that money is a form of memory.[180] They are referring primarily to credit money where money emerges from ways of keeping records of credit and debt; of who owes what to whom in the circulation of goods and services.[181] For example, in medieval China and early medieval Europe, credit and debt relations were tracked via tally sticks.[182] Historically there is a shift back and forth between virtual or credit money and commodity money: tokens of exchange such as gold or silver that were taken not simply to be a record of the exchange but as tokens with intrinsic value equivalent to what was received.[183] For Ingham, the key shift to a modern capitalist economy comes when signifiers of debt (e.g., a bill of exchange) could be anonymously transferred to third parties. The depersonalization of debt and the formation of an abstract monetary space emerge in Europe from the seventeenth century onward and involve a coalescence of commercial and monarchical interest as well as a delicate balance of power between them.[184]

Drawing attention to how money functions as much as a unit of accounting as it does as a means of exchange highlights how money serves as a way of remembering and mapping a history of relationships. So, for example, a credit card statement (credit cards themselves being simply a sophisticated form of ledger) is a kind of diary of what one has done, whom one has seen, and the places one has visited. And more than an itinerary of the people, places, and events that make up our lives, a credit card statement is a chart of what we invest our time and energy in. Hart argues that money, derived from Moneta (the name of the Roman goddess of memory and mother of the Muses) is "both a memento of the past and a sign of the future."[185] Envisaging it as "congealed desire" captures something of how money is both memory and aspiration.[186] Through money we invest in what we long for or want to see happen. Through the practices by which we store, exchange, and ascribe value to money, we articulate, symbolize, and embody our moral commitments, desires, and hopes. But as a means of doing this money can be highly reductive and occludes as much as it reveals. Without other ways of remembering and expressing our aspirations, ways that may not afford equivalence and therefore commensurability between items, but which reveal other dimensions of the events, people, and places that constitute a human life, life itself is reduced to an account of profit and loss, costs and benefits. Ritual meals, celebrations, storytelling, erecting monuments, acclamations, mourning rites, exchanging rings, ceremonial parades, pilgrimages, and other ways of memory keeping and covenanting are vital if a true and full account of what is due either to each or to the whole is to be given. Justice can involve monetary exchange as practices of *wergild* and compensation testify; but it cannot only be monetary and involves more than can be said with numbers.[187]

If liberal conceptions of justice and citizenship prioritize the exchange of equivalents, then consociational conceptions emphasize gift exchange, grace, and communion. Although equivalent exchange, whether in law or commerce, is a necessary antidote to the corruptions of consociational forms, in the contemporary context, contractual relations premised on the exchange of equivalents have themselves become the problem. When contractual rights occupy the entire canvas of citizenship, the underlying noncontractual and reciprocal nature of citizenship is eviscerated.[188] Within such a framework citizens cease to have equal moral worth; instead, failure to meet the quid pro quo of the contractual obligations of citizenship call into question the noncontributor's (and thus, malfeasant's) membership status within the political community. As Somers puts it, within the kind of "Hobbesian-inflected conception of the social contract, people with nothing to offer or exchange in the way of useful labor or personal assets – the poor, the very young, the infirm, the severely disabled – have no rights because they have no worth; they become rightless and excluded."[189]

A telling example of the processes whereby a contractual vision of citizenship undergirds the rendering of social relations into collateral for financial speculation is the fate of British football clubs. Formerly, they were institutions that combined civic, social, and economic dimensions and made a contribution to the upbuilding of a local common life. Now any identification with a football club is seen as a voluntaristic consumer choice and the institution itself is an abstracted commodity traded on financial markets and a piece of collateral used as a debt-leverage instrument. Any notion that a football club has meaning or civic purpose or generates noncontractual relations that demand loyalty and respect is entirely subordinated to and undermined by the demands of profit maximization. Framing all relations as contractual exacerbates commodification and financialization whereby the use value (and sacral/social value) of something is separated from its exchange value so that only its speculative and abstract exchange value is affirmed. Yet sustaining a common world of meaning and action depends on the connection being maintained between a thing's symbolic use (and the practices of remembrance and covenanting in which it participates) and its exchange value.

The counter to processes of contractualization, commodification, and financialized indebtedness is the restitution of forms of gift exchange, grace, and communion and the connections they forge between people and places over time as part of the canvas of citizenship. Such a restitution is vital if we are to recognize others – including the weak and vulnerable – as having inestimable dignity and as participants in a common life. Such forms of gift relation directly foster the social bonds that are the prerequisite for and the basis of a fuller vision of citizenship. In affirming the need to recognize the dignity of another, we must be aware of the kind of conceptual elision and confusion that frequently occurs with such an affirmation. It is easy to hear the call to recognize the dignity of all as the rendering of each having equivalent value or being the same, but this is to make each person exchangeable and therefore expendable. The philosopher Jean-Luc Nancy goes so far as to suggest that the emphasis on equivalence undergirds a practical nihilism that undermines democracy but that is, at the same time, an inherent possibility within its modern forms: if everything is of the same value and to be valued in the same way, then nothing and no one is of any particular value.[190] To affirm the dignity of all entails valuing the singularity of each and their infinite, incommensurable, and specific worth and therefore their nonequivalence. The building and sustaining of a common life entails being able to recognize and value the nonequivalence of each person and group and their unique contribution to the whole. Liberal egalitarian and contractualist political visions are ill-equipped to do this. As with capitalism, liberalism values direct equivalence and exchangeability: for example, Rawls's veil of ignorance is meant to strip away all vestiges of particularity and context so that every person can be counted the same. Political and moral judgments that seek to be proportional and appropriate according to the specificity of the person, the place, and the circumstances involved, and therefore to be mutable, appear on his account to be immoral. Yet forms of relation built around gift exchange, grace, and communion on "the land" are precisely ways of recognizing and valuing persons in nonequivalent ways. So although these forms of relation seem to contradict egalitarian commitments, the paradox is that they are a necessary means of upholding and affirming the dignity of each person as a unique and incommensurable human being.

THRESHOLD

One could argue that liberal political theory is premised on collapsing distinct patterns, habits, and forms of relationship into the exchange of equivalents. However, this would be to overstate the case. Yet liberal political theories do need more expansive conceptions of reciprocity and should include a broader range of forms of sociality as constitutive of democratic citizenship. Why this is so necessary becomes apparent when we consider the relationship between democratic citizenship and capitalism. There is something more at stake than the kind of civic republican critique put forward by Sandel: that is, that the collective liberty of self-governing citizens and their virtuous pursuit of the "common good" is undermined by commercial and competitive values that prioritize selfish interests.[191] Without a larger vocabulary of gift relations and with an exclusive focus on citizenship as a contract, we end up with two problems in response to pressure from the market: (1) the contractualization, commodification, and eventual financialization of citizenship and the subsequent suppression of modes of gift relation through which the specific and unique value of each person and group may be hallowed; and (2) the rendering licit of dehumanizing patterns of economic relation, notably debt bondage.

The exercise of covenantal forms of democratic citizenship at the points of production, distribution, and exchange is the antidote to the toxic effects of debt and the *pleonexia* for money. Community organizing is one form covenantal citizenship may take; mutuals, cooperatives, fair trade initiatives, and guild-like professional and vocational institutions represent other forms.

Conclusion

"Can there be a more fundamentally, democratic program than a democratically minded and participating people? Can man envisage a more sublime program on earth than the people having faith in their fellow men and themselves?"[1] There is a rich irony in this statement by Alinsky, for there are many things that are more sublime than keeping faith with oneself and another. People manage to keep faith with each other every day. Yet Alinsky's statement asks us to consider whether, if we could simply manage this seemingly mundane task, would not life be a great deal more neighborly? The acts of betrayal committed in the prioritization of profit and power over people point to the constant failure to answer his question in the affirmative. Alinsky's own answer, his own program for a more neighborly life, was to forge a distinctive form of democratic politics that still has much to teach us. It does not offer salvation, but it can provide some consolation for and a way of coping with the grief of living between the world as it is and the world as it should be. Alinsky was shrewd enough to realize that while democratic politics may well provide a means of developing *pietas* or a civic form of faithfulness, it is dependent on prior forms of piety; that is, the kinds of beliefs and practices that generate and renew faith, hope, and love. Nourishing faithful, hopeful, and loving people is vital if democracy is to be given the gift it cannot live without: time. Without people with the virtues necessary to take the time to listen to and build relationships with each other, democratic politics cannot be sustained over time.

DEMOCRACY, IRONY, AND TIME

Democracy and capitalism operate with different tempos and rhythms, what in Chapter 8 were identified as the different timescales of land and sea. In contrast to the ever-increasing speed and volatility of globalized forms of finance capitalism, democracy needs time and people capable of giving it time.[2] It is ordinarily slow. While democracy undoubtedly needs to be quickened on occasions by forms of agitation and a demotic impatience with the status quo, it is for the most part a slow and time-consuming business of patient deliberation, relationship building, and arriving at rather than making decisions.

More broadly, how we are orientated to and imagine the flux of time profoundly shapes our political vision.[3] Heuristically, we can name different stances to living with change that the passing of time involves as (1) *nostalgia* – living in the face of change and newness through looking back to the past and judging what is coming by reference to what was; (2) *fatalism* – seeing change as inevitable and oneself as powerless and passive in relation to the change, accepting loss of the familiar and the cherished as a given; (3) *irony* – recognizing the contingency of all times and things and acknowledging that change is disruptive and so demands a constant recalibration of one's existential orientation in the world; and (4) *progressivism* – the embrace of the new and of what is happening now as determinative of the good.[4] How we orientate ourselves to change (whether in a position of nostalgia, fatalism, irony, or progressivism), and in particular to profound change or cultural rupture, molds the way we respond to the conditions and possibilities of judgment and action.[5]

In many ways, democratic politics is an ironic approach to coping with what it means to be time-bound creatures caught betwixt and between continuity and change and who are complicit in creating, reinforcing, and mystifying our own structures of oppression. As already noted, democratic politics is a response to the grief generated by the distance between the world as it is and the world as it should be. So while all rulers want to celebrate and memorialize their achievements, a truly democratic politics necessitates remembering who was left behind, what was undone, and what is left to do. However, democratic politics also feeds off and is sustained by a hope that things can change for the better if we organize and act together. As a form of politics, it involves acting in time and in a way appropriate to the moment, while taking account of the inevitable limitations and ambiguities of any action. So democratic politics entails acting in recognition of what has gone before while leaving open the possibility of further change. The responsible lending campaign of London Citizens exemplifies this kind of action: it was appropriate to the moment and context and achieved a limited amount given the constraints it had to contend with while creating space for other kinds of political action that subsequently brought the campaign to a successful conclusion. Democratic politics neither suppresses those with whom one disagrees, nor is it a way of establishing a regime of control that excludes all other ways of addressing shared problems. It is a way of coming to judgment about how to pursue and sustain a common life among these people, in this place, at this time, while living with the reality that: (1) there will inevitably be unforeseen consequences; (2) "we" are part of the problem; (3) we cannot step "outside" to a different space and time but must generate change from "within" (both ourselves and our polity); and (4) that with different people in a different place, another way of proceeding might be more appropriate. When democracy ceases to be ironic and its proponents proclaim their own righteousness then a foolhardy and undemocratic politics quickly ensues. Part of what this book enumerates is how, given the possibilities of acting in time amid asymmetries of agency, conflicting loyalties, and our own culpability for what is wrong, community organizing constitutes a form of democratic politics that creates the conditions for making good political judgments.

The ironic stance of democracy to time can be contrasted with the progressive stance of capitalism. Capitalism is all about buying the new thing and throwing off the old as soon as it's past its sell-by date. Yet this commitment to innovation is born out of attempts to order, manage, and control time through scientific, bureaucratic, and industrial forms of production. Moreover, capitalism is premised not only on a progressive view of time and the attempt to micromanage time, but also on the buying and selling of time. The enclosure of common-pool resources and the commodification and collatoralization of people are preceded by the enclosure of time through debt and usury.[6] As noted in Chapter 8, part of the Scholastic prohibition against usury was that charging interest on a loan was an attempt to buy and sell time, which, as a gift of God, was a good in common to be shared by all. Yet the buying and selling of time through the charging of interest is now axiomatic of contemporary finance capitalism and our ability to sustain a life: to name but a few examples, buying a house or car, getting a degree, or obtaining medical care increasingly requires taking on debt and buying and selling time in the form of usury. In the process, we mortgage our future – literally, make a death pledge with it – so that both our personal and collective work now and to come is in bondage to the banks. Democratic politics is one means through which we might refuse to live as if the future is enclosed.

If on the one side we have various stances in relation to time that shape and color our response to change and rupture, then on the other side we have the processes of change themselves. We name these variously. Modernization names a particular assemblage of changes, an assemblage we can break down into various subprocesses we name as industrialization, urbanization, bureaucratization, societalization, rationalization, financialization, and so forth. Secularization used to be included as one of these processes, but part of what this book points to is the inadequacy of this term as a way of naming and identifying the changes we experience as an inherent aspect of modernization. However, while we may question whether secularization is an inherent part of modernization, of late, a new term has come to prominence and is taken to be an inherent part of the contemporary manifestation of modernization: globalization. This book has explored the ways in which broad-based community organizing (BBCO) is now both a creature of globalization and a way of negotiating the changes that globalization brings. We have seen how, in a context such as London, BBCO operates at the intersection of and is a way of mediating between democratic time and the revolutionary tempo of capitalism.

SECULARITY AND THE POLITICAL IMAGINARY

Different stances to time and their outworking in different visions of political and economic relations are premised on different social and ultimately cosmic imaginaries, each of which gives rise to different visions of secularity. A core theme explored in this book is the nature of the relationship between constructions of secularity and democratic politics. For the kind of complexly religious and nonreligious form of politics sketched here to be possible, the following are required. First, some kind of faith in a cosmic imaginary (whether "transcendent" or "immanent") in which material needs, violence, and unilateral power neither exhaust nor define all that politics entails. Second, an openness to a variety of forms of rationality, wisdom, and sources of knowledge other than the scientific and the technical. Third, recognition of ways of coming to political judgments other than those based on some form of rational choice theory or utilitarianism. Lastly, acknowledgment of the importance of forms of gift relations in shaping and sustaining a common life so that politics and economics are not all about equivalent exchange. The case study of how London Citizens constructs democratic citizenship as an identity, shared rationality, and performance of politics demonstrates not only what such a faithfully secular politics looks like in practice, but also that such a politics is possible in and profoundly relevant to the contemporary context.

Community organizing creates a political subjectivity that constructs and coordinates in distinctive ways faithfulness to religious commitments with the obligations incumbent on membership of and loyalty to an "earthly" polity. The process by which this subjectivity is formed involves the acquisition and enactment of a sequence of bodily and mental disciplines (particular conceptions of self-interest and anger, one-to-ones, the rules of organizing, etc.), narrative forms (testimony), aesthetics (dress, comportment), and repertoires of contention and ways of doing politics (the festive, working through institutions, popular education, etc.). Through involvement in iterations of this repertoire the participant gradually learns how to experience and perform democracy in faithfully secular ways: that is, ways that respect the myriad and at times conflicting obligations and commitments that citizens are faithful to (whether religious or otherwise) and which coexist and must be negotiated within a shared spatial and temporal civic realm. This political subjectivity is symbiotic with prior institutions and the moral visions, covenants, practices, and virtues they sustain over time. Given the nature of the relationship between organizing and institutions, it is not surprising that up to now the institutions in membership have been drawn primarily from Christianity, Judaism, and Islam. It is the interrelationship between organizing and institutions that provides a training ground in the arts and virtues necessary for ruling and being ruled, generating forms of practical rationality, sustaining patterns of gift relations, relativizing the claims of state and market, and producing relational power.

In pointing to the role of religious institutions in providing a horizon of reference beyond wholly materialistic and political concerns, and thereby de-totalizing political and economic life, I am not calling for the reassertion of a religious hegemony. One of the aims of this book is to provoke greater critical reflection on the question of what kinds of secularity are amenable and conducive to democratic politics. What is described and prescribed is a capacious secularity, one that is complexly religious and nonreligious, born out of a genuine plurality, and established and sustained by particular ways of doing democratic politics. A lesson of this book is that multiple forms of secular settlement are available and possible – the problem is that we tend to equate democracy with one rather pinched and anemic form of secularity that excludes religious beliefs and practices from public life. Moreover, rarely acknowledged is how this narrow form of secularity reinforces processes of commodification and undermines those forms of life that rethread the full-orbed texture of human life into capitalism and thereby disciplines and reconfigures it. The intersection of religious institutions and democratic politics means that BBCO is not merely a countermovement: it is a performance of time, space, and relationships that runs counter to those enacted within the institutional, symbolic, and representational forms of capitalism. As a counter-performance it contradicts and seeks to convert the enclosure of time and space and the commodification of people that capitalism produces if left unchecked.

For the kind of social and political imaginary described here to be possible there is a need for a genuine institutional plurality within the body politic. It requires also taking seriously forms of corporate life – and the faithfulness or loyalty these entail – as capable of making a constructive contribution to democratic politics, hence the emphasis on consociational democracy with its paradoxical admonition that through institutional plurality comes a common life. BBCO embodies this paradox through its use of wily wisdom, institutions with different and often rival visions of the good, particular political practices, and non-violent conflict to convert antagonism into a common life politics.

An outworking of the faithfully secular politics BBCO embodies is that rather than mobilize around abstract nouns such as "the environment," "justice," or "diversity," BBCO grabs people's attention through means of a populist politics that identifies, organizes, and constructively channels felt grievances about concrete concerns such as family life, neighborhood, work, wages, and debt. Part of what makes it a populist politics rather than antipolitical is that it incorporates forms of symbolic exchange and contestation orientated to building relationship and a common life. So instead of being simply a form of protest or replicating binary oppositions between black and white, rich and poor, and so forth, BBCO is a means through which to draw the "haves" into relationship with the "have-nots" in order to create the kind of "innovative milieu" that is vital to generating the productive adaptation and innovation necessary to solve collective problems in an equitable manner.[7]

INSTITUTIONAL IMAGINATION, POVERTY, AND DEMOCRATIC PROFESSIONALISM

Part of what Ella Baker called the "slow and respectful work" of democracy is building and sustaining institutions through which people can act collectively. Yet one of the challenges those concerned with strengthening democracy must address is a deficit not of people, ideas, or money, but of institutional imagination. We no longer trust the institutions we have, but we cannot imagine the institutions we need for the problems we face. For example, we know we have to educate our children, but there are basic disagreements about what schools are for, how to teach, who should be in the classroom, and how to train teachers. Addressing poverty and injustice is as much a question of institutional imagination as it is of distributing resources and securing political freedoms. Given the kinds of problems contemporary liberal democracies face, state-centric and social-democratic solutions – and the kind of large-scale institutional formations they engender – are now questioned by critics on both Left and Right.[8] A constructive alternative is to stimulate collaboration and coordination between a vast array of associations and institutions that have a variety of relationships to state and market and to remaster existing institutions using the kinds of "tools for conviviality" that organizing deploys.[9] Yet much political prognosis – of whatever stripe – pays little attention to the importance of institutions as means of solving collective problems and pursuing, fulfilling, and ordering the goods necessary to sustain a just and generous common life over time in the face of its erosion by "the sea."

Institutions are the point of integration that connect the consociational form and rationality of organizing, its populist performance of democratic politics, and the way organizing incorporates religious groups. Yet it is the intersection of these three elements that is also a point of creative tension within the practice of BBCO. Being populist in its performance of democratic citizenship means BBCO is structurally and discursively an "outsider." In their capacity as participants in BBCO, those involved cannot campaign for office or engage in party politics without compromising the identity and modus operandi of organizing. This is not to say these things do not happen and it may be strategic in certain contexts, but a shift to a different political repertoire has occurred when they are pursued.

Paradoxically, given its "outsider" location, what makes BBCO a populist but democratic politics (as against an antipolitical form of populism) is that it takes the institutional basis of a common life seriously and is committed to building distributed forms of leadership. In the world of democratic activism, BBCO is unusual in that it is profoundly concerned with the vitality of institutions and commits time and energy to renewing and strengthening them, whether they are congregations, schools, or clinics. As institutions are means of solving collective problems and pursuing goods necessary to sustain a common life trans-generationally they are vital for embedding change. The populist elements of BBCO challenge the status quo whereas commitment to popular agency (the iron rule) and to institutional renewal and creativity are means of seeking the kinds of simultaneously structural, interpersonal, and bottom-up transformation that means change is meaningful and resilient. However, such transformation needs virtuous leaders with sufficient courage, wily wisdom, and "ego" to work outside the comfort zones of their institutions in order both to initiate change and build a common life with others who are perceived as enemies by those within their institutions. Drawing together Chapters 1 and 6, we can say that the connection between a democratic populist politics, popular religion, an emphasis on virtuous leadership, and institutional imagination is a key feature of BBCO. In this respect, BBCO is an inheritor and mediator of the legacy of the populist and labor movements and the cooperatives, unions, adult education initiatives, and other institutional innovations that were central to the cultural and political impact of these movements.

Crucially, the institutions BBCO and the populist and labor movements worked with were self-generated. And echoing the vision of secularity portrayed here, many had a religious connection or character. Such institutions are particularly important to enabling those without access to the power of money or the institutions of the state to achieve their ends. To be sustained, institutions depend on gift relations and the kind of power that comes into being, as Arendt puts it, "when and where people would get together and bind themselves through promises, covenants, and mutual pledges."[10] The battle is to prevent these self-generated institutions from being co-opted and commodified and thereby transformed into programs based on equivalent exchange. The outcome of processes of co-option and commodification is that instead of addressing poverty, inequality, and injustice as a common work, to which all may contribute and have the agency to do so, "the poor" become clients and consumers of professional services. "We, the people" are divided between "the experts" and "the population" who are managed and governed through technocratic regimes of health, education, welfare, incarceration, and the like.[11]

The institutional emphasis in BBCO is vital for addressing the modern paradox of care. The paradox is that those you don't care about and don't have compassion for, you tolerate or leave alone, even if what they are doing is harmful or flies in the face of your own views. Those we care about or feel responsible for, when we see them doing something wrong or harmful or suffering in some way, we feel compelled to help, even at the expense of their agency. Yet the intervention prompted in such cases is more often than not an attempt to govern their lives and is paternalistic or even colonial in orientation. Therefore, while the impulse to rule is often a loving one born out of humanitarian concern for the welfare of others, it is distorted by the belief that we think we know better how those in need should live, and we remove their agency in order that they might conform to our notions of what is good and right and proper. We exercise *paideia* over them and this often involves strict forms of discipline – albeit usually "pastoral" in nature – in order that they might live well. Loving concern is then seen to produce modes of domination mediated through practices of governance. This paradox represents a central dilemma in all means of welfare provision and attempts to address poverty and inequality, whether through local, national, or international initiatives.

The reduction of the "public" face of love to altruism and humanitarianism and the almost exclusive emphasis on equivalent exchange and redistribution as ways of structuring welfare is part of the problem. In order to move beyond the stasis that is often produced by the paradox of care, it is vital to draw from the larger palette of gift relations outlined in Chapter 8 as ways of embodying and performing love for others and mixing these different forms together so as to counteract the pathologies of each. This broader canvas of gift relations enables the agency and wisdom of "ordinary" people to be part of addressing the problems of poverty, thereby putting people before program. But this represents a profound challenge to welfare, educational, health, and other services, and the professional identities of those who are paid to care. It also challenges how we conceptualize poverty. Poverty is not merely the condition of inequality and material scarcity; it is also a fracturing of the bonds of mutual recognition and respect that sustain a common world of meaning and action between different classes, races, genders, and a range of other potential friend-enemy relations. The problem of economic poverty and inequality is a political problem because it undermines and threatens the mutual recognition and gestures of neighborliness necessary for politics as the negotiation of a common life between distinct and often rival others. This was a fundamental insight of Alinsky, who understood the problem of poverty not simply as material lack but also as the need for participation in and a sense of responsibility for the body politic. In the context of "Vienna" – the liberal yet fragile state – the disintegration and disaggregation of associations, and thence the inability to form a consociationally organized "people," leads to either mob rule (antipolitical populism), rule by elites (whether financial or technocratic), or more often than not, a combination of the two.

Although BBCO represents a distinctive form of politics, it embodies an approach that resonates with those seeking non-state-centric and non-market based ways of reforming welfare provision and reconfiguring social democracy in the light of contemporary conditions. For example, based on empirical case studies, Fung and Wright identify core principles, properties, and enabling conditions that would foster more deliberative and empowering forms of governance.[12] They contrast their participatory model of decision making with more familiar methods: command and control by experts, aggregative voting, and strategic negotiation between interest groups. As Fung and Wright note, when reorganization along the lines they depict is successful, "participants have the luxury of taking some exercise of authority for granted; they need not spend the bulk of their energy fighting for power (or against it)."[13]

The following "rules" for the reform of public services and structures of governance can be deduced from the experience of broad-based community organizing:

1. Build relational power in order to challenge existing structures while simultaneously generating richer patterns of neighborliness;
2. Recruit an "organizer" figure to catalyze and agitate for relationship and shared learning between different groups in an area or silos within a large-scale institution such as a university or hospital;
3. Draw from people's customary practices, traditions, and common history to generate a transformative sense of being neighbors to each other;
4. Identify and develop "native" leaders who have a long-term self-interest and need for change;[14]
5. Identify strategic links, pressure points, or people in organizational networks and structures of provision where change can have a catalytic and more wide-ranging effect;
6. Organize in a number of strategic places or nodes that already have circuits connecting them to achieve lasting change;
7. Ensure forms of accountability can integrate repertoires of conflict and collaboration in the reform of institutions;
8. Work with a variety of stakeholders ranging from users (students, patients, etc.) to professionals and incorporate them into the governance of an institution at every level; and finally,
9. Invest in civic and political education and the generation of alternative communities of interpretation that can reframe or provide an alternative perspective to the orthodoxies and plausibility structures that are used to justify existing policy and practice. This last "rule" is particularly important if leaders are to understand, analyze, and make judgments about their situation while at the same time being attuned to their context.

All these "rules" can be summed up in the exhortation to put people before program. Such measures would enhance the skills, improvisational contribution, and active involvement of all citizens and strengthen and deepen the communicative dimensions of democratic politics across a range of fields. One aim of such "rules" is the improvement of public services and forms of governance; a corollary objective is to enable professionals and administrators to do good, meaningful work and resist the overweening demands of marketization and managerialism.

What is proposed in the kind of recommendations sketched here is not so much a series of amendments to social democratic forms of governance in order to refine and improve current practice, but a way of tilling the existing soil so that something different and better may grow. Simply put, we should ask of any policy or professional practice if it enhances the skills, responsibility, neighborliness, and agency of those it affects and if it allows for the contribution of the wisdom, knowledge, and experience of those affected in its formulation.[15] If not, not only will it not be resilient, but it will also undermine democratic citizenship. Democracy is premised on the basis that rulers and those being ruled should contribute to the formulation of the policies and practices that determine their common life. In the contemporary context this no longer relates solely to the domain of law and public policy, it includes also the vast array of institutions and programs that structure our life together. The practical reason, experience, consociational forms, and gift relations of ordinary people are a vital resource we ignore at our peril, leaving open the door to, on the one hand, brittle schemes of social engineering, and, on the other hand, the power of money and debt to overdetermine our common life.[16]

Citizens UK is beginning to explore some of what is proposed here in fledgling and sporadic ways. Since 2010 there have been experiments with organizers specifically tasked with organizing within a health care system (King's Health Partners), universities (the colleges that make up the University of London), and schools. A challenge such work faces is that large institutions such as a hospital or university cannot be treated simply as one more member within a broader coalition. Rather, as large-scale anchor institutions that connect people and capital to place in relatively stable configurations over time, they need to be conceptualized as a neighborhood or "natural area" in and of themselves. Different sections of the hospital or university are equivalent to different institutions in a coalition. And, as is the case with disorganized institutions in a neighborhood, there is often a lack of communication and relationship between those who work in the different sections (although not necessarily between those who manage them) so that those working in them experience each section as disconnected and frequently competitive silos. Yet as vocational institutions rooted in the history of a place there is, at least notionally, a common ethos and covenantal commitment to a shared purpose and vision. The commitment to delivering a substantive good such as health or education that sits above and beyond the institution can be used alongside more mundane place-based and convivial interests as a basis on which to organize.

DEMOCRACY, MONEY-POWER, AND WORK

So far the focus here has been on the linkages between organizing and the democratization of professional identities and practice, the delivery of public services, and the renewal of institutions. What is missing from, yet intrinsic to, this analysis is the importance of work and places of work to the practice of democratic citizenship.[17] As outlined in Chapters 6 and 8, work itself needs to be seen as part of a wider democratic endeavor and orientated to building a common life. Focusing on work necessarily entails attention to the conditions and possibilities of doing good work and ensuring that workplaces, as well as the neighborhoods of which they are a part, are contexts of human flourishing.

Moreover, central to upholding the dignity of labor is limiting the power of money and regimes of indebtedness in determining our life together, whether at home or at work. Only by taking work seriously as a means through which we learn to rule and be ruled and the workplace as a site of democratic practice can we begin to imagine accountability being brought to the power of money. The enactment of this accountability has three interrelated dimensions.

First, as discussed throughout this book, we must reinforce ways of embedding the institutions of capital – notably, banks and firms – within the body politic. Accountability entails the involvement of the state via external regulation, movements, and advocacy groups via civil society, the creation of unions and other forms of worker representation in corporate governance, and alternative forms of production such as worker-owned cooperatives. None of these measures on their own is sufficient, but all are necessary if a ceiling, floor, and furnishings are to be provided and thus a habitable space for living created. As has been detailed here, community organizing makes its own contribution to the task of re-embedding the institutions of capital in the body politic.

Second, we need to recover a conception of the dignity of the worker and of work itself. Beyond questions about the material conditions of work is its moral status. It is this moral status that undergirds notions of alienation, proletarianization, and other critiques of the indignity of modern work. As Catholic social teaching reiterates again and again, the principle of the priority of labor – and therefore the person – over capital is a necessary postulate of any moral vision.[18] The encyclical *Laborem Exercens* summarizes this insight as follows: "Since work in its subjective aspect is always a personal action, an *actus personae*, it follows that the whole person, body and spirit, participates in it, whether it is manual or intellectual work."[19] To make labor serve and be subject to capital is to invert the moral order by making humans serve money.[20] A parallel point has been explored throughout this book via the work of Polanyi for whom labor is nothing other than the interpersonal relationships that constitute society.[21] We must understand that work, of whatever kind and in whatever field, is not only toil, but also a gift. Like all gifts, the fruit of our labor is a way in which the person is symbolically present to and recognizes others.[22] Work, worker, and the objects and services produced are profoundly related. As part of the circulation of gifts that constitute our life together, in all its dimensions, work generates our *habitus* or form of life. To make work degrading is to desecrate the personhood of the workers and demean a way of life. Conceptualized as a gift, work points beyond class-based analyses that posit an inherent conflict between "labor" and "capital" to an understanding of work as constitutive of how we forge a common world of meaning and action amid enmity. Work can never be merely economic; it is always social and political as well.

Third, in order to take account of how work is constitutive of a form of life, there is a need to reconnect work-based and place-based organizing. The struggle to uphold the dignity of work and the worker is a central feature not only of the populist and labor movements, but also of a number of the IAF and Citizens UK's campaigns, notably the Living Wage campaign. Yet, while it was the initiatory context for the birth of the IAF, since Alinsky's death the importance of this struggle is often eclipsed by the attention paid to the relationship between organizing and civil society.[23] Indeed, rather than recognizing the complementarity of place-based and work-based organizing, there has been a tendency to focus on the former and disregard the latter. A striking feature of this disregard is the lack of small-to-medium-sized businesses in membership despite the fact that their concerns are often related to those of other institutions within an organizing coalition. The problem with the emphasis on how organizing is constitutive of civil society is that, as Boyte argues: "It consigns citizenship and civic action to the 'voluntary sector' separated from government and from work, work routines, and the workplace in ways that largely remove huge arenas from the possibilities of democratization."[24]

A judgment to be made when seeking to uphold the dignity of labor, embed capital, and limit debt is whether, as part of the dance of conflict and conciliation, there are occasions when what it means to act in time is for "outsiders" to become party political "insiders." It was a question about the need for such a shift that animated my coinvestigator Maurice Glasman in the research project out of which this book comes. Through our research he developed and initiated what came to be called "Blue Labour."[25] One result of Glasman's initiative and subsequent involvement at the heart of debates about the future of the Labour Party after its defeat in 2010 was the adoption of an explicit policy of training party officials and candidates in organizing and the emergence of a more populist politics at a local party level.[26] Key to the wider impact was the recruitment of the long-time IAF organizer Arnie Graf to work with the party and its affiliated unions.[27] The invitation from the Labour Party to Graf can be seen as an extension of the spirit of organizing into a more explicitly partisan arena. It is clearly a shift for Graf from being an "outsider" to that of an "insider"; with all the hazards that that can entail. However, it represents the opportunity to undertake "an action" on the Labour Party, and therefore party politics in the United Kingdom more generally, to adopt a more relational approach that is open to multiple sources of knowledge and experience and capable of engaging in reciprocal, noninstrumental relations with other kinds of association. The *kairos* moments for such interventions are rare but can make the difference between simply responding to the weather and changing the climate.[28]

The danger of any such move is that it might result in the over-alignment of party politics and community organizing. The capture of BBCO by one ideology or party platform represents a distortion of its primary purpose, which is to pursue not factional ends, but the dignity of work and the flourishing of places through training leaders and cultivating neighborly relations between as many different kinds of associations as possible.[29] In Arendtian terms there is an inherent conflict between the political form of the party, the interests of which are directed toward winning elections and ruling a nation-state, and the political form of popular councils and local associations, which constitute a realm of ongoing political freedom and deliberation.[30] The impetus of a political party operating within the constraints of an election cycle and responding to the administrative demands of governing a modern nation-state means there is an inevitable temptation to subordinate forms of popular, local association to the implementation of a policy program or an electoral strategy.[31] Moreover, what is achievable at a municipal level does not necessarily apply at the national level where the ability to be responsive to local conditions, histories, and traditions, and to engage in building meaningful relationships is obviated by the need to develop egalitarian, one-size-fits-all policies and procedures. Without radical commitment to decentralization and the reorganization of the public sector along consociational and mutualist lines the introduction of a more organizing-based approach to policy formulation and implementation will have only marginal impact.

POLITICAL FREEDOM AND A VIRTUOUS POLITICS OF A COMMON LIFE

In addition to time and institutions, democratic politics requires moral convictions: namely, the conviction that not just "the individual" but one's adversaries and those one fears are non-fungible and have irreducible worth. Thus, democratic politics requires moral traditions to sustain the kinds of practices and beliefs by which a commitment to the dignity of friends *and* enemies and a vision of a common life as something more than the aggregation of individual choices can be sustained and renewed through time. Yet too much moral conviction, combined with a belief in one's own innocence and the absolute rightness of one's cause, inhibits the kinds of negotiations, civic *pietas*, and neighborly relations necessary to forge a common life between friends and enemies. This is a point made by both Arendt and the Augustinian-Reformed tradition of political thought for which the use of political authority not simply to restrain evil but also to enforce virtue is as much of a problem as its use for corrupt and oppressive ends. Terror and totalitarianism are as often born of a zeal for righteousness as a desire to dominate. Yet if cooperation is so emphasized that any substantive moral claims are seen as a threat to it then the kinds of convictions that sustain democracy are undermined. Democratic politics cannot create these convictions, so it must find ways of creating space for the kinds of moral formation that are a condition of its own possibility. Therefore, democracy exists within a tension of conviction and cooperation. Community organizing bears witness to how this tension can be held in such a way that it generates a common life.

Undergirding the relationship between conviction and cooperation in democratic politics is a commitment to listening, talking, and acting together as ways to settle the inevitable conflicts that arise in complex societies. A commitment to democracy is a wager that politics as a form of shared speech and action and therefore communication and reciprocal relations can, over time, provide the antibodies necessary to keep in check the ever-present viruses of violence, domination, fear of others, envy, and asymmetries of power that arise when navigating the constraints imposed by necessity, finitude, and competing loyalties and obligations within a body politic. Democratic politics is not surgery that removes the gangrenous limb – that is the justification of revolutionary terror since the days of Robespierre. It is an immune system that enables the polity to maintain equilibrium and to rearrange itself so as to keep things steady (homeostasis), while combining this with the ability to grow, change shape, and adapt without breaking apart (morphogenesis). A healthy body politic involves a dynamic interplay between homeostasis and morphogenesis so as to live and act as a contingent, historical, time-bound form of shared life caught betwixt and between continuity and change. Analogous to an immune system, democratic politics is partially constituted by that which it opposes: that is, undemocratic and often vicious people inhabiting undemocratic and often dictatorial institutions. Democracy's paradox is that its pathogens are the source of its new life. Community organizing embodies a means through which such pathogens as antipolitical and antagonistic friend-enemy relations can be metabolized into a faithful, hopeful, and neighborly politics of a common life.

Appendix

A Note on Method

In order to research the Industrial Areas Foundation (IAF)/London Citizens, my research colleague Maurice Glasman and I drew from ethnographic approaches so as to pay close attention to the people, institutions, practices, and processes involved in community organizing.[1] In keeping with ethnographic research methods we became embedded within London Citizens. This enabled us to excavate how those involved conceptualized and enacted their involvement and learn what discourses and practices they utilized. The primary point of data collection was through being participant observers from 2008 to 2012.[2] This involved formally noting and assessing more than 100 events and meetings that themselves represented hundreds of hours and innumerable conversations in and around these gatherings. These mostly took place in London, but also included Chicago, Berlin, and Sydney. The meetings and events ranged in focus from the local, citywide, national, and international levels. They included internal organizational meetings, large public actions, training events (including the five-day training program), seminars, day-long retreats, as well as private meetings among participants and between representatives from Citizens UK and political or business leaders. In addition to those meetings and events specifically organized by London Citizens, we attended numerous meetings put on by other institutions that leaders and organizers from London Citizens attended as representatives of the organization. To supplement this process of apprenticeship in the craft of organizing, we undertook thirty-five in-depth interviews with key leaders, organizers, and critics of London Citizens' work and organizers from the IAF, DICO, and Sydney Alliance (some of whom were interviewed more than once).[3] The information and reflections based on this process of participant observation and interviews were then triangulated by references to archive material (both from Citizens UK's records and the IAF archive held by the University of Illinois in Chicago), video footage of assemblies, coverage of the work in the mainstream media and "blogosphere," and other academic studies of community organizing in the United Kingdom and the United States. The emerging conclusions were then checked with both long-established organizers and commentators on community organizing both within and outside of the IAF network.[4]

We focused on the work of London Citizens because it was the form of community organizing most immediately available to us. Since London Citizens, the primary and most established expression of Citizens UK and the largest and most established network of the community organizing coalitions in the United Kingdom, is affiliated with the IAF, this led to an inevitable focus on the history and context of the IAF. This twin focus turned out to be providential. London Citizens is a particularly generative example of community organizing within the context of a global city. Moreover, its response to the financial crisis that unfolded from 2008 onward and also to the 2010 General Election resulted in a hugely significant moment in the history of the organization: one that launched it, and by extension, Citizens UK, onto the national stage in Great Britain.

As a stem root of community organizing the IAF is historically significant. Added to this, its leadership training program and practices form the prototype on which the great majority of other contemporary community organizing networks have been built. This does not necessarily make it the best or the most effective model, but it does mean that the IAF is an important "telling case" from which we can learn a great deal about the field of organizing.

At the outset of the research we negotiated access to the work of London Citizens/Citizens UK with Neil Jameson, its lead organizer. The agreement we reached was that our access was conditional on commitment and involvement in the organization as leaders.[5] In order to be leaders, we had to be members of an affiliated institution. My local church was already a member of London Citizens, so I took part in events and meetings as a leader within St. Paul's, Hammersmith – an Anglican Church in West London. For my colleague, being a leader entailed bringing his university department into membership (which he did) and then subsequently, he brokered the entry of the Masorti synagogues, to which he belonged. However, it was made explicit that while we would seek the good of Citizens UK and actively take part in and contribute to the work to the best of our abilities, we would also be critical and use the research process to suggest changes in practice where this seemed appropriate.[6] What we were aiming for was a reciprocal, non-instrumental relationship; one that honored the particular but intertwined interests of each party and where we as researchers made a real contribution to the organization, while at the same time the organization actively contributed to and engaged with our research.[7] Negotiating this insider-outsider status required a constantly evolving combination of rapport, trust building, identification, and critical distance.[8] However, far from being innovative, such an approach fits an existing interpretive and participatory research method in which the line between researcher and research is fluid and there is a commitment to work collaboratively with those being researched to generate knowledge that is useful to and transformative of their practice.[9] Our method was also consistent with key practices of community organizing that trains people to identify their mutual interests and form a common work around the pursuit of that shared interest, critically evaluating everything that is done in that common work and engaging in constant learning and education in order to improve practices and deepen insight.

Another factor in adopting the approach outlined here was epistemological. Understanding the practice of community organizing was not possible simply through interviews and observation. Participants repeatedly used the language of conversion to describe the process of becoming involved in organizing. Such language captured for participants the way in which learning came by doing and involvement and how it was difficult to verbalize or describe community organizing in explicit and clear terms. This is partly explained by the unfamiliarity with organizing in the United Kingdom in contrast to the United States. But it is also partly explained by the nature of organizing as a form of craft knowledge as opposed to a rationally explicable technique that can be outlined in a manual. To learn a craft, one has to be apprenticed in its ways and means, but acquiring this knowledge is no guarantee of being able to give a theoretical account of it to the uninitiated. An apprentice or even a master carpenter cannot necessarily give a theoretical account of what they are doing and its rationale, but that does not mean they are not good at what they do.[10] Thus, immersion in the practice was the key to understanding broad based community organizing (BBCO); however, it was not sufficient for explaining it. Explanation required locating the practice within broader theoretical frameworks, engagement with its intellectual and social history, and comparing its practices with other case studies in order to bring the craft's knowledge to speech.

As a craft that requires entry into the "guild" as a full-orbed participant, BBCO points to the limits of interviews and observation as ways of gaining understanding. This is something that is increasingly recognized in broader methodological discussions.[11] Timothy Jenkins, in his own account of the relationship between fieldwork and knowledge generation, states:

> Knowledge of everyday life is not available to the disinterested gaze of an inquirer; rather, fieldwork is an apprenticeship of signs, the process of entry into a particular world, governed by a variety of factors, including the situation and previous experience of the anthropologist. During an apprenticeship, as well as skills and perceptions, memories and desires are altered, so that every actor, indigenous or ethnographer, is engaged in a personal and experiential capacity.[12]

Jenkins goes on to note that knowledge gained through such a process of apprenticeship is theoretically rich, providing the basis for the understanding of and reflection on action.[13] Apprenticeship as a form of learning suggests a different epistemological relationship to the subject of study than a positivist-empirical one.[14] Rather than autonomous distance and observation, it demands immersion and commitment to do the work well and to seek the best for the practice at all times. Through apprenticeship in what is studied and through practicing and even demonstrating flair at its proper practice – being judged a good practitioner by acknowledged masters in the craft – one can check whether one has understood the practice properly. But analogous to MacIntyre's conception of a tradition as an argument over time about what constitutes the good, this does not imply uncritical acceptance of the norms, rules, and behavioral sequences embedded within the practice. Rather, it entails listening and doing what one is told as well as argumentative collaboration. Broader validation of the personal perspective gained as constituting something of the "common sense" of the practice studied is enabled through triangulating one's own perspective with others, comparing it with other formal studies, reading archive material to gain a historical perspective, and engaging with criticisms of the work and the observations of those external to it.

An apprenticeship-based approach to research accords with research based primarily on practical rather than theoretical reason. Such research necessarily focuses on case studies, precedents, and exemplars.[15] In both philosophy and social science, empirical cases have generated key conceptual insights.[16] However, such empirical cases are different to the hypothetical case studies much loved by moral philosophers that are both too tenuously related to real dilemmas as to be of any practical value in guiding future judgment and fail to confront the complex nature of lived experience. In terms of political life, such an approach is best exemplified by Tocqueville, for whom observation of the dynamics and interrelation of political and social life forms the basis of generating conceptual categories and normative accounts of political life and action within a particular context of study. The case study method enables the formulation of normative judgments in dialogue with the concerns and practices of ordinary people and their judgments about what is meaningful and important. Ethnographic modes of attention (interview, participant observation, etc.) are vital for generating conceptual refinement and development in relation to lived practices, as the political life of ordinary people occurs not in texts but in contingent interactions among persons and groups.

Drawing from the sociologist Michael Burawoy's extended case study method, this book examined the macro world through the way it shapes and in turn is shaped and conditioned by the micro everyday world of face-to-face interactions.[17] Macro and micro are in a relation of codetermination rather than the micro simply being a paradigm or expression of the macro. For example, it would be easy to interpret the conditions of organizing in London as paradigmatic of wider forces of economic globalization. However, this would miss how the structures of economic globalization are themselves affected by the particular constellation of banking and politics in London and how community organizing in London is able to act on place-based banks and regulatory authorities. Any change accomplished feeds into broader global networks and flows. The broader point to draw out is that neither the religious groups involved nor community organizing itself should be read as simply a microcosm of broader political processes and structural forces; they have their own integrity that must be considered. Yet neither can an analysis of community organizing be separated from how organizing is in a relationship of codetermination (and at times co-construction) with its political environment. What I mean by codetermination is illustrated by the philosopher Charles Taylor's account of how secularity is the result not of external processes of modernization acting on belief and practice (i.e., wherein political and economic processes determine the nature of belief and practice) nor the internal logic of Christianity, but results from how belief and unbelief are themselves constantly interacting and changing (i.e., belief and unbelief codetermine and mutually constitute each other in an ongoing way).[18]

Burawoy's extended case study method points to how particular and often anomalous case studies can help enrich and develop conceptualizations of the interrelationship between religious and political discourses through ethnographic research of the kind undertaken for this book.[19] For Burawoy, theory is central to the process of analysis. It not only guides the focus of a study, but it also locates particular social processes in their wider context of determination.[20] However, in Burawoy's approach, the aim of research is not to confirm or refute a given theory. Rather, case studies are assessed for how they both present a crisis to a given theory – and so the more anomalous the case the better – but also how they are a resource by which a theory may be strengthened and developed.[21] The researcher, therefore, does work with theoretical frameworks, but these are continually evolving through attention to concrete cases, which themselves generate the conceptual resources for the repair and reformulation of the prior body of theory.[22] In the case of this study, the development of a consociational framework of analysis embodies this process of reformulation. Moreover, the combined focus on the IAF and the specific work of London Citizens in the context of a world city serves simultaneously as an act of memorialization as well as a demonstration of and a prescription for the vision of democratic politics the book articulates.

Notes

Introduction

1 There is no absolute opposition between faithfulness and treachery as true faith can paradoxically entail what appear to be acts of betrayal while what is claimed as faithful action can be hypocrisy. The Gospels have a rich theme examining the interplay between the paradoxical faithfulness of Jesus who fulfills the law and the prophets yet is seen as a traitor, the hypocrisy of the Pharisees and others who understand themselves to be paragons of faith yet who are "white washed sepulchers," and the straightforward betrayals of Judas and Peter. This theme builds on the prophetic tradition, which, long before the "masters of suspicion" – Nietzsche, Freud, and Marx – recognized suspicion and demystification as necessary adjuncts to true faithfulness and the formation of a just and generous polity (e.g., Amos 5:21–24). Suspicion is necessary to keep before us the tensional relationship between belief and practice, appearance and reality, knowledge and being, and the works of the flesh and those of the Spirit.

2 As well as broader debates in the study of citizenship since the 1990s, the framework set out here builds on and adapts parallel ones in Kevin O'Neill, *City of God: Christian Citizenship in Postwar Guatemala* (Berkeley: University of California Press, 2009); Aihwa Ong, "Citizenship in the Midst of Transnational Regimes of Virtue," *Political Power and Social Theory* 20 (2009): 301–07; and James Tully, "On Local and Global Citizenship: An Apprenticeship Model," in *Public Philosophy in a New Key*, vol. 2, *Imperialism and Civic Freedom* (Cambridge: Cambridge University Press, 2008), pp. 243–309. For an overview of key debates since the 1990s, see Will Kymlicka and Wayne Norman, "Return of the Citizen: A Survey of Recent Work on Citizenship Theory," in *Theorizing Citizenship*, ed. Ronald Beiner (Albany: State University of New York Press, 1995), pp. 283–322.

3 On the term "imagined community" and its relationship to identification with a nation-state, see Benedict Anderson, *Imagined Communities: Reflections on the Origin and Spread of Nationalism*, rev. ed. (London: Verso, 2006).

4 For a definition and discussion of the broader category of a "social imaginary," see Charles Taylor, *Modern Social Imaginaries* (Durham, NC: Duke University

Press, 2004); and Graham Ward, *Cultural Transformation and Religious Practice* (Cambridge: Cambridge University Press, 2005), pp. 119–47.

5 The term "common life" is used throughout in preference to a conception of "the common good." Although some notion of a "common good" may still operate as a regulative ideal, an all-encompassing "common good" can only ever be a deferred horizon of possibility rather than a plausible political reality under conditions of a fallen and finite political life. So while talk of particular "goods in common" or "common goods" is wholly appropriate for a generic way of denoting a shared realm of meaning and action and commitment to the good of political association amid enmity and rival visions of the good life, the term "common life" seems simultaneously more sober and hopeful. Where the term "common good" is used it is in quotation marks so as to denote its use as a quote or term deployed by those discussed.

6 Margaret Canovan, "The People, the Masses and the Mobilization of Power: The Paradox of Hannah Arendt's 'Populism,'" *Social Research* 69.2 (2002): 403–22, p. 411.

7 See Marc Stears, *Progressives, Pluralists, and the Problems of the State: Ideologies of Reform in the United States and Britain, 1909–1926* (Oxford: Oxford University Press, 2002), and Cécile Laborde, *Pluralist Thought and the State in Britain and France, 1900–25* (Basingstoke: Macmillan Press, 2000).

8 For an account of the secularization thesis as itself a product of this kind of interaction, such that it should be understood less as a scientific paradigm and more as a form of "epistemological anti-Catholicism," see Christopher Clark, "From 1848 to Christian Democracy," in *Religion and the Political Imagination*, eds. Ira Katznelson, Gareth Stedman Jones, and Walter Goode (Cambridge: Cambridge University Press, 2007), pp. 190–213.

9 Talal Asad, *Formations of the Secular: Christianity, Islam, Modernity* (Stanford, CA: Stanford University Press, 2003), p. 192.

10 This builds on Roland Robertson's suggestion that secularization is a transvaluation of Christian millennial categories and José Casanova's argument that processes of secularization are reiterations of developments within all axial religions that posit a duality between transcendent and mundane orders of space and time. A case in point is Augustine's division between the City of God and the earthly city, which together constitute the *saeculum*. Following Shmuel Eisenstadt, different axial religions give rise to "multiple modernities," each with their own construction of secularity that now, under conditions of globalization, contest and interact with each other (Roland Robertson, "Global Millennialism: A Postmortem on Secularization," in *Religion, Globalization and Culture*, eds. Peter Beyer and Lori Beaman [Leiden: Brill, 2007], pp. 9–34, and José Casanova, "Rethinking Secularization: A Global Comparative Perspective," in *ibid.*, pp. 101–20).

11 Key figures in developing this kind of theoretical approach include Talal Asad, José Casanova, Grace Davie, Danièle Hervieu-Leger, David Martin, Charles Taylor, and Peter van der Veer. Although there are differences and arguments between them (for example, Asad has been highly critical of the approach developed by Casanova), their combined questioning and cumulative deconstruction of the classic "secularization thesis" warrants locating them together.

12 For an overview of "post-secular" philosophical voices and the erasing of disciplinary boundaries between the study of religion and politics, see Ola Sigurdson,

"Beyond Secularism? Towards a Post-Secular Political Theology," *Modern Theology* 26.2 (2010): 177–96.

13 *Ibid.*, p. 180.

14 See, for example, the work of Oliver O'Donovan, Stanley Hauerwas, John Milbank, and Jürgen Moltmann.

15 An outline of the methodology used here is given in the Appendix.

16 See especially Luke Bretherton, *Christianity and Contemporary Politics: The Conditions and Possibilities of Faithful Witness* (Oxford: Wiley-Blackwell, 2010). In contrast to that book where I used the term "politics of the common good" but in keeping with its core argument, in this volume I use the term "politics of a common life."

17 There is no necessary opposition between these two forms. More often than not, what begins as a form of hospitality grows into a common life politics, and a common life politics may involve a guest-host dynamic wherein there is a process of mutual hospitality.

18 Peter Dreier, "Community Organizing for What? Progressive Politics and Movement Building in America," in *Transforming the City: Community Organizing and the Challenge of Political Change*, ed. Marion Orr (Lawrence: University Press of Kansas, 2007), p. 224.

19 Brad Fulton and Richard Wood, "Interfaith Community Organizing: Emerging Theological and Organizational Challenges," *International Journal of Public Theology* 6 (2012): 398–420, p. 402.

20 Robert Bailey, Jr., *Radicals in Urban Politics: The Alinsky Approach* (Chicago: University of Chicago Press, 1974), pp. 1–2.

21 On the origins of community organizing in the Philippines, see Jennifer Conroy Franco, *Elections and Democratization in the Philippines* (New York: Routledge, 2001), pp. 119–20. I am grateful to Mike Miller for drawing my attention to the work of Thomas Gaudette in India.

22 Nikolas Rose, "Governing Cities, Governing Citizens," in *Democracy, Citizenship and the Global City*, ed. Engin F. Isin (London: Routledge, 2000), pp. 95–109.

23 Whether it is a good or bad thing that London dominates the social imaginary and political economy of Britain is another question. For a critique of London understood as the "golden goose" on which Britain depends and the ways in which its dominance produces inequality both in Britain as a whole and within London itself, see Doreen Massey, *World City* (Cambridge: Polity Press, 2007; repr. 2010), pp. 97–129.

24 The two most notable journalistic treatments of Alinsky's work up to his death are Charles Silberman, *Crisis in Black and White* (New York: Random House, 1965) and Marion K. Sanders, *The Professional Radical: Conversations with Saul Alinsky* (New York: Harper & Row, 1970).

25 Bailey, *Radicals in Urban Politics*, p. 3.

26 A notable exception is Kim Bobo, Jackie Kendall, and Steve Max, *Organizing for Social Change: Midwest Academy Manual for Activists*, 4th ed. (Santa Ana, CA: Forum Press, 2010). However, as the name suggests, this is a training manual rather than an in-depth analysis of organizing. Moreover, although the approach advocated in the manual draws on the work of Alinsky and the IAF, it diverges from it in significant ways, particularly in relation to the tactics and strategies proposed.

27 Gregory Pierce, *Activism that Makes Sense: Congregations and Community Organization* (Chicago: ACTA Publications, 1997); Michael Gecan, *Going Public: An Organizer's Guide to Citizen Action* (New York: Anchor Books, 2002) and *After America's Midlife Crisis* (Cambridge, MA: MIT Press, 2009); Edward T. Chambers and Michael A. Cowan, *Roots for Radicals: Organizing for Power, Action, and Justice* (New York: Continuum, 2004); Kristin Layng Szakos and Joe Szakos, *We Make Change: Community Organizers Talk about What They Do – and Why* (Nashville, TN: Vanderbilt University Press, 2007); and Mike Miller, *A Community Organizer's Tale: People and Power in San Francisco* (Berkeley, CA: Heyday Books, 2009). Nicholas von Hoffman's portrait of Alinsky should also be counted within this genre as it is less a biography than an account of organizing itself. Hoffman was the first organizer Alinsky recruited to work with him: *Radical: A Portrait of Saul Alinsky* (New York: Nation Books, 2010). A further text that needs to be included but which stands halfway between academic analysis and autobiography is Marshall Ganz, *Why David Sometimes Wins* (Oxford: Oxford University Press, 2009). Ganz's account is focused on union organizing rather than community organizing, but Ganz himself has been an important influence in training organizers and informing the development of the practice.

28 In stark contrast to his right-wing detractors, Sanford D. Horwitt envisages Alinsky as a defender of and experimenter with U.S. democracy whose "relevance and legacy live on in no small part because he effectively advanced the great American radical ideal that democracy is for ordinary people" (*Let Them Call Me Rebel: Saul Alinsky, His Life and Legacy* [New York: Knopf, 1989], p. xvi). See also P. David Finks, *The Radical Vision of Saul Alinsky* (New Jersey: Paulist Press, 1984). Similar concerns animate Mary Beth Rogers's account of the work of the IAF in Texas (*Cold Anger: A Story of Faith and Power Politics* [Denton, TX: University of North Texas Press, 1990]). But it is a concern most clearly and forcefully articulated by Harry C. Boyte (*Commonwealth: A Return to Citizen Politics* [New York: Free Press, 1989]; and Sara M. Evans and Harry C. Boyte, *Free Spaces: The Sources of Democratic Change in America* [New York: Harper & Row, 1986]).

29 See Neil Betten, Michael J. Austin, and Robert Fisher, *The Roots of Community Organizing, 1917–1939* (Philadelphia: Temple University Press, 1990); Robert Fisher, *Let the People Decide: Neighborhood Organizing in America* (New York: Twayne Publishers, 1994); and Robert A. Slayton, *Back of the Yards: The Making of a Local Democracy* (Chicago: University of Chicago Press, 1986). In keeping with this stream is the work of Francesca Polletta, who analyzes and contrasts differing and interconnected styles of organization, relationship building, and leadership in grassroots and participatory democratic politics in the United States through the course of the twentieth century (*Freedom Is an Endless Meeting: Democracy in American Social Movements* [Chicago: University of Chicago Press, 2002]). Polletta closes her book by contrasting community organizing with contemporary anarchist forms of direct action. More recently, the public-interest lawyer, activist, and writer John Atlas has narrated the rise and fall of ACORN (Association of Community Organizations for Reform Now) as a community organizing network that reflects what he sees as the U.S. tradition of helping the poor help themselves through addressing structural inequalities and asymmetries of power (John Atlas, *Seeds of Change: The Story of ACORN, America's Most Controversial*

Antipoverty Community Organizing Group [Nashville, TN: Vanderbilt University Press, 2010]).

30 Ralph M. Kramer and Harry Specht, *Readings in Community Organization Practice* (Englewood, NJ: Prentice-Hall, 1969); Joan Lancourt, *Confront or Concede: The Alinsky Citizen-Action Organizations* (Lexington, MA: Lexington Books, 1979); Donald Reitzes and Dietrich C. Reitzes, "Alinsky in the 1980s: Two Contemporary Chicago Community Organizations," *The Sociological Quarterly* 28.2 (1987): 265–83; Marion Orr, *Transforming the City.* A more critical account is given in James DeFilippis, Robert Fisher, and Eric Shragge, *Contesting Community: The Limits and Potential of Local Organizing* (New Brunswick: Rutgers University Press, 2010). Significant among these studies is Heidi Swarts's comparison of the non-IAF networks, ACORN, Gamaliel, and PICO. Swarts locates different forms of community organizing strategies in the context of social movement theory and assesses the contrasting styles of political mobilization that had emerged among the divergent community organizing networks by the 1990s (*Organizing Urban America: Secular and Faith-Based Progressive Movements* [Minneapolis: University of Minnesota Press, 2008]).

31 For a summary and assessment of this debate, see Randy Stoecker, "The Community Development Corporation Model of Urban Redevelopment: A Critique and an Alternative," *Journal of Urban Affairs* 19.1 (1997): 1–23; and now in its fourth edition, see also Herbert Rubin and Irene Rubin, *Community Organizing and Development*, 2nd ed. (New York: Macmillan, 1992). The work of John Kretzmann and John McKnight, leading lights of the Asset-Based Community Development Institute, is an interesting fruit of this debate. The authors tried to integrate the developmental and organizing aspects of community activism. Kretzman and McKnight see their asset-based community development approach as a development of and improvement on Alinsky's approach ("Community Organizing in the Eighties: Toward a Post-Alinsky Agenda," in *The Careless Society: Community and Its Counterfeits* [New York: Basic Books, 1996], pp. 153–60). However, the accuracy of their portrayal of Alinsky's approach is highly questionable. Kretzmann and McKnight's work raises the question of the myriad paths community organizing has taken since Alinsky. There is not the space to map them here, but others have attempted to trace the rhizomatic connections between different organizers and organizing networks. See, in particular, David Walls, "Power to the People: Thirty-Five Years of Community Organizing," available at: http://www.sonoma.edu/users/w/wallsd/community-organizing.shtml (last accessed December 22, 2011). A related attempt is Mark Warren and Richard Wood, *Faith Based Community Organizing: The State of the Field* (Jericho, NY: Interfaith Funders, 2001), which has been updated, some of the results of which are given in Fulton and Wood, "Interfaith Community Organizing," pp. 398–420. In more direct continuity with the work of Bailey and Swarts are Jane Wills's studies of London Citizens within the field of urban geography and within debates about the construction of place and identity and their relationship to political activism and poverty alleviation in global cities. See, for example, Jane Wills, "Identity Making for Action: The Example of London Citizens," in *Theorizing Identities and Social Action*, ed. M. Wetherell (London: Palgrave Macmillan, 2009), pp. 157–76; Jane Wills et al., *Global Cities at Work: New Migrant Divisions of Labour* (London: Pluto, 2009).

32 More journalistic than scholarly, this stream of work was heralded by William Greider's *Who Will Tell the People? The Betrayal of American Democracy* (New York: Simon & Schuster, 1993). Political theorist and former organizer Harry Boyte's *Everyday Politics: Reconnecting Citizens and the Public Life* (2004) shares many of Greider's concerns but draws on the history and practice of community organizing to discuss a number of constructive responses to the perceived deracination of public life and civic education. Stephen Hart and Paul Osterman attend to similar concerns through empirically based studies of different broad-based community organizations.

33 Stephen Hart, *Cultural Dilemmas of Progressive Politics: Styles of Engagement Among Grassroots Activists* (Chicago: University of Chicago Press, 2001); and Paul Osterman, *Gathering Power: The Future of Progressive Politics in America* (Boston: Beacon Press, 2002). In a similar vein, see also Kristina Smock, *Democracy in Action: Community Organizing and Urban Change* (New York: Columbia University Press, 2004).

34 Mark R. Warren, *Dry Bones Rattling: Community Building to Revitalize American Democracy* (Princeton, NJ: Princeton University Press, 2001), idem, *Fire in the Heart: How White Activists Embrace Racial Justice* (Oxford: Oxford University Press, 2010); and Richard Wood, *Faith in Action: Religion, Race, and Democratic Organizing in America* (Chicago: University of Chicago Press, 2002). Warren's work is specifically focused on the IAF in Texas and the possibilities and limits of organizing at a regional and national scale. Wood's study is focused on the involvement of two Roman Catholic and one African-American Pentecostal congregation in the PICO network in California, contrasting this congregation-based form of organizing with the exclusively race-based form enacted by the Center for Third World Organizing. There is also some initial work along these lines relating to community organizing in the United Kingdom. See Robert Furbey et al., "Breaking with Tradition? The Church of England and Community Organising," *Community Development Journal* 32 (1997): 141–50; Lina Jamoul and Jane Wills, "Faith in Politics," *Urban Studies* 45.10 (2008): 2035–56; and Mark R. Warren, "Community Organizing in Britain: The Political Engagement of Faith-Based Social Capital," *City & Community* 8.2 (2009): 99–127.

35 C. Melissa Snarr, *All You That Labor: Religion and Ethics in the Living Wage Movement* (New York: New York University Press, 2011). Snarr focuses on a broad range of networks, including the IAF and ACORN, attending to the intersection of religion with gender and race in the context of organizing. Snarr draws on social movement theory to frame her account, while both Warren and Wood draw from the framework of "social capital" in order to discuss the interrelationships between religion and democratic politics. Use of a social capital framework is something I have resisted in my own work (Bretherton, *Christianity and Contemporary Politics*, pp. 39–42).

36 Wood's more recent work has addressed the interfaith dynamics of organizing in the U.S. context. See Fulton and Wood, "'Interfaith Community Organizing."

37 Other terms used to designate the kind of approach IAF's work represents include "institution-based community organizing" (Wood & Fulton); "power-based organizing" (Smock); and "faith-based community organizing" (Swarts).

38 Michael Sandel, *Democracy's Discontent: America in Search of a Public Philosophy* (Cambridge, MA: Belknap Press, 1996), pp. 336–38; Romand Coles, *Beyond Gated*

Politics: Reflections for the Possibility of Democracy (Minneapolis: University of Minnesota Press, 2005); and Jeffrey Stout, *Blessed Are the Organized: Grassroots Democracy in America* (Princeton, NJ: Princeton University Press, 2010).

39 Albert Dzur, *Democratic Professionalism: Citizen Participation and the Reconstruction of Professional Ethics, Identity, and Practice* (University Park: Pennsylvania State University Press, 2008).

40 On democracy as a form of collective problem solving and shared governance, see Xavier de Souza Briggs, *Democracy as Problem Solving: Civic Capacity in Communities across the Globe* (Cambridge, MA: MIT Press, 2008); and Carmen Sirianni, *Investing in Democracy: Engaging Citizens in Collaborative Governance* (Washington, DC: Brookings Institute, 2009). An equivalent practice of collaborative governance to community organizing that illustrates this approach is participatory budgeting. Gianpaolo Baiocchi, *Militants as Citizens: The Politics of Participatory Democracy in Porto Alegre* (Stanford, CA: Stanford University Press, 2005). For a range of other equivalent practices and how these constitute forms of participatory democracy, see Archon Fung and Erik Olin Wright, eds., *Deepening Democracy: Institutional Innovations in Empowered Participatory Governance* (London: Verso, 2003).

41 For a clear articulation of this nest of concerns, see Harry Boyte, "Reframing Democracy: Governance, Civic Agency, and Politics," *Public Administration Review* 65.5 (2005): 536–46, and *Civic Agency and the Cult of the Expert* (New York: Kettering Foundation, 2009).

42 Mark R. Warren, Karen L. Mapp, and The Community Organizing and School Reform Project, *A Match on Dry Grass: Community Organizing as a Catalyst for School Reform* (Oxford: Oxford University Press, 2011); Harry C. Boyte and Eric Fretz, "Civic Professionalism," *Journal of Higher Education Outreach and Engagement* 14.2 (2010): 67–90; Mark Warren, "Communities and Schools: A New View of Urban Education Reform," *Harvard Educational Review* 75.2 (2005): 133–73; and William Doherty and Tai Mendenhall, "Citizen Health Care: A Model for Engaging Patients, Families, and Communities as Coproducers of Health," *Families, Systems, & Health* 24.3 (2006): 251–63.

43 See, for example, Amanda Tattersall, *Power in Coalition: Strategies for Strong Unions and Social Change* (Ithaca, NY: Cornell University Press, 2010).

44 Jeffrey Hilmer, "The State of Participatory Democratic Theory," *New Political Science* 32.1 (2010): 43–63; Harry Boyte, *Reinventing Citizenship as Public Work: Citizen-Centered Democracy and the Empowerment Gap* (New York: Kettering Foundation, 2013).

1 The Origins of Organizing: An Intellectual History

1 Irving Cutler, *The Jews of Chicago: From Shtetl to Suburb* (Urbana: University of Illinois Press, 1996).

2 *Ibid.*, pp. 10–13.

3 von Hoffman, *Radical*, p. 124.

4 Jean Bethke Elshtain, *Jane Addams and the Dream of American Democracy* (New York: Basic Books, 2002); Maurice Hamington, "Jane Addams and a Politics of Embodied Care," *The Journal of Speculative Philosophy*, 15.2 (2001): 105–21.

5 Both of these assumptions drew on the work of George Herbert Mead.

6 For an account of how Alinsky and Addams's approach to community organizing overlaps and diverges and the indirect influence of Addams on Alinsky, see Maurice Hamington, "Community Organizing: Addams and Alinsky," in *Feminist Interpretations of Jane Addams*, ed. Maurice Hamington (University Park: Pennsylvania State University Press, 2010), pp. 255–74. While making a number of important points, particularly in relation to the sexism of Alinsky, Hamington's claim that Alinsky lacked a broader social and political vision is wholly inaccurate.

7 See Jane Addams, "The Settlement as a Factor in the Labor Movement," in *Hull House Maps and Papers* (Boston: Thomas Y. Crowell & Co, 1895), pp. 83–204; and "Trade Unions and Public Duty," *American Journal of Sociology* 4 (1899): 448–62.

8 Taylor Branch, *Parting the Waters: Martin Luther King and the Civil Rights Movement, 1954–63* (London: Macmillan, 1990), pp. 263–64; Charles M. Payne, *I've Got the Light of Freedom: The Organizing Tradition and the Mississippi Freedom Struggle* (Berkeley: University of California Press, 1995), pp. 70–77. Payne's work properly reminds us that while Highlander was important, the determinative influence on the early civil rights organizing efforts of Ella Baker, Fannie Lou Hamer, and others was the prior work of figures such as A. Philip Randolph and the Brotherhood of Sleeping Car Porters, and before that the long-standing, grassroots struggle since the days of slavery to resist white supremacy – a struggle that includes the involvement of African Americans in the nineteenth-century Populist movement.

9 Myles Horton with Judith Kohl and Herbert Kohl, *The Long Haul: An Autobiography* (New York: Teachers College Press, 1998), pp. 48–50. Horton did not meet Alinsky while at the University of Chicago, but did meet him later when Alinsky was establishing the Back of the Yards Neighborhood Council and they subsequently came to support each other in their work (175–80).

10 This was as true of the British settlement houses as their U.S. counterparts, although there were exceptions, most notably Kingsley Hall established in 1915 by the Lester sisters. In contrast to Toynbee Hall where the working classes entered as domestic servants, the Lester sisters did their own domestic labor, were heavily engaged in union organizing, and attempted to establish a more reciprocal relationship with those they lived among. Yet even in Kingsley Hall, despite their strenuous efforts at self-policing every area of their behavior, class distinctions were still reproduced (Seth Kovan, "The 'Sticky Sediment' of Daily Life: Radical Domesticity, Revolutionary Christianity and the Problem of Wealth in early 20th Century Britain," [unpublished paper]).

11 William Foote Whyte, *Street Corner Society: The Social Structure of an Italian Slum*, 2nd ed. (Chicago: University of Chicago Press, 1955), p. 99. Whyte details the disjuncture between the social structure and expectations of the settlement house workers and those of the local community.

12 *Ibid.*, p. 104.

13 Slayton, *Back of the Yards*, pp. 111–27 and 173–87.

14 Fisher, *Let the People Decide*, p. 13. By way of a case study of what Fisher discusses, see Slayton, *Back of the Yards*.

15 A quote that suggests how central this was to Alinsky comes from his critique of the lack of real followers and representativeness in the Black Power movement and their co-option by white elites: "They run around in circles. Somebody yells 'Black

Power!' So they call him in and say 'Ah, you're a Black Power leader. Sit down. Maybe we can work something out.' And they don't even know how to challenge, to check credentials. And, in desperation, they'll buy the kind of representation that they would never buy otherwise. The fact is that *that* representative doesn't have anything, really, to be representative *of*. You know the old Jewish expression, a minion? You know when Jews pray to God you've got to have ten Jews together, sort of collective bargaining with God. Well, a lot of these guys couldn't even get a minion together!" (Stephen C. Rose, "Saul Alinsky, the Industrial Areas Foundation and the Church's Millions," *Renewal* [March 1968]: 4–9, p. 7).

16 For an account of the shift from church-based welfare provision to "expert," "scientific" welfare provision and the role of Toynbee Hall in this shift, see Frank K. Prochaska, *Christianity and Social Service in Modern Britain: The Disinherited Spirit* (Oxford: Oxford University Press, 2006).

17 Michael J. Austin and Neil Betten, "The Intellectual Origins of Community Organizing," in *The Roots of Community Organizing, 1917–1939*, ed. Neil Betten and Michael J. Austin (Philadelphia: Temple University Press, 1990), pp. 16–31.

18 Roy Lubove, *The Professional Altruist: The Emergence of Social Work as a Career, 1880–1930* (New York: Atheneum Publishers, 1969), p. 180, quoted in Betten and Austin, *Roots of Community Organizing*, p. 5.

19 Horwitt, *Let Them Call Me Rebel*, p. 11.

20 The relationship between the work of Park and Mead and who influenced whom is a matter of some dispute (Donald C. Reitzes and Dietrich C. Reitzes, "Saul D. Alinsky: An Applied Urban Symbolic Interactionist," *Symbolic Interaction* 15.1 [1992]: 1–24).

21 Paul Atkinson, Amanda Coffey, Sara Delamont, John Lofland, and Lyn Lofland, *Handbook of Ethnography*, new ed. (London: Sage Publications, 2007), p. 19.

22 *Ibid.*

23 *Ibid.*, pp. 14–15, and Reitzes and Reitzes, "Saul D. Alinsky," pp. 8–12.

24 Slayton, *Back of the Yards*, pp. 6–7.

25 Marion Sanders, "The Professional Radical: Conversations with Saul Alinsky," reprinted from *Harper's Magazine*, June and July, 1965, p. 6.

26 *Ibid.*

27 Steven L. Schlossman and Michel W. Sedlak note that for Shaw the issue of recognizing and connecting to a wider social world were important parts of such work ("The Chicago Area Project Revisited," *Crime and Delinquency* 29.3 [1983]: 398–462, pp. 419–28).

28 Neil Betten and William E. Hershey, "The Urban Political Boss as Community Organizer," in *Roots of Community Organizing*, ed. Betten and Austin, p. 141. Echoing their analysis, Slayton comments that "loyalty and dependability in politics, as in every other aspect of life, was of paramount importance. Loyalty produced order out of chaos, as important in the political clubs as it was anywhere else" (Slayton, *Back of the Yards*, p. 151). For all its corruption, the party boss system was probably more democratic, less elitist, and more responsive than the liberal-minded settlement house residents and social workers. Jane Addams recognizes this in her own account of the role of the party boss in *Democracy and Social Ethics* (Chicago: University of Illinois Press, 2002), pp. 98–120. Her account is directly born out of her ongoing conflict with Alderman Johnny Powers of Chicago's 19th ward (Elshtain, *Jane Addams*, pp. 182–89).

29 *Ibid.*, p. 171.
30 Finks, *Radical Vision of Saul Alinsky*, pp. 6–10; Jon Snodgrass, "Clifford R. Shaw and Henry D. McKay: Chicago Criminologists," *The British Journal of Criminology* 16.1 (1976): 1–19, p. 2.
31 In an interview, Chambers says he received no training from Alinsky, but this is an overstatement that does not value the insistence Alinsky put on writing regular reports and engaging in sustained field work, which for Alinsky, with his urban ethnography background, was a training in how to listen and pay attention to what was going on. Interview with Ed Chambers (November 7, 2008, Chicago).
32 A key example of such a longitudinal study is Clifford Shaw's *The Jackroller: A Delinquent Boy's Own Story* (Chicago: University of Chicago Press, 1966 [1930]).
33 Snodgrass, "Clifford R. Shaw and Henry D. McKay," p. 3.
34 A parallel and complementary analysis can be seen in Jane Jacobs, *The Death and Life of Great American Cities* (New York: Modern Library, 1961) and her account of "street eyes": the informal surveillance that operates in some urban neighborhoods that prevents crime and facilitates the supervision of children's play. What Jacobs's analysis adds to social disorganization theory is how the material form and structure of urban buildings and streets affects the ability of a neighborhood to police itself. What social disorganization theory and Alinsky's subsequent work adds to Jacobs's account is that while improving streetscapes and the material form of cities is a necessary condition, it is insufficient by itself to improve the social and political conditions of a neighborhood. There is still the need to strengthen the civic life and reweave and reorganize the fabric of relationships between people within a place.
35 *Ibid.*, p. 8.
36 Michael J. Austin and Neil Betten, "The Roots of Community Organizing: An Introduction," in *Roots of Community Organizing*, p. 4.
37 Slayton's account of the Back of the Yards neighborhood self-consciously deconstructs Shaw's view by unveiling the dense fabric of associational life and the patterns of self-policing that emerged within it (Slayton, *Back of the Yards*, pp. 111–27). Slayton's account affirms Alinsky's analysis that the problem was not so much social disintegration, but the need to connect the divergent and disconnected forms of self-organization and strengthen existing forms of local leadership.
38 Clifford R. Shaw and Henry D. McKay, *Juvenile Delinquency in Urban Areas* (Chicago: University of Chicago Press, 1942).
39 Schlossman and Sedlak, "Chicago Area Project Revisited," *Crime and Delinquency*, p. 418.
40 Horwitt, *Let Them Call Me Rebel*, p. 26.
41 Snodgrass, "Clifford R. Shaw and Henry D. McKay"; and Shaw and McKay, *Juvenile Delinquency*.
42 Alinsky states: "There is no such animal as a disorganized community. It is a contradiction in terms to use the two words together of 'disorganized community.' ... Call it organized apathy or organized non-participation, but that is a community pattern. They are living under a certain set of arrangements, standards, accepted modus operandis and a way of life. ... Therefore, if your function is to attack apathy and create citizen participation it is in actual fact an attack upon the prevailing patterns of organized living in the community. Here I would like to state

my first proposition; the first function of community organization is community disorganization" (Saul Alinsky, "From Citizen Apathy to Participation," Paper Presented at the 6th Annual Fall Conference, Association of Community Councils of Chicago, Chicago, October 19, 1957, pp. 2–3. Box 32, file 523, Industrial Areas Foundation Archive, University of Illinois at Chicago).

43 For details of its present incarnation, see: www.chicagoareaproject.org.

44 Excerpt from Ernest Burgess, Joseph Lohman, and Clifford Shaw, "The Chicago Area Project," National Probation Association, *Yearbook*, 1937, pp. 8–10, quoted in Steven L. Schlossmann and Michael W. Sedlak, *The Chicago Area Project Revisited* (Santa Monica, CA: The Rand Corporation, 1983), pp. iii–iv.

45 Schlossman and Sedlak, "Chicago Area Project Revisited," *Crime and Delinquency*, p. 421

46 Slayton, *Back of the Yards*, pp. 202–03.

47 *Ibid.*, p. 203. What is not set out here is the vital importance of Joseph Meegan in the establishment and ongoing development of the Back of the Yards neighborhood. On this, see *ibid.*, pp. 193–205.

48 See the following essays in Betten and Austen, *Roots of Community Organizing*; Betten and Austin, "The Cincinnati Unit Experiment, 1917–1920," pp. 35–53; Robert Fisher, "Grass Roots Organizing in the Community Center Movement, 1907–1930," pp. 76–93; and Austin and Betten, "Social Planning and Physical Planning," pp. 109–22. There are striking parallels between the Back of the Yards Neighborhood Council and the work of the Cincinnati Social Unit, in particular their emphasis on local leaders and self-organization. Betten and Austin note that the Cincinnati Social Unit was a direct influence on Shaw (*ibid.*, p. 110). Conversely, as Betten and Austin point out, the Cincinnati Social Unit failed, in large part, because it did not address issues of power or sufficiently engage with the already existing local institutions and religious organizations. The Community Center Movement can also be seen as an antecedent of both CAP and the BYNC. However, Fisher notes that while it began with a strong emphasis on democratic self-government and self-expression as a way of addressing urban social problems, the trajectory of the Centers from 1907 onward was toward becoming increasingly centralized, professionalized, and bureaucratic.

49 Harry Boyte quotes Chambers as saying in an interview: "Saul thought experts studied communities theoretically but that their approaches were mostly bullshit. Talk about 'social disorganization' and social pathologies with no face to face analysis he saw as irrelevant" (*Everyday Politics*, p. 42). While in essence true, Alinsky and community organizing in general owes a great deal to theories of social disorganization. The direct influence is most explicitly reflected in an early article by Alinsky where he comments on the philosophical implications of "community organization" as a way of addressing "social pathology" (Saul Alinsky, "Youth and Morale," *The American Journal of Orthopsychiatry* 12.4 [1942]: 598–602).

50 Snodgrass, "Clifford R. Shaw and Henry D. McKay," p. 10.

51 Quoted in "Empowering People, Not Elites: Interview with Saul Alinsky," *Playboy Magazine*, March, 1972. See also Sanders, "Professional Radical," where Alinsky is even more dismissive of Chicago's sociology department, although in the same article he does distinguish between what he calls the "seminal minds" of figures such as Robert Ezra Park and the "sort of electronic breathing accessories to computers."

52 Snodgrass, "Clifford R. Shaw and Henry D. McKay," p. 14.

53 *Ibid.*, pp. 10–11.
54 *Ibid.*, p. 17.
55 Finks, *Radical Vision of Saul Alinsky*, p. 15.
56 Philip Yale Nicholson, *Labor's Story in the United States* (Philadelphia: Temple University Press, 2004), pp. 29–33. The 1785 and 1786 shoemakers' and printers' strikes in Philadelphia are also credited with being the first strikes in U.S. history.
57 *Ibid.*, p. 54.
58 Quoted *ibid.*, p. 91. Lincoln sets out what can be seen as an alternative economic vision to that which was pursued after his assassination in his 1865 statement on monetary policy.
59 In contrast to union membership among urban industrial workers, union membership among farm workers declined during World War I (Ganz, *Why David Sometimes Wins,* p. 29).
60 Robert H. Zieger, *American Workers, American Unions, 1920–1985* (Baltimore, MD: Johns Hopkins University Press, 1986), p. 40.
61 W. Willard Wirtz, *Brief History of the American Labor Movement*, 3rd ed. (Washington DC: Department of Labor, 1964), pp. 25–28.
62 Finks, *Radical Vision of Saul Alinsky*, p. 15. See also Betten and Austin, "The Conflict Approach to Community Organizing: Saul Alinsky and the CIO," in *Roots of Community Organizing*, pp. 152–61.
63 Sanders, "Professional Radical," p. 4.
64 Robert Fisher, *Let the People Decide: Neighborhood Organizing in America* (New York: Twayne Publishers, 1994), p. 61.
65 In the speech, Lewis is careful to distinguish his approach to that of the communists: "Unionization, as opposed to communism, presupposes the relation of employment; it is based upon the wage system and it recognizes fully and unreservedly the institution of private property and the right to investment profit. It is upon the fuller development of collective bargaining, the wider expansion of the labor movement, the increased influence of labor in our national councils, that the perpetuity of our democratic institutions must largely depend."
66 Quoted in Melvyn Dubofsky and Warren Van Tine, *John L. Lewis: A Biography* (Urbana: University of Illinois Press, 1986), p. 152.
67 Although not directly named in the novel, it is clear that the "party" Steinbeck had in view was the Communist Party.
68 von Hoffman, *Radical*, p. 33.
69 Saul Alinsky, *Rules for Radicals: A Practical Primer for Realistic Radicals* (New York: Vintage Books, 1989 [1971]), p. 9.
70 Saul Alinsky, *Reveille for Radicals* (New York: Vintage Books, 1969 [1946]), p. 85.
71 *Ibid.*, p. 50. It is worth noting that the Communist Party from 1930 onward engaged in neighborhood organizing under the auspices of the Communist Party Organizes the Unemployed. However, from 1937 onward, they began focusing all their energy away from local, place-based organizing toward union organizing (Fisher, *Let the People Decide,* pp. 38–48). As Fisher notes: "In essence there was never much real autonomy for the local councils. The party came to neighbourhood people with a prearranged ideology, program, and strategy – a 'line' they called it – that provided an analysis of current problems and their solutions" (p. 43). Alinsky

directly opposes such an approach in his writing. For him, "the foundation of a People's Organization is in the communal life of the local people" (*Reveille*, p. 76) and not a prior ideologically driven program.

72 Interestingly, Myles Horton echoes Alinsky's approach. While he opposed the CIO's insistence on including anticommunist commitments to those receiving official appointments in the union, and some of his early educational efforts focused on teaching farmers about collectivist measures in the Soviet Union, he vehemently rejected the ideologically driven nature of communism and the instrumentalization and subordination of people to theoretical ideas he found among its proponents. For an example of an incident that illustrates this, see Horton, *Long Haul*, pp. 140–43. For an account of Alinsky's involvement with the New Left and its failure to connect with the values and institutions of working-class Americans, see Michael Kazin, *The Populist Persuasion: An American History* (New York: Basic Books, 1995), pp. 196–218.

73 Alinsky, *Reveille*, p. 36. Arguably, Alinsky is simply extending the logic of John L. Lewis's original argument with the AFL union that led to the formation of the CIO, wherein unions could not simply protect the interests of particular crafts but needed to represent the general interests of all working men and women.

74 Alinsky, *Reveille*, pp. 200, 213.

75 Agnes Meyer in her article on the council reports a lunch she attended made up of officials and leaders of the Back of the Yards Council. These included a Polish Catholic priest, a German Lutheran pastor, a representative of the UPWA-CIO labor union (a Pole), the general manager of the local department store (a Jew), two Slovak Catholic priests, a German Catholic priest, a Mexican Catholic priest, the editor of the local paper, a German Lutheran, and Joe Meegan (an Irish Catholic who served as the council's executive secretary) (Agnes E. Meyer, "The Orderly Revolution," *The Washington Post* [June 4–9, 1945]).

76 This relationship-but-not-identification approach was even more pronounced in the work of Chambers and other white organizers within African-American communities in Rochester and in helping to set up The Woodlawn Organization in Chicago; and with Gerald Taylor, an African American working with white working-class Italian and Polish communities in Queens in the 1970s. On this, see von Hoffman, *Radical*, pp. 19–21.

77 For an account of how the kind of approach IAF adopts can work in practice and how it represents a powerful and more mutual way of addressing the difficult area of interracial political solidarity and common work, see Mark R. Warren, *Fire in the Heart: How White Activists Embrace Racial Justice* (Oxford: Oxford University Press, 2010). See, in particular, Warren's account of the work of Christine Stephens and Perry Perkins.

78 The symbiosis of Christianity and democracy in Alinsky's political vision is indicated in the following quotation: "Believing in people, the radical has the job of organizing them so that they will have the power to best meet each unforeseeable future crisis as they move ahead in their eternal search for those values for equality, justice, freedom, peace, a deep concern for the preciousness of human life, and all those rights and values propounded by Judeo-Christianity and the democratic political tradition. Democracy is not an end but the best means toward achieving these values. This is my credo for which I live and if need be, die" (Alinsky, *Rules*, pp. 11–12).

79 Bernard Sheil, the Auxiliary Roman Catholic Bishop of Chicago from 1928 to 1959, was a crucial figure when Alinsky was first developing his approach to community organizing (see Horwitt, *Let Them Call Me Rebel*). Ed Chambers, who took over the running of the IAF after Alinsky's death, had been a Benedictine seminarian and spent time with Dorothy Day from the Catholic Worker Movement before joining Alinsky as an organizer (*ibid*., p. 326); for an autobiographical account of his theological training, see Chambers, *Roots for Radicals*. This was not uncommon; many of the early organizers had theological training, for example, Richard Harmon and Jeff Williams (Horwitt, *Let Them Call Me Rebel*, p. 398).

80 This section builds on previously published work. See Bretherton, *Christianity and Contemporary Politics,* 91–94.

81 The 1966 statement is from Saul Alinsky, "The Tough Line on Poverty," *The United Church Observer*, February 15, 1966, p. 15. Recent research on those fighting for a decent wage for the low paid in London suggests Alinsky's comments are directly pertinent to the contemporary context. See Jane Wills, Kavita Datta, Yara Evans, Joanna Herbert, Jon May, and Cathy McIlwaine, "Religion at Work: The Role of Faith-Based Organizations in the London Living Wage Campaign," *Cambridge Journal of Regions, Economy and Society* 2.3 (2009): 443–61. Historical treatments of U.S. labor unions in the 1960s tend to share Alinsky's assessment. However, while he was critical of the unions, Alinsky was not uncritical of the churches. An early and particularly acute example of Alinsky's critique of the church is his speech, entitled "Catholic Leadership" presented before the National Conference of Catholic Charities, September 28, 1942. Box 16, file 239, IAF Archive. Alinsky retained much the same critique throughout his life. It was not a critique of Christianity per se, but of the ways in which Christians failed to live up to their own confession of faith.

82 See, in particular, Alexis de Tocqueville, *Democracy in America*, vol. 2, part 1, chapters 5–7.

83 On this, see Ronald Beiner, *Civil Religion: A Dialogue in the History of Political Philosophy* (Cambridge: Cambridge University Press, 2011), pp. 249–58; and Larry Siedentop, *Tocqueville* (Oxford: Oxford University Press, 1994), pp. 41–112.

84 Meyer, "The Orderly Revolution." It is interesting to note that such a dynamic can still form part of the appeal of community organizing to the Roman Catholic Church: for example, in Sydney, Catholic officials expressed real anxiety about how to integrate ethnic enclaves into multiethnic parishes and were looking to community organizing as one way of addressing this problem.

85 *The Philosopher and the Provocateur: The Correspondence of Jacques Maritain and Saul Alinsky*, ed. Bernard E. Doering (Notre Dame, IN: University of Notre Dame Press, 1994), p. 20.

86 *Ibid*., pp. xi–xxxviii.

87 Jacques Maritain, *Man and the State* (Chicago: University of Chicago Press, 1951); idem, *Integral Humanism: Temporal and Spiritual Problems of the New Christendom*, trans. Joseph Evans (New York: Charles Scribner's Sons, 1968), pp. 162–76.

88 Maritain and Alinsky, *The Philosopher and the Provocateur*, pp. xxii–xxiii. This was central to Alinsky's political vision and its rationale is clarified when he contends that "the concepts of the Industrial Areas Foundation are rooted in the democratic faith. It accepts the Madison and Monroe thesis of the Federalist Papers that

the common people, meaning the propertyless as well as those of limited formal education, are political equals and that they are competent and capable to be citizens in the fullest sense in the American body politic" (Saul Alinsky, "The I.A.F. – Why Is It Controversial?" *Church in Metropolis* 6 [Summer 1965], p. 13).

89 Maritain, *Integral Humanism*, pp. 108–11.

90 Maritain, *Man and the State*, pp. 54–75.

91 Doering, "Introduction," in Maritain and Alinsky, *The Philosopher and the Provocateur,* pp. xxxvi–xxxvii. Alinsky seems to take this on but frames what both Gandhi and Martin Luther King do as a form of moral self-interest and an appropriate political judgment that married means and ends in a realistic way. See Alinsky, *Rules for Radicals,* pp. 38–45. Maritain's contention that Alinsky's approach represents the use of repertoires of contention in order to appeal to moral ends can be seen as part of a wider reframing of adversarial political action from World War II onward. In contrast to an earlier generation of intellectuals, in particular Walter Lipmann and Reinhold Niebuhr, who saw the adversarial approach of the Depression-era CIO as a form of straightforward power politics, Maritain and many others saw adversarial politics as part of a moral appeal to core American values. On this see Marc Stears, *Demanding Democracy: American Radicals in Search of a New Politics* (Princeton, NJ: Princeton University Press, 2010).

92 Maritain, *Man and the State*, pp. 139–46. The analogy here is with Martin Luther King's rhetorical appeal to white America to live up to its own best insights and traditions rather than call for revolution, while at the same time profoundly reformulating many of those same traditions in new directions. Marc Stears rightly notes the mistaken interpretation and domestication of the civil rights movement (and equivalently, community organizing) by those who advocate either deliberative democracy or political liberalism. King was not simply appealing to an existent American creed but to a reformulation of that creed through the use of political strategies and behaviors that were judged illegitimate by the existing order (Stears, *Demanding Democracy*, pp. 146–47). The point of tactics of contention is not conflict per se, but the opening up of a space for new ways of relating or addressing an issue, ways that reconfigure the unjust status quo. As Alinsky puts it in his twelfth rule: "The price of a successful attack is a constructive alternative" (Alinsky, *Rules for Radicals,* p. 130). Political actions for Alinsky are to simultaneously declare the unjust way to be untrue and present a possible alternative through which all may flourish.

93 Fisher, *Let the People Decide*, pp. 231–33.

94 Saul Alinsky, "Is There Life after Birth?" Speech to the Centennial Meeting of the Episcopal Theological School, Cambridge, MA, June 7, 1967 (Chicago: IAF Reprint), p. 60.

95 Maritain, *Integral Humanism*, pp. 163 and 171.

96 *Ibid.*, pp. 169–71; 186–95. A parallel distinction is made by Pius XI in *Quadragesimo Anno* (1931), §§ 94–96 as a way of distinguishing a Christian corporatist vision of politics from fascist ones. On the Christian account, corporatist and personalist forms of civic association and economic organization are precisely a means of preventing the subsuming of all social relations to the political order.

97 See, for example, the critical comments by John Paul II of what he calls the "social assistance state" in *Centesimus Annus* (1991), §48. Sheldon Wolin develops a more comprehensive critique of the liberal welfare state in relation to his

problematic notion of "inverted totalitarianism" (Sheldon S. Wolin, *Politics and Vision: Continuity and Innovation in Western Thought* [Princeton: Princeton University Press, 2006 (1960)], pp. 591–95). Wolin argues that in fascism and communism the population is mobilized in order to serve the state. By contrast, within an inverted totalitarian state the population is depoliticized and demobilized via the mobility of money, goods, and people (p. 554). For Wolin, inverted totalitarianism is the paradigmatic form of "postmodern power" in that it is at once concentrated and disaggregated, combining centrifugal and centripetal forms of power. Part of the problem with Wolin's account is that it seems to preclude any possibility of constructive politics.

98 In a memo addressed to Right Reverend Monsignor John O'Grady for Dominico Cardinal Tardini, Cardinal Secretary of State, Vatican City dated August 27, 1959, Alinsky outlines how his approach represents a better way of relating church to politics and addressing the concerns and needs of the urban poor than the current strategies undertaken by the Roman Catholic Church in Italy. He is particularly critical of the church's over-alignment with the Christian Democratic Party. In the memo, Alinsky frames broad-based community organizing as the most effective way of diminishing the influence and rise of communism, citing his experience in the Back of the Yards as evidence for what he says (Box 9, file 128, IAF Archive).

99 Maritain and Alinsky, *Philosopher and the Provocateur*, p. 105. This is a recurrent theme in Maritain's response to Alinsky. He writes in a letter to the Ford Foundation (May 27, 1951): "I am writing this on a personal basis because I have known Saul Alinsky for about 10 years and because I admire and love him as a great soul, a man of profound moral purity and burning energy, whose work I consider the only really new and really important democratic initiative taken in the social field today, and whose natural generosity is quickened, though he would not admit it, by genuine evangelical brotherly love" (Box 12, file 179, IAF Archive). It was not just Maritain who made this connection, as the following quote from a letter (dated December 3, 1959) from Monsignor John O'Grady, then secretary to the National Conference of Catholic Charities, to the Cardinal-elect Most Reverend Albert G. Meyer, Archbishop of Chicago, puts it: "I am glad to know that you are showing a richly deserved appreciation of the kind of work that Saul Alinsky has been doing for some twenty years in the Back-of-Yards Neighbourhood Council, and in more recent years throughout the country. There is hardly any other person who has been more helpful to me in developing a truly Christian point of view in regard to Catholic Charities in the United States than Mr Alinsky" (Box 47, file 668, IAF Archive).

100 Maritain, *Philosopher and the Provocateur*, p. 109. This contests chambers's narration of how the IAF developed. For example, Chambers is quoted as saying: "I'd had a little training in philosophy. And I started forcing myself to look at what our kind of organizing meant to people. We worked with people in the churches, and their language was the language of the gospel. Their language was nothing like Alinsky's language [Alinsky, recall, was the IAF founder]. His language was power talk. Tough, abrasive, confrontational, full of ridicule. And those are really all non-Christian concepts. So I started looking at it. Here are the non-Christian concepts ... here are the Christian concepts. Are there any similarities? Is this just a different language for the same thing?" (quoted in "Gospel Values and Secular Politics," Mary Beth Rogers, *The Texas Observer*, November 22, 1990).

101 The thrust of the critique of Maritain's conception of the church in relation to the state is that he tends to spiritualize the church as a social body and thereby underemphasizes the extent to which the church is itself a polity or *res publica* that forms and socializes human bodies in ways that are very different to those of the modern nation-state. As Cavanaugh puts it: "[T]he key difficulty with Maritain's project is that he makes the Christian community the repository of purely supernatural virtues which stands outside of time, and thus interiorizes and individualizes the Gospel. Because he has sequestered political virtue from any direct habituation in Christian community, the state becomes that community of habituation, the pedagogue of virtue" (William Cavanaugh, *Torture and Eucharist: Theology, Politics and the Body of Christ* [Oxford: Blackwell, 1998], p. 195).

102 Maritain, *Man and the State*, pp. 108–14.

103 On Machiavelli's account these tensions are not so sharp for Judaism or Islam. For Machiavelli, the best prince is one who founds a state that integrates a political and religious order. Moses is his paradigm example of such a prince, but by extension, Mohammed meets the same high standard. Whereas Rousseau explicitly makes the connection between Moses and Mohammed ("the child of Ishmael") as exemplary legislators in *On The Social Contract*, bk II, ch. 7, the connection for Machiavelli is implied (see Ronald Beiner, *Civil Religion*, pp. 29–36).

104 On Machiavelli's republican conception of citizenship, power is based on the political community of citizens who constitute the state. For Christianity, in contrast, God is "sovereign" not humans; the basis of power is not citizenship, or the relationship between citizens, and the ultimate values are not self-government, self-sufficiency, and self-defense of a political community acting autonomously through time. (For a clear statement of this republican view, see J. G. A. Pocock, *The Machiavellian Moment: Florentine Political Thought and the Atlantic Republican Tradition* [Princeton, NJ: Princeton University Press, 1975], pp. 156–82). Neither is it freedom from foreign domination by sacrifice and obedience to laws given collectively to yourself that is to be valued above all else, but rather, obedience to the laws of God as revealed through Scripture. Human power is circumscribed by and derived from a relationship with God and what it means to participate rightly in the order of creation. Citizenship and "faith" thus seem incommensurable in terms of what really matters in politics: sovereignty, power, and authority. Citizenship locates power in human action within a self-sufficient political community that constitutes the ultimate good; whereas Christianity locates sovereignty outside the political community in divine revelation in which obedience to God is the ultimate value. In addition to this theoretical opposition, there is a second practical conflict, one that relates to the need for loyalty, solidarity, and obedience within a sovereign state. If one's ultimate loyalty is to God and one's primary solidarity with those who accept God's Word, then obedience lies not to the state but to the revealed Word and solidarity is with one's fellow believers, not with one's fellow citizens. The Romans who persecuted the early Christians understood this well enough. Porphyry, who provided philosophical legitimation to Diocletian's policy of repressing Christianity, saw that the claims of Christianity were opposed to and threatened the Roman religio-civil order and thus they were unpatriotic and should be punished accordingly. In many ways the Treaty of Westphalia (1648) and the rise of nation-states represents a return to the kind of order Porphyry

(and for that matter, Aristotle) sought to uphold, where religion served and was subordinate to the integrity of the polis.

105 Beiner asks: "What should define the relationship between politics and religion?" After interrogating the likes of Hobbes, Hume, Machiavelli, de Maistre, Mill, Montesquieu, Nietzsche, Rawls, Rousseau, and Spinoza on this question, he concludes: "The history of political philosophy has made available three possibilities: (1) the idea that politics and religion should be kept separate (liberalism); (2) the idea that politics and religion should be joined together but governed by the supremacy of religion (theocracy); and (3) the idea that politics and religion should be joined together but governed by the supremacy of politics (civil religion)" (Beiner, *Civil Religion*, p. 412). Whether these really are the only three options needs to be contested, as does Beiner's conception of theocracy. Part of my argument here is that attention to the practice of broad-based community organizing suggests a fourth option: a creative tension and reciprocal relation between "religion" and politics that disciplines both. However, this fourth option rests on a move that Beiner never considers: sovereignty itself might be plural. Beiner has a tacit conception of the indivisibility of sovereignty, so like those he interrogates from Machiavelli to Rawls, sovereignty becomes a zero sum game in which the church can only appear as a threat to political order.

106 For a discussion of the distinction between community organizing and social or protest movements, see Chambers, *Roots for Radicals*, pp. 129–31; and Leo Penta, "Islands of Democratic Practice: Organizing for Local and Regional Power in the USA," paper presented at the Biannual European Conference of the Inter-University Consortium for International Social Development in Cracow, Poland, September 24, 1999.

107 In addition to civic and place-based organizing, Harry Boyte suggests there is a need to rediscover workplace organizing, primarily in relation to professional groups, as a vital adjunct to community organizing and as a way of drawing the middle classes into what he calls a "commonwealth" or "everyday" politics (Boyte, *Everyday Politics*, pp. 64–76). Boyte does not include the role of labor organizing and its historic relationship with community organizing in his account of organizing developed in *Everyday Politics*. However, the importance of the labor movement to democratic populism is given in Sara M. Evans and Harry Boyte, *Free Spaces: The Sources of Democratic Change in America* (New York: Harper & Row, 1986).

108 David Harvey, *Spaces of Hope* (Edinburgh: Edinburgh University Press, 2000), pp. 124–30.

109 Mark R. Warren, *Dry Bones Rattling: Community Building to Revitalize American Democracy* (Princeton, NJ: Princeton University Press, 2001), p. 58.

110 For an account of this, see Bretherton, *Christianity and Contemporary Politics*, pp. 98–99.

111 I am grateful to Jonathan Lange and Leo Penta for this insight.

112 Contrary to the continuity I outline, Harry Boyte, Fisher, and Warren, along with most other academic commentators and key organizers within IAF, have a more disjunctive reading, seeing a distinct shift from 1972 onward when Ed Chambers took over the running of IAF. However, what evidence suggests is a process of consolidation, intensification, and a making explicit of elements already present with Alinsky rather than a distinctly new direction. For example, perhaps the most

significant shift is seen to be the move to see religious institutions as more than instruments for mobilizing resources and instead to organize around their values (for example, see Harry Boyte, *Commonwealth*, pp. 81–96; Fisher, *Let the People Decide,* pp. 192–93; and Warren, *Dry Bones Rattling*, p. 47). Yet, while Alinsky could be cavalier and rhetorically utilitarian about his relationship with churches and at times emphasize power and self-interest to the exclusion of all else, his correspondence with Jack Egan, Jacques Maritain, and other Catholic leaders reveals a deep sympathy between his political vision and developments in Catholic social teaching; a concern, for example, with how his work contributed to ecumenical relations; and above all else, deep personal friendship. A particularly striking example of this last point comes in a note from Jack Egan to Alinsky where he states: "Dear Saul, I miss you – Your face / Your wisdom / Your encouragement / Your irreverence / Your humor / Or just you – When can we have supper together? Faithfully, Jack" (Box 47, file 658, IAF Archive). Contrary to Boyte's view that Alinsky came to rescind his earlier commitments to democracy, adopting an overtly cynical and utilitarian view, there seems to be little evidence for this in his correspondence and other papers. Even if this were the case (and Boyte in personal correspondence insists that Alinsky and many of those influenced by him did take on an overly cynical view), it is not necessary to read *Reveille for Radicals* and *Rules for Radicals* as opposed to each other. Rather, they should be read together as complementary texts. Like the polarized statements of Biblical and Rabbinic judgment that Alinsky frequently mimicked, the books stand in fecund tension with each other (see, for example, his contrast between the prayer of St. Francis that calls on God to make one an instrument of peace counterpoised with Deuteronomy 32:41–42 that depicts God as a wrathful avenger [*Reveille for Radicals*, p. 18]). Boyte argues that those who came to Alinky's work in the 1970s developed an overly utilitarian and pragmatic approach through focusing on *Rules* and rarely, if ever, reading *Reveille.* This may well be right. Yet these texts should be read as complementary and thus the kind of intra-textual relationship that is consistent with Alinsky's own style is called forth. On the broader point, accounts of how the IAF developed after Alinsky's death are too dependent on Chambers' own somewhat self-referential version of events and fail to locate Alinsky within a historical account of his own intellectual points of reference.

113 von Hoffman, *Radical*, pp. 63–64.

114 *Ibid.*, pp. 43–45.

115 Gerald Taylor pointed out that a number of the most effective organizations from this period were initially mono-racial. These included East Brooklyn Congregations, Baltimoreans United in Leadership Development (BUILD) (which was African American), and Valley Interfaith (which was Latino/a) (interview May 21, 2013, Durham, NC).

116 Richard L. Wood, *Faith in Action: Religion, Race, and Democratic Organizing in America* (Chicago: University of Chicago Press, 2002), pp. 87–88.

117 Some of the fruit of this is captured in the document "Towards a Public Philosophy for the 1990's" that was authored by Leo Penta and Ed Chambers (Box 66, file 817, IAF Archive).

118 Interview with Ed Chambers (November 7, 2008, Chicago); Chambers, *Roots for Radicals*, p. 125. The introduction of Arendt owes much to Leo Penta who did his PhD thesis on the work of Hannah Arendt.

119 Bernard Crick, *In Defence of Politics* (London: Continuum, 2005 [1962]), pp. 3–4. We can align Crick's account with that of MacIntyre's conception of Aristotelean politics given in Alasdair MacIntyre, *Whose Justice? Which Rationality?* (London: Duckworth, 1988), pp. 33–34. However, MacIntyre pays far closer attention to the kinds of moral rationality needed to sustain politics as an architectonic master art that enables the integration of often conflicting and rivalrous arts and goods. I shall address the questions MacIntyre's work poses to the kind of account of politics developed in Chapter 5 of this book through a discussion of political judgment and practical reason.

120 Crick, *In Defence of Politics,* p. 7.

121 Boyte, *Civic Agency,* p. 15.

122 Quoted in *ibid.*, p. 18.

123 Wolin, *Politics and Vision,* p. 261.

124 Sheldon S. Wolin, "Contract and Birthright," in *The Presence of the Past: Essays on the State and the Constitution* (Baltimore, MD: John Hopkins University Press, 1989), p. 139.

125 An echo of this analysis is set out in the last section of Gecan's book, *Going Public*, in which he contrasts a market, a bureaucratic, and a relational culture (pp. 152–68). On a broader point, Craig Jackson Calhoun clarifies the sociological relationship between "archaic" traditions and the rejuvenation of a "radical" politic that challenges the status quo. Against Marx, Weber, and most other modern social theory, he contends there is no inherent incompatibility between tradition and rationality, and that political thinkers from left and right have failed to understand the "paradoxical conservatism" in revolution and the radicalism of tradition. He argues that traditional modes of corporatism provide the social foundations and means of organization for widespread popular mobilizations and that traditional values, particularly when these are threatened by rapid change and modern capitalist-dominated social formations, provide the rationality for legitimating radical political action that opposes elite centers of power (Craig Jackson Calhoun, "The Radicalism of Tradition: Community Strength or Venerable Disguise and Borrowed Language?" *American Journal of Sociology* 88.5 [1983]: 886–914). Calhoun's analysis helps explain the seemingly paradoxical yet consistent link between "conservative" religious congregations and the "radical" politics of community organizing.

126 Penta and Chambers, "Towards a Public Philosophy for the 1990's."

127 Hannah Arendt, "On Violence," in *Crises of the Republic* (Orlando, FL: Harcourt Brace & Co, 1972), p. 143. See also Hannah Arendt, *On Revolution* (London: Penguin, 1977), pp. 166–67. The contribution of Loomer will be discussed in Chapter 4.

128 Arendt's account, along with that of Bernard Loomer, directly informs both Ernesto Cortés and Leo Penta's conceptualization of power. See "Reweaving the Fabric: The Iron Rule and the IAF Strategy for Power and Politics," in *Interwoven Destinies: Cities and the Nation,* ed. Henry G. Cisneros (New York: W. W. Norton, 1993), pp. 294–319; Leo Penta, "Citizen Politics, Relational Organizing, and the Practice of Democracy," paper presented at the Community Empowerment and Economic Development Conference, University of Illinois, College of Law, April 23–25, 1993.

129 Hannah Arendt, *The Human Condition*, 2nd ed. (Chicago: University of Chicago Press, 1958), p. 198.

130 Fisher, *Let the People Decide*, p. 144.

131 Paul J. DiMaggio and Walter W. Powell, "The Iron Cage Revisited: Institutional Isomorphism and Collective Rationality in Organizational Fields," *American Sociological Review* 48.2 (1983): 147–60. For a discussion of the implications of institutional isomorphism for the churches, see Bretherton, *Christianity and Contemporary Politics*, pp. 37–45.

132 A key text is John P. Kretzmann and John McKnight, *Building Communities from the Inside Out: A Path Toward Finding and Mobilizing a Community's Assets* (Evanston, IL: The Asset-Based Community Development Institute, Northwestern University, 1993). For a helpful critique of their approach, see Mike Miller, "A Critique of John McKnight & John Kretzmann's 'Community Organizing in the Eighties: Toward a Post-Alinsky Agenda,'" *Comm-Org Papers* 15 (2009), available at: http://comm-org.wisc.edu/papers2009/miller.htm (last accessed August 21, 2010). For an account of the distinctions between community organizing and community development, see Stoecker, "Understanding the Development-Organizing Dialectic," *Journal of Urban Affairs* 25.4 (2003): 419–512; and idem, "Community Development and Community Organizing: Apples and Oranges? Chicken and Egg?" (2001), available at: http://comm-org.wisc.edu/drafts/orgdevppr2c.htm (last accessed June 6, 2012).

133 For an account of this relationship, see Warren, *Dry Bones Rattling*, pp. 175–81.

134 *Ibid.*, p. 179.

135 For a description of a community organization that faltered and fell apart as it tried to negotiate just such an arrangement, see Mike Miller's account of the Mission Coalition Organization in *A Community Organizer's Tale: People and Power in San Francisco* (Berkeley, CA: Heyday Books, 2009).

136 It has become almost axiomatic among practitioners and academics who write on this field that what distinguishes community organizing from both community development and other forms of community engagement is the emphasis on power. See, for example, the following introductory textbook to community organizing: Aaron Schutz and Marie Sandy, *Collective Action for Social Change: An Introduction to Community Organizing* (New York: Palgrave Macmillan, 2011).

137 Use of the term "'Populist" as a proper noun will be reserved for reference to the Populist movement of the nineteenth century; whereas, the term "'populism" will be used as a generic term.

138 For example, Myles Horton and the Highlander Folk School drew on populist themes and people from an earlier generation who had been involved in the Populist movement in its training of early CIO organizers. While Harry Boyte notes that in addition to African-American Christianity, Ghandi, and personalism, Martin Luther King, Jr. drew from Populist themes and, according to Boyte's recollection of a conversation with King, personally identified with the southern Populist tradition (Boyte, *Commonwealth*, p. 65 n. 5).

139 M. Elizabeth Sanders, *Roots of Reform: Farmers, Workers, and the American State, 1877–1917* (Chicago: University of Chicago Press, 1999), p. 135; Lawrence Goodwyn, *Democratic Promise: The Populist Moment in America* (New York: Oxford University Press, 1976), pp. 309–11. For a helpful conceptual analysis of this failure, see Ernesto Laclau, *On Populist Reason* (London: Verso, 2005), pp. 201–08. Laclau suggests that the Populists failed to generate the kind of symbolic and discursive forms of representation and social imaginary that allowed the

highly factional and heterogeneous movement to transcend its differences. The inability to connect with Catholic working classes is a key marker of this failure.

140 Much further work needs to be done on identifying and distinguishing the Protestant (and Evangelical) and Catholic strands of grassroots radicalism in nineteenth and twentieth century America, how they conflicted and converged over the years, and the different repertoires of contentions they deployed and developed.

141 For a treatment of Tocquevillian themes in Alinsky, see Andrew Sabl, "Community Organizing as Tocquevillean Politics: The Art, Practices, and Ethos of Association," *American Journal of Political Science* 46.1 (2002): 1–19.

142 On this, see John McCormick, "Machiavellian Democracy: Controlling Elites with Ferocious Populism," *The American Political Science Review* 95.2 (2001): 297–313.

143 Quoted in Kazin, *Populist Persuasion*, p. 142.

144 As Boyte notes: "To see emancipation as an intellectual shedding of the past produces a strong tendency toward condescension and a subjective distancing from large parts of the social fabric: religious institutions, ethnic groups, small business, geographically based identities, and so forth" (Boyte, *Commonwealth*, p. 40).

145 Boyte identifies what he calls the "commonwealth tradition" as having two key elements: an emphasis on rule by the people through a republican system of government and a view of property – both private goods and public resources – as having a social nature. In Boyte's view: "Together, ideas of popular government and the social quality of property combined in the term 'commonwealth' to suggest the concept of democratic government that sees as its aim tending to the general welfare, especially in opposition to selfish economic interests" (Boyte, *Commonwealth*, p. 17). Boyte does not explore the Calvinist roots of such a view. On this, see John Witte, *The Reformation of Rights: Law, Religion, and Human Rights in Early Modern Calvinism* (Cambridge: Cambridge University Press, 2007). Kazin does not explore the relationship between "pietistic revivalism" and Enlightenment rationalism and falls into the trap of seeing these as unrelated phenomenon. Although distinct, the origins of Evangelicalism and the Great Awakenings, which is what Kazin is referencing in his term "pietistic revivalism," are both part of and a response to intellectual and other developments during the eighteenth century (which he categorizes under the monolithic title "the Enlightenment," when it was in reality a much more diverse set of phenomena and intellectual developments with disparate outcomes in different contexts). For an account of the relationship between the birth of Evangelicalism and other intellectual streams in the United States, see Michael A. G. Haykin, Kenneth J. Stewart, and Timothy George, *The Advent of Evangelicalism: Exploring Historical Continuities* (Nashville, TN: B & H Academic, 2008); Mark A. Noll, *The Rise of Evangelicalism: The Age of Edwards, Whitefield and the Wesleys* (Nottingham: InterVarsity Press, 2004).

146 The shadow side of the opposition to elites is the tendency of populism to adopt conspiracy theories about how "hidden" elites operate.

147 Kazin, *Populist Persuasion*, pp. 11–17.

148 Kazin notes that Lewis's advocacy of antiracist measures was "a major advance in the history of white-dominated movements of producers. For the first time, racism was described as a malignant set of beliefs and not simply a nagging barrier to worker unity" (*ibid*., p. 147).

149 *Ibid*., p. 153.

150 Alinsky, *Reveille*, pp. 13–14.

151 During the Great Depression the Populists were portrayed by John D. Hicks as pragmatists seeking their fair share of America's wealth and opposing the corruption that led to high interest rates, unfair railroad practices, protective tariffs, and the manipulation of the nation's finances to suit the interests of the wealthy (John D. Hicks, *The Populist Revolt: A History of the Farmers' Alliance and the People's Party* [Minneapolis: University of Minnesota Press, 1931]). By contrast, Anna Rochester, herself a Marxist writing during World War II, envisaged the Populists as insufficiently radical proto-communists opposing monopoly capitalism – a view shared, incidentally, by Engels (Anna Rochester, *The Populist Movement in the United States: The Growth and Decline of the People's Party – A Social and Economic Interpretation* [New York: International Publishers, 1943]. Karl Marx and Frederick Engels, *Letters to Americans, 1848–1895: A Selection* [New York: International Publishers, 1953], pp. 239, 248–49, and 257). The contemporary historiographical debate begins with Richard Hofstadter's *Age of Reform*. Writing in the 1950s in reaction against McCarthyism, Hofstadter argued that the Populists were nostalgic, backward-looking petit bourgeois businessmen who were insecure about their declining status in an industrializing America. Additionally, he claimed that they were provincial, conspiracy minded, and tended to scapegoat others, a tendency that manifested itself in nativism and anti-Semitism (Richard Hofstadter, *The Age of Reform: From Bryan to F.D.R.* [New York: Alfred A. Knopf, 1955]). By contrast, Lawrence Goodwyn, writing in the wake of the 1960s, envisaged the Populists as precursors of the New Left who sought to structurally redesign U.S. capitalism and fulfill the ideal of America's democratic promise, but who were thwarted by a combination of modest reformers or "trimmers" (who for Goodwyn were equivalent to contemporary "liberals") and the combined hegemonic power of media, academy, banking, party political, and industrial interests (Goodwyn, *Democratic Promise*). More recently, Omar Ali casts the significant involvement of African Americans in and the complex and troubled biracial dimensions of Populism as a precursor to the civil rights movement (Omar Ali, *In The Lion's Mouth: Black Populism in the New South, 1886–1900* [Jackson: University of Mississippi Press, 2010]). Robert Fisher and Harry Boyte follow Goodwyn's account of Populism in their location of Alinsky and community organizing as inheritors of the Populist movement (Fisher, *Let the People Decide*, p. 273; Boyte, *Commonwealth*, pp. 27–33; Evans and Boyte, *Free Spaces*, pp. 168–81; Boyte, *Everyday Politics*, pp. 19–20). While not explicitly referencing Goodwyn, Manuel Castells also identifies Alinsky as continuing the Populist tradition (Manuel Castells, *The City and the Grassroots: A Cross-Cultural Theory of Urban Social Movements* [Berkeley: University of California Press, 1983], pp. 61–65).

152 Boyte, *Commonwealth*, pp. 45–44; Boyte, *Everyday Politics*, pp. 39–51. The account developed here differs from Boyte's in a number of ways: Boyte does not account sufficiently for the heterogeneity of the movement or its varied historiographic reception; he does not see the paradoxical link between conflict and the politics of a common life or what he calls a "commonwealth" politics; in his assessment, Alinsky lacked any larger political vision; he gives no account of the influence of Christian democratic thought on the development of community organizing; he overemphasizes the shift that took place in the IAF after Alinsky died in 1972; and

he tends to subsume community organizing to a set of prior programs, most notably what he comes to call "everyday politics" and "public work."

153 Goodwyn, *Democratic Promise*, p. xiii. The phrase "money power" was a frequent rhetorical term in labor and populist discourse from the 1890s onward. It is still used in IAF discourse to describe the concentrations of economic power within capitalism. The origins of the term lie in the rhetoric used by President Andrew Jackson and his allies in their "battle" with Nicholas Biddle and the Second Bank of the United States. As the historian Charles Postel notes: "On the lecture circuit Jefferson and Jackson figured as the historical godfathers of Populist reform, with Wall Street and the railroad corporations replacing King George and Nicholas Biddle's bank as the symbols of tyranny" (Charles Postel, *The Populist Vision* [New York: Oxford University Press, 2009], p. 142).

154 On the importance of theological discourse to populist rhetoric, see Joe Creech, *Righteous Indignation: Religion and the Populist Revolution* (Urbana: University of Illinois Press, 2006).

155 Sanders, *Roots of Reform*, p. 132.

156 As Theda Skocpol and colleagues note, "Classic American voluntary membership groups are widely presumed to have been spontaneous and particular creations, fashioned within relatively bounded local communities; neighbours and friends coalesced outside politics and apart from involvements with extralocal government" (Theda Skocpol, Marshall Ganz, and Ziad Munson, "A Nation of Organizers: The Institutional Origins of Civic Voluntarism in the United States," *American Political Science Review* 94.3 [2000]: 527–46, p. 527). They note the likes of Robert Putnam as the latest iteration of such a view and go on to develop a critique of it.

157 What is remarkable about Populism is that while it worked within the emerging consensus of the time in relation to gender and race, there flowered within it significant and extensive moments of biracial politics and it actively enabled and promoted women's involvement in public life. On this, see Postel, *Populist Vision* and Ali, *In the Lion's Mouth*.

158 This was adopted as the manifesto of the People's Party at its 1892 convention.

159 The aspirations of their platform are most easily expressed through what can be read as a parable of Populist policies and vision: *The Wonderful Wizard of Oz* by L. Frank Baum, published in 1900. Baum was, for a while, a silverite newspaper editor in South Dakota and wrote *The Wonderful Wizard of Oz* during the election of 1900 that pitted Williams Jennings Bryan against the Republican William McKinley in a rematch of the 1896 election. Interpretations of the book are many and varied but there is a strong case to be made for reading it as a political allegory, one that is filled with the kind of Protestant postmillennial optimism and cataclysmic imagery that was common to Populism (Rhys H. Williams and Susan M. Alexander, "Religious Rhetoric in American Populism: Civil Religion as Movement Ideology," *Journal for the Scientific Study of Religion* 33.1 [1994]: 1–15, p. 2). The reading given here is largely derived from Henry M. Littlefield, "The Wizard of Oz: Parable on Populism," *American Quarterly* 16.1 (1964): 47–58. "Oz" is, of course, short for "ounce," the measure for gold and silver. Dorothy comes from Kansas, a Populist stronghold, and represents the common person. She is transported by a cyclone – an image frequently used in the 1890s as a metaphor for the Populist movement's transformation of the political environment. Dorothy

forms a relationship with the Tin Woodsman, a trope for the industrial workers who are downtrodden, weak, and dependent on oil for their livelihood (both as a natural resource on which industry depended and as a motif of the large energy corporations such as Standard Oil), and a Scarecrow, a rural figure who lacks the ability to understand his situation. Their friendship is an allegory for the farmer-labor alliance that was the core of the Populist movement. Joining the company is the somewhat buffoon-like character of the Cowardly Lion, who stands for Williams Jennings Bryan (Baum himself was a political supporter of McKinley), whose roar is loud but who lacks any real power. The Good Witches represent the magical potential of the people of the North and the South. The cyclone kills the Wicked Witch of the East (the Eastern bankers) and frees The Munchkins (the plain people) from their debt slavery. With the witch's silver slippers (the silver standard), Dorothy sets out on the Yellow Brick Road (the gold standard) to the Emerald City (Washington), where they meet the Wizard (President McKinley), who appears powerful, but whose power is ultimately revealed to be an illusion: he is a little man dependent on mechanical procedures. Baum thereby parodies the Populist tendency to adopt conspiracy theories about hidden elites controlling the United States. When the real Wizard is exposed, the now enlightened Scarecrow denounces him. Dorothy goes on to drown the Wicked Witch of the West (the Darwinian forces of nature); the water being an allegory for the irrigation that would enable the Midwest farmers to escape the problems of drought. The Wizard flies away in a hot-air balloon, the Scarecrow is left to govern the Emerald City, the Tin Woodsman rules the West, and the Cowardly Lion returns to the forest where he becomes King of the Beasts after vanquishing a giant spider that was devouring the animals in the forest.

160 For an account of the devastating impact of the crop-lien and sharecropping system on both black and white farmers, how it created a system of debt peonage and the developments of efforts to break this system that culminated in the subtreasury plan, see Goodwyn, *Democratic Promise*, pp. 26–33; 110–73; and Ali, *In the Lion's Mouth*, pp. 15–77.

161 Williams and Alexander, "Religious Rhetoric in American Populism," p. 10.

162 Quoted in *ibid.*, p. 10. Given the rapid demise of the Populists after the mid-1890s, it is easy to miss the substantive nature of the threat the movement posed to global capitalism. Pegging a national currency to the gold standard was the centerpiece of an international economic consensus committed to a laissez-faire economic vision. As Jeffrey Frieden notes: "All those connected to the international financial and investing system saw the gold standard as central to its smooth functioning, and they shared a commitment to sustain it" (Jeffrey A. Frieden, *Global Capitalism: Its Fall and Rise in the Twentieth Century* [New York: W. W. Norton & Co, 2006], p. 48). Energizing and driving this commitment was the City of London, which accounted for nearly half of all international investment at the turn of the nineteenth century. And it was the City of London, spearheaded by Nathan Rothschild, then the most influential banker in the world, who pushed relentlessly from the mid-1870s for the United States to join the gold standard. When the United States finally put the dollar onto gold in 1879, it was Rothschild and his associate in the United States, August Belmont, who provided more than half the money the U.S. government needed to accumulate the necessary reserves (*ibid.*, p. 35). Coming off gold became a central focus of the Populist movement. In their view the gold

standard was a British-led scheme to "fatten usurers" at the expense of farmers and miners. A switch to silver at a depreciated exchange rate would raise farm prices and lower interest rates. Although it was controversial in the movement, the Populists voted to form an alliance with the Democrats and support the presidential campaign of Williams Jennings Bryan, who in turn adopted many parts of the Omaha platform for what became known as the Chicago platform adopted at the Democratic Party convention in Chicago. The closely fought 1896 election between the Democrat-Populist Bryan and the Republican McKinley was billed as the "battle of the standards" and can be seen as a serious democratic challenge to the dominance of finance capitalism. As Frieden summarizes it: "The financial leaders of Europe and the world watched in shock as the assault on the gold standard challenged the very structure of the international economic order. The United States was the world's largest economy, biggest borrower, and most important international destination for capital and people alike. Now it posed the greatest threat to the global economic order. ... If the Democrats won and implemented their platform, the gold standard everywhere would be in peril" (*ibid.*, p. 15). The northeastern business and financial elites contributed massive amounts of money to the McKinley campaign and the Democrat-Populist alliance was narrowly defeated. Despite the narrow defeat, *The Times* thought the McKinley victory would "suffice to bury Bryanism, Silverism, Socialism, and all the revolutionary proposals of the Chicago platform beyond hope of resurrection in this generation" (quoted in *ibid.*, p. 15). It did not, yet the electoral defeat, combined with a number of factors – such as changes in the wider global economy, which led to a lowering of gold prices, and a rise in the cost of wheat – helped drain Populism of much of its energy.

163 Conceptualizing populism as a countermovement accords with broader accounts of the conditions for the emergence of Populist movements (Francisco Panizza, *Populism and the Mirror of Democracy* [London: Verso, 2005], pp. 1–31).

164 Evidence for continuing to read community organizing as a countermovement that seeks to re-embed market relations in place-based social relations is outlined in Chapters 2 and 3 of this book.

165 Karl Polanyi, *The Great Transformation: The Political and Economic Origins of our Time* (Boston, MA: Beacon Press, 2001), pp. 247–49. Polanyi conflates fascism and populism. On the account developed here they need to be distinguished as distinct kinds of countermovement. As an aside, Sinclair Lewis's 1935 novel *It Can't Happen Here*, whose lead character Buzz Windrip is thought to be inspired by the figure of Huey Long, similarly conflates populism and fascism. By contrast, Robert Penn Warren's 1946 novel *All the King's Men*, whose central political figure, Willie Stark, is also thought to be based on Huey Long (although Warren himself played down the link), captures well the democratic and authoritarian mix of Long's manifestation of American populism.

166 An early and enduring influence on Polanyi himself was the Russian Populist Movement. As Michael Burawoy notes: "The influence of the Populists was surely one factor that led Polanyi to place a critique of the market at the center of his theorizing" (Michael Burawoy, "For a Sociological Marxism: The Complementary Convergence of Antonio Gramsci and Karl Polanyi," *Politics & Society* 31.2 [2003]: 193–261, p. 203). Moreover, Polanyi's last book, *The Plough and the Pen*, edited with his wife Ilona Duczynska, was devoted to the Hungarian

Populists. In Polanyi's view, these Populists, together with the Reform Communists, were the key movements behind the Hungarian Revolution of 1956.

167 Sabl, "Community Organizing as Tocquevillean Politics," pp. 2–5.

168 Defining populism is a notoriously difficult conceptual task. Margaret Canovan criticizes essentializing approaches to defining populism as being either too vague or too specific (Margaret Canovan, "Two Strategies for the Study of Populism," *Political Studies* 30.4 [1982]: 544–52). See also Laclau's discussion of the difficulties of defining populism (Laclau, *On Populist Reason*, pp. 3–20). Those that are too vague attempt to create one-size-fits-all accounts that fail to deal with the historical diversity and specificity of forms of populism. Laclau's sophisticated and insightful account of populism can be seen as an example of this tendency. (For Laclau's definition of populism and the term "political logic," see *ibid.*, p. 117–24). Conversely, those that are too specific seek to universalize theories derived from highly contextual accounts of one kind of populism. Michael Kazin's account of American populism referred to already is a good example of one that avoids both these pitfalls as it makes no claims beyond its specific context. In place of essentializing approaches, Canovan offers a phenomenological approach that makes only descriptive rather than explanatory claims. (Canovan develops seven categories of populism; see Margaret Canovan, *Populism* [New York: Harcourt Brace Jovanovich, 1981]. For a critique of her approach, see Laclau, *On Populist Reason*, pp. 5–8). However, drawing from Michael Oakeshott, Canovan herself subsequently developed her own "essential" theory of populism.

169 She states: "Populism understood in this structural sense can have different contents depending on the establishment it is mobilizing against. Where economic policy is concerned, for example, populists in one country with a hegemonic commitment to high taxation to fund a generous welfare state may embrace an agenda of economic liberalism, while other populists elsewhere are reacting against a free market hegemony by demanding protectionism and more state provision. This does not in itself demonstrate (as is sometimes claimed) that populists are either unprincipled or confused: merely that what makes them populist is their reaction to the structure of power. The values that are populist also vary according to context, depending upon the nature of the elite and the dominant political discourse" (Margaret Canovan, "Trust the People! Populism and the Two Faces of Democracy," *Political Studies* 47.1 [1999]: 2–16, p. 4). Kazin's account of Father Coughlin's shift from being an avid supporter of the New Deal and industrial trade unions to a fascist sympathizer by the late 1930s is an example of the phenomenon Canovan describes (Kazin, *Populist Persuasion*, pp. 109–33).

170 Canovan, "Trust the People!" p. 11.

171 What is given in this book is a *genetic* rather than a *generic* explanation. A genetic explanation does not first seek formal theory or abstract laws, which are then used to evaluate the historically specific context or phenomena, but instead seeks the historically specific causes and tries to explain particular outcomes. Moreover, whereas a generic strategy looks for similarities among disparate cases in order to develop a coherent, universal theory (Laclau and Canovan's approach), a genetic strategy focuses on differences between similar cases in order to regenerate and enrich existing theoretical frameworks. In this case, the specificity of American populism helps enrich and extend Polanyi's genetic explanation of the rise of the market system and the development of countermovements. It may be objected that

use of Polanyi here offends a genetic methodology. But Polanyi is using a parallel approach through attention to historical and anthropological sources in order to counter Hayek's account of economics that subsumes everything to a prior principle.

172 This would fit with one way of reading Arendt's own populist conception of "the people." On this, see Canovan, "The People, the Masses and the Mobilization of Power," pp. 403–22.

173 Horwitt, *Let Them Call Me Rebel*, pp. 530–31.

174 Alinsky, *Reveille*, p. 6. Elsewhere Alinsky uses the term "orderly revolution" to describe his approach (*ibid.*, p. 198).

175 Sheldon S. Wolin, "Archaism, Modernity, and *Democracy in America*," and "Tending and Intending a Constitution: Bicentennial Misgivings," in *Presence of the Past,* pp. 66–81 and 82–99. Wolin's work is a key reference point for many involved in community organizing. Ed Chambers goes so far as to describe Wolin as "America's finest political teacher" (Chambers, *Roots for Radicals*, p. 125).

176 For a critique of this tendency in modern, post-Enlightenment thought, see Alasdair MacIntyre, *After Virtue: A Study in Moral Theory* (London: Duckworth, 1994) and for a review of MacIntyre's broader position, see Luke Bretherton, *Hospitality as Holiness: Christian Witness Amid Moral Diversity* (Aldershot: Ashgate, 2006), pp. 9–33.

177 Wolin, *Politics and Vision*, pp. 604–05.

178 This suggests Wolin is best understood as attempting to develop a systematic populist democratic theory rather than a civic republican or radically democratic one.

179 Canovan, "The People, the Masses and the Mobilization of Power," pp. 403–22.

180 Antipolitical populism is a particular characteristic of the contemporary Tea Party movement. It would be interesting to compare the Tea Party with a resurgent antipolitical populism in Europe as evidenced in the popularity of the Front National in France, the Swiss People's Party, and the Freedom Party in the Netherlands.

181 A good example of this is the document produced by the IAF's black caucus in 1981 entitled *The Tent of the Presence*. The document drew on Numbers 11:10–18 to frame a call for a renewed engagement in public life and the development of new forms of collaborative leadership within broad-based organizations as distinct from 1960s style, top-down, movement leaders. On this, see Boyte, *Commonwealth*, pp. 108–09.

182 Alinsky, *Rules*, p. 59; see also Alinsky, *Reveille*, p. 228. In the Populist movement the decision to back the Democratic Party and the candidacy of Williams Jennings Bryan can be seen as an example of just such a compromise. In IAF training, teaching around this negotiation of a common life and the necessity of compromise is generated through an engagement with the Athenian-Melian dialogues in Thucydides's *History of the Peloponnesian War* 2.34–46. Those who refuse to compromise or who insist on putting principles before politics, even if it means complete failure or a breakdown of relationships with those who hold power, are often characterized as "Melians" within Citizens UK and IAF discussions.

183 Quoted in Boyte, *Commonwealth*, p. 114.

184 For a recent restatement of Kazin's declension narrative, see E. J. Dionne, *Our Divided Political Heart: The Battle for the American Idea in an Age of Discontent* (New York: Bloomsbury, 2012), pp. 189–212.

185 Whether the categories of political and antipolitical populism might be applied beyond the United States is another matter and beyond the scope of this present work.

186 Baroni was a key figure in the development of organizing and the application of its insights more broadly into legislative initiatives. Having been involved in the freedom movement, serving as Catholic coordinator for the 1963 March on Washington and leading the Catholic delegation to the 1965 Selma-to-Montgomery March, he went on to help found the Catholic Campaign for Human Development (CHD) in 1969. This initiative has been a key funding source for many community organizing initiatives. On the influence of Alinsky on Baroni and the founding of the CHD, see Lawrence Engel, "The Influence of Saul Alinsky on the Campaign for Human Development," *Theological Studies* 59 (1998): 636–61. Baroni was also a key figure in the development of the Community Reinvestment Act of 1977 when serving as Housing and Urban Development Assistant Secretary for Neighborhood Development, Consumer Affairs, and Regulatory Functions under President Carter. I am grateful to Harry Boyte to pointing out the importance of Baroni's work.

187 See, for example, Alinsky's critique of antipoverty programs that address economic poverty without addressing the poverty of power: Saul Alinsky, "Behind the Mask," in *American Child: Which Way Community Action Programs?* 47.4 (1965): 7–9. Wolin is equally critical of welfarism, noting how it has become an enemy of democratic participation: Wolin, "Archaism, Modernity and *Democracy in America,*" in *Presence in the Past,* p. 79.

188 Alinsky, *Reveille*, p. 175.

189 This is not to say there are not equivalent populist themes in British political discourse but, like Christian Democracy, these themes are not a central political tradition but a nascent one that is occasionally vivified. Margaret Canovan sees G. K. Chesterton as a populist and in the contemporary British context one could plausibly interpret Phillip Blond's "Red Tory" and Maurice Glasman's "Blue Labour" theses as attempts to construct different versions of a distinctly British political populism (Margaret Canovan, *G. K. Chesterton: Radical Populist* [New York: Harcourt Brace Jovanovich, 1977]; Phillip Blond and Maurice Glasman, "The Prospect Debate: Red Tory vs Blue Labour," *Prospect* [May, 2010]: 26–28).

190 Perhaps the equivalent discursive tradition to populism to be drawn on within the British context is that represented by the Labour movement. But of course, this poses the problem of political partisanship that is highly problematic for an avowedly nonpartisan organization.

2 Faith and Citizenship in a World City

1 London Citizens made this clear in public statements to the media. See in particular Jonathan Freedland, "Heard the one about a rabbi, an imam and a priest, who walk into a bank?" *The Guardian,* July 21, 2009, available at: http://www.guardian.co.uk/commentisfree/belief/2009/jul/22/debt-interest-religion-usury (last accessed November 15, 2010). The first formal representative from a synagogue did not attend a London Citizens meeting until January 7, 2010 as part of the preparations for the May 3 General Election Assembly. The Masorti synagogues formerly joined London Citizens in 2011.

2 At the Barbican assembly, Rabbi Asmoucha was publically thanked and applauded for his stand. He was also presented with a check from U.S. congregations in membership of the IAF in an act of international solidarity.

3 John McManus, "Rabbi Quits Job over City Protest," *BBC News*, October 17, 2009, available at: http://news.bbc.co.uk/1/hi/8311904.stm (last accessed November 13, 2010). *The Jewish Chronicle* confirmed this report, stating: "The row began after Rabbi Asmoucha allowed the demonstration to leave from the synagogue apparently without 'authority from or prior notification' from the community's spiritual head Rabbi Abraham Levy or the Community Security Trust. Some reports say that the congregation's executive, the mahamad, believed this to be a high security risk. Other sources said that there was concern because of the City financial interests of the leaders of the congregation" (Jessica Elgot, "Bevis Marks Rabbi Resigns," *The Jewish Chronicle Online,* October 19, 2009, available at: http://www.thejc.com/news/uk-news/21091/bevis-marks-rabbi-resigns (last accessed December 13, 2012).

4 I was one of the chairs. I was there as a representative "leader" from a local church in membership and helped organize the event.

5 Despite repeated attempts, no Anglican Bishop attended the event or agreed to be a participant.

6 More than 1,000 one-to-one meetings and more than 100 house-group meetings were held. The proposals put forward that evening were derived from this "listening campaign." This process culminated in September 2009 when about 100 different leaders from member institutions came together and debated and formulated the five proposals. The proposals were then taken to three assemblies involving more than 700 people from across London who voted to ratify them.

7 Quoted from Simon Clark, "Scrooge's Fate Is Lesson for London Bankers, Mayor Johnson Says," *Bloomberg.com,* November 26, 2010, available at: www.bloomberg.com/apps/news?pid=newsarchive&sid=a1qMzYeWoKwc (last accessed November 26, 2010).

8 Recording of the event, November 25, 2009.

9 The delicate matter of Jewish involvement in the public reading of Scripture with other religions and of a senior Jewish figure sharing the stage with a Muslim leader who refuses to attend Holocaust Memorial Day had almost caused Rabbi Wittenburg to pull out of participating in the event that morning, but he was persuaded of the importance of representing a clear Jewish presence at the event. The sensitivity over Wittenburg's need to stay faithful to the Masorti Jewish practices of Scriptural reading was negotiated by having him give a short introduction to the Nehemiah 5 text in which its context was outlined and he made clear that the Hebrew Scriptures were speaking of a conflict between Jews.

10 From the City of London website available at: www.cityoflondon.gov.uk/Corporation/LGNL_Services/Council_and_democracy/Council_departments/whatis.htm (last accessed September 28, 2010).

11 *Ibid.*

12 *Ibid.*

13 The meeting took place at Mansion House on May 28, 2009. It is important to distinguish the Lord Mayor of the City of London from the Mayor of the Greater London Authority, a role that was reinstated in 2000 after it had been abolished in 1986 by the then Conservative government led by Margaret Thatcher. The office

of the Lord Mayor is located in Mansion House within the historic and financial center of London whereas the Mayor of the Greater London Authority is located on the Southbank, the historic periphery of London: the spatial symbolism of this division is lost on most.

14 Available at: http://www.cityoflondon.gov.uk/Corporation/LGNL_Services/Council_and_democracy/Councillors_democracy_and_elections/The_Lord_Mayor/What_the_Lord_Mayor_does/international.htm (last accessed September 28, 2010).

15 Doreen Massey, *World City* (Cambridge: Polity Press, 2010 [2007]), p. x. An example of its significance is given by David Harvey who states: "It is worthwhile recalling that one of the conditions that broke up the whole Keynesian post-war Bretton Woods system was the formation of a Eurodollar market as US dollars escaped the discipline of its own monetary authorities." The banking sector of London was central in this development and benefited massively from it (David Harvey, *A Brief History of Neoliberalism* [Oxford: Oxford University Press, 2005], p. 141).

16 Peter Spufford traces how London's continuing significance as a place for financial transactions follows a broader pattern of European development from the thirteenth century onward whereby financial centers develop around centers of trade and industry, but when these shift elsewhere or decline, the financial sector continues to function as a major nexus of activity. London's continuing significance echoes the experience of Venice, Bruges, Antwerp, and Amersterdam (Peter Spufford, "From Antwerp and Amsterdam to London: The Decline of Financial Centres in Europe," *The Economist* 154.2 [2006]: 143–75).

17 Nicholas Shaxson, *Treasure Islands: Tax Havens and the Men Who Stole the World* (London: The Bodley Head, 2011), p. 247. Shaxson's important book builds on the work of my research partner Maurice Glasman and gives a good account of the origins and role of the City of London in economic globalization.

18 The term "state of exception" is adapted from a term first used by Carl Schmitt and then developed by Giorgio Agamben in *State of Exception* (Chicago: University of Chicago Press, 2005). My use of the term "state of exception" in relation to tax havens/secrecy jurisdictions deliberately problematizes Schmitt and Agamben's use. For a parallel but somewhat different use of the term, see Aihwa Ong, *Neoliberalism as Exception: Mutations in Citizenship and Sovereignty* (Durham, NC: Duke University Press, 2006), pp. 1–27.

19 The monarch cannot enter the City of London without permission and must wait to be met by the Lord Mayor of London before he or she can enter. The actual gates and bars are demolished, but the City retains a system of checkpoints and access is strictly controlled. In 1993 it reduced the number of entry points into the Square Mile to eight and the number of exit points to twelve (these were slightly increased in 1997). At times of security threats, these checkpoints can be put into effect and any vehicle can be stopped and searched by the City's own, independent police force: The City of London Police. The website states that "the Force introduced an Automatic Number Plate Recognition system at the zone's perimeter in 1997. The first of its kind in the world, the system automatically checks vehicle number plates against police records and alerts operators if a match is made" (available at: http://www.cityoflondon.police.uk/CityPolice/About/services/History/ [last accessed February 14, 2011]).

20 Neoliberalism is a term of abstraction, but there are enough family resemblances to its ideological iterations to posit such a thing as "neoliberalism." Neoliberalism can be characterized in the following way: it is based on a nominalist anthropology; a view of the economy as the sphere of free relations; sees markets as natural, spontaneous, self-regulating, efficient, and neutral mechanisms that best enable freedom of choice and equal distribution of resources; conceptualizes the state as a guarantor of property rights but a poor mechanism for social justice, welfare provision, or the redistribution of wealth, all of which is best achieved through market-based processes and entrepreneurial, philanthropic interventions. Neoliberalism looks back, reacting against the formation of welfare states, nationalized industries, and the dominance of Keynesian economic policies and so is an ideology that deploys a rhetorical repertoire of being a "conservative" corrective to a pendulum that swung too far toward the state. This corrective takes the form of the re-marketization of nationalized industries, utilities, and social services (notably, health, education, and welfare provision). But neoliberalism is Janus faced. It also looks forward, wearing the mantle of an emancipatory and progressive project that liberates individuals from both state policies and historical customary practices that are rhetorically constructed as overbearing, inefficient, and outdated. However, at its heart, neoliberalism is a utopian political project that claims to know best how to order our common life through refusing the possibility that there can be goods in common that determine and shape what should be done: there are only individuals and their self-interested choices and the aggregation of these determine what is good or bad, desirable and undesirable. This utopian core belief is constantly obscured and mystified by the positioning of neoliberalism as *Realpolitik*. Rather than claiming the mantle for itself as a revolutionary vision of the world as it should be, advocates of neoliberalism position it as simply dealing with the world as it is so that any attempt to contest its plausibility is positioned as idealistic whereas in actuality, neoliberalism is itself a highly idealistic program of social engineering. The plausibility of neoliberalism as a simultaneously "conservative" and progressive project is sustained through posing a false dichotomy: the choice is between the state or the market ordering our common life. It is a dichotomy that inherently produces the need for a "third way" that attempts to resolve the dichotomy, but this supposed "third way" is, in fact, a further iteration or combination of either neoliberalism or social democracy. What neoliberalism cannot countenance is the possibility of a common life: such a possibility is simply implausible within a neoliberal conceptuality because it entails countenancing something other than the individual and the state as social, economic, and political realities and something more than choice as a source of value. As a political project that constantly seeks to monopolize state processes to achieve its aims, neoliberalism gives rise to particular constellations or technologies of governing such as privatization, outsourcing government provision, "individual responsibilization," economic zoning, and the differentiated legal regimes affecting different zones in terms of tax and labor laws.

21 A version of the following history of the City of London was used as a briefing paper for leaders of London Citizens as part of the "Governance of London" campaign in 2009, the details of which are outlined in Chapter 4. This paper, entitled "Whatever Happened to London? A Tale of Two Cities" was based on unpublished work by my colleague Maurice Glasman. I have supplemented the original in places drawing from Reginald R. Sharpe, *London and the Kingdom: A History*

Derived Mainly from the Archives at Guildhall In the Custody of the Corporation of the City of London, III Volumes (London: Longmans, Green & Co, 1894–95). Glasman's paper and the work on which it is based was subsequently picked up by Nicholas Shaxson whose work is also referenced here. Both Glasman's and Shaxson's work on the City of London was itself a catalyst for some members of the Occupy London Stock Exchange group to call for the democratization of the City of London Corporation in November 2011. On this, see Shiv Malek, "Occupy London Protest Issues Demands to Democratise City of London," *The Guardian*, October 28, 2011. The article makes clear the connection to the work of Glasman and Shaxson. After considerable debate, and not without controversy within the broader Occupy group, a statement was released by the City of London Policy Group of Occupy London on November 8 calling for the democratization of the Corporation of the City (available at: http://occupylsx.org/?p=839 [last accessed November 10, 2011]). More specifically, the statement called for the corporation to: "Publish full, year-by-year breakdowns of the City Cash account, future and historic. Make the entirety of its activities subject to the Freedom of Information Act. Detail all advocacy undertaken on behalf of the banking and finance industries, since the 2008 financial crash." A fuller, but it seems erroneous, list of demands was reported in *The Guardian* that same day, available at: http://www.guardian.co.uk/uk/2011/nov/08/occupy-london-protesters-issue-demands?CMP=twt_gu (last accessed November 21, 2011).

22 Sharpe, *London and the Kingdom*, vol. 1, pp. 28–31.

23 The term "the ancient constitution" came to prominence in early modern political debates that preceded and flowed out of the English civil war. Technically the term "the ancient constitution" refers to any law, liberty, or customary practice that preceded Richard I's coronation in 1189 – the year that divided time before memory or time immemorial from time of memory. To be considered as valid, legal rights and customs that claimed to possess the status of time immemorial needed to have been exercised regularly before and after 1189 and importantly, proof needed to be given that they were not interrupted by the Norman Conquest. Debates about the ancient constitution were a key way of justifying the validity of parliamentary sovereignty and its claim to limit royal prerogative. The seminal work on the ancient constitution is J. G. A. Pocock, *The Ancient Constitution and the Feudal Law: A Study of English Historical Thought in the Seventeenth Century* (Cambridge: Cambridge University Press, 1987 [1957]). See also Corinne Weston, "England: Ancient Constitution and Common Law," in *The Cambridge History of Political Thought: 1450–1700*, ed. J. H. Burns (Cambridge: Cambridge University Press, 1991), pp. 374–411. It should be noted that neither Pocock nor Weston paid much attention to the status of the City of London in debates about the ancient constitution.

24 Sharpe, *London and the Kingdom*, vol. 1, pp. 61–66.

25 On this, see Antony Black, *Guild and State: European Political Thought from the Twelfth Century to the Present* (London: Transaction Publishers, 2003).

26 Glasman, "Whatever Happened to London?"

27 Sharpe, *London and the Kingdom*, vol. 1, pp. 99–112.

28 Clement Atlee, *The Labour Party in Perspective* (London: Gollanz, 1937), pp. 80–81.

29 The role of City-based banks and financial institutions in establishing tax avoidance schemes and regulation continues.

30 Shaxson, *Treasure Islands*, p. 248.
31 Quoted from *ibid*., p. 253.
32 Ken Livingstone, *Time Out*, July 13–20, 2005, p. 3. Quoted from Massey, *World City*, p. 4. It should be noted that London Citizens was directly involved in the process of bidding for the Olympics and subsequently secured a commitment for all workers employed at the games to be paid a living wage.
33 The term "world city" builds on the work of John Friedman's thesis that postulated that certain cities took on the status of being "world cities" by dint of: (1) the extent of their integration with the world economy; (2) their acting as "basing point" for global capital that results in them functioning as points of control in the organization of production and markets; (3) their being points of concentration for labor migration and resulting forms of spatial and economic polarization; and finally (4) their generating social costs that exceed the fiscal capacity of the nation-state in which they are located. John Friedman, "The World-City Hypothesis," in *World Cities in a World-System*, eds. Paul L. Knox and Peter J. Taylor (Cambridge: Cambridge University Press, 1995), pp. 317–31. Saskia Sassen has extended this work by developing the notion of "global cities" of which London is a prime example. According to Sassen, these global cities function in four new ways: "First, as highly concentrated command points in the organization of the world economy; second, as key locations for finance and for specialized service firms, which have replaced manufacturing as the leading economic sector; third, as sites of production, including the production of innovations, in these leading industries; and fourth, as markets for the products and innovations produced. … Cities concentrate control over vast resources, while finance and specialized service industries have restructured the urban social and economic order. Thus a new type of city has appeared. It is the global city. Leading examples are now New York, London, and Tokyo" (Saskia Sassen, *The Global City: New York, London, Tokyo* [Princeton, NJ: Princeton University Press, 1991], pp. 3–4).
34 The term "world" (*kosmos*) draws from the use of the term in the New Testament to denote either the unified order of created things, understood as a neutral description (John 17:5, 24; Romans 1:20; 1 Corinthians 4:9), or the worldly system that is hostile to God's good order (John 15:18–19; 17:14–16; 1 Corinthians 1:20; 5:10). In New Testament Greek a number of variations on these two basic connotations can be discerned. For example, Paul Ellingworth identifies six variations: (1) the universe, (2) the earth, (3) human beings and angels, (4) humanity as a whole, (5) humanity as organized in opposition to God, and (6) particular groups of human beings (Paul Ellingworth, "Translating Kosmos 'World' in Paul," *The Bible Translator* 53.4 [2002]: 414–21). See also David J. Clark, "The Word Kosmos 'World' in John 17," *The Bible Translator* 50.4 (1999): 401–06.
35 Hugh Pyper, "The Bible in the Metropolis," Ethel M. Wood Annual Lecture, King's College London, March 3, 2010.
36 Tikki Pang, Mary Ann Lansang, and Andy Haines, "Brain Drain and Health Professionals: A Global Problem Needs Global Solutions," *British Medical Journal* 324 (2002): 499–500. A report from 2001 estimated that in London 23 percent of its doctors and 47 percent of its nurses are born overseas (Stephen Glover et al., *Migration: An Economic and Social Analysis* [London: Home Office, 2001], p. 38). While a two-way relationship, it is also asymmetric and exploitative with London

gaining far more from the "client" states it draws from in order to staff its schools, hospitals, and other public sector services.

37 For an account of migrant labor in London, see Wills, *Global Cities at Work*.

38 Interview, September 8, 2009, London.

39 As Polanyi summarizes it: "Instead of economy being embedded in social relations, social relations are embedded in the economic system" (Polanyi, *Great Transformation*, p. 60). Polanyi argues that prior to the nineteenth century no market existed that was not embedded within or subservient to social and political relations. Arguably, Polanyi is correct in his normative account of the embedded nature of markets but wrong in his assertion that no disembedded markets existed prior to the early modern period. For an account of how Polanyi came to nuance his own position and distinguish between capitalistic markets (which existed prior to the modern period) and capitalism per se, see Gareth Dale, *Karl Polanyi: The Limits of the Market* (Cambridge: Polity Press, 2010), pp. 137–87.

40 A textbook example of such disdain is set out at the beginning of Gecan, *Going Public*. Accusations of being aligned with Marxism and socialism have been leveled at community organizing since its origin. An example of this accusation from the British context is given by Melanie Phillips who states: "For, incredible as it may seem, Mr Cameron himself said last spring that his 'Big Society' would be built on the model of America's 'community organisers' – and in a background briefing to that speech, the Conservative party actually paid homage to Saul Alinsky himself. Of course, the Tories' enthusiasm for Alinsky is most likely based on ignorance rather than a desire to subvert society. But the astounding fact remains that the Cameroons have endorsed a Marxist radical whose agenda was the covert destruction of the West" (Melanie Phillips, "Watch Out, Dave. Red Ed's Making a Cynical Grab for Your Big Society," *The Daily Mail*, January 17, 2011).

41 Interview, August 8, 2008, London.

42 Jeffrey Stout's analysis done in parallel to my own reaches a similar conclusion and identifies resistance to commodification as a central concern of BBCO. Stout, *Blessed Are the Organized*, pp. 218–26. Stout helpfully links this resistance to a concern to preserve a sense of the sacred.

43 Interview, August 8, 2008, London.

44 Likewise, the Nehemiah Homes projects in the United States and the proposals for community land trusts in the United Kingdom are about de-commodifying land so as to provide affordable, good-quality homes for low-income families.

45 For an account of Johnny Ray Youngland's ministry, see Samuel Freedman, *Upon This Rock: The Miracles of a Black Church* (New York: HarperCollins, 1994). For an account of the political battles and development of the Nehemiah Homes initiative, see Gecan, *Going Public*.

46 This phenomenon can be described as an example of "glocalization." The neologism "glocal" is a disruptive term meant to deconstruct false dichotomies that oppose the local and global and point to how each refracts and produces the other: a dynamic that, as will be seen, is a generic feature of London life. Roland Robertson, a key theorist of glocalization, notes globalization not only strengthens an emphasis on the local, but also gives the local global value. That is to say, kudos at a global level is given to having a local focus and identity such that the valuation of "local" should be regarded as itself a feature of globalization (Roland Robertson, *Globalization: Social Theory and Global Culture* [London:

Sage, 1992], p. 130). See also Roland Robertson, "Glocalization: Time-space and Heterogeneity-Homogeneity," in *Global Modernities*, eds. Mike Featherstone, Scott Lash, and Roland Robertson (London: Sage, 1995), pp. 25–44.

47 In terms of structure, the IAF network can be contrasted on the one hand with the segmented, polycentric network of the alter-globalization, "movement of movements"; and on the other, with centrally coordinated and administered forms of transnational organization (for example, the Salvation Army). The alter-globalization movement is often referred to as the "anti-globalization" movement. For example, Manuel Castells identifies the anti-globalization movement as "a global network of opposition to the value and interests embedded in the globalization process" (Manuel Castells, *The Power of Identity: The Information Age: Economy, Society and Culture*, vol. II, 2nd ed. [Oxford: Blackwells, 2004], p. 160). However, this is a misnomer. From its origins those within it identified it as, in the words of the 1997 Zapatista *encuentros*, "For Humanity and Against Neoliberalism." The rationale for this self-identification is that they are not against globalization per se, just one dominant form of globalization characterized as neoliberal. On this, see David Graeber, *Direct Action: An Ethnography* (Oakland, CA: AK Press, 2009); and Donatella Della Porta, *Globalization from Below: Transnational Activists and Protest Networks* (Minneapolis: University of Minnesota Press, 2006). For the genealogy of the term "alter-globalization," see Geoffrey Pleyers, *Alter-Globalization: Becoming Actors in the Global Age* (Cambridge: Polity Press, 2010), pp. 6–7.

48 Each affiliate pays an annual membership fee to the IAF in the United States. This pays for the mentoring and training of organizers and leaders by senior organizers from the United States. Another contrast to alter-globalization movements is the emphasis given to organization and hierarchy within the IAF. Each node in the IAF network can be described as at once *autocephalous* and *affiliated*. "Autocephalous" is primarily an ecclesial term that denotes a distinct and sovereign episcopal jurisdiction that is at the same time constitutive of the catholic whole whereas "affiliated" denotes a familial and paternal relation that at the same time marks the distinctness and independence of each participant in the relation. The paternity of the IAF marks an order of initiation and cause, although at times it also implied a hierarchy of value. As outlined in Chapter 1, loyalty and deference to those with more experience is a key value. Use of the term "affiliate" can be contrasted with parallel but subtly different terms such as "affinity" or "coalition" that denote a sense of less formal and less genealogical and more voluntaristic ties.

49 For an account of the centrality of institutions to the IAF, see Warren, *Dry Bones Rattling*, pp. 30–36.

50 See Anthony Giddens, *Modernity and Self-Identity: Self and Society in the Late Modern Age* (Cambridge: Polity Press, 1991); Ulrich Beck, *Risk Society: Towards a New Modernity*, trans. Mark Ritter (London: Sage, 1992); Ulrich Beck, Anthony Giddens, and Scott Lash, *Reflexive Modernization: Politics, Tradition and Aesthetics in the Modern Social Order* (Cambridge: Polity Press, 1994).

51 The booklet by Michael Gecan, *Effective Organizing for Congregational Renewal* (Chicago, IL: ACTA Publications, 2008) produced by one of the leading organizers in the IAF and widely distributed among leaders in London Citizens, specifically addresses the question of how to strengthen institutions through using the practices of organizing. Another expression of this concern was a booklet produced in

the same series and also distributed among London Citizens' organizers by Ernesto Cortés entitled *Rebuilding Our Institutions* (Chicago: ACTA Publications, 2010).

52 Tom MacInnes and Peter Kenway, *London's Poverty Profile* (London: New Policy Institute, 2009), p. 14.

53 Zygmunt Bauman, *Globalization* (Cambridge: Polity Press, 1998), pp. 12–26.

54 Polanyi, *Great Transformation*, p. 167.

55 Part of the resistance to London Citizens, and the anxiety it can generate both among members and nonmembers, is an unwillingness to see an inherent conflict between the demands of forming flourishing institutions and families and the demands of the market, because confronting this conflict puts members at odds with the status quo. Here we encounter the conflict between the critical and political process by which needs are addressed through London Citizens and the consensus-driven, pastoral, and service-orientated models that most churches adopt. The former challenges the power structures; the latter merely mitigates their effects while staying on good terms with those in power.

56 For example, Manuel Castells, in his analysis of the democratic aspirations of grassroots social movements in urban contexts – an analysis that includes a discussion of community organizing as a case study – concludes that such political forms cannot overcome the weakness of their structural position since they are too beholden to capital flows and elite political power (Castells, *City and the Grassroots*). In Castells's view, the only way for democratic politics to be effective is to move beyond the local to operate as networked global social movements. On this, see Castells, *The Power of Identity*, vol. II, 2nd ed. However, Castells is criticized as being too pessimistic and establishing a false dichotomy between a "space of flows" dominated by elite interests and a "space of places" in which social movements operate (Edward Soja, *Postmetropolis: Critical Studies of Cities and Regions* [Oxford: Blackwell Publishing, 2000], pp. 212–16). Castells can also be criticized for how he idealizes networks by rendering them reified, atemporal, and apolitical.

57 The framing of BBCO in terms of local versus global and the divergent conclusions drawn from such a framing need situating within a broader set of discourses about locality. Ever since the dawn of modernity there have been two basic responses to dealing with the detrimental impact of processes such as industrialization, urbanization, bureaucratization and the like. On the one hand there are those who advocate responding at a macro level so that either the national or the global becomes the scale at which to remedy the ills of modern life. On the other hand there are those who see the local community as the source of salvation from the dark satanic forces unleashed by modernity, either in the form of the Leviathan of the modern nation-state or the chaos monster of capitalism. For example, we can contrast Charles Fourier's localist form of communism with Marx and Engel's internationalist version; or Guild Socialism with the Fabians' technocratic and statist version. Whether it is socialism, the environmental movement, or various conservative theories and movements, all political ideologies have their localist variants. Advocacy of decentralization, localization, and community as bulwarks against the perils of either the state or the market is a stock-in-trade of social reformers and modernity critics on both "Left" and "Right" since the nineteenth century. Conversely, the dismissing of local forms of political action as parochial and failures to challenge broader structures goes hand in hand with their advocacy. The undercurrent of

lament sounded in Ferdinand Tönnies's analysis of the shift from *Gemeinschaft* to *Gesellschaft* is countered by the note of willing embrace heard in Max Weber's account of the iron cage of the bureaucratic state and its monopolization of violence. For an account of the contested nature of the local and community as arenas of political action in social theory and public policy, see DeFilippis, Fisher, and Shragge, *Contesting Community*.

58 Massey, *World City*, p. 84; Saskia Sassen, "Making Public Interventions in Today's Massive Cities," *Static* 4 (2006): 1–8, p. 6, available at: http://static.londonconsortium.com/issue04/ (last accessed December 13, 2013).

59 Massey calls for a move beyond a "scalar geographical imagination" (Massey, *World City*, p. 184). Massey advocates what she calls "local internationalism," positing it as an alternative to subsidiarity, which in her view still operates with a scalar geographical imagination that distributes tasks and decisions up and down the scale and thereby diminishes the significance and impact of local actions. For Massey, local authorities need a foreign policy: that is, some response to the ways in which their actions are interwoven into local economies and political processes elsewhere in the world. One could see the fair-trade movement and the development of fair-trade towns and procurement policies as an example of such "local internationalism." On this, see Nick Clark et al., "Fairtrade Urbanism? The Politics of Place beyond Place in the Bristol Fairtrade City Campaign," *International Journal of Urban and Regional Research* 31.3 (2007): 633–45.

60 As Massey puts it: "There is a need to rethink the 'place' of the local and to explore how we can rearticulate a politics of place that both meets the challenges of a space of flows and addresses head-on the responsibilities of 'powerful places' such as global cities" (Massey, *World City*, p. 15). Massey calls this a "politics of place beyond place." Massey points out that London as a place challenges notions of the local as either intrinsically good or simply a victim of globalization. Processes of globalization are not a set of abstract forces cut off from events and developments on the ground. Indeed, overly abstract accounts of globalization mystify and obscure how globalization is produced in particular places and avoid questions of power, agency, and responsibility. For a critique of globalization along these lines, see Doreen Massey, *For Space* (London: Sage Publications, 2005). What the experience of London Citizens suggests is that sometimes there is a need to blend neighborhood, citywide, national, and global scales through forms of action that are attuned to the nature of contemporary temporal and spatial relations (Jane Wills, "The Politics of Place," unpublished paper, "Colloquium on Community Organising," London, June 15–17, 2009). This is a lesson Citizens UK itself needs to learn: despite a commitment to neighborhood politics and reweaving civil society, organizers tended to operate with the citywide and the national as the predominant scales of political action and campaigns. Yet there were moves to counter this: all organizers were assigned a borough role to be combined with a campaign role in 2009.

61 A parallel account of a re-envisioned conception of urban citizenship is developed in Saskia Sassen, *Territory, Authority, Rights: From Medieval to Global Assemblages*, updated ed. (Princeton, NJ: Princeton University Press, 2008), pp. 314–19; idem, "The Repositioning of Citizenship: Emergent Subjects and Spaces for Politics," *Berkeley Journal of Sociology* 46 (2002): 4–25.

62 Without this recognition it is easy to miss the interconnections between local forms of organizing and wider social movements (whether national or global in scale). For example, the labor, civil rights, and feminist movements all grew out of local organizing. On this, see Polletta, *Freedom is an Endless Meeting*; and Robert Fisher and Eric Shragge, "Contextualizing Community Organizing: Lessons from the Past, Tensions in the Present, Opportunities for the Future," in Marion Orr, *Transforming the City: Community Organizing and the Challenge of Political Change* (Lawrence: University Press of Kansas, 2007), pp. 193–217.

63 London is not being held up as an exemplar of some universal process of development. Forms of "urban globality" are inevitably heterogeneous. For a critique of post-Marxist, postcolonial, and other singular theories of urban development and globalization, see Aihwa Ong, "Introduction: Worlding Cities, or the Art of Being Global," in *Worlding Cities: Asian Experiments and the Art of Being Global*, eds. Ananya Roy and Aiwha Ong (Oxford: Wiley-Blackwell, 2011), pp. 1–13.

64 The spatial turn has been an important feature of much social and cultural theory since the 1970s. Among others, the work of Henri Lefebvre, David Harvey, Manuel Castells, and Frederic Jameson are central figures in this turn. Their work draws attention to how, rather than being passive or neutral, space itself is produced and its representation is socially, economically, and politically contested, the outcomes of these struggles in turn affecting the conditions and possibilities of action within particular spatial/social configurations such as a cityscape or cyberspace. On the "spatial turn," see Barney Warf and Santa Arias, *The Spatial Turn: Interdisciplinary Perspectives* (London: Taylor & Francis, 2009); and John Pickles, "Review Article: Social and Cultural Cartographies and the Spatial Turn in Social Theory," *Journal of Historical Geography* 25.1 (1999): 93–98. Political theory must include some account of the production of space if it is to explain the conditions and possibilities of political action; and democratic political action has to engage in remaking geography if it is to really challenge the distribution of power.

65 The account of democratic citizenship that will be developed here moves beyond a "scalar geographical imagination" and instead generates a more spatially alert conception, capable of guiding political practice within contemporary conditions. One way of moving beyond myopic, self-limiting spatial frames is through a theological social/spatial imaginary in which the local is not absolutized or made an end in and of itself; instead, it is the necessary beginning point for the pilgrim's journey that culminates in communion with God and redeemed humanity. Within this Christian cosmopolitan vision the particularity of humans is constituted by their place; that is, our social, economic, political, and historical location in creation. Politics within this Christian cosmopolitan vision involves the formation of a common world of meaning and action within particular places but also locating these places within concentric circles of human sociality that culminate in an eschatological horizon of fulfillment. This horizon of fulfillment both draws in and constantly interrupts all attempts to make any place or scale of human interaction idolatrously self-sufficient or totally encompassing in terms of economic, political, and social relationships. On this account, various forms of localism, nationalism, and identity politics overvalue the particularity of a place whereas many cosmopolitan and global conceptions of citizenship and a neoliberal vision of economic globalization undervalue it. For a full account of a Christian cosmopolitan vision

and critique of other forms of cosmopolitanism, see Bretherton, *Christianity and Contemporary Politics*, pp. 126–74.

66 In 2013 Citizens UK adopted the opposite approach and created a centralized and national organizational form. With regard to developments within the IAF in the United States, broader organizational developments seem to be driven more by interpersonal conflict than any sustained attention to the practice itself. Part of exploring what a confederal structure may entail is encouraging a more collegial and collaborative culture among organizers and constituting them as a formal guild.

67 Sanford D. Horwitt, "Alinsky, Foreclosures and Holding Banks Accountable," *The Huffington Post*, January 1, 2012, available at: http://www.huffingtonpost.com/sanford-d-horwitt/alinsky-foreclosures-and-_b_1245449.html (last accessed August 23, 2013).

68 On this, see Gary Gereffi, "Global Value Chains in a Post-Washington Consensus World," *Review of International Political Economy* (2013): 1–29; Gary Gereffi, Joonkoo Lee, Michelle Christian, "US-Based Food and Agricultural Value Chains and Their Relevance to Healthy Diets," *Journal of Hunger & Environmental Nutrition* 4 (2009): 357–74.

3 Reimagining the Secular: Interfaith Relations as a Civic Practice

1 Historically religious institutions were the key component, but there are moves to make other kinds of groups and institutions such as schools, disability groups, and hospitals more central.

2 James Pitt and Maurice Keane, *Community Organising? The Challenge to Britain from the U.S.A.* (London: J & P Consultancy, 1984). See also Jay MacLeod, *Community Organising: A Practical and Theological Appraisal* (London: Christian Action, 1993).

3 Interview with Reverend Alan Green, June 25, 2009, London.

4 For a helpful historical overview of the emergence of community development as a field, and in particular its self-identified distinction from social work in the United Kingdom, see Gary Craig, "Introduction," in *The Community Development Reader: History, Themes and Issues*, ed. Gary Craig, Marjorie Mayo, Keith Popple, Mae Shaw, and Marilyn Taylor (London: The Policy Press, 2011), pp. 3–21. Craig notes that Alinsky was an important early influence and the *Reader* itself includes a section from *Rules for Radicals*. One point of convergence in the origins of community organizing and community development in the United Kingdom is the work of Alan Twelvetrees. See footnote 9 and Twelvetrees's important introductory text to community development – *Community Work* (London: Palgrave MacMillan, 2008 [1982]) – now in its fourth edition.

5 For example, the 2009 National Occupational Standards for Community Development Work in the United Kingdom defines community development in the following terms: "Community Development is a long-term value based process which aims to address imbalances in power and bring about change founded on social justice, equality and inclusion. The process enables people to organise and work together to: identify their own needs and aspirations; take action to exert influence on the decisions which affect their lives; improve the quality of their own lives, the communities in which they live, and societies of which they are a part"

(*National Occupational Standards for Community Development Work* [Federation for Community Development Learning, 2009], p. 4).

6 As one survey of community development workers in the United Kingdom notes: "The main source of funding for posts mentioned in the survey is government: 35% of posts were mainly funded by local government and 27% by central government programmes. Overall, European funding accounted for 8% of funds, but this figure was higher in Northern Ireland. Charitable trusts and the Community Fund are the main source of funds for 19% of posts" (*Survey of Community Development Workers in the UK – Summary Report* [Sheffield: Community Development Foundation, 2003], p. 2).

7 For a parallel history of Citizens UK, see Warren, "Community Organizing in Britain." It should be noted that Warren's account contains some inaccuracies and does not cover the process of Citizens UK's founding.

8 For example, Neil Jameson – lead organizer during the five-day London Citizens training at the Kairos Centre in Roehampton, October 6–10, 2008 – framed London Citizens as reviving prior traditions of organizing, especially Chartists and London Dockyard workers, but added there was a need to do it in a new way in response to the challenges of globalization.

9 Jameson originally encountered community organizing when researching the causes of vandalism and the work of community development corporations on a Churchill Fellowship in 1979. It was then that he met Edward Chambers and saw first-hand a number of community organizations. Sponsored by the Barrow Cadbury Trust, Jameson returned to North America in 1987 to undertake the Industrial Areas Foundation ten-day training course, having already arranged for a number of his colleagues at the Children's Society to attend training before him (letter from Ian Davies, Principal Officer [Neighborhoods and Congregations], The Children's Society, in response to his attendance at the ten-day training, December 29, 1986; Box 144, file 1513, IAF Archive). Ian Sparks, then Director of the Children's Society, actively encouraged and supported Jameson in his efforts to develop community organizing in the United Kingdom, recognizing it as a valuable complement to the Children's Society commitment to social justice but as too radical for the originally named Church of England's Children's Society (which had the Queen Mother as a Patron) to undertake themselves. Another figure involved in the early stages of COF's development was Alan Twelvetrees who investigated IAF in his research at UCLA and attended IAF training while working in the United States. In the 1980s he taught community work at the University of Wales. He wrote to Ed Chambers in 1984 about the possibility of setting up IAF in the United Kingdom. At the time, Jameson was working as Regional Director for the Children's Society in Wales and the West of England and met Twelvetrees when he set up a small working group to explore the relationship between community development work and community organizing. This group included Mary MacAleese, who subsequently became one of the first organizers Jameson recruited. Interestingly, Jameson notes that Twelvetrees never built an actual community organization – partly because of his resistance to involving faith groups, for which he was never able to locate an equivalent institutional basis for the work. Another parallel effort was undertaken in the late 1980s at the instigation of Victor Guazzelli, Roman Catholic Bishop of East London, who had sponsored the research by James Pitt and Maurice Keane into the viability of establishing community organizing work in the United Kingdom.

Guazzelli attempted to develop such a work in the East End just using the Roman Catholic churches. This did not work and quickly faded out. However, the Bishop subsequently funded Jameson to establish TELCO in 1992 (interview with Neil Jameson, June 24, 2010, London).

10 The deeds were changed early on when COF was trying to establish a broad-based community organization in Liverpool and work with Muslims there as COF was accused of being a "Christian conspiracy" (interview with Neil Jameson, June 24, 2010, London). The 1985 *Faith in the City* report by the Church of England provided the impetus and context in which the relationship with the Church Urban Fund, set up in the wake of the report, was developed. Along with the Barrow Cadbury Trust, the Church Urban Fund was a key financial backer and means of credentialing the fledgling organization.

11 Interview with Neil Jameson, June 24, 2010, London.

12 As George Thomas observes of the nineteenth-century U.S. context: "Revivalism radicalized ... mainstream Protestantism: A moral citizenry must actively construct the Kingdom of God. Viewing themselves blessed by God with foundational documents of democracy, Christians were to push forward and directly transform the nation. This led to an emphasis on social reform movements that had as their goal the defining of citizenship by building moral categories into the legal order, citizenship, education, and work. These reforms included temperance, abolition, observation of the Christian Sabbath, and public schools" (George Thomas, *Revivalism and Cultural Change: Christianity, Nation Building, and the Market in the Nineteenth-Century United States* [Chicago: University of Chicago Press, 1989], pp. 78–79. See also Dan McKanan, *Prophetic Encounters: Religion and the American Radical Tradition* (Boston: Beacon Press, 2012).

13 Contrary to the secularization thesis, processes of modernization in Europe and the United States did not directly correlate with the decline of the public significance of religion per se. However, modernization did coincide with a transmutation and redescription of theological categories such as sin and charity into more immanent and moralized ones such as vice and altruism. For a discussion of the secularization thesis in relation to social reform movements and a redescription of secularization as a process of immanentization, see Dominic Erdozain, "The Secularisation of Sin in the Nineteenth Century," *The Journal of Ecclesiastical History* 62.1 (2011): 59–88; and Mark Bevir, *The Making of British Socialism* (Princeton, NJ: Princeton University Press, 2011).

14 It is important to distinguish this more popular and practice-driven strand from the more elite and theoretically driven forms of Christian Socialism championed by figures such as Stewart Headlam, F. D. Maurice, Conrad Noel, and Saint John Groser. This latter form was a predominantly Anglican strain of thought and practice.

15 Sanders, *Roots of Reform*, pp. 157–58. On this, see also Michael Kazin, *A Godly Hero: The Life of William Jennings Bryan* (New York: Anchor Books, 2007). Bryan is a controversial figure and much lambasted for his role in the infamous Scopes "monkey" trial – now perceived as the harbinger of the contemporary U.S. culture wars. Yet rather than an atavistic "fundamentalist" reaction against modernity, his involvement in the trial was directly related to his reform impulse. As Sanders notes: "Bryan strongly objected to arguments that drew on the social implications of Darwinism to justify the exploitation of workers and consumers and to discourage reform movements. ... The Antimonopoly-Greenback-Populist creed that Bryan

embodied was naturally antithetical to Darwinism, whose founder, in *The Descent of Man*, had argued against reforms that checked the salutary processes of weeding out the weak and less fit. In addition, Bryan abhorred Nietzsche's Darwinist defense of war as both necessary and desirable for human progress. Such ideas, he believed, were important factors in the development of German militarism leading to World War I" (*ibid.*, p. 158). The contrast between the views of someone like Bryan and the views of later Evangelical Protestant political figureheads such as Pat Robertson and Jerry Falwell are striking.

16 See Nathan Hatch, *The Democratization of American Christianity* (New Haven, CT: Yale University Press, 1989); Ted Smith, *The New Measures: A Theological History of Democratic Practice* (Cambridge: Cambridge University Press, 2007); William Sutton, *Journeyman for Jesus: Evangelical Artisans Confront Capitalism in Jacksonian Baltimore* (University Park: Pennsylvania State University Press, 1998); and Taylor, *A Secular Age* (Cambridge, MA: Belknap Press, 2007), p. 451. Taylor notes how Evangelicalism, along with a reform-minded Catholicism in Europe, was part of a broader "age of mobilization."

17 Kazin, *Populist Persuasion*, p. 40. As already noted, Kazin draws out the "pietist" roots of Populism and how it drew on the forms and styles of the Evangelical "Great Awakenings."

18 As evidenced in his remarks on the Moral Majority, even Taylor seems to adopt this kind of view, thereby ignoring some of the more interesting implications of his own thesis. Taylor, *Secular Age*, pp. 487–88. The problem here is the overly disjunctive reading of the shift into the modern period that Taylor – while questioning it – does adopt as a governing paradigm.

19 Many scholarly identifications of fundamentalism see it as a negative or defensive reaction *against* modernity and as a religiously defined form of political mobilization. For example, Manuel Castells sees the political role of fundamentalist religious expressions as a form of what he calls "resistance identities" that build "trenches of resistance and survival on the basis of principles different from, or opposed to, those permeating the institutions of society" (Manuel Castells, *The Power of Identity* [Malden, MA: Blackwell, 1997], p. 8. The "Fundamentalist Project," a ten-year academic study of fundamentalism around the world was instrumental in developing this kind of perspective. While recognizing that fundamentalism was a diverse phenomenon, the project identified enough "family resemblances" to say the term could be used to describe different kinds of the same thing; see Martin E. Marty and R. Scott Appleby, eds., *Fundamentalisms Observed* (Chicago: University of Chicago Press, 1991). Others question whether there is such a thing as "fundamentalism," suggesting the term is an unhelpful academic construct that functions in the same way as the term "oriental" did: that is, it is used to delegitimize and stigmatize certain forms of discourse about the world. David Herbert points out that the use of the term represents a false ascription of a particular American Christian development to developments in other faith traditions that need to be interpreted in their own right. So, for example, we should not use the term Islamic fundamentalism but Islamist (David Herbert, *Religion and Civil Society: Rethinking Public Religion in the Contemporary World* [Aldershot: Ashgate, 2003], p. 48). Malise Ruthven, while recognizing the problems, defends the "family resemblances" approach (*Fundamentalism: The Search for Meaning* [Oxford: Oxford University Press, 2005], pp. 1–34). Building on the work of the

Fundamentalism Project, Gabriel Almond, Scott Appleby, and Emmanuel Sivan defined fundamentalism as referring to "a discernable pattern of religious militance by which self-styled 'true believers' attempt to arrest the erosion of religious identity, fortify the border of the religious community, and create viable alternatives to secular institutions and behaviours" (*Strong Religion: The Rise of Fundamentalisms around the World* [Chicago: University of Chicago Press, 2003], p. 17). Within this framework, a defining feature of fundamentalism is as a reaction against modernity and processes of secularization. However, this kind of conceptualization of fundamentalism can be seen as part of a wider reproduction of what William Cavanaugh identifies as a modern archetype – the religious fanatic – which is then used to reinforce a secularist hegemony ("The Invention of Fanaticism," *Modern Theology* 27.2 [2011]: 226–37). See also Alberto Toscano, *Fanaticism: On the Uses of an Idea* (London: Verso, 2010).

20 See, for example, Zygmunt Bauman, "Postmodern Religion?" in *Religion, Modernity and Postmodernity*, ed. Paul Heelas (Oxford: Blackwell, 1998), pp. 55–78. On Bauman's reading, fundamentalists are not against the fruits of modern culture, only its secularizing influences. According to Bauman, what fundamentalism does is mediate modernity so as to provide a total pattern of life. It thereby relieves the individual from the burden of choice and anxiety induced by uncertainty and insecurity. Richard Antoun takes a similar view, framing Jewish, Christian, and Islamic fundamentalism as modes of selective modernization and forms of what he calls "controlled acculturation" (Richard T. Antoun, *Understanding Fundamentalism: Christian, Islamic, and Jewish Movements*, 2nd ed. [Lanham, MD: Rowman & Littlefield Publishers, 2008]).

21 Shmuel Eisenstadt, "The Reconstruction of Religious Arenas in the Framework of 'Multiple Modernities,'" *Millennium: Journal of International Studies* 29:3 (2000): 591–611.

22 On this, see Luke Bretherton, "A Postsecular Politics? Inter-faith Relations as a Civic Practice," *Journal of the American Academy of Religion* 79.2 (2011): 346–77.

23 Almond et al., *Strong Religion*, p. 18; and Ruthven, *Fundamentalism*, pp. 26–29. For a case study in this kind of innovative and entrepreneurial appropriation, see recent work on the globalization of Pentecostalism and charismatic Christianity and the ways in which past and present are negotiated in this religious tradition: Simon Coleman, *The Globalization of Charismatic Christianity: Spreading the Gospel of Prosperity* (Cambridge: Cambridge University Press, 2000); David Martin, *Pentecostalism: The World Their Parish* (Oxford: Blackwell, 2002); and Joel Robbins, "The Globalization of Pentecostal and Charismatic Christianity," *Annual Review of Anthropology* 33 (2004): 117–43.

24 See, for example, Kevin Phillips, *American Theocracy: The Peril and Politics of Radical Religion, Oil, and Borrowed Money in the 21st Century* (New York: Viking Press 2006) and Chris Hedges, *American Fascists: The Christian Right and the War on America* (New York: Free Press, 2008). These are examples of what Louis Bolce and Gerald De Maio, in their content analysis of the *New York Times* and *Washington Post* articles and editorials between 1987 and 2004, see as a distinct bias against Christian fundamentalists in reporting. They conclude that "[A]nti-Christian fundamentalism has become a very fashionable prejudice of the sophisticated classes" ("A Prejudice for the Thinking Classes: Media Framing, Political Sophistication, and the Christian Fundamentalist," cited in Jon A. Shields,

The Democratic Virtues of the Christian Right [Princeton, NJ: Princeton University Press, 2009], p. 62).

25 Shields, *Democratic Virtues*, pp. 1–2; see also pp. 115–46. Perhaps the irony is not quite so sharp given that many of those who helped initiate the pro-life movement, in particular its most controversial element – Operation Rescue – were veterans of the 1960s antiwar movement and inspired to take direct action by figures such as David Thoreau, Mahatma Gandhi, Martin Luther King, Jr., and Thomas Merton (Shields, *Democratic Virtues*, p. 50).

26 Clyde Wilcox and Carin Robinson, *Onward Christian Soldiers? The Religious Right in American Politics*, 4th ed. (Boulder, CO: Westview Press, 2011), p. 148. Whether the increased turnout of white Evangelicals is a result of the actions of the Christian Right is an open question.

27 He states that: "Christian Right leaders in the pro-life movement overwhelmingly emphasize four important deliberative norms: promoting public civility, practicing careful listening and dialogue, avoiding theological arguments, and embracing moral reasoning" (Shields, *Democratic Virtues*, p. 44). He goes on to outline how rank-and-file participants in pro-life campaigning uphold these commitments in practice. Wilcox and Robinson contend there is evidence to suggest that Shields's findings are echoed more broadly across the Christian Right as a movement for those involved in it over the long term and at some level of engagement whereas those on the periphery may become less tolerant (Wilcox and Robinson, *Onward Christian Soldiers?* pp. 155–56).

28 For an account of and contrast between models of "translation" and "conversation" as ways of relating religious and political discourse, see Bretherton, "Translation, Conversation, or Hospitality? Approaches to Theological Reasons in Public Deliberation," in *Religious Voices in Public Places*, eds. Nigel Biggar and Linda Hogan (Oxford: Oxford University Press, 2009), pp. 85–109. For an account and example of the process of hybridization of Christian and other discursive frames, see Susan Friend Harding, *The Book of Jerry Falwell: Fundamentalist Language and Politics* (Princeton, NJ: Princeton University Press, 2000). Harding describes how the Christian Right draws on motifs of linguistic practices such as Disney, corporate management, and Hollywood yet converts them within a Christian setting.

29 The event took place on Friday, February 26, 2010. The event was somewhat atypical of London Citizens' public gatherings as it was not an assembly or contentious action. It was framed as an internal "action" by organizers – the action being in the education of leaders and in the recognition and thereby credentializing of the work of London Citizens by a leading philosopher.

30 Gordon Rayner, "Muslim Groups Linked to September 11 Hijackers Spark Fury over Conference," *The Telegraph*, December 27, 2008, available at: http://www.telegraph.co.uk/news/uknews/3966501/Muslim-groups-linked-to-September-11-hijackers-spark-fury-over-conference.html (last accessed October 21, 2010). Dilowar Khan contends that despite the commitment of *Jamaat-e-Islami* to the implementation of Sharia and the development of an Islamic state, it is a mainstream political party in Bangladesh and committed to the democratic process. He makes no secret of figures involved in *Jamaat-e-Islami* having a voice in the leadership of the mosque but holds that given the overwhelming majority of those who attend the mosque come from Bangledesh, it is inevitable that *Jamaat-e-Islami* will be an influence, but that they are only one of a number of political parties

supported by leaders in the mosque. For example, Khan pointed out that his own brother was a Conservative Party candidate in the 2010 General Election. As for Anwar al-Awlaki, Kahn does not deny that he preached in the mosque in 2003 but argues that it was before al-Awlaki became an extremist after time spent in a Yemeni jail from 2006 to 2007. He admits also that a video sermon of al-Awlaki was shown in the mosque in January 2009 but says that was before al-Awlaki was well known as a supporter of al-Qaeda and violent jihad (interview, April 20, 2011, London). Some contest whether this is a viable defense, although there is some evidence to support Khan: al-Awlaki was invited to the Pentagon weeks after the attacks of 9/11 as part of an outreach program to Muslim leaders. Yet at the same time, the 9/11 Commission Report found that key members of those involved in the attacks had met with al-Awlaki a number of times before the attacks (Martha Raddatz, "Radical Cleric Al-Awlaki Invited to Private Lunch at Pentagon," October 21, 2010, available at: http://abcnews.go.com/Politics/Blotter/al-qaeda-cleric-awlaki-invited-pentagon-911/story?id=11935006 [last accessed April 28, 2011]). Al-Awlaki was killed in a joint Yemeni-U.S. operation on September 30, 2011.

31 Muslim Council of Britain, press release, December 17, 2007, available at: http://www.mcb.org.uk/article_detail.php?article=announcement-702 (last accessed October 21, 2010).

32 Organizers and leaders were exhorted to read the book before the event and reduced-price copies of the book were available for purchase from the offices of London Citizens. However, many leaders commented in evaluations of the event that they could not see how Sandel's work was relevant to organizing, and in contrast to the work of political thinkers such as Sheldon Wolin and Hannah Arendt, it is difficult to discern any influence of Sandel's work on the thinking of organizers in the United Kingdom or the United States. At the event itself, Glasman presented a short paper that set out a critique of Sandal's approach, arguing that it contrasted sharply with that encapsulated in community organizing. The salient points of this critique were Sandel's lack of attention to processes of commodification and the importance of institutions in resisting them; divergent conceptions of power, self-interest, leadership, and conflict; and how broad-based community organizing rejects a politics motivated by a commitment to a singular and inherently abstract value such as justice or equality and is instead committed to a diverse, reciprocal, and place-based politics of the common good that draws on multiple traditions, institutions, beliefs, and practices and is organized around concrete issues. Subsequent to this critique, Sandel has published work addressing some of the issue of commodification: Michael Sandel, *What Money Can't Buy: The Moral Limits of Markets* (New York: Farrar, Status, and Giroux, 2012).

33 There are a range of explanations that can be given for this. Although I focus on issues of belief and practice that might or might not inhibit greater participation, a number of material factors are also present. These are identified and summarized by Muslim leaders themselves in the following statement from a document they produced in 2011 (Ali, Ruhana, Lina Jamoul, and Yusufi Vali, "A New Covenant of Virtue: Islam and Community Organising," Citizens UK and IAF, available at: http://www.citizensuk.org/wp-content/uploads/2012/08/Islam-and-Community-Organising-V3-singles.pdf [last accessed December 13, 2012]). It states: "Muslims in the West find themselves in a unique position. While interactions between Muslims and the West have a very long history, it has been two and a half generations since

we settled here. The first generation of our parents, uncles, and aunts who settled here had an experience similar to other immigrants who settled in Europe and the United States. They had to find jobs, housing, good schools for their children, build places of worship that they felt comfortable and welcome in, and figure out how to pass on rich cultural and religious heritages to their children born in a foreign land. In addition to the familiar pressures experienced by most immigrant families, the Muslim community certainly in recent years, has faced other unique pressures. We have seen an increased (and mostly unwanted) scrutiny from government, law enforcement agencies, and the media. Muslims, and our institutions, receive more than our fair share of unwanted and negative attention." As the quote suggests, the creation of new institutions and the inevitably insecure and insular position of first-generation immigrants is further exacerbated by the securitization of Islam post-9/11 so that the confrontational approach of community organizing can be perceived as making more difficult an already tense and vulnerable situation.

34 Other interfaith practices such as Scriptural reasoning do not have to face such questions, as those involved tend to be self-selecting and not have participants who support such things as apostasy laws.

35 Ahmed was cited as paying tribute to Hamas founder Sheikh Ahmed Yassin (its present leadership) and Sheikh al-Qassam (after whom the military wing of Hamas was named) in a speech shown on YouTube and recorded in January 2009 (Martin Bright, "Rabbi 'in pain' over London Citizens link," *The Jewish Chronicle*, June 2, 2011). The first article highlighting Ahmed's views in the video and his links with London Citizens was Martin Bright's "London Citizens Stand by Islamist Hardliner," *The Jewish Chronicle*, May 26, 2011.

36 The Northwest Bronx Community and Clergy Coalition – a non-IAF broad-based community organization – explicitly used the notion of a community of shared fate to frame their work, particularly in the area of school reform (Paul Kuttner, Amanda Taylor, and Helen Westmoreland, "'Cement between bricks': Building Schools and Communities in New York City," in *A Match on Dry Grass: Community Organizing as a Catalyst for School Reform*, eds. Mark R. Warren and Karen L. Mapp [Oxford: Oxford University Press, 2011], pp. 197–226).

37 It must, of course, be recognized that "areas" can become coded in terms of class, race, and culture leading to the homogenization of that area. However, the proximity to other areas must still be negotiated, even if it is a suburban-inner city division.

38 As Ataullah Siddiqui notes, when it comes to other religious traditions, "[t]he fulfilment of revelations to the Prophet Muhammed it seems sealed all opportunities to look even with curiosity at 'the otherness of the other'" (*Christian-Muslim Dialogue in the Twentieth Century* [Basingstoke: Macmillan, 1997], p. 196). There are attempts within Islam to construct a distinctively Islamic rationale for engagement with religious others. A notable example of such a move emerged within the South African context of the struggle against Apartheid when Muslims worked alongside people of other faith. See, for example, Farid Esack, *Qur'an, Liberation and Pluralism: An Islamic Perspective on Interreligious Solidarity Against Oppression* (Oxford: Oneworld, 1997).

39 On this, see Yohanan Friedmann, *Tolerance and Coercion in Islam: Interfaith Relations in the Muslim Tradition* (Cambridge: Cambridge University Press, 2003).

40 Key in this shift was responses to the Holocaust. An important milestone was Pope Paul VI's *Nostra Aetate* (1965), coupled with the expansion at a popular level of Christian Zionism among Evangelical and Pentecostal Christians driven in large part by a particular form of premillennial eschatology. This same development among Protestants problematizes Christian-Islamic relations, as it tends to frame the conflict in the Middle East in terms of a cosmic battle between good and evil, with Muslims seen as being on the side of evil.

41 It is an open question as to whether the quest for interfaith dialogue is actually a kind of crypto-Christian theological concern. Christian mission has often taken an exclusivist, colonizing, derogatory, and at times demonizing attitude toward other religions. However, this is not a necessary or inevitable stance. Even a highly "exclusivist" approach to mission can entail listening to and learning from other religions as a theological imperative to hear from potential bearers of divine presence. For an example of this kind of approach to mission, see either Lesslie Newbigin, *The Open Secret: An Introduction to the Theology of Mission* (London: SPCK, 1995) or Gavin D'Costa *Christianity and World Religions: Disputed Questions in the Theology of Religions* (Oxford: Wiley-Blackwell, 2009). For a broader discussion of the difficulties in interreligious dialogue and of not overlaying a Christian reading of other faiths but allowing their otherness to stand in any encounter, see Michael Barnes, *Theology and the Dialogue of Religions* (Cambridge: Cambridge University Press, 2002).

42 Dilwar Hussain, "Muslim Political Participation in Britain and the 'Europeanisation' of *Fiqh*," *Die Welt des Islams* 44.3 (2004): 376–401.

43 In Islamic jurisprudence the notion of the common good is equated with *maslaḥah* or *maslaḥah 'amma*. On this, see Muhammad Qasim Zaman, "The 'Ulama' of Contemporary Islam and Their Conceptions of the Common Good," in *Public Islam and the Common Good*, eds. Armando Salvatore and Dale Eickelman (Leiden: Brill, 2004), pp. 129–55; and Armando Salvatore, *The Public Sphere: Liberal Modernity, Catholicism, Islam* (New York: Palgrave Macmillan, 2007), pp. 156–71.

44 Interview, July 15, 2008, London. The multiple use of double em-dashes within brackets designates a break in thought or pause within the interview.

45 The question of the minority status of Muslims in what are seen as non-Islamic societies is one that is severely contested and debated within Islam. For an overview of responses to minority status by Muslims, see Muhammad Khalid Masud, "Being Muslim in a Non-Muslim Polity: Three Alternative Models," *Journal of the Institute of Muslim Minority Affairs* 10.1 (1989): 118–28. However, the question in relation to the East London Mosque is slightly different as at a local level – that of Hackney – where Muslims constitute a major power and influence within the borough. The same can be said for other local contexts in Great Britain such as Bradford. More broadly, it is a mistake to think of this as simply a contemporary issue for Muslims and one peculiar to those living in majority non-Muslim societies. As the situation of the Copts in Egypt and other Christian and Jewish populations in majority Muslim societies makes clear, the need to conceptualize relations with non-Muslim others has been a constant and ongoing challenge within Islam since its foundation.

46 Tariq Ramadan, *Western Muslims and the Future of Islam* (Oxford: Oxford University Press, 2004).

47 Muhammad Muslih, "Democracy," in *Oxford Encyclopedia of the Modern Islamic World*, ed. John L. Esposito et al. (Oxford: Oxford University Press, 2001), pp. 356–60. Another approach, not discussed here, are the attempts to relate the traditions of Islamic juristic theology to modern conceptions of human rights. On this, see Ebrahim Moosa, "The Dilemma of Islamic Rights Schemes," *Journal of Law and Religion* 15.1–2 (2000–01): 185–215.

48 Official statement quoted in Rachel M. Scott, *The Challenge of Political Islam: Non-Muslims and the Egyptian State* (Stanford, CA: Stanford University Press, 2010), p. 151. As Scott notes, quite what this statement implies is a matter of some dispute, both within and without the party. A parallel with the Wasat Party is suggested by a comment during a conversation with Dilowar Khan who mentioned that when he visited Egypt he had tried to meet the leader of the party. Although its future after the "Arab Spring" is uncertain, the party did have significant involvement of Coptic Christians in its leadership as part of a shared platform. Scott notes: "For most of the twentieth century, Islamists associated citizenship with the prerevolutionary secular order and viewed it as a particularly Western concept. Citizenship, along with values such as democracy, was rejected by the Islamicists of the 1970's. However, there has been a shift towards accepting the idea of citizenship as, on some level, compatible with the Islamic revival. The change is illustrated by the fact that political groups such as the Muslim Brotherhood and the al-Wasat Party have been using the discourse of citizenship to define relations between Muslims and non-Muslims in Egypt" (*ibid.*, p. 139). The significance of Egypt and the developments there in the formation of modern political Islam cannot be underestimated, home as it was to Sayid Qutb and the formation of the Muslim Brotherhood.

49 Although he has lived in exile in the United States since 2000, the movement's founder, Fethullah Gülen, is credited by some with providing the intellectual and moral framework for the internalization of democracy and the separation of mosque and state among the conservative Islamic populations in Turkey. For example, Gülen writes: "Democracy and Islam are compatible. Ninety-five percent of Islamic rules deal with private life and the family. Only five percent deals with matters of the state, and this could be arranged only within the context of democracy. If some are thinking something else, such as an Islamic state, this country's history and social conditions do not allow it. Democratization is an irreversible process in Turkey" (interview in *Sabah*, January 27, 1995, quoted in Helen Rose Ebaugh, *The Gülen Movement: A Sociological Analysis of a Civic Movement Rooted in Moderate Islam* [London: Springer, 2009], p. 42). Ebaugh does not address the question of how the Gülen Movement conceptualizes interfaith relations but does see it as a civic rather than a religious movement. Personal conversations with leading figures in the movement in the United Kingdom suggest that the movement departs from the mainstream tradition of Islam in its approach to apostasy laws that stipulate those who convert out of Islam should die, seeing these as no longer having the force of law in a context where Islam and the state are no longer identified.

50 Chambers and Cowan, *Roots for Radicals,* pp. 121–23.

51 Initial funding for the process came from the Charles Stewart Mott Foundation and was catalyzed by organizers rather than initiated by Islamic leaders. However, by all accounts, key leaders soon emerged who were committed and gave energy to the process. A separate but related event was held in London in June 2009 for British Muslim leaders and included a dinner to raise funds for an organizer specifically

focused on drawing more mosques into membership of London Citizens. The East London Mosque hosted both the event and dinner. Presentations on the relationship between organizing and Islam were given by Dr. Manazir Ahsan, The Islamic Foundation; Dr. Zahid Parvez, Islamic Society of Britain; Dilowar Khan, London Muslim Centre/East London Mosque; Dr Abdulkarim Khalil, Muslim Cultural Heritage Centre; and Farooq Murad, The Islamic Foundation. Subsequent events were held in 2011, again, to try and recruit more mosques in East London to join TELCO.

52 It is significant that although the paper draws from many different periods of the prophet's life, it is the Meccan/Makkahn period, when Muslims were in the minority, rather than the Medinan period that is used as the best analogy for Islamic involvement in broad-based community organizing. It could be argued that this is a departure from the mainstream tradition of interpretation. However, it does have parallels in the tradition. Although those involved in drafting the document seem unaware and uninfluenced by them, the emphasis on the Meccan/Makkahn period directly parallels moves made by the Sudanese Islamic scholars Mahmoud Mohammed Taha and Abdullahi Ahmed An-Na'im. These scholars suggest that in the formation of Islam and the Qur'an as a text, the Meccan rather than Medina period is to be prioritized. They argue that in this period the prophet emphasized the equal dignity of all "children of Adam." See in particular Abdullahi Ahmed An-Na'im, *Toward an Islamic Reformation: Civil Liberties, Human Rights and International Law* (Syracuse, NY: Syracuse University Press, 1990). In a related development, Citizens UK and the IAF sent an organizer from London and a Muslim leader from Chicago to Egypt in March 2011 in order to establish contact with the leadership of the democratic movement there to discuss how community organizing as an approach could contribute to the momentum for reform.

53 Since 2012, liberal and reformed synagogues have begun joining London Citizens.

54 Interview, March 31, 2011, London.

55 Plen was made aware of Pesner's work, but his initiative was a wholly independent one. Pesner is director of Just Congregations, an initiative of the Union for Reform Judaism in the United States. Just Congregations seeks to apply what it calls the "congregation-based community organizing model" to synagogues and their social engagement activities. Their Web site gives the following rationale for this work: "The Union for Reform Judaism is committed to having our congregations explore congregation-based community organizing, because: It makes our synagogues stronger, helping us find and develop each other as leaders, and strengthening the fabric of our community. It brings us into sacred relationships across lines of race, class, and faith. It enables us to act powerfully on our most deeply held Jewish values in order to bring about a redeemed world" (available at: http://urj.org/socialaction/training/justcongregations/ [last accessed April 18, 2011]).

56 The Masorti training material was written over the course of 2010 with funding from the Lottery Fund and the PAIRS Foundation.

57 Jessica Elgot, "I Can Do More as an Organiser than as a Politician," *The Jewish Chronicle Online,* March 17, 2011. Available at: http://www.thejc.com/46695/i-can-do-more-organiser-a-politician (last accessed March 18, 2011).

58 Osterman notes how leaders in Texas IAF, having spent time in Latin America and worked with *communidades de base,* critically appropriated and incorporated elements of liberation theology into organizing (*Gathering Power,* pp. 96–100).

59 See Austen Ivereigh, *Faithful Citizens: A Practical Guide to Catholic Social Teaching and Community Organising* (London: Darton, Longman & Todd, 2010).

60 Horwitt, *Let Them Call Me Rebel*, p. 531. Niebuhr and Alinsky met when Alinsky gave the Auburn Lectures at Union Theological Seminary in New York in 1966. Niebuhr invited Alinsky back to his apartment and to Alinsky's great surprise, Niebuhr asked Alinsky to sign copies of Alinsky's books. In a letter to Niebuhr's widow, where he discusses this incident, Alinsky cites Niebuhr as an influence (Saul Alinsky to Ursula M. Niebuhr, February 4, 1972, letter, *Reinhold Niebuhr Papers*, Library of Congress). Although Alinsky saw his conception of self-interest as consonant with Niebuhr's work, the extent of the influence appears limited. While parallels can be drawn, the influence of Maritain is more direct.

61 *Tent of the Presence: Black Church Power in the 1980s* (New York: Industrial Areas Foundation, 1981). In a pattern that exactly follows that of the writing of the "New Covenant of Virtue: Islam and Community Organising" statement, the "Tent of the Presence" statement emerged from a retreat that included key Black church leaders in membership of the IAF, including Vernon Dobson, Douglas Miles, Clarence Williams, and Johnny Ray Youngblood. During the retreat, the pastors brainstormed the themes that became the "Tent of the Presence." Subsequent to the retreat, Arnie Graf and Michael Gecan discussed and then wrote up a draft of the paper. The paper then went back to the clergy for comments and improvements, and then Gecan wrote the final draft, which the pastors unanimously approved. I am grateful to Michael Gecan for outlining the process (personal correspondence, April 19, 2011).

62 London Citizens continue to actively engage in developing the black clergy caucus in London, but the theological dialogue is embryonic. A key point of distinction from the U.S. situation is the size and importance of the African diaspora church, particularly from West Africa. The experience of the civil rights movement and the voice of Black theologians and intellectuals such as James Cone and Cornel West are a point of reference for Black church leaders in the United States. London Citizens has tended to try and find analogies with this experience through either using reflections based on Martin Luther King or drawing from UK theologians who work within the framework of Black Liberation Theology, such as Robert Beckford. What is needed, however, is an engagement with African theology and the experience of being a diaspora church as this is the context and background of the larger congregations engaged with London Citizens. Leaders from this West African diaspora background within the caucus are themselves beginning to undertake such work. Arguably, the same is needed in the U.S. context, which itself has a growing number of African diaspora churches. For a case study of such churches, see Mark R. Gornik, *Word Made Global: Stories of African Christianity in New York City* (Grand Rapids, MI: Eerdmans, 2011).

63 See http://www.cscoweb.org/ (last accessed April 4, 2011). However, as Osterman notes, the IAF has had limited success in recruiting Evangelical congregations to date (*Gathering Power*, p. 118). However, senior U.S. organizers are confident that this may change and are actively engaging with a number of "mega-churches."

64 Richard Wood's recent work addresses exactly this dynamic. He assesses what leads to the strengthening of congregations via engagement in community organizing. The key research question addressed in Wood's study is: When congregations become politically engaged in community organizing, what dynamics drive the

resulting impact on the congregations? And how does this vary across traditions and settings? Wood identifies a constellation of factors that contribute to a mutually beneficial relationship between community organizing and congregational development. Key for Wood is identifying factors that neither instrumentalize and burn out a congregation nor disempowers the political work of community organizing. See Richard Wood, *The Fire of Public Life: Congregational Development through Civic Engagement* (forthcoming).

65 This is reflected in the following comment from Arnie Graf, one the IAF's most experienced organizers: "You get to combine your intellectual growth with putting it into action and so as an organizer I've been forced to, in a good way, learn about Christianity, something I knew nothing about, or even some of my own Jewish scripture, you know, Old Testament Scripture, Hebrew scripture, now we're learning [about] Islam" (interview, February 10, 2009, London).

66 Chapter 6 explores in detail how broad-based community organizing constitutes an ideologically porous or open practice of politics that allows for multiple interpretative configurations.

67 This was taught explicitly in the five-day leadership training program.

68 Neil Jameson, "British Muslims – Influencing UK Public Life: A Case Study," *British Muslims: Loyalty and Belonging*, eds. Mohammad Siddique Seddon, Dilwar Hussain, and Nadeem Malik (Markfield, UK: The Islamic Foundation, 2003), pp. 47–48.

69 Obviously, there are those institutions that do not want to contribute and are suspicious of building relationships with others not like them. In the context of London, the example of the Hasidic community is a case in point. The positive contribution of something like Hasidism is to stand as a sign of contradiction that questions the normative commitments and patterns of shared life that have emerged within the body politic. This is to be distinguished from antipolitical and politically antagonistic forms of consociation that actively undermine the formation of a common life. The task of BBCO is to enable *all* groups – whether they are a sign of contradiction, or political or antipolitical in orientation – to identify their convivial and place-based interest in building a common life with their neighbors. Yet organizers need to be more attuned to the kinds of involvement possible for certain groups given their religious or other commitments. In the case of the Hasidic community, this might entail messages of goodwill rather than active engagement.

70 Organizers regularly grade every institution in membership on a scale of A–D according to the criteria of whether an institution: (1) has an active leadership team in the institution-coordinating activity (ideally, 5–10 members), (2) pays dues, (3) attracts people to actions and meetings, (4) has members actively involved in campaigns, and (5) sends members on training.

71 There were signs that this was beginning to happen, but organizers need to engage with this question much more self-consciously and deliberately.

72 See, for example, Jeffrey Stout, *Democracy and Tradition* (Princeton, NJ: Princeton University Press, 2004).

73 On this account, to talk of democratic politics could be seen as tautological. However, it makes sense to retain the term "democratic politics" as we can posit other kinds of politics in which diverse interests and loyalties are considered and involved in the formation of a common life, only the circle of those interests and loyalties is much more limited. Thus "aristocratic politics," where only the diverse

interests and loyalties of privileged groups are considered and involved, is distinguishable from "democratic politics" that seeks to draw into the forging of a common life the interests and loyalties of all groups who live in a particular place.

74 Interview, September 11, 2008, London.

75 For example, at a meeting immediately prior to the May 3, 2010 General Election Assembly, instead of focusing on crucial organizational issues, most of the meeting was dominated by a discussion of how to accommodate Muslim sensibilities in any after-the-assembly party. In the event, this proved impossible given the limited range and expense of venues in the Westminster area.

76 It must also be recognized that involvement in broad-based community organizing by its nature rules out certain religious groups: in the case of London Citizens it was Orthodox and Hasidic Jews. Yet this does not invalidate the proposal to affirm interfaith relations understood as a civic practice. As my colleague Maurice Glasman witnessed, the elders of the Hasidic Jewish community and Muslims from a very conservative mosque in East London would meet regularly to collaborate on matters of common concern, namely, navigating relations with the local authorities regarding matters to do with burial and birthing practices and schooling. When it was proposed that they might undertake some form of externally orientated common action, both sets of elders readily agreed: the Muslims would clean up one park and the Jews another, both on the same day.

77 For a parallel account, see Coles, *Beyond Gated Politics,* p. 222.

78 Bretherton, *Christianity and Contemporary Politics*, pp. 86–88.

79 Crick, *In Defence of Politics*, p. 4.

80 Bretherton, *Christianity and Contemporary Politics*, pp. 32–45.

81 The promotion of dialogue and joint humanitarian endeavors is encapsulated in the 2008 white paper entitled *Face to Face and Side by Side: A Framework for Partnership in our Multi Faith Society* published by the Department for Communities and Local Government. At a global level, the central idea of this white paper received a direct echo in President Barack Obama's 2009 Cairo speech in which he called for both greater dialogue between Jews, Christians, and Muslims and what he named "interfaith service." The term "interfaith relations" is used in place of "interreligious relations" for no other reason than it is the more common term.

82 Examples of the kinds of specialist academic and institutional processes include colloquia organized by the World Council of Churches Office on Interreligious Relations in 1992 and 1993; the day of prayer for world peace at Assisi in 1986 and 2002 hosted by Pope John Paul II; the emergence of Scriptural Reasoning as a practice of Jews, Christians, and Muslims reading their Scriptures together; and the C-1 Dialogue process that has emerged in response to the 2007 statement by 138 Muslim scholars, clerics, and intellectuals, *A Common Word between Us and You*, available at: www.acommonword.com (last accessed December 12, 2012). For an account of contemporary Christian-Muslim dialogue initiatives, see Hugh Goddard, *A History of Christian-Muslim Relations* (Edinburgh: Edinburgh University Press, 2000), pp. 177–98. For an overview of developments in Britain specifically, see Ataullah Siddiqui, "Inter-Faith Relations in Britain since 1970 – An Assessment," *Exchange* 39.3 (2010): 236–50.

83 Jameson, "British Muslims – Influencing UK Public Life," p. 52.

84 Interview, December 16, 2008, London.

85 For example, Augustine contrasts two cities and the kinds of devotion that characterize each of them. The "earthly city," while commanding a proper *pietas*, is at root in opposition to God and is made up of members whose wills are orientated toward self and away from God (De. Civ. XV.7). The city of God consists of those whose primary *pietas* is toward God and whose wills are orientated away from themselves. Hence, Augustine relativizes the *pietas* that might be shown towards one's earthly *res public*.

86 On this, see Susan Bickford, *The Dissonance of Democracy: Listening, Conflict and Citizenship* (Ithaca, NY: Cornell University Press, 1996), pp. 25–53.

87 For a contemporary example of a cosmopolitan vision of citizenship, see Andrew Linklater, *Critical Theory and World Politics: Citizenship, Sovereignty and Humanity*, new ed. (London: Routledge, 2007).

88 Mrs. Jellyby is a character in Charles Dickens's *Bleak House* who is a "telescopic philanthropist" more concerned with an obscure African tribe than her duty of care to her family to the extent that she nearly destroys herself and them.

89 My use of the term *pietas* is more restricted than Stout's more expansive "Emersonian" use of the term piety (Stout, *Democracy and Tradition*, pp. 19–41). I see *pietas* as a synonym for the civic virtue of faithfulness, which, while more than a "splendid vice," can only ever subsist on and must be chastened by prior and more extensive forms of piety such as Christianity, Judaism, or Islam. In an echo of the "Euthyphro dilemma," the question is whether civic virtues are good in and of themselves or good insofar as they conform to a prior and superordinate tradition of belief and practice. If the former, then religious groups are bound to conform to a prior and superordinate democratic "creed" or "piety"; if the latter, then democracy can be jettisoned as simply an instrumental good when it conflicts with religious beliefs and practices. I do not propose to resolve this dilemma here, but I do want to suggest that an abstract philosophical consideration of this problem is no substitute for mapping ways in which this dilemma is constructively negotiated in practice. On this I take it that Stout and I entirely concur.

90 For examples of republican theorists who call for a national vision of citizenship, see David Miller, *On Nationality* (Oxford: Oxford University Press, 1995); Ross Poole, *Nation and Identity* (London: Routledge, 1999); and Charles Taylor, "Why Democracy Needs Patriotism," in *For Love of Country?* eds. Martha C. Nussbaum and Joshua Cohen (Boston: Beacon Press, 1996).

91 For parallel accounts of urban citizenship, see Murray Bookchin, *From Urbanization to Cities: Towards a New Politics of Citizenship*, rev. ed. (London: Cassell, 1995); Engin F. Isin, *Being Political: Genealogies of Citizenship* (Minneapolis: University of Minnesota Press, 2002); and Robert Beauregard and Anna Bounds, "Urban Citizenship" in *Democracy, Citizenship and the Global City*, ed. Engin F. Isin (London: Routledge, 2000), pp. 243–56.

92 Interview, September 8, 2009, London.

93 *Ibid.*

94 In the debate about what characterizes a faith-based organization as distinct from other kinds of nongovernmental social welfare providers, a number of factors determine the extent to which religiously affiliated organizations have an explicitly religious identity. These include the internal culture, organizational structure, and program of service delivery. Variations in how these characteristics are related determine whether an organization appears to be religious or not. On this, see

Thomas H. Jeavons, "Identifying Characteristics of 'Religious' Organisations: An Exploratory Proposal," in *Sacred Companies: Organisational Aspects of Religion and Religious Aspects of Organisations*, eds. N. J. Demerath III, Peter Dobkin Hall, Terry Schmitt, and Rhys H. Williams (Oxford: Oxford University Press, 1998), pp. 79–95. London Citizens itself is very careful not to identify itself as a religious organization. Instead, the organization describes itself as an alliance of civil society or as representing civil society of which religious groups are a key part.

95 Harding, *Book of Jerry Falwell*, p.166.

96 Taxpayers Alliance Web site article, March 31, 2010.

97 This is made explicit in Gecan, *Effective Organizing for Congregational Renewal.*

98 In the United States, a distinction is sometimes drawn between faith-based community organizing and broad-based community organizing. However, even self-identified faith-based community organizing networks such as PICO are not necessarily identified as "religious" by external observers. Rather, they are often framed as "progressive" despite the involvement of many conservative congregations.

99 Talal Asad, "The Construction of Religion as an Anthropological Category," in *Genealogies of Religion: Discipline and Reasons of Power in Christianity and Islam* (Baltimore, MD: Johns Hopkins University Press, 1993), pp. 27–54. See also William Cavanaugh, *The Myth of Religious Violence: Secular Ideology and the Roots of Modern Conflict* (Oxford: Oxford University Press, 2009).

100 Here we can draw a contrast with conservative Protestants in the United States prior to the 1980s and the emergence of the Christian Right (Harding, *Book of Jerry Falwell,* p. 79). Harding argues that the New Christian Right activism from the 1980s onward ruptured an earlier cycle of engagement followed by marginalization by forming a new mode of engagement that also refused the terms and conditions of secular modernity and the self-marginalizing process (*ibid.*, p. 81). Whether it really did mark the kind of rupture Hardings suggests it did is another matter. Jon Shields's study of the pro-life movement in the 1990s and 2000s suggests many conservative Protestants (and Roman Catholics) intentionally avoid overtly theological speech in public settings and train activists in using "secular" discourses when making arguments for pro-life and other policy positions.

101 There is a widespread literature and debate about the nature of secularization in Britain since 1945. Most of it is focused on whether or not external processes of modernization do or do not lead to the decline in the public significance of religious belief and practice. Relatively little attention has been paid to the self-marginalizing effects of stances adopted by the churches.

102 For an example of self-censoring in practice, see the following analysis of the contributions of Anglican Bishops to debates in the House of Lords: Andrew Partington and Paul Bickley, *Coming Off the Bench: The Past, Present and Future of Religious Representation in the House of Lords* (London: Theos, 2007).

103 On this, see José Casanova, "Immigration and the New Religious Pluralism: A European Union/United States Comparison," in *Democracy and the New Religious Pluralism*, ed. Thomas F. Banchoff (Oxford: Oxford University Press, 2007), p. 63.

104 Arguably the same applies in the United States as well, where there was a distinct increase in the number and variety of broad-based community organizations from the 1990s onward (see Warren and Wood, *Faith-Based Community Organizing*).

This also mirrors developments among Evangelicals, for whom, as Jon Shields's analysis reveals, the real engagement in political life did not begin and end with the rise and fall of the Moral Majority in the 1980s (which on Shields's account was little more than a form of checkbook activism that failed to build a broad base). Rather, widespread conservative Evangelical involvement only really rose from 1992 onward (Jon Shields, *Democratic Virtues of the Christian Right* [Princeton, NJ: Princeton University Press, 2009], pp. 117–46).

105 Interview, March 31, 2011, London.

106 For an account of the intrinsic link between capitalism and the emergence of a disenchanted or simplistically secularist public sphere, see John Milbank, *Theology and Social Theory: Beyond Secular Reason* (Oxford: Blackwell, 1993), pp. 25–45; and John Milbank, "'On Baseless Suspicion: Christianity and the Crises of Socialism," in *The Future of Love: Essays in Political Theology* (Eugene, OR: Cascade Books, 2009), pp. 112–29. For Milbank, any true critique of capitalism has to begin with a moral critique.

107 For a critique of how an emphasis on consensus denies the inherently political and contestable nature of the existing hegemony in liberal democracy and thereby excludes religious and other discourses, see Chantal Mouffe, *The Democratic Paradox* (London: Verso, 2000), pp. 17–35.

108 Although there is a debate as to how to relate the different New Testament uses of the term *kosmos*, I contend that these uses can be integrated within the overarching notion of cosmopolis: each term is an element of and a synecdoche for the whole order of the cosmos, with each usage denoting a different set of relations (including a sinful set of relations) within the overall relationship set that constitutes the whole. I have chosen to use the New Testament conception of *kosmos* (κόσμος) as distinct from Augustine's term, the *saeculum,* because, as the wide-ranging exegetical debates that surround Augustine's use of the term *saeculum* reveal, Augustine is much more ambiguous than the New Testament about the possibility of common objects of love being forged between Christians and non-Christians in the non-eschatological order. Arguably, the very concept of the secular is itself a theological construct, determined as it is in contradistinction to either the *eschaton* (its original theological meaning), the institutional church or, as it came to be known, "'religion." For an account of the secular as a theological category determined by its relationship to eschatology, see Robert A. Markus, *Christianity and the Secular* (Notre Dame, IN: University of Notre Dame Press, 2006). For my engagement with the use of the term *saeculum,* see Bretherton, *Christianity and Contemporary Politics*, pp. 81–88.

109 For a comparison of Plato's influential conceptualization of cosmos in the *Timaeus* and how it contrasts with the Pauline use of the term, see Edward Adams, *Constructing the World: A Study in Paul's Cosmological Language* (Edinburgh: T & T Clark, 2000).

110 Such a view is implicit in Taylor's account of the relationship between cosmos and chaos: the domestication and healing of deserts and wilderness spaces, which are seen as subject to the forces of chaos (whether bestial or demonic), involves making them part of the cosmic order (*Secular Age*, pp. 335–37). The openness of what is subject to chaos to healing and redemption is in no way to domesticate the kind of threat chaos poses as a form of nonbeing within Christian theology. As Karl Barth notes, "'Why is it that the being of the creature is menaced by nothingness,

menaced in such a way that it needs the divine preservation and sustaining and indeed deliverance if it is not to fall victim to it and perish? Obviously it is menaced by something far more serious than mere non-being as opposed to being, although it is of course menaced by non-being too. But what makes non-being a menace, an enemy which is superior to created being, a threatened destroyer, is obviously not its mere character as non-being, but the fact that it is not elected and willed by God the Creator, but rather rejected and excluded. It is that to which God said No when He said Yes to the creature. And that is chaos according to the biblical term and concept" (*Church Dogmatics: The Doctrine of Creation*, vol. III.3, trans, G. W. Bromiley and R. J. Ehrlich [Edinburgh: T & T Clark, 1960], pp. 75–76).

111 It is at precisely this point that there is a need to develop the New Testament conceptuality further and engage with the kind of theological framework developed by Augustine. Augustine wrestles with how to integrate a Platonic conception of what it meant to participate in the *kosmos* understood as a harmonious order and Christian understandings of the *kosmos* as something created yet fallen and redeemed.

112 Axial Age theory posits a similar, sociologically driven account of how Judaism and thence Christianity come to delineate a gulf between a true and good order and the order realized concretely by any given society. The distinction then serves to provide a horizon against which a real, existing political order can be criticized. On this, see Salvatore, *Public Sphere*, pp. 53–67. Salvatore goes on to outline how the tension between a transcendent vision of the good and concrete political order shapes overlapping notions of the public sphere in Islam, Judaism, and Christianity and their shared Aristotelian inheritance.

113 For the Pauline basis to this claim, see John M. G. Barclay, *Pauline Churches and Diaspora Jews* (Tübingen: Mohr Siebeck, 2011), pp. 363–87.

114 For an account of Augustine's view of slavery, see Peter Garnsey, *Ideas of Slavery from Aristotle to Augustine* (Cambridge: Cambridge University Press, 1996). For an analysis of the New Testament and early church's attitude to slavery along Augustinian lines, see Oliver O'Donovan, *The Desire of the Nations: Rediscovering the Roots of Political Theory* (Cambridge: Cambridge University Press, 1996), pp. 184–86, 264–66.

115 The key distinction here is between a Platonic notions of *epistrophē*, entailing a protological sense of recollection, return to origin, refinement, and perfection of what is already present at the point of origin, and a Christian sense of *metanoia*, denoting an eschatological sense of rebirth or recapitulation of the origin in new ways and a rupture with existing patterns through a radical recalibration and redirection. Foucault's insightful discussion of this distinction misses the protological and eschatological distinction between the Platonic and Christian visions of conversion. See Michel Foucault, *The Hermeneutics of the Subject: Lectures at the College de France, 1981–82*, trans. Graham Burchill (New York: Palgrave MacMillan, 2005), pp. 205–66. Hence, he is overly focused on kenotic forms of self-cultivation and it would seem is unable to encompass or even notice forms that combine ascetic holiness with ecstatic worship, healing practices, and millenial fervor such as Montanism and, most recently, Pentecostalism.

116 Peter Brown's magisterial study of the gradual shift in conceptions of poverty under the influence of Christianity is a case study of such radical yet incremental change over time. Peter Brown, *Through the Eye of a Needle: Wealth, the Fall of*

Rome, and the Making of Christianity in the West, 350–550 AD* (Princeton, NJ: Princeton University Press, 2012).

117 Taylor, *Secular Age*, pp. 123–30. Although Taylor also makes reference to the term cosmos, he does not pay sufficient heed to the important differences between the Christian and Platonic conceptions, neither does he account for the range of uses of the term in the New Testament (see *ibid.*, p. 158).

118 *Ibid.*, p. 323.

119 *Ibid.*, p. 284.

120 *Ibid.*, p. 349.

121 *Ibid.*, p. 351.

122 The irony is that Weber himself was sensitive to the interrelationship and symbiosis between the construction of political and economic orders and religious traditions of belief and practice, as is evidenced in his account of the relationship between Protestantism and capitalism. That being said, the impact of Weber's teleological account of processes of modernization, rationalization, and disenchantment is to close off the contemporary context from experiencing a parallel symbiosis.

123 What all such contradictions share is an animus toward capitalism and processes of commodification since such processes sever the link between the meaning of a thing and its exchange value. Such a severing depends on the view that meanings are only ever ascribed rather than inherent to a thing. Thus, whether it is ping-pong or playing fields, everything can be bought and sold as units of equivalent value within the market and nothing is sacred or priceless. One of the differences between the Christian Right in the United States and broad-based community organizing is, on this account, that the Christian Right, for all its assertion of religious discourse in public, actually mirrors the flat and mechanistic view of reality of its atheist counterparts (on this, see Taylor, *Secular Age*, pp. 330–32). To the Christian Right, capitalism does not appear problematic because it is understood as a providential mechanism within an enclosed system without mystery. The parallel myopia regarding the negative consequences of capitalism by the new atheists and the Christian Right is striking in this regard.

124 Stanley Marrow, "κόσμος in John," *The Catholic Biblical Quarterly* 64 (2002): 90–102.

125 Some will criticize what has just been said as an initiative to renew a form of metaphysical humanism that is inconsistent with liberal "ends" such as autonomy, freedom, and equality. Whether it is inconsistent or not with such ends is a matter of dispute, but the charge as regards the advocacy of some form of metaphysical humanism is counted here a virtue rather than a vice.

4 An Anatomy of Organizing I: Listening, Analysis, and Building Power

1 For an account of how IAF goes about forming a BBCO in a particular place, see Gecan's account of the formation of East Brooklyn Congregations in Gecan, *Going Public*, pp. 9–46. For an account of a process of refounding a BBCO where previous ones had gone into abeyance, see Chambers, *Roots for Radicals*, pp. 112–21.

2 In distinction from primary or key leaders, straightforward "leaders" were defined simply as those who had followers: that is, other people who trusted them and would attend events or meetings if that leader asked them. This could be anyone within an institution.

3 Stout, *Blessed Are the Organized*, p. 95.
4 *Ibid.*, p. 105.
5 For a comparison of the two approaches in practice see Celina Su, *Streetwise for Book Smarts: Grassroots Organizing and Education Reform in the Bronx* (Ithaca, NY: Cornell University Press, 2009).
6 Su notes that contemporary Freirean organizers in New York no longer subscribe to an exclusively Marxist framework and the approach has been adapted in recent years to include a number of interpretative frameworks, most notably, race (*ibid.*, pp. 80–81).
7 The City Bridges Trust began disbursing money for charitable works in Greater London in 1995 but its origins date back to 1097 when William Rufus, second son of William the Conqueror, raised a special tax to help repair London Bridge. The original aim of the trust was the building and upkeep of the bridges across the Thames, and it is on the basis of money accumulated over the centuries from legacies, bequests, and revenues related to these bridges that it makes its grants. Available at: www.bridgehousegrants.org.uk/CityBridgeTrust/TheTrust/History.htm (last accessed April 27, 2011).
8 For a discussion of how, even today, looking like a "punk" or "'hippie" recodes class and racial privilege among anarchists and alternative culture activists, see Graeber, *Direct Action*, pp. 239–41.
9 Horwitt, *Let Them Call Me Rebel*, p. 274; von Hoffman, *Radical*, p. 6.
10 The colloquium was jointly hosted by London Citizens; DICO; the Faith & Public Policy Forum, King's College London; The City Centre, Queen Mary, University of London; and the Faith & Citizenship Programme, London Metropolitan University, and was partly funded with money from my Arts and Humanities Research Council grant. It was a follow-on event from one organized in Berlin in June 2008, funded by the Volkswagon Foundation and organized by the Catholic Technical University; the Frei University, Berlin; the Great Cities Institute, University of Illinois in Chicago; The City Centre, Queen Mary, University of London; and the Industrial Areas Foundation.
11 Nick Mathiason, "Bring Back Usury Law to Control Interest Rates, Campaign Urges," *The Observer*, July 19, 2009.
12 Alice Fishburn, "Could Safe Havens Prevent Teenage Stabbings?" *The Times of London*, November 18, 2009.
13 Sean Coughlan, "Self-Help Plan to Make the Streets Safer," *BBC News*, August 10, 2010, available at: www.bbc.co.uk/news/education-10869719 (last accessed August 11, 2010).
14 For an account of the original Living Wage campaign in Baltimore, see Harvey, *Spaces of Hope*, pp. 124–30 and Snarr, *All You That Labor*; and of its adoption by other IAF affiliates in the United States, see Osterman, *Gathering Power*, pp. 150–57.
15 For a regularly updated chronology of the Living Wage campaign, see information at Queen Mary University of London, available at: http://www.geog.qmul.ac.uk/livingwage/chronology.html (last accessed November 8, 2010). For an extensive analysis of the campaign, see Jane Wills, "Campaigning for Low Paid Workers: The East London Communities Organisation (TELCO) Living Wage Campaign," in *The Future of Worker Representation*, eds. Geraldine Healy, Edmund Heery, Phil Taylor, and William Brown (Oxford: Oxford University Press, 2004), pp. 264–82; and Wills et al., "Religion at Work," pp. 443–61.

16 Constant J. Mews and Ibrahim Abraham, "Usury and Just Compensation: Religious and Financial Ethics in Historical Perspective," *Journal of Business Ethics* 72.1 (2007): 1–15, p. 6.
17 The precise ways in which interest rate ceilings are calculated vary from country to country, with some having a relative and others an absolute ceiling.
18 A similar criticism of the "10% is Enough" campaign was given by one of the U.S. advisors to that initiative: the Center for Responsible Lending.
19 Alinsky, *Reveille*, p. 54.
20 Interview November 7, 2008, Chicago. See also Chambers, *Roots for Radicals*, p. 47.
21 Gecan, *Effective Organizing*, p. 7. Gecan discusses the one-to-one in a pamphlet published by ACTA. This small, Chicago-based, Roman Catholic publishing house directly contributes to IAF's organizational culture of self-reflection. The ACTA pamphlets are written by key leaders and organizers and widely distributed for free among affiliates, including those in Britain, Germany, and Australia. The pamphlets are often used as the basis for reflection on organizing by organizers and by organizers with leaders. ACTA describes itself in the following terms: "ACTA Publications began in 1957 as a publisher of books and audio/video resources for Catholic religious education and marriage preparation. It has since broadened its editorial scope to include a wide variety of materials for those attempting to live out the Christian faith in their daily lives, on their jobs, with their families, and in their communities" (available at: www.actapublications.com/about/ [last accessed May 9, 2011]).
22 The other three he cites are: power (relational) analysis, teaching and training, and action and evaluation (*ibid.*, p. 7).
23 *Ibid.*, pp. 8–11. See also Chambers, *Roots for Radicals*, pp. 44–54.
24 Cortés, *Rebuilding Our Institutions,* pp. 12–13. Cortés echoes Chambers's analysis. See Chambers, *Roots for Radicals*, pp. 16–19.
25 For a parallel and more expansive reading of the importance of face-to-face meetings for the IAF, see Stout, *Blessed Are the Organized*, pp. 148–64.
26 Gecan defines public action as "when more than one person, focused on a specific issue, engages a person in power directly for that issue, for the purpose of getting a reaction. Twenty seniors meeting with a powerful politician about the cost of prescription drugs is an action. Eight parents pressing the local school principal to improve pedestrian safety about the local school is an action" (Gecan, *Going Public,* pp. 50–51).
27 Alinsky, *Rules*, p. 21.
28 Alinsky, *Reveille*, p. 156.
29 See, in particular, Rogers, *Cold Anger,* pp. 188–92; and Stout, *Blessed are the Organized*, pp. 64–69.
30 Citizens UK, "The Tent of Presence: The Church in the United Kingdom in the 1990's (Revised 2010)," pp. 4–5.
31 Chambers, *Roots for Radicals*, p. 108. A contrast can be drawn between the IAF vision of grief/anger and the more melancholic and quietist vision put forward by Judith Butler in *Precarious Life: The Powers of Mourning and Violence* (London: Verso, 2004).
32 The "mothers of the disappeared" refers to the "Mothers of the Plaza de Mayo" a social movement in Argentina formed by the mothers of those who were "disappeared" in what was called the "dirty war" in Argentina (1976–83).

33 Taylor, *Secular Age*, pp. 215–18.

34 Stout, *Blessed Are the Organized*, p. 65. For a broader critique of consensus as a key value in political liberalism and deliberative democracy, see Danielle S. Allen, *Talking to Strangers: Anxieties of Citizenship since Brown v. Board of Education* (Chicago: University of Chicago Press, 2004), pp. 53–68.

35 Gordon Wood argues that a crucial innovation in the American Revolution was the shift to a notion of representative democracy where the representative was seen to have a mutual interest with those being represented. He cites the arguments of William Findley in 1786 against those seeking to recharter the Bank of North America. Findley contended that those in favor of rechartering were trying to pose as disinterested gentleman of the classical, magnanimous mold who were above financial interests and concerned only with the public good. But they were in fact "interested in it personally, and therefore by promoting it they were acting as judges in their own cause." Findley sees nothing wrong in this as long as they come clean and admit their interest and did not protest when others, with different interests, advocated their own causes. As Wood notes: "If representatives were elected to promote the particular interests and private causes of their constituents, then the idea that such representatives were simply disinterested gentlemen, squire worthies called by duty to shoulder the burdens of public service, became archaic" (Gordon Wood, "Democracy and the American Revolution," in *Democracy: The Unfinished Journey, 508 BC to AD 1993*, ed. John Dunn [Oxford: Oxford University Press, 1992], p. 103). The kind of discourse Findley articulates undermined the classical republican tradition of political leadership by a disinterested leisured aristocracy and opened the doors to political office for the laboring classes and the direct representation of their interests in the governance of the land.

36 Saul Alinsky, "The War on Poverty – Political Pornography," *The Journal of Social Issues* 21.1 (1965): 41–47, p. 43. On the importance of interrelating conflict and consensus in democratic approaches to problem solving see Briggs, *Democracy as Problem Solving*, pp. 42–45.

37 In 2003 Gibbons identified the grounds for a Competition Commission inquiry into the home credit or door-to-door lending market and in 2008 his paper, written with Sir Ian McCartney, concerning the position of low-income borrowers in the current financial crisis led directly to the Office of Fair Trading High Cost Credit Review.

38 Politicians and journalists repeatedly use the phrase "the goose that lays the golden egg" as a description of the City of London and the financial services industry in order to justify the importance of the banking sector to the British economy and tax revenues, and thereby delegitimize attempts to limit or regulate it. It continues to be used even after the financial crisis. For a representative example of the kind of arguments the phrase became a touchstone for, see Chris Blackhurst, "Don't Kill the City Goose that Lays the Golden Egg," *Evening Standard*, December 16, 2010.

39 For a parallel account of a power analysis, this time of New Orleans, see Stout, *Blessed Are the Organized*, pp. 55–64.

40 For a more extensive critique of the dualistic conception of power used by the IAF and the need to take account of cultural power/"organized knowledge" as a source, if not a mode, of power that is a vital complement to the emphasis on "organized people" and "organized money," see Boyte, *Everyday Politics*, pp. 54–56, 179–82; Boyte, *Civic Agency*; and Harry Boyte and Eric Fretz, "Civic Professionalism," *Journal of Higher Education Outreach and Engagement* 14.2 (2010): 67–90. Boyte

notes that unless organized knowledge is addressed directly, then what he calls "the cult of the expert" and the ways in which professional and academic knowledge production pacifies and undermines active citizenship cannot be addressed. However, the emphasis on popular education and the actual ways in which organizers work with academics suggests the practice of organizers is ahead of their theory of organizing.

41 Stout, *Blessed Are the Organized*, pp. 105–06.

42 *Ibid.*, p. 104.

43 This is not the whole story; U.S. initiatives such as Public Achievement, Campus Compact (and the Wingspread Declaration), and the American Commonwealth Project point to attempts to recover a vision of universities "as agents and architects of democracy." For details, see the Center for Democracy and Citizenship (available at: www.augsburg.edu/democracy/index.html [last accessed May 20 2013]) and Campus Compact (available at: www.compact.org [last accessed May 20, 2013]).

44 George J. Stigler, "The Theory of Economic Regulation," *The Bell Journal of Economics and Management Science* 2.1 (1971): 3–21.

45 "Groupthink" as a term dates back to the work of William H. Whyte but was most fully articulated by the social psychologist Irving Janis. Janis understood groupthink to occur when peer and time pressures lead to a deterioration of "mental efficiency, reality testing, and moral judgment" (*Victims of Groupthink: A Psychological Study of Foreign Policy Decisions and Fiascoes* [New York: Houghton Mifflin, 1972], p. 9). Groups affected by groupthink ignore alternatives and tend to take irrational actions that dehumanize other groups based on a desire for consensus and the suppression of critical evaluations and dissenting voices. A group is especially vulnerable to groupthink when its members are similar in background and when the group is insulated from outside opinions.

46 Community auditing and "community-based" action research projects represent parallel ways of generating an independent community of interpretation. For examples of this kind of work, see the work of the Community Audit and Evaluation Centre, available at: http://www.ioe.mmu.ac.uk/caec/ (last accessed May 26, 2011).

47 Albert O. Hirschman, *Exit, Voice, and Loyalty: Responses to Decline in Firms, Organizations, and States* (Cambridge, MA: Harvard University Press, 1970).

48 On the relationship between the IAF and the "iron law of oligarchy," see Osterman, *Gathering Power*, pp. 67–73.

49 Alinsky, *Rules*, p. 119.

50 For a critical reflection on Foucault and the IAF's related but divergent conceptions of power, see Stout, *Blessed Are the Organized*, pp. 301–03, n. 33.

51 Amy Gutmann and Dennis F. Thompson, *Democracy and Disagreement* (Cambridge, MA: Harvard University Press, 1996), p. 77. In fairness to Gutmann and Thompson, they are not calling citizens to revoke strong moral convictions. Rather, as they put it, they seek the kind of people who are "morally committed, self-reflective about their commitment, discerning of the difference between respective and merely tolerable differences of opinion, and open to the possibility of changing their minds or modifying their position at some time in the future if they confront unanswerable objections to their point of view" (*ibid.*, pp. 79–80).

52 Shields, *Democratic Virtues*, p. 153.

53 *Ibid.*, p. 3
54 For an account of how many forms of associational life can produce the opposite effect and depoliticize participants, see Nina Eliasoph, *Avoiding Politics: How Americans Produce Apathy in Everyday Life* (Cambridge: Cambridge University Press, 1998). The implications of Eliasoph's work underscores the need for community organizers and undermines the assumption that forms of voluntary and other association necessarily or inevitably contribute to promoting a democratic public life.
55 Shields, *Democratic Virtues*, p. 16.
56 Alinsky, *Rules*, p. 59.
57 The tension between the demands for achieving "insider" and maintaining "outsider" status frequently manifested itself in internal debates in Citizens UK and came to a head when the IAF organizer, Arnie Graf, began working directly with the Labour Party in 2011.
58 For Alinsky's discussion of power, see *Rules*, pp. 49–53. For an overview of different conceptions of power, see Steven Lukes, "Power and Authority," in *A History of Sociological Analysis*, eds. Tom Bottomore and Robert Nisbet (New York: Basic Books, 1978), pp. 633–76.
59 As noted in Chapter 1, Arendt sketched an initial conception of relational power ("On Violence," pp. 105–98; *On Revolution* [London: Penguin, 1977], pp. 166–67). For a critique of Arendt's concept of relational power as insufficiently attentive to the nonviolent but nevertheless coercive dimensions of relational power, see Jane Mansbridge, "Using Power/Fighting Power: The Polity," in *Democracy and Difference*, ed. Seyla Benhabib (Princeton, NJ: Princeton University Press, 1996), pp. 46–66. Cortés developed his distinction between unilateral and relational power through drawing on the work of Bernard Loomer whose account explores some of the theological issues from the perspective of process theology ("Two Conceptions of Power," *Process Studies*, 6.1 [1976]: 5–32). For his account of relational power, see Cortés, "Reweaving the Fabric," pp. 295–319. Chambers further specifies this distinction (Chambers, *Roots for Radicals*, pp. 27–31). The distinction between "power with" and "power over" originates with Mary Parker Follett, *Creative Experience* (New York: Longman, Green & Co, 1930 [1924]). Most modern political thought, with its emphasis on the nature of sovereign power, has focused almost exclusively on unilateral power. Interestingly, although Steven Lukes identifies the two conceptions of power outlined here, he fails to develop this distinction in his own account of power, thus conforming to the general emphasis on sovereign/unilateral power already noted. See Steven Lukes, *Power: A Radical View*, 2nd ed. (New York: Palgrave Macmillan, 2005).
60 Chambers, *Roots for Radicals*, p. 28.
61 Alinsky, *Reveille*, p. 17. There is a strong overlap between what Alinsky is saying here and the emphasis on the importance of participation in society in modern Roman Catholic social teaching. See, for example, United States Conference of Catholic Bishops, *Economic Justice for All: Pastoral Letter on Catholic Social Teaching and the U.S. Economy* (Washington, DC: U.S. Catholic Conference, 1986), section 77 that states: "These fundamental duties can be summarized this way: *basic justice demands the establishment of minimum levels of participation in the life of the human community for all persons.* The ultimate injustice is for a person or group to be treated actively or abandoned passively as if they were

nonmembers of the human race. To treat people this way is effectively to say they simply do not count as human beings. This can take many forms, all of which can be described as varieties of marginalization, or exclusion from social life." The letter goes on to describe acts of exclusion as a social sin.

62 On the ways technocratic professionals depoliticize and monopolize tasks, disable popular agency, and act as a barrier to lay participation in solving shared problems, see Dzur, *Democratic Professionalism*, pp. 85–101.

63 Rose, "Saul Alinsky, the Industrial Areas Foundation and the Church's Millions," pp. 4–9.

64 Horwitt, *Let Them Call Me Rebel*, p. 531.

65 Stears, *Demanding Democracy*, p. 15.

66 *Ibid.*, p. 208. This anxiety about the use of coercive means in democratic politics is expressed by many who become involved in organizing. See, for example, Swarts, *Organizing Urban America*, pp. 12–13. It is also widespread among advocates of participatory democracy. See, for example, Mark Warren, "Deliberative Democracy and Authority," *American Political Science Review* 90 (1996): 46–60; and Benjamin R. Barber, *Strong Democracy: Participatory Politics for a New Age* (Berkeley: University of California Press, 1984).

67 For an account of how the IAF's relational view of power relates to and can extend Foucault's analysis of power, see Stout, *Blessed Are the Organized*, pp. 302–03 n. 33.

68 For an account of the centrality and adoption of Roman law into Western political and social conceptions of sovereignty and the theological debates that mediated this, see Jean Bethke Elshtain, *Sovereignty: God, State, and Self* (New York: Basic Books, 2008).

69 For an enormously helpful discussion of the differing conceptions of public and private on which this account draws, see Jeff Weintraub, "The Theory and Politics of the Public/Private Distinction," in *Public and Private in Thought and Practice: Perspectives on a Grand Dichotomy*, eds. Jeff Weintraub and Krishan Kumar (Chicago: University of Chicago Press, 1997), pp. 1–42.

70 For an account of legislation as limiting domination so as to ensure freedom from domination, see Ian Shapiro, *The State of Democratic Theory* (Princeton, NJ: Princeton University Press, 2003), pp. 51–55.

71 In this respect, the IAF and other networks contrast sharply with advocates of deliberative democracy who are extremely wary of notions of leadership. For example, Benjamin Barber states that leadership is "opposed to participatory self-government; it acts in place of or to some degree encroaches on the autonomy of individual actors" (*Strong Democracy*, p. 238).

72 This is parallel to but distinct from Stout's concept of an "earned entitlement to deference." Stout, *Blessed Are the Organized*, p. 100.

73 A good account of how leadership within the IAF works is given in Warren, *Dry Bones Rattling*, pp. 228–37.

74 Barbara Cruikshank, *The Will to Empower: Democratic Citizens and Other Subjects* (Ithaca, NY: Cornell University Press, 1999), pp. 23–24.

75 Sheldon Wolin, "What Revolutionary Action Means Today," in *Dimensions of Radical Democracy: Pluralism, Citizenship, Community*, ed. Chantal Mouffe (London: Verso, 1992), p. 245.

76 I am not claiming BBCO represents the only way of ushering in this movement, but it is a particularly generative example. The movement from private or group

self-interest to seeking the public interest through forms of what Boyte calls "public work" can be ushered by a diverse range of agencies from educational institutions, "social" businesses, and professional commitments entailed in such areas of expertise as medicine or engineering or design. What is vital is some sense of the work being undertaken and the institutional and organizational priorities attending to how the action strengthens the common life and civic agency of all those involved.

77 The definition and particular use of the term "self-interest" is something the IAF has in common with other community organizing networks. Other networks can frame the nature of self-interest in more overtly theological terms while sharing the same basic conception. On this, see Hart, *Cultural Dilemmas,* pp. 66–73.

78 Alinsky, *Rules*, p. 58; and *Reveille*, p. 93.

79 On this, see Merold Westphal, *Suspicion and Faith: The Religious Uses of Modern Atheism* (New York: Fordham University Press, 1998).

80 Alinsky, *Rules*, p. 23.

81 Alinsky, *Reveille*, p. 94.

82 The term "'Machiavellian" is being used here in its rhetorical and polemical sense. Machiavelli's civic republicanism effectively subsumes the pursuit of individual glory to the pursuit of the needs and glory of the republic.

83 Alexis de Tocqueville, *Democracy in America*, trans. Gerald Bevan (London: Penguin, 2003), p. 612. Tocqueville distinguishes between egoistic or brutal self-interest and *l'intérêt bien entendu* or what in English translates as "'self-interest rightly understood." For Tocqueville, self-interest rightly understood refers not to disinterested actions (although he notes that this is, in fact, what is actually going on) but to helping others recognize that one's own welfare is bound up in the welfare of others, and conversely, the pursuit of one's own interest to the exclusion of all others is likely to lead to losing everything (pp. 611–12). Rather than deploy the inherently usurious term "'interest" to interpersonal relations, the term "'mutual aid" can be posited as a more accurate one for describing what Tocqueville is attempting to articulate in the term "self-interest rightly understood." However, with the spread of capitalist and contractual relations as paradigmatic of all human relations, it is precisely relations of mutual aid that are having to be justified and framed within the new logic of "interest." This issue is discussed further in Chapter 8.

84 This is an aperçu borrowed from Roy Porter, *English Society in the Eighteenth Century*, 2nd ed. (London: Penguin, 2001), p. 145.

85 Arendt, *Human Condition*, p. 182. Chambers explicitly links the IAF conception of self-interest to that developed by Arendt. See Chambers, *Roots for Radicals*, p. 25.

86 Arendt, *Human Condition*, p. 183.

87 As C. B. Macpherson observed, for Hobbes, the state of nature is: "A statement of the behaviour to which men as they now are, men who live in civilised societies and have the desires of civilised men, would be led if all law and contract enforcement (i.e. even the present imperfect enforcement) were removed. To get to the state of nature, Hobbes has set aside law, but not the socially acquired behaviour and desires of men" (*The Political Theory of Possessive Individualism: Hobbes to Locke* [Oxford: Oxford University Press, 1962], p. 22). On Macpherson's controversial reading, Hobbes's "state of nature" is not a reconstruction or postulation

of a prehistorical condition, but a *Lord of the Flies* vision in which those socialized within the social mores of a market society are left without restraint. For Hobbes, the social logic of a market society without a strong sovereign power is "solitary, poor, nasty, brutish and short."

88 For an account of the importance of "office" as a regulatory institution of the civil sphere that carries certain procedural norms and moral obligations that transcend the individual and their personal interests or political views and which office holders can be held accountable to by other actors within the civil sphere, see Jeffrey Alexander, *Civil Sphere* (Oxford: Oxford University Press, 2006), pp. 132–50. Alexander outlines the ecclesial origins of contemporary political and bureaucratic conceptions of office as a regulatory institution.

89 The formulation of contradiction in this way was first set out in Bretherton, *Christianity and Contemporary Politics,* p. 79.

90 It should be noted that issues – and the contradictions they articulate – are always under a process of evaluation, revision, and refinement in community organizing. Thus, they are likely to evolve and change over time.

91 On the dynamics of mimetic rivalry, see René Girard, *Violence and the Sacred*, trans. Patrick Gregory (Baltimore, MD: Johns Hopkins University Press, 1977).

5 An Anatomy of Organizing II: Rules, Actions, and Representation

1 In Sydney Alliance, there is a division between soft and hard money; however, it functions differently. There are very few foundations funding the work of Sydney Alliance, so it is not dependent on soft money. The majority of its funds come from membership dues; however, these dues are paid by national or regional organizations and not by local institutions. This means that union or denominational officials pay them, yet these same people cannot generate turnout and are not directly accountable to locally embedded organizations. Organizers and leaders reported that these officials are anxious about letting go of control to local institutions, yet they dominate the overarching leadership of the alliance. The effect is that hard money functions like soft money in determining the agenda and also leads to a focus on issues rather than putting people before program.

2 Interview, June 3, 2008, London.

3 The lead trust behind this initiative was the Diana Princess of Wales Memorial Fund.

4 From 2006 to 2008 the commission reviewed the UK asylum system and came up with 180 recommendations to safeguard refugees seeking sanctuary. These recommendations are contained in the following reports by the commission: *Saving Sanctuary: How we restore public support for sanctuary and improve the way we decide who needs sanctuary*; *Safe Return: How to improve what happens when we refuse people sanctuary*; and *Deserving Dignity: How to improve the way we treat people seeking sanctuary.*

5 See Marshall Ganz, "Why David Sometimes Wins: Strategic Capacity in Social Movements," in *The Psychology of Leadership: New Perspectives and Research*, eds. David M. Messick and Roderick M. Kramer (Mahwah, NJ: Lawrence Erlbaum Associates, 2005), pp. 209–38; and Ganz, *Why David Sometimes Wins.*

6 Ganz, *Why David Sometimes Wins*, p. 14.

7 *Ibid.*, p. 19.

8 In her extensive study of deliberative and decision-making styles in different forms of participatory democracy, Polletta identifies this kind of decision making as involving a "complex equality" that allows people "to learn from each other without feeling patronized or imposed on" (*Freedom Is an Endless Meeting*, p. 208). The paradigm is one of friendship rather than legal process. Such an approach relies on a high degree of trust. As Polletta points out, the danger with it is that it can tend toward the formation of cliques and the creation of oligarchies.

9 Of the thirty-two organizers surveyed, twenty had attended a Russell Group university and of them, seven had attended Oxford or Cambridge.

10 In turn, this was further intensified in a parallel initiative called the Jellicoe Society that established a link between Oxford University and London Citizens. Reverend Dr. Angus Ritchie, who was simultaneously Fellows Chaplain at Magdalene College, Oxford, and ran the Centre for Contextual Theology in Shadwell, East London, set it up to create links between Christian students and institutions in membership of London Citizens. Instead of focusing on a specific campaign, as in the Summer Academy, the students would focus on strengthening the links between congregations and London Citizens. This initiative was part of a self-conscious attempt to revive a link between Oxford and London's East End established by Father John Basil Jellicoe, an alumnus of Magdalene and vicar of St. Mary's, Somers Town, in the 1920s. Father Jellicoe was actively involved in housing reform.

11 Osterman, *Gathering Power*, p. 55.

12 Alinsky, *Rules*, pp. 60–61; von Hoffman, *Radical*, p. 81. For an account of what is involved in being an organizer, see Osterman, *Gathering Power*, pp. 54–58.

13 Taking advantage of an emphasis in policy discourses on localism and the devolution of parliamentary institutions to Scotland and Wales, Citizens UK made renewed efforts from 2009 onward to establish affiliates outside of London, notably in Milton Keynes, Cardiff, Glasgow, and Nottingham. It also worked to reestablish an organization in Birmingham, while at the same time expanding and further localizing its efforts in London, through, for example, the establishment of a neighborhood-specific organization in 2011: Shoreditch Citizens.

14 Alinsky, *Rules*, p. 165.

15 By way of contrast, see Graeber's discussion of anarchist styles of direct action (Graeber, *Direct Action*, pp. 359–434). In contemporary anarchism, an emphasis on the festive has been key and, through the influence of such things as Situationist notions of psychogeography, so has an attention to place.

16 For an example of the disempowering effects of de-spatialization on the conditions and possibilities of democratic politics and the efforts to re-spatialize democratic power under acute conditions, see Stout's account of the IAF's work in post-Katrina New Orleans (Stout, *Blessed Are the Organized*, pp. 21–52).

17 Alinsky, *Rules*, p. 128.

18 For an example that illustrates how Alinsky's rules both operate in practice and contain inherent tricksterism, see Alinsky, *Rules*, p. 141.

19 See Romand Coles, "Of Tensions and Tricksters: Grassroots Democracy between Theory and Practice," *Perspectives on Politics* 4.03 (2006): 547–61.

20 For a parallel account of the role of the festive and religious ritual in living wage actions in the United States, see Snarr, *All You That Labor*, pp. 122–39.

21 The action took place on Wednesday, December 17, 2008.

22 The song was adapted by Bernadette Farrell, the lead organizer of South London Citizens and herself a noted writer of contemporary Catholic hymns. Songs are a prevalent feature of community organizing, among networks that work mostly with religious groups and those that do not. For example, the Midwest Academy, founded by Heather Booth, is primarily focused on working with nonreligious groups. Its widely used manual devotes an appendix to "Songs for Organizers," a number of which are overtly Christian, such as "Amazing Grace," or adapted from Christian songs (Bobo, Kendall, and Max, *Organizing for Social Change*).

23 As I have argued elsewhere, there is always the danger in the relationship between churches and community organizing that worship becomes subservient to effective political action rather than forming the People of God and shaping their witness in the world. Worship is thereby made subservient to its impact on society and reduced to a "'resource" for the moralization of the world. This does happen in community organizing (see, for example, Dennis Jacobsen's description of a "'pray-in" at the county courthouse in Milwaukee in *Doing Justice: Congregations and Community Organizing* [Minneapolis: Augsburg Fortress, 2001], pp. 36–37). For my critique of such an approach and the role of worship in community organizing more generally, see Bretherton, *Christianity and Contemporary Politics*, pp. 96–104. In anthropological terms, what is problematic about making political use of worship is that it takes what is most treasured and what in any event cannot be given, but only received as a gift – communion with God – and presumes to make of it an alienable thing that can be circulated among strangers.

24 See especially Alberto Melucci, *Challenging Codes: Collective Action in the Information Age* (Cambridge: Cambridge University Press, 1996); Karl-Dieter Opp, *Theories of Political Protest and Social Movements* (London: Routledge, 2009); and Jeffrey S. Juris "Performing Politics: Image, Embodiment, and Affective Solidarity during Anti-Corporate Globalization Protests," *Ethnography* 9.1 (2008): 61–97.

25 For a critique of this tendency in social movement theories that attend to the cultural dynamics of political mobilization, see Alexander, *Civil Sphere*, pp. 221–24.

26 Interview, September 24, 2008, London.

27 Interview, December 16, 2008, London.

28 *Ibid.*

29 At the meeting on April 27, 2010 at Conservative Party Headquarters in London a compromise was reached whereby it was agreed no direct yes-or-no answers would be demanded. Subsequent discussions among leaders and organizers as part of the evaluation of the meeting concluded that the primary goal of the assembly, in contrast to more local assemblies, was establishing a working relationship and not obtaining agreement to specific points of policy. This was felt to warrant relinquishing the demand of unequivocal responses. A solution proposed by Matthew Bolton was that on those questions the party leaders disagreed with the position of London Citizens, the person questioning them would clearly state the position of London Citizens as a contrast but not demand further response. At the actual event on May 3 the process was much more fluid, and although Cameron gave a clear indication where he disagreed with the Citizens UK manifesto and was "pinned" on his responses, there was considerable consternation at the event, and in subsequent evaluations it was judged that Gordon Brown was not as clear in his responses and was not pinned on all the issues.

30 Stout, *Blessed Are the Organized*, p. 121.

31 This was a rhetorical contrast as organizers are increasingly dependent on mobile phones and email. Organizers systematically collect email addresses from participants in meetings and actions in order to facilitate further communication and mobilization. From April 2010 they even began to employ an organizer, one of whose main responsibilities was mobilizing through online social networking sites such as Facebook and Twitter. Interestingly, the rhetorical tension between the online and face-to-face communication was negotiated at the launch of the Citizens UK blog on April 30, 2010 through the following statement: "Online social networking is no substitute for the face-to-face meetings (one-to-ones) which are the staple of community organising. Citizens UK is all about reweaving the fabric of society. But once relationships are formed, social networking is a great way of maintaining and deepening relationships" (available at: www.citizensukblog.org [last accessed April 30, 2010]).

32 As political theorist Jodi Dean puts it: "Uncoupled from contexts of action and application – as on the Web or in print and broadcast media – the message is simply part of a circulating data stream. Its particular content is irrelevant. Who sent it is irrelevant. Who receives it is irrelevant. That it need be responded to is irrelevant. The only thing that is relevant is circulation, the addition to the pool. Any particular contribution remains secondary to the fact of circulation. The value of any particular contribution is likewise inversely proportionate to the openness, inclusivity or extent of a circulating data stream – the more opinions or comments that are out there, the less of an impact any one given one might make (and the more shock, spectacle or newness is necessary for a contribution to register or have an impact). In sum, communication functions symptomatically to produce its own negation" ("Communicative Capitalism: Circulation and the Foreclosure of Politics," *Cultural Politics,* 1.1 [2005]: 51–74, p. 58).

33 It is Durkheim who first fully articulates such a conception of democracy as political communication. See Emile Durkheim, *Professional Ethics and Civic Morals* (London: Routledge, 2001 [1957]), pp. 76–109. For a contemporary account of democracy as political communication, see Paul Hirst, *Associative Democracy: New Forms of Economic and Social Governance* (Cambridge: Polity Press, 1994), pp. 35–43.

34 Use of the term "estates" draws on formulations of the medieval polity as constituted by those classes with property, power, and public rank or status (notably, the nobles, clergy, and townsmen or commons) that together constitute the body politic. It also has a theological register. The medieval conceptuality was used by Luther to describe that which structures the created order (Luther uses various terms ranging from *ordo*, *stand*, *genus vitae* to *hierarchia*). He names these estates as church (*ecclesia*), the household (*oeconomia*) and the civic life (*politia*). These spheres are distinct yet mutually constitutive and co-inhering spheres of communication and responsibility in which humans take up the tasks, offices, and vocations through which we love God and our neighbor.

35 Interview, June 5, 2009.

36 *Standing for the Whole* (Chicago: Industrial Areas Foundation, 1990), p. 1.

37 *Ibid.*, p. 2.

38 Mouffe, *Democratic Paradox,* p. 82.

39 Oliver O'Donovan, *Ways of Judgment* (Grand Rapids, MI: Eerdmans, 2005), p. 179.

40 *Ibid.*, p. 167.

41 On the importance of ongoing arenas of collective deliberation for sustaining political freedom and the role of self-organized associations in this, see Arendt, *On Revolution*, pp. 223–40.

42 O'Donovan, *Ways of Judgment*, p. 150.

43 Allen, *Talking to Strangers*, pp. 70–71.

44 *Ibid.*, p. 20.

45 For the genealogy of acclamation as a juridical-political act that mediates consent, enacts a procedure of legitimation, and constitutes a people, see Giorgio Agamben, *The Kingdom and the Glory: For a Theological Genealogy of Economy and Government* (Stanford, CA: Stanford University Press, 2011), pp. 169–93. However, Agamben does not distinguish its reciprocal, call-and-response forms from its unidirectional ones and therefore, following Schmitt, sees an emphasis on acclamation as necessarily "conservative" rather than democratic.

46 Stout, *Blessed Are the Organized*, p. 109.

47 The "notes" or marks of BBCO identified here overlap and complement those identified by Warren and Osterman. Warren, in his sociological study of the IAF, identifies five key component parts to it. It is focused on: (1) institutions, (2) relationship building, (3) being broad-based, (4) being independent and unaligned with any political party or government agency (particularly through an emphasis on being independently funded), and (5) has a clear authority structure, with professional organizers and leaders drawn from affiliated institutions making decisions (Warren, *Dry Bones Rattling*, pp. 30–36). Likewise, Osterman identifies five core "processes" that vary slightly from Warren's: (1) its relational techniques of one-to-one and house meetings, (2) listening and dialogue, (3) a particular conception of self-interest, (4) being broad-based (and how this constitutes a basis for being pragmatic), and (5) its religious values base (Osterman, *Gathering Power*, pp. 172–77).

48 These included a commitment by all three to meet regularly with Citizens UK. In addition, the Conservative Party leader committed to include Community Land Trusts as part of the Olympic Park, train 5,000 community organizers, and introduce a cap on interest rates on store cards. The Liberal Democrat leader committed to end the detention of children scheduled for deportation, as well as provide support for an initiative to regularize the status of undocumented migrants who were resident for ten or more years in the United Kingdom. The Labour Party leader committed to implement the living wage in Whitehall, make land available in order to establish Community Land Trusts, and explore an interest-rate cap alongside establishing a People's Bank to provide local affordable credit.

49 Will Heaven, "Gordon Brown's speech to Citizens UK Was Weird, Not a 'Barnstormer,'" *The Telegraph*, available at: http://blogs.telegraph.co.uk/news/willheaven/100037879/gordon-browns-speech-to-citizens-uk-was-weird-not-a-barnstormer/ (last accessed December 16, 2013).

50 For example, in collaboration with Marshall Ganz at the Kennedy School of Government, the National Health Service's Institute for Innovation and Improvement developed an extensive program using community organizing practices to address strategic issues such as end-of-life care.

51 Available at: http://www.movementforchange.org.uk/ (last accessed December 21, 2011).

52 See Maurice Glasman, "Labour As a Radical Tradition," in *The Labour Tradition and the Politics of Paradox*, eds. Maurice Glasman, Jonathan Rutherford, Marc Stears, and Stuart White (London: Soundings, 2011), pp. 14–34.

6 Civil Society as the Body Politic

1 Hannah Arendt, *Lectures on Kant's Political Philosophy*, ed. Ronald Beiner (Chicago: University of Chicago Press, 1982), pp. 76–77.
2 This is an important point as, according to Gareth Stedman Jones, socialism itself is better understood "as a self proclaimed, science-based post-Christian religion or as a novel cosmology to which diverse forms of politics were at different time attached" ("Religion and the Origins of Socialism," in *Religion and the Political Imagination*, eds. Ira Katznelson, Gareth Jones, and Walter Goode [Cambridge: Cambridge University Press, 2007], p. 187). For Jones, such a definition applies equally to its "utopian" and "scientific" forms. However, Jones does not account for the emergence and persistence of various strands of explicitly Christian rather than "religious" socialism.
3 Graeber, *Direct Action*, pp. 11 and 328.
4 Graeber states: "Direct action represents a certain ideal – in its purest form probably unattainable. It is a form in which means and ends become effectively, indistinguishable; a way of actively engaging with the world to bring about change, in which the form of the action – or at least, the organization of the action – is itself a model for the change one wishes to bring about. At its most basic, it reflects a very simple anarchist insight: that one cannot create a free society through military discipline, a democratic society by giving orders, or a happy one through joyless self-sacrifice. At its most elaborate, the structure of one's own act becomes a kind of micro-utopia, a concrete model for one's own vision of a free society" (*ibid.*, p. 210).
5 *Ibid.*, p. 328.
6 For an account of Graeber's involvement in the initial stages of the Occupy movement and how he helped to establish the General Assemblies as the standard form adopted for decision making, see Drake Bennett, "David Graeber, the Anti-Leader of Occupy Wall Street," *Businessweek*, October 26, 2011 (available at: http://www.businessweek.com/magazine/david-graeber-the-antileader-of-occupy-wall-street-10262011.html [last accessed Dec. 3, 2011]). Graeber gives his own account of how the Occupy movement conforms to core anarchist principles and of his own involvement in it in David Graeber, *The Democracy Project: A History, a Crisis, a Movement* (New York: Spiegel & Grau, 2013).
7 Hakim Bey, "The Temporary Autonomous Zone, Ontological Anarchy, Poetic Terrorism" (available at: http://hermetic.com/bey/taz3.html#labelTAZ [last accessed November 4, 2011]). Although in contrast to Bey's conception of a TAZ, the St. Paul's Cathedral encampment was highly visible.
8 These reflections are based both on what those involved in the movement said of their actions in the "blogosphere," on observation of the Occupy London camp, and conversations with key figures involved. However, Pleyer confirms this analysis, identifying a consistent strategy of the alter-globalization movement from the 1990s onward as involving creating alternative spaces of experience and thence of subjectivity to those dominated by global corporations and processes of

commodification. Direct action – in all its forms – is being said to contrast with the passivity of consumerism. See Pleyers, *Alter-Globalization*, pp. 35–54.

9 Available at: http://occupyLSX.org/?page_id=575 (last accessed April 11, 2011).

10 Graeber, *Direct Action*, pp. 28 and 211.

11 Ya Basta! Collective and Direct Action Network press release, quoted in Graeber, *Direct Action*, p. 53.

12 *Ibid.*, p. 212.

13 *Ibid.*, p. 213. There is a strong historical warrant for Graeber's point. See Black, *Guild and State*, p. 184.

14 Graeber, *Direct Action*, p. 214.

15 A further historical parallel for BBCO as a practice-driven politics, one that is directly related to the development of anarchism and consociationalism via the work of Otto von Gierke, is that of the medieval guilds and communes. As Antony Black argues, the guilds were very influential on the political practices and governance of towns and cities throughout medieval Europe but, with the notable exception of Marsiglio of Padua, were almost entirely ignored in the theoretically driven political thought of the Scholastics and their contemporaries (*Guild and State*, pp. 66–95).

16 Proudhon famously remarks: "Il est surprenant qu'au fond de notre politique nous trouvions toujours la théologie" (*Les Confessions d'un Révolutionnaire* [Paris, 1849], p. 61). For a study of the theological significance of Proudhon's work, see Henri de Lubac, *The Un-Marxian Socialist: A Study of Proudhon*, trans. R. E. Scantlebury (London: Sheed and Ward, 1948).

17 Peter Marshall, *Demanding the Impossible: A History of Anarchism* (London: HarperCollins, 2008), p. 85. On the intersections of anarchism and religion, see also Lisa Kemmerer, "Anarchy: Foundations in Faith," in *Contemporary Anarchist Studies*, eds. Randall Amster, Abraham DeLeon, Luis Fernandez, Anthony J. Nocella II, and Deric Shannon (London: Routledge, 2009), pp. 200–12.

18 Graeber, *Direct Action*, pp. 43–44, 129, and 394. See also Polletta, *Freedom Is an Endless Meeting*.

19 Graeber, *Direct Action*, p. 487. The emphasis on imagination can be seen as a legacy of situationism on contemporary anarchism. Marshall echoes Graeber's emphasis on imagination in his evaluation on contemporary developments in anarchism (*Demanding the Impossible*, pp. 671–72).

20 For a detailed study of the place of ludic dimensions of contemporary political activism, see Benjamin Shepard, *Play, Creativity, and Social Movements* (London: Routledge, 2011).

21 Graeber hints at another connection between the sacred, the possibility of radical politics, and critiques of the status quo. He notes how early anarchism drew from those groups with some experience of non-alienated labor and some measure of autonomy over their means of production such as craftsman (by contrast, Marx dismissed the nineteenth-century anarchist base as a combination of "petty bourgeoisie" and "*lumpenproletariat*"). Likewise, in the twentieth century, bohemians such as writers, musicians, and artists, who also had some experience of non-alienated labor, were key to radical politics and creating alternative social imaginaries. We could postulate that another arena through which people generate alternative social imaginaries and experience a realm of non-alienated labor and a degree of autonomy from state and market procedures is in the experience of producing

worship. This is in accord with a key development in contemporary Christian political thought that envisages liturgy as a counter-performance to the politics of domination and oppression we experience in the nation-state. Worship as *leitourgia* represents a nonmonetized, noncompetitive form of work outside of the capitalist economy. On this, see Luke Bretherton, "Sharing Peace: Class, Hierarchy and Christian Social Order," in *The Blackwell Companion to Christian Ethics*, eds. Stanley Hauerwas and Sam Wells, rev. ed. (Oxford: Wiley-Blackwell, 2011), pp. 329–43.

22 Graeber, *Direct Action*, p. 222.

23 See, for example, Gecan, *Going Public*, pp. 49–53; and Chambers, *Roots for Radicals*, pp. 130–31.

24 Payne, *I've Got the Light of Freedom*, pp. 67–264.

25 Stears, *Demanding Democracy*, p. 169. See also Payne, *I've Got the Light of Freedom*, pp. 363–90.

26 Alexander, *Civil Sphere*, pp. 275–76. Alexander is here referring to the prehistory of the civil rights movement, but it can be applied equally to the cultural politics that emerged in the wake of Black Power. However, Alexander fails to recognize how Black Power and the formation of singular, nonwhite counterpublics was an intensification and further development of earlier dynamics within the civil rights movement itself. The early civil rights movement drew on particularist counterpublics, albeit one's that were constructed as nonwhite for reasons of circumstance and external hostility rather than because of ideological commitments.

27 Alexander, *Civil Sphere*, pp. 275–77. Alexander's position represents a critique of what he calls "radical, separatist" conceptions of multiculturalism of which he takes Iris Marion Young as a paradigmatic example (p. 400). He charges that not only are such conceptions normatively and theoretically mistaken in his view, they are also sociologically naïve and empirically wrong. Against both separatist conceptions and conservative critics of multiculturalism such as Samuel Huttington, Alexander presents a positive account of multiculturalism as a strategy of incorporation and integration.

28 *Ibid.*, p. 276.

29 What we can call *incorporative* social movements can be contrasted with *non-incorporative* forms that seek not acceptance but to change the system as such. Some anarchist, Marxist, and radical Islamic groups fit such a category.

30 Wood, *Faith in Action*, pp. 153–71.

31 David Harvey, "Contested Cities: Social Process and Spatial Form," in *Transforming Cities: Contested Governance and New Spatial Divisions*, eds. Nick Jewson and Susanne MacGregor (London: Routledge, 1997), p. 19.

32 Sassen, *Territory, Authority, Rights*, pp. 115–19.

33 Chicago was a child of the railroads and the industrial revolution, growing from fewer than 298,877 people within 35 square miles in 1870 to 1,698,575 in 190 square miles by 1900 and doubling its population again by 1930 (Slayton, *Back of Yards*, p. 11).

34 Alinsky, *Reveille*, pp. 43–50. As already noted, those he trained quickly saw its relevance to parallel contexts. The disaggregating and disorganized urban conditions were mirrored among migrant farm workers who, like factory workers, experienced acute forms of modern industrialization, this time of mass agriculture rather than mass industry, and whose livelihood and physical presence as immigrants

likewise depended on the money flows of global capitalism. It is notable that where community organizing has proved to have the least traction is in suburbia and among the middle classes. On this, see Osterman, *Gathering Power*, pp. 81–84.

35 Richard White defines the middle ground in the following terms: "The middle ground is the place in between: in between cultures, peoples, and in between empires and the nonstate world of villages. ... On the middle ground diverse peoples adjust their differences through what amounts to a process of creative, and often expedient, misunderstandings. People try to persuade others who are different from themselves by appealing to what they perceive to be the values and practices of those others. They often misinterpret and distort both the values and the practices of those they deal with, but from these misunderstandings arise new meanings and through them new practices – the shared meanings and practices of the middle ground" (*The Middle Ground: Indians, Empires and Republics in the Great Lakes Region, 1650–1815* [Cambridge: Cambridge University Press, 1991], p. xxvi).

36 Margaret R. Somers, *Genealogies of Citizenship: Markets, Statelessness, and the Right to Have Rights* (Cambridge: Cambridge University Press, 2008), pp. 63–117.

37 "Leaving it all up to the market" in reality means imposing the market through deregulation and delegitimizing or outlawing customary practice. Federal policy with regard to urban poverty since the Progressive Era onward is a lamentable case study in this regard. See Alice O'Conner, "Swimming Against the Tide: A Brief History of Federal Policy in Poor Communities," in *Urban Problems and Community Development*, eds. Ronald Ferguson and William Dickins (Washington, DC: Brookings Institute, 1999), pp. 77–138.

38 John Rawls, "The Idea of Public Reason Revisited," in *The Law of Peoples*. (Cambridge, MA: Harvard University Press, 2001), p. 141; *Political Liberalism* (New York: Columbia University Press, 1993), pp. 214–15. Although the need to translate a comprehensive doctrine into public reasons only applies to decisions that involve the coercive use of force to achieve public ends, it is difficult to see how this does not affect most areas of public policy, resting as it ultimately does on appeal to law and the threat of coercion.

39 Oliver O'Donovan is an example of a theologian who expresses this concern. See his *Desire of the Nations*.

40 See, for example, William E. Connolly, *Pluralism* (Durham, NC: Duke University Press, 2005).

41 Coles, *Beyond Gated Politics*.

42 By my account, Coles is taking one particular tradition – the nepantalist one – and making of this the dominant interpretative framework. Given the crucial contribution of Latino communities in his context, this is an appropriate dialogic incorporation of BBCO into a particular tradition. However, it is problematic on empirical grounds, as should be clear from the previous chapters. My account would locate Coles's interpretation as a very sophisticated version of what was observed in relation to Roman Catholic social teaching, Islam, Judaism, liberal Protestant theology, the Black churches, and Evangelicalism. It is the establishment of a critically dialogic and mutually educational relationship between nepantalism/agonistic democracy and BBCO by a leader within the IAF. A key point of difference between our accounts is the attention given in mine to how community organizing constitutes a means of forging a shared arena of rationality based on practical reason.

43 See Peter J. Steinberger, *The Concept of Political Judgment* (Chicago: University of Chicago Press, 1993), pp. 67–69; Ronald Beiner, *Political Judgement* (London: Methuen, 1983), p. 141.
44 MacIntyre, *After Virtue*, pp. 30–31.
45 Beiner, *Political Judgment*, p. 16.
46 John Rawls is a contemporary exponent of such an approach. For Rawls, we cannot develop what he calls "nonideal theory" without first working out ideal theory (*A Theory of Justice*, rev. ed. [Cambridge, MA: Harvard University Press, 1999], p. 8).
47 A parallel charge can be leveled at Kant who developed an account of judgment that intellectualizes and abstracts judgment and aestheticizes the faculty of taste that prior to Kant was largely understood as a social-moral faculty. For Kant, judgment becomes about abstract reason, not communally formed decisions that demand the cultivation of persons able to make appropriate judgments within a *sensus communis*. Similarly, as Beiner notes, utilitarianism precludes a concept of practical reason because it subsumes all policy under a universal rule: that of the quantitative calculus of utility (*Political Judgment*, p. 110). Stout notes that from the perspective of grassroots democracy, "utilitarianism and egoism are the two forms that commodity fetishism takes in public philosophy. The two forms differ on what perspective one should adopt when calculating costs and benefits. But both are focused strictly on maximising the utility of consequences, rather than on other forms and bearers of value – utility for everybody, in the one case, and utility for the calculator, in the other. Both reflect the current prestige of economic practices that reduce practical reasoning to cost benefit calculation, rather than providing a radical critique of them. Grassroots democrats, in contrast, speak as if there are kinds of value that are distinct from utility and as if there are bearers of intrinsic value (such as persons and some acts and things) that are distinct from consequences (resulting states of affairs)" (Stout, *Blessed Are the Organized*, p. 225).
48 "In my view, he who conforms his course of action to the quality of the times will fare well, and conversely he whose course of action clashes with the times will fare badly" (Machiavelli, *The Prince*, trans. Peter Constantine [New York: Modern Library, 2008], p. 116). The quote comes from chapter 25 where Machiavelli discusses the need for prudence in identifying the right course of action in relation to the changing of fortune's wheel; that is, the contingency and flux of history. There is a wide-ranging debate about the relationship between *virtu* and *fortuna* in Machiavelli that need not concern us here. Suffice it to say that Machiavelli's insights about politics as involving action in time can be adopted without having to be committed to his entire philosophy and vision of political order.
49 As we shall see in Chapter 8 in the discussion of how the state is caught between land and sea, there is certain irony to Aristotle and others' choice of a sea captain as an image for political rule and the ship of state as a trope for the polis.
50 The recognition of the unpredictable nature of political life is not to assert it is a realm of total chaos. It is simply to recognize political judgments address modes of action different from those of the chemist or engineer and no amount of "evidence-based policy" can circumvent this.
51 My use of the term "practical reason" in the context of forming political judgments should be understood as combining *phronēsis* and *mētis*. *Mētis*

encompasses the kind of wily wisdom, shrewdness, or cunning needed in politics, especially when trying to outmaneuver those with greater power. Alinsky clearly possessed a great deal of *mētis* and I have argued elsewhere that organizing can be seen as a form of tricksterism (*Christianity and Contemporary Politics*, pp. 78–81). However, in contrast to *phronēsis, mētis* is more a semantic field than a clearly definable term. According to Marcel Detienne and Jean-Pierre Vernant, it entails a body of attitudes and behaviors that combines flair, wisdom, forethought, perspicuity, subtlety, resourcefulness, vigilance, opportunism, and experience acquired over years that enables one to navigate circumstances of conflict, change, and instability (*Cunning Intelligence in Greek Culture and Society*, trans. Janet Lloyd [Chicago: University of Chicago Press, 1991]). By contrast, *phronēsis,* at least for Aristotle, more directly emphasizes the moral dimensions of practical reasoning. As an aside, when combined, *mētis* and *phronesis* are parallel in meaning to key Hebrew terms for wisdom: *hokmâ* and *hakam*. On the importance of *mētis* as an alternative and rival to state and capitalist forms of scientific management and control, see James C. Scott, *Seeing Like a State: How Certain Schemes to Improve the Human Condition Have Failed* (New Haven, CT: Yale University Press, 1998), pp. 309–41. However, Scott neither relates *mētis* and *phronēsis*, nor does he discuss the need to connect *mētis* and virtue in order to generate just and generous political action. The form of the virtues and vision of the good life in which *mētis* is embedded is crucial: there is, afterall, a world of difference between Jesus and Odysseus as exemplars of *mētis*.

52 For a critique of Aristotle's conception of *phronēsis* and how this problematizes an account of political judgment based on an Aristotelian conception, see Steinberger, *Concept of Political Judgment*, pp. 106–27.

53 Bent Flyvbjerg, *Making Social Science Matter: Why Social Inquiry Fails and How it Can Succeed Again*, trans. Steven Sampson (Cambridge: Cambridge University Press, 2001), p. 59. Flyvbjerg also draws from Aristotle to argue that social science has ignored *phronēsis* and overly focused on *episteme* and *technē* as modes of analysis in its attempt to model itself on the natural sciences. See also Scott, *Seeing Like a State*, pp. 309–28.

54 See Scott, *Seeing Like a State*, pp. 11–83.

55 *Ibid.*, p. 95. It should be noted that the positive appraisal of the potential for relating Aristotle and Foucault goes against MacIntyre's counterposing of Aristotle and Nietzsche/Foucault as necessarily rival and incommensurable interpretative frameworks. Flyvbjerg does not address the conflict MacIntyre identifies. However, Flyvbjerg's drawing from Foucault's conception of power to enhance his Aristotelian conception of *phronēsis* does not necessitate the full-scale adoption of genealogy. For an account of *phronēsis* that seeks to integrate MacIntyre's conception of tradition and *phronēsis* with Foucault's notion of genealogy via Vico's more charitable conception of genealogy, see Salvatore, *Public Sphere*.

56 See, for example, Michel Foucault, "Preface," in Gilles Deleuze and Félix Guattari, *Anti-Oedipus: Capitalism and Schizophrenia*, trans. Robert Hurley, Mark Seem, and Helen R. Lane (New York: Penguin Books, 2007), pp. xi–xiv.

57 The imagery of entanglement and weaving stem from the origins of the terminology associated with *mētis*, which is rooted in practices of hunting and fishing. As Denant and Vernant note, *mētis* as a term is related to ancient techniques "that

use the pliability and torsion of plant fibres to make knots, ropes, meshes and nets to surprise, trap and bind and that exploit the fact that many pieces can be fitted together to produce a well-articulated whole" (*Cunning Intelligence*, p. 46).

58 As Paul Kelly notes: "The critique of ideological forms and discourses of power is too often divorced from any more positive conception of the role and task of political theory" – or, we might add, of politics itself ("Political Theory – The State of the Art," *Politics* 26.1 [2006]: 47–53, at p. 51).

59 Alinsky, *Rules for Radicals*, p. 36.

60 See George Ritzer, *The McDonaldization of Society* (Thousand Oaks, CA: Pine Forge Press, 2000); and Alan Bryman, *Disneyization of Society* (Thousand Oaks, CA: Sage, 2004).

61 Jürgen Habermas, "Social Action and Rationality," in *Jürgen Habermas on Society and Politics: A Reader*, ed. Steven Seidman (Boston: Beacon Press, 1989), p. 157.

62 See Alexander, *Civil Sphere*, pp. 214–21.

63 Alinsky, *Rules for Radicals*, p. 46.

64 *Ibid.*, p. 47.

65 Aristotle, *Nicomachean Ethics* 3.31112b15–19; 6.11.1143a29-b1.

66 On Jesus' actions and teachings as trickster-like, see Kathleen M. Ashley, "The Guiler Beguiled: Christ and Satan as Theological Tricksters in Medieval Religious Literature," *Criticism: A Quarterly for Literature and the Arts* 24.2 (1982): 126–37; and Walter Wink, *Engaging the Powers: Discernment and Resistance in a World of Domination* (Minneapolis, MN: Fortress Press, 1992), pp. 175–93.

67 See Cary Nederman, "Men at Work: *Poesis*, Politics and Labor in Aristotle and Some Aristotelians," *Analyse & Kritik* 30 (2008): 17–31; Kelvin Knight, *Aristotelian Philosophy: Ethics and Politics from Aristotle to MacIntyre* (Cambridge: Polity, 2007), pp. 176–79; and Keith Breen, "Work and Productive Reason: Rival Visions of Production and the Workplace," paper delivered at the Contemporary Aristotelian Studies in Politics Conference, London Metropolitan University, June 3, 2011.

68 As Knight notes, for MacIntyre "it is where the social activity of production is free from capitalist management that producers can best think and act for themselves. Where this is the case, they are often motivated to defend their shared practices against the depredations of state and capital" (*Aristotelian Philosophy*, p. 174).

69 MacIntyre, "Three Perspectives on Marxism: 1953, 1968, 1995," in Alasdair MacIntyre, *Selected Essays*, vol. 2, *Ethics and Politics* (Cambridge: Cambridge University Press, 2006), p. xxvi.

70 For an account of the contrast between Aristotle and Althusius's consociational conception of what it means to be a political animal, see Thomas O. Hueglin, *Early Modern Concepts for a Late Modern World: Althusius on Community and Federalism* (Waterloo, Canada: Wilfrid Laurier University Press, 1999), pp. 56–82. To date, MacIntyre has not engaged with the work of Althusius but there are striking parallels between the kind of account of a politics he is trying to develop and that given by Althusius.

71 *Ibid.*, pp. 95–96. Hueglin argues that Althusius developed his political theory from three mutually reinforcing strands: political Calvinism, the *Politics* of Aristotle (in particular, the affirmation of the cooperative sociability inherent within human nature), and the tradition of Germanic communitarianism and fellowship (*ibid.*, p. 56).

72 This is a distinction borrowed from Hueglin (*ibid.*, p. 113).

73 Alinsky, "Is There Life after Birth?" *Anglican Theological Review* 1 (1968), p. 59. Alinsky is quoting from Tocqueville, *Democracy in America,* IV.6. It is not just Aristotle who had this insight. One can read the book of Exodus as a commentary on the problem of how a formerly enslaved people can come to rule themselves wisely and justly. The need to move from revolution to education in order to generate a people capable of self-rule rather than replicating the structures of oppression they are liberated from is a central theme of Michael Walzer's reflections on Exodus (see Michael Walzer, *Exodus and Revolution* [New York: Basic Books, 1985]). However, what Walzer misses from his account is the place of organization and the distribution of authority in the formation of a people with the experience of self-rule. A theme that is also present in the book of Exodus.

74 Alexander, *Civil Sphere*, pp. 98–99.

75 MacIntyre, *Whose Justice, Which Rationality?* p. 44. See also Knight, *Aristotelian Philosophy*, p. 179. MacIntyre countenances politics as enabling the pursuit of a "common good," although its contingent and fugitive nature suggests it is perhaps better to talk of "common goods" and the formation of a proximately just and generous common life.

76 For a summary of MacIntyre's "politics of virtuous resistance," see Kelvin Knight and Paul Blackledge, "Introduction: Towards a Virtuous Politics," in *Virtue and Politics: Alasdair MacIntyre's Revolutionary Aristotelianism*, eds. Kelvin Knight and Paul Blackledge (Notre Dame, IN: University of Notre Dame Press, 2011), pp. 1–10. MacIntyre's revolutionary Aristotelianism helps delineate how distant his thought is from what is labeled communitarianism. MacIntyre is much closer to the syndicalism of Proudhon and Sorel who rejected capitalism, corporatism, state socialism, and liberal parliamentary democracy, advocating instead the need for a new social and political order founded on the occupational group or *syndicat*.

77 On the need for such a conception in democratic theory, see Jeff Weintraub, "Democracy and the Market: A Marriage of Inconvenience," in *From Leninism to Freedom: The Challenges of Democratization*, ed. Margarat Latus Nugent (Boulder, CO: Westview Press, 1992), pp. 47–66.

78 That being said, his approach to case studies is more generic than genetic. For an account of the centrality of case studies to his approach, see Jeffrey Alexander, "On the Interpretation of *The Civil Sphere*: Understanding and Contention in Contemporary Social Science," *Sociological Quarterly* 48 (2007): 641–59.

79 Alexander, *Civil Sphere*, p. 24. Marvin Becker notes that what civil society and capitalism in particular were seen as undermining was a concept of society as a by-product of the correct performance of duties and obligations incumbent on each order or estate. Marvin B. Becker, *The Emergence of Civil Society in the Eighteenth Century* (Bloomington: Indiana University Press, 1994).

80 See Albert Hirschman, *The Passions and the Interests: Political Arguments for Capitalism before Its Triumph*, anniversary ed. (Princeton, NJ: Princeton University Press, 1997).

81 Alexander, *Civil Sphere*, p. 25.

82 Charles de Montesquieu, *The Spirit of the Laws*, trans. Anne Cohler, Basia Miller and Harold Stone (Cambridge: Cambridge University Press, 1989 [1748]), p. 338.

83 For example, see Deirdre N. McCloskey, *The Bourgeois Virtues: Ethics for an Age of Commerce* (Chicago: University of Chicago Press, 2006).

84 Luc Boltanski and Eve Chiapello's *The New Spirit of Capitalism* (London: Verso, 2007).

85 Georg Simmel in his *The Philosophy of Money* (London: Routledge and Kegan Paul, 1978) powerfully articulated the emancipatory effects of money. However, it is not just a question of money but also of property. For example, Erik J. Olsen points to the importance of property rights and the ability to act independently in the market to the civic agency of impoverished Indian women. He notes: "Whether in land or its movable forms, property can provide resources – *dominium* in the neoclassical republican sense of the word – in support of personal and civic independence and therefore dignity as well. By supporting independence, property can also play a role in securing the terms of civic equality" (*Civic Republicanism and the Properties of Democracy* [Langham, MD: Lexington Books, 2006], p. 264). However, as will be argued in Chapter 8, whether it is a social or exclusivist vision of property that is operative makes a vital difference.

86 Alexander, *Civil Sphere*, p. 27.

87 Macpherson, *Political Theory of Possessive Individualism*, p. 106. Drawing from Marx, Macpherson defines what he means by a "possessive market society" in the following terms: "By possessive market society I mean one in which, in contrast to a society based on custom and status, there is no authoritative allocation of work or rewards, and in which, in contrast to a society of independent producers who exchange only their products in the market, there is a market in labour as well as in products. If a single criterion of the possessive market society is wanted it is that man's labour is a commodity, i.e. that a man's energy and skill are his own, yet are regarded not as an integral part of his personality, but as possessions, the use and disposal of which he is free to hand over to others for a price. It is to emphasise this characteristic of the fully market society that I have called it the *possessive* market society. Possessive market *society* also implies that where labour has become a market commodity, market relations so shape or permeate all social relations that it may properly be called a market society not merely a market economy" (*ibid.*, p. 48). In sum, what individuals possess is not commodities but their own labor, which becomes a property that can be alienated and sold as a commodity, which in turn puts all individuals in competition with each other. In contrast to Marx and Polanyi, Macpherson's account of market society does not require any particular account of origin or historical development. Macpherson's point is that it is only in a fully market society that the state of nature as conceptualized by Hobbes can be envisaged. Older forms of society with different economic and social arrangements do not allow for the kind of competition and threat Hobbes ascribes to the state of nature and which thereby justify the need for Leviathan. Macpherson's argument parallels that of Polanyi for whom the emergence of capitalism heralded a new form of economic relation disembedded from gift-based patterns of sociality.

88 See Ian Baucom, *Specters of the Atlantic: Finance Capital, Slavery, and the Philosophy of History* (Durham, NC: Duke University Press, 2005).

89 Alexander, *Civil Sphere*, p. 28.

90 Burawoy, "For a Sociological Marxism," pp. 193–261. For an example of a post-Marxist critique of civil society much influenced by Foucault, see Michael Hardt, "The Withering of Civil Society," *Social Text* 45 (1995): 27–44.

91 On Polanyi's concept of dis/embeddedness and its contested interpretation, see Dale, *Karl Polanyi*, pp. 188–206. Dale rightly questions Burawoy's co-option of

Polanyi as a "sociological Marxist" on the grounds that Burawoy's own conception hardly constitutes a form of Marxism (*ibid.*, pp. 240–43).

92 *Ibid.*, p. 7.

93 *Ibid.*, pp. 229–31.

94 See Somers, *Genealogies of Citizenship*, pp. 213–88.

95 For an extensive critique of Putnam and the use of the term "social capital" in the social sciences and how it compares with and differs from conceptions of civil society, see Somers, *Genealogies of Citizenship*, pp. 213–53. Somers explicitly draws on Polanyi to develop her critique and sees social capital as a "Trojan horse" that ideologically legitimizes the marketization of social relationships.

96 For a critique of the neo-Tocquevillian view of civil society represented by Putnam, see Mark Warren, *Democracy and Association* (Princeton, NJ: Princeton University Press, 2001), pp. 32–37.

97 Alexander, *Civil Sphere*, p. 30. See Jean L. Cohen and Andrew Arato, *Civil Society and Political Theory* (Cambridge, MA: MIT Press, 1992).

98 For an extensive critique of Habermas's misconception of religion, tradition, and customary practices in his account of civil society, see Salvatore, *Public Sphere*, pp. 33–98. Salvatore locates his critique within a broader critique of modern sociological conceptions of "'religion."

99 Alexander, *Civil Sphere*, p. 31.

100 *Ibid.*

101 Arendt, *Human Condition,* pp. 38–49; and *On Revolution*, pp. 49–105. As will be seen in Chapter 8, central to the thesis developed here is a rejection of Arendt's view that the customs, habits, and manners of society are irrelevant to the constitution of the body politic and that the realm of "the social" is necessarily a threat to political freedom. For a contrasting account of the emergence and role of a "social order" amenable to study and distinct from the orders of nature and politics, see Polanyi, *Great Transformation*, pp. 116–35. For a critique of Arendt's conception of the social as inherently depoliticizing, see Cruikshank, *Will to Empower*, pp. 54–58.

102 Alexander, *Civil Sphere*, p. 31. Alexander is, in effect, inverting Hegel so that rather than the state constituting the universal sphere which civil society presupposes and is subsistent on, civil society becomes the sphere in which universal values and forms of solidarity are realized, but these values and forms of solidarity, rather than being all encompassing, as in a nation-state, are necessarily contested and in flux.

103 *Ibid.*, p. 33. The linking of the intellectual and the religious by Alexander is right, but his rationale for their linkage is partly wrong. The linkage is a filial one. Athens and Jerusalem may be rivals but they are also brothers and as the ancients teach us, sibling rivalry – whether that of Cain and Abel or Romulus and Remus – can be the fiercest, most bitter, and deadliest of rivalries. Alexander identifies such conceptual labor as directed to transcendent and abstract goods, but use of the term of "religion" here conflates orthodoxy and orthopraxy, the cognitive and the performative, and is thereby in danger of reinscribing certain assumptions about religion as subjective, inner, and private.

104 Jeffrey Alexander, "Civil Sphere, State, and Citizenship: Replying to Turner and the Fear of Enclavement," *Citizenship Studies* 12.2 (2008): 185–94.

105 He states it is a sphere of solidarity "in which individual rights and collective obligations are tensely intertwined. It is both a normative and a 'real' concept. It allows the relationship between universalism and particularism, so central to philosophical thinking, to be studied empirically, as a condition that determines the status of civil society itself" (Alexander, *Civil Sphere*, p. 53).

106 I am grateful to Dan Rhodes for helping me formulate the reweaving of civil society as a form of "binding and loosing." The phrase draws from Matthew 16:19 and is developed by John Howard Yoder as a particular practice of the church in *Body Politics: Five Practices of the Christian Community before the Watching World* (Scottdale, AZ: Herald Press, 2001).

107 Alexander, *Civil Sphere*, pp. 33–34, 193–95.

108 *Ibid.*, pp. 203–09.

109 *Ibid.*, p.208.

110 Alexander, "On the Interpretation of *The Civil Sphere*," p. 647.

111 Martin Buber, "To the Clarification of Pacifism," in *A Believing Humanism: My Testament, 1902–1965* (New York: Simon and Schuster, 1967), pp. 212–13. Buber is another figure organizers have drawn from in their reflections and writing. Buber is here wrestling with a core paradox of democracy: how to build a virtuous and democratic people and set of institutions out of undemocratic and immoral individuals and structures. For an examination of this paradox, see Bonnie Honig, "Between Decision and Deliberation: Political Paradox in Democratic Theory," *American Political Science Review* 101.1 (2007): 1–17.

112 Alexander, *Civil Sphere*, p. 103.

113 These factors are echoed in Sirianni's case studies of more state-centric collaborative governance. He identifies, in particular, the role of an organizer figure as vital. What he does not assess is the function of different kinds of communities of virtue, although this is often implicit in the case studies analyzed (Sirianni, *Investing in Democracy*, especially pp. 66–116).

114 For a critique of Alexander on this, see Bryan Turner, "Civility, Civil Sphere and Citizenship: Solidarity versus the Enclave Society," *Citizenship Studies* 12:2 (2008): 177–84.

115 *Ibid.*, p. 183. Contrary to "postsecular" thinkers such as Habermas, Alexander does not maintain that the secular, and in particular the secular civil sphere, is something from which religious discourses must be excluded.

116 See Alexander, *Civil Sphere*, pp. 503–47. Elsewhere he clarifies his position, stating: "My argument ... is that the civil sphere should not be controlled by any single religion, or, for that matter, by any particular group. The solution to religious sectarianism is not secularity but incorporation and multiculturalism. The *parole* (speech) of public life can be religious, as long as the diverse religious groups physically co-present in the national community are allowed to speak the *langue* (language) of civil society" ("Civil Sphere, State, and Citizenship," p. 190).

117 Turner, "Civility, Civil Sphere and Citizenship," p. 183.

118 For a summary of contemporary democratic theory and how it relates to these concerns, see Stears, *Demanding Democracy*, pp. 5–12.

119 See, for example, Weintraub, "Democracy and the Market," p. 63.

120 Alexander, *Civil Sphere*, p. 55.

121 *Ibid.*, p. 198.

122 *Ibid.*, p. 110. There is overlap here between Alexander's account of civil power and Habermas's conception of civil society. Habermas states: "The public opinion that is worked up via democratic procedures into communicative power cannot 'rule' of itself but can only point the use of administration power in specific directions" (Jürgen Habermas, *Between Facts and Norms: Contributions to a Discourse Theory of Law and Democracy* [Cambridge, MA: MIT Press, 1998], p. 300). The primary point of difference is that Habermas does not see civil society as a sphere of political relations.

123 For Alexander, civil society has an internal symbolic structure that varies from context to context. This symbolic structure of in-groups and out-groups contains within itself its own resources of critique and repair: there are universalistic ideals, visions of a better world, practices and narratives that can be mobilized to extend and expand the civil sphere so as to include those previously judged as unworthy, or for holding accountable those who are deemed to have polluted the civil sphere and are now deemed unworthy of inclusion. Scandals concurrent with the period described in the book including bankers (the financial crisis the emerged from 2008 onward), politicians (the 2009 Parliamentary expenses scandal), journalists and police (the 2011 News of the World/News Corps hacking scandal), and young people (the 2011 riots in the United Kingdom) are all instances of the mobilization of these resources of critique and repair and the regulatory institutions of "civil power" within civil society to hold to account those deemed to have acted irresponsibly.

124 For a parallel account of the body politic, see Maritain, *Man and the State*, pp. 9–19, 148–54. Maritain's conception of the body politic is too organicist, but he rightly distinguishes it from the state and as the basis and bearer of a vision of what he calls "the common good." For Maritain the body politic is political society as a whole as distinct from the state, which is the political authority and which is only ever an instrumental good subordinate to and meant to serve the body politic.

125 It is important to clarify what he means by this. If one is to judge a particular situation as pertaining to the political as against some other sphere of judgment, such as the moral or aesthetic, then the specific criterion for a political judgment is whether a particular relation constitutes a friend or an enemy, but not of an individual but of an association or people. Other antitheses such as whether something is ugly or beautiful, profitable or unprofitable, moral or immoral are distinct from the criteria of political judgment. On Alexander's terms, they pertain to the logics at work within differing spheres.

126 Carl Schmitt, *The Concept of the Political*, trans. George Schwab, expanded ed. (Chicago: University of Chicago Press, 2007), p. 27.

127 *Ibid.*

128 Given Schmitt's Nazi sympathies, there is a hollow ring to this claim. In his later work Schmitt distinguishes between the "'real enemy" and the "absolute enemy." The latter is one who is declared to be totally criminal and inhuman, "to be a total non-value" (*Theory of the Partisan: Intermediate Commentary on the Concept of the Political*, trans. G. L. Ulman [New York: Telos Press Publishing, 2007], p. 94). The notion of the absolute enemy is identified as a distinctly modern phenomenon that arises with the advent of absolute or total war conducted by both revolutionary regular and irregular forces.

129 Schmitt recognizes that given the centrality and force of the political distinction other distinctions become emotionally aligned with it.

130 For Schmitt, part of the problem with liberalism is its refusal to admit the reality of enemies. For him, liberalism subsumes enemies to another category entirely such as making the enemy an economic competitor or a debating adversary and thereby denying the existence of the political (Schmitt, *Concept of the Political*, p. 28). The attempt to replace political with moral or economic categories leads to what Schmitt saw as the depoliticization of public life (*ibid.*, pp. 69–73). By this account, an emphasis on dialogue and consensus as paradigms of public discourse are attempts to avoid and suppress political conflicts. Moreover, the refusal to take seriously the friend-enemy distinction results in widespread conceptual confusion. For Schmitt, words such as state, republic, class, and sovereignty only make sense when one knows "who is to be affected, combated, refuted, or negated by such a term" (*ibid.*, p. 31). Or as he puts it most sharply: "The enemy is he who defines me" (*Theory of the Partisan*, p. 85, n. 89).

131 Schmitt, *Concept of the Political*, pp. 40–45; and Carl Schmitt, "State Ethics and the Pluralist State," in *Weimar: A Jurisprudence of Crisis*, eds. Arthur J. Jacobson and Bernhard Schlink (Berkeley: University of California Press, 2000), pp. 300–12.

132 Carl Schmitt, *The Leviathan in the State Theory of Thomas Hobbes: Meaning and Failure of Political Symbol*, trans. George Schwab and Erna Hilfstein (Westport, CT: Greenwood Press, 1996), p. 73.

133 Schmitt, *Theory of the Partisan*, p. 6. Schmitt's state-centric view of the political is partly driven by the fact that he conflates the political and the juridical in order to justify a conception of political sovereignty as involving the monadic will of the one who decides the exception. Schmitt himself seems to step back from this assertion in his later work, conceding that it is the "degree of intensity of an association and dissociation" that constitutes the basis of making the friend-enemy distinction rather than whether such an association constitutes a state or not (*Political Theology II: The Myth of the Closure of Any Political Theology*, trans. Michael Hoelzl and Graham Ward [Cambridge: Polity Press, 2008], p. 45).

134 Schmitt himself notes that evolution of the economically based power of workers and capitalists into political power through their assuming political representation (*Roman Catholicism and Political Form*, trans. G. L. Ulman [Westport, CT: Greenwood Press, 1996], p. 24).

135 See also Mouffe, *Democratic Paradox*, pp. 36–59.

136 This typology is derived from an analogous one given by Anthony Waterman, *Political Economy and Christian Theology since the Enlightenment: Essays in Intellectual History* (New York: Palgrave Macmillan, 2004), p. 199.

137 Chantal Mouffe, "Religion, Liberal Democracy, and Citizenship," in *Political Theologies: Public Religions in a Post-Secular World*, ed. Hent de Vries and Lawrence Sullivan (New York: Fordham University Press, 2006), p. 338. See also, idem, *Democratic Paradox*, p. 101.

138 Mouffe, *Democratic Paradox*, p. 13.

139 Mouffe, "Religion, Liberal Democracy, and Citizenship," p. 339.

140 See Mouffe, *The Return of the Political* (London: Verso, 1993), p. 30–33.

141 For a critique of strict separation of church and state as antidemocratic and the development of a constructive account based on an associative democratic vision consonant with the kind of consociational account I am developing, see Veit Bader,

"Religious Diversity and Democratic Institutional Pluralism," *Political Theory* 31.2 (2003): 265–94; idem, "Religions and States: A New Typology and a Plea for Non-Constitutional Pluralism," *Ethical Theory and Moral Practice* 6.1 (2003): 55–91.

142 Likewise, along with other agonistic pluralists such as William Connolly and Bonnie Honig, Mouffe also ignores the examples of consociational democracies such as the Netherlands and Switzerland, which despite being characterized by deep social, cultural, and religious cleavages, achieve something that could be characterized as a politics of the common life. For a comparison between agonistic and consociational approaches to dealing with deeply divided societies, see John Dryzek, "Deliberative Democracy in Divided Societies: Alternatives to Agonism and Analgesia," *Political Theory* 33.2 (2005): 218–42. Dryzek is critical of both agonistic and consociational approaches while defending deliberative democracy. However, he calls for a substantially modified deliberative approach, one that takes on elements of both agonism and consociationalism. My own approach is different and attempts a more direct marriage of agonism and consociationalism. As already noted in the Introduction, the kind of consociational and agonistic democratic politics of a common life I envisage differs markedly from the elite orientated, consensus focused, polyarchic, and state-centric form that, following the work of Arend Lijphart, is generally denoted by the term "consociational democracy" and applied to a country like the Netherlands.

143 Schmitt, *Leviathan in the State Theory of Thomas Hobbes*, p. 74. As Schwab notes for Schmitt: "To prevent the societal sphere from becoming a political battleground, with all that that implies, including, in the most extreme case, civil war, Schmitt insisted on the depoliticisation of society; that is, the state must prohibit politically centrifugal forces from operating within its domain" (*ibid.*, p. xii).

144 For an exposition of Arendt's conception of the link between democratic politics and the need for political elites who are precisely *not* vanguards claiming to represent the "general will," see Arendt, *On Revolution*, pp. 247–72; and Jeffrey Isaac, "Oases in the Desert: Hannah Arendt on Democratic Politics," *The American Political Science Review* 88.1 (1994): 156–68.

7 Sovereignty and Consociational Democracy

1 Jürgen Habermas and Jacques Derrida, *Philosophy in a Time of Terror: Dialogues with Jürgen Habermas and Jacques Derrida*, ed. with commentary by Giovanna Borradori (Chicago: University of Chicago Press, 2003), p. 113; and Jacques Derrida, *Rogues: Two Essays on Reason* (Stanford, CA: Stanford University Press, 2005).

2 For Agamben's discussion of "bare life," see Giorgio Agamben, *Homo Sacer: Sovereign Power and Bare Life* (Stanford, CA: Stanford University Press, 1998). For one articulation of Foucault's notion of "bio-politics," see Michel Foucault, "The Political Technology of Individuals," in *Technologies of the Self: A Seminar with Michel Foucault*, eds. Luther Martin, Huck Gutman and Patrick Hutton (Amherst: University of Massachusetts Press, 1988), pp. 145–62.

3 See especially Michael Gillespie, *Theological Origins of Modernity* (Chicago: University of Chicago Press, 2008).

4 The distinction between God as Logos and God as sovereign will is drawn from Elshtain, *Sovereignty: God, State, and Self*.

5 Another shift is the eclipse of Trinitarian theology and the emergence of Deist, Unitarian, and rationalist conceptions of God. Immanuel Kant both exemplifies and intensifies the marginalization of Trinitarian theology. He drew from the pietism in which he was educated and the rationalism of Leibniz, Reimarus, and Christian Wolff, but in the place of revelation was reason, and law governs what should be said and done. There is a God, but parallel to the development of Deism in Britain, Kant conceives God as a supremely perfect being: immutable, indivisible, and timeless. The right political order of perpetual peace is the analogue of the right ontological order of a rule-governed, rational deity. The church, including its liturgies, rituals, and institutional form, is to be tolerated but can have no public presence in the rationally administered state. In the move away from Trinitarian to more monarchical, voluntarist, and rationalist doctrines of God, there is an almost inescapable process of mimesis whereby sovereignty itself takes on the pattern of being one substance, indivisible, set apart, nonparticipative, and defined by the exercise of a single will, the sole function of which is to secure an immanent rational mechanism.

6 For the genealogy of this conflict over who is the anointed and supreme representative of Christ on earth, see Ernst Kantorowicz, *The King's Two Bodies: A Study in Mediaeval Political Theology* (Princeton, NJ: Princeton University Press, 1957).

7 Against Milbank and Gillespie, Agamben sees an emphasis on the sovereign will of God in the creation and rule of the cosmos as a basic development in the emergence of Patristic Trinitarian theology born out of the fracturing of the being and acting of God. See Agamben, *Kingdom and the Glory*, pp. 56–57.

8 Quoted from Gelasius I, "'The Bond of Anathema," in *From Irenaeus to Grotius: A Sourcebook in Christian Political Thought, 100–1625*, eds. Oliver O'Donovan and Joan Lockwood O'Donovan (Grand Rapids, MI: Eerdmans, 1999), pp. 178–79.

9 John Milbank, "On Complex Space," in *The Word Made Strange: Theology, Language, Culture* (Oxford: Blackwell Publishers, 1997), pp. 268–92.

10 This conception came to preeminence among Protestant political thinkers through their engagement with Talmudic scholarship. On this, see Eric Nelson, *The Hebrew Republic: Jewish Sources and the Transformation of European Political Thought* (Cambridge, MA: Harvard University Press, 2010); and Adrian Hastings, *The Construction of Nationhood: Ethnicity, Religion and Nationalism* (Cambridge: Cambridge University Press, 1997).

11 Agamben, *Kingdom and the Glory*, pp. 109–42.

12 Scott, *Seeing Like a State*, p. 27. Scott explains: "If we imagine a state that has no reliable means of enumerating and locating its population, gauging its wealth, and mapping its land, resources, and settlements, we are imagining a state whose interventions in that society are necessarily crude. A society that is relatively opaque to the state is thereby insulated from some forms of finely tuned state interventions" (*ibid.*, p. 77).

13 Benjamin Constant, *De l'esprit de conquête* (1815), quoted in *ibid.*, p. 30.

14 *Ibid.*, p. 32.

15 Prior to Immanuel Kant, Thomas Paine, and Rousseau were James Harrington, John Milton, and a host of Protestant political polemicists who viewed monarchy as idolatrous and sinful. This republican position was in turn opposed by the assertion of the divine right of kings: an equally simple and singular early modern conception of political space. As Arendt notes, both republicanism and absolute

monarchy prepared the way for the rise of the "secular" nation-state (Arendt, *On Revolution,* pp. 149–56). For both "Hebrew Commonwealthsmen" and the proponents of absolute monarchy, the key texts were Deuteronomy 17:14 and 1 Samuel 8 and the question of whether Scripture marks kingship as inherently wicked or positively required (Nelson, *Hebrew Republic*, pp. 23–56). What neither side would countenance was a mixed constitutional order. Agamben in his discussion of the place of monarchy and *oikonomia* in political theology in *Kingdom and the Glory* completely misses both the significance of this early modern debate and the Scriptural verses in the development of political theology.

16 See Julian Franklin, "Sovereignty and the Mixed Constitution: Bodin and his Critics," in *The Cambridge History of Political Thought: 1450–1700*, eds. J. H. Burns and M. Goldie (Cambridge: Cambridge University Press, 1991), pp. 298–344.

17 Jean Bodin, *On Sovereignty: Four Chapters from "The Six Books of the Commonwealth,"* trans. Julian Franklin (Cambridge: Cambridge University Press, 1992), p. 11.

18 *Ibid.*, p. 92.

19 Jacques Maritain, "The Concept of Sovereignty," *The American Political Science Review* 44.2 (1950): 343–57, p. 346.

20 Schmitt, *Concept of the Political.*

21 See Thomas Hueglin, *Early Modern Concepts for a Late Modern World: Althusius on Community and Federalism* (Waterloo: Wilfrid Laurier University Press, 1999); and Black, *Guild and State.*

22 Thomas Hobbes, *Leviathan* (Cambridge: Cambridge University Press, 1996), p. 127 (XVIII).

23 The account given here is in many ways parallel to that developed by Pierre Manent, but Manent's involves a slightly different cast of characters, most notably Locke and Montesquieu, and is not focused on the question of sovereignty per se (Pierre Manent. *An Intellectual History of Liberalism*, trans. Rebecca Balinski [Princeton, NJ: Princeton University Press, 1994]).

24 Schmitt, *Concept of the Political*, p. 52.

25 Schmitt, *Leviathan in the State Theory of Thomas Hobbes*, p. 33.

26 *Ibid.*

27 Jean Jacques Rousseau, *The Social Contract and Other Later Political Writings* (Cambridge: Cambridge University Press, 1997), p. 146.

28 Schmitt, *Leviathan in the State Theory of Thomas Hobbes*, p. 57.

29 *Ibid.*, p. 73.

30 Rousseau, *Social Contract,* p. 45.

31 *Ibid.*

32 *Ibid.*, p. 50.

33 The original theological problem, beginning with the dispute between Augustine and Pelagius, related to the Pauline assertion in 1 Timothy 2:4 that "God wills that all men be saved." The theological question was how could a general will for universal salvation be related to the election of particular humans for salvation? To analyze this problem, the Scholastics distinguished between the antecedent and the consequent will of God. As Patrick Riley explains: "God willed 'antecedently' (or generally) that all men be saved, but after the Fall of Adam He willed 'consequently' (or particularly) that only some be saved" (*The General Will before Rousseau: The Transformation of the Divine into the Civic* [Princeton, NJ:

Princeton University Press, 1986], p. 6). Riley argues that in the seventeenth century the Jansenist Arnaud "invented" the idea of the general will for examining this question. See also Christopher Brooke, "Rousseau's Political Philosophy: Stoic and Augustinian Origins," in *The Cambridge Companion to Rousseau*, ed. Patrick Riley (Cambridge: Cambridge University Press, 2001), pp. 94–123.

34 Riley, *General Will before Rousseau*, p. 19.

35 See Beiner, *Civil Religion*, pp. 73–83.

36 Bernard Cullen, *Hegel's Social and Political Thought* (Dublin: Gill and MacMillan, 1979), p. 42.

37 This is not to say there was an absolute rejection of the medieval inheritance. As Cary Nederman argues, traces of the gothic constitution were incorporated into Hegel's political theory. Cary Nederman, "Sovereignty, War and the Corporation: Hegel on the Medieval Foundations of the Modern State," *The Journal of Politics* 49.2 (1987): 500–20.

38 Agamben, *State of Exception*.

39 Hegel, *Hegel's Philosophy of Right*, trans. T. M. Knox (Oxford: Oxford University Press, 1967), p. 177 (§273).

40 *Ibid.*, p. 188 (§286).

41 *Ibid.*, p185 (§280).

42 *Ibid.*, p. 166 (§270).

43 Paul Lakeland, *The Politics of Salvation: The Hegelian Idea of the State* (Albany: State University of New York Press, 1984), p. 53.

44 Hegel, *Hegel's Philosophy of Right*, pp. 170–71 (§270).

45 The church does not disappear for Hegel; instead, it is divided into state churches that support the state and provide an integrating function, and voluntary sects, such as Quakers, who are reduced to being part of civil society and tolerated by the state (*ibid.*, p. 168 [§270]).

46 Medieval constitutionalists were building on distinctions in Roman law between *ius scriptum* and *ius non scriptum*. The principal text that justified custom as legally binding was taken to be *Digest* 1.3.32.1, which was ascribed to the Emperor Julian. See P. G. Stein, "Roman Law," in *The Cambridge History of Medieval Political Thought c. 350–c. 1450*, ed. J. H. Burns (Cambridge: Cambridge University Press, 1988), p. 45. See also, Howell Lloyd, "Constitutionalism," in *The Cambridge History of Political Thought 1450–1700*, ed. J. H. Burns (Cambridge: Cambridge University Press, 1991), pp. 267–68.

47 James Tully, *Strange Multiplicity: Constitutionalism in an Age of Diversity* (Cambridge: Cambridge University Press, 1995), p. 125.

48 For example, to advocates of discontinuity such things as bishops in the House of Lords appear as irrational and must be expunged, whereas for those who see value in continuity and honoring customary practice, such phenomena can open space for further negotiation and the recognition and incorporation of other forms of corporate and religious association into the upper chamber.

49 Allen, *Talking to Strangers*, p. 72.

50 *Ibid.*, pp. 72–75.

51 Purdy notes the paradoxes of such an approach, stating: "In their insistence on a white Protestant settler hegemony over the continent, which they opposed to Britain's willingness to govern a multicultural empire of commerce, the Americans were imperialists par excellence. On the other hand, the American Revolution was

a colonialists' revolt against the world's leading imperial power" (Jedediah Purdy, *The Meaning of Property: Freedom, Community and the Legal Imagination* [New Haven, CT: Yale University Press, 2011], pp. 70–71). Given the importance of the prior experience of covenants and "cosociation" to Arendt's account of the success of the American Revolution, it is notable she misses the paradox Purdy points to (*On Revolution*, pp. 156–70).

52 Tully, "On Local and Global Citizenship: An Apprenticeship Model," pp. 243–309.

53 Of particular significance was the Royal Proclamation of October 7, 1763 that was based on the Royal Commissions on Indian Affairs since 1665, Royal instructions to colonial administrators from 1670 onward, and the Board of Trade's recognition of aboriginal sovereignty in 1696. In contrast to the subsequent U.S. government, the British understood themselves as immigrants who needed to recognize and accommodate themselves to the existing sovereign authorities. The Declaration of Independence of 1776 represents the nonrecognition of preexisting forms of aboriginal sovereignty (Tully, *Strange Multiplicity*, p. 118). The British Crown was not alone in taking this approach. Also of significance was the Two Row Wampum Treaty between the Dutch and the *Haudenosaunee* (Iroquois) in 1613, later renewed by the British when they established the Province of New York. It is also important to note that the British frequently did not take such an approach: British-Irish relations being a particularly intense, bitter and significant example of the nonrecognition of the sovereign status of other groups.

54 Tully, *Strange Multiplicity*, p. 120.

55 *Ibid.*, p. 82.

56 Michael Hardt and Antonio Negri, *Commonwealth* (Cambridge, MA: Belknap Press, 2009). See also Tully, "On Local and Global Citizenship: An Apprenticeship Model," pp. 249–67.

57 Martin Buber, *Paths in Utopia* (New York: Syracuse University Press, 1996). For a parallel critique, see Scott, *Seeing Like a State*, pp. 193–222. Hardt and Negri do not see forms of state communist and state socialist expropriation as intrinsic to these projects but as part of ongoing and eventually victorious forms of capitalist development (Hardt and Negri, *Commonwealth*, pp. 89–95). However, they do recognize the inherently eurocentric perspective of Marx himself (Hardt and Negri, *Empire* [Cambridge: MA: Harvard University Press, 2000], p. 120).

58 In addition to Tully, the connections between liberalism and justifications of colonialism are also explored in Bikhu Parekh, "Liberalism and Colonialism: A Critique of Locke and Mill," in *The Decolonization of Imagination: Culture, Knowledge and Power*, eds. Jan Nederveen Pieterse and Bhikhu Parekh (London: Zed Books, 1995), pp. 81–98; and Anthony Pagden, "Human Rights, Natural Rights, and Europe's Imperial Legacy," *Political Theory* 31.2 (2003): 171–99.

59 On Locke's vested interests in such a project, see David Armitage, "John Locke, Carolina, and the 'Two Treatises of Government,'" *Political Theory* 32.5 (2004): 602–27; and Barbara Arneil, *John Locke and America: The Defense of English Colonialism* (Oxford: Oxford University Press, 1996).

60 Tully, *Strange Multiplicity*, pp. 73–74.

61 See Purdy, *The Meaning of Property*, pp. 67–86.

62 Althusius, *Politica* I.1. It is probable that Althusius derived his use of the term from Cicero (*De Re Publica* 1.25–27), although in Cicero's usage its meaning is

restricted to the legal bond for the organized conduct of public life rather than an all-encompassing term for social relations. See Hueglin, *Early Modern Concepts,* p. 79.

63 James Skillen, *The Development of Calvinistic Political Theory in the Netherlands, with Special Reference to the Thought of Herman Dooyeweerd* (PhD dissertation, Duke University, 1973), pp. 191–217.

64 As Robert Latham notes: "While commentators since the seventeenth century have read Althusius as an early formulator of ideas about popular sovereignty, they have generally overlooked how he was actually vesting sovereignty or supreme power in the webs of relations that shape the possibilities for agency across a body politic ... rather than a collective of persons" (Robert Latham, "Social Sovereignty," *Theory, Culture and Society* 17.4 [2000]: 1–18, p. 6).

65 I am grateful to Davey Henreckson for helping me clarify this point.

66 Philip Stern, *The Company-State: Corporate Sovereignty and the Early Modern Foundations of the British Empire in India* (Oxford: Oxford University Press, 2012), pp. 4–6. We may speculate that firms such as the East India Trading Company are the points of transition from the medieval, city-based mercantile republics such as Venice and Genoa to the modern mercantile republics that now take the form of transnational corporations such as Halliburton, Honda, or Apple.

67 Tully, "On Local and Global Citizenship: An Apprenticeship Model," p. 279. How such an approach connects with Foucault's influential account of "governmentality" is that a diffuse range of authoritative agencies (professionals, academic experts, corporations, lawyers, civic groups, public administrators, etc.) participate in reproducing and contesting the construction, communicative formations, and structures of sovereignty (Latham, "Social Sovereignty," p. 8).

68 Otto von Gierke, *Community in Historical Perspective*, ed. Antony Black, trans. Mary Fischer (Cambridge: Cambridge University Press, 1990); and for the English Pluralists, see Paul Q. Hirst, ed., *The Pluralist Theory of the State: Selected Writings of G. D. H. Cole, J. N. Figgis, and H. J. Laski* (London: Routledge, 1993).

69 There were substantive differences between the frameworks developed by those associated with the English Pluralist/Guild Socialist "school." For example, unlike the historian of political thought, John Neville Figgis, G. D. H. Cole and Harold Laski, two key intellectuals in the development of the Labour Party, had a decidedly voluntaristic anthropology. For an account of the conceptual differences between the English Pluralists (and those who subsequently developed Guild Socialism), see Laborde, *Pluralist Thought and the State,* pp. 45–100; and Marc Stears, "Guild Socialism," in *Modern Pluralism: Anglo-American Debates Since 1880*, ed. Mark Bevir (Cambridge: Cambridge University Press, 2012), pp. 40–59. Stears uses the term "Guild Socialist" to include the English Pluralists, but this blanket designation more directly relates to the work of Cole and Laski rather than Figgis. For the differences between the English Pluralists and the U.S. traditions of political pluralism, notably that of Robert Dahl, see Avigail Eisenberg, *Reconstructing Political Pluralism* (New York: SUNY Press, 1995). However, Eisenberg conflates forms of U.S. political pluralism with an aligned but distinct tradition of consociational thought to which the English Pluralists are more directly related.

70 See Jonathan Chaplin, *Herman Dooyeweerd: Christian Philosopher of State and Civil Society* (Notre Dame, IN: University of Notre Dame Press, 2011).

71 In the Latin of the encyclicals the word for "function" is *munus*, meaning service, gift, or vocation. Pius XI introduces it to contrast with rights-based or contractual notions of recognition. *Munera* are how the laity participates in the offices/*munera* of Christ who is the paradigmatic human. The state is to facilitate/serve the development of these munera/offices/vocations. The theo-logic behind the consociational conception of plurality in Catholic social teaching means it has a very different basis to most modern notions of devolution and delegation, both of which imply that the state grants, distributes, and concedes public authority to subsidiary agencies. Instead, the logic envisaged in the encyclicals accords much more closely with notions of federal/covenantal pluralism found in the likes of Kuyper and Figgis. On this dimension of Catholic social teaching, see Russell Hittinger, "Social Pluralism and Subsidiarity in Catholic Doctrine," *Christianity and Civil Society: Catholic and Neo-Calvinist Perspectives*, ed. Jeanne Heffernan Schindler (Lanham, MD: Lexington Books, 2008), pp. 11–30.

72 See, for example, Hirst, *Associative Democracy*.

73 See Cavanaugh, *Torture and Eucharist*, p. 195.

74 Such tendencies have been criticized in more recent papal encyclicals. See, for example, the critical comments by John Paul II of what he calls the "social assistance state" in *Centesimus Annus*, §48.

75 See Brian Z. Tamanaha, "'Understanding Legal Pluralism: Past to Present, Local to Global," *Sydney Law Review* 30 (2008): 375–411; and William Twinning, *General Jurisprudence: Understanding Law from a Global Perspective* (Cambridge: Cambridge University Press, 2009).

76 Through numerous case studies, Ostrom demonstrates that addressing the efficient management of common resources, either through their marketization via the imposing of property rights or through centralized control by the state, can have adverse consequences for resource management. This is because both marketization and centralization undermine the capacity of people to govern themselves and lead to the depletion and destruction of important forms of local collective wisdom and the institutions and patterns of relationship that sustain this knowledge over time. Elinor Ostrom, *Governing the Commons: The Evolution of Institutions for Collective Action* (Cambridge: Cambridge University Press, 1990). David Harvey criticizes Ostrom for being too localist in orientation, but this is not a necessary implication of her work (*Rebel Cities: From the Right to the City to the Urban Revolution* [London: Verso, 2012], pp. 68–88).

77 Arend Lijphart, *The Politics of Accommodation: Pluralism and Democracy in the Netherlands*, 2nd ed. (Berkley: University of California Press, 1975), pp. 1–2.

78 See Arend Lijphart, *Democracy in Plural Societies: A Comparative Exploration* (New Haven, CT: Yale University Press, 1980); and *Thinking about Democracy: Power Sharing and Majority Rule in Theory and Practice* (London: Routledge, 2008).

79 For a summary of these, see M. P. C. M. Van Schendelen, "Consociational Democracy: The Views of Arend Lijphart and Collected Criticisms," *Political Science Reviewer* 15 (1985): 143–83. See also Kenneth McRae, "The Plural Society and the Western Political Tradition," *Canadian Journal of Political Science* 12.4 (1979): 675–88; Jürg Steiner, "Review: The Consociational Theory and Beyond," *Comparative Politics* 13.3 (1981): 339–54.

80 Peter Gourevitch and Gary Jacobson, "Arend Lijphard, A Profile," *PS: Political Science and Politics* 28.4 (1995): 751–54. On the reception history of Althusius and the rival interpretations of his political theory, see Stephen Grabill, *Rediscovering the Natural Law in Reformed Theological Ethics* (Grand Rapids, MI: Eerdmans, 2006), pp. 122–30.

81 See Shapiro, *State of Democratic Theory* and David Held, *Models of Democracy*, 3rd ed. (Cambridge: Polity, 2006). However, neither Shapiro nor Held discuss consociational conceptions of democracy and only briefly mention the different varieties of pluralist approaches.

82 The term "association" is used here in a generic way and encompasses both voluntary and nonvoluntary (rather than involuntary) forms of association. For a discussion of the distinction between voluntary, nonvoluntary, and involuntary, see Warren, *Democracy and Association*, pp. 96–103. There are extensive debates about: (1) how to distinguish various forms of associative relation such as contractual, covenantal, and corporate forms of relationship; (2) the corporate personality of groups as these relate to the state; and (3) a sociological debate about what happens to different forms of social relations within processes of modernization stemming from Tönnies' distinction between *Gemeinschaft* (community) and *Gesellschaft* (society/association). These sociological distinctions echo a distinction in Roman law between *societas* (partnership/voluntary association) and *universitas* (a corporation with a common identity and which is capable of common action) brought to prominence in political theory by Michael Oakeshott. As important as these debates and distinctions are, for the purposes of this book, a generic use of the term association suffices.

83 Arendt, *On Revolution*, p. 162.

84 Tocqueville made voluntary associations the beginning point of his conception of the proper nature and form of democracy. More recently, Joshua Cohen and Joel Rogers, Paul Hirst, and Mark E. Warren have explored the intrinsic nature of the relationship between association and collective self-rule (Joshua Cohen and Joel Rogers, *Associations and Democracy* [London: Verso, 1995]; Hirst, *Associative Democracy*; Warren, *Democracy and Association*).

85 Indicative of this position are the following: Arendt, *Human Condition*; Barber, *Strong Democracy*; Beiner, *What's the Matter With Liberalism?*; Philip Pettit, *Republicanism: A Theory of Freedom and Government* (Oxford: Clarendon, 1997); Michael Sandel, *Democracy's Discontent* (Oxford: Oxford University Press, 1996); Quentin Skinner, *Liberty before Liberalism* (Cambridge: Cambridge University Press, 1998); Charles Taylor, *Multiculturalism and the "Politics of Recognition": An Essay*, ed. Amy Gutmann (Pinceton, NJ: Princeton University Press, 1992), pp. 25–73; idem, *The Ethics of Authenticity* (Cambridge, MA: Harvard University Press, 1992); and idem, *Modern Social Imaginaries*. A primary contribution of civic republicanism to modern democratic theory is to sensitize it to traditional republican themes eclipsed by late-modern liberal democratic thought and practice. For Olsen, these themes include "the importance of cultivating habits of responsible citizenship, the public dimensions of liberty, the connection between corruption and tyranny, the patriotism of virtuous resistance to tyranny, and ... the threat to civic virtue and public liberty that is posed by excessive acquisitiveness and commercialism" (Olsen, *Civic Republicanism*, p. 146).

86 Iseult Honohan, *Civic Republicanism* (London: Routledge, 2002), pp. 8–11.

87 Sandel, *Democracy's Discontent*, p. 26.
88 For a review of the problematic relationship between republican theory, liberalism, and the emergence of citizenship studies and sociological accounts of citizenship, see Somers, *Genealogies of Citizenship*. Although the book as a whole addresses this relationship, see especially pp. 147–70.
89 For a discussion of such concerns, see Michael Walzer, *Politics and Passion: Toward a More Egalitarian Liberalism* (New Haven, CT: Yale University Press, 2005).
90 For example, Hirst uses the term "associative" to describe his conception of democracy.

8 Economy, Debt, and Citizenship

1 John Dunn follows the view established by M. I. Finley and other scholars who suggest it was a result of the latter (*Setting the People Free*, p. 32), whereas Edward Harris argues Solon's reforms and the emergence of democracy arose because of the former. On the distinction between debt bondage and debt slavery in ancient Athens and the ancient world more generally, as well as his discussion of Solon's reforms, see Edward Harris, "Did Solon Abolish Debt-Bondage?" in *Democracy and the Rule of Law in Classical Athens: Essays on Law, Society and Politics*, ed. Edward Harris (Cambridge: Cambridge University Press, 2006), pp. 249–69.
2 Aristotle, *The Constitution of Athens*, trans. J. M. Moore, in *The Politics* and *The Constitution of Athens*, ed. Stephen Everson (Cambridge: Cambridge University Press, 1996), II.2–3, VI.1–4; pp. 211, 214.
3 Whether or not Aristotle had what in modern terms would be called a distinctively economic analysis, and more specifically an analysis of a monetary economy, is a matter of some dispute. On this, see Scott Meikle, "Aristotle and the Political Economy of the Polis," *The Journal of Hellenic Studies* 99 (1979): 57–73.
4 Paul Millett, *Lending and Borrowing in Ancient Athens* (Cambridge: Cambridge University Press, 1991), pp. 151–58.
5 Usury in ancient Athens was mostly limited to small-time moneylenders who amounted to little more than local hustlers (*ibid.*, pp. 180–88). However, much larger scale interest-bearing loans were lent for purposes of maritime trade. Such loans entailed huge sums (*ibid.*, p. 195).
6 Aristotle, *The Nicomachean Ethics*, trans. David Ross (Oxford: Oxford University Press, 1980), p. 84 (1121b.34).
7 Plato, *Laws*, in *The Dialogues of Plato*, trans. Benjamin Jowett (Oxford: Oxford University Press, 1953), IV.705a, pp. 273–74.
8 The port of trade par excellence in the ancient maritime economy was Alexandria, which existed as a kind of political no-man's-land.
9 Cicero, *On Duties*, eds. M. T. Griffin and E. M. Atkins (Cambridge: Cambridge University Press, 1991), p. 58 (1, 151). In his advice, Cicero demarcates the twofold process of making money honorable: the first step was to obtain cash via trade in the unregulated ancient maritime economy and bring this into port: an occupation which, if done on a large scale was "not entirely to be criticised." The second stage involved a movement from the port, via a process of rustication, into the land-based and regulated political economy.

10 To quote Aristotle: "And the avarice of mankind is insatiable ... men always want more and more without end; for it is of the nature of desire to be unlimited, and most men live only for the gratification of it" (*The Politics*, ed. Stephen Everson [Cambridge: Cambridge University Press, 1996], p. 45 [1267b.1]).

11 Marcel Hénaff, *The Price of Truth: Gift, Money, and Philosophy* (Stanford, CA: Stanford University Press, 2010), p. 90.

12 Scott Meikle, "Aristotle on Money," *Phronesis* 39.1 (1994): 26–44, pp. 30–31.

13 In our own day philosophers like Michael Sandel and Alasdair MacIntyre reiterate this lament and use it as a critique of liberalism and capitalism.

14 Francis Watson, *Text, Church and World: Biblical Interpretation in Theological Perspective* (Edinburgh: T & T Clark, 1994), pp. 68–70.

15 Genesis 47:18–19. It is worth noting that, as Odd Langholm points out, the question of what constitutes compulsion and the issue of whether a voluntary act was really done under duress is central to the definitions of and debate around usury (*Legacy of Scholasticism in Economic Thought: Antecedents of Choice and Power* [Cambridge: Cambridge University Press, 1998]).

16 Gregory Chirichigno, *Debt-Slavery in Israel and Ancient Near East* (Sheffield: Sheffield Academic Press, 1993); Isaac Mendelsohn, *Slavery in the Ancient Near East: A Comparative Study of Slavery in Babylonia, Assyria, Syria and Palestine from the Middle of the Third Milennium to the End of the First Milennium* (New York: Oxford University Press, 1949).

17 The linkage between liberation from Egypt and debt slavery is made explicit in Leviticus 25:35–46. In this text the prohibitions against usury and limits placed on debt slavery through the institution of Jubilee are grounded in the relationship established between God and the people through the act of liberation from Egypt.

18 For an extended reading of this text as a declaration of Jubilee, see John Howard Yoder, *The Politics of Jesus*, 2nd ed. (Grand Rapids, MI: Eerdmans, 1994), pp. 60–75. Yoder includes the Lord's Prayer as a call for the proper practice of Jubilee with its use of the word *aphiēmi* in the statement: "remit us our debts as we ourselves have also remitted them to our debtors" (*ibid.*, p. 62).

19 See Nathan Eubank, *Wages of Cross-Bearing and the Debt of Sin: The Economy of Heaven in Matthew's Gospel* (Göttingen: De Gruyter, 2013). On the centrality of the metaphor of debt to conceptualizations of sin in early Judaism and Christianity, see Gary Anderson, *Sin: A History* (New Haven, CT: Yale University Press, 2009). In patristic theology, the theme of liberation from debt bondage is most developed in Ambrose's *De Tobia*, which constitutes a complex allegory of sin and salvation that uses freedom from debt bondage and the practice of usury as a central motif.

20 Here the parables of the rich man and Lazarus (Luke 16:19–31) and of the rich fool (Luke 12:16–20) are instructive. In these parables the wealthy who hoard their riches, using them for their own aggrandizement and benefit instead of giving and lending to others in need, are condemned as not only foolish but damned (David Mealand, *Poverty and Expectation in the Gospels* [London: SPCK, 1980], pp. 46–53).

21 There is much debate on the relationship between the texts specifically addressed to the issue of usury, in particular Exodus 22:25, Leviticus 25:35–38, and Deuteronomy 23:19–20. There is strong evidence of redactional unity between these texts and that the differences between them represent an unfolding line of development rather than one of disjunction. On this, see Adrian Schenker, "The Biblical Legislation on the Release of Slaves: The Road from Exodus to Leviticus,"

Journal for the Study of the Old Testament 78 (1998): 23–41. The Hebrew word used in Exodus and Psalm 15 is *nešek*, which is probably derived from the proto-semitic root of *ntk* or *nsk* meaning "bite" (Samuel Loewenstamm, "neshek and ma/tarbît," *Journal of Biblical Literature* 88:1 [1969]: 78–80; D. L. Baker, *Tight Fists or Open Hands?: Wealth and Poverty in Old Testament Law* [Grand Rapids, MI: Eerdmans, 2009], p. 260). There is some dispute over what kind of interest *nešek* represented and how it differed from *tarbît*. On this, see Jacob Milgrom, *Leviticus 23–27* (New York: Doubleday, 2000), pp. 2209–10.

22 Not charging interest is a way of demarcating Israel from the other nations. As Gerhard von Rad notes, charging interest was common in the surrounding countries at the time (von Rad, *Deuteronomy* [London: SCM, 1966], p. 148).

23 The patristic conceptualization of usury seems to be consistent with this, as is early Rabbinic Judaism. For a discussion of patristic teachings on usury, see Malony, "The Teaching of the Fathers on Usury," 241–65. If anything, as Jacob Neusner argues, the Mishnah inflates the prohibition on charging interest to equate it with all forms of non-barter based, monetary economic transactions that resulted in a profit (Jacob Neusner, "Aristotle's and the Mishnah's Economics: The Matter of Wealth and Usury," *Journal for the Study of Judaism in the Persian, Hellenistic and Roman Period* 21.1 [1990]: 41–59).

24 Although as Milgrom notes, sexual and other violations of the law also connect to the proper treatment of the land. For Milgrom, Sabbath rest is part of the expiation that purifies the land from sin (Milgrom, *Leviticus 17–22*, p. 1404).

25 *Ibid.*, 1404; and Albino Barrera, *God and the Evil of Scarcity: Moral Foundations of Economic Agency* (Notre Dame, IN: University of Notre Dame Press, 2005), p. 54.

26 Chirichigno, *Debt-Slavery in Israel*, p. 142.

27 Milgrom, *Leviticus 23–27*, pp. 2204–28. This is parallel to the situation that pertained in ancient Athens (Harris, "Did Solon Abolish Debt-Bondage?").

28 Walter Houston, "What's Just about the Jubilee? Ideological and Ethical Reflections on Leviticus 25," *Studies in Christian Ethics* 14:1 (2001): 34–47. On the debate surrounding the interpretation and dating of the Jubilee legislation, see Baker, *Tight Fists or Open Hands?*, pp. 166–73.

29 Barrera, *God and the Evil of Scarcity*, p. 67.

30 Leviticus 25:35–38; Deuteronomy 15:1–11. On the provisions for mandatory lending, see Barrera, *God and the Evil of Scarcity*, pp. 97–99.

31 For such a reading, see David Graeber, *Debt: The First 5,000 Years* (New York: Melville House, 2011), pp. 271–82. For an account of the basis for the prohibition against paying or receiving *riba* and its connections to broader accounts of justice in Islamic law, see Mohammad Fadel, "*Riba*, Efficiency and Prudential Regulation: Preliminary Thoughts," *Wisconsin International Law Journal* 25.4 (2008): 655–703.

32 Barrera, *God and the Evil of Scarcity*, p. 46. See also David Novak, "Economics and Justice: A Jewish Example," in *Jewish Social Ethics* (Oxford: Oxford University Press, 1992), p. 210.

33 Daniel Elazar, *Covenant and Polity in Biblical Israel: Biblical Foundations and Jewish Expressions* (New Brunswick, NJ: Transaction Publishers, 1995), pp. 86–91. Elazar helpfully summarizes the overall structure of the polity within which the *edah* and *shevet* function.

34 *Ibid.*, p. 133. The ultimate punishment for failure to fulfill covenant obligations is exile from the land.

35 On the roots of modern republicanism in the Scriptural polity, see Nelson, *Hebrew Republic.*

36 Hardt and Negri, *Commonwealth*, p. 282.

37 Hardt and Negri are not unique in their binary opposition between property ownership and the cultivation of democratic virtues. Olsen notes that advocates of civic republicanism also refuse to countenance alternative visions of property ownership, and how what he calls the "placeful" aspects of property ownership can be a formative context of moral and civic responsibility (*Civic Republicanism and the Properties of Democracy*, pp. 81–90).

38 Thomas Aquinas, *Political Writings*, trans, R. W. Dyson (Cambridge: Cambridge University Press, 2002), pp. 205–20 (*Summa Theologiae*, IIa–IIae, Q66). See also John Finnis, *Aquinas: Moral, Political, and Legal Theory* (Oxford: Oxford University Press, 1998), pp. 187–210. A parallel account of property as a communicable and shared good can be found in the work of John Wesley and early Methodism. Wesley, while in many respects a Tory, rejected an account of property as an inviolable right. On this, see Randy Maddox, "'Visit the Poor' John Wesley, the Poor, and the Sanctification of Believers," in *The Poor and the People Called Methodists*, ed., Richard P. Heitzenrater (Nashville, TN: Kingswood Books, 2002), pp. 59–81.

39 John Paul II, *Laborem Exercens*, §14. See also John Paul II, *Centesimus Annus*, § 43. Although it is modified in subsequent encyclicals (see, for example, *Quadragesimo Anno*, §§ 44–49), *Rerum Novarum* grounds private property in nature. However, the prior common gift and orientation of property to common use is still emphasized (Leo XIII, *Rerum Novarum*, §§ 8–9). For an account of the twin currents in Catholic social thought – one Lockean, emphasizing an absolute right to private property, and the other Thomistic – and the gradual eclipse of the former and the reassertion of the latter, see Waterman, *Political Economy and Christian Theology*, pp. 169–74.

40 Harvey, *Rebel Cities*, pp. 67–88. Building on Ostrom and Hardt and Negri's works, Harvey comes close to something similar to a social conception of property with his account of the constructive interaction between enclosure and the building of the commons.

41 Creative Commons, available at: http://creativecommons.org.

42 See, for example, Edward Neufeld, "The Prohibitions against Loans at Interest in Ancient Hebrew Laws," *Hebrew Union College Annual* 26 (1955): 355–412.

43 For an example of this kind of analysis, see John Calvin, *Commentarii in Libros Mosis necum in Librum Josue* (Amsterdam, 1567). Quoted from and translated by Kerridge, *Usury, Interest and the Reformation*, appendix 1.

44 Although, as Calvin perceived, "[u]sury has almost always these two inseparable accompaniments, viz. tyrannical cruelty and the art of deception" (from Calvin's 1575 letter to Claude de Sachin, quoted from translation by André Biéler, *Calvin's Economic and Social Thought*, trans. James Greig [Geneva: WCC Publications, 2005], p. 404). In arguing that usury is not an exceptionless moral norm, my position is closer to that of Calvin than the Scholastics. However, as Biéler and Kerridge point out, Calvin was in practice, if not in principle, very close to the Scholastics. Kerridge argues that under the Reformers there were no substantial changes to

Christian attitudes to usury, remedies for it, or laws against it (Kerridge, *Usury, Interest and the Reformation*, p. 23). Specifically in relation to Calvin, Biéler suggests that charging interest became lawful in principle while being forbidden whenever it contradicted the rule of justice and charity, whereas for the Scholastics, charging interest was forbidden in principle, but allowed in many specific instances (Biéler, *Calvin's Economic and Social Thought*, p. 445).

45 Derrida points to the ambiguity in the word *pharmakon* in his study of Plato's *Phaedrus*. He notes how the term *pharmakon* – meaning a drug – can signify both a remedy and/or a poison. A *pharmakon* can be – alternately or simultaneously – beneficent and maleficent (Derrida, *Dissémination*, trans. Barbara Johnson [London: Athlone Press, 1981], p. 70).

46 Hayek defines catallaxy as the order "brought about by the mutual adjustment of many individual economies in a market. A catallaxy is thus the special kind of spontaneous order produced by the market through people acting within the rules of the law of property, tort and contract" (Friedrich A. von Hayek, *Law Legislation and Liberty*, vol. 2, *The Mirage of Social Justice* [Chicago: University of Chicago Press, 1978], pp. 107–08). The friend-enemy distinction plays a role in Hayek's account and he explicitly cites Schmitt (*ibid.*, p. 144, n. 11). For Hayek, the market represents the means of overcoming the political as defined by the friend-enemy distinction.

47 Stout is referring to chattel slavery in the United States. However, what characterizes the kind of slavery he discusses was not just that the slave was treated as the property of, and therefore entirely subject to, another person and so could be bought and sold, but also its hereditary nature and that as a system it originated in acts of violent capture. By contrast, while debt slavery means one is entirely subject to another in perpetuity and can be sold, it results from a "voluntary" act and, in principle, one's children do not automatically inherit the status of being a slave (although in practice, this is often the case). Moreover, if the debt is paid (e.g., by a family member), the debt slave is free. In addition, debt slavery does not entail being part of a caste or class of people denoted as slaves, which in the United States was racially defined. Debt slavery is distinguished from debt bondage in that it is not a permanent condition and the creditor does not have all the rights exercised by an owner, just the right to specific services or labor for a certain period of time or until the debt is paid. However, the status of someone in debt bondage is often opaque and stands between slavery and freedom. Slavery (of all kinds) and debt bondage must also be distinguished from forced labor; all slavery and debt bondage entail forced labor but not all forced labor is slavery (e.g., prison labor) or arises from indebtedness.

48 Marx and Weber both posited a fundamental conflict between chattel slavery and industrial capitalism, despite, as Marx argued, chattel slavery constituting part of the primitive accumulation and expropriation on which capitalism was founded. Recent work has extended this latter insight, outlining how the emergence of industrialization and, in particular, finance capitalism within the "Atlantic system" depended on and was intimately bound up with the slave trade and slavery as a means of economic production. On this, see Baucom, *Specters of the Atlantic*; and Cedric Robinson, *Black Marxism: The Making of the Black Radical Tradition* (London: Zed Press, 1983). For case studies of the U.S. context that work with the grain of Marx and Weber's oppositional relationship between slavery and capitalism,

see John Ashworth, "The Relationship between Capitalism and Humanitarianism," *The American Historical Review* 92.4 (1987): 813–28; and Robin Blackburn, *The American Crucible: Slavery, Emancipation and Human Rights* (London: Verso, 2011), pp. 304–27. Ashworth links the rise of wage labor and the kind of workforce demanded by industrialization as key factors connecting capitalism and the abolitionist movement, while Blackburn develops a more nuanced and modified version of Marx and Weber's arguments about the opposition between an agrarian and craft-based mode of production based on chattel slavery and the needs, production methods, patterns of consumption and aspirations of an industrializing economy. However, against Marx and Weber, it would be wrong to posit an inherent opposition between "southern" chattel slavery and a "northern" industrial economy: the cotton plantation and the textile factory were part of the same process. For a review of recent work in this area, see Seth Rockman, "Slavery and Capitalism," *The Journal of the Civil War Era* 2.1 (2012): 5.

49 The term financialization is defined here as the emphasis on profits generated through financial means rather than commodity production and trade and the valuing and conversion of substantive assets such as buildings into instruments that can then be either traded in financial markets or used to leverage debt. The conversion of mortgages into credit default swaps being a case in point.

50 Stout, *Blessed Are the Organized*, pp. 59, 213.

51 *Ibid.*, p. 61.

52 *Ibid.*, p. 62.

53 *Ibid.*, p. 63.

54 *Ibid.*, p. 110.

55 *Ibid.*, p. 141.

56 *Ibid.*, p. 142.

57 *Ibid.*, pp. 143–44.

58 For Stout's account of how this vision of "grassroots democracy" contrasts with other conceptions of democracy, see *ibid.*, pp. 247–59. Stout goes against Pettit as the latter contrasts and puts in conflict what he calls a populist vision of democracy (which he conflates with participatory democracy) with a republican one (Pettit, *Republicanism*, pp. 8–10).

59 International Labour Organization, *ILO 2012 Global Estimate of Forced Labour Executive Summary* (Geneva: International Labour Office, 2012).

60 One can even make the case that access to credit is the new determiner of class relations and basic structures of socioeconomic inequality. For Geoffrey Ingham, society is divided between the "relatively poor majority of debtor 'classes' that borrows from the minority of net creditors and the owners and controllers of the means of producing credit-money" (Geoffrey Ingham, "Class Inequality and the Social Production of Money," in *Renewing Class Analysis*, eds. Rosemary Crompton, Fiona Devine, Mike Savage and John Scott [Oxford: Blackwell Publishers, 2000], p. 73). By this account, power over money and the power of money is key, with the expropriating class being the moneylenders not the bourgeoisie. Credit and risk rating constitute the real class system and reveal both the true structure of power and of inequality. It is the banks, not the factory owners, who hold real power and the highest class are the low-risk, "high net worth" individuals who receive favorable terms for borrowing money. The lowest class are the financially excluded who are considered high-risk borrowers and have neither access to bank accounts

nor credit cards and are locked into a cash economy. Here we see the "Matthew effect" come into operation: to those who have, more will be given but from those who have the least, it will be taken away (i.e., the rich get richer while the poor get poorer). Lack of access to credit means the financially excluded pay more for utilities or household items because they miss out on the discounts available to those who pay direct from a bank account or by credit card; they pay more for loans as they have to resort to high interest rate sub-prime lenders such as payday lenders; and become locked into impoverished localities because they cannot borrow money to cover a move to where better work is available or draw in investment to start new businesses. However, unlike in a factory system where class consciousness could develop and collective action was possible through unionization, the "underclass" of the financially excluded are disaggregated and individually isolated with few means of social organization. The result is that they lack political voice and struggle to establish forms of mutual aid and alternative provisions such as a credit union. In this context, religious congregations and forms of democratic politics such as community organizing become incredibly important.

61 Pettit himself sees debt relations as instances of domination (Pettit, *Republicanism*, pp. 5, 61). Pettit also makes the point that contractual relations can mask the asymmetries of power embedded within them and mask the ways in which contractual relations can be relations of domination (*ibid.*, p. 62).

62 For developments in the theological analysis of usury and its development in Scholastic and Reformational thought, see John T. Noonan, *The Scholastic Analysis of Usury* (Cambridge, MA: Harvard University Press, 1957); Langholm, *Legacy of Scholasticism*; Diane Wood, *Medieval Economic Thought* (Cambridge: Cambridge University Press, 2002), pp.159–205; Jacques Le Goff, *Your Money or Your Life: Economy and Religion in the Middle Ages*, trans. Patricia Ranum (New York: Zone Books, 1990); Kerridge, *Usury, Interest and the Reformation*; and Joan Lockwood O'Donovan, "The Theological Economics of Medieval Usury," *Studies in Christian Ethics* 14.1 (2001): 48–64. Against those who argue for a radical disjuncture between the Reformers and the Scholastic view of usury such as R. H. Tawney and Max Weber, Kerridge and O'Donovan are right in arguing for a consistency between the two. For a summary of the changes in Rabbinic teaching on charging interest, see Novak, "Economics and Justice," pp. 223–24.

63 Noonan, *Scholastic Analysis of Usury*, p. 407.

64 This is seen most explicitly in the shift away from a strict view of usury in the later Scholastics such as Cajetan where the social usefulness of exchange banking forms the basis of Cajetan's arguments in its favor (Noonan, *Scholastic Analysis of Usury*, p. 313).

65 Langholm, *Legacy of Scholasticism*, pp. 62–76. As Langholm notes, the issue of compulsion was not restricted to the debate over usury but was central to discussions of the just price and the justice of market exchanges (*ibid.*, pp. 77–99).

66 Aquinas's arguments render any such distinction problematic even though Aquinas himself allows for partnership and risk-sharing arrangements. See Noonan, *Scholastic Analysis of Usury*, pp. 43–54, 143–45. See also Christopher Franks, *He Became Poor: The Poverty of Christ and Aquinas's Economic Teaching* (Grand Rapids, MI: Eerdmans, 2009), pp. 70–83.

67 In instances where the ownership of money was transferred, variations on two arguments were used in adjudicating whether charging interest was unjust or not.

The first argument centered on the issue of consumptibility. With certain things (for example, a house), the use and ownership of the item were separable and so its use could be rented without the transfer of ownership. By contrast, in the case of other items (for example, wine), use and ownership were inseparable. To use it was to consume it and so wine could not be rented. As Aquinas puts it: "Somebody who wanted to sell wine and the use of the wine separately would be selling the same thing twice over or be selling something non-existent. And this would obviously be to commit the sin of injustice" (Thomas Aquinas, *Summa Theologiæ*, 2a2æ. 63–79, vol. 38 *Injustice*, trans. Marcus Lefébure [Cambridge: Cambridge University Press, 2006], 78.1; p. 235). Money was seen to be comparable to wine and not a house; therefore, it could not be rented. The second argument was built around Aristotle's contention that money was sterile. Unlike a cow or a fruit tree, when left on its own, money could not grow or bear fruit. Likewise, a bag of gold could be given to someone and it could be returned exactly as it was at the time of giving for it is unlike a house or a pig that are changed by time and use. Thus, to seek interest or make a charge for the loan of money was to make money an end in and of itself rather than a means to an end, and this was to make money act against its own nature. Conversely, where legitimate cost, risk, or some other title could be claimed, then a charge could be made. Legitimate charges related, broadly speaking, to questions of: *damnum emergens* (where a payment was delayed; a charge was incurred as a form of compensation, analogous to a modern credit card arrangement); *indemnity* (where there was danger of losing one's capital; a charge could be made as a form of insurance against loss); *lucrum cessans* (interest could be charged where greater profit could have been earned by using the money for something else, so the interest was a form of restitution for lost earnings); and *remuneration* or *stipendium laboris* (a charge could be made for the work in managing a loan). The question then becomes what constitutes an excessive charge.

68 Although, as Christopher Franks argues, it is important to be mindful of the very different assumptions about the relationship between the human and natural order informing the premodern debates compared to those that inform contemporary economics (Franks, *He Became Poor*, pp. 35–66).

69 Graeber, *Debt*, p. 120.

70 *Ibid.*, p. 121.

71 For a parallel but very different account of the relationship between debt and morality, see Friedrich Nietzsche, "Second Essay," *On the Genealogy of Morality and Other Writings*, trans. Carol Diethe (Cambridge: Cambridge University Press, 1994), pp. 38–71. The account of the relationship between gifts and debt given here is in many ways a direct counter to how Nietzsche conceives the origins of morality in credit-debt relations.

72 MacIntyre directly criticizes Aristotle's "illusion" of self-sufficiency, contrasting it with a Thomistic account of how dependency is a condition of the virtuous life (MacIntyre, *Dependent Rational Animals: Why Human Beings Need the Virtues* [London: Duckworth, 1999], p. 127).

73 Novak, "Economics and Justice," p. 210. The drive to equality of status and mutual service is echoed in St. Paul's "economic" vision (Gordon Mark Zerbe, *Citizenship: Paul on Peace and Politics* [Winnipeg: Canadian Mennonite University Press, 2012], pp. 75–92).

74 It must be recognized that within a Christian account, especially from Augustine on, the basis and prospect of civic friendship changes from classical conceptions. The earthly polis is no longer the context of human fulfillment; nevertheless, citizenship is still a form of fellowship, albeit a distorted one based on a false ordering of loves. On this, see Eric Gregory, *Politics and the Order of Love: Augustinian Ethic of Democratic Citizenship* (Chicago: University of Chicago Press, 2008), and John von Heyking, "The Luminous Path of Friendship: Augustine's Account of Friendship and Political Order," *Friendship and Politics: Essays in Political Thought*, eds. John von Heyking and Richard Avramenko (Notre Dame, IN: University of Notre Dame Press, 2008), pp. 115–38.

75 When and where this shift takes places and whether Macpherson is correct in identifying Hobbes and Locke as the ideologues of the shift is a matter of some dispute. So, for example, in relation to Locke there are broadly two schools of thought regarding the interpretation of Locke's social contract theory and his understanding of property rights. The first school (what we might call the "C. B. MacPherson school") considers Locke's understanding of property to be a precursor of a capitalist hegemony with its central tenets of self-interest, individualism, alienable wage labor, robust private property rights, and an inevitable inequality of material goods. The second school (what we might call the "Jeremy Waldron school") locates Locke's theory of property within his theological worldview and a natural-law tradition. For Locke this included such premises as the inherent purposefulness of God's design, the fundamental equality of men and the correlate obligation to preserve mankind, and the priority of the common good and the claims of charity over private property rights. For an account of the development of a view of political relations as based on contract and property rights that reaches back further than the early modern period, see Langholm, *Legacy of Scholasticism*, pp. 139–57.

76 Oliver O'Donovan, *Desire of the Nations*, p. 248; and pp. 278–81; Brian Tierney, *The Idea of Natural Rights: Studies on Natural Rights, Natural Law, and Church Law, 1150–1625* (Atlanta, GA: Scholars Press, 1997). Against Michel Villey's contention that subjective rights originate with Ockham, Tierney suggests that the conceptualization of individual subjective rights has its origins among twelfth-century canon lawyers.

77 Macpherson, *Political Theory of Possessive Individualism*.

78 While contesting Macpherson's dating and genealogy of the emergence of notions of "possessive individualism," Pocock narrates the impact and importance of speculative finance capitalism and a national debt to the emergence of contractual concepts of citizenship. As Pocock points out, initially contractual conceptions were partly developed as a negative reaction to the emergence of financial speculation and public credit. J. G. A. Pocock, *Virtue, Commerce, and History: Essays on Political Thought and History, Chiefly in the Eighteenth Century* (Cambridge: Cambridge University Press), pp. 51–71; 91–102; 103–24; and 193–212. For an account of the importance of debt to the emergence of the modern state, see Geoffrey Ingham, *The Nature of Money* (Cambridge: Polity, 2004), pp. 69–85.

79 Jeremy Bentham, "Defence of Usury," in *Economic Writings*, vol. 1, ed. Werner Stark (London: Allen and Unwin, 1952), pp. 123–207.

80 Wolin, *Politics and Vision*, p. 261. Wolin's arguments have a direct parallel in Schmitt's critique of liberalism and what Schmitt identifies as the fallacious attempt

by liberalism to overcome the political by the economic. According to Schmitt's account, the political always, of necessity, reasserts itself. Similar to Wolin, Schmitt identifies the reduction of politics to categories of consumption and production (Schmitt, *Roman Catholicism and Political Form*, pp. 14–17) and the synchronicity between liberalism, capitalism, and communism. Schmitt states: "I reiterate that the materiality of economic-thinking capitalists is very close to that of radical communism. Neither persons nor things require a 'government' if the economic-technical mechanism is allowed its own immanent regularity" (*ibid.*, pp. 36–37). Schmitt contrasts the "juridical foundation of the Catholic Church on the public sphere" with "liberalism's foundation on the private sphere" (*ibid.*, p. 29).

81 Wolin states: "The free politics of a liberal society allows, indeed presumes, that those who control economic power are naturally entitled and expected to promote corporate or self-interest through the political process" (*Politics and Vision*, p. 526).

82 *Ibid.*, p. 271.

83 For Macpherson, Hobbes's political philosophy was the ideological articulation of England's seafaring, mercantilist state. According to this reading, Hobbes is not attempting to reconstruct a prehistorical state of nature but instead is giving an account of what would happen to a market society like England if sovereign power were removed. By way of contrast, Carl Schmitt takes exactly the opposite view. For Schmitt, there is a paradoxical relationship between the mythic symbol of the Leviathan and its relationship to what he sees as the Prussian and French process of state building. Hobbes's sea monster becomes the trope for European land powers whose absolutist monarchies, positivist law state, standing army, and bureaucracy contrast with the seafaring, commercial power and mixed, parliamentary constitution of England. For Schmitt: "[Hobbes's] concepts contradicted England's concrete political reality" (Schmitt, *The Leviathan in the State Theory of Thomas Hobbes*, p. 85). Like Schmitt, Karl Barth also sees Hobbes's Leviathan as the mythic embodiment of modern European "political absolutism," from the sun-king Louis XIV to the fascism and Stalinism of his own day. See Karl Barth, *The Christian Life: Church Dogmatics IV.4 Lecture Fragments*, trans, Geoffrey Bromiley (Edinburgh: T & T Clark, 1981), p. 221. I contend that what Macpherson and Schmitt identify are two sides of the same coin.

84 Scott points out that not only are modern regimes of freehold tenure a creation of the state, they are also required by the state for fiscal clarity; a centralized system for evaluating who, how much, and what to tax required a singular and standardized property system. This system therefore creates the conditions necessary for a national real estate market (*Seeing Like a State*, pp. 33–52).

85 This is a point drawn from Keith Hart who notes: "One side reminds us that states underwrite currencies and that money is originally a relation between persons in society, a token perhaps. The other reveals the coin as a thing, capable of entering into definite relations with other things, as a quantitative ratio independent of the persons engaged in any particular transaction. In this latter respect money is like a commodity and its logic is that of anonymous markets. Heads and tails stand for social organisation from the *top* down and from the *bottom* up, epitomised in modern theory by the state and the market respectively. Most theories of money give priority to one side over the other. ... The coin has two sides for a good reason – both are indispensable. Money is at the same time an aspect of relations

between persons and a thing detached from persons. If we forget this, we encourage social disasters and perpetuate the wild oscillation between extremes which has dogged monetary policy over the last century" (Keith Hart, "Heads or Tails? Two Sides of the Coin," *Man* 21.3 [1986]: 638–39).

86 The reference to Revelation is not as anachronistic as it might appear. Graeber suggests that the ambiguous role of centralized political authorities in both fostering the commodification of persons and intervening to ameliorate its effects is a constant feature of states dating back to ancient Mesopotamia (Graeber, *Debt*, pp. 176–85). Something of the ambiguity of the state is captured in the Biblical depiction of political authority as both a demonic beast (Revelation 13) and divinely ordained (Romans 13). Indeed, the Roman Empire itself struggled to maintain the boundaries between the land-based and regulated political economy and the sea-based ancient maritime economy. On this, see Maurice Glasman, "Landed and Maritime Markets in Ancient Rome: The Polanyi Paradigm Reconsidered" (unpublished paper).

87 Carl Schmitt, *Land and Sea*, trans. Simona Draghici (Washington, DC: Plutarch Press, 1997), pp. 1–9.

88 *Ibid.*, pp. 9–17.

89 This helps explain some of the differences of political outlook between the British political establishment and those of France and Germany, which tend to look from the land to the sea. From their perspective, the land – which symbolizes identity and language, as well as trade and industry – must be protected. You may indebt yourself to save your land or to ensure you can work it another year, but you don't view it as part of a planetary system where the wind and tides rather than the land are the primary points of reference. Britain is a ship, with the City of London at the helm. As a maritime power, it looked from the sea to the land. To keep things solid and earthbound is to be shipwrecked financially. As exemplified in its unwavering commitment to free trade, Imperial Britain realized it must be open to the currents and the winds of the market if it was to remain at the center of the global economy. This commitment is symbolized in the Guildhall of the Corporation of the City of London where images of the sea as a cornucopia abound. The sea is envisaged as a source of bounty, not chaos.

90 Contrary to what Maurizio Lazzarato, Gilles Deleuze, and Félix Guarttari suggest (Maurizio Lazzarato, *The Making of Indebted Man: An Essay on the Neoliberal Condition*, trans., Joshua David Jordon [Los Angeles: Semiotext(e), 2011]), the inherent intersection of finance and production did not emerge from the 1970s onward but was always integral to capitalism. The symbiosis of maritime insurance, the Atlantic slave trade, and industrialization is but one example of this. See Baucom, *Specters of the Atlantic*, pp. 80–112.

91 The virtual world of the Internet, with its dependence on oceanic cables and orbiting satellites, is an extension and intensification of the greater velocity and time-space compression possible within the kinds of planetary economic and political relations available to British, U.S., and Soviet forms of rule.

92 Hardt and Negri's account of "empire" illuminates the nature of political authority in the spatial shift from land to air and why the United States is both at the center of and peripheral to this new form of "global" empire. Hardt and Negri's thesis is that we are moving beyond either a unipolar or multipolar global system dominated by a sovereign nation-state such as Great Britain. Instead of one sovereign

power asserting dominance, what has emerged since 1989 is "empire" – a distributed and networked form of sovereignty. Rather than a single center of power, global governance is "a process of continual negotiation, an arrangement of instruments for consensual planning and coordination in which a multiplicity of state and non-state actors with vastly unequal powers work together. And only the collaboration among these actors can determine the process of policymaking on the global terrain." They conclude that "[t]he global order today is defined by a varied set of norms, customs, statutes, and laws that constitute a heterogeneous ensemble of demands and powers on the global horizon" (Hardt and Negri, *Commonwealth*, p. 225). However, contrary to Hardt and Negri, we should be cautious of thinking this shift heralds the end of state sovereignty. It just as easily provides opportunities for new assemblages and configurations of state sovereignty. China and the growing importance of sovereign wealth funds being cases in point.

93 These measures were supplemented by experiments in economic democracy such as factory and worker councils. However, much of this program was top-down and technocratic, and disregarded existing forms of working-class self-organization. At the same time, it was destabilized by rampant inflation, high unemployment, ethnic tensions, anti-Semitism, and actively opposed by Catholic authoritarian and nationalist forces with support in the surrounding provinces (Helmut Gruber, *Red Vienna: Experiment in Working Class Culture 1919–1934* [Oxford: Oxford University Press, 1991]).

94 For overviews of the debate, see Günther Chaloupek, "The Austrian Debate on Economic Calculation in a Socialist Economy," *History of Political Economy* 22.4 (1990): 659–75; and Don Lavoie, *Rivalry and Central Planning: The Socialist Calculation Debate Reconsidered* (Cambridge: Cambridge University Press, 1985).

95 This is a central argument of Hayek's *The Road to Serfdom* (London: Routledge, 1944), which emerged from his reflections on the socialist calculation debate and his response to the rise of Nazism.

96 For Hayek and Mises's initial responses to this debate, see Friedrich Hayek, *Collectivist Economic Planning: Critical Studies on the Possibilities of Socialism* (London: Routledge, 1935).

97 Polanyi's key arguments appear in "Sozialistische Rechnungslegung," *Archiv für Sozialwissenschaft und Sozialpolitik* 49.2 (1922): 377–420; "Die funktionelle Theorie der Gesellschaft und das Problem der sozialistischen Rechnungslegung," *Archiv für Sozialwissenschaft und Sozialpolitik* 52 (1924): 218–228; "Über die Freiheit," and "Zur Socialisierungsfrage," in *Chronik der großen Transformation*, vol. 3, eds. Michele Cangiani, Karl Polanyi-Levitt, and Claus Thomasberger (Marburg: Metropolis-Verlag, 2005). For a summary of his position, see Dale, *Karl Polanyi*, pp. 20–31.

98 Cited in Jeremy Shearmur, "Hayek's Politics," *The Cambridge Companion to Hayek*, ed. Edward Feser (Cambridge: Cambridge University Press, 2006), p. 159.

99 Contemporary advocates of "participatory economics" set out parallel versions of the kind of approach Polanyi envisages. See, for example, Michael Albert, *Parecon: Life After Capitalism* (London: Verso, 2003); and Robin Hahnel, *Of the People, By the People: The Case for a Participatory Economy* (Portland: Soapbox Press, 2012).

100 A parallel argument is made by Cohen and Rogers who argue that whether it is workplace regulation or welfare provision, "on-the-ground" forms of democratic association can provide more accurate and contextually attuned information and implementation in contrast to centralized forms of regulation and service provision (*Association and Democracy*, pp. 55–63).

101 As Arendt argues in relation to the insights of the American Revolutionaries, insights that she notes were sadly ignored in much subsequent modern political thought, "[f]or them, power came into being when and where people would get together and bind themselves through promises, covenants, and mutual pledges; only such power, which rested on reciprocity and mutuality, was real power and legitimate, whereas the so-called power of kings or princes or aristocrats, because it did not spring from mutuality but, at best, rested on consent, was spurious and usurped" (*On Revolution*, p. 173).

102 Central to Polanyi's position is that money is not a neutral commodity. Polanyi thought that the creation and use of money involved power relations and could not be taken as merely a neutral indicator of prior economic relations. Although Polanyi did not develop a fully fledged theory of money, something like Ingham's account is implicit in his understanding of economics. For Ingham, "[a]ll money is constituted by credit-debt relations" (*Nature of Money*, p. 72). Chrematistics (which leads to the commodification of money) is to give the symbol greater value than the prior social relations of credit and debt.

103 Whether a living wage, as distinct from a minimum wage, should be legally enforced or not is another matter. There is a case to be made that to achieve a wage rate set to reflect the real cost of living rather than the market rate, it should involve an element of organizing. To organize and achieve a living wage – rather than a minimum wage – entails not doing for others what they can do for themselves so as to ensure their agency, and therefore dignity, is recognized.

104 For a historical survey of working-class and labor militancy and its linkage to war and colonial and postcolonial struggles, see Beverly J. Silver, *Forces of Labor: Workers' Movements and Globalization Since 1870* (Cambridge: Cambridge University Press, 2003).

105 One such distortion that has come to prominence since 2008 is the so-called "Minsky moment" that draws from the work of the economist Hyman Minsky.

106 To reciprocity, exchange, and redistribution must be added a further, somewhat anomalous category: householding. On the anomalous nature of householding in Polanyi's schema, see Dale, *Karl Polanyi*, pp. 118–19. Householding consists in production for one's own use. As Polanyi puts it: "Its pattern is the closed group. Whether the very different entities of the family or the settlement or the manor formed the self-sufficient unit, the principle was invariably the same, namely, that of producing and storing for the satisfaction of the wants of the members of the group" (*Great Transformation*, pp. 55–56).

107 *Ibid.*, pp. 51–53.

108 *Ibid.*, p. 59. Polanyi sets market relations in opposition to reciprocity. However, those who build on Polanyi's work point to the complex interplay of market and reciprocal relations in forms of commercial exchange. For numerous examples of this interplay, see Stephen Gudeman, "Necessity or Contingency: Mutuality

and Market," in *Market and Society: The Great Transformation Today*, eds. Chris Hann and Keith Hart (Cambridge: Cambridge University Press, 2009), pp. 17–37.

109 Polanyi, *Great Transformation*, p. 60.

110 *Ibid.*, p. 57.

111 *Ibid.*, p. 55.

112 For an analysis of Polanyi's concept of the embedded economy, see Mark Harvey, Sally Randles, and Ronnie Ramilogan, "Working with and beyond Polanyian Perspectives," in *Karl Polanyi: New Perspectives on the Place of the Economy in Society*, eds. Mark Harvey, Ronnie Ramlogan, and Sally Randles (Manchester: Manchester University Press, 2007), pp. 3–7.

113 T. H. Marshall, *Citizenship and Social Class* (Cambridge: Cambridge University Press, 1950).

114 On the question of whether "welfare capitalism"/"embedded liberalism" constitutes a form of re-embedding or a perpetuation of a dialectic between liberalization and protectionism, see Hannes Lacher, "The Slight Transformation: Contesting the Legacy of Karl Polanyi," in *Reading Karl Polanyi for the Twenty-First Century: Market Economy as Political Project*, eds. Ayşe Buğra and Kaan Ağartan (New York: Palgrave Macmillan, 2007), pp. 49–64.

115 Margaret Somers synthesizes Arendt, Marshall, and Polanyi in a contemporary analysis of social citizenship and civil society under conditions of what she calls "'market fundamentalism." Counter to what is said here, rather than as a form of redistribution, Somers envisages welfare provision as an aspect of citizenship conceptualized as a form of noncontractual, generalized reciprocity (*Genealogies of Citizenship*, p. 87). Likewise, Mauss envisaged social insurance legislation as enshrining a principle of reciprocity (*The Gift: The Form and Reason for Exchange in Archaic Societies* [London: Routledge, 2001], pp. 86–87). One can go further and posit different models of welfare provision as accenting different types of gift relations. For just such an account, see Steffan Mau, "Welfare Regimes and the Norms of Social Exchange," *Current Sociology* 52.1 (2004): 53–74. However, while I concur with the ways in which these accounts locate welfare provision within a broader account of citizenship as a form of generalized reciprocity, what they fail to reckon with is how the logic of redistribution has come to dominate forms of welfare provision and either exclude forms of reciprocal relation operating in the production of welfare itself or convert them into forms of equivalent exchange. On this, see Jacques Godbout in collaboration with Alan Caillé, *The World of the Gift* (Montreal: McGill-Queen's University Press, 1998), pp. 51–64. Interestingly, Michael Walzer develops a constructive account of the relationship between gifts and redistribution and sees both as limiting the power of money. However, his primary concern is with developing an account of redistributive justice with the role of gifts dealt with only in passing (*Spheres of Justice: A Defense of Pluralism and Equality* [New York: Basic Books, 1983]).

116 Their work can be seen as parallel to and an extension of the "heterodox" U.S. school of thought known as "institutional economics" initiated by the likes of Thorstein Veblen and John R. Commons.

117 Luigino Bruni and Stefano Zamagni, *Civil Economy: Efficiency, Equity, Public Happiness* (Bern: Peter Lang, 2007), pp. 20–21.

118 In a separate work, Luigino Bruni develops a different taxonomy: *Reciprocity, Altruism and the Civil Society: In Praise of Heterogeneity* (London: Routledge, 2008). I draw from Bruni's account in subsequent discussions but have focused primarily on his joint work with Zamagni as this more directly parallels Polanyi's and is less concerned with highly technical discussions in game theory. A consequence of Bruni framing discussion in terms of game theory is that there is an underlying mathmaticalization of human relations and methodological individualism in his account of reciprocity. Likewise, Bruni and Zamagni, perhaps as is inevitable for those working in the discipline of economics, locate their account of sociality before a bench of judges whose criteria of evaluation are utilitarian and who see the world through the prism of an economistic rationality. Although it may be a proper apologetic strategy, it is not something I think is either necessary or even desirable as it reinscribes the problem that economic anthropology and theology contest: namely, the overly reductive nature of economistic rationalities and their voluntaristic anthropology as a dominant form of public reason.

119 *Ibid.*, p. 177. See also Graeber, *Debt*, pp. 102–08.

120 Christian theology often resorts to the language of gift to examine the meaning and nature of love and recently, a number of theologians have explored connections between conceptions of gift, theology, and economic and political relations. See, for example, John Milbank, *Being Reconciled: Ontology and Pardon* (London: Routledge, 2003); and Kathryn Tanner, *Economy of Grace* (Minneapolis, MN: Fortress Press, 2005). The most prominent theological account that brings together love, gift, and an integrated account of economic and political relations in the contemporary context is that given in Catholic social teaching. This is particularly apparent in the 2009 papal encyclical *Caritas in Veritate*. We find in the encyclical, and more broadly the tradition of reflection it is responding to and grows out of, a critique of capitalism in which concern for the common good and the importance of the transformation of capitalism through loving relations is central. Although published amid the growing financial crisis from 2008 onward, *Caritas in Veritate* was not intended to be a direct response to the crisis. Rather, its occasion was the fortieth anniversary of Pope Paul VI's encyclical, *Populorum Progressio* (1967). Thus, it stands in a tradition of marking the anniversaries of previous encyclicals addressing economic questions, a tradition initiated by Leo XIII's *Rerum Novarum* (1891). In modern Protestantism, a common way of framing a theological analysis of love distinguishes its forms through a taxonomy involving some or all of the following categories: *eros*, *philia*, *agapē*, *cupiditas*, *caritas*, and *fraternitas*. The work of the Swedish Lutheran theologian Anders Nygren was a crucial catalyst for this approach in the twentieth century. Central to the debate Nygren's work sparked was the question of how to interpret Augustine's doctrine of love and his eudaimonistic conception of ethics. Recent responses to this debate, most notably by Charles Mathewes and Eric Gregory, have developed an Augustinian ethics of citizenship in which love is a central virtue (Gregory, *Politics and the Order of Love*; and Charles T. Mathewes, *A Theology of Public Life* [Cambridge: Cambridge University Press, 2007]).

121 As Peter McMylor notes of Polanyi: "It would be hard not to notice the presence here of a partially secularised Christian conscience" ("Moral Philosophy and Economic Sociology: What MacIntyre Learnt from Polanyi," in *Karl Polanyi: New*

Perspectives on the Place of the Economy in Society, eds. Mark Harvey, Ronnie Ramlogan, and Sally Randles [Manchester: Manchester University Press, 2007], p. 116). Although his family converted from Judaism to Protestant Christianity, as an adult Polanyi was never a confessing Christian. Yet he was actively involved in Christian socialist circles; for example, he helped to found the Christian Auxiliary Left, a group that was, as Gareth Dale notes, "dedicated to forging a social current within Christianity and to infusing the communist and socialist movements with the Christian spirit" (Dale, *Karl Polanyi*, p. 40).

122 Initiated by Karl Bücher and much influenced by Mauss, Polanyi's work is nevertheless key to the development of economic anthropology. Despite engaging with the same anthropological sources as Mauss, Polanyi does not directly discuss Mauss's work. However, there are strong parallels between Polanyi's and Mauss's political positions. For an exploration of these, see Philippe Steiner, "The Critique of the Economic Point of View: Karl Polanyi and the Durkheimians," in *Market and Society: The Great Transformation Today*, eds. Chris Hann and Keith Hart (Cambridge: Cambridge University Press, 2009), pp. 56–71.

123 For example, see Warren, *Dry Bones Rattling*; Chambers, *Roots*, p. 68.

124 On the different emphasis given within conceptions of gift relations within different world religions, see Jonathan Parry, "The Gift, the Indian Gift and the 'Indian Gift,'" *Man* 21.3 (1986): 453–73.

125 For a catalogue of instances where market values crowd out nonmarket and moral considerations, see Sandel, *What Money Can't Buy*, pp. 93–130.

126 On the continuing importance yet occluded status of gift relations to modern societies, see Godbout, *World of the Gift*.

127 Hénaff, *Price of Truth*, pp. 386–87.

128 The identification of this last corruption draws from the work of René Girard. The implication of his account of mimetic rivalry is to highlight the ambiguity of sacrifice – which I take to be a form of ceremonial gift exchange – as a means of either resolving or forestalling violent conflicts through processes of scapegoating and victimization that lead to violence being directed against the one rather than it erupting between the many.

129 This is a point that both Graeber and Hénaff are at pains to emphasize. See Hénaff, *Price of Truth*, p. 153; Graeber, *Debt*, pp. 298–302.

130 Hénaff, *Price of Truth*, p. 397.

131 *Ibid.*, pp. 154, 397.

132 For numerous instances of this kind of misinterpretation, particularly by economists, see Sandel, *What Money Can't Buy*. The advocacy that Christmas presents should be monetized being a striking example (pp. 98–107).

133 MacIntyre identifies this capacity as the virtue of *misericordia*. For MacIntyre, *misericordia* directs one to include the stranger within one's communal relationships. It is thus the basis for extending the bounds of one's communal obligations, and thereby including the other in one's relations of giving and receiving characterized by just generosity. He states: "*Misericordia* is that aspect of charity whereby we supply what is needed by our neighbour and among the virtues that relate us to our neighbour *misericordia* is the greatest" (MacIntyre, *Dependent Rational Animals*, p. 125). In Latin it denoted pity, compassion, and mercy and was used as the term to translate the Hebrew word *hesed* or loving-kindness, a key attribute ascribed to God.

134 As Bruni notes, "[t]he agapic logic can renounce all forms of conditionality, but still remains a form of reciprocity" (*Reciprocity, Altruism and the Civil Society,* p. 50, n. 8).

135 For a more extensive discussion of Greco-Roman and New Testament conceptions of grace and the responses appropriate to it, see David deSilva, *Honor, Patronage, Kinship and Purity: Unlocking New Testament Culture* (Downers Grove, IL: InterVarsity Press, 2000), pp. 106–48.

136 Numerous parables in the New Testament illustrate these expectations. For example, in the parable of the unforgiving servant in Matthew 18:23–35, the servant who is forgiven a great debt by his master fails to act appropriately by similarly forgiving a fellow servant a small amount and so is judged harshly.

137 A number of New Testament stories play with or against this pattern. See, for example, the parable of the sower (Matthew 13:1–9); the feeding of the 5,000, where a gift is given out of compassion, which subsequently produces an abundant surplus (Matthew 14:13–21); or 1 Corinthians 15:3, where the corollary of receiving the gift of faith is to pass it on.

138 On the relationship between humanitarianism and processes of secularization, see Michael N. Barnett, *Empire of Humanity: A History of Humanitarianism* (Ithaca, NY: Cornell University Press, 2011); Gilbert Rist, *The History of Development: From Western Origins to Global Faith* (London: Zed Books, 2002); and Erica Bornstein and Peter Redfield, *Genealogies of Suffering and the Gift of Care: A Working Paper on the Anthropology of Religion, Secularism, and Humanitarianism,* SSRC Working Papers, Social Science Research Council, New York (2007).

139 The kinds of language used to describe such forms of renunciation need careful discernment. Use of terms such as self-emptying, kenosis, sacrifice, and self-dispossession can be deployed within the logic of self-ownership and a voluntaristic anthropology. Such a logic runs counter to the kind of relational anthropology that undergirds the account of gift relations set out here, wherein an individual's personhood is constituted through relations with others. Acts of self-renunciation (as distinct from self-dispossession) are not premised on giving up my absolute sovereign control over myself. To assume one has a sovereign control to give up is a subspecies of a broader problem: the need to recognize that I am destructively turned in on myself and pridefully seek to dominate others. Such prideful domination of others is buttressed and reinforced by material possessions. As a condition, it can only be healed by becoming free for others and therefore free to truly be in relation with others.

140 Contrary to Graeber, who seems to envisage acts of divine grace as establishing a relationship of debt and obligation, I build on a specifically Christian theological reading of grace and see it as the antidote to debt. The proclamation of Jubilee, which is how Jesus' mission and ministry are framed in Luke, represents the cancellation of debt. This theme is picked up in the use of the word forgiveness/*aphesis* (e.g., Matthew 26:28; Ephesians 1:7; Colossians 1:14; Hebrews 10:8), which means the cancellation or release from a debt or obligation. Yet it is precisely the need for a Biblical-style Jubilee that Graeber calls for at the end of his book (*Debt,* p. 390).

141 In New Testament terms, communion is the fulfilment of the Jubilee we hear of in Acts 2:44–45: "All who believed were together and had all things in common; they

would sell their possessions and goods and distribute the proceeds to all, as any had need." It is a sign of the Holy Spirit's work and foundational to the initiation of the church.

142 In distinction from Aristotle's conception of friendship as only possible between equals, a Christian theological account suggests we can be friends of God and in the New Testament, the paterfamilias is called on to see women, slaves, and children as both "brothers" and as citizens. This involves a subtle departure from the kind of view Aristotle outlines, such that in the New Testament, despite conditions of inequality pertaining, we are to treat all people as equals.

143 This, of course, echoes Marx's formulation of justice as involving giving to each according to ability and need. MacIntyre, in his discussion of Marx's more-developed version, gives direct expression to what I have in mind here. He states: "Between those capable of giving and those who are most dependent and in most need of receiving – children, the old, the disabled – the norms will have to satisfy a revised version of Marx's formula for justice in a communist society, 'From each according to her or his ability, to each, so far as is possible, according to her or his needs' (*Critique of the Gotha Program,* I). Marx of course understood his second formula as having application only in an as yet unrealizable future. And we must recognise that limited economic resources allow only for its application in imperfect ways. But without its application, even if imperfectly, even if *very* imperfectly, we will be unable to sustain a way of life characterized both by effective appeals to desert and by effect appeals to need, and so by justice to and for both the independent and the dependent" (MacIntyre, *Dependent Rational Animals,* p. 130).

144 The interplay between the golden rule and the love command in the New Testament is one that leads to the constant and mutual reinterpretation and thence transfiguration of both. On this, see Paul Ricoeur, "Ethical and Theological Considerations on the Golden Rule," in *Figuring the Sacred: Religion, Narrative, and Imagination*, ed. Mark I. Wallace, trans. David Pellauer (Minneapolis, MN: Augsburg Fortress, 1995), pp. 293–302; and idem, "The Golden Rule: Exegetical and Theological Perplexities," *New Testament Studies* 36.3 (1990): 392–97.

145 Ricoeur, "Love and Justice,' in *Figuring the Sacred*, p. 328. For Ricoeur, the golden rule is a necessary ethical maxim that must nevertheless stand in a dialectical relation to the command to "love thy neighbor." On this dialectical relation and how it creates a "genuine reciprocity," see Alan Kirk, "'Love Your Enemies,' the Golden Rule, and Ancient Reciprocity [Luke 6:27–35]," *Journal of Biblical Literature* 122.4 (2003): 667–86.

146 Indeed, one implication of community organizing is to suggest that noncontractual patterns of sociality are vital to the proper functioning of citizenship.

147 The taxonomy just outlined should be read as a piece of informed but conjectural hypothesizing or what Charles Sanders Peirce called abductive reasoning, as distinct from the primarily deductive and inductive forms deployed up to now.

148 Such an endeavor was an important dimension of Mauss's and Durkheim's work.

149 *A Vindication of the Rights of Woman: With Strictures on Political and Moral Subjects* (1797). Mauss draws attention to the demeaning aspects of accepting "the injurious patronage of the rich almsgiver" and sees modern morality as an attempt to do away with such forms of charity (*The Gift,* pp. 81–82).

150 Alinsky, *Reveille*, p. 59.

151 For an account of the shift away from an Aristotelian conception of virtue and the development of notions of self-interest in the emergence of civil society, see Becker, *Emergence of Civil Society in the Eighteenth Century*. In light of the persistent confusions around the use of the term "self-interest," a better term to describe the IAF's theory and practice of interests is perhaps "mutual interest." This makes explicit commitments of reciprocity and loyalty between distinct others, shows forth the importance of trust in the other, and signals the investment in the capacity of relationships to sustain a common life amid competing interests.

152 For an account of the multivalent uses of the term self-love in Augustine, see Oliver O'Donovan, *The Problem of Self-Love in St. Augustine* (London: Yale University Press, 1980). Augustine's framing of the problem was crucial for subsequent debates, particularly in the early modern period between those seeking to find a universal, rational basis for political order not on the basis of revelation but on the basis of self-preservation (for example, Grotius) and their critics (for example, the Jansenists). Rousseau's account of the relationship between *amour propre* and *amour de soi* can be seen as an attempt to reconcile these two sides of the debate.

153 For an intellectual history of the shift, see Harry Liebersohn, *The Return of the Gift: European History of a Global Idea* (Cambridge: Cambridge University Press, 2011).

154 For example, although Adam Smith uses the term "self-love" twice in the *Wealth of Nations*, both times it is as a synonym for self-interest. By contrast, the term "interest" and its cognates are used 557 times. On this and for an account of how Smith inverts an Augustinian theodicy into a providentialist natural theology, see Waterman, *Political Economy and Christian Theology*, pp. 88–106.

155 Despite this, in politics and commerce people often act for reasons not reducible to material gain or calculating self-regard. For an account of the shift, from Hobbes, Mandeville, and Locke onward, from conceptions of economic relations as reciprocal and as relations in which virtue was central to the proper ordering of commercial exchange to the dominance of conceptions of economic relations as driven by selfish interests divorced from the pursuit of the common good/notions of public happiness, see Bruni and Zamagni, *Civil Economy*. See also, Mauss, *The Gift*, pp. 97–98.

156 Parry, "The Gift, the Indian Gift and the 'Indian Gift,'" p. 466.

157 Kant's notion of "duty" (*Pflicht*) exemplifies this false dichotomy (see, in particular, Immanuel Kant, *Groundwork of the Metaphysics of Morals*, trans. Mary Gregor, 2nd ed. [Cambridge: Cambridge University Press, 2012]). Just as significant as Kant in separating a concept of moral action from mutual benefit is the emergence of the notion of altruism and its place at the forefront of moral discourse in the nineteenth century. On this, see Thomas Dixon, "The Invention of Altruism: Auguste Comte's *Positive Polity* and Respectable Unbelief in Victorian Britain," in *Science and Beliefs: From Natural Philosophy to Natural Science, 1700–1900*, eds. David M. Knight and Matthew D. Eddy (Aldershot, UK: Ashgate, 2005), pp. 195–211; and Stefan Collini, *Public Moralists: Political Thought and Intellectual Life in Britain, 1850–1930* (Oxford: Clarendon Press, 1991), pp. 60–90.

158 For an account of Mauss's political vision, see Liebersohn, *The Return of the Gift*, pp. 139–63.

159 There are real points of tension between a full-orbed account of Christian love and mutuality and the kind of temporal political obligations that the IAF conception of self-interest encapsulates. I have delineated elsewhere these points of tension and set out a theological framework for how they might be coordinated with an Augustinian account of the relationship between the City of God and the earthly city. See Bretherton, *Christianity and Contemporary Politics*, pp. 71–125.

160 Altruism is a term developed by Comte in explicit rejection of Christian notions of love. It is not to be confused with notions of magnanimity and economies of gift exchange. Charles Taylor sees an emphasis on benevolence and altruism as ideals as a key feature in the development of what he calls "exclusive humanism," identifying these notions as the trace of the prior Christian emphasis on *agapē*, yet in "exclusive humanism" they are located in an atomistic conception of agency (*Secular Age*, pp. 246–80). See also Collini, *Public Moralists*, pp. 60–90.

161 Sheldon Wolin, *Tocqueville between Two Worlds: The Making of a Political and Theoretical Life*, new ed. (Princeton, NJ: Princeton University Press, 2003), p. 422. By way of contrast, the purpose of Christ's sacrifice was not philanthropic donation but the public renewal of communion through an exceptional act of radical hospitality. This exceptional act kick-starts a subsequent chain of gift exchange and mutuality.

162 John Rawls, *Political Liberalism*, pp. 16–17. Another, parallel example is R. M. Titmuss, *The Gift Relationship: From Human Blood to Social Policy* (London: George Allen and Unwin, 1970).

163 Rawls, *Political Liberalism*, p. 50. See also John Rawls, "Justice as Reciprocity," in *Collected Papers*, ed. Samuel Freeman (Cambridge, MA: Harvard University Press, 1999), pp. 190–224.

164 One implication of the inattention to symbolic exchange in public life is to obscure the ways in which the gift of the severely disabled are gestures and forms of being in the world that challenge the pace and structure of so much of modern life. Instead, they are rendered entirely passive subjects of altruism. The need to take seriously the reciprocal nature of the relationship between able bodies and the disabled is a theme Jean Vanier, founder of the L'Arche communities, constantly reiterates in his writings. For a more systematic rendition of this point, see Hans S. Reinders, *Receiving the Gift of Friendship: Profound Disability, Theological Anthropology, and Ethics* (Grand Rapids, MI: Eerdmans, 2008), pp. 312–78.

165 They note also that "[t]he reciprocal action can be directed toward a third party" (Bruni and Zamagni, *Civil Economy*, p. 168). One can read MacIntyre's account of what it means to be a dependent rational animal as representing one attempt to take the transitivity of human relations over time seriously. See MacIntyre, *Dependent Rational Animals*.

166 For a critique of Rawls as reducing the golden rule to the logic of equivalence, see Paul Ricoeur, *The Just*, trans. David Pellauer (Chicago: University of Chicago Press, 2000), pp. 36–57; idem, "Love and Justice," *Figuring the Sacred*, pp. 315–29. For a more positive appraisal, see Thom Brooks, "Reciprocity as Mutual Recognition," *The Good Society* 21.1 (2012): 21–35.

167 Jacques Derrida, *Politics of Friendship*, trans. George Collins (London: Verso, 1997), pp. 93–99, 197–98. For Derrida, such a linkage also inscribes patriarchal relations into democratic ones: the circle of brothers excludes women and is what he calls a "phallogocentric" schema.

168 *Ibid.*, pp. 83–89.
169 *Ibid.*, p. 83.
170 *Ibid.*, p. 22.
171 John Caputo, "Who is Derrida's Zarathustra? Of Fraternity, Friendship, and a Democracy to Come," *Research in Phenomenology* 29 (1999): 184–98, p. 187. Derrida states: "Pure hospitality consists in leaving one's house open to the unforeseeable arrival, which can be an intrusion, even a dangerous intrusion, liable eventually to cause harm. This pure or unconditional hospitality is not a political or juridical concept. Indeed, for an organized society that upholds its laws and wants to maintain the sovereign mastery of its territory, its culture, its language, its nation, for a family or for a nation concerned with controlling its practices of hospitality, it is indeed necessary to limit and to condition hospitality. This can be done with the best intentions in the world, since unconditional hospitality can also have perverse effects" (Jacques Derrida and Elisabeth Roudinesco, *For What Tomorrow ...: A Dialogue*, trans. Jeff Fort [Stanford, CA: Stanford University Press, 2004], p. 59).
172 Caputo, "Who is Derrida's Zarathustra?" p. 192.
173 Derrida, *Politics of Friendship*, p. 105.
174 Jacques Derrida, "The Villanova Roundtable: A Conversation with Jacques Derrida," in *Deconstruction in a Nutshell*, ed. John D. Caputo (New York: Fordham University Press, 1997), p. 18.
175 Derrida, "Villanova Roundtable," p. 13.
176 Milbank criticizes Derrida's "other-regarding" ethics for reintroducing forms of self-possession and invulnerability and refusing the contingent and therefore open-ended and uncertain nature of the moral life. See Milbank, *Being Reconciled*, pp. 138–61.
177 Hénaff, *Price of Truth*, p. 316
178 *Ibid.*, p. 323.
179 As Michael Walzer notes, the animus toward, and at times the advocacy of, abolishing the family in egalitarian political visions rests on the insight that the family is a perennial source of inequality and special relations (*Spheres of Justice*, p. 229).
180 Ingham, *The Nature of Money*; Keith Hart, *The Memory Bank: Money in an Unequal World* (London: Profile Books, 1999).
181 This builds on what is called the "chartalist" view of money established by Georg Friedrich Knapp. Knapp contrasts "fiat" or chartalist money, which was a creature of the law, with "metallism" or a commodity theory, wherein money had to actually contain or represent (as in the Gold Standard) something of equivalent value.
182 Graeber, *Debt*, pp. 48–49, 268–69.
183 Ingham suggests that in the shift from credit to commodity money or cash, a crucial role is played by centralizing sovereign, often imperial authorities: they monopolize the issuing and production of money for the purposes of tax and the provisioning of armies. Money moves from being a way of tracking credit and debt relations between persons (and thereby interpersonal) to becoming a way for sovereigns to manage what subjects are said to owe the state, backed up by violent force if necessary (*The Nature of Money*, pp. 97–101; see also Hart, *The Memory Bank*, pp. 233–72). Arguably, credit money emerges in relatively stable,

high-trust contexts whereas commodity money becomes desirable in unstable, often violent low-trust contexts where wealth needs to be easily transportable and exchangeable.

184 Ingham, *The Nature of Money*, p. 125. Ingham postulates that this coalescence took place within the unique conditions of England.

185 Hart, *The Memory Bank*, p. 256.

186 James Buchan, *Frozen Desire: An Inquiry into the Meaning of Money* (London: Picador, 1997), p. 108.

187 The ways in which money redescribes the world in numerical and therefore quantifiable and by implication homogenizing, rationalizing, and liquefying ways is a common feature of Marx's, Simmel's, and Weber's theories of money. However, building on the work of Viviana Zelizer, Bill Maurer argues that numbers and money do not always do this. They can re-sacralize exchanges, and reintroduce and reinforce material and social practices. Bill Maurer, "The Anthropology of Money," *Annual Review of Anthropology* 35 (2006): 15–36. It is important to note Zelizer and Maurer address themselves to embedded markets rather than the highly speculative financial markets of "the sea."

188 Somers, *Genealogies of Citizenship*, pp. 88–89.

189 *Ibid.*, p. 89. Somers examines how the process of "contractualization" manifested itself in New Orleans in the response to Hurricane Katrina. *Ibid.*, pp. 92–113.

190 Jean-Luc Nancy, *The Truth of Democracy*, trans. Pascale-Anne Brault and Michael Naas (New York: Fordham University Press, 2010), pp. 19–25. Nancy recognizes, albeit tangentially, the place of gift relations as ways of recognizing the singularity of others. However, he sees such gestures of recognition as nonpolitical. Democratic politics for him is the means through which such gestures are given space and possibility. Although he is right in one sense – such gestures constitute the space and possibility of democratic politics – by my account, there is a mutual relation between the two. It is this mutually constitutive relation between democratic politics and gift relations that configures a common space in which multiple visions of the good life can be heard and valued.

191 Sandel, *Democracy's Discontent* and *What Money Can't Buy.*

Conclusion

1 Alinsky, *Reveille*, p. 197

2 This is a point drawn from Sheldon Wolin, "Agitated Times," *Parallax* 11.4 (2005): 2–11, p. 8. This article represents a development of Wolin's earlier reflections on democratic temporality in "What Time Is It?" *Theory & Event* 1.1 (1997). For a critical assessment of Wolin's shifting views in relation to democratic temporality, see Mario Feit, "Wolin, Time, and the Democratic Temperament," *Theory & Event* 15.4 (2012).

3 As Agamben notes: "Every conception of history is invariably accompanied by a certain experience of time which is implicit in it, conditions it, and thereby has to be elucidated. Similarly, every culture is first and foremost a particular experience of time, and no new culture is possible without an alteration in this experience. The original task of a genuine revolution, therefore, is never merely to 'change the world', but also – and above all – to 'change time'" ("Time and History: Critique

of the Instant and the Continuum," in *Infancy and History: On the Destruction of Experience*, trans. Liz Heron [London: Verso, 1993], p. 91).

4 I am here drawing from Jonathan Lear's Kierkegaardian conception of irony (*The Case for Irony* [Cambridge, MA: Harvard University Press, 2011]).

5 In terms of Christian theology, none of these human, immanent, and earthly responses are adequate, governed as they are by finitude and fallenness. None of these stances toward time are equivalent to the radically reconfiguring impact of the posture of *hope in Christ*, with its paradoxical injunction to remember our future.

6 Marx pointed to the role of primitive accumulation in the form of the enclosure of common lands and the enslavement of colonial peoples in the emergence of industrial capitalism. Hardt and Negri draw from this insight to argue that capitalism can only sustain itself through repeated acts of enclosure – whether of the gene pool or language itself. It could be argued that Marx does include an account of the enclosure of time within his labor theory of value. By Marx's account, capitalism is largely built on the coercive extraction of surplus time from the producing classes and the use of technology to make ever more efficient use of time and thereby extract greater value from labor. The homogenization of time and the overcoming of time as a limit are central to Marx's critique of capitalism. On this, see William James Booth, "Economies of Time: On the Idea of Time in Marx's Political Economy," *Political Theory* 19.1 (1991): 7–27. However, Marx does not discuss the temporal dimensions of usury in his analysis of it.

7 This term is taken from Briggs, *Democracy as Problem Solving*, pp. 136–39.

8 See, for example, Cohen and Rogers, *Associations and Democracy*, pp. 236–63.

9 The term "tools for conviviality" is taken from Ivan Illich who was one of the most penetrating critics of modern institutional arrangements for delivering public goods such as education, health, and welfare. His contribution is a vital if neglected resource for reimagining the production and delivery of goods in common. Briefly put, Illich calls for less capital intensive, agency centric and more widely distributable "tools," by which he means institutions and systems as well as material technologies. Alinsky and Illich knew each other and corresponded and Illich himself can be seen as part of the broader transatlantic conversation about consociational forms of democracy outlined in Chapters 7 and 8.

10 Arendt, *On Revolution*, p. 173.

11 Foucault's critique of modern regimes of "governmentality" becomes pressingly salient at this point. Michel Foucault, *Security, Territory, Population: Lectures at the College de France, 1977–1978*, trans. Graham Burchell (New York: Picador, 2007).

12 Fung and Wright's *principles* are the following: a focus on specific, tangible problems; bottom-up participation through the involvement of those people directly affected by these problems and officials close to them; and a deliberative approach to planning, problem solving, and strategizing. The *properties* they identify are: the devolution of decision making to "empowered local units"; the creation of formal linkages of legitimation, responsibility, resource distribution, coordination, and communication that connect these units to each other and to superordinate, centralized public authorities; and a key role for formal, state authorities but in such a way as to allow for the transformation of governance institutions through the institutionalization of ongoing participation by ordinary citizens. Finally, the *enabling*

conditions discussed include such things as education levels and the equality of power held by different groups involved (Fung and Wright, *Deepening Democracy*, pp. 15–29). Similarly, Sirianni identifies eight core principles for designing policy so as to ensure it allows for collaborative governance. Sirianni's eight principles are: the coproduction of public goods, the identification and mobilizing of community assets, the sharing of professional expertise, the enabling of public deliberation, the promotion of sustainable partnerships, building fields and governance networks strategically, transforming institutional cultures, and ensuring reciprocal accountability (*Investing in Democracy*, pp. 41–65).

13 Fung and Wright, *Deepening Democracy*, p. 22. Common features of such approaches involve: (1) advocacy of the co-governance and coproduction of public services; (2) re-envisaging professional identities and practice as enabling "lay" participation and facilitating access to multiple sources of knowledge; (3) conceiving problem solving as common work involving multiple stakeholders with a shared sense of purpose; and (4) the renewal of workplace democracy as part of the extension of democratic practices beyond an apolitical vision of civil society. Experts and specialist knowledge continue to play a vital role. However, they cease to have a monopoly on the decision-making process. Conversely, what is envisaged here is shared responsibility rather than the delegation of decision making to a "consumer." For case studies from different fields of civic professionalism in practice, see Doherty and Mendenhall, "Citizen Health Care"; Dzur, *Democratic Professionalism*, chaps. 5–7; and Sirianni, *Investing in Democracy*, chaps. 3–5.

14 For example, in the context of a hospital, through listening to those patients with a permanent condition that requires regular engagement with health care facilities and staff, leaders with knowledge of the system and a long-term self-interest in change can be identified.

15 It is the involvement of such elements that stops coproduction and co-governance from becoming a reproduction of what Gilles Deleuze calls the "control society"; that is, the co-option, commodification, and liquefication of the productive and communicative agency of ordinary people so that their creative energies are turned against them in order that they help generate their own subjection ("Postscript on the Societies of Control," *October* 59 [1992], pp. 3–7).

16 The kinds of proposals outlined here pose a question to the practice of BBCO: Can existing coalitions work to create and participate in forms of collaborative governance? This question confronted London Citizens when it had the opportunity to bid for a government contract to train 5,000 community organizers in 2010. The possibility sparked a vehement internal debate; the primary issue being whether winning such a contract was worth compromising the commitment to bipartisanship, independence, and not taking state money. In its favor, the contract was felt to offer a strategic opportunity to expand Citizens UK nationally, establish Citizens UK's approach to organizing as best practice in the still embryonic world of organizing in the United Kingdom, and place Citizens UK on a firmer financial footing. Various proposals had been discussed with the Conservative Party before the 2010 Election. The one put forward by Citizens UK was for an institute for organizing and leadership development endowed by government and thereby semiautonomous. In the event, the proposals actually put forward by the Office for Civil Society, which was tasked with managing the contract, were a pale shadow of what was discussed and rendered the delivery wholly subject to

centralized control. Citizens UK did submit a proposal but despite strong indications to the contrary, it did not win the bid. "Locality," which was the agency awarded the contract, had a track record in community development rather than organizing and, as an organization, grew out of the coalition of the remaining settlement houses in the United Kingdom. Given the history of community organizing outlined in Chapter 1, there was a certain irony to this outcome. However, the difficulties and limitations Locality subsequently experienced in working with the government to deliver the contract meant that the retrospective judgment of organizers and leaders in Citizens UK was one of relief. I should note that I sat on a panel entitled the "Community First and Community Organising Programme Advisory Panel" that was appointed by the Office for Civil Society to advise on the delivery of the bid by Locality from 2011 to 2012. The nature and process of delivering the contract highlighted how, despite rhetoric to the contrary, there is a strong aversion among UK civil servants and politicians to enacting the kind of reform of public services suggested here, with public sector reform still captive to visions determined by redistribution and equivalent exchange (whether neoliberal, social democratic, or a mélange of the two). However, given the nature of the kind of measures proposed here, their enactment is not dependent on directives by central government. So, for example, the National Health Service has experimented with introducing elements of organizing practice into its operations at various levels. Perversely, neoliberal reform processes can create space for such experimentation while at the same time eroding the relational, financial, and institutional means necessary to do it.

17 Boyte, *Reinventing Citizenship as Public Work*; see also Cynthia Estlund, *Working Together: How Workplace Bonds Strengthen a Diverse Democracy* (Oxford: Oxford University Press, 2003).

18 This is set out explicitly in John Paul II's encyclical *Laborem Exercens* (1981) that sees the nature and purpose of human work as the key to what it calls "the social question"; that is, how, in the modern period, to make life more humane.

19 *Laborem Exercens*, §V.24.

20 This is also a central insight of Marx's analysis of "commodity fetishism." See especially Karl Marx, *Capital: A Critique of Political Economy*, vol. I, trans. Ben Fowkes (London: Penguin Books, 1990).

21 Polanyi, *Great Transformation*, p. 75.

22 Drawing from Mauss, Parry points out that in conceptions of gifts, "[i]t is because the thing contains the person that the donor retains a lien on what he has given away and we cannot therefore speak of an alienation of property; and it is because of this participation of the person in the object that the gift creates an enduring bond between persons" ("The Gift, the Indian Gift and the 'Indian Gift'," p. 457).

23 The reverse is true for much left-wing politics, which has historically tended to prioritize sites of production rather than places as the key emphasis for political action. This is exemplified in the Marxist emphasis on the factory as the womb of the proletariat and the anarchist emphasis on autonomous production and syndicates. As Harvey points out, paradoxically, an almost exclusive attention to workplaces fails to engage the ways in which social conditions and urban living point to the importance of money and finance capital (*Rebel Cities*, pp. 128–30).

24 Boyte, *Reinventing Citizenship as Public Work*, p. 15. Although, as should be clear from the analysis presented here, Boyte is wrong to suggest that the emphasis by

organizers on associative democracy necessarily "takes substantial institutional transformation off the map, ruling out the possibility of re-invigorating the public cultures and purposes and work practices of institutions such as higher education, professional systems, businesses, and government" (p. 17). However, what it does require is an extension of some of the insights of organizing to these other areas.

25 For an initial statement and discussion of what Blue Labour stood for, see Glasman et al., eds., *The Labour Tradition and the Politics of Paradox*. Something of the story of Blue Labour's rapid rise to prominence is told in Rowenna Davis, *Tangled Up in Blue: Blue Labour and the Struggle for Labour's Soul* (London: Ruskin Publishing, 2011).

26 A significant fruit of the incorporation of community organizing and a more populist, less technocratic and top-down approach being engaged with was the adoption of a cap on interest rates as Labour policy. For a description of the introduction of community organizing into policy formulation in the lead-up to adopting a cap on interest rates as party policy, see James Scott, "This Is What Happens When Community Organising and Policy Combine," available at: http://labourlist.org/2013/02/this-is-what-happens-when-community-organising-and-policy-combine/ (last accessed August 8, 2013).

27 Although initially contacted via Glasman in 2010, Graf was only directly involved in the party from 2011 onward. Even though Graf is officially retired from the IAF, he is still strongly associated with it and the linkage is reiterated in media coverage of his involvement in the Labour Party. Moreover, he enjoys the full backing of Gecan and the other senior organizers in Metro IAF (although Cortés, leader of Southwest IAF, opposes the connection). Jameson strongly opposed the move. For him, Graf's involvement overidentified organizing with the Labour Party in such a way as to compromise the commitment to nonpartisanship central to BBCO and make working with the Conservative Party very difficult. At a stretch, it was felt to raise questions about the charitable status of Citizens UK as a nonpartisan organization. The tension was also the fruit of twenty years of frustration on Jameson's part with the hostility and suspicion often expressed by figures within the Labour Party and the unions toward community organizing.

28 Earlier in his career Graf had undertaken analogously transformative political engagements when organizing for Communities Organized for Public Service (COPS) in San Antonio. On the transformative impact of COPS on the municipal politics of San Antonio in the late 1970s see Heywood Sanders, "Communities Organized for Public Service and Neighborhood Revitalization in San Antonio," in *Public Policy and Community: Activism and Governance in Texas*, ed. *Robert Wilson* (Austin: University of Texas Press, 1997), pp. 36–68.

29 Citizens UK has marginalized itself from engagement with developments in the Labour Party and its connection to the IAF. The danger for Citizens UK is that it interprets the rules of organizing too legalistically and reifies organizing as a practice. Organizing is always a work in progress, capable of innumerable riffs and adaptations. Conversely, there is a risk that in discussions of Blue Labour, community organizing and what it means to be a political party are elided. Much greater attention needs to be given to what the analogies and dis-analogies between the two are.

30 For Arendt's analysis of this conflict, see Arendt, *On Revolution*, pp. 240–70.

31 This was the fate of "Organizing for America" after 2008: instead of being the seedbed of myriad organizing initiatives attuned to local needs, it was rendered

moribund after the moment of election by being entirely subordinated to the needs of the Democratic Party.

Appendix: A Note on Method

1 Use of the term ethnography here is understood to mean "social research based on the close-up, on-the-ground observation of people and institutions in real time and space, in which the investigator embeds herself near (or within) the phenomenon so as to detect how and why agents on the scene act, think and feel the way they do" (Loïc Wacquant, "Ethnografeast: A Progress Report on the Practice and Promise of Ethnography," *Ethnography* 4.1 [2003]: 5–14, p. 5).

2 All data (including notes, interviews, and archival material) were coded and analyzed using QSR International's NVivo 8 (2008) software.

3 We made a purposeful selection so as to achieve a representative sample of leaders of member institutions and organizers. We also interviewed those organizers within the IAF who were some of the most influential on its development of organizing as a practice. We recognize that this approach suffers from a degree of "key informant bias" as it focuses on leaders and not a sample of ordinary members of the institutions involved. However, this bias is offset in part by the extensive participant observation of London Citizens. This means the research is informed by many conversations with non-leaders about community organizing. The primary approach taken is warranted as a strategic research decision as we were looking at the meaning-making aspects of the practice and hence, a key focus was on gatekeepers and interpreters of organizing within institutions. Richard Wood identifies this in his research as a key variable in determining the level and capacity of involvement of congregations in the political work of organizing.

4 I am extremely grateful for the conversation, patient feedback, and comments on the research from those outside of the IAF, in particular Harry Boyte, Marshall Ganz, Mike Miller, Heidi Swarts, Mark Warren, Jane Wills, and Richard Wood; and to those from within the IAF, in particular Mike Gecan, Arnie Graf, Neil Jameson, Jonathan Lange, Leo Penta, and Gerald Taylor.

5 In contrast to "action research" approaches, our research process was not part of the conscientization of the members of the organization nor did it engage in a problem-solving process with a particular group (Ernest T. Stringer, *Action Research*, 2nd ed. [London: Sage Publications, 1999], p. 10). For Stringer, in action research, the knowledge-production process is a collective process whereby the "subjects" of the research "are engaged in the process of defining and redefining the corpus of understanding on which their community or organizational life is based." It thus involves "collective investigation" (ibid., p. 11). In contrast, our investigation was researcher-led and directed. So although we were active participants in the practice and contributed to its flourishing, the design and implementation of the research was not itself participatory.

6 The study had to constantly negotiate (not always successfully) key tensions associated with participant observation: the tension between impartial observation and advocacy, the tension between identification with and becoming a supporter of the group studied, and the tension between the demands of active participation and the need to observe, take notes, and raise questions.

7 S. Lawrence-Lightfoot and J. Davis criticize the tendency, even in qualitative research, to treat relationships as a tool or strategy for gaining access to data, rather than as a means through which to establish a real relationship. They argue that "relationships that are complex, fluid, symmetric, and reciprocal – that are shaped by both researchers and actors – reflect a more responsible ethical stance and are likely to yield deeper data and better social science." They go on to emphasize the continual creation and renegotiation of the trust, intimacy, and reciprocity involved in building real research relationships (*The Art and Science of Portraiture* [San Francisco: Jossey-Bass, 1997], pp. 137–38).

8 It must be recognized that such a relationship is either not always possible in research of this kind or even appropriate given the subject of the research. Research on neo-fascists or groups with links to terrorist activities could adopt a similar approach, but this would obviously raise many questions about the "ethics" of such research.

9 A classic precedent for such an approach can be found in Eric Redman's *The Dance of Legislation* (New York: Simon & Schuster, 1973). Redman traces the passage of a bill that created the National Health Service Corps during the 91st Congress in 1970. He was a member of Senator Warren Magnuson's staff and actively involved in campaigning for the bill and making decisions in the political work. More contemporary equivalents to the kind of project undertaken here include: Cruikshank, *The Will to Empower*; Graeber, *Direct Action*; and Polletta, *Freedom is an Endless Meeting*.

10 This is not meant to apply an opposition between theory and the development of craft-based knowledge. Indeed, as Christopher Winch argues, under conditions of modern industrialization, theoretical learning becomes essential to the development of craft-based apprenticeships. See Christopher Winch, "Georg Kerschensteiner – Founding the Dual System in Germany," *Oxford Review of Education* 32.3 (2006): 381–96; and Linda Clarke and Christopher Winch, "Apprenticeship and Applied Theoretical Knowledge," *Educational Philosophy and Theory* 36.5 (2004): 509–21.

11 See, for example, Charles Briggs, *Learning How to Ask: A Sociolinguistic Appraisal of the Role of Interview in Social Science Research* (Cambridge: Cambridge University Press, 1986).

12 Timothy Jenkins, "Fieldwork and the Perception of Everyday Life," *Man* 29.2 (1994): 433–55, p. 445.

13 *Ibid.*, p. 452.

14 From a theological perspective, the positivist thrust of most social science is highly problematic. See Milbank, *Theology and Social Theory*. For an account of the centrality of apprenticeship in theological learning, see Stanley Hauerwas, "The Politics of Church: How We Lay Bricks and Make Disciples," in *After Christendom? How the Church is to Behave if Freedom, Justice and a Christian Nation are Bad Ideas* (Nashville, TN: Abingdon, 1991), chap. 4; and "Carving Stone or Learning to Speak Christian," in *The State of the University: Academic Knowledges and the Knowledge of God* (Oxford: Wiley-Blackwell, 2007), chap. 7.

15 A key exponent of such an approach is Bent Flyvbjerg. Flyvbjerg himself builds on the work of Robert Bellah, who first proposed reconceptualizing social science as a form of *phronesis* (Robert Bellah, "Social Science as Practical Reason," in *Ethics, Social Sciences, and Policy Analysis*, eds. Daniel Callahan and Bruce Jennings [New

York: Plenum Press, 1983], pp. 37–64). Flyvbjerg states: "Practical rationality and judgment evolve and operate primarily by virtue of deep-going case experiences. Practical rationality, therefore, is best understood through cases – experienced or narrated – just as judgment is best cultivated and communicated via the exposition of cases" (Flyvbjerg, *Making Social Science Matter*, p. 135).

16 Flyvbjerg gives the examples of Foucault's Panopticon and Freud's "Wolfman" as having strategic importance in the development of these thinkers' works. Likewise, David Thatcher, in his parallel account of what he calls the "normative case study" gives a long array of other such examples ("The Normative Case Study," *American Journal of Sociology* 111.6 [2006]: 1631–76).

17 See especially Michael Burawoy, *Ethnography Unbound: Power and Resistance in the Modern Metropolis* (Berkeley: University of California Press, 1991). This study can be seen as a contribution to Burawoy's and his students' call for a "global ethnography" in order to show how "ethnography's concern with concrete, lived experience can sharpen the abstractions of globalization theories into more precise and meaningful conceptual tools" (Burawoy et al., *Global Ethnography: Forces, Connections, and Imaginations in a Postmodern World* [Berkeley: University of California Press, 2000], xiv).

18 Taylor, *Secular Age*.

19 A fuller account of the methodology that undergirds this book is given in Luke Bretherton, "Coming to Judgment: Methodological Reflections on the Relationship between Ecclesiology, Ethnography and Political Theory," *Modern Theology* 28.2 (2012): 167–96.

20 Michael Burawoy, "The Extended Case Method," *Sociological Theory* 16:1 (1998): 4–33, p. 21. See also Michael Burawoy, "Revisits: An Outline of a Theory of Reflexive Ethnography," *American Sociological Review* 68 (2003): 645–79.

21 Burawoy, *Ethnography Unbound*, p. 9.

22 Burawoy, "Extended Case Method," p. 5.

Bibliography

ACTA. "About Us." Available at: www.actapublications.com/about/

Adams, Edward. *Constructing the World: A Study in Paul's Cosmological Language*. Edinburgh: T & T Clark, 2000.

Addams, Jane. *Democracy and Social Ethics*. Chicago: University of Illinois Press, 2002.

"The Settlement as a Factor in the Labor Movement." In *Hull House Maps and Papers*. Boston: Thomas Y. Crowell & Co., 1895.

"Trade Unions and Public Duty." *American Journal of Sociology* 4 (1899): 448–62.

Agamben, Giorgio. *Homo Sacer: Sovereign Power and Bare Life*. Translated by Daniel Heller-Roazen. Stanford, CA: Stanford University Press, 1998.

The Kingdom and the Glory: For a Theological Genealogy of Economy and Government. Translated by Lorenzo Chiesa and Matteo Mandarini. Stanford, CA: Stanford University Press, 2011.

State of Exception. Translated by Kevin Attell. Chicago: University of Chicago Press, 2005.

"Time and History: Critique of the Instant and the Continuum." In *Infancy and History: On the Destruction of Experience*. Translated by Liz Heron. London: Verso, 1993.

Albert, Michael. *Parecon: Life after Capitalism*. London: Verso, 2003.

Alexander, Jeffrey. "Civil Sphere, State, and Citizenship: Replying to Turner and the Fear of Enclavement." *Citizenship Studies* 12.2 (2008): 185–94.

"On the Interpretation of *The Civil Sphere*: Understanding and Contention in Contemporary Social Science." *Sociological Quarterly* 48 (2007): 641–59.

The Civil Sphere. Oxford: Oxford University Press, 2006.

Ali, Omar. *In The Lion's Mouth: Black Populism in the New South, 1886–1900*. Jackson: University of Mississippi Press, 2010.

Ali, Ruhana, Lina Jamoul, and Yusufi Vali. "A New Covenant of Virtue: Islam and Community Organising." Citizens UK and IAF, 2012. Available at: http://www.citizensuk.org/wp-content/uploads/2012/08/Islam-and-Community-Organising-V3-singles.pdf

Alinsky, Saul. "Behind the Mask." In *American Child: Which Way Community Action Programs?* 47.4 (1965): 7–9.

"Catholic Leadership." Speech presented to the National Conference of Catholic Charities, September 28, 1942. Box 16, file 239. Industrial Areas Foundation Archive, University of Illinois at Chicago.

"Empowering People, Not Elites: Interview with Saul Alinsky." *Playboy Magazine*. March, 1972.

"From Citizen Apathy to Participation." Paper Presented at the 6th Annual Fall Conference, Association of Community Councils of Chicago, October 19, 1957. Box 32, file 523. Industrial Areas Foundation Archive, University of Illinois at Chicago.

"Is there life after birth?" *Anglican Theological Review* 1 (1968).

"Is there life after birth?" Speech to the Centennial Meeting of the Episcopal Theological School, Cambridge, MA, June 7, 1967. Chicago: Industrial Areas Foundation Reprint.

"The I.A.F.—Why Is It Controversial?" *Church in Metropolis* 6 (Summer 1965): 13–16.

Letter to the Ford Foundation, May 27, 1951. Box 12, file 179. Industrial Areas Foundation Archive, University of Illinois at Chicago.

Letter to Ursula M. Niebuhr, February 4, 1972. *Reinhold Niebuhr Papers*, Library of Congress.

Memo addressed to Rt. Rev. Msgr. John O'Grady for Dominico Cardinal Tardini, Cardinal Secretary of State, Vatican City, August 27, 1959. Box 9, file 128. Industrial Areas Foundation Archive, University of Illinois at Chicago.

Reveille for Radicals. New York: Vintage Books, 1969 [1946].

Rules for Radicals: A Practical Primer for Realistic Radicals. New York: Vintage Books, 1989 [1971].

"The Tough Line on Poverty." *The United Church Observer*, February 15, 1966.

"The War on Poverty – Political Pornography." *The Journal of Social Issues* 21.1 (1965): 41–47.

"Youth and Morale." *The American Journal of Orthopsychiatry* 12.4 (1942): 598–602.

Allen, Danielle S. *Talking to Strangers: Anxieties of Citizenship since Brown v. Board of Education*. Chicago: University of Chicago Press, 2004.

Almond, Gabriel A., R. Scott Appleby, and Emmanuel Sivan. *Strong Religion: The Rise of Fundamentalisms around the World*. Chicago: University of Chicago Press, 2003.

Anderson, Benedict. *Imagined Communities: Reflections on the Origin and Spread of Nationalism*. Rev. ed. London: Verso, 2006.

Anderson, Gary. *Sin: A History*. New Haven, CT: Yale University Press, 2009.

An–Na'im, Abdullahi Ahmed. *Toward an Islamic Reformation: Civil Liberties, Human Rights and International Law*. Syracuse, NY: Syracuse University Press, 1990.

Antoun, Richard T. *Understanding Fundamentalism: Christian, Islamic, and Jewish Movements*, 2nd ed. Lanham, MD: Rowman & Littlefield Publishers, 2008.

Aquinas, Thomas. *Political Writings*. Translated by R. W. Dyson. Cambridge: Cambridge University Press, 2002.

Summa Theologiae: Volume 38, Injustice. Edited by Marcus Lefébure. Cambridge: Cambridge University Press, 2006.

Arendt, Hannah. *The Human Condition*. 2nd ed. Chicago: University of Chicago Press, 1958.

Lectures on Kant's Political Philosophy. Edited by Ronald Beiner. Chicago: University of Chicago Press, 1982.

On Revolution. London: Penguin, 1977.

"On Violence." In *Crises of the Republic*. Orlando, FL: Harcourt Brace & Co., 1972.

Aristotle. *The Constitution of Athens*. Translated by J. M. Moore. In *The Politics* and *The Constitution of Athens*. Edited by Stephen Everson. Cambridge: Cambridge University Press, 1996.

The Nicomachean Ethics. Translated by David Ross. Oxford: Oxford University Press, 1980.

The Politics. Edited by Stephen Everson. Cambridge: Cambridge University Press, 1996.

Armitage, David. "John Locke, Carolina, and the 'Two Treatises of Government.'" *Political Theory* 32.5 (2004): 602–27.

Arneil, Barbara. *John Locke and America: The Defense of English Colonialism*. Oxford: Oxford University Press, 1996.

Asad, Talal. "The Construction of Religion as an Anthropological Category." In *Genealogies of Religion: Discipline and Reasons of Power in Christianity and Islam*. Baltimore, MD: Johns Hopkins University Press, 1993.

Formations of the Secular: Christianity, Islam, Modernity. Stanford, CA: Stanford University Press, 2003.

Ashley, Kathleen M. "The Guiler Beguiled: Christ and Satan as Theological Tricksters in Medieval Religious Literature." *Criticism: A Quarterly for Literature and the Arts* 24.2 (1982): 126–37.

Ashworth, John. "The Relationship between Capitalism and Humanitarianism." *The American Historical Review* 92.4 (1987): 813–28.

Atherton, John. *Transfiguring Capitalism: An Enquiry into Religion and Global Change*. London: SCM-Canterbury, 2008.

Atkinson, Paul, Amanda Coffey, Sara Delamont, John Lofland, and Lyn Lofland. *Handbook of Ethnography*. New ed. London: Sage Publications, 2007.

Atlas, John. *Seeds of Change: The Story of ACORN, America's Most Controversial Antipoverty Community Organizing Group*. Nashville, TN: Vanderbilt University Press, 2010.

Atlee, Clement. *The Labour Party in Perspective*. London: Gollanz, 1937.

Austin, Michael J. and Neil Betten, eds. *The Roots of Community Organizing, 1917–1939*. Philadelphia, PA: Temple University Press, 1990.

Bader, Veit. "Religions and States: A New Typology and a Plea for Non–Constitutional Pluralism." *Ethical Theory and Moral Practice* 6.1 (2003): 55–91.

"Religious Diversity and Democratic Institutional Pluralism." *Political Theory* 31.2 (2003): 265–94.

Bailey, Robert, Jr. *Radicals in Urban Politics: The Alinsky Approach*. Chicago: University of Chicago Press, 1974.

Baiocchi, Gianpaolo. *Militants as Citizens: The Politics of Participatory Democracy in Porto Alegre*. Stanford, CA: Stanford University Press, 2005.

Baker, D. L. *Tight Fists or Open Hands?: Wealth and Poverty in Old Testament Law*. Grand Rapids, MI: Eerdmans, 2009.

Barber, Benjamin R. *Strong Democracy: Participatory Politics for a New Age*. Berkeley: University of California Press, 1984.

Barclay, John M. G. *Pauline Churches and Diaspora Jews*. Tübingen: Mohr Siebeck, 2011.

Barnes, Michael. *Theology and the Dialogue of Religions*. Cambridge: Cambridge University Press, 2002.

Barnett, Michael N. *Empire of Humanity: A History of Humanitarianism*. Ithaca, NY: Cornell University Press, 2011.

Barrera, Albino. *God and the Evil of Scarcity: Moral Foundations of Economic Agency*. Notre Dame, IN: University of Notre Dame Press, 2005.

Barth, Karl. *The Christian Life: Church Dogmatics IV.4 Lecture Fragments*. Translated by Geoffrey Bromiley. Edinburgh: T & T Clark, 1981.

Church Dogmatics: The Doctrine of Creation, Vol III. Translated by G. W. Bromiley and R. J. Ehrlich. Edinburgh: T & T Clark, 1960.

Baucom, Ian. *Specters of the Atlantic: Finance Capital, Slavery, and the Philosophy of History*. Durham, NC: Duke University Press, 2005.

Bauman, Zygmunt. *Globalization*. Cambridge: Polity Press, 1998.

"Postmodern Religion?" In *Religion, Modernity and Postmodernity*. Edited by Paul Heelas. Oxford: Blackwell, 1998.

Beauregard, Robert and Anna Bounds. "Urban Citizenship." In *Democracy, Citizenship and the Global City*. Edited by Engin F. Isin. London: Routledge, 2000.

Beck, Ulrich. *Risk Society: Towards a New Modernity*. Translated by Mark Ritter. London: Sage, 1992.

Beck, Ulrich, Anthony Giddens, and Scott Lash. *Reflexive Modernization: Politics, Tradition and Aesthetics in the Modern Social Order*. Cambridge: Polity Press, 1994.

Becker, Marvin B. *The Emergence of Civil Society in the Eighteenth Century*. Bloomington: Indiana University Press, 1994.

Beiner, Ronald. *Civil Religion: A Dialogue in the History of Political Philosophy*. Cambridge: Cambridge University Press, 2011.

Political Judgement. London: Methuen, 1983.

What's the Matter with Liberalism? Berkeley, CA: University of California Press, 1992.

Bellah, Robert. "Social Science as Practical Reason." In *Ethics, Social Sciences, and Policy Analysis*. Edited by Daniel Callahan and Bruce Jennings. New York: Plenum Press, 1983.

Benedict XVI. *Caritas in Veritate*. Available at: http://www.vatican.va/holy_father/benedict_xvi/encyclicals/documents/hf_ben-xvi_enc_20090629_caritas-in-veritate_en.html

Bentham, Jeremy. "Defence of Usury." In *Economic Writings*, vol. 1. Edited by Werner Stark. London: Allen and Unwin, 1952.

Betten, Neil, Michael J. Austin, and Robert Fisher. *The Roots of Community Organizing, 1917–1939*. Philadelphia, PA: Temple University Press, 1990.

Betten, Neil and William E. Hershey. "The Urban Political Boss as Community Organizer." In *The Roots of Community Organizing, 1917–1939*. Edited by Neil Betten and Michael J. Austin. Philadelphia, PA: Temple University Press, 1990.

Bevir, Mark. *The Making of British Socialism*. Princeton, NJ: Princeton University Press, 2011.

Bey, Hakim. "The Temporary Autonomous Zone, Ontological Anarchy, Poetic Terrorism." Available at: http://hermetic.com/bey/taz3.html#labelTAZ

Bickford, Susan. *The Dissonance of Democracy: Listening, Conflict, and Citizenship*. Ithaca, NY: Cornell University Press, 1996.

Biéler, André. *Calvin's Economic and Social Thought*. Translated by James Greig. Geneva: WCC Publications, 2005.

Black, Antony. *Guild and State: European Political Thought from the Twelfth Century to the Present*. London: Transaction, 2002.

Blackburn, Robin. *The American Crucible: Slavery, Emancipation and Human Rights*. London: Verso, 2011.

Blackhurst, Chris. "Don't Kill the City Goose that Lays the Golden Egg." *Evening Standard*. December 16, 2010.

Blond, Phillip and Maurice Glasman. "The Prospect Debate: Red Tory vs. Blue Labour." *Prospect* (May 2010): 26–28.

Bobo, Kim, Jackie Kendall, and Steve Max. *Organizing for Social Change: Midwest Academy Manual for Activists*. 4th ed. Santa Ana, CA: Forum Press, 2010.

Bodin, Jean. *On Sovereignty: Four Chapters from "The Six Books of the Commonwealth."* Translated by Julian Franklin. Cambridge: Cambridge University Press, 1992.

Bolce, Louis and Gerald De Maio. "A Prejudice for the Thinking Classes: Media Framing, Political Sophistication, and the Christian Fundamentalist." Paper presented at the annual meeting of the Southern Political Science Association, New Orleans, LA, January 3, 2007.

Boltanski, Luc and Eve Chiapello. *The New Spirit of Capitalism*. London: Verso, 2007.

Bookchin, Murray. *From Urbanization to Cities: Towards a New Politics of Citizenship*. Rev. ed. London: Cassell, 1995.

Booth, William James. "Economies of Time: On the Idea of Time in Marx's Political Economy." *Political Theory* 19.1 (1991): 7–27.

Bornstein, Erica and Peter Redfield. *Genealogies of Suffering and the Gift of Care: A Working Paper on the Anthropology of Religion, Secularism, and Humanitarianism*. SSRC Working Papers. New York: Social Science Research Council, 2007.

Boyte, Harry C. *Civic Agency and the Cult of the Expert*. New York: Kettering Foundation, 2009.

Commonwealth: A Return to Citizen Politics. New York: Free Press, 1989.

Everyday Politics: Reconnecting Citizens and the Public Life. Philadelphia: University of Pennsylvania Press, 2004.

"Reframing Democracy: Governance, Civic Agency, and Politics." *Public Administration Review* 65.5 (2005): 536–46.

Reinventing Citizenship as Public Work: Citizen–Centered Democracy and the Empowerment Gap. New York: Kettering Foundation, 2013.

Boyte, Harry C. and Eric Fretz. "Civic Professionalism." *Journal of Higher Education Outreach and Engagement* 14:2 (2010): 67–90.

Branch, Taylor. *Parting the Waters: Martin Luther King and the Civil Rights Movement, 1954–63*. London: MacMillan, 1990.

Breen, Keith. "Work and Productive Reason: Rival Visions of Production and the Workplace." Paper delivered at the Contemporary Aristotelian Studies in Politics Conference, Metropolitan University, London, June 3, 2011.

Bretherton, Luke. *Christianity and Contemporary Politics: The Conditions and Possibilities of Faithful Witness*. Oxford: Wiley–Blackwell, 2010.

"Coming to Judgment: Methodological Reflections on the Relationship between Ecclesiology, Ethnography and Political Theory." *Modern Theology* 28.2 (2012): 167–96.

Hospitality as Holiness: Christian Witness Amid Moral Diversity. Aldershot, UK: Ashgate, 2006.

"A Postsecular Politics? Inter–faith Relations as a Civic Practice." *Journal of the American Academy of Religion* 79.2 (2011): 346–77.

"Sharing Peace: Class, Hierarchy and Christian Social Order." In *The Blackwell Companion to Christian Ethics*. Edited by Stanley Hauerwas and Sam Wells. Rev. ed. Oxford: Wiley–Blackwell, 2011.

"Translation, Conversation, or Hospitality? Approaches to Theological Reasons in Public Deliberation." In *Religious Voices in Public Places*. Edited by Nigel Biggar and Linda Hogan. Oxford: Oxford University Press, 2009.

Briggs, Charles L. *Learning How to Ask: A Sociolinguistic Appraisal of the Role of Interview in Social Science Research*. Cambridge: Cambridge University Press, 1986.

Briggs, Xavier de Souza. *Democracy as Problem Solving: Civic Capacity in Communities across the Globe*. Cambridge, MA: MIT Press, 2008.

Bright, Martin. "London Citizens Stand by Islamist Hardliner." *Jewish Chronicle*, May 26, 2011. Available at: http://www.thejc.com/news/uk-news/49505/london-citizens-stand-islamist-hardliner

"Rabbi 'In Pain' Over London Citizens Link." *Jewish Chronicle*, June 2, 2011. Available at: http://www.thejc.com/news/uk-news/49791/rabbi-pain-over-london-citizens-link

Brooke, Christopher. "Rousseau's Political Philosophy: Stoic and Augustinian Origins." In *The Cambridge Companion to Rousseau*. Edited by Patrick Riley. Cambridge: Cambridge University Press, 2001.

Brooks, Thom. "Reciprocity as Mutual Recognition." *The Good Society* 21.1 (2012): 21–35.

Bruni, Luigino. *Reciprocity, Altruism and the Civil Society: In Praise of Heterogeneity*. London: Routledge, 2008.

Bruni, Luigino and Stefano Zamagni. *Civil Economy: Efficiency, Equity, Public Happiness*. Bern: Peter Lang, 2007.

Bryman, Alan. *Disneyization of Society*. Thousand Oaks, CA: Sage, 2004.

Buber, Martin. "To the Clarification of Pacifism." In *A Believing Humanism: My Testament, 1902–1965*. New York: Simon and Schuster, 1967.

Paths in Utopia. New York: Syracuse University Press, 1996.

Buchan, James. *Frozen Desire: An Inquiry into the Meaning of Money*. London: Picador, 1997.

Burawoy, Michael. *Ethnography Unbound: Power and Resistance in the Modern Metropolis*. Berkeley: University of California Press, 1991.

"The Extended Case Method." *Sociological Theory* 16.1 (1998): 4–33.

"Revisits: An Outline of a Theory of Reflexive Ethnography." *American Sociological Review* 68 (2003): 645–79.

"For a Sociological Marxism: The Complementary Convergence of Antonio Gramsci and Karl Polanyi." *Politics & Society* 31.2 (2003): 193–261.

Burawoy, Michael, et al. *Global Ethnography: Forces, Connections, and Imaginations in a Postmodern World*. Berkeley: University of California Press, 2000.

Burgess, Ernest, Joseph Lohman, and Clifford Shaw. "The Chicago Area Project." In *Yearbook*. National Probation Association, 1937.

Butler, Judith. *Precarious Life: The Powers of Mourning and Violence*. London: Verso, 2004.

Calhoun, Craig Jackson. "The Radicalism of Tradition: Community Strength or Venerable Disguise and Borrowed Language?" *American Journal of Sociology* 88.5 (1983): 886–914.

Calvin, John. *Commentarii in Libros Mosis necum in Librum Josue*. Amsterdam: 1567.

Canovan, Margaret. *G. K. Chesterton: Radical Populist*. New York: Harcourt Brace Jovanovich, 1977.

"The People, the Masses and the Mobilization of Power: The Paradox of Hannah Arendt's 'Populism.'" *Social Research* 69.2 (2002): 403–22.

Populism. New York: Harcourt Brace Jovanovich, 1981.

"Trust the People! Populism and the Two Faces of Democracy." *Political Studies* 47.1 (1999): 2–16.

"Two Strategies for the Study of Populism." *Political Studies* 30.4 (1982): 544–52.

Caputo, John. "Who is Derrida's Zarathustra? Of Fraternity, Friendship, and a Democracy to Come." *Research in Phenomenology* 29 (1999): 184–98.

Casanova, José. "Immigration and the New Religious Pluralism: A European Union/United States Comparison." In *Democracy and the New Religious Pluralism*. Edited by Thomas F. Banchoff. Oxford: Oxford University Press, 2007.

"Rethinking Secularization: A Global Comparative Perspective." In *Religion, Globalization and Culture*. Edited by Peter Beyer and Lori Beaman. Leiden: Brill, 2007.

Castells, Manuel. *The City and the Grassroots: A Cross-Cultural Theory of Urban Social Movements*. Berkeley: University of California Press, 1983.

The Power of Identity. Malden, MA: Blackwell, 1997.

The Power of Identity: The Information Age: Economy, Society and Culture. Volume II, 2nd ed. Oxford: Blackwells, 2004.

Cavanaugh, William. "The Invention of Fanaticism." *Modern Theology* 27.2 (2011): 226–37.

The Myth of Religious Violence: Secular Ideology and the Roots of Modern Conflict. Oxford: Oxford University Press, 2009.

Torture and Eucharist: Theology, Politics and the Body of Christ. Oxford: Blackwell, 1998.

Chaloupek, Günther. "The Austrian Debate on Economic Calculation in a Socialist Economy." *History of Political Economy* 22.4 (1990): 659–75.

Chambers, Edward T. and Michael A. Cowan. *Roots for Radicals: Organizing for Power, Action, and Justice*. New York: Continuum, 2004.

Chaplin, Jonathan. *Herman Dooyeweerd: Christian Philosopher of State and Civil Society*. Notre Dame, IN: University of Notre Dame Press, 2011.

Chirichigno, Gregory. *Debt-Slavery in Israel and Ancient Near East*. Sheffield: Sheffield Academic Press, 1993.

Cicero, Marcus Tullius. *On Duties*. Edited by M. T. Griffin and E. M. Atkins. Cambridge: Cambridge University Press, 1991.

Citizens UK. "The Tent of Presence: The Church in the United Kingdom in the 1990's." Rev. ed. 2010.

City of London. "Common Questions about the City Corporation." Available at: www.cityoflondon.gov.uk/Corporation/LGNL_Services/Council_and_democracy/Council_departments/whatis.htm

"History." City Bridge Trust Web page. Available at: www.bridgehousegrants.org.uk/CityBridgeTrust/TheTrust/History.htm

City of London Police. Available at: http://www.cityoflondon.police.uk/CityPolice/About/services/History/

Clark, Christopher. "From 1848 to Christian Democracy." In *Religion and the Political Imagination*. Edited by Ira Katznelson, Gareth Stedman Jones, and Walter Goode. Cambridge: Cambridge University Press, 2007.

Clark, David J. "The Word Kosmos 'World' in John 17." *The Bible Translator* 50.4 (1999): 401–06.

Clark, Nick, Alice Malpass, Paul Cloke, and Clive Barnett. "Fairtrade Urbanism? The Politics of Place Beyond Place in the Bristol Fairtrade City Campaign." *International Journal of Urban and Regional Research* 31.3 (2007): 633–45.

Clark, Simon. "Scrooge's Fate Is Lesson for London Bankers, Mayor Johnson Says." *Bloomberg.com*, November 26, 2010. Available at: www.bloomberg.com/apps/news?pid=newsarchive&sid=a1qMzYeWoKwc

Clarke, Linda and Christopher Winch. "Apprenticeship and Applied Theoretical Knowledge." *Educational Philosophy and Theory* 36.5 (2004): 509–21.

Cohen, Jean L. and Andrew Arato. *Civil Society and Political Theory*. Cambridge, MA: MIT Press, 1992.

Cohen, Joshua and Joel Rogers. *Associations and Democracy*. London: Verso, 1995.

Coleman, Simon. *The Globalisation of Charismatic Christianity: Spreading the Gospel of Prosperity*. Cambridge: Cambridge University Press, 2000.

Coles, Romand. *Beyond Gated Politics: Reflections for the Possibility of Democracy*. Minneapolis: University of Minnesota Press, 2005.

"Of Tensions and Tricksters: Grassroots Democracy between Theory and Practice." *Perspectives on Politics* 4.3 (2006): 547–61.

Collini, Stefan. *Public Moralists: Political Thought and Intellectual Life in Britain, 1850–1930*. Oxford: Clarendon Press, 1991.

Connolly, William E. *Pluralism*. Durham, NC: Duke University Press, 2005.

Cortés, Ernesto. *Rebuilding Our Institutions*. Chicago: ACTA Publications, 2010.

Cortés, Ernesto and Leo Penta. "Reweaving the Fabric: The Iron Rule and the IAF Strategy for Power and Politics." In *Interwoven Destinies: Cities and the Nation*. Edited by Henry G. Cisneros. New York: W. W. Norton, 1993.

Coughlan, Sean. "Self–help plan to make the streets safer." BBC News, August 10, 2010. Available at: www.bbc.co.uk/news/education–10869719

Craig, Gary. "Introduction." In *The Community Development Reader: History, Themes and Issues*. Edited by Gary Craig, Marjorie Mayo, Keith Popple, Mae Shaw, and Marilyn Taylor. London: The Policy Press, 2011.

Creech, Joe. *Righteous Indignation: Religion and the Populist Revolution*. Urbana: University of Illinois Press, 2006.

Crick, Bernard. *In Defence of Politics*. London: Continuum, 2005.

Cruikshank, Barbara. *The Will to Empower: Democratic Citizens and Other Subjects*. Ithaca, NY: Cornell University Press, 1999.

Cullen, Bernard. *Hegel's Social and Political Thought*. Dublin: Gill and Macmillan, 1979.

Cutler, Irving. *The Jews of Chicago: From Shtetl to Suburb*. Urbana, IL: University of Illinois Press, 1996.

Dale, Gareth. *Karl Polanyi: The Limits of the Market*. Cambridge: Polity Press, 2010.

Davies, Ian. Letter, December 29, 1986. Box 144, file 1513. Industrial Areas Foundation Archive, University of Illinois at Chicago.

Davis, Rowenna. *Tangled up in Blue: Blue Labour and the Struggle for Labour's Soul*. London: Ruskin Publishing, 2011.

D'Costa, Gavin. *Christianity and World Religions: Disputed Questions in the Theology of Religions*. Oxford: Wiley-Blackwell, 2009.

Dean, Jodi. "Communicative Capitalism: Circulation and the Foreclosure of Politics." *Cultural Politics* 1.1 (2005): 51–74.

DeFilippis, James, Robert Fisher, and Eric Shragge. *Contesting Community: The Limits and Potential of Local Organizing*. New Brunswick, NJ: Rutgers University Press, 2010.

Deleuze, Gilles. "Postscript on the Societies of Control." *October* 59 (1992): 3–7.

Della Porta, Donatella, Massimillano Andretta, Lorenzo Mosca, and Herbert Reiter. *Globalization from Below: Transnational Activists and Protest Networks*. Minneapolis: University of Minnesota Press, 2006.

Department for Communities and Local Government. *Face to Face and Side by Side: A Framework for Partnership in our Multi Faith Society*. White Paper. London, 2008.

Derrida, Jacques. *Dissémination*. Translated by Barbara Johnson. London: Athlone Press, 1981.

Politics of Friendship. Translated by George Collins. London: Verso, 1997.

Rogues: Two Essays on Reason. Translated by Pascale-Anne Brault and Michael Naas. Stanford, CA: Stanford University Press, 2005.

"The Villanova Roundtable: A Conversation with Jacques Derrida." In *Deconstruction in a Nutshell*. Edited by John D. Caputo. New York: Fordham University Press, 1997.

Voyous: deux essais sur la raison. Paris: Galilée, 2003.

Derrida, Jacques and Elisabeth Roudinesco. *For What Tomorrow ...: A Dialogue*. Translated by Jeff Fort. Stanford, CA: Stanford University Press, 2004.

deSilva, David. *Honor, Patronage, Kinship and Purity: Unlocking New Testament Culture*. Downers Grove, IL: InterVarsity Press, 2000.

Detienne, Marcel and Jean-Pierre Vernant. *Cunning Intelligence in Greek Culture and Society*. Translated by Janet Lloyd. Chicago: University of Chicago Press, 1991.

DiMaggio, Paul J. and Walter W. Powell. "The Iron Cage Revisited: Institutional Isomorphism and Collective Rationality in Organizational Fields." *American Sociological Review* 48.2 (1983): 147–60.

Dionne, E. J. *Our Divided Political Heart: The Battle for the American Idea in an Age of Discontent*. New York: Bloomsbury, 2012.

Dixon, Thomas. "The Invention of Altruism: Auguste Comte's *Positive Polity* and Respectable Unbelief in Victorian Britain." In *Science and Beliefs: From Natural Philosophy to Natural Science, 1700–1900*. Edited by David M. Knight and Matthew D. Eddy. Aldershot, UK: Ashgate, 2005.

Doherty, William and Tai Mendenhall. "Citizen Health Care: A Model for Engaging Patients, Families, and Communities as Coproducers of Health." *Families, Systems, & Health* 24.3 (2006): 251–63.

Dreier, Peter. "Community Organizing for What? Progressive Politics and Movement Building in America." In *Transforming the City: Community Organizing and the Challenge of Political Change*. Edited by Marion Orr. Lawrence: University Press of Kansas, 2007.

Dryzek, John. "Deliberative Democracy in Divided Societies: Alternatives to Agonism and Analgesia." *Political Theory* 33.2 (2005): 218–42.

Dubofsky, Melvyn and Warren Van Tine. *John L. Lewis: A Biography*. Urbana: University of Illinois Press, 1986.

Dunn, John. *Setting the People Free: The Story of Democracy*. London: Atlantic Books, 2005.

Durkheim, Emile. *Professional Ethics and Civic Morals*. London: Routledge, 2001 [1957].

Dzur, Albert. *Democratic Professionalism: Citizen Participation and the Reconstruction of Professional Ethics, Identity, and Practice*. University Park: Pennsylvania State University Press, 2008.

Ebaugh, Helen Rose. *The Gülen Movement: A Sociological Analysis of a Civic Movement Rooted in Moderate Islam*. London: Springer, 2009.

Egan, Jack, Rev. Note to Saul Alinsky. Box 47, file 658. Industrial Areas Foundation Archive, University of Illinois at Chicago.

Eisenberg, Avigail. *Reconstructing Political Pluralism*. New York: SUNY Press, 1995.

Eisenstadt, S. N. "The Reconstruction of Religious Arenas in the Framework of 'Multiple Modernities.'" *Millennium: Journal of International Studies* 29.3 (2000): 591–611.

Elazar, Daniel. *Covenant and Polity in Biblical Israel: Biblical Foundations and Jewish Expressions*. New Brunswick, NJ: Transaction Publishers, 1995.

Elgot, Jessica. "Bevis Marks Rabbi Resigns." *The Jewish Chronicle Online*, October 19, 2009. Available at: http://www.thejc.com/news/uk-news/21091/bevis-marks-rabbi-resigns

"I can do more as an organiser than as a politician." *The Jewish Chronicle Online*, March 17, 2011. Available at: http://www.thejc.com/46695/i-can-do-more-organiser-a-politician

Eliasoph, Nina. *Avoiding Politics: How Americans Produce Apathy in Everyday Life*. Cambridge: Cambridge University Press, 1998.

Ellingworth, Paul. "Translating Kosmos 'World' in Paul." *The Bible Translator* 53.4 (2002): 414–21.

Elshtain, Jean Bethke. *Jane Addams and the Dream of American Democracy*. New York: Basic Books, 2002.

Sovereignty: God, State, and Self. New York: Basic Books, 2008.

Engel, Lawrence. "The Influence of Saul Alinsky on the Campaign for Human Development." *Theological Studies* 59 (1998): 636–61.

Erdozain, Dominic. "The Secularisation of Sin in the Nineteenth Century." *The Journal of Ecclesiastical History* 62.1 (2011): 59–88.

Esack, Farid. *Qur'an, Liberation and Pluralism: An Islamic Perspective on Interreligious Solidarity Against Oppression*. Oxford: Oneworld, 1997.

Estlund, Cynthia. *Working Together: How Workplace Bonds Strengthen a Diverse Democracy*. Oxford: Oxford University Press, 2003.

Eubank, Nathan. *Wages of Cross-Bearing and the Debt of Sin: The Economy of Heaven in Matthew's Gospel*. Göttingen: De Gruyter, 2013.

Evans, Sara M. and Harry C. Boyte. *Free Spaces: The Sources of Democratic Change in America*. New York: Harper & Row, 1986.

Fadel, Mohammad. "*Riba*, Efficiency and Prudential Regulation: Preliminary Thoughts." *Wisconsin International Law Journal* 25.4 (2008): 655–703.

Feit, Mario. "Wolin, Time, and the Democratic Temperament." *Theory & Event* 15.4 (2012).

Finks, P. David. *The Radical Vision of Saul Alinsky*. New York: Paulist Press, 1984.

Finnis, John. *Aquinas: Moral, Political, and Legal Theory*. Oxford: Oxford University Press, 1998.

Fishburn, Alice. "Could Safe Havens Prevent Teenage Stabbings?" *The Times of London*. November 18, 2009.

Fisher, Robert. "Grass Roots Organizing in the Community Center Movement, 1907–1930." In *The Roots of Community Organizing, 1917–1939*. Edited by Neil Betten and Michael J. Austin. Philadelphia, PA: Temple University Press, 1990.

Let the People Decide: Neighborhood Organizing in America. Updated ed. New York: Twayne Publishers, 1994.

Fisher, Robert and Eric Shragge. "Contextualizing Community Organizing: Lessons from the Past, Tensions in the Present, Opportunities for the Future." In Marion Orr, *Transforming the City: Community Organizing and the Challenge of Political Change*. Lawrence: University Press of Kansas, 2007.

Flyvbjerg, Bent. *Making Social Science Matter: Why Social Inquiry Fails and How it Can Succeed Again*. Translated by Steven Sampson. Cambridge: Cambridge University Press, 2001.

Follett, Mary Parker. *Creative Experience*. New York: Longman, Green & Co, 1930 [1924].

Foucault, Michel. "The Political Technology of Individuals." In *Technologies of the Self: A Seminar with Michel Foucault*. Edited by Luther Martin, Huck Gutman and Patrick Hutton. Amherst: University of Massachusetts Press, 1988.

"Preface." In Gilles Deleuze and Félix Guattari, *Anti-Oedipus: Capitalism and Schizophrenia*. Translated by Robert Hurley, Mark Seem, and Helen R. Lane. New York: Penguin Books, 2007.

Security, Territory, Population: Lectures at the College de France, 1977–1978. Transcribed by Graham Burchell. New York: Picador, 2007.

Franco, Jennifer Conroy. *Elections and Democratization in the Philippines*. New York: Routledge, 2001.

Franklin, Julian. "Sovereignty and the Mixed Constitution: Bodin and His Critics." In *The Cambridge History of Political Thought: 1450–1700*. Edited by J. H. Burns and M. Goldie. Cambridge: Cambridge University Press, 1991.

Franks, Christopher. *He Became Poor: The Poverty of Christ and Aquinas's Economic Teaching*. Grand Rapids, MI: Eerdmans, 2009.

Freedland, Jonathan. "Heard the One about a Rabbi, an Imam and a Priest, Who Walk into a Bank?" *The Guardian*, July 21, 2009. Available at: http://www.guardian.co.uk/commentisfree/belief/2009/jul/22/debt-interest-religion-usury

Freedman, Samuel G. *Upon This Rock: The Miracles of a Black Church*. New York: HarperCollins, 1994.

Frieden, Jeffrey A. *Global Capitalism: Its Fall and Rise in the Twentieth Century*. New York: W. W. Norton & Co., 2006.

Friedman, John. "The World-City Hypothesis." In *World Cities in a World-System*. Edited by Paul L. Knox and Peter J. Taylor. Cambridge: Cambridge University Press, 1995.

Friedmann, Yohanan. *Tolerance and Coercion in Islam: Interfaith Relations in the Muslim Tradition*. Cambridge: Cambridge University Press, 2003.

Fulton, Brad and Richard Wood. "Interfaith Community Organizing: Emerging Theological and Organizational Challenges." *International Journal of Public Theology* 6 (2012): 398–420.

Fung, Archon and Erik Olin Wright, eds. *Deepening Democracy: Institutional Innovations in Empowered Participatory Governance*. London: Verso, 2003.

Furbey, Robert, et al. "Breaking with Tradition? The Church of England and Community Organising." *Community Development Journal* 32 (1997): 141–50.

Ganz, Marshall. *Why David Sometimes Wins: Leadership, Organization, and Strategy in the California Farm Worker Movement*. Oxford: Oxford University Press, 2009.

"Why David Sometimes Wins: Strategic Capacity in Social Movements." In *The Psychology of Leadership: New Perspectives and Research*. Edited by David M. Messick and Roderick M. Kramer. Mahwah, NJ: Lawrence Erlbaum Associates, 2005.

Garnsey, Peter. *Ideas of Slavery from Aristotle to Augustine*. Cambridge: Cambridge University Press, 1996.

Gecan, Michael. *After America's Midlife Crisis*. Cambridge, MA: MIT Press, 2009.

Effective Organizing for Congregational Renewal. Skokie, IL: ACTA Publications, 2008.

Going Public: An Organizer's Guide to Citizen Action. New York: Anchor Books, 2002.

Gelasius, "The Bond of Anathema." In *From Irenaeus to Grotius: A Sourcebook in Christian Political Thought, 100–1625*. Edited by Oliver O'Donovan and Joan Lockwood O'Donovan. Grand Rapids, MI: Eerdmans, 1999.

Gereffi, Gary. "Global Value Chains in a Post-Washington Consensus World." *Review of International Political Economy* (2013): 1–29.

Gereffi, Gary, Joonkoo Lee, and Michelle Christian. "US-Based Food and Agricultural Value Chains and Their Relevance to Healthy Diets." *Journal of Hunger & Environmental Nutrition* 4 (2009): 357–74.

Giddens, Anthony. *Modernity and Self-Identity: Self and Society in the Late Modern Age*. Cambridge: Polity Press, 1991.

Giddens, Anthony, and Scott Lash. *Reflexive Modernization: Politics, Tradition and Aesthetics in the Modern Social Order*. Cambridge: Polity Press, 1994.

Gierke, Otto von. *Community in Historical Perspective*. Edited by Antony Black. Translated by Mary Fischer. Cambridge: Cambridge University Press, 1990.

Gillespie, Michael. *Theological Origins of Modernity*. Chicago: University of Chicago Press, 2008.

Girard, René. *Violence and the Sacred*. Translated by Patrick Gregory. Baltimore, MD: Johns Hopkins University Press, 1977.

Glasman, Maurice. "Labour as a Radical Tradition." In *The Labour Tradition and the Politics of Paradox*. Edited by Maurice Glasman, Jonathan Rutherford, Marc Stears, and Stuart White. London: Soundings, 2011.

"Landed and Maritime Markets in Ancient Rome: The Polanyi Paradigm Reconsidered." Unpublished paper.

Glasman, Maurice, Jonathan Rutherford, Marc Stears, and Stuart White. *The Labour Tradition and the Politics of Paradox*. London: Soundings, 2011.

Glover, Stephen, et al. *Migration: An Economic and Social Analysis*. London: Home Office, 2001.

Godbout, Jacques with Alan Caillé. *The World of the Gift*. Montreal: McGill–Queen's University Press, 1998.

Goddard, Hugh. *A History of Christian–Muslim Relations*. Edinburgh: Edinburgh University Press, 2000.

Goodwyn, Lawrence. *Democratic Promise: The Populist Movement in America*. New York: Oxford University Press, 1976.

Gornik, Mark R. *Word Made Global: Stories of African Christianity in New York City*. Grand Rapids, MI: Eerdmans, 2011.

Gourevitch, Peter and Gary Jacobson. "Arend Lijphard: A Profile." *PS: Political Science and Politics* 28.4 (1995): 751–54.

Grabill, Stephen. *Rediscovering the Natural Law in Reformed Theological Ethics*. Grand Rapids, MI: Eerdmans, 2006.

Graeber, David. *Debt: The First 5,000 Years*. New York: Melville House, 2011.

The Democracy Project: A History, a Crisis, a Movement. New York: Spiegel & Grau, 2013.

Direct Action: An Ethnography. Edinburgh and Oakland, CA: AK Press, 2009.

Gregory, Eric. *Politics and the Order of Love: An Augustinian Ethic of Democratic Citizenship*. Chicago: University of Chicago Press, 2008.

Greider, William. *Who Will Tell the People? The Betrayal of American Democracy*. New York: Simon & Schuster, 1993.

Gruber, Helmut. *Red Vienna: Experiment in Working Class Culture 1919–1934*. Oxford: Oxford University Press, 1991.

Gudeman, Stephen. "Necessity or Contingency: Mutuality and Market." In *Market and Society: The Great Transformation Today*. Edited by Chris Hann and Keith Hart. Cambridge: Cambridge University Press, 2009.

Gülen, Fethullah. Interview in *Sabah*, January 27, 1995. Quoted in Helen Rose Ebaugh, *The Gülen Movement: A Sociological Analysis of a Civic Movement Rooted in Moderate Islam*. London: Springer, 2009.

Gutmann, Amy and Dennis F. Thompson. *Democracy and Disagreement*. Cambridge, MA: Harvard University Press, 1996.

Habermas, Jürgen. *Between Facts and Norms: Contributions to a Discourse Theory of Law and Democracy*. Cambridge, MA: MIT Press, 1996.

"Social Action and Rationality." In *Jürgen Habermas on Society and Politics: A Reader*. Edited by Steven Seidman. Boston: Beacon Press, 1989.

Habermas, Jürgen and Jacques Derrida. *Philosophy in a Time of Terror: Dialogues with Jürgen Habermas and Jacques Derrida*. Edited and with commentary by Giovanna Borradori. Chicago: University of Chicago Press, 2003.

Hahnel, Robin. *Of the People, By the People: The Case for a Participatory Economy*. Portland, OR: Soapbox Press, 2012.

Hamington, Maurice. "Community Organizing: Addams and Alinsky." In *Feminist Interpretations of Jane Addams*. Edited by Maurice Hamington. University Park: Pennsylvania State University Press, 2010.

"Jane Addams and a Politics of Embodied Care." *The Journal of Speculative Philosophy* 15.2 (2001): 105–21.

Harding, Susan Friend. *The Book of Jerry Falwell: Fundamentalist Language and Politics*. Princeton, NJ: Princeton University Press, 2000.

Hardt, Michael, "The Withering of Civil Society." *Social Text* 45 (1995): 27–44.

Hardt, Michael and Antonio Negri. *Commonwealth*. Cambridge, MA: Belknap Press, 2009.

Empire. Cambridge: MA: Harvard University Press, 2000.

Harris, Edward. "Did Solon Abolish Debt-Bondage?" In *Democracy and the Rule of Law in Classical Athens: Essays on Law, Society and Politics*. Edited by Edward Harris. Cambridge: Cambridge University Press, 2006.

Hart, Keith. "Heads or Tails? Two Sides of the Coin." *Man* 21.3 (1986): 637–56.

The Memory Bank: Money in an Unequal World. London: Profile Books, 1999.

Hart, Stephen. *Cultural Dilemmas of Progressive Politics: Styles of Engagement among Grassroots Activists*. Chicago: University of Chicago Press, 2001.

Harvey, David. *A Brief History of Neoliberalism*. Oxford: Oxford University Press, 2005.

"Contested Cities: Social Process and Spatial Form." In *Transforming Cities: Contested Governance and New Spatial Divisions*. Edited by Nick Jewson and Susanne MacGregor. London: Routledge, 1997.

Rebel Cities: From the Right to the City to the Urban Revolution. London: Verso, 2012.

Spaces of Hope. Edinburgh: Edinburgh University Press, 2000.

Harvey, Mark, Sally Randles, and Ronnie Ramilogan. "Working with and beyond Polanyian Perspectives." In *Karl Polanyi: New Perspectives on the Place of the Economy in Society*. Edited by Mark Harvey, Ronnie Ramlogan, and Sally Randles. Manchester: Manchester University Press, 2007.

Hastings, Adrian. *The Construction of Nationhood: Ethnicity, Religion and Nationalism*. Cambridge: Cambridge University Press, 1997.

Hatch, Nathan O. *The Democratization of American Christianity*. New Haven, CT: Yale University Press, 1989.

Hauerwas, Stanley. "The Politics of Church: How We Lay Bricks and Make Disciples." In *After Christendom?: How the Church Is to Behave if Freedom, Justice and a Christian Nation Are Bad Ideas*. Nashville, TN: Abingdon, 1991.

The State of the University: Academic Knowledges and the Knowledge of God. Oxford: Wiley-Blackwell, 2007.

Hayek, Friedrich A. von. *Law Legislation and Liberty*. Vol. 2, *The Mirage of Social Justice*. Chicago: University of Chicago Press, 1978.

The Road to Serfdom. London: Routledge, 1944.

Hayek, Friedrich A. von, et al. *Collectivist Economic Planning: Critical Studies on the Possibilities of Socialism*. London: Routledge, 1935.

Haykin, Michael A. G., Kenneth J. Stewart, and Timothy George. *The Advent of Evangelicalism: Exploring Historical Continuities*. Nashville, TN: B & H Academic, 2008.

Heaven, Will. "Gordon Brown's speech to Citizens UK Was Weird, Not a 'Barnstormer.'" *The Telegraph*, May 4, 2010. Available at: http://blogs.telegraph.co.uk/news/willheaven/100037879/gordon-browns-speech-to-citizens-uk-was-weird-not-a-barnstormer/

Hedges, Chris. *American Fascists: The Christian Right and the War on America*. New York: Free Press, 2008.

Hegel, Georg W. F. *Hegel's Philosophy of Right*. Translated by T. M. Knox. Oxford: Oxford University Press, 1967.

Held, David. *Models of Democracy*. 3rd ed. Cambridge: Polity, 2006.

Hénaff, Marcel. *The Price of Truth: Gift, Money, and Philosophy*. Stanford, CA: Stanford University Press, 2010.

Herbert, David. *Religion and Civil Society: Rethinking Public Religion in the Contemporary World*. Aldershot: Ashgate, 2003.

Hicks, John D. *The Populist Revolt: A History of the Farmers' Alliance and the People's Party*. Minneapolis: University of Minnesota Press, 1931.

Hilmer, Jeffrey. "The State of Participatory Democratic Theory." *New Political Science* 32.1 (2010): 43–63.

Hirschman, Albert O. *Exit, Voice, and Loyalty: Responses to Decline in Firms, Organizations, and States*. Cambridge, MA: Harvard University Press, 1970.

The Passions and the Interests: Political Arguments for Capitalism before Its Triumph. Anniversary ed. Princeton, NJ: Princeton University Press, 1997 [1977].

Hirst, Paul. *Associative Democracy: New Forms of Economic and Social Governance*. Cambridge: Polity Press, 1994.

Hirst, Paul, ed. *The Pluralist Theory of the State: Selected Writings of G. D. H. Cole, J. N. Figgis, and H. J. Laski*. London: Routledge, 1993.

Hittinger, Russell. "Social Pluralism and Subsidiarity in Catholic Doctrine." In *Christianity and Civil Society: Catholic and Neo-Calvinist Perspectives*. Edited by Jeanne Heffernan Schindler. Lanham, MD: Lexington Books, 2008.

Hobbes, Thomas. *Leviathan*. Cambridge: Cambridge University Press, 1996.

Hofstadter, Richard. *The Age of Reform: From Bryan to F.D.R.* New York: Alfred A. Knopf, 1955.

Honig, Bonnie. "Between Decision and Deliberation: Political Paradox in Democratic Theory." *American Political Science Review* 101.1 (2007): 1–17.

Honohan, Iseult. *Civic Republicanism*. London: Routledge, 2002.

Horton, Myles, with Judith Kohl and Herbert Kohl. *The Long Haul: An Autobiography*. New York: Teachers College Press, 1998.

Horwitt, Sanford D. "Alinsky, Foreclosures and Holding Banks Accountable." *The Huffington Post*, January 1, 2012. Available at: http://www.huffingtonpost.com/sanford-d-horwitt/alinsky-foreclosures-and-_b_1245449.html

Let Them Call Me Rebel: Saul Alinsky, His Life and Legacy. New York: Knopf, 1989.

Houston, Walter. "What's Just about the Jubilee?: Ideological and Ethical Reflections on Leviticus 25." *Studies in Christian Ethics* 14.1 (2001): 34–47.

Hueglin, Thomas. *Early Modern Concepts for a Late Modern World: Althusius on Community and Federalism*. Waterloo: Wilfrid Laurier University Press, 1999.

Hunter, James Davidson. *To Change the World: The Irony, Tragedy and Possibility of Christianity in the Late Modern World*. Oxford: Oxford University Press, 2010.

Hussain, Dilwar. "Muslim Political Participation in Britain and the 'Europeanisation' of *Fiqh*." *Die Welt des Islams* 44.3 (2004): 376–401.

Industrial Areas Foundation. *Standing for the Whole*. Chicago: Industrial Areas Foundation, 1990.

Tent of the Presence: Black Church Power in the 1980s. New York: Industrial Areas Foundation, 1981.

Ingham, Geoffrey. "Class Inequality and the Social Production of Money." In *Renewing Class Analysis*. Edited by Rosemary Crompton, Fiona Devine, Mike Savage, and John Scott. Oxford: Blackwell Publishers, 2000.

The Nature of Money. Cambridge: Polity, 2004.

International Labour Organization. *ILO 2012 Global Estimate of Forced Labour Executive Summary*. Geneva: International Labour Office, 2012.

Isaac, Jeffrey. "Oases in the Desert: Hannah Arendt on Democratic Politics." *The American Political Science Review* 88.1 (1994): 156–68.

Isin, Engin F. *Being Political: Genealogies of Citizenship*. Minneapolis: University of Minnesota Press, 2002.

Ivereigh, Austen. *Faithful Citizens: A Practical Guide to Catholic Social Teaching and Community Organising*. London: Darton, Longman & Todd, 2010.

Jacobs, Jane. *The Death and Life of Great American Cities*. New York: Modern Library, 1961.

Jacobsen, Dennis A. *Doing Justice: Congregations and Community Organizing*. Minneapolis: Augsburg Fortress, 2001.

Jameson, Neil. "British Muslims—Influencing UK Public Life: A Case Study." In *British Muslims: Loyalty and Belonging*. Edited by Mohammad Siddique Seddon, Dilwar Hussain, and Nadeem Malik. Markfield, UK: The Islamic Foundation, 2003.

Jamoul, Lina and Jane Wills. "Faith in Politics." *Urban Studies* 45.10 (2008): 2035–56.

Janis, Irving L. *Victims of Groupthink: A Psychological Study of Foreign Policy Decisions and Fiascoes*. New York: Houghton Mifflin, 1972.

Jeavons, Thomas H. "Identifying Characteristics of 'Religious' Organisations: An Exploratory Proposal." In *Sacred Companies: Organisational Aspects of Religion and Religious Aspects of Organisations*. Edited by N. J. Demerath III, Peter Dobkin Hall, Terry Schmitt, and Rhys H. Williams. Oxford: Oxford University Press, 1998.

Jenkins, Timothy. "Fieldwork and the Perception of Everyday Life." *Man* 29.2 (1994): 433–55.

Jennings, Willie James. *The Christian Imagination: Theology and the Origins of Race*. New Haven, CT: Yale University Press, 2010.

John Paul II. *Centesimus Annus*. 1991. Available at: http://www.vatican.va/holy_father/john_paul_ii/encyclicals/documents/hf_jp-ii_enc_01051991_centesimus-annus_en.html

Laborem Exercens. 1981. Available at: http://www.vatican.va/holy_father/john_paul_ii/encyclicals/documents/hf_jp-ii_enc_14091981_laborem-exercens_en.html

Jones, Gareth Stedman. "Religion and the Origins of Socialism." In *Religion and the Political Imagination*. Edited by Ira Katznelson, Gareth Jones, and Walter Goode. Cambridge: Cambridge University Press, 2007.

Juris, Jeffrey S. "Performing Politics: Image, Embodiment, and Affective Solidarity during Anti-Corporate Globalization Protests." *Ethnography* 9.1 (2008): 61–97.

Kant, Immanuel. *Groundwork of the Metaphysics of Morals*. Translated by Mary Gregor. 2nd ed. Cambridge: Cambridge University Press, 2012.

Kantorowicz, Ernst. *The King's Two Bodies: A Study in Mediaeval Political Theology*. Princeton, NJ: Princeton University Press, 1957.

Kazin, Michael. *A Godly Hero: The Life of William Jennings Bryan*. New York: Anchor Books, 2007.

The Populist Persuasion: An American History. New York: Basic Books, 1995.

Kelly, Paul. "Political Theory—The State of the Art." *Politics* 26.1 (2006): 47–53.

Kemmerer, Lisa. "Anarchy: Foundations in Faith." In *Contemporary Anarchist Studies*. Edited by Randall Amster, Abraham DeLeon, Luis Fernandez, Anthony J. Nocella II, and Deric Shannon. London: Routledge, 2009.

Kerridge, Eric. *Usury, Interest and the Reformation*. Aldershot, UK: Ashgate, 2002.

Kirk, Alan. "'Love Your Enemies,' the Golden Rule, and Ancient Reciprocity (Luke 6:27–35)." *Journal of Biblical Literature* 122.4 (2003): 667–86.

Knight, Kelvin. *Aristotelian Philosophy: Ethics and Politics from Aristotle to MacIntyre*. Cambridge: Polity, 2007.

Knight, Kelvin and Paul Blackledge. "Introduction: Towards a Virtuous Politics." In *Virtue and Politics: Alasdair MacIntyre's Revolutionary Aristotelianism*. Edited by Kelvin Knight and Paul Blackledge. Notre Dame, IN: University of Notre Dame Press, 2011.

Kovan, Seth. "The 'Sticky Sediment' of Daily Life: Radical Domesticity, Revolutionary Christianity and the Problem of Wealth in Early 20th Century Britain." Unpublished paper.

Kramer, Ralph M. and Harry Specht. *Readings in Community Organization Practice*. Englewood, NJ: Prentice-Hall, 1969.

Kretzmann, John P. and John McKnight. *Building Communities from the Inside Out: A Path toward Finding and Mobilizing a Community's Assets*. Evanston, IL: The Asset-Based Community Development Institute, Northwestern University, 1993.

Kuttner, Paul, Amanda Taylor, and Helen Westmoreland. "'Cement between bricks': Building Schools and Communities in New York City." In *A Match on Dry Grass: Community Organizing as a Catalyst for School Reform*. Edited by Mark R. Warren and Karen L. Mapp. Oxford: Oxford University Press, 2011.

Kymlicka, Will and Wayne Norman. "Return of the Citizen: A Survey of Recent Work on Citizenship Theory." In *Theorizing Citizenship*. Edited by Ronald Beiner. Albany: State University of New York Press, 1995.

Laborde, Cécile. *Pluralist Thought and the State in Britain and France, 1900–25*. Basingstoke: Macmillan Press, 2000.

Lacher, Hannes. "The Slight Transformation: Contesting the Legacy of Karl Polanyi." In *Reading Karl Polanyi for the Twenty-First Century: Market Economy as Political Project*. Edited by Ayşe Buğra and Kaan Ağartan. New York: Palgrave Macmillan, 2007.

Laclau, Ernesto. *On Populist Reason*. London: Verso, 2005.

Lakeland, Paul. *The Politics of Salvation: The Hegelian Idea of the State*. Albany: State University of New York Press, 1984.

Lancourt, Joan. *Confront or Concede: The Alinsky Citizen-Action Organizations*. Lexington, MA: Lexington Books, 1979.

Langholm, Odd Inge. *The Legacy of Scholasticism in Economic Thought: Antecedents of Choice and Power*. Cambridge: Cambridge University Press, 1998.

Latham, Robert. "Social Sovereignty." *Theory, Culture and Society* 17.4 (2000): 1–18.

Lavoie, Don. *Rivalry and Central Planning: The Socialist Calculation Debate Reconsidered*. Cambridge: Cambridge University Press, 1985.

Lawrence-Lightfoot, S. and J. Davis. *The Art and Science of Portraiture*. San Francisco: Jossey-Bass, 1997.

Lear, Jonathan. *The Case for Irony*. Cambridge, MA: Harvard University Press, 2011.

Le Goff, Jacques. *Your Money or Your Life: Economy and Religion in the Middle Ages*. Translated by Patricia Ranum. New York: Zone Books, 1990.

Leo XIII. *Rerum Novarum*. 1891. Available at: http://www.vatican.va/holy_father/leo_xiii/encyclicals/documents/hf_l–xiii_enc_15051891_rerum–novarum_en.html

Liebersohn, Harry. *The Return of the Gift: European History of a Global Idea*. Cambridge: Cambridge University Press, 2011.

Lijphart, Arend. *Democracy in Plural Societies: A Comparative Exploration*. New Haven, CT: Yale University Press, 1980.

The Politics of Accommodation: Pluralism and Democracy in the Netherlands. 2nd ed. Berkeley: University of California Press, 1975.

Thinking about Democracy: Power Sharing and Majority Rule in Theory and Practice. London: Routledge, 2008.

Linklater, Andrew. *Critical Theory and World Politics: Citizenship, Sovereignty and Humanity*. New ed. London: Routledge, 2007.

Littlefield, Henry M. "The Wizard of Oz: Parable on Populism." *American Quarterly* 16.1 (1964): 47–58.

Lloyd, Howell. "Constitutionalism." In *The Cambridge History of Political Thought 1450–1700*. Edited by J. H. Burns. Cambridge: Cambridge University Press, 1991.

Loewenstamm, Samuel. "neshek and ma/tarbît." *Journal of Biblical Literature* 88:1 (1969): 78–80.

Loïc Wacquant, Loïc. "Ethnografeast: A Progress Report on the Practice and Promise of Ethnography." *Ethnography* 4.1 (2003): 5–14.

Loomer, Bernard. "Two Conceptions of Power." *Process Studies* 6.1 (1976): 5–32.

Lubac, Henri de. *The Un–Marxian Socialist: A Study of Proudhon*. Translated by R. E. Scantlebury. London: Sheed and Ward, 1948.

Lubove, Roy. *The Professional Altruist: The Emergence of Social Work as a Career, 1880–1930*. New York: Atheneum Publishers, 1969.

Lukes, Steven. "Power and Authority." In *A History of Sociological Analysis*. Edited by Tom Bottomore and Robert Nisbet. New York: Basic Books, 1978.

Power: A Radical View. 2nd ed. New York: Palgrave Macmillan, 2005.

MABDA. *A Common Word between Us and You*. Amman, Jordan: The Royal Aal Al-Bayt Institute for Islamic Thought, 2012. Available at: www.acommonword.com

Machiavelli, Niccolo. *The Prince*. Translated by Peter Constantine. New York: Modern Library, 2008.

MacInnes, Tom and Peter Kenway. *London's Poverty Profile*. London: New Policy Institute, 2009.

MacIntyre, Alasdair. *After Virtue: A Study in Moral Theory*. London: Duckworth, 1994.

Dependent Rational Animals: Why Human Beings Need the Virtues. London: Duckworth, 1999.

"Three Perspectives on Marxism: 1953, 1968, 1995." In *Selected Essays*. Vol. 2, *Ethics and Politics*. Cambridge: Cambridge University Press, 2006.

Whose Justice? Which Rationality? London: Duckworth, 1988.

MacLeod, Jay. *Community Organising: A Practical and Theological Appraisal*. London: Christian Action, 1993.

Macpherson, C. B. *The Political Theory of Possessive Individualism: Hobbes to Locke*. Oxford: Oxford University Press, 1962.

Maddox, Randy. "'Visit the Poor': John Wesley, the Poor, and the Sanctification of Believers." In *The Poor and the People Called Methodists*. Edited by Richard P. Heitzenrater. Nashville, TN: Kingswood Books, 2002.

Malek, Shiv. "Occupy London Protest Issues Demands to Democratise City of London." *The Guardian*, October 28, 2011.

Manent, Pierre. *An Intellectual History of Liberalism*. Translated by Rebecca Balinski. Princeton, NJ: Princeton University Press, 1994.

Mansbridge, Jane. "Using Power/Fighting Power: The Polity." In *Democracy and Difference*. Edited by Seyla Benhabib. Princeton, NJ: Princeton University Press, 1996.

Maritain, Jacques. "The Concept of Sovereignty." *The American Political Science Review* 44.2 (1950): 343–57.

Integral Humanism: Temporal and Spiritual Problems of the New Christendom. Translated by Joseph Evans. New York: Charles Scribner's Sons, 1968.

Letter to the Ford Foundation. May 27, 1951. Box 12, file 179. Industrial Areas Foundation Archive, University of Illinois at Chicago.

Man and the State. Washington, DC: Catholic University of America Press, 1998 [1951].

Maritain, Jacques and Saul Alinsky. *The Philosopher and the Provocateur: The Correspondence of Jacques Maritain and Saul Alinsky*. Edited by Bernard E. Doering. Notre Dame, IN: University of Notre Dame Press, 1994.

Markus, Robert A. *Christianity and the Secular*. Notre Dame, IN: University of Notre Dame Press, 2006.

Marrow, Stanley. "κόσμος in John." *The Catholic Biblical Quarterly* 64 (2002): 90–102.

Marshall, Peter. *Demanding the Impossible: A History of Anarchism*. London: HarperCollins, 2008.

Marshall, T. H. *Citizenship and Social Class*. Cambridge: Cambridge University Press, 1950.

Martin, David. *Pentecostalism: The World Their Parish*. Oxford: Blackwell, 2002.

Marty, Martin E. and R. Scott Appleby, eds. *Fundamentalisms Observed*. Chicago: University of Chicago Press, 1991.

Marx, Karl. *Capital: A Critique of Political Economy*. Vol. 1. Translated by Ben Fowkes. London: Penguin Books, 1990.

Marx, Karl and Frederick Engels. *Letters to Americans, 1848–1895: A Selection*. New York: International Publishers, 1953.

Massey, Doreen. *World City*. Cambridge: Polity Press, 2010.

Masud, Muhammad Khalid. "Being Muslim in a Non-Muslim Polity: Three Alternative Models." *Journal of the Institute of Muslim Minority Affairs* 10.1 (1989): 118–28.

Mathewes, Charles T. *A Theology of Public Life*. Cambridge: Cambridge University Press, 2007.

Mathiason, Nick. "Bring Back Usury Law to Control Interest Rates, Campaign Urges." *The Observer*, July 19, 2009.

Mau, Steffan. "Welfare Regimes and the Norms of Social Exchange." *Current Sociology* 52.1 (2004): 53–74.

Maurer, Bill. "The Anthropology of Money." *Annual Review of Anthropology* 35 (2006): 15–36.

Mauss, Marcel. *The Gift: The Form and Reason for Exchange in Archaic Societies*. London: Routledge, 2001.

McCloskey, Deirdre N. *The Bourgeois Virtues: Ethics for an Age of Commerce*. Chicago: University of Chicago Press, 2006.

McCormick, John. "Machiavellian Democracy: Controlling Elites with Ferocious Populism." *The American Political Science Review* 95.2 (2001): 297–313.

McKanan, Dan. *Prophetic Encounters: Religion and the American Radical Tradition*. Boston: Beacon Press, 2012.

McKnight, John (with John Kretzmann). "Community Organizing in the Eighties: Toward a Post-Alinsky Agenda." In *The Careless Society: Community and Its Counterfeits*. New York: Basic Books, 1996.

McManus, John. "Rabbi Quits Job Over City Protest." *BBC News*, October 17, 2009. Available at: http://news.bbc.co.uk/1/hi/8311904.stm

McMylor, Peter. "Moral Philosophy and Economic Sociology: What MacIntyre Learnt from Polanyi." In *Karl Polanyi: New Perspectives on the Place of the Economy in Society*. Edited by Mark Harvey, Ronnie Ramlogan, and Sally Randles. Manchester: Manchester University Press, 2007.

McRae, Kenneth. "The Plural Society and the Western Political Tradition." *Canadian Journal of Political Science* 12.4 (1979): 675–88.

Mealand, David. *Poverty and Expectation in the Gospels*. London: SPCK, 1980.

Meikle, Scott. "Aristotle and the Political Economy of the Polis." *The Journal of Hellenic Studies* 99 (1979): 57–73.

"Aristotle on Money." *Phronesis* 39.1 (1994): 26–44.

Melucci, Alberto. *Challenging Codes: Collective Action in the Information Age*. Cambridge: Cambridge University Press, 1996.

Mendelsohn, Isaac. *Slavery in the Ancient Near East: A Comparative Study of Slavery in Babylonia, Assyria, Syria and Palestine from the Middle of the Third Millennium to the End of the First Millennium*. New York: Oxford University Press, 1949.

Mews, Constant J. and Ibrahim Abraham. "Usury and Just Compensation: Religious and Financial Ethics in Historical Perspective." *Journal of Business Ethics* 72.1 (2007): 1–15.

Meyer, Agnes E. "The Orderly Revolution." *The Washington Post*. June 4–9, 1945.

Milbank, John. *Being Reconciled: Ontology and Pardon*. London: Routledge, 2003.

"On Baseless Suspicion: Christianity and the Crises of Socialism." In *The Future of Love: Essays in Political Theology*. Eugene, OR: Cascade Books, 2009.

"On Complex Space." In *The Word Made Strange: Theology, Language, Culture*. Oxford: Blackwell Publishers, 1997.

Theology and Social Theory: Beyond Secular Reason. Oxford: Blackwell Publishers, 1993.

Milgrom, Jacob. *Leviticus 23–27*. New York: Doubleday, 2000.

Miller, David. *On Nationality*. Oxford: Oxford University Press, 1995.

Miller, Donald E. and Tetsunao Yamamori. *Global Pentecostalism: The New Face of Christian Social Engagement*. Berkeley: University of California Press, 2007.

Miller, Mike. *A Community Organizer's Tale: People and Power in San Francisco*. Berkeley, CA: Heyday Books, 2009.

"A Critique of John McKnight & John Kretzmann's 'Community Organizing in the Eighties: Toward a Post–Alinsky Agenda.'" *Comm–Org Papers* 15 (2009). Available at: http://comm–org.wisc.edu/papers2009/miller.htm

Millett, Paul. *Lending and Borrowing in Ancient Athens*. Cambridge: Cambridge University Press, 1991.

Montesquieu, Charles de. *The Spirit of the Laws*. Translated by Anne Cohler Basia Miller and Harold Stone. Cambridge: Cambridge University Press, 1989 [1748].

Moosa, Ebrahim. "The Dilemma of Islamic Rights Schemes." *Journal of Law and Religion* 15.1–2 (2000–2001): 185–215.

Mouffe, Chantal. *The Democratic Paradox*. London: Verso, 2000.

"Religion, Liberal Democracy, and Citizenship." In *Political Theologies: Public Religions in a Post–secular World*. Edited by Hent de Vries and Lawrence Sullivan. New York: Fordham University Press, 2006.

The Return of the Political. London: Verso, 1993.

Movement for Change. Available at: http://www.movementforchange.org.uk/

Muslih, Muhammad. "Democracy." In *Oxford Encyclopedia of the Modern Islamic World*. Edited by John L. Esposito, et al. Oxford: Oxford University Press, 2001.

Muslim Council of Britain. Press release, December 17, 2007. Available at: http://www.mcb.org.uk/article_detail.php?article=announcement-702

Nancy, Jean–Luc. *The Truth of Democracy*. Translated by Pascale–Anne Brault and Michael Naas. New York: Fordham University Press, 2010.

National Occupational Standards for Community Development Work. Federation for Community Development Learning, 2009.

Nederman, Cary. "Men at Work: *Poesis*, Politics and Labor in Aristotle and Some Aristotelians." *Analyse & Kritik* 30 (2008): 17–31.

"Sovereignty, War and the Corporation: Hegel on the Medieval Foundations of the Modern State." *The Journal of Politics* 49.2 (1987): 500–20.

Nelson, Eric. *The Hebrew Republic: Jewish Sources and the Transformation of European Political Thought*. Cambridge, MA: Harvard University Press, 2010.

Neufeld, Edward. "The Prohibitions against Loans at Interest in Ancient Hebrew Laws." *Hebrew Union College Annual* 26 (1955): 355–412.

Neusner, Jacob. "Aristotle's and the Mishnah's Economics: The Matter of Wealth and Usury." *Journal for the Study of Judaism in the Persian, Hellenistic and Roman Period* 21.1 (1990): 41–59.

Newbigin, Lesslie. *The Open Secret: An Introduction to the Theology of Mission*. London: SPCK, 1995.

Nicholson, Philip Yale. *Labor's Story in the United States*. Philadelphia: Temple University Press, 2004.

Nietzsche, Friedrich. *On the Genealogy of Morality and Other Writings*. Translated by Carol Diethe. Cambridge: Cambridge University Press, 1994.

Noll, Mark A. *The Rise of Evangelicalism: The Age of Edwards, Whitefield and the Wesleys*. Nottingham: InterVarsity Press, 2004.

Noonan, John T. *The Scholastic Analysis of Usury*. Cambridge, MA: Harvard University Press, 1957.

Novak, David. "Economics and Justice: A Jewish Example." In *Jewish Social Ethics*. Oxford: Oxford University Press, 1992.

O'Conner, Alice. "Swimming Against the Tide: A Brief History of Federal Policy in Poor Communities." In *Urban Problems and Community Development*. Edited by Ronald Ferguson and William Dickins. Washington, DC: Brookings Institute, 1999.

O'Donovan, Joan Lockwood. "The Theological Economics of Medieval Usury." *Studies in Christian Ethics* 14.1 (2001): 48–64.

O'Donovan, Oliver. *The Desire of the Nations: Rediscovering the Roots of Political Theology*. Cambridge: Cambridge University Press, 1996.

The Problem of Self-Love in St Augustine. London: Yale University Press, 1980.

The Ways of Judgment. Grand Rapids, MI: Eerdmans, 2005.

O'Grady, John, Msgr. Letter to Cardinal–elect Most Rev. Albert G. Meyer, Archbishop of Chicago. Box 47, file 668. Industrial Areas Foundation Archive, University of Illinois at Chicago.

Olsen, Erik J. *Civic Republicanism and the Properties of Democracy*. Langham, MD: Lexington Books, 2006.

O'Neill, Kevin. *City of God: Christian Citizenship in Postwar Guatemala*. Berkeley: University of California Press, 2009.

Ong, Aihwa. "Citizenship in the Midst of Transnational Regimes of Virtue." *Political Power and Social Theory* 20 (2009): 301–07.

"Introduction: Worlding Cities, or the Art of Being Global." In *Worlding Cities: Asian Experiments and the Art of Being Global*. Edited by Ananya Roy and Aiwha Ong. Oxford: Wiley-Blackwell, 2011.

Neoliberalism as Exception: Mutations in Citizenship and Sovereignty. Durham, NC: Duke University Press, 2006.

Opp, Karl–Dieter. *Theories of Political Protest and Social Movements*. London: Routledge, 2009.

Orr, Marion. *Transforming the City: Community Organizing and the Challenge of Political Change*. Lawrence: University Press of Kansas, 2007.

Osterman, Paul. *Gathering Power: The Future of Progressive Politics in America*. Boston: Beacon Press, 2002.

Ostrom, Elinor. *Governing the Commons: The Evolution of Institutions for Collective Action*. Cambridge: Cambridge University Press, 1990.

Pagden, Anthony. "Human Rights, Natural Rights, and Europe's Imperial Legacy." *Political Theory* 31.2 (2003): 171–99.

Pang, Tikki, Mary Ann Lansang, and Andy Haines. "Brain Drain and Health Professionals: A Global Problem Needs Global Solutions." *British Medical Journal* 324 (2002): 499–500.

Panizza, Francisco. *Populism and the Mirror of Democracy*. London: Verso, 2005.

Parekh, Bikhu. "Liberalism and Colonialism: A Critique of Locke and Mill." In *The Decolonization of Imagination: Culture, Knowledge and Power*. Edited by Jan Nederveen Pieterse and Bhikhu Parekh. London: Zed Books, 1995.

Parry, Jonathan. "The Gift, the Indian Gift and the 'Indian Gift.'" *Man* 21.3 (1986): 453–73.

Partington, Andrew and Paul Bickley. *Coming off the Bench: The Past, Present and Future of Religious Representation in the House of Lords*. London: Theos, 2007.

Paul VI. *Nostra Aetate*. 1965. Available at: http://www.vatican.va/archive/hist_councils/ii_vatican_council/documents/vat-ii_decl_19651028_nostra-aetate_en.html

Populorum Progressio. 1967. Available at: http://www.vatican.va/holy_father/paul_vi/encyclicals/documents/hf_p-vi_enc_26031967_populorum_en.html

Payne, Charles M. *I've Got the Light of Freedom: The Organizing Tradition and the Mississippi Freedom Struggle*. Berkeley: University of California Press, 1995.

Penta, Leo. "Citizen Politics, Relational Organizing, and the Practice of Democracy." Paper given at the Community Empowerment and Economic Development Conference, University of Illinois, College of Law. April 23–25, 1993.

"Islands of Democratic Practice: Organizing for Local and Regional Power in the USA." Paper presented at the Biannual European Conference of the Inter–University Consortium for International Social Development in Cracow, Poland. September 24, 1999.

Penta, Leo and Ed Chambers. "Towards a Public Philosophy for the 1990's." Box 66, file 817. Industrial Areas Foundation Archive, University of Illinois at Chicago.

Pettit, Philip. *Republicanism: A Theory of Freedom and Government*. Oxford: Clarendon, 1997.

Phillips, Kevin. *American Theocracy: The Peril and Politics of Radical Religion, Oil, and Borrowed Money in the 21st Century*. New York: Viking Press, 2006.

Phillips, Melanie. "Watch Out, Dave. Red Ed's Making a Cynical Grab for Your Big Society." *The Daily Mail*, January 17, 2011.

Pickles, John. "Review Article: Social and Cultural Cartographies and the Spatial Turn in Social Theory." *Journal of Historical Geography* 25.1 (1999): 93–98.

Pierce, Gregory. *Activism That Makes Sense: Congregations and Community Organization*. Chicago: ACTA Publications, 1997.

Pitt, James and Maurice Keane. *Community Organising?: The Challenge to Britain from the U.S.A.* London: J & P Consultancy, 1984.

Pius XI. *Quadragesimo Anno*. 1931. Available at: http://www.vatican.va/holy_father/pius_xi/encyclicals/documents/hf_p-xi_enc_19310515_quadragesimo-anno_en.html

Plato. *Laws*. In *The Dialogues of Plato*. Translated by Benjamin Jowett. Oxford: Oxford University Press, 1953.

Pleyers, Geoffrey. *Alter–Globalization: Becoming Actors in a Global Age*. Cambridge: Polity, 2010.

Pocock, J. G. A. *The Ancient Constitution and the Feudal Law: A Study of English Historical Thought in the Seventeenth Century*. Cambridge: Cambridge University Press, 1987 (1957).

The Machiavellian Moment: Florentine Political Thought and the Atlantic Republican Tradition. Princeton, NJ: Princeton University Press, 1975.

Virtue, Commerce, and History: Essays on Political Thought and History, Chiefly in the Eighteenth Century. Cambridge: Cambridge University Press, 1985.

Polanyi, Karl. "Die funktionelle Theorie der Gesellschaft und das Problem der sozialistischen Rechnungslegung." *Archiv für Sozialwissenschaft und Sozialpolitik* 52 (1924): 218–28.

The Great Transformation: The Political and Economic Origins of Our Time. 2nd ed. Boston, MA: Beacon Press, 2001.

"Sozialistische Rechnungslegung." *Archiv für Sozialwissenschaft und Sozialpolitik* 49.2 (1922): 377–420.

"Über die Freiheit" and "Zur Socialisierungsfrage." In *Chronik der großen Transformation*. Vol. 3. Edited by Michele Cangiani, Karl Polanyi-Levitt, and Claus Thomasberger. Marburg: Metropolis-Verlag, 2005.
Polletta, Francesca. *Freedom is an Endless Meeting: Democracy in American Social Movements*. Chicago: University of Chicago Press, 2002.
Poole, Ross. *Nation and Identity*. London: Routledge, 1999.
Porter, Roy. *English Society in the Eighteenth Century*. 2nd ed. London: Penguin, 2001.
Postel, Charles. *The Populist Vision*. New York: Oxford University Press, 2009.
Prochaska, Frank K. *Christianity and Social Service in Modern Britain: The Disinherited Spirit*. Oxford: Oxford University Press, 2006.
Proudhon, Pierre–Jospeh. *Les Confessions d'un Révolutionnaire*. Paris, 1849.
Purdy, Jedediah. *The Meaning of Property: Freedom, Community and the Legal Imagination*. New Haven, CT: Yale University Press, 2011.
Pyper, Hugh. "The Bible in the Metropolis." Ethel M. Wood Annual Lecture, King's College London. March 3, 2010.
Queen Mary University of London. Living Wage Research. Available at: http://www.geog.qmul.ac.uk/livingwage/chronology.html
Raddatz, Martha. "Radical Cleric Al-Awlaki Invited to Private Lunch at Pentagon." October 21, 2010. Available at: http://abcnews.go.com/Politics/Blotter/al-qaeda-cleric-awlaki-invited-pentagon-911/story?id=11935006
Ramadan, Tariq. *Western Muslims and the Future of Islam*. Oxford: Oxford University Press, 2004.
Rawls, John. "The Idea of Public Reason Revisited." In *The Law of Peoples*. Cambridge, MA: Harvard University Press, 2001.
"Justice as Reciprocity." In *Collected Papers*. Edited by Samuel Freeman. Cambridge, MA: Harvard University Press, 1999.
Political Liberalism. New York: Columbia University Press, 1993.
A Theory of Justice. Rev. ed. Cambridge, MA: Harvard University Press, 1999.
Rayner, Gordon. "Muslim Groups 'Linked to September 11 Hijackers Spark Fury Over Conference'." *The Telegraph*, December 27, 2008. Available at: http://www.telegraph.co.uk/news/uknews/3966501/Muslim-groups-linked-to-September-11-hijackers-spark-fury-over-conference.html
Redman, Eric. *The Dance of Legislation*. New York: Simon & Schuster, 1973.
Reinders, Hans S. *Receiving the Gift of Friendship: Profound Disability, Theological Anthropology, and Ethics*. Grand Rapids, MI: Eerdmans, 2008.
Reitzes, Donald C. and Dietrich C. Reitzes. "Alinsky in the 1980s: Two Contemporary Chicago Community Organizations." *The Sociological Quarterly* 28.2 (1987): 265–83.
"Saul D. Alinsky: An Applied Urban Symbolic Interactionist." *Symbolic Interaction* 15.1 (1992): 1–24.
Ricoeur, Paul. *Figuring the Sacred: Religion, Narrative, and Imagination*. Edited by Mark I. Wallace. Translated by David Pellauer. Minneapolis: Augsburg Fortress, 1995.
"The Golden Rule: Exegetical and Theological Perplexities." *New Testament Studies* 36.3 (1990): 392–97.
The Just. Translated by David Pellauer. Chicago: University of Chicago Press, 2000.
Riley, Patrick. *The General Will before Rousseau: The Transformation of the Divine into the Civic*. Princeton, NJ: Princeton University Press, 1986.

Rist, Gilbert. *The History of Development: From Western Origins to Global Faith*. London: Zed Books, 2002.

Ritzer, George. *The McDonaldization of Society*. Thousand Oaks, CA: Pine Forge Press, 2000.

Robbins, Joel. "The Globalization of Pentecostal and Charismatic Christianity." *Annual Review of Anthropology* 33 (2004): 117–43.

Robertson, Roland. "Global Millennialism: A Postmortem on Secularization." In *Religion, Globalization and Culture*. Edited by Peter Beyer and Lori Beaman. Leiden: Brill, 2007.

Globalization: Social Theory and Global Culture. London: Sage, 1992.

"Glocalization: Time-Space and Heterogeneity-Homogeneity." In *Global Modernities*. Edited by Mike Featherstone, Scott Lash, and Roland Robertson. London: Sage, 1995.

Robinson, Cedric J. *Black Marxism: The Making of the Black Radical Tradition*. London: Zed Press, 1983.

Rochester, Anna. *The Populist Movement in the United States: The Growth and Decline of the People's Party—A Social and Economic Interpretation*. New York: International Publishers, 1943.

Rockman, Seth. "Slavery and Capitalism." *The Journal of the Civil War Era* 2.1 (2012): 5.

Rogers, Mary Beth. *Cold Anger: A Story of Faith and Power Politics*. Denton, TX: University of North Texas Press, 1990.

"Gospel Values and Secular Politics." *The Texas Observer*, November 22, 1990.

Rose, Nikolas. "Governing Cities, Governing Citizens." In *Democracy, Citizenship and the Global City*. Edited by Engin F. Isin. London: Routledge, 2000.

Rose, Stephen C. "Saul Alinsky, the Industrial Areas Foundation and the Church's Millions." *Renewal* (March 1968): 4–9.

Rousseau, Jean Jacques. *The Social Contract and Other Later Political Writings*. Cambridge: Cambridge University Press, 1997.

Rubin, Herbert and Irene Rubin. *Community Organizing and Development*. 2nd ed. New York: Macmillan, 1992.

Ruthven, Malise. *Fundamentalism: The Search for Meaning*. Oxford: Oxford University Press, 2005.

Sabl, Andrew. "Community Organizing as Tocquevillean Politics: The Art, Practices, and Ethos of Association." *American Journal of Political Science* 46.1 (2002): 1–19.

Salvatore, Armando. *The Public Sphere: Liberal Modernity, Catholicism, Islam*. New York: Palgrave Macmillan, 2007.

Sandel, Michael. *Democracy's Discontent: America in Search of a Public Philosophy*. Cambridge, MA: Belknap Press, 1996.

What Money Can't Buy: The Moral Limits of Markets. New York: Farrar, Straus, and Giroux, 2012.

Sanders, Elizabeth. *Roots of Reform: Farmers, Workers, and the American State, 1877–1917*. Chicago: University of Chicago Press, 1999.

Sanders, Heywood. "Communities Organized for Public Service and Neighborhood Revitalization in San Antonio." In *Public Policy and Community: Activism and Governance in Texas*. Edited by Robert Wilson. Austin: University of Texas Press, 1997.

Sanders, Marion. "The Professional Radical: Conversations with Saul Alinsky." *Harper's Magazine*, June and July, 1965.

The Professional Radical: Conversations with Saul Alinsky. New York: Harper & Row, 1970.

Sassen, Saskia. *The Global City: New York, London, Tokyo*. Princeton, NJ: Princeton University Press, 1991.

"Making Public Interventions in Today Massive Cities." *Static* 4 (2006): 1–8. Available at: http://static.londonconsortium.com/issue04/

"The Repositioning of Citizenship: Emergent Subjects and Spaces for Politics." *Berkeley Journal of Sociology* 46 (2002): 4–25.

Territory, Authority, Rights: From Medieval to Global Assemblages. Princeton, NJ: Princeton University Press, 2008.

Schenker, Adrian. "The Biblical Legislation on the Release of Slaves: The Road from Exodus to Leviticus." *Journal for the Study of the Old Testament* 78 (1998): 23–41.

Schlossman, Steven L. and Michel W. Sedlak. "The Chicago Area Project Revisited." *Crime and Delinquency* 29.3 (1983): 398–462.

Schmitt, Carl. *The Concept of the Political*. Translated by George Schwab. Exp. ed. Chicago: University of Chicago Press, 2007.

Land and Sea. Translated by Simona Draghici. Washington, DC: Plutarch Press, 1997.

The Leviathan in the State Theory of Thomas Hobbes: Meaning and Failure of Political Symbol. Translated by George Schwab and Erna Hilfstein. Westport, CT: Greenwood Press, 1996.

Political Theology II: The Myth of the Closure of Any Political Theology. Translated by Michael Hoelzl and Graham Ward. Cambridge: Polity Press, 2008.

Roman Catholicism and Political Form. Translated by G. L. Ulman. Westport, CT: Greenwood Press, 1996.

"State Ethics and the Pluralist State." In *Weimar: A Jurisprudence of Crisis*. Edited by Arthur J. Jacobson and Bernhard Schlink. Berkeley: University of California Press, 2000.

Theory of the Partisan: Intermediate Commentary on the Concept of the Political. Translated by G. L. Ulman. New York: Telos Press Publishing, 2007.

Schutz, Aaron and Marie Sandy. *Collective Action for Social Change: An Introduction to Community Organizing*. New York: Palgrave Macmillan, 2011.

Scott, James. "This Is What Happens When Community Organising and Policy Combine." Available at: http://labourlist.org/2013/02/this-is-what-happens-when-community-organising-and-policy-combine/

Scott, James C. *Seeing Like a State: How Certain Schemes to Improve the Human Condition Have Failed*. New Haven, CT: Yale University Press, 1998.

Scott, Rachel M. *The Challenge of Political Islam: Non–Muslims and the Egyptian State*. Stanford, CA: Stanford University Press, 2010.

Shapiro, Ian. *The State of Democratic Theory*. Princeton, NJ: Princeton University Press, 2003.

Sharpe, Reginald R. *London and the Kingdom: A History Derived Mainly from the Archives at Guildhall In the Custody of the Corporation of the City of London*. III vols. London: Longmans, Green & Co., 1894–95.

Shaw, Clifford. *The Jackroller: A Delinquent Boy's Own Story*. Chicago: University of Chicago Press, 1966 [1930].

Shaw, Clifford and Henry D. McKay. *Juvenile Delinquency in Urban Areas*. Chicago: University of Chicago Press, 1942.

Shaxson, Nicholas. *Treasure Islands: Tax Havens and the Men Who Stole the World*. London: The Bodley Head, 2011.

Shearmur, Jeremy. "Hayek's Politics." In *The Cambridge Companion to Hayek*. Edited by Edward Feser. Cambridge: Cambridge University Press, 2006.

Shepard, Benjamin. *Play, Creativity, and Social Movements*. London: Routledge, 2011.

Shields, Jon A. *The Democratic Virtues of the Christian Right*. Princeton, NJ: Princeton University Press, 2009.

Siddiqui, Ataullah. *Christian–Muslim Dialogue in the Twentieth Century*. Basingstoke: Macmillan, 1997.

"Inter-Faith Relations in Britain since 1970—An Assessment." *Exchange* 39.3 (2010): 236–50.

Siedentop, Larry. *Tocqueville*. Oxford: Oxford University Press, 1994.

Sigurdson, Ola. "Beyond Secularism? Towards a Post-Secular Political Theology." *Modern Theology* 26.2 (2010): 177–96.

Silberman, Charles. *Crisis in Black and White*. New York: Random House, 1965.

Silver, Beverly J. *Forces of Labor: Workers' Movements and Globalization since 1870*. Cambridge: Cambridge University Press, 2003.

Simmel, Georg. *The Philosophy of Money*. London: Routledge and Kegan Paul, 1978.

Sirianni, Carmen. *Investing in Democracy: Engaging Citizens in Collaborative Governance*. Washington, DC: Brookings Institute, 2009.

Skillen, James. *The Development of Calvinistic Political Theory in the Netherlands, with Special Reference to the Thought of Herman Dooyeweerd*. PhD dissertation, Duke University, 1973.

Skinner, Quentin. *Liberty before Liberalism*. Cambridge: Cambridge University Press, 1998.

Skocpol, Theda, Marshall Ganz, and Ziad Munson. "A Nation of Organizers: The Institutional Origins of Civic Voluntarism in the United States." *American Political Science Review* 94.3 (2000): 527–46.

Slayton, Robert A. *Back of the Yards: The Making of a Local Democracy*. Chicago: University of Chicago Press, 1986.

Smith, Ted A. *The New Measures: A Theological History of Democratic Practice*. Cambridge: Cambridge University Press, 2007.

Smock, Kristina. *Democracy in Action: Community Organizing and Urban Change*. New York: Columbia University Press, 2004.

Snarr, C. Melissa. *All You that Labor: Religion and Ethics in the Living Wage Movement*. New York: New York University Press, 2011.

Snodgrass, Jon. "Clifford R. Shaw and Henry D. McKay: Chicago Criminologists." *The British Journal of Criminology* 16.1 (1976): 1–19.

Soja, Edward. *Postmetropolis: Critical Studies of Cities and Regions*. Oxford: Blackwell Publishing, 2000.

Somers, Margaret R. *Genealogies of Citizenship: Markets, Statelessness, and the Right to Have Rights*. Cambridge: Cambridge University Press, 2008.

Spufford, Peter. "From Antwerp and Amsterdam to London: The Decline of Financial Centres in Europe." *The Economist* 154.2 (2006): 143–75.

Stears, Marc. *Demanding Democracy: American Radicals in Search of a New Politics*. Princeton, NJ: Princeton University Press, 2010.

"Guild Socialism." In *Modern Pluralism: Anglo-American Debates Since 1880*. Edited by Mark Bevir. Cambridge: Cambridge University Press, 2012.

Progressives, Pluralists, and the Problems of the State: Ideologies of Reform in the United States and Britain, 1909–1926. Oxford: Oxford University Press, 2002.

Stein, P. G. "Roman Law." In *The Cambridge History of Medieval Political Thought c. 350–c. 1450*. Edited by J. H. Burns. Cambridge: Cambridge University Press, 1988.

Steinberger, Peter J. *The Concept of Political Judgment*. Chicago: University of Chicago Press, 1993.

Steiner, Jürg. "Review: The Consociational Theory and Beyond." *Comparative Politics* 13.3 (1981): 339–54.

Steiner, Philippe. "The Critique of the Economic Point of View: Karl Polanyi and the Durkheimians." In *Market and Society: The Great Transformation Today*. Edited by Chris Hann and Keith Hart. Cambridge: Cambridge University Press, 2009.

Stern, Philip J. *The Company-State: Corporate Sovereignty and the Early Modern Foundations of the British Empire in India*. Oxford: Oxford University Press, 2012.

Stigler, George J. "The Theory of Economic Regulation." *The Bell Journal of Economics and Management Science* 2.1 (1971): 3–21.

Stoecker, Randy. "Community Development and Community Organizing: Apples and Oranges? Chicken and Egg?" 2001. Available at: http://comm–org.wisc.edu/drafts/orgdevppr2c.htm

"The Community Development Corporation Model of Urban Redevelopment: A Critique and an Alternative." *Journal of Urban Affairs* 19.1 (1997): 1–23.

"Understanding the Development–Organizing Dialectic." *Journal of Urban Affairs* 25.4 (2003): 493–512.

Stout, Jeffrey. *Blessed are the Organized: Grassroots Democracy in America*. Princeton, NJ: Princeton University Press, 2010.

Democracy and Tradition. Princeton, NJ: Princeton University Press, 2004.

Stringer, Ernest T. *Action Research*. 2nd ed. London: Sage Publications, 1999.

Su, Celina. *Streetwise for Book Smarts: Grassroots Organizing and Education Reform in the Bronx*. Ithaca, NY: Cornell University Press, 2009.

Survey of Community Development Workers in the UK—Summary Report. Sheffield: Community Development Foundation, 2003.

Sutton, William. *Journeyman for Jesus: Evangelical Artisans Confront Capitalism in Jacksonian Baltimore*. University Park: Pennsylvania State University Press, 1998.

Swarts, Heidi J. *Organizing Urban America: Secular and Faith–based Progressive Movements*. Minneapolis: University of Minnesota Press, 2008.

Szakos, Kristin Layng and Joe Szakos. *We Make Change: Community Organizers Talk About What They Do—And Why*. Nashville, TN: Vanderbilt University Press, 2007.

Tamanaha, Brian Z. "Understanding Legal Pluralism: Past to Present, Local to Global." *Sydney Law Review* 30 (2008): 375–411.

Tanner, Kathryn. *Economy of Grace*. Minneapolis, MN: Fortress Press, 2005.

Tattersall, Amanda. *Power in Coalition: Strategies for Strong Unions and Social Change*. Ithaca, NY: Cornell University Press, 2010.

Taylor, Charles. *The Ethics of Authenticity*. Cambridge, MA: Harvard University Press, 1992.

Modern Social Imaginaries. Durham, NC: Duke University Press, 2004.

Multiculturalism and the "Politics of Recognition": An Essay. Edited by Amy Gutmann. Princeton, NJ: Princeton University Press, 1992.

A Secular Age. Cambridge, MA: Belknap, 2007.

"Why Democracy Needs Patriotism." In *For Love of Country?* Edited by Martha C. Nussbaum and Joshua Cohen. Boston: Beacon Press, 1996.

Thatcher, David. "The Normative Case Study." *American Journal of Sociology* 111.6 (2006): 1631–76.

Thomas, George M. *Revivalism and Cultural Change: Christianity, Nation Building, and the Market in the Nineteenth-century United States*. Chicago: University of Chicago Press, 1989.

Tierney, Brian. *The Idea of Natural Rights: Studies on Natural Rights, Natural Law, and Church Law, 1150–1625*. Atlanta, GA: Scholars Press, 1997.

Titmuss, R. M. *The Gift Relationship: From Human Blood to Social Policy*. London: George Allen and Unwin, 1970.

Tocqueville, Alexis de. *Democracy in America*. Translated by Gerald Bevan. London: Penguin, 2003.

Toscano, Alberto. *Fanaticism: On the Uses of an Idea*. London: Verso, 2010.

Tully, James. "On Local and Global Citizenship: An Apprenticeship Model." In *Public Philosophy in a New Key*. Vol. 2, *Imperialism and Civic Freedom*. Cambridge: Cambridge University Press, 2008.

Strange Multiplicity: Constitutionalism in an Age of Diversity. Cambridge: Cambridge University Press, 1995.

Turner, Bryan. "Civility, Civil Sphere and Citizenship: Solidarity versus the Enclave Society." *Citizenship Studies* 12:2 (2008): 177–84.

Twelvetrees, Alan. *Community Work*. 4th ed. London: Palgrave Macmillan, 2008.

Twinning, William. *General Jurisprudence: Understanding Law from a Global Perspective*. Cambridge: Cambridge University Press, 2009.

United States Conference of Catholic Bishops. *Economic Justice for All: Pastoral Letter on Catholic Social Teaching and the U.S. Economy*. Washington, DC: U.S. Catholic Conference, 1986.

Van Schendelen, M. P. C. M. "Consociational Democracy: The Views of Arend Lijphart and Collected Criticisms." *Political Science Reviewer* 15 (1985): 143–83.

von Gierke, Otto. *Community in Historical Perspective*. Edited by Antony Black. Translated by Mary Fischer. Cambridge: Cambridge University Press, 1990.

von Heyking, John. "The Luminous Path of Friendship: Augustine's Account of Friendship and Political Order." In *Friendship and Politics: Essays in Political Throught*. Edited by John von Heyking and Richard Avramenko. Notre Dame, IN: University of Notre Dame Press, 2008.

von Hoffman, Nicholas. *Radical: A Portrait of Saul Alinsky*. New York: Nation Books, 2010.

von Rad, Gerhard. *Deuteronomy*. London: SCM, 1966.

Walls, David. "Power to the People: Thirty-five Years of Community Organizing." Available at: http://www.sonoma.edu/users/w/wallsd/community-organizing.shtml

Walzer, Michael. *Exodus and Revolution*. New York: Basic Books, 1985.

Politics and Passion: Toward a More Egalitarian Liberalism. New Haven, CT: Yale University Press, 2005.

Spheres of Justice: A Defense of Pluralism and Equality. New York: Basic Books, 1983.

Ward, Graham. *Cultural Transformation and Religious Practice*. Cambridge: Cambridge University Press, 2005.

Warf, Barney and Santa Arias. *The Spatial Turn: Interdisciplinary Perspectives*. London: Taylor & Francis, 2009.

Warren, Mark R. "Communities and Schools: A New View of Urban Education Reform." *Harvard Educational Review* 75.2 (2005): 133–73.

"Community Organizing in Britain: The Political Engagement of Faith-Based Social Capital." *City & Community* 8.2 (2009): 99–127.

"Deliberative Democracy and Authority." *American Political Science Review* 90.1 (1996): 46–60.

Democracy and Association. Princeton, NJ: Princeton University Press, 2001.

Dry Bones Rattling: Community Building to Revitalize American Democracy. Princeton, NJ: Princeton University Press, 2001.

Fire in the Heart: How White Activists Embrace Racial Justice. Oxford: Oxford University Press, 2010.

Warren, Mark R., Karen L. Mapp, and The Community Organizing and School Reform Project. *A Match on Dry Grass: Community Organizing as a Catalyst for School Reform*. Oxford: Oxford University Press, 2011.

Warren, Mark R, and Richard Wood. *Faith Based Community Organizing: The State of the Field*. Jericho, NY: Interfaith Funders, 2001.

Waterman, A. M. C. *Political Economy and Christian Theology since the Enlightenment: Essays in Intellectual History*. New York: Palgrave Macmillan, 2004.

Watson, Francis. *Text, Church and World: Biblical Interpretation in Theological Perspective*. Edinburgh: T & T Clark, 1994.

Weintraub, Jeff. "Democracy and the Market: A Marriage of Inconvenience." In *From Leninism to Freedom: The Challenges of Democratization*. Edited by Margarat Latus Nugent. Boulder, CO: Westview Press, 1992.

"The Theory and Politics of the Public/Private Distinction." In *Public and Private in Thought and Practice: Perspectives on a Grand Dichotomy*. Edited by Jeff Weintraub and Krishan Kumar. Chicago: University of Chicago Press, 1997.

Weston, Corinne. "England: Ancient Constitution and Common Law." In *The Cambridge History of Political Thought: 1450–1700*. Edited by J. H. Burns. Cambridge: Cambridge University Press, 1991.

Westphal, Merold. *Suspicion and Faith: The Religious Uses of Modern Atheism*. New York: Fordham University Press, 1998.

White, Richard. *The Middle Ground: Indians, Empires and Republics in the Great Lakes Region, 1650–1815*. Cambridge: Cambridge University Press, 1991.

Whyte, William Foote. *Street Corner Society: The Social Structure of an Italian Slum*. 2nd ed. Chicago: University of Chicago Press, 1955.

Wilcox, Clyde and Carin Robinson. *Onward Christian Soldiers? The Religious Right in American Politics*. 4th ed. Boulder, CO: Westview Press, 2011.

Williams, Rhys H. and Susan M. Alexander. "Religious Rhetoric in American Populism: Civil Religion as Movement Ideology." *Journal for the Scientific Study of Religion* 33.1 (1994): 1–15.

Wills, Jane. "Campaigning for Low Paid Workers: The East London Communities Organisation (TELCO) Living Wage Campaign." In *The Future of Worker Representation*. Edited by Geraldine Healy, Edmund Heery, Phil Taylor, and William Brown. Oxford: Oxford University Press, 2004.

"Identity Making for Action: The Example of London Citizens." In *Theorizing Identities and Social Action*. Edited by M. Wetherell. London: Palgrave Macmillan, 2009.

"The Politics of Place." Unpublished paper presented at "Colloquium on Community Organising," London, June 15–17, 2009.

Wills, Jane, et al. *Global Cities at Work: New Migrant Divisions of Labour*. London: Pluto, 2009.

Wills, Jane, and Kavita Datta, Yara Evans, Joanna Herbert, Jon May, and Cathy McIlwaine. "Religion at Work: The Role of Faith-Based Organizations in the London Living Wage Campaign." *Cambridge Journal of Regions, Economy and Society* 2.3 (2009): 443–61.

Winch, Christopher. "Georg Kerschensteiner—Founding the Dual System in Germany." *Oxford Review of Education* 32.3 (2006): 381–96.

Wink, Walter. *Engaging the Powers: Discernment and Resistance in a World of Domination*. Minneapolis, MN: Fortress Press, 1992.

Wirtz, W. Willard. *Brief History of the American Labor Movement*. 3rd ed. Washington, DC: Department of Labor, 1964.

Witte, John. *The Reformation of Rights: Law, Religion, and Human Rights in Early Modern Calvinism*. Cambridge: Cambridge University Press, 2007.

Wolin, Sheldon S. "Agitated Times." *Parallax* 11.4 (2005): 2–11.

Politics and Vision: Continuity and Innovation in Western Thought. Princeton, NJ: Princeton University Press, 2006 [1960].

The Presence of the Past: Essays on the State and the Constitution. Baltimore, MD: Johns Hopkins University Press, 1989.

Tocqueville between Two Worlds: The Making of a Political and Theoretical Life. New ed. Princeton, NJ: Princeton University Press, 2003.

"What Revolutionary Action Means Today." In *Dimensions of Radical Democracy: Pluralism, Citizenship, Community*. Edited by Chantal Mouffe. London: Verso, 1992.

"What Time Is It?" *Theory & Event* 1.1 (1997).

Wood, Diane. *Medieval Economic Thought*. Cambridge: Cambridge University Press, 2002.

Wood, Gordon. "Democracy and the American Revolution." In *Democracy: The Unfinished Journey, 508 BC to AD 1993*. Edited by John Dunn. Oxford: Oxford University Press, 1992.

Wood, Richard. *Faith in Action: Religion, Race, and Democratic Organizing in America*. Chicago: University of Chicago Press, 2002.

The Fire of Public Life: Congregational Development through Civic Engagement. Forthcoming.

Yoder, John Howard. *Body Politics: Five Practices of the Christian Community before the Watching World.* Scottsdale, AZ: Herald Press, 2001.

The Politics of Jesus: Vicit Agnus Noster. 2nd ed. Grand Rapids, MI: Eerdmans, 1994.

Zaman, Muhammad Qasim. "The 'Ulama' of Contemporary Islam and Their Conceptions of the Common Good." In *Public Islam and the Common Good.* Edited by Armando Salvatore and Dale Eickelman. Leiden: Brill, 2004.

Zerbe, Gordon Mark. *Citizenship: Paul on Peace and Politics*. Winnipeg: Canadian Mennonite University Press, 2012.

Zieger, Robert H. *American Workers, American Unions, 1920–1985*. Baltimore, MD: Johns Hopkins University Press, 1986.

Index